COLLISHAW & COMPANY

COLLISHAW & COMPANY

CANADIANS *IN THE*
ROYAL NAVAL AIR SERVICE
1914 -1918

02 DEC 12

TO LEE WEBER
A FELLOW NAVAL AVIATOR

Yours ay
J. Allan Snowie

By
J. ALLAN SNOWIE

FOREWORD BY

REAR-ADMIRAL BOB WELLAND, DSC & BAR, RCN (RETIRED)

COLLISHAW & COMPANY
FIRST PRINTING

J. ALLAN SNOWIE

Book & Cover Design: Cynthia J. Snowie

Cover Painting: "Hairy Do and First Two' by Geoff Bennett

25Oct16 – FSLt Raymond COLLISHAW
(Nanaimo BC) – First Victories

In what he describes as a 'hairy do' Collishaw becomes lost over the Western Front while ferrying a Sopwith Strutter. Jumped by six enemy machines, his goggles are shattered by gunfire but he manages to send down two of the attackers. Partially blinded, he lands at an aerodrome and taxiing in, his sight clears enough to find that the aircraft all bear Iron Cross markings. Collishaw immediately powers up and escapes in heavy rain.

NIEUPORT PUBLISHING, Inc.

4152 Meridian Street
Suite 105-221
Bellingham, WA 98226

nieuportxi@gmail.com

Library of Congress Control Number: 2010936929

International Standard Book Number: 978-0-69200989-5

Printed in the United States of America and available through:

Village Books
1200 11th Street
Bellingham, WA 98225

www.villagebooks.com

TABLE of CONTENTS

*Note: Consult Appendix A for the alphabetical listing of ALL North American members of the RNAS. This listing also gives the date (in bold) of individual narratives in the Chapters.

to my friend, my sweetie, my bride,

Cynthia

ROYAL NAVAL AIR SERVICE
SWEETHEART WINGS

FOREWORD

COLLISHAW & COMPANY

Allan Snowie asked me to write the Foreword to this book perhaps because he was aware I am old enough to have known some of the remarkable characters he describes; besides that he and I served on board the aircraft carrier *Bonaventure*, he as a submarine-hunting, deck-landing pilot and I fleet commander.

When Air Marshal Wilf Curtis was Chief of the RCAF in 1947 and stationed in Ottawa I was a junior Lieutenant Commander. Because of his naval beginnings Curtis frequently visited our Naval Mess, a popular haunt of naval aviators. The Air Marshal began his flying career as a naval Sub Lieutenant and was not shy about letting us know that he, and many other Air Force officers originated naval flying. On the other hand it was an equally honest argument that the Navy created the Air Force by equipping and training the hundreds of pilots whose names are mentioned in this book. I recall one of our Admirals stating, in the spirit of interservice rivalry, that the Navy invented the Air Force. "A major mistake, torpedoing ones own ship".

I also had the privilege of meeting Air Chief Marshal Breadner in the informal atmosphere of the mess. Also Air Marshals Leckie and Edwards and Cowley, all of who began their careers as naval Sub Lieutenants. I was well aware these men had pioneered military flying, faced the enemy, got away with it, and then led our Royal Canadian Air Force throughout the Second World War to its great achievements—And that they carried the responsibility for the enormous sacrifices of Canadian aircrew.

The nature of air warfare is that only a few engage in the actual combat, as did the knights and champions of ancient times; this book has identified our Canadian Naval Knights of the First World War, told us who they were, what they did, and what happened to them. All Canadians will feel a surge of pride to learn about our early fighting aviators, our Royal Naval Air Service Sub Lieutenants, who made Canada's greatest Naval contribution to winning that War. These men then went on to form the Royal Canadian Air Force, of whom all Canadians are rightfully proud.

Allan Snowie first learned to fly as a naval cadet while attending HMCS *Venture*, and he was a Sub Lieutenant, like Curtis and Breadner and the others when he won his naval wings; he knows of what he speaks. He has written a memorable and valuable book.

HMCS Venture

Well done.

Rear Admiral Robert P. Welland, DSC & Bar, CD
Royal Canadian Navy (Retired)

PREFACE

One of my Squadron Commanders in the aircraft carrier HMCS *Bonaventure*, Robbie Hughes, co-edited a book in 1994 titled *Canada's Naval Aviators*. It contains the biographies of over 1,600 flying personnel, mainly from the Second World War through to the Canadian Armed Forces integration of 1966. Robbie and his 'partner-in-crime', John MacFarlane, admitted that they had scant materiel on Royal Naval Air Service Canadians and only about a hundred or so are mentioned. So, thought I, the perhaps hundred or so others should be fun to trace down…

And here we are, only sixteen years and 943 names later…

Today, the Public Records Office at Kew Gardens in London, England, maintains the service files of all Royal Navy personnel, and specific information on aviators is preserved by the Fleet Air Arm Museum at Yeovilton Naval Air Station. In Canada, the Hitchins Collection at Western University in London, Ontario, and the Creghan Collection at the National Aviation Museum in Ottawa provide further source materiel. The Directorate of History and Heritage of the Canadian Armed Forces holds the correspondence of Air Vice Marshal Raymond Collishaw and Mr. Ronald V. Dodds. The two collaborated on the official Collishaw biography *Air Command, A fighter pilot's story*. Initially published in the United Kingdom in 1973, this aviation treasure was finally launched in Canada during 2008 as *The Black Flight* by CEF Books.

The genesis of this manuscript, *Collishaw & Company*, took root from these resources. The fruition was inspired by the exceedingly kind assistance of archivists, historians, and from knowledge shared by families and friends of the RNAS lads. The educational institutions attended by many of the young men were also very helpful with materiel and the Royal Aeronautical Club Trust supplied the bulk of the photographs.

This book contains a fair number of stories of the 943 told in a chronological flow of individual experiences—for flying was pretty much a solo adventure in this, the second decade of flight. As these collective tales from across multiple war fronts are broad and diverse, insightful observations of Raymond Collishaw are spliced throughout to link the narratives. Further, the term 'Canadian' is expanded somewhat to include the colony of Newfoundland, not yet a part of Confederation in 1914; and also to speak for some dozen United States citizens who travelled north of the 49th parallel to join the RNAS.

When the Great War opened in August 1914, the British Royal Navy believed that they had an opportunity for glory in a Trafalgar-style sea battle and kept their trained personnel in the fleet. Loath to release these experienced officers to flying duties, they readily recruited Canadians and other 'Colonials' as aviators. The 943 North Americans herein all joined the colours before April First 1918, the date on which the new Royal Air Force was formed by the political marriage of the Navy's RNAS to the Army's Royal Flying Corps.

This is not a chronicle of tactics or strategy or even about aeroplanes or ships; it is rather a compendium of short character bios that aims to increase knowledge and appreciation about a spectacular company of men who flew in the First World War. Some pages may read like a litany of the dead; but it is most important to honour all losses. Other entries could be expanded into fascinating particulars for few Canadians know very much about this era other than the Vimy Ridge victory, or about pilots—with the possible exception of RFC ace Billy Bishop—in other words, something about the Army, a little about Aviation, but nothing about the Navy.

J. Allan Snowie, CD

The last living Canadian Naval Aviator was Henry Botterell who passed in 2003. Always a gentleman, Henry would lapse into what had to be an Edwardian manner of speech during an interview. (Who knows today?) It was one of life's highlights to make his acquaintance and I thank his son Edward and aviation historian Warren Carroll for enabling that privilege. I owe a huge debt of gratitude to so many…

The extended family of Raymond Collishaw was most kind in providing information; the Collishaw-Smiths of Calgary, and 'first cousin twice-removed' David Jones of Cardiff Wales. A stout friend of RNAS Canadians is Brian Costello, former Mayor of Carleton Place, Ontario, who provided materiel on Roy & Horace Brown, RP Abbott, LS Breadner, WJ Sussan, ST Edwards, DMB Galbraith and DD Findlay. The historic town of Carleton Place is nicknamed 'Nursery of the Air Force.'

Further family and friend acknowledgements go to Doug Seagrim, who also provided information on Roy Brown; to Bill Campbell, who inquired about his father Ewan. Don Cumming, East Pennant, NS, for HWM Cumming. Mrs. Mary Varill, of London, England, and her brother John Dawson of Victoria, BC, regards news about their father FGT Dawson. Tony Delamere on his uncle Rudolf. Son Windy Geale of Nowra, Australia, told about his dad CN Geale. Brian Pettit, Nanaimo, BC, on CRR Hickey. Bill Hughes, Victoria BC, on uncle Robbie RNAS/RFC. Joe MacBrien of Mississauga provided for his friend JH Keens. Robin Leckie of Ottawa, son of Air Marshal Bob Leckie. Daughter Betty Stewart, Brockville ON, on her life saving father GK Lucas. Bill Mulock happily shared the family album of Great Uncle Redford, named in 2010 to the Canadian Aviation Hall of Fame. Douglas Munn sent fascinating photographs of his flying boat grandfather James. John Pendergast, Calgary, for WK Pendergast. Wayne Robinson had all the files on his grandfather WE Robinson. Douglas Salter, Ottawa, for background on his POW father HP Salter. Arthur E. Jones, Waterloo ON, for in-law JI Sanderson; and Bill Windrum of Vancouver on his dad William. Mike Fall of Nanaimo took me to visit the humble gravesite of his father Joe and provided poignant detail on this great Canadian.

The Canadian Navy's Air Branch veterans helped in so many subtle and indirect ways providing assistance about our naval air forefathers: Ted Cruddas, who edits the group's annual newsletter, Rod Bays and Ralph Fisher, always urbane with their encouragements, as is Rolfe Monteith. Dave Bayne is a literal scrounger and so too is Jack Ford, for his volumes of the Canada Gazette 1914-1919. Then there is George Plawski, who 'opens the hangar deck hatches' with an annual RCN mess dinner. Bob Drader, Bob Murray, Scottie Grant, Glen Cook, Dave Tate and Ed L'Heureux – Volunteers all at the National Air Museum in Ottawa. From the Canadian Naval Air Group: Paul Baiden, Bud MacLean, Al Whalley, Chip Milson, and Stu Soward, himself an author of books on naval air. At Nova Scotia's Shearwater Air Museum: Ted Keiser, Ken Millar, and Base Commander Colonel Sam Micheaud, who marvelously represents our modern generation of naval airmen. Former RCN pilot, Dr. Peter Lawson of Halifax, provided an initial military content proofread. Any errors remaining are absolutely mine alone and I'll be expressing deep regret and standing a round for any of this paragraph's 'Nazal Radiators' whose names I've missed. (That statement could be costly). The Canadian Navy's Jack Arrowsmith, Bill Farrell and Gord Moyer, have passed beyond a proper thanks on this earth. Their contributions are, one hopes, properly enshrined in these pages.

Other assists were made by Ray Pollard of Guelph, whose father 'Polly' was an RNAS photographer during the Gallipoli campaign. Ray most kindly made these albums available as a resource. Paul Donnellan, Isle of Wight, discovered a Bembridge photo collection at a 'car boot' sale and shared same. Jon Straw for his 'collections'. Peter Pigott, yet another author; as is Stewart Taylor, a *Cross & Cockade* Journal contributor. From the Air Force Heritage and History in Winnipeg: Brendan Bond, Don Pearson, and Leo Pettipas. In Ottawa, Michael Whitby, Senior Naval Historian, Directorate of History and Heritage. Also in the capital city, the Ottawa Chapter of the Canadian Aviation Historical Society: Timothy Dube and Hugh Halliday who are professional military archivists and unrepentant boosters and encouragers of all matters relating to Canada's 100-plus years of flight.

To publicly acknowledge and gratefully thank contributing Museums, I'm taking the liberty of adding their website addresses; reason being that ALL museums are underfunded and most have charitable tax status. Might I be even more liberal (or cheeky) in suggesting to readers that such institutions heartily deserve both volunteer energies and financial support.

West to East, here are but a few of these keepers of our aviation heritage starting from the hometown of Raymond Collishaw. The Vancouver Island Military Museum, Nanaimo, is one of Canada's lesser-known military archival sites but it is a gem of a resource. Thanks for all the sheer kindnesses to Chairman Roger Bird, and the late Ted Brothers. **vimm@nanaimo.ark.com/**

The Comox Air Force Museum, CFB Comox, houses one of the finest aviation libraries in Canada.
www.comoxairforcemuseum.ca/

Also on Vancouver Island, The BC Aviation Museum: appreciations to Jeff Phillips. **www.bcam.net/**

The Bomber Command Museum of Canada, honouring the memory of over 10,000 airmen lost during the Second World War is located and operated in the tiny Prairie town of Nanton, Alberta.
www.lancastermuseum.ca/

The Canadian Aviation Hall of Fame, Wetaskiwin Alberta carries out a formal national recognition of airmen and women who have 'Led the Way.' I thank Curator David Crone and Volunteers John Chalmers, Rosella Bjornson and Bill Pratt. **www.cahf.ca/**

Edmonton is a city fortunate to have a downtown commercial airfield. One of the historic RCAF hangars now houses the Alberta Aviation Museum and supports 504 Squadron, Royal Canadian Air Cadets. **www.albertaaviationmuseum.com/**

The Tiger Boys at the Guelph, Ontario, airstrip have a most eclectic collection of unique early flying machines. Tom Dietrich and Bob Revell truly 'Keep Them Flying.' **www.tigerboys.com/**

Guelph is also the birthplace museum of Colonel John McCrae, who penned the poppy poem 'In Flanders Fields.' A few miles east, the Great War Flying Museum in Brampton, builds, maintains, and most importantly flies reproduction First World War aircraft. Appreciations to Chairman and Pilot, Air Canada Captain Richard Sowden, and to the more grounded David Steel, a stealth finder of RNAS facts, assisted I'm told by Darcy the curious cat. **www.greatwarflyingmuseum.com/**

In Toronto the Royal Canadian Military Institute has a superb reference library. Bless you, Honourary Librarian Arthur Manvell, for years of assistance. An item of interest in this military club is the seat from Manfred von Richthofen's red Fokker Triplane together with an iron cross fabric patch stripped from his wing and signed by the pilots of 209 Squadron on 21 April 1918. **www.rcmi.org/**

Eastbound along the shore of Lake Ontario is Canadian Forces Base Trenton and the National Air Force Museum of Canada. Director Chris Coulton has a brilliant restoration Team.
www.airforcemuseum.ca/

The Canadian Aviation and Space Museum, in Ottawa, contains the Harry E. Creagen Collection on First World Aviators and much, much more in their Archives—Not to mention Canada's most outstanding aircraft art collection—and then there are the aircraft... Thank you Stephen Quick and Marc Ducharme. **www.aviation.technomuses.ca/**

Across the Ottawa River in Gatineau, Quebec, is Vintage Wings of Canada. Among their flying aircraft is a Fleet Air Arm Corsair in the colours of Lt. Robert Hampton Gray, RCNVR, last Canadian to win the Victoria Cross. **www.vintagewings.ca/**

Shearwater Aviation Museum, Nova Scotia, is the bedrock for Canadian Naval Air: The Chairman, Rear Admiral Gord Edwards, along with Kay Collacutt, Christine Hines; Christine Dunphy, Historian Ernie Cable, all deserve recognition. Currently the Museum's Restoration Team is heavily involved in making a Fairey Firefly airworthy. **www.shearwateraviationmuseum.ns.ca**

Overseas the Royal Navy's Fleet Air Arm Museum at RNAS Yeovilton, England, harbours Europe's largest Naval Aviation collection. Commander David Hobbs, Jan Keohane, Catherine Cooper and the late Duncan Black provided kindness and hospitality when my wife Cynthia and I scoured their files many years ago. Today Barbara Gilbert and Susan Dearing continue this welcoming tradition.

http://www.fleetairarm.com

PHOTO CREDITS

Schools attended by the RNAS lads were exceedingly kind in permitting ready access to files of their former students. I specifically wish to thank the archivist(s) of Upper Canada College; the University of Toronto, and Queen's University.

Also the Special Collections and Archives, Wright State University, Dayton, Ohio was a source for photographs from their William H. Chisam holdngs

As the book came to a close I despaired of not having enough images of the Naval Aviators. One appreciates the stories of these lads most when a visage looks back from the page. My sister-in-law, Sallie Stuart, has been a resource par excellence for finding esoteric information on the internet and she discovered that the Royal Aeronautical Club had recently made available early pilot certificates, containing the photographs of aviators, through the Ancestery.com website. Thus it is that the RAeC Trust provides an eye-to-eye contact with our past. Thank you Sallie, and also Andrew Dawrant of the Trust. **www.royalaeroclubtrust.org**

On the subject of the Internet, please note the work being done by Ms. Marika Pirie who is cataloging and retouching photographs for the Canadian Virtual War Memorial, an online database covering wartime deaths. She is also a contributor to the Canadian Great War Project that is working towards a database and photo entry for every serviceman. Volunteers add the names and images.

Since this book layout is in a 'yearbook' like format, space for photo captions is limited. The aviator description is in name and initials only; the source, 'Courtesy of', is shortened as follows:

CAHF – Canadian Aviation Hall of Fame

CB of C – *Letters From the Front,* Canadian Bank of Commerce publication, 1920

Comox – CFB Comox Air Force Museum

CVWM – Canadian Virtual War Memorial, Marika Pirie **www.virtualmemorial.gc.ca/**

DND – Department of National Defense

FAAM – Fleet Air Arm Museum, Yeovilton

GWFM – Great War Flying Museum

MHR – *McGill Honour Roll, 1914–1918,* publication, 1926

PRO – Public Records Office Kew, London, England

Queen's – Queen's University Archives, Kingston, ON: **http://archives.queensu.ca/Exhibits.html**

RAeC – The Royal Aeronautical Club Trust

UCC – Upper Canada College, Toronto

UofT – University of Toronto

VIMM – Vancouver Island Military Museum

WSU – Special Collections and Archives, Wright State University, Dayton, Ohio

RE, A and e-numbered – Library and Archives Canada

Other Contributors are shown as: Delamere Family/Tony Delamere,Paul Donnellan, Windy Gaele, Bill Mulock, Mary Varill, Wayne Robinson, Douglas Munn, Ray Pollard and Mike Fall

EXAMPLE OF AN EXTRACT FROM THE PUBLIC RECORDS OFFICE:
ADM/273 RNAS OFFICERS 1914 TO APRIL 1918
THIS IS FILE NUMBER 37814: COLLISHAW

SQUADRON COMMANDER RAYMOND COLLISHAW

1916

10Jan16	Entry into the Air Service as Probationary Flight SubLieut. RCN to RNAS Redcar. Graduated FSLt – 13Jul16
14Jul16	Accident to Avro 1487 owing to forced landing. Pilot sustained cut lip & shock.
16Jul16	Eastchurch Gunnery School
02Aug16	No. 3 Wing Manstone; to France

1917

01Jan17	Report: Ability to command Very Good Indeed being steady & reliable pilot. Has shown great resource as a fighter pilot. Recommended for promotion.
01Feb17	Dunkirk – Sick – Frostbite
26Apr17	No. 10 Naval Rank: A/FLt - 03Jun17; FLt – 30Jun17; A/FCdr - 02Jul17
27Apr17	Insignia of Croix de Guerre with Star conferred by France.
15Jun17	DSC Awarded for displaying great gallantry & skill in all his combats. From June 1st to 6th he shot down in flames 5 Albatross enemy M/C's, & killed the Pilot of another. C-in-C France.
30Jun17	Report: Exceptionally capable Flight Commander with exceptional ability to command and organize.
07Jul17	DSO – For conspicuous skill in leading attacks against hostile aircraft.
03Aug17	Canada Leave Reverted in rank to FLt while on Leave.

VIMM

R Collishaw, August 1917

Report: In my opinion this Officer is quite capable of running a Squadron, and I strongly recommend him for early promotion to Acting Squadron Cdr. FLt Collishaw has been on active service for a long time and he thoroughly deserves a few weeks leave. B. Bell, CO 10 Naval.

Report: Has performed exceptionally good work during the last three months and is an Officer of exceptional skill, courage & ability. It is submitted that this Officer be granted three months leave with permission to visit Canada. C.L. Lambe, Wing Captain. Dunkirk.

29Nov17	Seaplane Defence Flight Dunkirk (later 13 Naval). Rank: A/FCdr – 29Nov17; FCdr - 31Dec17.

1918

01Jan18	Report: Invaluable experience. Great command & capable organizer. Marvellous fighting Pilot whose energy never tires.
02Jan18	Promoted to Acting Squadron Commander.
17Apr18	Recommended for promotion to Squadron Commander by G.O.C. 7th Brigade, Royal Air Force.

Air Vice Marshal Raymond Collishaw, CB, DSO & Bar, OBE, DSC, DFC
Royal Air Force (Retired)
22 November 1893 – 28 September 1976

During the last two decades of his life, Retired Air Vice Marshal Raymond Collishaw developed a keen interest on research of First World War aviators. In a 28 November 1964 letter to the (then) Royal Canadian Air Force Historical Section, he wrote:

"I think you will agree that it is very difficult to create an interesting story when the materiel to be dealt with is confined to bare-bone official facts. It seems to me that these historic stories could be improved, so as to capture the average readers interest, by the introduction of some elements of a character study."

In his Biography 'Air Command', Collishaw states.

"At the outbreak of the war Canada had no air service. There was not a single aerodrome in the country and no flying schools. Canadians themselves were doing very little flying and there was no aircraft manufacturing industry in the Dominion.

"Canadians were enthusiastic about aviation but were spectators rather than participants. If they wanted to buy an aircraft or learn to fly they had to do so outside of their own country. In view of these conditions and the country's limited population Canada contributed in a remarkable degree to the war in the air. Accurate figures are impossible to determine but it would seem that of all the RNAS, RFC and RAF airmen who flew against the enemy between 15 and 20 percent were Canadians."

"I have always been very conscious of being a Canadian and I feel that my countrymen should look back with a great deal of pride on the part played by Canadian flyers in the First World War. Their accomplishments form a part of our national heritage and should never be forgotten. At the same time I must acknowledge that many attempts have been made to gild the lily and that a tremendous amount of sheer bilge has appeared in print since the end of the First World War concerning Canadian flyers."

In an interview with the national newspaper's *Weekend Magazine* in 1966 he said:

"The truth of the matter is there were some excellent pilots and some indifferent pilots."

In keeping with Air Vice Marshal Collishaw's writings and words, here then are all of Canada's Naval Airmen 1914 – 1918 ...

Courtesy of Fleet Air Arm Museum, 2000/0065/0035

'STARTING OFF'
A Nieuport Scout (Fighter) at Breguet

Each aeroplane has a crew of three:
> the Pilot,
> the Fitter (Engine Mechanic)
> and the Rigger (Airframe Technician)

PROLOGUE

1867 to JULY 1914

The years from Canadian Confederation up to the opening of the First World War are a time of innovation and growth unlike any other period in history. Among the events, the world's most powerful armed force, the British Royal Navy, modernizes; man finally achieves his dream to fly; and the new Dominion of Canada matures towards nationhood. In this trilogy of events, the future and the fate of Nine Hundred and Forty-three young Canadian lads is cast.

16Feb1873 – Arthur John O'REILLY (Victoria) – Date of Birth

Born this day in the capital of British Columbia, O'Reilly will be over forty years of age when the First World War erupts. Nevertheless, having grown up in the glory days of the British Empire, and having served in the Royal Navy as a young man, O'Reilly will be determined to re-enter. In doing so he will become the oldest Canadian to fly with the Royal Naval Air Service.

O'Reilly's birth year is the approximate mid-point of one hundred years of 'Pax Britannia', a relatively international war-free period enforced by the British Royal Navy after the defeat of Napoleon at Waterloo. Sending in a battleship or transporting an Army regiment to the scene of a problem easily controls small bush-fire conflicts. One such example is the American Fenian Raids into Canada that are put down by British Army regulars assisted by local volunteer militias. This leads to the northern country becoming a self-governing Dominion in 1867 and promotes the myth that Canada can protect itself with militia units. These volunteer groups are more a community-based social organization and camaraderie of chums than a fearsome force, however they are considered the country's military might. Many of the militias affiliate with British Regiments, taking great pride in wearing the tartans or the redcoat uniforms of the old country at annual parades.

At the time of the 1867 Confederation, Canada has the world's fourth-largest merchant marine. But during the years following, the new Dominion invests and grows internally rather than externally, building railways from sea to sea. These are the great years of Queen Victoria and although Canadians consider the Royal Navy as 'Our Navy', very few join. When young boys from middle-class families such as O'Reilly's grow out of infant dresses they are often clothed in sailor suits. It will take the opening of a major war in August 1914 for Canadians to put on real naval uniforms. *(Read 29Jul15)*

05Jan1893 – John Edward 'Jack' COLLISHAW and Sarah 'Sadie' JONES
(Wales – USA – Canada) – Marriage

Both Welsh speakers, Jack and Sadie marry after having met in Oakland, California. Born in Wrexham, Wales, the son of an innkeeper, Jack was a coal miner who entered the United States via Ellis Island. Sadie, one of a family of eleven children, came from Newport, Monmouthshire, and had immigrated with two of her sisters to America.

Together with the sisters, the young couple travel north to Canada and take on a small farm near Vancouver, British Columbia. By all accounts from their letters home to Wales, flooding plagues the low-lying lands. They uproot and moved to Nanaimo, also known as 'Coal Town,' on Vancouver

Island. There, on the 22nd of November 1893, **Raymond 'Ray' Collishaw** is born. He will become the best-known Naval Airman of the First World War and will attain the rank of Air Vice Marshal with the Royal Air Force during the Second World War.

Raymond is the first of a family that will expand to four brothers and two sisters. His mother Sadie had to leave a son behind with her parents in Wales and she keeps her Canadian children aware of their elder half-brother. Raymond's father Jack is a bit of a dreamer with a restless nature and as a result, travels for extended periods. Having panned for gold in California, and prospected in the Klondike, Jack will die during the early 1920's in the Western Australia gold fields. Son Raymond inherits both his mother's sense of responsibility and his father's spirit of adventure.

At age 15, Ray joins the Canadian Fisheries Protection Services as a cabin boy. In response to American poaching in Canadian fishing waters and the Royal Navy's refusal to 'send in a gunboat', Ottawa has built up a specialized maritime militia. This is the line from which a Canadian Navy will eventually surface – or, as one naval historian quips: 'It all began with fish & ships.' By 1914, Raymond Collishaw, after working his way up the ladder to First Officer, has earned his shipmaster's papers. Tellingly, in the opening paragraph of his autobiography, *Air Command*, he remarks that had it not been for the First World War: "I might have become the captain of the *Queen Elizabeth*. On the other hand I might have ended up skippering a tugboat hauling sawdust or lumber barges…" *(Read 28Apr17)*

16Jun1900 – James Edwin JACKSON (Port Perry ON) – Date of Birth

Jackson will be the youngest Canadian to join the RNAS. Leaving his Ontario home in January 1918, he will travel to England and train initially with the Royal Navy at the Greenwich Officer's College before moving on to flying training. On the first of April 1918, the RNAS is integrated with the British Army's Royal Flying Corps to create the Royal Air Force. When Jackson graduates from flight school he is commissioned into this new service as a Second Lieutenant and will complete his War with 28 Squadron, RAF, operating Sopwith Camels on the Italian and Adriatic Front.

Although Jackson's military aviating is less than eighteen years away, at the time of his birth, powered flight, much less in such sophisticated machines as the Sopwith Camels, is unimaginable. The British Empire is presently embroiled in a situation in South Africa against the Boers, a conflict fought with cavalry and cannon. A scant few observation balloons are utilized but that is the extent of any long-range aeronautical conception.

17Dec03 – First Flight – Orville & Wilbur Wright

The world's first heavier-than-air human flight is achieved by the Wright Brothers at Kitty Hawk, North Carolina. Bicycle mechanics Wilbur (1867-1912) and Orville (1871-1948) make four separate and very brief flights. Taking turns operating with Orville going first, they are acknowledged as the inventors of the first successful flying machine.

The brothers fly intermittently for two years following these inaugural hops and then retire to patent their invention. In 1908 they will begin to fly again and at the same time initiate litigation against anyone who infringes upon 'their' creation – the aeroplane, and in particular, the longitudinal control known as wing warping – the ability to turn an aircraft in flight. These legal battles will not only hamper the development of aviation in the United States, but will contribute to that nation's woeful lack of preparedness when they enter the Great War in 1917.

For Canada, the dawn of aviation will arrive six years after the Wright Brother's first flight when Douglas McCurdy flies at Baddeck, Nova Scotia, during 1909. Yet, it will be a further six years before flying truly becomes a force in the Dominion. Driven by the British Empire's need for aircraft and aviators in a world war, young Canadians will flock to join the Royal Naval Air Service and the Royal Flying Corps in 1915. The demand on manufacturing and services that this creates will play a pivotal role in both the establishment of an aircraft industry in Canada and in the expansion of flying training throughout North America. Meanwhile, during these years, the Royal Navy is modernizing.

1905 – Royal Navy First Sea Lord – Admiral 'Jackie' Fisher

The overall command and control of the Royal Navy is vested in the Admiralty, a hierarchy composed of The First Lord, a civilian and member of the House of Parliament, and six Sea Lords, or Admirals. Admiral Fisher is now the senior Admiral in this group known throughout the Navy as 'Their Lordships'.

This is the year that witnesses end of the Russo-Japanese War. At Tsushima, in the strait between Korea and Japan, the first modern-day clash of ironclads is won by a small island nation against the world's largest land empire. The Imperial Japanese Navy, whose modern ships are equipped with large caliber guns, is well led, and the officers and sailors respect and trust one another. In contrast, the Russian Navy, with older vessels and smaller weapons, is officered by noblemen's sons ignorant of their men. The Tsushima Battle is won by dignity and strength and lost through stupidity and frailty.

It has been one hundred years since Lord Nelson's victory at Trafalgar and this latest battle serves to confirm beliefs held by senior sailors about the 'romance' of war at sea. But Admiral Fisher, a maverick in a Victorian-thinking Navy, recognizes the realities of a modern war on the water. He decommissions scores of obsolete ships and encourages the development of HMS *Dreadnought*. When launched in late 1906, this first new 'big-gun' battleship outclasses the existing ships of all other navies. An arms race ensues led by a German Kaiser anxious to build a dominant surface fleet for a yet-to-be-created overseas empire.

1907 – Mother of Canadian Aviation – Mabel Bell

The inventor of the telephone, Dr. Alexander Graham Bell, has become fascinated with aviation and determines to build an engine-powered kite capable of lifting a man. Needing help to realize this dream, Bell is encouraged by his wife Mabel to find additional enthusiasts. During the summer, he recruits Douglas McCurdy, an engineer who had grown up on Bell's estate in Cape Breton, Nova Scotia. One of McCurdy's fellow classmates from the University of Toronto, Frederick 'Casey' Baldwin, is also invited along.

With his high-level contacts, Bell asks American President Teddy Roosevelt for Lieutenant Thomas Selfridge, an officer with an interest in powered flight, to be seconded to the project as an official observer for the U.S. Army. Another American, Glenn Curtiss, a self-made designer, builder, and racer of motorcycles, joins the team as an engine expert. "He has only to look at the engine to get it to run well," Bell wrote in admiration.

The 59-year-old Bell also writes: "So, there we were, living in my house, myself, an elderly man, surrounded by brilliant young men, each an expert in his own line. We became very friendly. My wife became very much attracted to them all. She suggested that we form an association…" Mabel Bell, recently the beneficiary of a sizeable inheritance, offers $20,000 to finance the goal of building a practical flying machine. (One hundred years later this amount of money would be valued at over $400,000). On the first of October 1907, the Aerial Experiment Association (AEA) is established for one year. The men travel to the Glen Curtiss factory at Hammondsport in New York State. There, Bell directs each of the four AEA members to design an individual aircraft:

• March 1908 – *Red Wing* – by Selfridge

Casey Baldwin becomes the first Canadian to fly when he lifts Selfridge's *Red Wing* into the air off the frozen surface of Lake Keuka, near Hammondsport. This initial effort by the Association is important, as it is the first open demonstration of flight. After the relative secrecy of the Wright

Brothers, the general public is finally shown that the dream of powered flight has become a reality. The red-silk-covered aircraft crashes without pilot injury a few days later. The failure was the result of a lack of a means of turning.

• May 1908 – *White Wing* – by Baldwin

Each member of the Association takes a turn to fly this second successful effort. *White Wing* has two unique innovations: the body is mounted on a tricycle undercarriage rather than sled runners; and, triangular hinged-flaps are located at the tips of the wings to assist longitudinal control. It will be claimed that this aileron device was inspired by Bell and perfected by the AEA but the actual inventor will remain in dispute throughout history.

• June 1908 – *June Bug* – by Curtiss

June Bug flies during the month for which it is named but it is in the following month that the aircraft achieves a lasting legacy. The AEA enters *June Bug* in the Scientific American Trophy competition for the first successful public straight-line flight of one kilometer. At Hammondsport on July 4, pilot Curtiss wins the prestigious cup, exceeding the goal by more than half.

The Aero Club of America had invited the Wright Brothers to compete and had offered to allow them time to enter. However the Wrights refused. They would have had to mount wheels on their aircraft and count on having a field open enough for the Trophy requirement of an unassisted takeoff.

The Wrights do however, put Curtiss on notice that they did not issue permission for the use of 'their' control system for exhibitions or commercial purposes. Litigation is in the air.

17Sep08 – First Aviation Passenger Death – Lt Thomas Selfridge

At Fort Meyer, Virginia, Selfridge is tragically killed in a crash while riding aboard an aircraft flown by Orville Wright. The machine impacts just a few hundred feet from Arlington National Cemetery where Selfridge will be buried with full military honors. Becoming the first passenger fatality in an aircraft accident is a grim distinction for the young Army officer. It remains a question whether his loss also means an end to any chance of a more amiable relationship with the Wright Brothers.

The Aerial Experiment Association is devastated by the death of their friend. Regrouping, they resolve to continue the work for a further six months. Mabel Bell unstintingly contributes an extra ten thousand dollars.

• Dec 1908 – *Silver Dart* – by McCurdy

McCurdy writes to Mabel Bell: "The surfaces are silvered on one side, that suggested the 'Silver', and the word 'Dart' will explain itself … She certainly is a beauty."

During the summer at the Hammondsport, the AEA had assisted with the building of a Curtiss-engined dirigible for the American military. The gasbag, designated the SC-1, is the US Army's first powered lighter-than-air craft. Excess rubberized silk from the project becomes the fabric for the wings of McCurdy's aeroplane design. Following several successful test flights, the proven *Silver Dart* is dismantled and shipped to Nova Scotia for a Canadian debut.

23Feb09 – First Flight In Canada
– John Alexander Douglas McCurdy

Alexander Graham Bell chose the 'open ice and steady winds' of Baddeck, Nova Scotia, for this epic event. The AEA, known locally as 'Bell's Boys' have reassembled the *Silver Dart* and today the weather is perfect. McCurdy surveys the aircraft while Curtiss checks the engine.

In what has been described as the quintessential Canadian winter setting, 22-year-old McCurdy soars off the ice and into the skies. Forty years later, McCurdy, now the Lieutenant-Governor of Nova Scotia, will recall:

> "With an extra special snort from the motor, we scooted off down the ice. Behind came a crowd of small boys and men on their skates, most of them still doubtful I would fly.

> "With a lurch and a mighty straining of wires we were in the air. It was amusing to look back and watch the skaters. They seemed to be going in every direction, bumping into each other in their excitement at seeing a man actually fly."

McCurdy executes a wide, shimmering arc across the blue sky, returning to the spot from whence he launched. He describes the experience as: "just like being on a high after a couple of shots of whisky", and he wants to repeat the event three or four more times. But Alexander Graham Bell, aware of the significance of the flight, decides that it is sufficient for the day to *not* tempt fate. His protégé McCurdy has just completed the first powered, heavier-than-air, controlled flight by a British subject in Canada and the Empire. A celebration is called for and Bell invites everyone, including the school children and local citizens who had come to watch, back to his mansion *Beinn Bhreagh*. In succeeding days, McCurdy will fly his design more than eight miles at a stretch, a remarkable occurrence in the Americas of 1909.

At the end of March, the Aerial Experiment Association will bring their work to a close. Bell wants to keep his Canadian-American team together, but Glen Curtiss is anxious to strike out on his own. In France during the summer, Curtiss competes against Europe's top aviators of the day and wins the Gordon Bennett cup for flying the fastest speed. He returns to the United States to build his aircraft manufacturing business and to deal with a patent infringement lawsuit launched against him by the Wright Brothers.

McCurdy and Baldwin will go on to form Canada's first aviation business, the Canadian Aerodrome Company, at Baddeck. Hoping to sell aircraft to the Canadian Army, they crash during a demonstration at Camp Petawawa in Ontario and the military demurs. A Parliamentary cabinet minister calls it 'The work of the devil.' Canada's aircraft industry will not take off until the First World War.

25Jul09 – First Flight across the English Channel – Louis Bleriot

The *London Daily Mail* offered a £1000 prize to the first aviator to fly across the English Channel. Now Frenchman Bleriot succeeds and the public is absolutely delighted by the accomplishment. However, the Admiralty is in shock and horror. Apparent that Britain is 'no longer an island,' the Royal Navy recognizes a need for powered flight to continue their historic role as defenders of the realm. Previously the navy had experimented with man-lifting kites simply as a way to assist a ship's over-the horizon capabilities.

The Admiralty invests in the construction of dirigible airships but the first prototype is back-broken in a wind gust and never becomes operational. When an English gentleman arranges the loan of two aircraft to train Naval Officers as aviators the RN is truly set on the path to becoming an airborne force.

04May10 – Royal Canadian Navy – Rear Admiral Charles Kingsmill

On this day, the Canadian Parliament formally authorizes the Naval Service of Canada. Two political schools of thought have clashed over this issue: The Conservatives feel that Canada should remain a partner with Britain and provide men and money as an Imperial Defense contribution. The Liberals believe that military spending must benefit the country, and that Canada must raise and equip her own forces for her own purposes. This latter view is in direct contradiction to the British Empire's Imperial Foreign policy. However, the Liberals are in power and under the leadership of Prime Minister Wilfrid Laurier, they advance their agenda for the creation of what will receive the King's assent to be called the Royal Canadian Navy.

At the behest of Laurier, Rear Admiral Charles Kingsmill of Guelph, Ontario, having spent a career with the Royal Navy, accepts an appointment as Director of the new Canadian Service. Kingsmill will lead for eleven years and will guide and grow the nascent Navy through a global conflict. One unanticipated task for the Admiral will be the selection of aviators for that War.

23Apr11 – William 'Bill' TEMPLETON (Vancouver) – Aviator

Together with a brother and a cousin, Templeton designs and builds a Curtiss-type biplane in British Columbia. The trio moves their creation from a basement workshop to Minoru Park on Lulu Island, south of the city of Vancouver, where Bill successfully flies the machine.

In 1915, Templeton will become one of a new breed of naval officers—an aviator—when Admiral Kingsmill accepts him as a Candidate for the Royal Navy Air Service. *(Read 1929)*

October 1911 – First Lord of the Admiralty – Winston Churchill

Appointed to the Royal Navy's highest position, the young and energetic Churchill more than rises to occasion. Once a parliamentary non-believer in the costs of armaments, he becomes an absolute advocate after the Germans send a gunboat to the Moroccan port of Agadir in a display of force. Recognizing the threat to British naval supremacy, Churchill carries on with the program of modernization begun by Admiral Fisher. Indeed, he eventually brings the old Admiral out of retirement to resume the post of First Sea Lord. Churchill also conducts a complete reorganization of the Navy into four fleets; three for home waters and a fourth based in Gibraltar to work with the French Mediterranean Fleet. He recognizes the importance of oil versus coal as fuel and that the vital links to the Persian petroleum fields through the Suez Canal must be protected.

By 1912, a Royal Flying Corps is formed with a Naval Wing and a Military (Army) Wing. Interested in all things new, Churchill is a strong proponent of using aircraft and undertakes flying lessons. An enthusiastic but not in any way a natural pilot, he finally bows to the wishes of his family and friends to cease and desist. He will remain keenly involved—but safely for all concerned—on the ground.

The two Wings of the RFC hold distinct differences on several levels. Philosophically, the Military Wing views aircraft as simply a standby method of reconnaissance, an adjunct to their prized troops of cavalry. They focus on slow and stable aircraft for this purpose, a decision that will cost hundreds of young lives in the realities of aerial combat. The Navy, from the outset, sees aviation as a means of carrying the fight to the enemy; in other words, an offensive weapon. Through the past decade of Fleet modernization, the Navy is also much more technologically developed in mind and machinery than is the Army.

Another disparity is seen with regards to personnel. The Military Wing recruits their pilots from various British Army battalions. These appointments are regarded as temporary postings with the individual expecting to return to his regiment in due course. The first leaders of the military wing are also fairly bureaucratic and staff-minded. The Naval Wing, on the other hand, consists of, in part, some individuals who ship's captains are perhaps quite happy to disembark. However, the new and outgoing First Lord, Churchill, happily views his aviators as being fellow adventurers: "What is wanted for this dangerous service is a young gentleman and a good animal."

Not surprisingly, the Navy and Military Wings soon go their separate ways and the Royal Naval Air Service (RNAS) is formally named in July 1914. Older Victorian-era naval officers claim that RNAS means Really Not A Sailor: the young Edwardian-era-raised pilots counter that the initials stand for Rather Naughty After Sunset.

WRIGHT AVIATION SCHOOL, DAYTON OHIO, JUNE 1915

The first Canadian 'Candidates' to join the RNAS and the RFC in 1915 had to have an official Federation Aeronautique International Pilot Certificate in order to be accepted into the services. With only one flying school in Canada, the United States of America trained the bulk of these early applicants.

The flight establishments were: The Wright Schools in Dayton, Ohio, Minneola and Hempstead Plains in New York State, as well as Augusta, Georgia. Curtiss Schools operated in Newport News, Virginia, and Buffalo NY. The Stinston sisters ran a school in San Antonio, Texas, and the Thomas brothers operated in Ithaca, NY. On the California West Coast, Martin in Griffith Park, Burns of Los Angeles and Christofferson at Alameda.

This photograph is of the first class at the Wright School in Dayton. Unfortunately names are not noted,however, many of the faces look familiar from RNAS photographs; those most readily identified are:

L to R standing rear row, 2nd and 3rd are ST Edwards and AR Brown. 6th is LS Breadner and the two Magor brothers are at the far right-hand side.

In the center row: 2nd 3rd, 4th, and 5th are JA Shaw, WH Chisam, WJ Sussan, and BD Hobbs; 9th is DMB Galbraith.

Front row: 3rd is WE Robinson.

Also in this photo are other RNAS graduates of the school at this time. In the order of their American Aeronautical Certificate (AAeC) Number they are: JM Alexander (335), WB Evans (339), GH Simpson (346), GF Ross (347), KG Macdonald (348), PE Beasley (349), KF Saunders (353), AG Woodward (357), JO Galpin (364), JL Gordon (366), PS Kennedy (383), RM Weir (386), C McNicoll (398), JR Bibby (403), TC Wilkinson (414), JG Ireland (415), AH Pearce (416), and G. Breadner (417).

CHAPTER 1

AUGUST 1914 – DECEMBER 1915

CANDIDATES & PROBATIONARIES

On August 4th, Britain declares war with Germany. One month beforehand a Serbian nationalist shot and killed the heir to the Austro-Hungarian Empire at Sarajevo. This 'damned foolish thing' in the Balkans sets a world conflict in motion through a domino-like chain reaction of alliances and mobilizations.

The British have pledged to uphold Belgian neutrality and this is now compromised by German troops advancing through that small nation to attack France. Canada, a self-governing colony of the British Empire, is immediately embroiled in the conflict. When new Conservative Prime Minister Robert Borden offers a Canadian contingent of 25,000 men; Great Britain readily accepts. With a regular army of just 3,000, Canada can claim a volunteer militia of over 60,000.

The Minister of Militia, Colonel Sam Hughes, a bombastic individual, ignores the existing plan for mobilization and conducts an ad-hoc one-man show to raise the promised contingent. Known as the Canadian Expeditionary Force (CEF), this body will eventually grow into a Canadian Corps of four divisions. A fearsome nationalist, Hughes will keep the Canadian troops together as a single force and not allow them to be broken up as reinforcements for British regiments.

Canada's Navy consists of two obsolete vessels, one on each coast. On the Atlantic, HMCS *Niobe* is stationed at Halifax, Nova Scotia. HMCS *Rainbow* operates out of Esquimalt, British Columbia. A month before the declaration of war, this Pacific coast ship had forcefully persuaded the SS *Komagata Maru*, with its load of illegal East Indian immigrants, to leave Vancouver harbour. *Rainbow* now sails more operationally, bravely steaming forth to seek out the German East Asiatic Squadron's SMS *Leipzig* reportedly in their waters. To the good fortune of all aboard, the ancient RCN ship does not encounter the Kaiser's modern cruiser.

Rather than expand the RCN, the British Admiralty and the Conservative government in Ottawa jointly come to a decision that Canadians should be allowed to enter the Royal Navy directly if they wish. Many will do so and Candidates for Royal Naval Air Service will make Canada's biggest naval effort in the 1914-1918 War. Those who join the Royal Navy's surface fleet will learn the Watchkeeping trade and go on to become the leaders of the RCN in the 1939-1945 conflict.

August 1914 figures on the RNAS show a strength of 138 Officers and 589 Ratings. The naval air service operates some 93 aircraft of various types; however, only about 50 are in any kind of a usable condition. The immediate wartime responsibilities for the RNAS are patrols off the east coast of England and over Channel as a British Army Expeditionary Force and the Royal Flying Corps embark for France.

SEPTEMBER 1914

In spite of the chaotic coast-to-coast mobilization caused by the Canadian Minister of Militia, some 32,000 recruits are gathered at a hastily-erected camp near Valcartier, Quebec. The confusion caused by disregard for the regimental cohesion of pre-war militia units only adds to the problem of trying to create soldiers. However, the enthusiastic spirit of the raw human materiel is high and the First Canadian Contingent coalesces thanks to the many former British Army-types who had immigrated to the Dominion and now join the ranks 'for a free visit home'.

A small Canadian Aviation Corps is authorized consisting of two officers and one mechanic. By the end of the month a Burgess-Dunne biplane is purchased from Massachusetts and flown to Quebec City. It is Canada's first military flying machine. In England this month, the first Canadian joins the RNAS:

16Sep14 – Francis Gilmer Tempest DAWSON (Chester NS) – First RNAS Canadian

The initial 'War Batch' of Royal Navy pupils for the Eastbourne Aviation Company School commences training. One member of this class is Dawson from Nova Scotia, he entered as a Probationary Flight Sub-Lieutenant (PFSLt), thus becoming Canada's number one naval aviator.

Nicknamed 'Wuffy', young Dawson was an engineering student at Montreal's McGill University in 1910 when he developed a strong interest in flying. Coming from a prosperous family, he was able to pursue this fascination by entering Cambridge University to study aeronautical

FGT Dawson

Mary Varill

engineering. There, he spent his weekends and summers at Eastchurch, the Royal Aeronautical Club (RAeC), flying field, on the Isle of Sheppy. In collaboration with two other undergraduates, he constructed a biplane glider. Now a wartime navy pilot, Dawson earns RAeC Pilot Certificate Number 937 in October and, based on his previous practical knowledge of flying, is promoted to Flight Lieutenant (FLt). With a total of seven hours solo experience, young Dawson is sent to Number 2 Naval Wing for the Dover Patrol escorting troopships across Channel. Flying out of both Dover and Dunkirk, he will also carry out bombing missions over German gun emplacements on Belgium's coast. In July 1915 Dawson is appointed to the books of HMS *Ark Royal* in the Dardanelles. *(Read 09Jul15)*

At this time, the RNAS operates a three Wing system of aircraft organization. Number 1 Wing, like Dawson's Number 2 is engaged in cross-Channel activities. Number 3 Wing has been dispatched to Antwerp in Belgium. While the front lines are fluid and ever changing, this Wing roves like 20th century pirates, using aircraft and armour-rigged cars to harass the enemy. The Officers and Sailors of the mini-expeditionary force bolt boilerplate to the sides of their vehicles to create a mobile, bullet-proof means of transport. The audacity of the group's creation catches the imagination of Winston Churchill who will expand their novel concept into future battlefield tanks.

On September 22nd, four of 3 Wing's aircraft conduct the first British air raid on Germany by attempting to bomb the Cologne and the Dusseldorf Airship Sheds. This is an effort to dismiss the growing 'Zeppelin Fear' that many English civilians have of skies darkened by German dirigibles. The worry is unfounded, as there are very few Zeppelins in actual operation, but the press has whipped up a public hysteria. Although this first RNAS raid is unsuccessful, a follow-up attack in early October destroys an airship at Dusseldorf. The Zeppelin myth receives its first deflation.

Commander Charles Romney Samson, an Englishman and the first Royal Navy aviator to gain a RAeC Certificate (No. 71), leads 3 Wing. He will figure in many RNAS operations involving Canadians throughout what will become the Great War.

OCTOBER 1914

Despite the lack of an embarkation plan, the Canadian Expeditionary Force has thirty poorly-weight-and-balanced vessels steaming down the St. Lawrence by the first of October. To date, this is the largest convoy to ever sail the Atlantic, and it reaches Plymouth Harbour by mid month. The amateurish lading of ships in Quebec leads to a mountainous mess on the English docks, which takes weeks to clear. Meanwhile, the damp British winter weather commences. Among the items deteriorating dock side is the sole aircraft of the new Canadian Aviation Corps. It will never fly and is soon written off. With no aircraft and few personnel, the tiny aviation corps decommissions.

Stationed on Salisbury Plain for training, the CEF Camp is within eyesight of the ancient rocks of Stonehenge but the view is oft obscured by one of the worst winters in living memory. The troops are housed 'under canvas' in what is described as an appalling environment of rain and mud. They little know that this experience will do much to battle-harden them for much worse ahead in the trenches of Flanders.

In Western Europe, a deadlock begins between the combatant armies. As each tries to outflank the other in a so-called 'race to the sea,' a line of entrenchments is created from the border of Switzerland up through France to the English Channel coastline. A salient around the city of Ypres keeps a tiny part of Belgium on the Allied side of what will be called the Western Front.

Beyond anyone's imagination, Armies will stalemate along the 440-mile zigzag trench line on this Front for the next two years. Killing grounds at Verdun, Loos, and on the Somme will darken spirits and devastate families until the Canadian Victory at Vimy Ridge in early 1917 offers a glimmer of hope.

Meanwhile, in the Channel and the North Sea, the Royal Navy is suffering ship casualties at an alarming rate to a new menace, the German *Unterseeboot* or U-Boat. One vessel, HMS *Hermes*, the RN's only seaplane carrier, is torpedoed and sunk inside the Dover Straits. This submarine threat causes the Royal Navy to wisely settle into a dreary war of long-distance 'watch and wait' blockade against Germany.

Naval prestige also suffers when two modern German cruisers, SMS *Goben* and *Breslau* slip through a Mediterranean gauntlet to Constantinople and bring Turkey into the War. On far distant seas, the German Cruiser *Emden* harasses the Empire in the Pacific until destroyed by the Royal Australian Navy at the Cocos Islands. Another cruiser, *Konigsberg* is creating concerns around Zanzibar; and the *Leipzig* is still haunting the North American West Coast.

01Oct14 – Radio Telegraphist Guy Duncan SMITH (Oakland CA; b. ENG) – *Leipzig*

Working aboard German merchant steamer *Mazattan* out of San Francisco, Telegraphist Smith is told by his Captain to contact the German cruiser *Leipzig*. The *Leipzig* has been harassing British merchant ships traveling up and down the Pacific coast and *Mazattan* is secretly carrying coal for her to rebunker. Smith pretends to transmit but in reality renders the wireless crystals useless. When his ship docks in Mexico, the young radio operator is fortunate to escape with his life. Smith's evidence leads to the capture of *Mazattan* by HMS *Kent* and the arrest of the German Consul in Mexico for non-neutral acts.

In July 1915, Smith will make his way to HMC Dockyard, Esquimalt, British Columbia. There he is interviewed by the RCN Flag Officer, West Coast, and accepted as a Candidate pilot for the RNAS. Smith returns to California and takes flying lessons with the Christofferson Flying School. He is the lead man of over a dozen United States citizens who will enter Canada in order to join the RNAS. *(Read 6May17)*

24Oct14 – Enlisted RNAS Canadians

– Private Frank Lince FETHEWAY, CEF (Vancouver)

Soldiers of the Canadian Expeditionary Forces, drilling on the muddy Salisbury Plain, have began taking a keen interest of the flying machines jousting overhead in the cloudy but clean skies.

A farmer from the Vancouver area of British Columbia, Fetheway becomes the initial enlisted Canadian in the RNAS. He transfers from the CEF and is 'taken on strength' as an Airman First Class, Engineer.

– Alfonse AILLOUD,

A motor circuit mechanic from Montreal enlists in early November and, based on his civilian skills, is given the immediate rank of Petty Officer Mechanic.

It is not within the parameters of this manuscript to include the names of Canadians who served in the ranks of the RNAS. Although rather few, their service records are with the total enlisted naval airmen, Service Numbers F1 to F55,000, held in 86 volumes by the British Public Records Office (File series ADM/188). These records give the date and place of birth, physical description, date of enlistment, rating, ships or stations served, assessment of character and conduct as well as date of discharge. The names of Fetheway and Ailloud come from the first volume of these rolls, the original of which is held by the Royal Navy's Fleet Air Arm Museum at Yeovilton. *(Read Brock, DFM, 01Jan19)*

NOVEMBER 1914

On November 1st, off the coast of Chile, the Royal Navy's West Indies Squadron is lost to the same German East Asia Cruiser Squadron that HMCS *Rainbow* had optimistically set out to engage in August. At this Battle of Coronel, four Canadian Midshipmen completing their 'Big Ship' time with the RN are drowned. One is the Midshipman term's Chief Cadet Captain; all had promising futures in the Canadian Fleet. Their deaths will be avenged in early December when the German Squadron is spotted and sunk by a British battle cruiser fleet at the Falkland Islands.

In France, the RNAS continues to take the fight to the enemy. Shipping new Avro 504 aircraft by railroad to Belfort in Southern France, the machines are assembled and flown across Lake Constance to attack the Friedrichshafen Zeppelin factory sheds. This long-range round-trip mission of 125 miles creates awareness for Germany that security behind her own borders is not assured.

DECEMBER 1914

07Dec14 – Theodore Douglas HALLAM (Toronto)–RNAS Applicant

Hallam had taken flying lessons at the Glen Curtiss School in Hammondsport, New York in early 1914. At the outbreak of the War he cabled both the British Admiralty and the British War Office offering his services as an aviator. Understandably, given the nature of the War's furious beginnings, he received no reply. As with so many others

TD Hallam

RAeC Trust

caught up in patriotic fervor, Hallam was anxious to serve in an adventure that is predicted to be sharp and quick and 'over by Christmas'. He enlisted in the rapidly forming CEF as a Private in the Sifton Machine-Gun Battery and shipped overseas with the First Canadian Contingent. Now in England, Hallam makes a personal application to the Admiralty:

> "I was informed that Colonials were not required, as they made indifferent officers, that the service had all the fliers that they wanted, and besides all this, that I was too old."

Thirty-one years of age and a University of Toronto science graduate, Hallam tries a different tack. In his first attempt he had proudly presented himself at the Admiralty in the ill-fitting uniform of a Private soldier. He applies again in person, this time wearing a well-tailored suit and bearing letters of introduction from important Canadians.

He is duly offered a Commission as a machine-gun Officer with the Royal Navy Volunteer Reserve (RNVR) attached to the RNAS. Believing that this is the right step to get into flying, he accepts. In March of 1915, Sub-Lieutenant Hallam is ordered to duty in Gallipoli. *(Read 04Jun15)*

On Christmas Day, three Royal Navy seaplane carriers launch seven RNAS aircraft against the Cuxhaven shipyards and Zeppelin sheds at the mouth of the Elbe River. These carriers are cross-Channel steamers converted to support seaplanes. They are commissioned as HMS *Empress*, *Engadine* and *Riviera*. The results of this, the world's first ship-borne air strike, is negligible but a new manner of warfare is created—the concept of the Carrier Task Force.

JANUARY 1915

20Jan15 – Corporal Redford Henry MULOCK, CEF (Winnipeg) - DOJ

Mulock is the second Canadian to join the Royal Naval Air Service but it will be a reputation for 'firsts' that dominates his flying. He will be rightfully named Canada's most versatile and experienced airman of the First World War.

Born in Peterborough, Ontario, in 1888, Mulock was raised in Winnipeg, Manitoba. An electrical engineering graduate from McGill University in Montreal, he, like many patriotic Canadians, 'joins the colours' in August 1914. Although holding a Lieutenant's commission in the Militia, in order to get overseas sooner Mulock enlists in the First Contingent of the Canadian Expeditionary Force as a Corporal. Following training with the artillery at Valcartier he shipped out to England in October.

RH Mulock

Bill Mulock, via CAHF

By March 1915, Mulock qualifies and receive his pilot's certificate, RAeC 1103, and his confirmation as a Flight Sub Lieutenant. Initially nicknamed 'Canada', this moniker is soon changed to 'Red' as more Canadians enter naval aviation. Mulock is the first of nearly four hundred CEF Officers and NCOs who will transfer to the RNAS while serving overseas.

In April 1915, German airships begin to carry out raids on southern England. During the night of 16th–17th May, Mulock makes the first interception of a Zeppelin raider over England. Patrolling in an Avro 504 out of Westgate, he discovers LZ.38 casually floating over the Thames at an unusually low altitude of 2,000 feet. Swiveling his peg-mounted Lewis machine gun on target, Mulock opens fire. However, after a couple of

rounds, the weapon jams and, while Mulock struggles to clear the stoppage, the startled dirigible crew dumps ballast and soars aloft to safety. *(Read 08Jul15)*

FEBRUARY 1915

The immobile trenches system of the Western Front is a stark contrast to the mobile Eastern Front where Czarist troops are being routed. To break this situation of impasse/retreat, the Admiralty, chiefly Winston Churchill and his First Sea Lord 'Jackie' Fisher, prepare and mount a naval attack from the Mediterranean at Germany's ally Turkey. Their plan is to bombard the Gallipoli Peninsula, steam through the Dardanelles Straits and capture Constantinople. This strategy, it is considered, will cause the surrender of Turkey and open a supply route to Russia.

HMS *Ark Royal*, a new aircraft carrier is sent along with the attacking fleet. Also, Wing Commander Sampson and his RNAS 3 Wing 'pirates' of Antwerp armoured car notoriety are dispatched to the Eastern Mediterranean.

Forcing the Dardanelles turns into another failure for the Royal Navy. The British Army has to be brought in to take Gallipoli and these soldiers, including Australian, New Zealand and Newfoundland troops, are soon in desperate need of air support.

At this point the Admiralty becomes severely pressed to fulfill three wartime assignments: the Dardanelles campaign, anti-submarine operations, and, the aerial protection of Great Britain. Submarines have grown to be more of a threat than any Admiral could have imagined. Tramp cargo steamers and pristine battleships alike are in peril from German U-boat efforts to blockade the island nation. Additionally, the scant few Zeppelin raids on England have caused widespread panic and a public clamor for protection. With the Army and its Royal Flying Corps completely enmeshed in Flanders, it is up to the RNAS to provide overhead protection. As is usual in such scenarios, more pilots and aircraft are needed yesterday.

Britain is not the only country that suffers from 'Zeppelinitis'. On the 14th of February, a series of unidentified aerial lights are spotted over Ogdensburg, New York, across the St. Lawrence River from Prescott, Ontario. An alarm is sent to Ottawa and all illumination devices in the Canadian Parliament buildings are darkened. It transpires that the 'fire balloons' were part of an American St. Valentines Day celebration but the

Wartime Order for lights out in government buildings will stand throughout the war.

MARCH 1915

17Mar15 – A/SLt John Augustus BARRON, RCN (Stratford ON) – Airships

On this date Barron is one of 20 Acting Sub-Lieutenants lent from the RN to the RNAS as airship pilot trainees. He is the only Canadian in the group.

Barron had joined the Canadian Marine Service in 1908 at the age of 14, and became a Midshipman in the new Royal Canadian Navy when it was formed in 1910.

Appointed to the Royal Navy in 1914, he is already a trained watch-keeper and thus fits the profile required for airship piloting: knowledge of navigation and signaling.

Shortly after graduating from Kingsnorth airship school in May, Barron will operate anti-submarine patrols out of Barrow-in-Furness, Lancashire.

JA Barron

GWFM

Floating over the Irish Sea and the North Channel, he is carried aloft in a BE2c aircraft fuselage that is slung as a gondola below the non-rigid 'Submarine-Scout' airships. Patrols in these SS dirigibles can last for eight hours at speeds only as high as 50 miles-per-hour. *(Read 19Sep16)*

APRIL 1915

Recognizing the acute 'wastage' of men and machines, Churchill minutes the War Council on April 3rd. 'Every effort should be made to reach 1,000 aeroplanes and 300 seaplanes as early as possible before the end of the present year. 400 pilots will be required, and all arrangements should be made to procure and train them.'

In America, Glen Curtiss's interest in aviation has engendered a conglomerate of aircraft and aero-engine companies. Now, like many others, he is being hamstrung by Wright Brothers' lawsuits. Ailerons have taken the place of wing-warping wires but the brothers,

Orville and Wilbur, contend that their original patent covers all means of longitudinal control. Legally however, their 1908 patents have not been filed in Canada and therefore have no standing. To avoid the usury fees being demanded by the Wrights, Curtiss happily sets about manufacturing ailerons north of the border. Employing his former *Silver Dart* associate Douglas McCurdy as his Canadian representative, he opens the Curtiss Aeroplanes and Motors Limited (Toronto) in April 1915. The plant quickly grows beyond ailerons when a British Admiralty Mission to Canada places an immediate order for eighteen aircraft.

The Naval Mission has also come to Ottawa to seek potential pilots. Canadian Prime Minister Robert Borden in concert with the Royal Navy grants Rear Admiral Kingsmill, Chief of Canadian Naval Staff, approval to carry out this recruitment. In brief, volunteers are to be interviewed by Kingsmill in the capital or by his Flag Officers at Halifax and Esquimalt. Applicants deemed suitable are given a medical and the healthy are formally registered with the Admiralty as RNAS 'Candidates'. But herein lies a catch: Candidates must secure flying certificates with their own funds before they will be accepted into the Royal Navy as Chief Petty Officer Pilots. Naval aviators will be obliged to pay rather than accept, the King's shilling.

During this same period, the British Royal Flying Corps begins a separate recruiting program in Canada under much the same terms but offers a commission to 2nd Lieutenant upon certification. The upgrade to officer status causes some Candidates to switch armed-forces loyalties. This is quickly reversed when the Royal Navy initiates a midshipman-style rank for new pilots. Receiving commissions as Probationary Flight Sub Lieutenants, they will complete their probation period upon graduation from 'advanced' flying schools in England.

There is no shortage of Canadian volunteers for the RNAS. By the close of the 1915 Admiral Kingsmill will have accepted hundreds of Candidates—all of whom will need to secure the required Federation Aeronautique Internationale (FAI) flying certificate issued by the Britain's Royal Aeronautical Club (RAeC).

Seeing this accelerating demand for pilots, McCurdy opens the Curtiss Aviation School at Hanlans' Point on Toronto Island. The fee for achieving the FAI certificate is four hundred dollars, about a dollar a minute. The first phase of the training, on Curtiss flying boats, is followed with airfield training on Curtiss JN-3 'Jennies' at Long Branch, a converted rifle range just west of Toronto. These efforts by McCurdy represent three firsts for Canada: the first seaplane base, the first airfield, and the Dominion's first flying school. On May 10th, an initial class of ten students—seven RNAS and three RFC—will begin training, fulfilling the required four hours in 'flying leaps' of ten- to twelve-minute increments.

MAY 1915

07May15 – 2Lt Hugh ALLAN, CEF (Montreal) – *Lusitania*

The Cunard liner *Lusitania* is torpedoed in sight of the south coast of Ireland with a loss of 1,198 lives. For Canadian Expeditionary Force 2nd Lieutenant Allan, the news is heartbreaking: his mother and two sisters are aboard and en route to visit him in England.

Young Hugh, the son of Sir H. Montague Allan of the Allan Ship Line soon learns that his sisters have drowned in the sinking, and that his mother is one of the very few rescued. Now more than anxious to 'do his bit', he will take machine-gun training and then, chafing to get into action, applies to become an RNAS pilot. *(Read 12Jun16)*

H Allan
RAeC Trust

JUNE 1915

04Jun15 – Lt Theodore Douglas HALLAM, RNVR (Toronto) – WIA/DSC

(From 07Dec14) Serving in the Dardanelles with an RNAS Armored Car Unit, Hallam is Wounded in Action and invalided back to England. He has distinguished himself while in charge of two machine-guns at an important forward position. For six days, he and his men continuously repelled all attempts by Turkish troops to overrun them. In Hallam's own words:

"After forty days in Gallipoli in command of a traveling circus of machine-guns… being attached in turn to the Australians in Shrapnel Valley, sundry units at Cape Helles and finally to the 29th Division in Gully Ravine, where I worked with the 13th Sikhs until they were practically wiped out on June 4–I again found myself in England in July, my arm in a sling and feeling very thin as the result of sand colic, a horrid complaint which seized me the moment I set foot on Turkish soil at Gaba Tepe."

Following a recuperation "and sundry visits to the Admiralty" Hallam will finally achieve his primary goal when he joined the RNVR–he is transferred to the RNAS. Posted to Hendon he serves as the air station's First Lieutenant and is in charge of the aircraft-assembling shed. During this time he becomes more fully fit and discretely re-learns how to fly.

In December 1915 he will be Gazetted the DSC for his signal gallantry at Gallipoli and then appointed Officer Commanding Hendon. Forbidden by doctors to fly at any altitude, and recognizing the acute submarine situation requiring low flying reconnaissance, Hallam requests and receives a transfer to the Felixstowe Seaplane Station. *(Read 23Apr17)*

19Jun15 – William Cope POWER (Winnipeg MB) – RNVR

While Hallam manages to get into flying, other Canadians are joining the Navy to contribute to the air effort from the ground. Prairie lad Power joins the Royal Navy Volunteer Reserve as a Temporary Lieutenant for engineering duties. Following a shortened officer's course at the Crystal Palace just south of London, he is assigned to Chingford Naval Air Station in December. A first report on Power, dated April 1916, remarks that he is: 'A very efficient engine Officer, very keen and hardworking'. He is recommended for advancement and by early 1917 sent to 1 Wing, Dunkirk. There he is further noted for: 'V.G. command, shows great keenness and ability'. Power will be promoted to Lieutenant Commander on the First of January 1918 Naval appointments list.

JULY 1915

08Jul15 – FSLt Redford Henry MULOCK (Winnipeg) – 1 Wing

(From 20Jan15) Mulock is sent to Number 1 Naval Wing at Dunkirk. Flying Nieuport model 10 and 11 aircraft, he carries out scouting (fighter) patrols, bombing missions, photoreconnaissance flights, and directs naval gunfire. He also pioneers the use of parachute flares to spot for artillery at night. In September, Mulock becomes the first Canadian to attack a submarine when he drops five 20lb bombs on a U-boat. Later that same month he makes a lone bombing raid on the Zeppelin sheds at Berchem Ste Agathe near Brussels. His Squadron Commander calls the night action: '… a remarkable incident of cross-country flying as he had to depend almost entirely on compass and timing.'

By the close of 1915 Mulock will be Mentioned in Despatches (MID). He will also score his first aerial victory, sending an enemy aircraft out of control on the 30th of December. In January of the New Year he downs another two enemy machines and by March 1916 FLt Mulock will be promoted to Acting Flight Commander and Gazetted for another 'Mention'. *(Read 21May16)*

09Jul15 – FLt Francis Gilmer Tempest DAWSON (Chester NS) – Dardanelles

(From 16Sep14) Dawson has arrived in the middle of the Dardanelles Campaign and is taken on a familiarization flight by Squadron Commander Richard Bell-Davies to see the trenches and gun positions. They fly from the Island of Tenedos to the Gallipoli Peninsula and back. On return the engine stops and a forced landing ensues on Rabbit Island; it turns out that Dawson has inadvertently knocked off the petrol switches. No harm done, they swing the propeller to restart and continue the flight home.

(SCdr Bell-Davies will win the Victoria Cross in Bulgaria on the 19th of November. When his wingman is forced down by gunfire, Bell-Davies lands alongside the crippled craft and in spite of approaching enemy, carries out a rescue, taking off safely over the uneven ground: 'A feat of airmanship that can seldom have been equaled for skill and gallantry.')

Dawson has joined Wing Commander Charles Sampson's 3 Wing, which is now conducting support of Eastern Mediterranean Army and Navy operations by aerial reconnaissance, artillery spotting, and bombing.

Due to Turkish guns, airfields cannot exist on the Peninsula and flights to Gallipoli have to be based out of Tenedos—a feat similar to crossing the English Channel *and back*. Dawson's new Wing consists of a mix of aeroplanes and seaplanes of five different types and six different engines. Standardization is not an issue—it simply does not exist. He is soon operating a daily gun-spotting flight to and from the Peninsula in Voisin aeroplanes, each flight averaging two hours.

This was not an easy assignment by any count. Although enemy air power is minimal, the weather can be forbidding; even clear days assault aircraft with unrelenting wind, sand and heat. It is only sheer tenacity on the part of the Royal Navy ground crews that keeps the equipment operational.

'Gallipolitis,' an intestinal bug, ravages the Wing—over one-third of the sailors and officers are sick at any given time. With the short supply of water and ample supply of flies and scorpions, no one gets away unscathed. Comfort is a relative term: sleeping quarters are tents or wooden aircraft packing cases pitched alongside the rudimentary airstrip.

As great as these operational challenges can be, they are overshadowed by a lack of understanding on the part of the Admiralty and the Army's War Office regarding the tactical abilities and inabilities of aircraft. The slow, heavy seaplanes operating from the new and untested HMS *Ark Royal* are entirely unsuited to the task of ranging naval guns. In most cases the seaplanes can only climb to a sufficient spotting altitude by catching a thermal of rising air.

When the Australia-New Zealand Army Corps (ANZAC) is brought in to attack and hold the flanks at Gallipoli, 3 Wing moves their land-based aeroplanes to the Island of Imbros, closer to that action. In early August just before a British Landing to support the ANZAC breakout, they reconnoiter over Suvla Bay and report an absence of Turkish troops. With consequences of tragic proportions, the commanding English General does not use that information to immediately capture the high ground.

In addition to the stress of sustained operations, by late August 'Wuffy' will become the victim of the unhealthy living. Diagnosed with sand in his stomach and a murmur in his heart, he is evacuated to hospital, first in Malta then onward to England. His naval commission ends with a medical release in October 1915. *(Read 1982)*

11Jul15 – Candidate Arthur Strachan INCE (Toronto) – PFSLt

An RNAS Candidate and university engineering student, Ince is the first pilot to graduate from the Curtiss Flying School in Toronto. An official of the new Aero Club of Canada, acting for the Royal Aeronautical Club of Great Britain, conducts the examination. The test consists of three solo flights while the examiner observes safely from the ground.

The first two circuits require figure eight maneuvers with landings at a designated spot. The third flight is a climb above 300 feet, followed by an engine cut and a glide down to another spot landing. Earning RAeC Certificate number 1519 establishes Ince as the first pilot to be licensed in Canada. *(Read 14Dec15)*

The **Canadian Curtiss School** alone cannot solve the overwhelming problems of the Navy's supply and demand regarding pilot training. With 284 RNAS Candidates registered in 1915 and only three seaplanes with an equal number of American instructors, it was evident that there would be a substantial logjam just for phase one flying. By July 1915 that saturation point is reached with a mass of these aspiring pilots assembled in Toronto.

One of those wait-listed is future Air Vice Marshal Raymond Collishaw. In a letter some fifty years later to Department of National Defense historians, Collishaw writes that the pilots organized themselves into an assembly and bombarded both the Admiralty and Ottawa with letters and telegrams demanding that something be done. For one thing, money was running out; Collishaw noted that to be a pilot required finding a minimum of $2,000. Flying instruction could cost up to $500 and $700 was needed to pay for the RNAS uniforms that were compulsory upon being commissioned. Then there was food and lodging…

The Admiralty agrees to accept a limited number of the Candidates directly into the RNAS and calls them to England as training facilities permit. Once overseas they join fellow countrymen who are transferring from the CEF to naval flying. Ottawa, in turn, arranges travel for approximately 25 Candidates to Halifax for naval training in HMCS *Niobe*. In November 1915, Collishaw is appointed a temporary Petty Officer to lead this Nova Scotia contingent, a rank that he loses immediately

THE 'FIRST'—THE INITIAL CURTISS AVIATION SCHOOL STUDENTS AT HANLAN'S POINT, TORONTO.

Six of these nine are entered as Candidates for the RNAS (in **bold**):
Sitting, from left to right are **AS Ince, C MacLaurin,** EH McLachlin (RFC), **WH Peberdy, GA Gooderham, DA Hay**
Reclining, from left to right are **HF Smith,** CI VanNostrand (RFC), DG Joy (RFC)
The photograph was taken by fellow classmate **CN 'Charlie' Geale**

Windy Geale

upon arrival, when real Petty Officers take over—as only they can do.

More than one hundred Candidates head south of the border to earn their certificates at American flying schools. For the next year, over half of all FAI certificates issued by the American Aero Club will go to these Canadians. As an example, the first four students of aviatrix sisters Katherine and Marjorie Stinson at their mother's new flying school in San Antonio, Texas, are all RNAS types.

Those attending the various Wright Schools in Ohio, Georgia, and New York might note the typewritten addendum to the official School pamphlet stating 'Wheel control used exclusively.' This is a direct reference to the Wright patent on flight controls. Wilbur had passed away from typhoid in 1912, a death possibly exacerbated by the pressures of litigation. By late 1916, Orville will relinquish his case as a 'contribution to the war effort.'

On the subject of contributions to the cause, it may be said that the so-called 'Canadian invasion' into the American flying schools actually does much to help in the buildup and preparation of their southern neighbors for entry into the war

11Jul15 – SLt Harwood James ARNOLD, RNVR (Queen Charlotte Isls BC; b. ENG) – DSO

HJ Arnold
DND

Arnold has the distinction of being the first Canadian aviator to receive a decoration. On this day, he is flying with his English Flight Commander JT Cull, as an Observer against the enemy cruiser *Konigsberg* in German East Africa. When their Henry Farman aircraft is hit and going down, Arnold distinguishes himself by coolly continuing to send Morse code fall-of-shot directions to attacking Royal Navy Monitors. Thrown clear on a crash landing into the Rufiji River, Arnold swims back under the wreckage to rescue his trapped pilot. *Konigsberg* is completely disabled by the accurate spotting and Arnold is Gazetted the

Distinguished Service Order (DSO) for his part in the action.

A civilian radiotelegraph operator with the Canadian Naval Service when war broke out, Arnold had sailed single-handed in January 1915 from the Queen Charlotte Islands to Victoria to join the RNVR with an ambition of 'wirelessing' from aeroplanes.

This entire African expedition is an outstanding effort for the RNAS operating so far from Europe. Among the problems to be overcome is the warping of propellers and wings in the moist heat. Often too, the aircraft, both seaplanes and land planes could not become 'unstuck' to get airborne in the soupy atmosphere. Sand flies and dysentery continue to inflict debilitating problems for personnel. Following the *Konigsberg* crippling, part of the now-acclimatized aviation force was sent to Mesopotamia to assist British and Indian forces against the Turks. They are to operate Short 184 aircraft off the River Tigris.

Observer Arnold will return to England to commence pilot training. Age 26, his maturity and background mark him out for teaching and he is retained at Eastchurch as a flying instructor. Sadly, on the 20th of March 1918, he is killed during a target shoot. His student's bullets strike their aircraft's propeller causing the Maurice Farman S.11 Shorthorn N6312 to catch fire and crash. The Able Seaman student, GHG Walker is also lost. *(Read 1940).*

23Jul15 – Candidate Hugh Adderley PECK (Montreal) – PFSLt

Peck becomes a Probationary Flight Sub-Lieutenant when he achieves his FAI Certificate at the Thomas School of Aviation in Ithaca, New York. His American Aeronautical Club (AAeC) license is number 29 'Hydro'. The unusually low number is due to it being granted for flying water-borne aircraft. The School proprietors, brothers William and Oliver Thomas operate their 'hydro-aeroplanes' from the surface of Cayuga Lake. The term 'seaplane,' coined by the great wordsmith Winston Churchill, is soon more universally accepted.

Peck will sail for England in January 1916 to complete his probation at Felixstowe. He is subsequently appointed to Calshot, and in April reported as: 'A sound & capable Officer & Assistant Instructor.' An accident in Maurice Farman Seaplane 113 in June does not diminish his stature. The Calshot Commander writes: 'There being a Northerly wind blowing & a strong ebb tide, and as this

M/C was difficult to control on water, I do not consider Pilot to blame. M/C is an old type & hardly worth repairing.'

Instructing on seaplanes and flying boats will be Peck's main work during the War and his Report of January 1918 will contain the highest praise of the Royal Navy—the

HA Peck

UCC

term VGI—Very Good Indeed: 'VG Command Indeed; VGI S'plane Pilot. Experienced Instructor & carries out duties of 1ˢᵗ Lieut. & Chief Instructor with conspicuous success.'

23Jul15 – Candidate Frank Scholes McGILL (Montreal) – PFSLt

Also taking his flying training at the Thomas School, McGill receives AAeC number 30 'Hydro' and proceeds to England for further training at Calshot. Located on The Solent, this air station is one of the first RNAS seaplane bases. Here, on the 13ᵗʰ of September, McGill will wreck FBA Pusher Flying Boat 3203. By November, he is flying out of Sheerness Station at the mouth of the River Thames when he force lands Short 184 Seaplane 8034. Crashing into the Thames he suffers a broken arm and scraps the machine.

These incidents of aircraft write-offs are not unusual at this budding point in flying, let alone operating machines off water. Even so, it is likely not an understatement that when McGill finally passes his Royal Navy examinations his report will read: 'Has improved considerably. Shows great keenness.'

With the term 'Probationary' removed from his rank title, FSLt McGill is appointed to the new air station at Tresco, on the Scilly Islands off Land's End. In October 1917 he will twice bomb enemy submarines but with inconclusive results. During the summer of 1918, and by now a Flight Commander, McGill is sent to the American Naval Aircraft Factory in Philadelphia to test the prototype Felixstowe F5L Flying Boat. He completes his war service as Senior Flying Officer of the Southwest Group, England and is rated: 'A good Executive Officer. Extremely keen Pilot, handles men well & carries out

stores duties satisfactorily.' It would seem that the stores duties are his forte. During the Second World War, Air Vice Marshal McGill becomes the RCAF's Air Member for Supply and Organization.

29Jul15 – Arthur John O'REILLY (Victoria) – DOJ

(From 16Feb1873) Now 42 years of age, O'Reilly has purchased his own passage to England and, based on previous RN service obtains a new commission in the Royal Navy Volunteer Reserve. The British Admiralty has established a Balloon School at Roehampton and O'Reilly becomes one of the first students. It is Navy policy to appoint older, more mature types to Balloons and Dirigibles. Considered steadfast in their duties, the reports that they send down can save a great many lives from attack, and their precise gunnery spotting can kill scores of the enemy.

O'Reilly will be shipped across Channel to France and Belgium with No. 11 Kite Balloon Section. His CO's Report of the 31ˢᵗ of December 1916 describes him as: 'Most dependable and reliable in every way. Has good executive ability and is well liked by both Officers and Men. Good Observer, who has done much useful work with his Section. His observations can always be relied upon for great accuracy. Being considerably older than average he has a very helpful influence with his fellow Officers.'

In the spring of 1917 O'Reilly will receive a break from front line duties when he is appointed to command the Balloon Section at Milford Haven in South Wales. By Armistice Day 1918 he will have risen to the rank of Captain in the new Royal Air Force.

AUGUST 1915

02Aug15 – PFSLt Arthur Thomas Noel COWLEY (Victoria), &
– Cdt Douglas Alex Hardy NELLES (Simcoe ON) – Crash – Toronto

Aloft in a Curtiss JN4 'Jenny' off Toronto's Longbranch Rifle Range, the two novice aviators recover from a low altitude steep bank only to have the biplane 'dished'. The local newspaper uses this single-word description to try to explain the hard landing to a public unfamiliar with aviation terms—but keen for aeronautical information.

PFSLt Cowley has just received his Certificate, Number 1566, but his experience is strictly limited to flying boats and this is his first flight in a wheeled machine. Furthermore, he has taken along new RNAS Candidate Nelles for a familiarization hop. Both are badly shaken up but none the worse for the mishap. Nelles limps away with 'Hurt shins on gas tank.' When Cowley departs a few days later for England, Nelles completes his 'Ticket', plaintively noting in his flying log 'No more Cowley!'

The Canadian Curtiss School is saturated with students. Sending an RNAS applicant up with an inexperienced pilot is no safe procedure, however; the School is attempting to expedite the pupils through the curriculum. The British Admiralty have now informed Admiral Kingsmill that 'No more aviators are needed at present' but, nearly three hundred have been accepted as Candidates and are awaiting processing. While there are a few exceptions, for the most part the quality of the Candidates is high. As examples: 27-year-old Cowley is a McGill Engineering Graduate; the 23-year-old Nelles a University of Toronto Law Student and Lieutenant in the Canadian Militia. *(Cowley – Read 06May16; Nelles – Read 22Apr17)*

08Aug15 – PFSLt Warner Hutchins PEBERDY (Toronto; b. ENG) – Crash

In training at Chingford, Peberdy has a peculiar accident. His Curtiss JN3 'Jenny' runs away when he starts the engine by swinging his own propeller. The pilot-less machine takes off, flies over a river and crashes. Deemed a forgivable incident, Peberdy graduates in September and is assigned to the Dover Patrol with Number 1 Wing, Dunkirk. By December it will be noted that: 'He has been continually employed on reconnaissance work & hostile aircraft patrols over the enemy's lines. Specially recommended for promotion.'

Peberdy was with the original class of RNAS Candidates at the Curtiss School in Toronto. An Englishman, he is one of only six British-born pilots who will eventually train at the school, all others being native-born Canadians. An electrical engineer from Oxford University, Peberdy had been working with the Curtiss Hammondsport factory in New York when war was declared and traveled north to Canada to join and fly.

On the 3rd of March 1916, Peberdy will have a more serious accident at the Navy's St. Pol Field near Dunkirk. Arriving from Paris in a twin-engine Caudron he lands heavily, sustaining neck injuries. Resurveyed fit in early September he is sent to the Eastchurch War

WH Peberdy

Flight and then assigned to Number 2 Wing being sent to the Eastern Mediterranean to relieve 3 Wing.

On the fourteenth of January 1917, recently-promoted Flight Lieutenant Warner Hutchins Peberdy will go missing over Macedonia. In Nieuport XI 3983, he fails to return from a scouting flight out of Thasos Island. The Wing's 'A' Squadron laments the 'Loss of a capable & zealous officer.'

17Aug15 – FSLt Walter Brodgin LAWSON (Barrie ON) – Mesopotamia

A 1913 Royal Military College graduate, Lawson had gone overseas with Toronto's 48th Highlanders in the First Canadian Contingent. Having transferred to the RNAS and completed the Eastchurch Flying School in July, he is now sent on Foreign Service to the Persian Gulf. Lawson's assignment is to join the Seaplane Flight being shipped to Basra from East Africa following the *Konigsberg* crippling. This unit, consisting of three Short 827 machines, is placed on loan to an Indian Expeditionary Force moving up the Tigris River to capture the Turkish-held town of Kut. The overall campaign strategy is to protect the Anglo-Persian Oil Company pipeline and to stop German agents from implementing a Jihad, or Holy War.

Lawson arrives to find a mix of support RNAS and RFC air detachments, operating from a steamer towing three barges of aircraft. Innovation is everything in these severe climatic conditions. When it is recognized that the prevailing wind does

WB Lawson

not always favor an adequate takeoff run on the Tigris, the underpowered seaplanes are converted by means of improvised undercarriages to be flown from even more improvised fields ashore.

By the end of September, aeroplane reconnaissance reports have assisted in the capture of Kut and the British General commanding the Expedition then continues further upstream towards Baghdad. This, however, proves to be a classic 'bridge too far'. Advance is halted 25 miles south of the Arab capital at Ctesiphon on the 22nd of November. The Allies are counterattacked by the Turks and forced to fall back to Kut. Desperate shortages of medical staff and supplies decimate the retreating force. On reaching Kut, Lawson and some of his fellow aviators are ordered to fly out to Basra. Kut is surrounded, bombarded and besieged. Gallant attempts at aerial food drops prove insufficient and the beleaguered garrison is starved into surrender. After capitulation, one third of the 12,000 taken captive will die on a 700 mile forced-march to Turkish prison camps in Anatolia. Of 44 aviator POW's, only six survive.

In Basra, Lawson, like many others, becomes sick with dysentery and is evacuated to Bombay via hospital ship. Eventually he will be transported to England, arriving at Davenport in mid May 1916. By July 1916 he will be Resurveyed Fit—'But not for East or Mediterranean service.' *(Read 25Nov18)*

SEPTEMBER 1915

12Sep15 – PFSlt James Morrow ALEXANDER (Toronto) – KIC - Midair

Alexander was the first Canadian RNAS graduate of an American flying School, achieving USA license 335 at the Wright School at Dayton, Ohio, in early July 1915. Now, he has the tragic distinction of becoming the first Canadian naval aviation casualty. Flying Caudron G.III 3282 at NAS Eastchurch, he is killed in a mid-air collision with another student pilot. Age 23, Alexander is buried with full naval honours in the Isle of Sheppey Cemetery, Kent, near the air base. A mid-air is an unusual accident at this early point in the war and the funeral of the two pilots is attended by the Admiral commanding the Nore, together with a large number of officers and men, including a detachment from the Rifle Brigade. Unfortunately, in-flight collisions will become a more frequent occurrence.

19Sep15 – PFSLt Douglas Archibald HAY (Owen Sound ON) – Lost at Sea

A scant two days after 'logging in' to Whitley Bay costal defense station in Northumberland, Hay is missing. His Royal Aircraft Factory BE2c, 1133, has become lost over the North Sea. The third graduate of the Curtiss School in Toronto, he had achieved his Certificate on the 13th of July and left for England on the SS *Scandinavian*. After completing a five-week Royal Navy training period at Chingford, an RNAS school in Essex, Hay was appointed to Whitley Bay. Because

DA Hay

Geale Family

he was engaged in a training flight, Hay's death is recorded as accidental. He is Canada's second naval aviation casualty. Like the many lost at sea who will sadly follow, he is listed on the Admiralty Memorial at Chatham.

OCTOBER 1915

03Oct15 – FSLt James Errol Durnsford BOYD (Toronto ON) – Interned, Holland

An Amsterdam newspaper, the *Tyd*, of October 4th reports: 'Five English aviators from Dunkirk dropped bombs on Zeebrugge at 6 am on Sunday, October 3rd. German anti-aircraft guns shelled them heavily. One machine, flown by a naval officer named Boyd, had just dropped its last bomb when, at an altitude of 14,000 feet, shrapnel hit the motor. To save himself from falling into the hands of the Germans, the pilot made for Dutch territory and landed at Nieuwvliet [Zeeland].'

Boyd's forced landing in Holland results in his internment for the duration of the war by a nation anxious to remain neutral. His 5 Naval Wing mission was to attack the enemy seaplane sheds situated on the Zeebrugge Mole. Now the REP Parasol aircraft 8460 is taken by his captors and becomes Netherland's LA-23. Interned at Wierickerschaus, Big-Boderganeu, it becomes a long war for Boyd. Although not a prisoner, he chafes at the interminable detainment and runs afoul of his senior British Naval Officer. Boyd is written up in The Hague in May 1917: 'This Officer's conduct during his stay in Holland has not been satisfactory. Had reference been made to Rear Admiral he would decidedly have reported against him.'

In June 1917 Dutch authorities grant Boyd a six-month parole from Holland to the USA. Back in America the ever-keen aviator is involved in an aircraft accident at Mineola and in November he is granted extension of leave until well into the following year. *(Read 09Oct30)*

13Oct15 – Candidate George Howard SIMPSON (Toronto) – PFSLt

Simpson graduates from the Wright Flying School in Dayton Ohio, attaining his probationary officer status. Before departing Canada for England, he registers a change to his Next-of-Kin form replacing his mother's name with that of a new wife from Dayton; he is one of very few RNAS pilots to be married during the conflict.

Simpson's war will be spent as a seaplane pilot aboard various HM Ships with the Grand Fleet, the Royal Navy's combined Atlantic and Home Fleets, based at the Scapa Flow anchorage in the Orkney Islands. The large fleet remains on ready standby to engage the German High Seas Fleet should it venture forth from Wilhelmshaven. The Germans have attempted a strategy of raids into the North Sea aiming to draw out and destroy sections of the British Fleet but these battles—Heligoland Bight in August 1914, and Dogger Bank in January 1915—have been inconclusive.

Later serving with a Naval detachment to the Russian White Sea, Simpson will be Mentioned in Despatches in October 1918. Returning to Canada, he continues to fly and in July 1920 will walk out of the bush to Sudbury after a forced landing a week prior.

NOVEMBER 1915

13Nov15 – FSLt Frank Homer SMITH (Toronto) – REL to RNVR

Smith has entirely lost his nerve for flying and requests to have his appointment as a Flight Sub-Lieutenant terminated, asking for a transfer to any other duty but flying. He is re-appointed as a Lieutenant RNVR for armament duties with the RNAS.

A former Lieutenant in the Queen's Own Rifles of Canada Militia Regiment, Smith was the second graduate of the Toronto Curtiss School. Anxious to serve, he had left immediately for England in HMS *Baltic* upon attaining

FH Smith

UCC

his Aeronautical Certificate.

By September he was flying out of Dunkirk with 1 Wing. He wrote home describing a bomb-dropping raid some 30 miles across the German lines at Ypres:

"…at 12,000 feet, the enemy anti-aircraft guns got my range. In spite of circling and dipping on my part they put two holes in the seat of the aircraft and four in the wings."

A successful businessman and financier between the Wars, Smith will serve as an RCAF Wing Commander during the second global conflict 1939-1945. He has broad ties to the USA and helps to encourage hundreds of qualified American pilots north of the border.

14Nov15 – PFSLt Ronald John McDOUGALL (Port Hawkesbury, NS) – Crash & REL

Smashing Curtiss JN3 3403 at the Chingford Flying School is only a part of McDougall's problems. The following day his Commanding Officer writes up a report: 'This officer is in my opinion quite unsuited to be an officer in the RNAS. […] he yesterday totally wrecked a machine through the greatest stupidity, ruddering & banking in opposite directions with the result that he side-slipped 300ft.'

When McDougall ignores the formal Caution and continues to run afoul of Naval authority, his career is considerably shortened: 'Probationary FSLt McDougall shows no promise of ever becoming even a moderate flier & his general appearance, conduct, etc, makes it necessary for me to recommend his removal from the Service.' McDougall's Royal Navy appointment is terminated on the 12th of December 1915.

15Nov15 – PFSLt Louis William NURSE (Toronto) – Report & REL

Although he graduated from Canada's Curtiss Aviation School, Nurse has demonstrated neither pilot nor officer potential to the Royal Navy. His Flight Commander at Chingford reports: 'This officer is exceedingly dirty, has no manners & has objectionable habits. In addition to this, he shows no sign of ever becoming a reliable pilot & I have the honour to submit that he may be discharged to Shore.'

LW Nurse

RAeC Trust

The Rear Admiral, Director of Air Service, then requests a more detailed report from the Chingford Station Commander. This proves to be the finish of Nurse's short naval career: 'This officer was brought up before me for spitting on the floor of his dormitory, the state of which will perhaps be better understood when I mention the fact that a Boy-Servant who was responsible for the cleanliness thereof, reported that he wished to be taken off that duty in consequence of the filthy mess he has to clear up every morning.' Nurse, like **McDougall**, is released from the Royal Navy on the 12th of December.

18Nov15 – PFSLt Arthur Cecil HARLAND (Canada) – REL

The Naval appointment of Harland is terminated and he too is released from service. His Chingford Flying School squadron commander writes: 'I consider this Officer too slow & dull-witted to be of any use in the RNAS, & the CO of his flight informs me that he is quite impossible to teach. He has shown no improvement whatever since he joined this Station.'

Harland was one of the many 'Candidates' selected by the Department of Naval Services of Canada and sent directly to Greenwich for pilot training. He had arrived in England only two months previously and is now shipped home.

18Nov15 – FSLt John Turner BONE (Calgary AB) – KIA, Belgium

Bone does not return from a raid on the Zeppelin airship sheds at Berchem Ste. Agathe, near Brussels. His aircraft, Nieuport 10 3177 goes down in the English Channel and Bone's body washes up at Zuydcote. The Wing surgeon conducts an autopsy and reports no gun shot wounds and that death was due to drowning; however, this is a

death on an operational mission and John Turner Bone is Canada's first naval air combat loss.

Making his own way to England to join the RNAS, Bone had attained his flying certificate at Hendon during May 1915. He was then assigned to Number 1 Wing out of Dunkirk. On one mission he was launched on a Hostile Aircraft Patrol, after an unknown enemy intruder was reported, but nothing was sighted. The aircraft he flew that day was a Morane, the same machine used in the destruction of Zeppelin LZ.37 over Bruges on the 7th of June, winning a Victoria Cross for English pilot FSLt RAJ Warneford.

JT Bone

FAAM

Morane Sulnier 3253 is taken out of service in early 1916 and with great foresight, preserved for exhibition. It is on display to this day at the RAF Museum at Hendon.

19Nov15 – PFSLt Bert Sterling WEMP (Tweed ON) – Crash

Training on Curtiss JN3 8394 at the primary flying school in Killingholme, Linconshire, Wemp has an engine failure and side-slips into the Humber River. The machine is salvaged although found to be completely wrecked; Wemp is uninjured and only slightly shaken. The incident is not considered a reflection of his flying skills as the Station Commanding Officer reports: 'He has made several excellent solo flights and promises to turn out a really first class Pilot. He is very keen indeed & will make an excellent Officer as well as Pilot.'

Wemp was the first Chairman of the Aero Club of Canada, a group that had held their inaugural banquet at Toronto in July 1915, dining with Honourary President Sir John Eaton. As well as Wemp, Club Secretary **ATN Cowley** and members **ER Grange** and **RG Delamere** are now all in RNAS service.

At the advanced flying school Redcar, Wemp goes on to receive another outstanding report: 'This Officer is very promising all round. Has completed 30 Hrs 42 Mins flying on Caudrons, Bleriots, Avro's and Curtis Machines. Is a V.G. Pilot, has V.G. knowledge of

80HP Gnome & Renault engines & Theory of Flight. At Signaling he is fair. I submit that he be confirmed in rank.'

Promoted out of his probationary status in early March 1916, FSLt Wemp and three other Canadians, **MG Dover, CE Moore**, and **KM Smith**, are sent to RNAS Yarmouth. This particular station's Commanding Officer does not much care for Canadian pilots and makes a remark in the Wardroom that they need half-an-hour's instruction in English every morning. When an overly keen First Lieutenant takes the comment seriously and parades the foursome for lecture, all furiously threaten to tender their resignations. The CO responds to this with a reading of the Naval Articles of War regarding 'Mutiny'. In the Inquiry that follows however, it will be the Commander who is reprimanded for being tactless. *(Read 25Apr16)*

BS Wemp

RAeC Trust

21Nov15 – FSLt Rudolph Dawson DELAMERE (Toronto), &

– PFSLt Charles Eldridge BURDEN (Toronto) – Crash

Just two weeks earlier, Burden, a Lieutenant in the Eaton Machine Gun Brigade, had resigned his Canadian Expeditionary Force commission to join the RNAS. Today's flight, as a passenger with Pilot Delamere, a fellow University of Toronto student, is one of his first—and nearly last. Delamere himself had only just graduated from the Curtiss School in Toronto on the 30th of July.

On takeoff, their Hendon-based Burgess Gunbus 3660 collides with an airfield shed. Delamere is unhurt, but Burden, sitting up front in the 'bathtub' of the pusher biplane, suffers severe shock as well as slight injuries to the knees and face. He will recover and go on to attain his pilot certificate by the end of January 1916. *(Delamere – Read 07Feb16; Burden – Read 22Jan18)*

26Nov15 – FSLt Harold Spencer KERBY (Calgary) – Sick Gallipoli

Growing up in Calgary where his father, Rev. W.G. Kerby was Mayor, Harold had studied mechanical engineering at the University of Toronto. Together with **JT Bone**, he made his own way to England to enter the RN Air Service, joining at Hendon in March 1915. Shortly after achieving his Royal Aeronautical Certificate in May, he was assigned to the Dardanelles with **'Wuffy' Dawson**. Now Kerby is sick with enteric fever and sent to Malta for hospitalization before being invalided back to England and discharged from the Service as physically unfit.

Following recovery of his health in Canada, Kerby will apply once again to the RNAS and by November 1916 is resurveyed as fit for flying. His Cranwell Flying School Report of January 1917 will read: 'Since re-joining to re-qualify, he has been through a complete course. He is a VG Pilot & perfectly fit to return to flying duties, though I should recommend Home Service at present.' In spite of the recommendation of locality, Kerby is appointed to Dunkirk for Scouts—a term used to describe First World War fighter aircraft. *(Read 06May17)*

HS Kerby

FAAM

27Nov15 – FSLt Lewis Ewing SMITH (Mystic QB) – Crash

Flying from Hendon to Detling in Curtiss Jenny 3423, Smith becomes lost and crashes in marshes two miles from Wrotham. His aeroplane is returned in bits to Hendon by lorry. It is later repaired at Eastchurch only to be written off by Canadian **AB Shearer** in January 1916. The majority of the RNAS Canadians are not yet in action, but they are managing to cut a swath through the training machines of the Royal Navy. *(Read 25Feb17)*

DECEMBER 1915

01Dec15 – PFSLt Clarence Earl MOORE
(Fort William ON) – DOJ

Today, Moore is entered in the RNAS by the Department of Naval Service, Ottawa, but his initial Report out of the Flying School at Calshot will be unpromising: 'Not a very good Officer; has not had previous experience in handling men or any responsibility.' The Royal Navy values an Officer's leadership qualities more highly than flying abilities. This inauspicious start notwithstanding, Moore will graduate by early May 1916 as a 'Good & steady Pilot' and it is noted that he has accomplished 'extended patrols'.

Subsequently appointed to Grain Naval Air Station in Kent, Moore is evaluated as: 'Promises well, but very raw' and during August he will crash twice. In the first instance, while maneuvering to engage a U-boat, he stalls and falls into the sea. His Short 827 3112 is a total loss and Moore and his Petty Officer Mechanic WH Hodgson are fortunate to be rescued by a trawler. In the second incident he damages Curtiss JN4 8831.

In October 1916 Moore is sent to the Mediterranean for Number 2 Wing. By April 1917, in spite of a crash of a Short S.90 Seaplane his report reads: 'A very capable Officer'; and by the end of June: 'Keen & Zealous Officer. Good Command.' In early July Moore nosedives and damages Sopwith Schneider 3792 while landing alongside HMS Ark Royal and by now he is sick with neurasthenia: 'constitutional causes aggravated by service.'

Neurasthenia is the term used for a condition suffered by a great many First World War aviators. It is generally defined as: An emotional and psychological disorder characterized by impaired functioning, utter fatigue, headache depression, noise and light hypersensitivity as well as psychosomatic symptoms. For soldiers in the trenches, this exhaustion of the nervous system is more commonly called 'Shell Shock.' Today it would be diagnosed as Post-Traumatic Stress Disorder.

Fit again by September 1917, Moore, the initial 'Not a very good Officer' will be appointed to the naval air unit on the Island of Mudros—in Command. By the end of that year, before going on a Canada Leave, he is described as: 'Extremely capable CO. Very Good Pilot.' His Reports are a prime example of how the Navy matches keenness and ability to bring a young man to maturity—and in Moore's case—in spite of all the aircraft damage.

He will return to England in April 1918 and fly the Large America Flying Boats out of Felixstowe with 202 Squadron RAF.

06Dec15 – Candidate Melville Grant DOVER
(Winnipeg) – PFSLt

An onslaught of harsh Canadian weather causes the Toronto Curtiss School to close down for the winter. The last two students were graduated in late November but there remains the sizeable backlog of Candidates waiting to be trained. In consultation with the Royal Navy, DNS Canada enrolls eight as PFSLt's and ships them directly overseas to the Chingford Flying School in England. Six will prove to be unsuitable and are released by July 1916. The seventh, Melville Grant Dover, a contractor from Winnipeg, is injured

MG Dover

in training but will finish the War as a Captain, RAF, with service in the Aegean. *(Read 23Aug16)*

– Candidate Robert 'Bob' LECKIE
(Toronto; b. SCT) – PFSLt

The eighth member of the group proves eminently suitable: 'Bob' Leckie, a Glasgow-born Scot who immigrated to Canada in 1907, will eventually retire as Chief of Air Staff, RCAF, in 1947.

His first military rank, that of Probationary Flight Sub-Lieutenant, will become substantive in June 1916 upon his graduation from Chingford. After undergoing advanced training on the Large America flying boats at Felixstowe in September, he is considered an: 'Extremely efficient Pilot of these Boats. Exceptionally capable Officer.' Leckie is appointed to the Yarmouth Naval Air Station. *(Read 14May17)*

14Dec15 – FSLt Alfred James NIGHTINGALE
(Mount Dennis ON) – MIA

Out of Westgate Seaplane Station in Kent, Nightingale's Short 827 3067 is declared missing on patrol. His machine is a presentation aircraft, 'Hong Kong Britons

No. 3' powered by a 150 horsepower Sunbeam engine.

The following evening, Nightingale reports back aboard Westgate. His engine had failed, after which he was rescued by the French trawler *Printemps*. An attempt had been made to salve the machine but the high seas and the wrecked condition of the seaplane rendered the task impossible. This, the third aeroplane war gift from the British residents of Hong Kong, was lost. The Westgate Station CO now re-telegraphs the Admiralty to cancel the Missing report, adding the comment: 'I consider it is much to Pilot's credit that he succeeded in first instance restarting engine under difficult circumstance, & having done all in his power to save

AJ Nightingale

machine, only abandoning her when complete wreck, & in sinking condition.'

It is the second positive report that Nightingale has received. Another of the first dozen graduates of the Curtiss Aviation School in Toronto, he had completed his flying training in England with the write up: 'He is of a very good stamp, has flown a machine from Hendon to Eastbourne three times successfully, & I consider him to be of the right type for the Service.'

During the summer of 1916, Nightingale will be appointed to Port Said, Egypt, for pilot duties in HMS *Ben-my-Chree*. This ship is one of nine cross-channel steamers converted to service as a seaplane carrier. *Ben-my-Chree* (Woman of my Heart), the former flagship of the Isle of Man Steam Packet fleet, is the fastest of these carriers with a top speed of over 24 knots. Nicknamed 'The Ben' she is considerably more efficient than the Royal Navy's first carrier, the modified collier HMS *Ark Royal*, that has a speed of only 10 knots. Whereas 'The Ark' launched aircraft in trolleys over the bow, The Ben must heave-to in order to hoist out seaplanes by crane. Even so, a fully worked-up flight deck crew can embark and disembark a seaplane in less than a minute. In these evolutions Nightingale will again fly the Short 184 aircraft but now with the power of a 225HP Sunbeam engine. *(Read 02Dec16)*

14Dec15 – FSLt Arthur Strachan INCE (Toronto) – DSC Action

(From 11Jul15) On his arrival in England, Ince, the first Curtiss Canada graduate, was sent to Naval Air Station Chingford for further flying training. While there he suffered the rigors of two flying accidents before graduating to 1 Wing at Dunkirk. On this day, taking a turn flying as the observer/gunner in Nieuport 10 3971 Ince shoots down a large German seaplane just off La Panne on the Belgian coast. Following the stricken enemy down, the Nieuport engine chokes and Ince must ditch with the aircraft. Striking the water, it overturns and sinks trapping him. Rescued by his Pilot FSLt CW Graham, Ince emerges with a bruised head and is severely shaken by the immersion. Fortunately, a nearby minesweeper, HMS *Balmoral Castle,* quickly picks up the two airmen.

Ince's flying confidence is now completely shattered, and reflecting on his three crashes he requests a release. His decision is not deterred by the award of a Distinguished Service Cross (DSC) for his actions in shooting down an enemy aircraft, the first by a Canadian aviator. Granted release in February 1916, Ince will immediately commission with the RNVR for armament duties. He serves the remainder of the war at NAS Calshot as Station Gunnery Officer.

16Dec15 – PFSLt Benjamin Nelson HARROP (Indian Head SK) – DOJ

On this date, Harrop is entered by DNS Canada as a PFSLt and by mid January of 1916 he will have achieved his Pilot Certificate at Eastbourne; however, his graduation Confidential Report (CR) reads: 'Uncertain but might improve.' In June this statement changes to 'Promises very well' on his first appointment, Grain Island. By October it becomes: 'Steady Pilot. Improving as an Officer', and at the end of December: 'VG Pilot, Keen & capable Officer. Can take charge of men.'

The following year will find Harrop with the Malta

BN Harrop

Group, serving in HMS *Riviera*. He continues to grow in stature as an officer and is 'Specially recommended for promotion'. Adding a Flight Lieutenant's stripe to his uniform in June, he assumes additional duties. His September report speaks of them: 'Excellent Pilot. Very steady & performs Executive duties very well.' The 1917 year-end report confirms with the comment: 'Excellent Pilot. Is a steady & thoroughly reliable Officer. Very attentive to his duties as Executive Officer.'

Again these Confidential Reports display the strong attention that the Royal Navy gives to encouraging Officer Leadership Qualities of young men. Prairie lad Harrop proves well and will see out the war flying from HMS *Vindex* in the Mediterranean.

17Dec15 – FSLt Charles Norman GEALE
(Peterborough ON) – Ditching

Charlie Geale's very first operational flight is a bit of a non-starter. As Second Pilot in Curtiss H4 'Small America' 3555, the mission ends with an Anzani engine failure and a forced landing off Dungeness. This is followed by a tow back to Dover behind HMS *Amazon*—a duty considered by many Destroyer Commanders to be an all-too-frequent headache. However, Geale, going on to become very adept at seaplane handling, will be selected to instruct on the new Curtiss twin-engine H-12 'Large America' flying boats.

Medically grounded for a period in 1917 and early 1918, he serves as Gunnery Officer at the RNAS Eastbourne training school, earning an accolade from the Commanding Officer: 'He has conducted himself with sobriety and to my entire satisfaction.

CN Geale

Windy Geale

A capable and hard working Officer. Carried out the duties of 1st Lieut during above period with great zeal… & especially has contributed in no small way to the efficiency of the Station.'

By War's end, Geale's logbook will list time on seventeen different aircraft types from the early pushers up to modern Sopwith Snipe scouts. The University of

Toronto graduate will return to Canada in November 1918 and resume his civil engineering profession. Charles Norman Geale is the father of Commander Bob 'Windy' Geale who serves in the Royal Navy, the Royal Canadian Navy and the Royal Australian Navy. Son 'Windy' retires in Australia and is the founding curator of the RAN's Fleet Air Arm Museum at Nowra, New South Wales.

27Dec15 – SLt Aubrey Mansfield TIDEY, RNVR
(Vancouver) – Observer

AM Tidey, in foreground, at Bembridge

Paul Donnellan

Tidey attaches from the Royal Navy's Volunteer Reserve to take training as an aerial Observer. His duties will include navigation over water as well as signaling, seamanship, photography and aircraft gunnery. Wireless telegraphy is also being introduced.

Stationed at Bembridge after graduation, Tidey cross trains as Pilot in January 1917. He will be awarded the Air Force Cross in June 1919 for his years of HAPs (Hostile Submarine Patrols).

30Dec15 – FSLt Howard Vincent REID
(St Johns NF) – Gallipoli

A son of Sir William Duff Reid, Howard was a 2nd Lieutenant in the Royal Newfoundland Regiment. The First Contingent of these 'Blue Puttees', so-named for their uniquely coloured leggings, shipped out to England in mid 1915. On arrival, Reid applied for and was accepted into the RNAS.

Reid has been sent to the Dardanelles for Number 2 Wing, RNAS. This is a reinforcement and relief unit for 3 Wing, which has been in the Eastern Mediterranean operation from the beginning. Reid's Newfoundland Regiment has also been in action at Gallipoli since

September. Now, at the close of 1915, British Empire troops are ordered to withdraw from the Peninsula. During the evacuation Newfoundland soldiers provide a rearguard and are among the last to depart They leave behind 49 members in graves alongside over ten thousand Australian and New Zealand dead. Britain has lost twenty-one thousand.

Captured German reports later confirm that the RNAS successfully camouflaged the evacuation by keeping the Turkish artillery exhausted with all-night bombing attacks. In their nine months of operations, 3 Wing's total flying time was an amazing 2,600 hours.

Reid's decision to join the naval flying service has probably saved his life. In France on the First of July 1916, the Royal Newfoundland Regiment will 'go over the top' of their trenches at Beaumont-Hamel with 801 soldiers. Only 69 men will answer the roll call the following day. Every officer is either wounded or dead. Reid's brother Bruce is among the lost in this first day of the Battle of the Somme.

Meanwhile, on the Eastern Mediterranean Front, Reid will be described as having done much good flying on Active Service. He is sent as part of a relief flight to Roumania in late 1916. Instructed to return to England that December he sets out overland via Petrograd, Archangel and Yaroslavl, finally arriving on the 6th of February 1917. Taking a well-earned home leave in March, he will be retained in Canada for special service and as a Captain, Administration Officer, with the RAF in the Dominion.

December 1915

First Lord of the Admiralty, Churchill, is made to pay the price for the bloody failure of the Dardanelles Campaign. Held responsible, he is dismissed from his post in the Navy and joins the Army. As a Lieutenant Colonel, Churchill commands a battalion of the Royal Scots Fusiliers on the Western Front until May 1916.

Extract:

A booklet titled HINTS FOR FLIGHT SUB-LIEUTENANTS will be made readily available to Candidates and Probationary Officers during 1916. It mentions the Pay and Allowance of 10/ shillings a day with the addition of 4/- shillings for Flying Risk and that the first notifications of appointments appear in the London Gazette. Other sections give advice on Kit and Uniform and an update on Who's Who in the Naval Air Service.

Perhaps the most important read for new RNAS Officers is headed :

A Little Friendly Advice:

'When you receive your first appointment as a Probationary Flight Sub-Lieutenant you will become entitled to wear practically the same uniform as a Sub-Lieutenant R.N. and you must not forget that in the Navy this takes an immense amount of hard work and some five years to attain.

'If you remember this, and behave accordingly, everything will be made as pleasant as possible for you; but if, on the other hand, you do not, you will be sure to find someone in authority who will do his best to remove that too self-satisfied feeling from you.

Probably you won't like the process, but if it happens you will only have yourself to blame for it.'

PROBATIONARY FSLᴛs TAKE LEWIS GUN TRAINING

Paul Donnellan

The Vendome Primary Flying School's firing range in France

THE GALLIPOLI EXPERIENCE – DARDANELLES 1915

Ray Pollard

Sailors help extract the crew of a Nieuport 10 that has come to grief.

3 WING, LUXEUIL, FRANCE

Photo taken by AB Shearer about two days before the Oberndorf Raid
12OCT16

Standing left to right (Canadians in bold):

Flight Sub Lieutenants (FSLts) **R. Collishaw, GS Harrower, PG McNeil** [or **KG MacDonald**], **CE Burden**, **ST Edwards**, NM MacGregor, SLt LV Pearkes (RNVR), FCdr CB Dallison, SLt CN Downes (RNVR), FSLts **FC Armstrong, JA Glen**, SCdr CM Murphy, FSLts **JE Sharman** and **LE Smith**.

Seated left to right:

Wing Captain WL "Daddy" Elder and Wing Commander R Bell-Davies VC, DSO.

CHAPTER 2
THE YEAR 1916

FLIGHT SUB LIEUTENANTS

In early January, **Raymond Collishaw** finally reaches the United Kingdom and is entered into books of the RNAS as a Probationary Flight Sub Lieutenant.

"I noted with some interest that after arriving in England, without ever having got into the air, I was given exactly the same flying training as those others who had gained their pilot certificates in Canada or the United States. Both the RNAS and the RFC dropped the requirement for a certificate during the latter half of 1916 as regards their Canadian recruiting. It seems odd that it took them so long to get around to this."

Some fifty years later, Collishaw still felt strongly about this early period and corresponded these feelings to his biographer Ronald Dodds.

"The naval pilots would have made a bigger impact on the War, had the Canadians arrived a year sooner. The RNAS pilots lost a year in Canada because the Admiralty blundered in not ordering an expansion of its Flying Training schools in England at the end of 1914; instead of hoping that flying training civil training facilities in Canada could do the job for them. As matters turned out, the, RFC in France lost Air Superiority to the Germans at the end of 1915. The whole history of Military aviation in Great Britain in the early years, was of almost incredible stupidity and the general result was that England entered the 1914 War with only 50% of the air strength of the Germans.

"Ps. Incidentally, exactly the same thing occurred again in 1939." (*Letter 24Apr64 to Dodds*)

Operational in early August, Collishaw is sent to Number 3 Wing which is being reformed at Manston. The 1915 Gallipoli 3 Wing has been relieved by 2 Wing in the Eastern Mediterranean, and a new 3 Wing is raised in retaliation to the German Zeppelin raids on England with the sole purpose of striking at industrial plants in the Saar.

English Wing Commander, Captain WL 'Daddy' Elder, had begun recruitment of Canadian Candidates for the RNAS in 1915 when he was in the Dominion arranging the purchase of Curtiss aircraft. Now, with the first wave of these aviators completing flying training the Wing Commander plans to keep them together as a cohesive force. Carrying British Gunners, some 47 Canadian Flight Sub Lieutenants will fly with 3 Wing before it is disbanded yet again in April 1917. Gaining combat experience with the unit, many will become prominent on the front lines of the Navy's air war effort.

Flying Sopwith Strutters, the Wing sends the aircraft out as single-pilot bombers escorted by 'fighter' aircraft crewed with both a pilot and an enlisted Air-Gunner. Collishaw will be chosen for the fighter role and flies his first mission in October.

"Anyone who says he was not nervous during his first operational flight is either a completely insensitive idiot or he has forgotten what it was really like. There are so many things to look after that you don't have time to worry about being frightened but you are definitely twitchy about mistakes that you might make…Later on these things come automatically but on your first flight you think about them."

During 1916, the opposing navies will finally clash their dreadnoughts at Jutland, off the west coast of Denmark, The combatants suffer a controversial draw rather than an all out victory. Aviation wise, bad weather; misusage of Zeppelins by the German Navy; and, insufficient of aeroplane operations by the Royal Navy: all contribute to the fiasco. Jutland is no glorious second Trafalgar for the British Grand Fleet but it will essentially retire the German High Seas Fleet for the duration. The Kaiser turns his naval ambitions to unrestricted submarine warfare.

JANUARY 1916

10Jan16 – PFSLt Gordon Ezra DUKE
(Toronto) – KIC

Operating Short S38, 3148 on a training flight at Eastbourne, 19-year-old Duke crashes near a brickfield at Hampden Park. Both he and his instructor, Warrant Officer Percival Victor Fraser, a 30-year-old Australian, are killed. During the subsequent coroner's inquest, an RNAS witness who had watched the machine in flight believes that something must have gone wrong with the elevator controls: 'I thought it was flying rather irregularly. Watched it turn to the left, right itself, and then make a mad dive from a height which I put at from 150ft to 200ft.' Another witness, Commander Philip Shepherd states he had examined the remains of the machine and found that one wire had slipped off the elevator control pulley. In reply to a particularly leading question, Commander Shepherd responded: 'You do not find your men from Canada losing their heads very easily.' The panel of adjudicators will return a verdict of accidental death.

10Jan16 – FSLt Clarence 'Claire' MacLAURIN
(Lachine PQ) – Base Command

Although only six months since graduating from Curtiss Canada, the twenty-six-year-old MacLaurin is recognized by the Royal Navy as having strong leadership ability. Following training in England he is placed in command of RNAS Bembridge, a seaplane base on the Isle of Wight. This is the first air station command appointment for a Canadian.

Bembridge is a sub-station of RNAS Calshot, Portsmouth, and the CO of the senior base writes in MacLaurin's initial report: 'I consider this officer is exceptionally

suitable for promotion to Flt Lieut. He is a very skilful Seaplane pilot, & His ability to command is exceptional. Has been in charge of Sub-Station at Bembridge for some months, has carried out his duties in every way satisfactorily.'

FSLt MacLaurin will prove his mettle on the 28th of February 1916 when flying Sopwith Schneider Seaplane 3735. After a normal landing the tail float splits and fills with water, somersaulting the machine over backwards. Remaining afloat for about three hours, MacLaurin is at last picked up by the Destroyer HMS *Wizard*. Every

C MacLaurin, at Bembridge
Paul Donnellan

attempt is made to salvage the aircraft and hoist it aboard, but the fuselage breaks adrift and sinks. Again the CO of Calshot reports on his sub-station Commander: 'I submit that this Officer behaved throughout with coolness & courage although suffering from extreme cold & exposure, he did everything he could to assist in salving the m/c after he had been picked up.'

On the first of October 1917, MacLaurin will be Gazetted the DSC with the citation that he is: 'especially deserving of the decoration. Since November 1915 has carried out 262 patrols. On all occasions when patrols have been necessary in bad or doubtful weather has invariably undertaken them himself. Has never hesitated to carry out a patrol.' This same month 'Mac' sights and bombs a U-boat, leaving it with suspected damage.

In his 1917 end-of-year Report, the Wing Commander of the Portsmouth Group will state that his Canadian CO of Bembridge: 'Has done the most valuable patrol work of any air stn in this cmd during the year & I consider that it is entirely due to the very great energy & capability shown by him that this air stn; though only a small sub air stn, has carried out more patrols & flown more hours than almost any other in the RNAS.' During 1918, now–Major MacLaurin, DSC, RAF, is sent to Canada to help in the organization and development of a Royal Canadian Naval Air Service (RCNAS). *(Read 11Sep22)*

**16Jan16 – PFSLt Cavanagh Nixon SOMERVILLE
(Georgetown ON) – RIP**

Somerville dies in Augusta, Georgia. He had just completed his RNAS Candidate flying training at the Wright Flying School. Cause of death for the 29-year-old former bank clerk is unknown and Somerville's name will be entered on Page 574 of the First World War Book of Remembrance on public display at the Peace Tower on Parliament Hill, Ottawa.

FEBRUARY 1916

**07Feb16 – FSLt Rudolf Dawson DELAMERE
(Toronto ON) – Zanzibar**

(From 21Nov15) Delamere is detailed for Squadron Commander Cull's Party, the part of the *Konigsberg* force remaining in German East Africa. This unit, later numbered as 7 Squadron Dar es Salaam, flies BE2c aircraft. Cull soon rates his new addition as: 'Canadian Pilot of good type & appears to be quite sound and reliable. Zealous with plenty of common sense.' The Commander in Chief, Cape Town, recommends promotion.

RD Delamere
Tony Delamere

But, by December, after several months reconnaissance and bombing operations over the jungle, Delamere 'blots his copy-book'. Sent to an advanced base aerodrome recently completed at Alt Iringa, he becomes lost enroute. To make matters worse, he totally wrecks the machine, BE2c 8715, fifteen miles short of the destination. His fitness reports now read: 'This pilot is considered careless and incompetent in cross country flying.'

Transferred to 8 Squadron based in Zanzibar, Delamere commences flying Short 827 types in co-operation with the Monitor HMS *Manica*. The squadron's aerodrome,

recently established at Lindi is a difficult field to operate from, being unhealthy and by no means a satisfactory landing strip. The recce and artillery-spotting work done out of here by Delamere is doubly valuable. In August 1917, ground troops, supported by monitor bombardment, will force the enemy in the vicinity to retire. While RNAS aircraft conduct fall-of-shot spotting, the monitor floods its ballast tanks to manage the necessary shell trajectory.

In October 1917, the Lindi aerodrome will be abandoned and a move made to Mtwa, where the RNAS machines cooperate in driving the enemy out of Makiwa. This engagement is the heaviest of the Defense of Zanzibar Campaign. As the German officers and their native Askari soldiers retreat, the naval airmen are employed flying low in search of water holes for the supply of friendly troops. Working ahead of the advancing soldiers, Delamere and his Observer, Fitzherbert, conduct photo work and draft maps of the countryside. During this time, the Squadron contends with shortages of everything: 'planes, personnel and parts.' Fever and dysentery are rampant but despite all setbacks, the unit runs several small and isolated operations with an unvarying success.

Delamere returns to England in January 1918 and thence goes on Canada Leave, taking along a DSC awarded for good work in East Africa. Returning to Felixstowe in mid-June of that year, he finishes his war operating Large America flying boats. *(Read 21Nov18)*

**07Feb16 – FSLt John 'Jack' ROBINSON
(Toronto) – Africa**

Like **Delamere**, Robinson joins Number 7 Squadron in Africa. There, Commander Cull describes him as a: 'Safe and Reliable Pilot & should develop into a skilful one & a good Officer.' In one year's time, by February 1917, Robinson will be Gazetted a MID by none-other than General Smuts, Commander East Africa, for Meritorious Service.

J Robinson
RAeC Trust

As with Delamere and everyone assigned to Africa, Robinson is taken aboard the books of HMS *Hyacinth*, flagship of the Cape and East Africa Station. A listing 'on the books' is a formality, primarily for administrative and accounting purposes. Prior to this appointment, and like all other Probationary FSLt's, Robinson has been carried on the books of HMS *President II* since acceptance in the Royal Navy. Tied up alongside on the River Thames in London, *President*'s staff implements the documentary matters of RNAS Pilots unless they are assigned overseas. All RN personnel must belong to a Commissioned warship, so as to be subject to Naval orders and discipline. Completing his African tour in May 1917, Robinson will depart Durban for England. *(Read 13Nov17)*

08Feb16 – FSLt Thomas Gordon Mair STEPHENS (Toronto) – Crash(es)

According to Stephens' own account: "I left Bembridge at 3:30pm 8th Inst. in Nieuport Seaplane 3190 for patrol. Owing to bursting of induction pipe was forced to land in rough sea. Was eventually picked up about 5:30pm by Hospital Ship *St.Andrew*, which took the machine in tow with rope I made fast to the boss of propeller. The sea becoming so rough, the m/c broke away and disappeared. I was conveyed to Rouen in *St. Andrew* & returned in her to Southampton on Feb 11th, & sent to Haslar Hospital suffering from exposure & chill." One week later Stephens will report fit and by March is flying Hostile Aircraft Patrols out of Dover. There, the cold weather takes its toll and he is down with neurasthenia in June, but recovers by mid September. However, in yet another incident on October 23rd, he sustains slight shock following the forced landing and loss of Short Seaplane 8558 near the Long Sand Light Vessel. Once more Stephens and his Air Mechanic are fortunate to be rescued by a friendly ship.

Fit yet again by the end of November, Stephens will have the pleasure of experiencing the warmer waters of Egypt with an appointment to Port Said. He will crash twice more—and be injured twice—in operations from the seaplane carriers HMS *Raven II*, and HMS *Empress*, but he will also be twice Mentioned in Despatches for his efforts with the East Indies Group.

13Feb16 – PFSLt Neil Howard McDIARMID (Victoria) – INJ/REL

A McGill student, McDiarmid earned his flying 'ticket' on the Curtiss Flying Boats in Toronto Harbour. Now in

NH McDiarmid

England he is operating another flying boat, FBA Pusher Bi-plane 3205 at Calshot, when he crashes. The Air Station reports: 'Machine was apparently being handled well. Pilot attempted then to turn sharply, & with too much bank, with result that m/c sideslipped & nose-dived into the water. Pilot rescued from wreckage but there was no sign of Passenger, Air Mechanic FG Haynes. Pilot sustained injuries to nose & forehead, back slightly bruised & severe shock. He has been dispatched to Haslar Hospital. Although not having flown much at this station, was considered quite a good pilot.'

McDiarmid needs a good three months to recover from the trauma of the crash and the loss of his passenger. Finally resurveyed as fit, he graduates a fully-fledged Flight Sub-Lieutenant at the end of June. Subsequently assigned to Air Station Yarmouth, he becomes noted for carrying out Hostile Aircraft Patrols (HAPs) in Avro 504C night fighters, looking for enemy intruders. However by October he will suffer from the effects of the aggravated nervous breakdown, neurasthenia, and is 'Released to Shore' as Medically Unfit. It is a Honourable Release, with an expression of TL's regret and the granting of a free passage back to Canada. McDiarmid is also awarded a gratuity of £35 in compensation for his 'unfitness'.

Ever keen to serve, McDiarmid rejoins the RNAS in a draft of aviators from Toronto in March 1918 but is again Honourably Released in May of that year.

15Feb16 – FSLt Herbert Joseph PAGE (Saturna Island BC) – MIA

When a hostile enemy seaplane is reported, Yarmouth Station launches new pilot Page to intercept. This is a winter patrol and the weather closes. Page, only six weeks since wings graduation, together with his Observer, FSLt RB Lee, fails to return. The following morning, Yarmouth telegrams the Admiralty: 'Regret to report this officer who ascended for patrol in Short Seaplane No 8220 at 4pm 15th Inst, is missing. Have sent all available ships in search, but in view of SW gale blowing, have ordered them to return, as further search seems hopeless.'

The Commander-in-Chief Naval Base Lowestoft orders an investigation. This Court of Enquiry finds: 'No blame is attributable to anyone. All necessary precautions were made previous to the flight, machine being in perfect order before leaving. The OC of the Station was quite justified in allowing this patrol to be carried out, the weather conditions at the time being suitable. It is presumed the machine was forced to descend, & apparently sunk, causing the crew to be drowned.'

The missing seaplane, Short Admiralty 827 8220, had been a presentation aircraft *New York Britons No. 1*. Another paid-and-presented machine from the same Short 827 construction lot is *Shanghai Britons No. 3*. Such aircraft are becoming more common in the RNAS inventory, as gifts to the War effort from overseas contributors continue to arrive.

29Feb16 – PFSLt Albert Oswald BRISSENDEN (Nova Scotia) – Probation

Brissenden is not endearing himself to the Royal Navy. Since taking his ticket in Canada, he has displayed an indifferent attitude to further flying examinations in England. He continually executes bad landings and on one occasion runs into another aircraft after touchdown. Achieving only nineteen percent on a simple paper on engines, he is sent for further examination in 'E' subjects. The Engineering Lieutenant Commander reports: 'He stated that he did not expect when he left Canada, that he would be expected to take any exams, & conveyed the impression that he did not like exams, & thought they were quite unnecessary, since he had come over here to fly.'

In spite of such poor reports, Brissenden does eventually graduate from Probation in May, although reported as 'Inclined to be careless & casual.' In August, flying with 3 Wing in France, he will completely wreck Sopwith Strutter 9747

AO Brissenden

RAeC Trust

near Beauvais. Sustaining a double fracture of his left leg and hip, he is medically released as being unfit for any further service.

MARCH 1916

23Mar16 – PFSLt Thomas William WEBBER (Toronto) – REL Unsuitable

Although he graduated from the Curtiss Canada School in September 1915, Webber has been found Unsuitable for the Royal Navy. The termination process for his appointment began with his Flight Commander's unfavourable report from the Eastchurch Flying School the previous December: 'I do not consider that this Officer is at all suitable to hold a commission in H.M. Service. He is quite unfit socially, & unable to talk or write English correctly.

TW Webber

RAeC Trust

'He fails in conversation to aspirate his H's, and constructs his sentences ungrammatically. He does not appear to have previously associated with gentlemen on terms of equality.

'I regret that I cannot give a very impartial opinion on his value as a pilot. Owing to constant bad weather & lack of sound machines, I have not had much opportunity to watch him fly. He has, however, made four flights on Curtiss machines, on two of which he damaged the machine when landing. Although this does not mean that he might not eventually develop into a good pilot, I am of the opinion that at present he is considerably below the average. I would submit that he may be removed from this station. It is very unsatisfactory to have an officer who is considerably less educated than a number of the men.'

By March this same English Flight Commander, Reginald Matrix, has been promoted to Squadron Commander and he again reports on the Probationary Webber: 'As an Officer he has proved most unsatisfactory.

I have watched him carefully, & am fully convinced he will never develop into even a moderate Officer. In a recent exam held after a fortnights instruction, he was unable to answer a single question, & could not even define "a true course" although all the other Officers answered the questions.

'I consider his general behaviour brings discredit upon the Service, as he cannot understand that Officers in uniform do not behave like the people he has obviously associated with. I have never been able to entrust any duties to him, & he has proved quite useless in every way. As a Pilot he cannot be depended upon, as after several months in the Air Service, he is still unable to work out a course correctly, & generally loses his way as soon as he gets out of sight of the Aerodrome.'

Webber is duly Released. Astoundingly, by early summer he is back in Canada and holding a position as an instructor pilot with the Curtis School in Toronto. Claiming to have been flying costal patrols and delivering aircraft to the front, Webber is readily taken into the Long Branch operation to teach new students. It is perhaps not surprising that he is involved in the only crash reported in the 1916 Toronto newspapers, when a Jenny falls just after takeoff. The undercarriage and wings are smashed and pilot and pupil severely shaken. The newspaper reports the cause to have been gusty wind conditions. The insouciant Webber is back on the job within two weeks; no record exists that his student J. Harley Shaw ever became a graduate of the school.

24Mar16 – FSLt Richard Eldon BUSH (Canadian; b. ENG) – INJ; Later KIC

Landing Bristol Scout 3023 at Westgate, Bush misjudges the approach, touches down too late and fails to stop before the aircraft reaches the edge of the cliffs and plunges to the sea. Fortunately the tide is high and the water cushions the aircraft's fall. Bush sustains cuts on the head and severe shock. He is reported as having 'Nothing broken – progressing favourably.'

The Westgate aerodrome is very small and its surroundings do not offer a pilot much margin for error at the most critical moments of flight; that is, during landing or taking off. This accident, coupled with frequent storm damage to the airfield, spurs the development of an alternate field at Manston. Westgate had been selected in August 1914 as an expedient site from which to fly anti-submarine cover for the British Expeditionary Force crossing the Channel.

RE Bush

Described as a very good pilot, 'Keen & Plucky' Bush had joined the Royal Canadian Navy in August 1914, and transferred to the Army's 28th London Regiment in early 1915. He then entered the RNAS in July of that year.

Eventually appointed to Naval Air Station Fishguard, Bush is lost in April 1917. Leaving the water in Sopwith Baby N1033 during test flight, he banks to port and strikes a cliff, bursting into flames. The two sixteen-pound bombs aboard explode, rendering machine a total wreck. Although pulled from the fire by a military sentry, Bush sustains severe burns over much of his body and cuts about the head.

The 26-year-old succumbs to his injuries at five in the morning on 24 April and his body is interred at the Keynsham Cemetery, Somerset. A Court of Enquiry will find that FLt Bush made an error in judgment in not having the machine overhauled, and that the: 'Accident was primarily due to attempting to fly in a confined space'.

APRIL 1916

01Apr16 – PFSLt Arthur Gerald WOODWARD (Victoria) – Crash

In training at Calshot, Woodward crashes Short 184, 8001. His CO reports: 'Pilot apparently failed to look ahead before opening out to get off water, with result that he hit the Black Jack Buoy, completely wrecking machine. Pilot practically unhurt & was picked up by emergency Motor Boat. M/C was towed to Calshot Pier & salved. This Officer has been flying very well, so I do not consider that accident due to bad flying, but to extreme carelessness.'

One week later, Woodward overturns Sopwith Schneider 3779 on takeoff. This second crash might spell termination of an appointment but Woodward had arrived from basic training at Eastbourne as a 'very sound and promising officer.' The former medical student finishes the seaplane course on the 12th of April and his Probationary title is removed.

FSLt Woodward's graduation report is a good example of the training that the new pilots receive and of the selection process for scouts or seaplanes: 'He has now flown a total of 9 hours 37 minutes & is a good Pilot on the bigger machines & flying boats. Did not prove quick enough to properly control a Sopwith Schneider, & appeared too nervous of this type to continue. Did well in exams on Navigation, Hints on Flying, Construction & Rigging of Seaplanes, Types of Vessels, Map reading & Aero Engines; but did not do so well on Seamanship, W/T, Signaling, & Meteorology. His drilling & attention to classes has been good. Generally he is a good Officer, keen and reliable. Should be most useful abroad flying 225-hp Shorts.'

In August Woodward will depart for Gibraltar and the Mediterranean. Gaining experience, he overcomes the 'nervousness' and by mid-1917 is flying the lighter 'fast scouts' out of the Greek islands to good effect.

02Apr16 – FSLt George Cyril Van HEWSON (Port Hope ON) – Crash(es)

A crash on landing at Dunkirk's Coudekerque aerodrome results in a dislocated left shoulder for Hewson. His Caudron G.IV 9115 is written-off and Hewson granted sick leave from 5 Wing to proceed to Canada for convalescence.

Returning to France and joining 1 Wing in December, Hewson will be ferrying Nieuport 12 8914 to England when he crashes at the Dover Royal Flying Corps airfield. This time he is very badly injured and later in 1917 will be declared fit for ground duties only.

GCV Hewson

24Apr16 – FSLt Alexander MacDonald SHOOK (Tioga ON) – MID

Flying with 5 Wing out of Dunkirk, Shook takes part in an air raid on Mariakerke Aerodrome at Ostend. The Vice Admiral, Dover 'Mentions' Shook for his attack: 'well pressed home.'

A Red Deer, Alberta schoolteacher, Shook joined the Dunkirk Wing in February and was first reported as: 'Will probably do well. Has flying confidence although he appears nervous in manner.' Now two months later he

AM Shook

is rated a: 'thoroughly conscientious. Good Pilot.' An accident at the end of the month renders him unfit until September but, re-qualified by October he is back in France. On Sopwith Pups with 4 Naval Squadron, the future Ace will bring down his first enemy machine in April 1917. *(Read 04Jun17)*

25Apr16 – PFSLt John Keith WAUGH (Whitby ON) – FSLt

The *Globe and Mail* newspaper of Toronto reports: 'Writing to his parents in Whitby, John Keith Waugh of Calshot Camp, England, a prominent Toronto hockey player, tells of having been successful in winning first place in the examinations for the Royal Naval Air Service. This gives him his rank as Flight (Sub) Lieutenant and also an instructorship at Calshot. Waugh commenced his course last June in Toronto and went to England last fall.'

By January 1917, Waugh, 'A capable Officer & Instructor in every way,' will be placed in command of the Calshot Sub-Station at Portland in Dorset. There, he has a patrol area of 6,000 square miles, covering the western reaches of the English Channel. His unit consists of three other pilots, three armourers acting as observers, and four different, and old, machine-types with which to carry out his missions. Made an Acting Flight Commander in July, he will have his first crack at the enemy on the 23rd of September 1917. In Wight Seaplane 9848 he drops three 100lb bombs on position where he and his Air

Mechanic crewman, Laycock, sight a diving U-boat, ten miles West of Portland Bill. Waugh reports: "It would appear probably from the disturbance produced that the submarine was damaged or sunk."

These long overwater missions can take a toll on an airman's health and by the end of September 1917 Waugh is ailing and in hospital. The 'Very capable CO & excellent Patrol Pilot' is eventually sent to the Peebles Convalescent Center in Scotland. Recovering by the spring of 1918, he will be Gazetted for the DSC for his zeal and devotion to duty. *(Read 20Aug18)*

25Apr16 – FSLt Garnet Nelson HUGHES (Picton ON) – INJ/REL

Flying Breguet DeChasse 3210, Hughes crashes at the flying school in Coudekerque France, sustaining a severe injury to his right shoulder. This is his second accident in twenty days, having suffered burns and cuts to both legs during the previous crash. His unit, Number 5 Wing, considers that it is undesirable, from a medical standpoint, that he fly again. Hughes is resurveyed in September and found to be medically unfit for further service. Diagnosed as having neurasthenia, he is released from the Navy.

GN Hughes

25Apr16 – FSLt Bert Sterling WEMP (Tweed ON) – Action

(From 19Nov15) In an effort to support the Easter Uprising in Ireland, the German High Seas Fleet raids the Scarborough East Coast area of England. Accompanied by Zeppelins, enemy battle cruisers shell the town of Lowenstoft. Wemp is one of several pilots who get airborne in retaliation. Pursuing a German Cuiser Squadron out to sea, he attacks the rear-most ships in line, dropping his eight puny 16lb bombs on the armoured vessels below. It is a brave, if foolhardy attempt, as every German gun that can be brought to bear takes a shot at Wemp's tiny BE2c, Number 8612.

BS Wemp

Wemp survives his brazen foray and will also survive a perhaps more hazardous duty – assignment to instruct at RNAS Redcar. In July he sustains cuts on the face and shock during a forced landing in a Caudron GIII. Then, in August, his student overshoots an approach and collides with a cottage. This Caudron is completely wrecked but the crew unhurt. In January 1917 Wemp suffers the indignity of an undercarriage collapse and broken propeller in a Curtiss Jenny landing. About this time he applies to be transferred to an alleged Naval Flying School in Canada but the rumor comes to naught. *(Read 03Jun18)*

25Apr16 – PFSLt William Fulton CLEGHORN (Toronto) – WIA

Probationary Pilot Cleghorn is performing his required 'G' (Gunnery) Course in the light cruiser HMS *Conquest* when he is wounded. His ship is in action during the night of 24th–25th of April, when the German heavy cruisers carry out the hit-and-run bombardment on Yarmouth and Lowestoft. Cleghorn receives a shrapnel wound to his face, fracturing his lower jaw and tearing away several teeth.

He is awarded a gratuity of seven-months' pay (£106) for compensation and he spends the next few months at Eastbourne Naval Air Station on ground duties.

'Cleggy' will at last graduate as a Pilot in early February 1917 and joins 5 Naval in Dunkirk. By January 1918 he will have earned Canada Leave, which is inadvertently extended by a telegraph company who then must forward their sincere apologies to the Admiralty, saving Cleghorn from certain Court Martial for being Absent Without Leave. By April of that year, he will return to Dunkirk for 218 Squadron RAF as a DH-4 Pilot. *(Read 02Oct18)*

WF Cleghorn
'Petite Synthes – 1918'
FAAM, E01085

27Apr16 – PFSLt Gerald Arthur MacLEAN (Toronto) – REL

Early in January, MacLean had reported aboard HMS *Riviera* out of Dunkirk to fly the Short 184 Seaplane-type, making him one of the first Canadians to operate ship-borne aircraft. However, a collision with a trawler during takeoff in February rendered him ill and he missed the strike by aircraft from *Riviera* and *Vindex* on the Zeebrugge Mole on the 20th of March. Now he is released from the service as Medically Unfit.

GA MacLean
RAeC Trust

A ship's report on MacLean had noted that he was: 'a zealous & promising young Officer. Has good bearing.' He will certainly prove to be zealous. After recovering his health in Canada he is hired by the Curtiss Flying School in Toronto as an Instructor. At the same time, he also begins to pester the Canadian Department of Naval Service. In January 1917, Ottawa sends a telegram to the Admiralty requesting that FSLt MacLean be reinstated. When the Royal Navy replies to the negative on medical grounds, MacLean promptly joins the Royal Flying Corps in Canada.

By April 1918, he is a fully qualified pilot and Captain, Royal Air Force. Although injured in May 1917 and again in May 1918, he does survive the War.

27Apr16 – FSLt Andrew John BODDY (Toronto) – KIC

The young Torontonian has been at Killingholme Naval Air Station just nine days and today, operating off the North Sea, he is killed in the wreck of Sopwith Baby 8147. A Curtiss Canada-trained aviator, he had recently graduated from Eastchurch with a glowing report: 'As a pilot, shows promise of being very good indeed. He has very good hands & plenty of nerve & pluck. Taking up a Bristol Scout for the first time, he made a perfect flight & landing, without using the air speed indicator. He has flown about 18 hours on all school types, including Farman, Bristol, Sopwith, & Bleriot machines, and has made no serious mistake.

'Recommended for High Speed Scout work, for which he is particularly suitable.'

AJ Boddy
RAeC Trust

30Apr16 – PFSLt Thomas Robson LIDDLE (Grimsby ON) – KIC

For any new pilot, the transitional period from post-solo caution to pre-graduate competence can be treacherous. This learning curve proves fatal for Liddle. While attempting a loop in Canadian-built Curtiss JN4, 3431, he loses control of the air craft and crashes into the Angel Railway Station Goods Yard in North London. The Chingford Base Inquest finds that: 'The Pilot, who was of considerable skill & ability was practicing the carrying-out of very heavily banked turns at a height of 3000 feet or more. During one of these the machine side-slipped downwards, after which it assumed an upside down position, which it retained for some time. The engine stopped, & machine got into a vertical nose-dive at 1000 feet, from which it did not recover before striking the earth. We do not consider that the blame is attributable

TR Liddle

RAeC Trust

to anyone.' Because he was killed in England, the body of the 20-year-old is permitted shipment back to Canada and Liddle is buried at St. Andrew's Anglican cemetery in Grimsby, Ontario. Later in the War, such overseas recovery of bodies from the United Kingdom by grieving families will not be allowed.

MAY 1916

04May16 – FSLt Kenneth Marsden VanALLEN (Brantford ON) – POW/DOW

Flying Caudron G.IV 9118 with 5 Wing, VanAllen fails to return from a night bombing raid on Mariakerke Aerodrome, Belgium. Heavy anti-aircraft fire was experienced during the attack and he has been shot down and taken prisoner. Severely wounded, VanAllen succumbs seven days later and is buried at Ingoyghem Military Cemetery, near the city of Bruges.

KM VanAllen

U of T

An 'old boy' of Lakefield Prep School and Trinity College School VanAllen had taken Applied Science at the University of Toronto (UofT), graduating in 1911 as an electrical engineer. His initial operational flying with the RNAS was out of Dover on costal patrols. New at the game, his first report read 'Started very well but has greatly depreciated. Very uncertain & has no confidence.' One month later the former UofT Rugby player has learned how to play this new sport and he is noted as being a: 'Reliable & serious hard worker.' He had been sent to Dunkirk for 5 Wing on April 26th.

The RNAS is still using the 'Wing' system of aircraft organization at this point of the war. VanAllen's Number 5 is based at Cloudekerque on the Belgian frontier. By late 1916 these Wings will be subdivided into more easily workable squadron formations in order to operate effectively with the RFC Squadrons on the Western Front.

06May16 – FSLt Arthur Thomas Noel COWLEY (Victoria) – POW

(From 02Aug15) Out of Dunkirk, Short 184 8038 suffers engine failure. According to an Official Communiqué from the Berlin Admiralty received the next day, a German Torpedo Boat at Nordsee has captured both seaplane and crew. Cowley and his Observer, Lt RM Inge, are eventually listed as Prisoners Of War at Heidelberg. For the Royal Navy, this is the loss of an aviator of great potential. Seven months beforehand,

ATN Cowley

RAeC Trust

Cowley's graduation report from Eastbourne stated: 'Entered by DNS Canada, has flown 75 HP Shorthorn M. Farnham; 70 HP BE2c; 80 HP Bleriot monoplane; 90HP Curtiss + 80 HP Farman. He is of a very good stamp, has flown a machine from Hendon to Eastbourne & if an Officer should be required for Foreign Service, I should recommend him. I consider him of the right type for the Service. His Naval Instructor also reports very well of him.' Cowley was duly appointed to Dunkirk Seaplanes.

In February, he conducted an early morning seaplane attack against the German Seaplane base on the Mole at Zebrugge, and was further described as '[…] an exceptional Seaplane Pilot. He is level headed & steady, & has great ability to command. He has a good technical training in engineering, & has great ability in application of this to matters of aviation.'

Capture puts a halt to a promising pilot's progress, and for the next two years Cowley is a POW at Mainz, Germany. In April 1918, he will be granted parole and transferred to internment in Holland.

Following the War, Cowley elects to stay in service with the new Canadian Air Force and during the 1920's flies out of Jericho Beach, Vancouver. These duties are in HS2L Flying Boats performing preventative patrols for the suppression of smuggling and illegal fishing: prohibition in USA gives him 'active service.' During the Second World War he will rise to the rank of Air Vice Marshal, RCAF.

21 May16 – FLt Redford Henry MULOCK (Winnipeg MB) – ACE

(*From 08Jul15*) Flying a solo mission in Nieuport XI 3992 from 1 Wing, Dunkirk, Mulock sends down two German aircraft out of control. Scoring this double victory makes him not only the first Canadian Ace but also the first RNAS pilot to achieve five enemy machines down—indeed, he is the world's first naval ace.

Mulock's feat is accomplished during a period in the War known as 'The Fokker Scourge'. Since the autumn of 1915, French and British aircraft have taken a severe beating from the Germans and their Fokker Eindeckker, the first aircraft armed with a machine-gun synchronized to fire through the turning propeller; a technology not yet possessed by the Allies. Mulock's machine, the French-built Nieuport biplane was originally designed as a peacetime air racer. It is equipped with a single Lewis gun mounted above the top wing in order to shoot over the propeller arc, giving the Allied pilots the same advantage as the Fokker aviators—that of simply aiming their aircraft. Also, the nimble Nieuport XI 'Bebe' is highly maneuverable, using aileron controls versus the awkward wing warping mechanism of the Eindekker. In experienced hands, the Naval Nieuports can easily out-fly the enemy.

Canada's first Royal Flying Corps Ace is Lieutenant Alan Duncan Bell-Irving of Vancouver, who will bring down his first enemy machine on the 28th of August

'Mulock sighting a gun on a Nieuport Scout'
Note the watchful mascot, lower left

FAAM, Album 441 2000/065/0222

1916 and in just over one month, attain a fifth victory on the 30th of September. He too will fly the Nieuport XI. Other RFC squadrons employ the DeHavilland 2 pusher-type aircraft, which have a rear-mounted engine, giving the pilot a chilly but unobstructed firing platform. By the time of the disastrous Somme ground battles in the summer of 1916, the RNAS and the RFC will have regained control of the skies through a policy of Offensive Patrol—taking the fight to the enemy.

The London Gazette cites Mulock in June 1916 naming him to the Distinguished Service Order (DSO): 'This officer has been constantly employed at Dunkirk since July 1915 and has displayed indefatigable zeal and energy. He has on several occasions engaged hostile aeroplanes and seaplanes, and attacked submarines, and has carried out attacks on enemy air stations and made long distance reconnaissance.' (*Read 06Feb17*)

22May16 – FSLt Grant Armstrong GOODERHAM (Toronto) – Action

Airborne in a Nieuport scout, Gooderham spots five hostile aircraft in close formation with yet another further behind. He closes and attacks the tail-end machine from underneath at very close range. When his tracers enter the German fuselage, the enemy Observer ceases return fire. As Gooderham breaks off to change his now-empty 47-round Lewis gun magazine tray, the hostile aircraft draws away.

'Gooderham and Lutz'

FAAM, 2000/065/0085

Gooderham was the fourth graduate of the Curtiss Flying School in Canada. A University of Toronto civil engineer, he has become proficient at flying Hostile Submarine Patrols (HSPs) after reported U-boat contacts and Hostile Aircraft Patrols (HAPs) against enemy intruders, including Zeppelins.

Recommended for single-seat Nieuports he, like Mulock, becomes one of the Royal Navy's first true fighter pilots. His 1 Wing Dunkirk Report in April described him as: 'VG & careful Pilot & good night flyer. Very keen, zealous & hard working on the ground. Is a good all-round Officer.'

Short in stature, Gooderham's fellow pilots have cheerfully nicknamed him 'Stumpy'.

Throughout 1916, Gooderham will experience many other non-scoring engagements. Often the enemy machines are superior in speed and escape, or else it is the limited firepower and frequent stoppages of the Lewis Gun that hinders results. In early December, flying the prototype Sopwith Triplane N500, Gooderham engages an Enemy Aircraft over the floods near Pervyse. As he opens fire with the new synchronized Vickers gun, the EA disappears into clouds. By February 1917, the winter months of front line flying will sorely tell on Gooderham's health, and he is admitted to the Haslar Naval Hospital with a diagnosis of neurasthenia. *(Read 02May19)*

30May16 – FSLt William Herbert MacKENZIE (Victoria) – U-boat

Off Felixstowe, MacKenzie carries out a patrol of over five-and-a-half hours' duration. His Short Seaplane 8347 is equipped with the standard war load of a Lewis machine-gun, three trays of ammunition, and two 65 lb bombs. In addition, his English Observer, FSLt Ball, is operating a new wireless device. Together they spot and attack an enemy submarine from a height of 800 feet, dropping one bomb, which misses the U-boat by only a few feet, causing it to submerge. They immediately send a wireless transmission to all ships in the vicinity warning them of submarine activity in the area. The tenacity of the patrol is both a proof and repudiation on MacKenzie's assessment of the previous month when he was judged as: 'Tries, but at present does not show much promise.' He continues to try and is soon re-considered as a 'Hardworking Officer and good Pilot' by the time of his June report.

Almost one year later, in February 1917, the pre-War British Columbia building contractor will receive appointment to 2 Naval, a bomber squadron in Taranto, Italy. His enthusiasm for his work is recognized as invaluable and MacKenzie is assessed as: 'A natural leader of men, VG organizer. Would make excellent 1st Lieutenant for a Station.' This report is acted upon by the Navy and MacKenzie is sent to the Calshot Torpedo School in February 1918, and thence to East Fortune in Scotland where he helps to develop torpedo bombing tactics. He refuses to take the Canadian Leave that he has earned from two-years overseas duty. In April 1919, Major WH Mackenzie, RAF, will be awarded the Air Force Cross for distinguished services during the War.

JUNE 1916

10 Jun 16 – FSLt George Knox WILLIAMS (Port Credit ON) – KIC – Midair

GK Williams

U of T

Williams is killed while flying in a joint-aerodrome training session with the French 4th bomber group at Luxeuil-les-Bains. Carrying a French gunner (Soldat Beaucourt) on a familiarization flight, his Sopwith Strutter collides with a French two-seater Nieuport. All four aviators are lost. A University of Toronto graduate and a teacher before entering the RNAS, Williams had served as the Secretary of the Aero Club of Canada. He was 28 years of age and is the first casualty of the newly reactivated 3 Wing.

12 Jun 16 – PFO Hugh ALLAN (Montreal, PQ) – Release Request

(From 07May15) Allan joined the RNAS in England two short days ago. He had been serving as Lieutenant, Machine-gun Instructor, at the Canadian Military School in Shorncliffe. Now, as the awful news from the Somme battlefield begins to trickle across the Channel, he telegrams the Admiralty that he: "Desires to remain with the Canadian Infantry to replace casualties in the field." However, his Naval appointment is ordered to stand.

Still grieving the loss of his two sisters drowned in the sinking of the *Lusitania,* Allan more than ever wants to get into action. Remaining with the RNAS, he trains on scout aircraft and is sent to 3 Naval Squadron in France. Described as a 'daring fighter' he will receive a Mention for good work while serving with 3 Naval 'in the field.' Despite his fighting spirit, and with his desire for battle yet unfulfilled, Hugh Allan's life will end on the 6th of July 1917, when his Sopwith Pup N6181 dives into the ground near Furnes. The only son of Sir Montague Allan of Montreal is buried at Coxyde (Koksijde) Military Cemetery, Belgium.

13 Jun 16 – PFSLt Ken Chesborough FREEMAN (Wallaceburg ON) – REL

Freeman forwards his request to be allowed to resign from the Naval Air Service. His Chingford instructors agree, stating that: 'He is not making satisfactory progress, & is unlikely to be of use in the Service.' By the 19th of July, Freeman has apparently reconsidered his options about returning home without Rank. He is charged with offering a consideration as an inducement to the grant of a Commission. The Public Prosecutor's Department hands down a severe admonition.

JULY 1916

09 Jul 16 – PFSLt Paul Oliver GADBOIS (Montreal) – INJ

In training at Calshot, Gadbois slips into a spinning seaplane propeller and sustains a cerebral concussion, his second accident in a matter of weeks. Less than one month earlier, at the Northern Aircraft Company School at Windermere, he had taken FBA Flying Boat 3650 for a short hop and nose-dived into the lake. He was then only slightly shaken, but the aircraft had to be deleted from inventory. By September Gadbois, recovered from his propeller scalping, returns and graduates from flying school.

PO Gadbois

RAeC Trust

Months later, in March 1917 Gadbois will experience a forced landing while ferrying a recently repaired Curtiss Jenny, 8831, from Grain Island to Chingford. The aircraft is surveyed off the books and this time Gadbois is quite badly shaken and, subsequently, requests to be relieved from flying duties for nervous reasons. Sent back to Canada for sick leave, he is resurveyed unfit and invalided, but to retain Rank. His release will include a service gratuity for disability.

10Jul16 – FSLt Wm Malcom Colin MATHESON (Winnipeg) – HMS *Manxman*

Upon graduation in May, Matheson was appointed to the Seaplane Carrier HMS *Campania* for deck-flying tests. Now follows an appointment to HMS *Manxman* at the Scapa Flow in the Orkneys, a natural deep-water harbour, and home to the Royal Navy's Grand Fleet.

Consisting of nearly forty modern capital ships, the anchorage was formed in 1914 by Sea Lord Churchill's amalgamation of the British Home Fleet and the Atlantic Fleet.

In early November, Matheson is described as 'Good S'plane Pilot & zealous Officer. Displays initiative powers of command.' However, winter

WMC Matheson

RAeC Trust

flying over frigid waters will cost him his health and by March 1917, Matheson is suffering from heart disease & neurasthenia. Sent home on Canadian Sick Leave, he is resurveyed in Winnipeg and diagnosed with an 'irregularity of heart and pulse.' In early 1918, the Department of Naval Service Canada terminates his appointment and Matheson is awarded a Gratuity of 150 Pounds Sterling per year for the 'Disability of Vertigo, aggravated by Service.'

15Jul16 – FSLt Dan Murray Bayne GALBRAITH (Carleton Place ON) – DSC & Cd'G

Patrolling ten miles out to sea in Nieuport XI 3963, Galbraith encounters a German seaplane at 12,000 feet off Ostend. The outcome is reported in a Dunkirk Communiqué: 'The enemy manoeuvered for position behind the Nieuport, both M/C's meanwhile executing a steep glide. Our Pilot then looped over & above the hostile M/C, which passed underneath, thus giving the Nieuport the desired position behind, empting one tray into the enemy at 100 yards range. Bullets were observed to pass in behind the pilot's seat. The German Pilot being palpably hit, made a vertical nose-dive and the M/C was last seen in flames falling headlong downwards.'

Galbraith has been flying with 1 Naval Wing just one month, and this is his first victory. On the 28th of September, in **Red Mulock's** Nieuport 3992, he scores again: 'This officer, whilst patrolling the sea, sighted a large enemy two-seater seaplane. The enemy machine blew up in the air, probably caused by his bombs having been struck and exploded. From the position, it appears probable that this machine was on its way to attack the southeast coast of England. Flight Sub-Lieutenant Galbraith's machine was severely damaged by gunfire from the enemy; his windscreen and gun sight being shot away in the early part of the encounter, but the pilot continued his attack. This was witnessed by the pilot and observer of a French seaplane.' For this second action, Galbraith is conferred the Croix de Guerre (Cd'G) by the Commander of the French air forces and Gazetted the Royal Navy's DSC. By October, he is flying Sopwith Pups and will have brought down a third German Seaplane. *(Read 16Nov16)*

16Jul16 – FSLt Arthur York WILKS (Westmount PQ) – Crash

Wilks falls afoul of his Station Commander at NAS Calshot when he completely wrecks Short Admiralty 827 Seaplane 8557: 'Cause of the accident was because the Pilot attempted to fly the machine, and actually got off the water, with the wheel control pillar locked by the locking bar. I can find no excuse for this Officer's accident, which I put down to gross carelessness. Had my written orders been obeyed, it would have been impossible for him not to have noticed that the pillar was locked.'

At sea off Killingholme in February 1917, Wilks will wreck yet another aircraft, Short 184, 9082. By that July, he will leave England for the Mediterranean and fly out of the Island of Thasos without further (recorded) incident. His reports while there describe him as a very good pilot and a well-disciplined officer.

18Jul16 – PFSLt William Brodie EDMONDS (Toronto) – REL to CEF

Edmonds' Commission is terminated with the comment: 'This Officer will never make a useful aeroplane Pilot but is satisfactory in all other respects & has a good general education. Grant passage back to Canada if he so desires.' Edmonds, a University of Toronto man, does not so desire; rather, he wishes to serve and transfers to the Canadian Expeditionary Force. As an Infantry Officer he will be Wounded in Action at Ypres during July 1917. Following the war, he returns to school and becomes a physician.

20Jul16 – FSLt Douglas H. WHITTIER (Victoria BC) – KIC

A member of 3 Wing awaiting orders to Luxeuil, France, Whittier attempts a low level loop in Bristol Scout C1245 at Manston, England. His machine loses speed, and twists into a sideslip, which tightens into a spiraling nosedive. There is simply not enough altitude to recover: Death from Misadventure is the verdict of the Court of Inquiry, as all controls are found in good order. The inquest also notes: 'This Officer was a good Pilot and his death is deeply felt amongst the Officers & Men of the Wing'. Arrangements are made with the Army to provide a gun carriage, band and firing party for the funeral. Age 24, Whittier is buried at Thanet, Kent.

20Jul16 – FSLt William Ross WALLACE (Westmount, PQ) – KIC

From the Telephone Log of Naval Air Station Calshot it is learned that Wallace has been very badly injured in an accident to Short 827 Seaplane 8556 at Southampton Docks. His machine failed to clear the mainmast of the transport ship *Paucras,* and crashed

onto the deck of the vessel. Wallace, flying as a passenger, has been conveyed to Netley Hospital. It is reported that he is not expected to live and the following day a Naval signal from Calshot informs that he has passed away during the night. Aged 20, Wallace is buried at Haslar Royal Naval Cemetery, in Hampshire.

WR Wallace

RAeC Trust

30Jul16 – FSLt James Alpheus 'Jimmy' GLEN (Enderby BC) – First Action

Number 3 Wing has been ferrying Sopwith Strutters from England to the south of France in order to begin bombing operations. However, the Battle of the Somme has created a severe shortage of RFC pilots and machines and the War Office has begged aircraft from the Admiralty. Only today is the newly-formed Wing able to mount its first attack, a three-ship effort.

Glen flies the sole Strutter bomber (Pilot only), escorted by two Strutter fighters (Pilot & Gunner), and drops four 65lb bombs on the German fuel storage tanks at Mulheim.

By April 1917, Glen will be conferred the Cd'G avec Palm by General Nollet, Number 36 French Army Corps, for assisting the French at Verdun. *(Read 07Jul17)*

AUGUST 1916

04Aug16 – PFSLt Albert Ed. Ernest BLACKBURN (Lower Truro NS) – REL

Blackburn is Released and appointed to the RNVR as Temporary Sub Lieutenant. His Cranwell CO writes: 'This Officer has applied to transfer to Motor Boats, I concur in his request as I consider he will never become an efficient Pilot. He has considerable experience in small boats in the Bay of Fundy & he may be of use. I am satisfied with his conduct.'

Blackburn achieves the RN rank of full Lieutenant and

AEE Blackburn

RAeC Trust

commands Motor Launch 504, serving until September 1917 when he is invalided out of the Navy.

23Aug16 – FSLt Melville Grant DOVER (Winnipeg) – Palestine Action

(From 06Dec15) Dover takes part in bombing raids flown by ten seaplanes from *Ben-my-Chree,* the former Isle of Man steamer, and *Raven II* and *Anne,* both one-time German cargo vessels that had been seized and converted to carrier service. The target is El Afuleh, on the railway line inland and south of Nazareth. Attack aircraft strike Turkish stores and rolling stock despite heavy AA fire. Dover and his observer make two sorties from *Ben-my-Chree,* scoring hits on a railway station and wagons on both occasions. The Vice Admiral C-in-C East Indies & Egypt writes: 'This operation was

well organized and gallantly carried out. The GOC in Command Egypt, expressed his grateful thanks for these flights, which he considered to be of great military value.'

By November and into early December, Dover will be noted for making reconnoiter flights along the coast to Bursir, Gaza, Cesaria, Tul Keram and Samaria. He will fly out of Italy during 1917 and then return to Canada on Leave in early 1918, remaining in the Dominion for instructional duties pending amalgamation of the services. Dover completes his war service with the RAF's Canadian training organization.

31 Aug16 – FSLt John Alfred HARMAN (Uxbridge ON) – INJ

In a practice flight at the Detling Night Landing Ground, Harman strikes a treetop and nose-dives onto the airfield. Both he and his airman passenger suffer cuts and bruises. They are fortunate to be alive, as the aircraft, Curtiss JN3 N3420, is a write-off.

JA Harman, still smiling
'FSLt Harman after forced landing, Detling 1916'
FAAM, 1991/235/101

Harman's Curtis 'Jenny'
FAAM, 1991/235/44

Harman had taken his initial license with the Stinson School in San Antonio, Texas, in December 1915 and had graduated from Probationary Sub Lieutenant status at Cranwell during July 1916.

Following recovery from his mishap at Detling, Harman is sent via an overland route through France to join 2 Wing in the Eastern Mediterranean. Initially based on the Island of Mudros, he will be badly shaken in a May 1917 accident when returning from a reconnaissance mission. Then, in August, flying Short 184 N1261 off the Seaplane Carrier Ark Royal, he overturns on a downwind water landing. His Report reads: 'Hard-working Officer. Keen on flying. Has had continual bad luck as a Pilot and needs a rest'.

Harman submits a request to transfer to the Canadian Expeditionary Forces on medical grounds but then elects to resign his Commission. He will be released from the Royal Navy in November 1917 with the rank of Flight Lieutenant and a gratuity of £150. He records his Canadian destination as Medicine Hat, Alberta.

Many Canadians fly with 2 Wing in the Eastern Mediterranean. They operate out of seaplane carriers, from bases ashore in Macedonia and from the Classical Greek lands that they had read about as boys - Homer's fabled islands of the Aegean.

SEPTEMBER 1916

07Sep16 – FSLt Charles Beverley SPROATT (Toronto) – MIDx2

In France, Sproatt has received a Mentioned in Despatches for a tenacious attack on Ghistelle Aerodrome on the third of September. Now, four days later, he bombs the St. Denis Westrem airfield and is again Mentioned. He completes the month with a raid on the Airship Sheds at Evere in Brussels. For the past five months, Sproatt has been flying the twin-engine Caudron G.IV bombers with 5 Wing, Dunkirk. In spite of ditching one machine in July and being rated for lacking in experience, he was also noted as being a 'Promising' officer. Now, his double Mention fulfills the promise.

CB Sproatt

RAeC Trust

One year later, Sproatt will fly the De Havilland DH-4 with 5 Naval Squadron and earn a DSC. On September 4th 1917, while subjected to heavy and accurate anti-aircraft fire, he presses home a determined attack on the Bruges Docks although his machine is very much shot about and the radiator pierced. An Acting Flight Commander by October 1917, Sproatt is described as a 'Brilliant 2-seater Pilot.'

Following a well-deserved Canada Leave in January 1918, he returns to an assignment at Yarmouth for Home Service, flying the new DH-9 with 212 RAF. Returning again to Canada at war's end, he takes up architecture and becomes known for Ontario Hydro designs. During the Second World War Sproatt is a Director for the building of Mosquito and Lancaster aircraft.

13Sep16 – Telegram
From Aircraft Westrand To Naval Ottawa:

'Twenty-four pilots for RNAS may be entered per month until further notice under usual conditions. STOP. Request entries may be spread out as evenly as possible. STOP.

[signed] E. Vaughn Lee, Rear Admiral
Director of Air Services, Royal Navy'

The Admiralty is now fully cognizant of the continuing 'wastage of war' on pilots and 'planes. The telegram to Admiral Kingsmill of the Royal Canadian Navy gives clear direction to continue to enroll Candidates with the RNAS.

19Sep16 – FSLt John Augustus BARRON (Stratford ON) – MID

(From 17Mar15) In Coastal Airship C10 out of NAS Mullion, Cornwall, Barron is working with the Destroyer HMS *Foyle* when he comes upon two burning sailing ships and a surfaced German submarine. The surprised U-boat submerges before the airship can attack but leaves behind the stores stolen from the French ships that it had plundered before torching. For this rescue action, Barron is Mentioned in Despatches.

By the following June, Barron is appointed to 6 Wing based in Taranto, Italy. From there he will fly anti-submarine airship patrols over the Otranto Strait and the Adriatic. Within months of his arrival, he is promoted to Flight Commander and given charge of the Wing's Airship Squadron. In recognition of his efforts, Italy will decorate Barron as a Cavaliere, Order of St. Maurice and St. Lazarus. *(Read 08Feb18)*

20Sep16 – FSLt James Douglas SCOTT (Regina; b. Montreal) – KIC

Lost on a 3 Wing training flight near Luxeuil, France, Scott's navigational error costs him his life. The crash of Sopwith Strutter 9726 also costs the Navy a good man: 'A very sound, keen & promising Officer. Fine all round Pilot of great courage. Should do excellently abroad.'

Age 27, the former Regina real estate manager is buried at Luxeuil. One of the very few married Canadians, Scott's widow will be informed that no gratuity is payable to his estate.

JD Scott

RAeC Trust

23Sep16 – FSLt David Douglas FINDLAY
(Carleton Place ON) – Dardanelles

Findlay graduated from the Stinson Flying School in San Antonio, Texas, with American license 463. He will later recall:

"I got my ticket about March 28th. The fee was $240.00 for four hours flying – a dollar a minute. Our aeroplane was a Wright twin-prop pusher. After about 15 hours further flying in England I was posted to No. 2 Wing on the *Ark Royal* at Mudros Harbour on the Greek island of Lemnos in September. [We] were sent to replace old experienced pilots diverted to help the hard-pressed Roumanians. Our wing had squadrons deployed on the islands of Crete, Lemnos, Lesbos, Imbros, Thasos and on the Macedonian mainland at Stavros. Our job was to harry the Turks and Bulgarians and, in particular, to watch for the German warships *Goeben* and *Breslau*, berthed at Constantinople. To this end the Imbros-based squadron made a dawn and dusk flight the whole length of the Dardanelles every flying day.

"In September 1916, 'first line machines' were B.E.2C's, Henri Farmans and two-seater Nieuports. Then we got Sopwith Strutters and later Pups.

"In the spring of 1917, some of the more experienced pilots were hand-picked to form 'F' Squadron. Canada was well represented and I am proud to say I was among those present. We practiced the then unused technique of flying formation in Sopwith Strutters. When we got proficient we went into action and literally ruled the skies. We bombed enemy shipping, bridges, railway centers, troop concentrations and, I am ashamed to say, burned the ripe grain crops in Bulgarian Macedonia with petroleum bombs.

"I think it is accurate to say that the RNAS and RFC (on the Struma and Vardar fronts) had virtual control of the air in 1917 and 18 and made life miserable for the enemy. I like to think that is one reason why the Bulgars and Turks decided they were on the losing side and were the first the throw in the sponge."

Findlay flies with No. 2 Wing for over a year and is described as: 'A Very Good Pilot & Good Officer. Has carried out many long night raids. Shows great keenness.' However, service in the Eastern Mediterranean brings him down with malaria and he is sent on Canada Leave. To add further inconvenience, the liner in which he sets sail is torpedoed and all his personal effects are lost. Rescued back to England, he is furnished with a duplicate letter authorizing him to proceed. Findlay will return from Leave in May 1918 and become an instructor at Portholme Meadow Air Station. *(Read 1933)*

25Sep16 – FSLt James Curtis WATSON
(Victoria) – Ditched

On patrol out of Dunkirk, Watson cannot avoid a water-landing when his 240 horsepower Sunbeam Gurkha engine fails. He is adrift in Short 184 9049 until rescued the next day.

Watson will endure yet another engine failure and another chilling experience in February 1917.

JC Watson

Taking off to bomb Ostende, he pancakes 9047 in Dunkirk Harbour, beaching the machine amid snow and ice. Surveyed unfit, he is sent on Canadian sick leave to recover from frostbite. Watson returns to duty with an appointment to NAS Felixstowe in July 1917.

26Sep16 – PFSLt Patrick Sylvester KENNEDY
(South Porcupine ON) – KIC – Midair

PS Kennedy

Kennedy took his early flying training at the Wright Flying School in Augusta, Georgia. Achieving American Flying Certificate No. 383 in December 1915, he cabled the RNAS and was 'promoted' from Candidate status to Probationary FSLt.

Kennedy has almost completed additional flying at Cranwell when today's midair mishap takes his life. The Naval Board of Inquiry will state: 'Accident occurred as a consequence of Bristol Scout 3016 colliding with an Avro 504. Impossible to attach blame to anybody.' Age 25, the former McGill student is buried at Cranwell, Linconshire.

OCTOBER 1916

02Oct16 – FSLt Arnold Jacques CHADWICK (Toronto) – Escape

A Sopwith Strutter pilot with 5 Wing, Chadwick is compelled to land with a motor defect during a raid on the Zeppelin sheds of Brussels. Finding himself behind enemy lines, he attempts to set fire to his machine, but discovers he has no matches. A carload of German troops arrives on scene and he runs for cover. Donning a peasant's cap and blouse

AJ Chadwick

via M Pirie

at the house of a priest, Chadwick is 'taken in hand' by a woman to a public cafe to meet the local resistance leader. He is then hidden in a nearby Chateau for three weeks while a 'Committee' in Liege arranges escape. German spies visit the Chateau on several occasions but in the end Carter manages to leave, disguised as a woman. Hiding with seventeen others he tries to cross the Dutch frontier and succeeds on the third attempt. Traveling next to The Hague he arrives in London on the 10th of November.

This is Chadwick's second escape. As a student of music and languages in Germany in August 1914 he had managed to evade internment for five weeks after war was declared, eventually finding his way to England. *(Read 28Jul17)*

03Oct16 – FSLt David Moair 'Bill' BALLANTYNE (Winnipeg) – Episode

Ballantyne graduated from Cranwell and was appointed to NAS Westgate Seaplane Base where the duties include keeping the shipping channel of the River Thames clear. Soon he is considered to be an experienced pilot, as is illustrated by the following narrative from his station's

First Lieutenant AH Sandwell: 'Normally deskbound, I found some free time to fly. Joyfully the old Short was warmed up, and I taxied out before a full gallery on to a sea as calm as the proverbial millpond. Do you think that machine would unstick? Not by a jugful! I squattered about on the glassy surface like a wounded duck for twenty minutes or more, until the water in the radiator was boiling and the cockpit was like a Turkish Bath, with a strong flavour of sulphur from my remarks. Finally I taxied back to the slipway, feeling very crestfallen. And here's where the psychological angle comes in, which caused me to do some heavy thinking. If ordered the machine put away, there was always to be the possibility of doubt as to whether a really first-class pilot might not have got it off. On the other hand, if I got one of the Sub Lieutenants to try it, and he succeeded where I had failed, where would my reputation be? I am glad to say I had enough confidence in myself to send out Flt Sub Lt Ballantyne, of Winnipeg, a fine Short pilot. And he couldn't get it off either, so the day was saved.'

Arnold Hugh Sandwell, the Westgate Station 'Adjutant,' or 'Jimmy-the-One' in Naval terminology, immigrates to Canada post-war. He was a technical writer at *Flight* prior 1914 and he continues as a contributor to the *Canadian Aviation* Magazine in the 1930s.

In May 1917, Ballantyne is entered on the books of HMS *Ark Royal* for flying with 2 Wing in the Mediterranean. *(Read 22Jan18)*

12Oct16 – FSLt Chs. H. Stanley BUTTERWORTH (Ottawa ON) – WIA/POW

Fully operational at last, 3 Wing joins a combined RNAS and French operation from Luxeil, in the Voges, against the Mauser rifle factories at Oberndorf. This bombing attack represents a return distance of over 220 miles. Altogether some 55 aircraft take part, with 3 Wing providing 21 machines – six Breguets, nine Sopwith Strutter single-seat bombers, and six two-seater Strutters as escort scouts.

The RNAS loses two Bruguets and also Butterworth's bomber to enemy machines. Flying Sopwith Strutter 9660, Butterworth is shot down by *Feldwebel* Ludwig Hanstein. **Raymond Collishaw**, flying as escort, goes to Butterworth's aid and drives off the attacking aircraft. However, the bomber has been hit in the engine and loses altitude, disappearing into low cloud. Butterworth, wounded in the neck, manages to glide down to the German aerodrome at Freiburg where he is immediately taken prisoner.

CHS Butterworth

GWFM

After his recovery from the wound, he is dispatched to the *Gefairgenenfager,* or Fallen Airmen, POW Camp at Claustenhal.

Collishaw's machine, Strutter 9407, was also damaged in the engagement but he is able to nurse about 900 rpm from the ailing Clerget engine, and limps home over the fog-shrouded River Rhine to Luxeuil. The Oberndorf Raid is a first in strategic bombing and for many of the combatants, their debut mission. Eighteen fledgling Canadian RNAS pilots take part.

The Raid includes a French fighter-escort of four Nieuport XI 'Bebe' scouts. Part of the newly formed *Escadrille américaine* (later named the *Lafayette Escadrille*), the aircraft are flown by freelance American volunteers. They account well of themselves on this first combined offensive, driving down three enemy machines. Sadly, the founder of the Escadrille, Norman Prince of Massachusetts, is killed when attempting to land in the gathering dusk.

The Escadrille shares the same airfield with Collishaw's 3 Wing: "Over the years the *Escadrille Lafayette* has received a tremendous amount of publicity, to a point indeed where the unit has gained a degree of immortality. I don't begrudge them this at all, for they were a good bunch of fellows, but it has always struck me as peculiar and rather unfair that the Americans who flew with the *Lafayette* Squadron should have received such great public acclaim whereas the many hundreds of Americans who flew as members of the British air forces, mostly with the RFC and the RAF, remain almost completely ignored...there were only a few in the RNAS but some of them were very good indeed..."

On the German side, a young NCO, Ernst Udet, is also flying one of his first missions and is forced down by a French machine. He crash-lands safely on the East side of the Rhine and lives on to become the second-highest scoring German pilot of the War, with 62 victories. Udet will be one of the leaders of the Nazi Luftwaffe in the initial stages of the Second World War. However, by the end of 1941, political infighting will ultimately lead to *Generaloberst* Udet's suicide.

In February 1918, after sixteen-months at Claustenhal, POW Butterfield will be transferred to internment in Holland and finally repatriated on 18Nov18. In 1942, Butterworth's son, Charles Edgar, will continue the family's military tradition and join the Fleet Air Arm. Serving in the Far East he is awarded the DSC while flying Corsairs with 1842 Squadron in HMS *Formidable*.

The Oberndorf area will become well known to Canadians serving with the RCAF and CAF in NATO during the Cold War. The future Canadian military bases at Lahr and Baden, Germany, lie beneath the October 1916 flight path.

12Oct16 – FSLt Mostyn LEWIS (Montreal) – INJ

M Lewis

RAeC Trust

On takeoff Short 827 Seaplane 8639 stalls and side-slips, falling into the River Medway just opposite the Grain Naval Air Station pier. Pilot Lewis is quite badly bruised and his passenger, a Petty Officer Mechanic, W H Hodgson, is drowned.

The Inquest finds that: 'The evidence is not sufficiently strong to definitely attribute blame to anyone.' Lewis is very shaken and when he later smashes an undercarriage on landing a Be2c he is found to have shown 'bad Pilotage'. He requests a transfer to Rigid Airships but before this happens he develops traumatic neurasthenia and is given Canada Leave to recover. Returning to England in mid 1917, the former McGill student takes up an appointment for non-flying work as an RNAS Armament Officer.

18Oct16 – FSLt Walter James SUSSAN (Carleton Place ON) – REL

Sussan is the fourth member of the *Hobo Quartet*, a self-named group of hometown Carleton Place hockey players who entered the RNAS together as Candidates in 1915. The foursome, **Roy Brown**, **Murray Galbraith**, **Sterne Edwards** and Walt Sussan had all achieved their Aeronautical Certificates within a month of each other at the Wright School in Dayton Ohio. However, Sussan's path through the RNAS differs from that of the rest of his friends. While training in England for operational flying with 3 Wing, Sussan damages two of the new Sopwith Strutter bombers.

By early autumn he has not proven to posses as strong a constitution as his hockey teammates for the severities of high-altitude, open-cockpit, wartime flying. Now, with the Wing gone to France, FSLt Sussan

WJ Sussan

RaeC Trust

leaves for Canada. He has been invalided out of the service as medically unfit due to neurasthenia. Brown, Galbraith and Edwards will eventually become fighter-pilot Aces, but each in turn will also fall ill from this same exhaustion of the nervous system. Early cases like Sussan are released and shipped home.

Unlike other commission-terminated individuals, Sussan returns to England in March 1917 at his own expense to request a re-survey from the Admiralty medical Board. Successfully re-instated with original seniority, he is sent to Cranwell where his flying is evaluated as: 'very disappointing considering previous experience'. He is, however, dispatched onwards to Mullion Seaplane Station in Cornwall and by September is described as an 'apparently a capable pilot.' The low-level work scouting for submarines has steadied his somewhat frayed nerves. As he cannot fly at more than 9,000 feet of altitude, a submission is put forward that he be exchanged; and Sussan is sent to 2 Wing in the Eastern Mediterranean during September 1917. Operating out of the islands of Stavros and Marsh he will be reported as 'Conscientious in the air' and 'Very Good Pilot.'

In a 1918 letter home, he writes about one incident:

> "Had a very exciting and trying experience last week. My engine fell to pieces when I was about 30 miles out to sea and about 4,000 feet high. There was no boat around and it was quite misty. I managed to

land safely in the water. I then fired danger signals and inflated my life belt. After a short time, the aeroplane sank, leaving my Observer and myself floating around the sea, which we did successfully for about 4 hours, eventually being picked up by a destroyer, which happened to spot us by luck. It was just getting dark at the time. So such is life in war time." As well as the dunking, Sussan survives the War and returns to Canada in the rank of Captain RAF with the award of a Greek Military Cross for his Aegean efforts.

23Oct16 – FSLt George BREADNER (Winnipeg) – Ditched

While involved in deck flying trials aboard HMS *Campania*, Breadner has an engine failure in Sopwith Schneider 3798 that force lands him in the sea. When the 100hp Gnome Monosoupape quits, Breadner has no choice but to put the aircraft down in the water. As it has been flown off the deck on wheels, the machine quickly capsizes on contact with the liquid surface.

Breadner is one of Canada's first test pilots and this is his second damp landing. In June he had an accident in an FBA Flying boat off Cowes. That Court of Enquiry noted: 'Under the circumstance I do not think Pilot could have landed better, but both wings were severely damaged'. Deemed a 'promising, very painstaking and reliable Officer' Breadner is well suited for the rigors of flying untried machines.

In January 1918, after nearly two years testing and operating seaplanes off *Campania*, Breadner will requalify on scouts at Cranwell. There, he is reported as: 'A very steady Pilot, but inclined to be heavy handed, due to having flown Seaplanes before which seemed to affect his landings. Was rapidly improving at the end of his time here.' Breadner returns to *Campania* and is: 'Specially recommended for promotion. A most zealous & capable Officer.'

NOVEMBER 1916

02Nov16 – PFSLt Horace Owen MERRIMAN (Hamilton ON) – REL to RNVR

A University of Toronto graduate Electrical Engineer, Merriman, after several months at the RNAS Flying School in Chingford, cannot make the Probation cut and submits an application for a Royal Navy Volunteer

Reserve commission. His Commanding Officer writes: 'This Officer's application for transfer is forwarded here within. He is an exceedingly good electrical engineer, & I submit it would be useful if given a Commission in the RNVR. He is very slow at learning to fly, & I consider it would be far more use if he could be employed where his undoubted talent could have scope to carry on, on lines of which he has worked all his life.'

HO Merriman

RAeC Trust

Merriman is released from the RNAS on the 2nd of November 1916 and immediately appointed a Sub-Lieutenant RNVR for Experimental Gunnery Duties on the 3rd of November. He is sent on to Grain Island with the Ministry of Munitions as a Technical Officer for the Station Test Flight.

By 1919, Merriman and another technical type, Lionel Guest, a former Canadian governor-general's aide, have begun experimenting with electrical recording using a microphone. Through their efforts, the first commercial recording anywhere is made by the duo at the ceremony for the burial of the Unknown Warrior in Westminster Abbey on the 11th of November 1920. Their work ushers in a new era of recording.

12Nov16 – FSLt Francis Arthur Rivers MALET (Vancouver; b. ENG) – KIC

In a Sopwith Baby launched from HMS *Riviera* on a strafing run practice, Malet is killed by a ricocheting bullet. The aircraft, No. 8181, smashes into the sea just 300 yards from the ship – a freak, non-synchronized round had struck his propeller.

FAR Malet

RAeC Trust

Malet transferred from the Canadian Expeditionary Force (Engineers) in September 1915. Assessed on graduation as: 'An indifferent Officer, & does not understand discipline', Malet found his forte in weaponry at Dundee Air Station, and his next report was much more positive: 'Performing duties of Armament Officer very well indeed & is exceptionally keen on his work. Ability to command very much above the average. Is desirous of being transferred to permanent List, for which favourable consideration is strongly recommended.'

In early July, Malet had been part of an extensive RNAS effort to range the 12-inch gun of the Dominon Battery against the 11-inch guns of the Tirpitz Battery defending the Ostend dockyard. It is ironic that now Malet's own weapon brings him down.

15Nov16 – FSLt Edward Bloomfield WALLER (Toronto) – Force Landing

Waller is ferrying the Royal Navy's seventh, and newest, Handley-Page bomber, 1461, from Manston to Luxeuil when he has an engine failure and force-lands safely near Abbeville. Eventually, he delivers the giant twin-engine machine to the 3 Wing base. The Naval Air Service has been asking for a 'Bloody Paralyzer of a Bomber' and now they have them.

One of the very first aviators qualified on the Handley-Page, Waller later pens a narrative of a bombing operation in 1917:

"On the night of 5th/6th April I was piloting Handley Page No. 1460. It was originally intended to raid the iron works at Hagendingen, but owing to adverse weather, high winds, the objective was changed before leaving the aerodrome to the railway junction at Arnaville. This change in the objective was made on the advice of Lt. Le Couteau, acting as guide.

"The machine left the aerodrome at 23.40 and after reaching an altitude of 3,000 feet proceeded on course climbing to an altitude of 7,200 feet by the time of reaching the objective. Twelve 100 lb bombs were released at 00.05. Four circuits were made over the objective, during which time it was observed that the bombs had exploded on the station and surrounding buildings. While in the vicinity of the objective the machine was subjected to well directed anti aircraft fire, which appeared to be approximately equal quantities of

EB Waller, with a Handley Page Bomber.

Flak-torn fabric is being replaced.

FAAM, 1998/047/0072

H.E. and shrapnel. Although on one occasion the searchlights passed over the tail of the machine, they failed to locate it. Landing was effected at 01.20 at the aerodrome. During the course of the raid a very strong wind was experienced and the mist was more intense after passing over the line. The guide Lt Le Couteau of the French Aviation Service proved to be invaluable, owing to his thorough knowledge of the surrounding country."

– SLt Douglas Ross Cameron WRIGHT RNVR (New Westminster BC) – OBS

The new heavy bomber carries a four-man crew. On the mission described, in addition to the French co-pilot, the Observer was Wright, RNVR, who will later train as a pilot. A fourth crewman, the Gunlayer, is an English Leading Mechanic. *(Read 23Dec17)*

16Nov16 – FSLt Dan Murray Bayne GALBRAITH DSC, MID (Carleton Place ON) – ACE

(From 15Jul16) Galbraith brings down his fifth German aircraft and in so doing becomes Canada's second Naval Ace. At this point in the War, the Allies do not yet officially recognize the term 'Ace', however, an action one week later on the 23rd of November brings Galbraith to the attention of Field Marshal Haig, British Commander-in-Chief, France. With no other friendly machines in his vicinity, Galbraith single-handedly takes on a formation of half-a-dozen enemy at 16,000 feet, destroying one and driving another down. The remaining aircraft break away and fly to safety behind

their own lines. The Field Marshal recommends a decoration for conspicuous gallantry and Galbraith is Gazetted a bar to his DSC.

Galbraith was one of the original members of Naval 8 Squadron when it was formed in October for the specific purpose of assisting the RFC. At that time, he had three victories to his credit and soon made the new Squadron's first kill when he sent a Roland out of control over Bapaume on the 10th of November.

DMB Galbraith

via M Pirie

By early winter, high altitude actions begin to tell on Galbraith's health. He has been in continual front line flying since May. His Squadron Commander later writes: 'On December 1st, we lost the services of Galbraith who had a breakdown in health and was sent away for a rest. He came to the Squadron with an established reputation as a fighting pilot and his work with us was beyond praise. No Hun retreated too far behind the line and no formation was too formidable for this stout hearted Canadian to attack. He had remarkable courage and brains and, although a curious sort of fellow who took a bit of understanding, he was a jolly good chap right through.'

Galbraith is invalided to Dover for light duties. Diagnosed with neurasthenia in April he is granted a long Canada Leave (without flying pay) and will return to England in October 1917. He is then surveyed as fit to return to duty but 'should not be allowed to fly at a greater altitude than 8,000'. To this end Galbraith will be appointed to Italy for Anti-submarine operations – all low altitude work. *(Read 29Mar21)*

20Nov16 – FSLt Harold DRUMMOND (Toronto) – REL Unsuitable

Calshot Confidential Report: 'I now consider this Officer to be unsuitable for further service in RNAS. When he first joined this Station, I was of opinion that he might in time become a capable Officer. However, he appears unable to behave properly, either in the Mess or during instruction & has always been slovenly & dirty in his appearance & habits, & altogether a very bad example to the other Officers. He persistently refuses to pay attention to the classes & lectures, & takes every opportunity to skulk from them. I have warned him & resorted to very strict measures on several occasions, but without effect. As a Seaplane Pilot he is only fair & seems to take very little interest in flying, so, I do not consider him sufficiently valuable to be retained from a flying point of view.'

H Drummond

UCC

Following his Release, Drummond joins the British Army and completes a war service in Singapore.

24Nov16 – FSLt Fredrick Stanley MILLS (Toronto) – MID Romania

In August, Romania finally made the decision as to which side it was on and joined the Allies, hoping to make territorial gains. This declaration of war against the Central Powers turns out to be badly timed and the RNAS now must send support aircraft from Salonika. Mills is part of this special flight and carries essential medicines for the failing forces in Bucharest. The long-distance effort earns him a Mention in Despatches.

The adventure for this former Toronto Argonaut Rugby player begins in earnest in the Romanian capital. King Ferdinand's army is being routed and falls back towards the Russian border. Mills escapes with them just ahead of the invading German and Bulgarian forces. Upon his arrival in England – via Petrograd – in early January 1917, he is immediately hospitalized with appendicitis, which fortunately did not burst during his circuitous route home.

FS Mills

RAeC Trust

Described during initial flying training at Eastchurch as 'Very keen & plucky', Mills had lived-up to these words shortly after graduation. On the 9th of July 1916, in Bristol Scout 8957, he chased a German Seaplane off North Foreland and then engaged the enemy within a few miles of Ostend. Although the fight itself was inconclusive, for this, his first flight under actual war conditions, Mills received an Admiralty Expression of Their Lordship's appreciation.

Following his appendectomy and subsequent Canada Leave to recover, he will be appointed to Eastbourne and in May 1918 is Gazetted the DSC for zeal and devotion to duty.

30Nov16 – FSLt George Samuel ABBOTT (Ottawa) – WIA Turkey

On reconnaissance in Short S90 Seaplane 9758 with 2 Wing, Eastern Mediterranean, Abbott is slightly wounded by AA fire near Karjam. An officer considered 'very reliable, plenty of initiative,' he is flying from the island of Mudros when he suffers this gunshot wound to the right leg.

The Mudros missions consist of co-operation flying with the Fleet, anti-submarine and reconnaissance patrols, and harassment of enemy countryside within reach of the coast.

GS Abbott
RAeC Trust

Abbott survives to fly and fight another day. Following Canada recovery leave, he returns to the Mediterranean and spends the duration of the War with 62 and 63 Wings in the Mesopotamia theatre. Duties with 62 Wing include contact offensive patrols; with 63 Wing he flies aerial co-operation patrols in the advance on Mosul, bombing and ground-strafing the Turkish positions.

In 1928, Abbott joins the Civil Air Branch of the Department of Transportation, eventually becoming its Chief Inspector.

DECEMBER 1916

02Dec16 – FSLt Alfred James NIGHTINGALE (Mount Dennis ON) – POW Palestine

(From 14Dec15) Launched from alongside HMS *Ben-my-Chree* off the coast of Palestine, Nightingale's mission is a reconnaissance of Ramleh, a railroad town located between Jaffa and Jerusalem. The Turkish anti-aircraft defenses prove accurate and Short 184 Seaplane 8372 receives a direct hit. Last seen going down out of control, Nightingale and his Observer, Lt PM Woodland RNVR, are considered as missing, probably killed. However, that evening, a German wireless message is intercepted stating that the crew is safe in captivity.

This is the second time that Nightingale has been shot down. On the 17th of September during a three-plane spotting operation for a Naval monitor, he was chased out of the sky by a German scout. The enemy fighter had attacked the three seaplanes as they arrived on station over El Arish and flamed one. Then, in the words of English Squadron Commander Sampson: 'Nightingale immediately engaged the German; but the latter flew rings round him, being immensely faster and far handier. Nightingale put up a stubborn fight; but he was soon forced to alight on the water with his petrol tank riddled with holes. It was only by the mercy of God he didn't get on fire.'

Following this latest crash, the Turks officially report Nightingale as a POW on the 8th of December. He will spend the remainder of the war at Yozgat Camp in central Turkey. During the Second World War he flies again, this time as an Elementary Flying Training School instructor with the British Commonwealth Air Training Plan – in Canada.

04Dec16 – FSLt Charles Torryburn BRIMER (Toronto) – MIA Channel

Brimer fails to return from a patrol in FBA Flying Boat 3639 out of Naval Sub-Station Bembridge. The Station signals: 'Search having been made & no trace of either m/c or Pilot, it seems likely that both are lost, Missing and presumed drowned.'

Brimer was two days short of his nineteenth birthday. Earlier that year, in June, he received American license No. 491 after paying for his own flying lessons at Newport News, Virginia. Accepted as a Probationary Flight Sub Lieutenant, he graduated from Cranwell in early November: 'A very good pilot and a promising

CT Brimer

Officer, being zealous & keen.' On the 30th of November, just four days before his misfortune, this keen new officer had written to his parents "I'll be the happiest boy alive if I can bag a submarine." Brimer is listed on the Chatham Naval Memorial to the Missing, England. Because he was confirmed in rank prior to being reported lost, a refund for his United States flight tuition fee, £75, is paid to next of kin.

05Dec16 – Lt Forrest Henry MITCHELL, RNVR (Halifax NS) – POW/DOS Turkey

Mitchell, an RNAS Armoured Car and Aeroplane Support Officer, is captured by Turkish troops in the Dardanelles. The former Nova Scotia broker will succumb to septic tonsillitis at Afiou-Kara-Hissar Prison Camp on the 6th of February 1917.

11Dec16 – FSLt Stanley Valentine TRAPP, MIDx2 (New Westminster BC) – KIC

With Naval 8 Squadron, FSLt SV Trapp dies in a test flight of Sopwith Pup N5192 over the Somme. Age 26, he is buried at Beauval, France.

Trapp has been twice Mentioned in Despatches. In the first instance he was immediately on the scene at a Cranwell training accident in February 1916:

SV Trapp

RAeC Trust

'Specially mentioned by Members of Court of Enquiry into the accident which occurred on 20th inst, resulting in the death of PFSLt F.W. Toms for the splendid manner in which he behaved in trying to free the Pilot from the burning machine.' His second MID is for good work with No. 8 Squadron while attached to RFC.

(Read 12Nov17 for Brother G.L. Trapp)

17Dec16 – Candidate Norman Graham FRASER (Toronto) – PFSLt

As the Curtiss Canada Flying School closes down for the winter, Candidate Fraser graduates with RAeC 4058. Although 27-years-old, he had been accepted as a Candidate prior to the age limit being reduced from 30 to 25 years: he is duly appointed Probationary Flight Sub Lieutenant.

Following what has now become the usual training pattern in England, Fraser attends Crystal Palace for naval officer indoctrination, after which, he is sent to Vendome, France, for initial flying and then back to England for advanced flying at Cranwell. He graduates from his probationary status in July 1917 and is streamed for Seaplane instruction at Killingholme and Calshot. By September Fraser is a qualified seaplane pilot. His report states that he: 'Did well in all subjects in examination except Seamanship & Discipline.' Although seemingly lacking in these two important criteria, Fraser will go on to

NG Fraser

RAeC Trust

excel at Cattewater, his first station, and is then sent to Felixstowe for Large America flying boats. In March 1918, he is appointed as second in command of this, the largest training station in England—and will, paradoxically, be placed in charge of discipline.

The January 1919 Awards List recognizes him with an AFC for his work. By that March, he will be back in action once again, carrying-out reconnaissance and bombing patrols for Russia's White forces. This will earn Fraser the Czarist Order of St Anne, 3rd Class, with Swords and Bow. AMember of the British Empire (MBE) is bestowed upon him in December 1919 for services in North Russia

20Dec16 – Candidate Roy Clark WHITFIELD (Hamilton ON) – Last Grad

RC Whitfield

RAeC Trust

Whitfield achieves RAeC 4067 and is the last to graduate from the Curtiss Flying School in Toronto. However, he will sustain a concussion as the result of a crash at Eastchurch in May 1917 and that, coupled with neurasthenia, leads to his release as being permanently unfit to fly.

Although Toronto's Curtiss Flying School operated only during the summer and fall of 1915 and again throughout 1916, it established a legacy for air training in Canada. In its relatively short history, the school had no fatalities or serious accidents, and one hundred and thirty Candidates achieved their flying certificates. Forty-eight of the sixty-seven 1915 graduates joined the RNAS together with fifty-eight of the sixty-three in 1916. Eighteen however, failed to pass their probationary training in England and, like Whitfield, are released. Approximately one third of the remaining eighty-eight will perish: nine killed in aircraft accidents and twenty lost in action. Twelve become fighter Aces and account for a total of 109 enemy aircraft. Five are captured and become prisoners of war and one is interned in Holland. In total, these eighty-eight first-Canadian-trained aviators will win 25 British gallantry awards and ten foreign awards for bravery.

By the end of 1916, The Curtiss School, managed by Canada's first aviator, Douglas McCurdy, has been unable to obtain the federal assistance needed to continue operating. Although the country is on a solid war footing, it is more a matter of a lack of political support, rather than financial, as the Canadian Parliament remains unsure about flying. This is in sharp contrast to the Australian government that founded an Australian Flying Corps in 1914.

Curtiss Aeroplanes and Motors Limited (Toronto) is sold to the British Government. They establish a new Toronto company, Canadian Aeroplanes Ltd and begin building aircraft and training RFC pilots. In many ways it is a prelude to the Second War's Commonwealth Air Training Plan. From this point onward, all Royal Naval Air Service pilots will be trained in Great Britain and France, where large flying schools had been developed.

In his 1960's correspondence, Air Vice Marshal Collishaw summed up a feature of the Curtiss School that has often been overlooked:

> "It was the good bearing and devotion to duty of the 1915 Canadians that prompted the War Office and the Admiralty to go in later for Canadians, in a big way. The RFC in Canada in 1917 and 1918 had and important impact upon industrializing Ontario; and in 1918 the Imperial Treasury was spending about $1,000,000 a day [in the Province]."

via M Pirie

The Royal Naval Air Service

A limited number of men are required for the ROYAL NAVAL AIR SERVICE.

Very high physical and educational standards are required, and applicants must be natural born British subjects. and the sons of natural born British subjects.

All the training is done in England. Usual age from 17½ to 23; extreme age 25th birthday. Pay on entry $2.50 per day; while undergoing training $3.50

For further particulars apply to the Chief Naval Recruiting Officer

305 Wellington Street, • • OTTAWA

1-11-17

RNAS recruiting advertisement placed in the Ottawa newspapers, November 1917

'SUNDAY MORNING AFTER SERVICE ON THE FLYING DECK'

Ray Pollard

HMS *Ark Royal*, Dardanelles.
The aircraft in the background is a Short 184.

'HMS MANXMAN AT STAVROS'

Courtesy of Fleet Air Arm Museum, 2003/040/0097

'HMS MANXMAN, AT MUDROS'

Courtesy of Fleet Air Arm Museum, 2003/040/0064

The early aircraft carriers had to 'Hoist Out' and 'Hoist In', a laborious procedure next to impossible in heavy seas. The aircraft secured alongside has its wings folded, awaiting the hoist-aboard and trundle into the hangar. Both aircraft are Short 184s.

'HOISTING INBOARD CRASHED SEAPLANE'

...in this case, a Sopwith Schneider

Courtesy of Fleet Air Arm Museum, 2003/040/0117

Courtesy of Fleet Air Arm Museum, Album 153

THE "DALLAS CIRCUS" NUMBER 1 NAVAL AT BAILLEUL

Squadron Commander R.Stanley Dallas of Australia stands tall 5th from the right with his Sopwith Triplane pilots. Twenty Canadians will fly with 1 Naval during 1917. Owing to the rapid 'wastage' of pilots during the year, only four are present in this photograph, taken 28Oct17.

Left toRight:

SM Kinkhead* (South Africa), **JH Forman***, N Wallace, **AJA Spence***, L Everett, HV Rowley*, P Luard, MacGrath, WF Crundell, WH Sneath*, E Burton, HR McArdee, **SW Rosevear***, RP Minifie (Australia)*,RS Dallas (Australia)*, CB Ridley*, R DeWilde, **JB White***, WH Holden.

* Are, or will become, Aces.

CHAPTER 3
THE YEAR 1917

FLIGHT LIEUTENANTS

The aerial assistance of Naval 8 Squadron over the Western Front since October 1916 has proven so successful that the Army's War Office urgently appeals to the Admiralty for additional help. Scout squadrons are badly needed, primarily to provide cover for RFC reconnaissance aircraft exploring and mapping the German lines in preparation for an Allied Spring Offensive—One that includes the Canadian Corps assault on Vimy Ridge.

The Royal Navy responds by raising new squadrons slated for RFC operational control. This initiative takes place over a few short months during what is recorded as a very cold and depressing winter. A tremendous amount of logistical and physical effort goes into the build-up and to provide aviators, Number 3 Wing will be disbanded. Raymond Collishaw, after recovering from frostbite in an action where his goggles were shot apart, is transferred to one of the new units.

> "I do not think that the part played by the RNAS fighter squadrons during the critical spring, summer and early-autumn period of 1917 on the Western Front has ever been generally appreciated. In all, six Naval fighting squadrons were attached to the RFC and five were maintained on attachment throughout the whole of this time. Without them the aerial war on the Western Front might well have taken a different turn."

Collishaw also expounds that:

> "The fighter pilot emerged from the First World War as the top glamour boy of the conflict and he has since been the subject of innumerable magazine articles, books and motion pictures. Rarely has comparable publicity been given to the many others who flew on artillery observation work, reconnaissance, bombing and a host of other duties. The reason for this is simple. (Their) work … was highly technical."

> "The jobs that they did represented the main reasons for maintaining an air force and the work of the fighters was completely subsidiary to their role."

Years later, as he delved in aviation history during the 1960's Collishaw noted that fighter pilot mission recordings also:

> "… seems to me to tend to be humdrum with a succession of perhaps uninteresting combat reports. One has to recollect that these reports were taken down by a Recording Officer the moment the pilot landed … when the pilot was fatigued after the patrol. Scant imagination could be expected … when all the pilot was thinking of was to get out of his heavy flying clothes and into the Mess. Consequently it is dull reading matter". *(11May63 to R.V.Dodds)*

Shortage of aviators is yet another concern of the RFC and again the RNAS fills a gap. During early 1917, some sixty-nine Canadians entered in the books of HMS *President* are 'Appointment Teminated' and involuntarily transferred directly to the Army's air corps. *(Appendix B)*

JANUARY 1917

04Jan17 – FSLt John Roland Secretan DEVLIN (Ottawa) – DSC Salonica

Operating in a flight of three Sopwith machines on the Turkish-Bulgarian Frontier, Devlin is immediately Mentioned for this day's bombing attack. The target is the Maritza railway bridge at Kuleli Burgas south of Adrianople, and several hits are scored. The raiding aircraft are exposed to anti-aircraft, rifle and machine-gun fire during the attack, and again on the return journey across Thrace to their 2 Wing Base. When the extent of the considerable damage done to the bridge is recognized Devlin is further awarded a DSC.

An aviator trained at Eastchurch he was: 'Very keen & capable young Officer. Has started very well & takes charge absolutely. Excellent Pilot.' Devlin has been flying in the Aegean (Salonika) and Mesopotamia (Balkan) Front since October 1916.

He is noted as being capable of command of a small station and is promoted to Flight Lieutenant. Towards the end of 1917, a letter to the Admiralty from Prime Ministers office, Canada, asks 'for leave for this officer'. Granted permission to proceed, Devlin has to disembark in Plymouth and be admitted to hospital with Mediterranean 'Malaria and Debility.' He finishes his convalescence in Canada and remains there on Special Service with the RFC-RAF Canadian Training Scheme. He will be Gazetted the new Air Force Cross for his aviation service in the Dominion.

JRS Devlin
RAeC Trust

04Jan17 – FLt Edward Rochfort GRANGE, Cd'G (Toronto; b. USA) – Triple Victory DSC

In Sopwith Pup N5194, Grange destroys one enemy Albatros D.II and sends down two others 'out of control'. This triple victory results in his being: 'Recomd'd for award of Naval Decoration for Conspicuous gallantry & skill on several occasions, in attacking & bringing down hostile machines, particularly on Jan 4th, when during one flight he had 3 separate engagements, bringing the enemy M/C down each time.' Fittingly, the Royal Navy's Distinguished Service Cross is Gazetted.

Grange has come a long way from his first flight over enemy lines in early 1916. On that mission, his Bristol scout was armed with a shotgun, roped to the fuselage. Now, with a synchronized Vickers machine gun, Grange claims four German machines to his credit. The previous September, while escorting a French photo mission, he shot down an attacking Sablatnig SF2, which broke up and fell into the sea off Ostend. The grateful French conferred the Croix d'Guerre on him for that effort. The Commendation read: 'Chargé le 25 septembre 1916 d'escorter un appareil au cours d'une mission photographique lointaine, a attaqué un hydravion ennemi au large des cotes. L'appareil ennemi est tombé en vrille dans la mer d'une hauteur de 2,000 mètres.'

ER Grange
U of T

On January 7th, Grange achieves Ace status. Then, having just driven down his fifth German machine, he observes two other enemy aircraft attacking another scout. On the way to assist, Grange is set upon by a third hostile. Hit in the shoulder by a bullet, he still manages to land his Sopwith safely at the closest RNAS aerodrome. Sent on Canada Leave to recover, Grange is further awarded with a Mention in Despatches for good work with Naval 8 Squadron while attached to the RFC.

Grange will return to England to instruct for the remainder of the War and in the 1920's becomes an Examiner for the Canadian Air Board. A successful businessman and engineer, he joins the civilian arm of the RCAF in the Second World War and serves as an inspector and auditor. Described by fellow Canadian RNAS pilot **ST Edwards** as 'Big Chap, very nice, quiet.' Grange lives to the grand age of 96 and attends the last First World War Ace's Reunion in Paris in 1981. During an interview with the CAF Historical Branch at that time he expressed a thought on nervous breakdowns—that it could have been caused by the evening discussions in the Wardroom Mess, explaining that reliving the day's experience did not help morale. He himself wisely avoided such nightly debate after he found things starting to get to him.

Many Americans believe that their first airmen in combat during the 1914-1918 conflict had fought with French escadrilles such as the highly publicized Lafayette unit, or with their own squadrons in the American Expeditionary Forces. In fact, a few were in action with the RNAS, and a great many more with the RFC and the RAF. By virtue of his 1892 birthplace in Lansing, Michigan, Grange is the unacknowledged first American-born Naval Ace. He is, though, recognized in the 2007 Book, *Wolverines in the Sky: Michigan's Fighter Aces of World War I, World War II and Korea*, by Andrew Layton.

Sixteen-years-old when his Canadian parents and family moved back to Canada in 1908, Grange never lays claim to any American status. He was an engineering graduate of the University of Toronto and joined the RNAS in September 1915, after learning to fly with the Curtiss Canada School.

04Jan17 – FLt Allan Switzer TODD (Georgetown ON) – MIA Red Baron

Todd of Naval 8 offensively takes on three enemy aircraft over Bapaume. During the engagement, he is shot down by Manfred von Richthofen, and becomes the Red Baron's 16th victim and first Canadian kill. In an after-action report, Richthofen writes: '…the English plane attacked us and we saw immediately that the enemy plane was superior to ours. Only because we were three against one did we detect the enemy's weak points. I managed to get behind him and shot him down. The plane broke apart whilst falling.' Previously, on 20Dec16 and in this same Sopwith Pup, Todd had shot down a Type K Albatros 'Out Of Control'.

The German Air Services has recovered from their slump of the summer of 1916 and have reorganized into large *Jagdstaffel* or '*Jasta*' squadrons. The pilots of the Pups are on somewhat equal terms with these new enemy fighting units. The small Sopwith, although underpowered with an 80-hp Le Rhone and under-armed with only a single Vickers machine gun, is a highly responsive and maneuverable machine in the hands of an aggressive aviator such as Todd.

AS Todd

Missing at age 30, Todd's downing is a significant victory for von Richthofen. The prized *Pour le Merité*, or Blue Max, is highly sought-after by German aviators. The requirement for this decoration was eight victories but had been raised to sixteen. Richthofen is now accorded the medal. Indeed, the importance of this kill to the future German Ace of Aces is revealed in a famous photo of his study at the family home in Schweidnitz, where a poignant trophy is prominently displayed: the fabric remnants bearing Todd's aircraft registration, N5193.

Trophy Wall, von Richthofen's Study
Todd's aircraft numbers displayed in lower center

Windy Geale

07Jan17 – FSLt Albert Herbert Stanton LAWSON (Little Current ON) – WIA

Fired upon and hit while on an offensive patrol with Naval 8, Lawson nurses his bullet-riddled Pup, N5198, back across the lines. His Squadron Commander telegraphs the Dunkirk Admiral: 'This officer performed a very creditable performance in bringing back his machine safely as she was badly shot about & pilot suffering considerable pain, owing to the bullet being still in his body.' The awkward wound to the buttocks effectively takes Lawson out of battle. He is approved for sick leave to Canada and awarded a gratuity of £163 in compensation for the gunshot injury.

An 'Extremely plucky Pilot', Lawson will be back in England by early summer but declared fit for ground duties only. Such work notwithstanding,

AHS Lawson

he is recorded to have been the Observer/Gunner on an Anti-Gotha Patrol out of Eastchurch in a Henry Farman on the 5th of June 1917. Following that latest experience, he does retrain as an Observer at NAS Eastchurch in September 1917.

11Jan17 – FSLt Frederick Cecil HENDERSON (Toronto) – Sunk

HMS *Ben-my-Chree* is resting at anchor in Castellorizo Harbour in the Dodescanese Islands when Turkish shore batteries find her range. An enemy round ignites a petrol fire in the hangar, and it quickly rages out of control. The order to abandon ship is given and performed efficiently. No one is lost out of the crew of two hundred and fifty—due in no small part to

FC Henderson

the vessel's RNAS Captain, Charles Sampson's standing order that all hands learn to swim. Pilot Henderson had joined ship at Port Said, Egypt, in November 1916, and today, he is one of the swimmers.

Operating along the Coast of Palestine the 3,880-ton *Ben* had carried out artillery spotting and bombardment missions. These tasks included reconnaissance around Jaffa as well as flights over Turkish-occupied Jerusalem.

The previous December 22nd, Henderson had flown Short 184 Seaplane 8080 out of *Ben* on a bombing attack up the Haifa Valley against enemy troops advancing on the Suez Canal. Five days later on the 27th, flying Sopwith Schneider Seaplane 3770, he took part in an attack on the Chikaldi Bridge, an important Baghdad railway crossing of the Jeihan River near the Gulf of Alexandretta—a source of reinforcements for the Turks. Henderson, on the third wave of the attack hit the iron structure with two 16lb bombs and rendered the span temporarily unusable. Now, following the loss of the *Ben*, Henderson becomes shore-based and continues his flying with 6 Wing out of Taranto, Italy.

23Jan17 – FSLt Maurice Hugh STEPHENS (Toronto; b. ENG) – Bomb INJ

Stephens, in Sopwith Strutter N5121, returns from a raid on the Burbach iron works and blast furnaces at Saarbruke. He lands and taxis; unaware that one of his weapons had half launched and become lodged in the bomb bay hatch. FSLt **MR Kingsford** of Toronto has landed ahead of Stephens, and noticing the snagged device, passes along a warning. Alerted, Stephens jumps out and tugs at the weapon. As it does not budge, he climbs back in the cockpit and taxies on. Approaching the hangar line, two air mechanics, his Fitter and his Rigger run alongside, each grabbing a wingtip to help guide the Strutter to its dispersal point. As they draw near the hangar sheds, the bomb slips free and explodes.

The Sopwith is blown to pieces. The engine and fore part of the fuselage, including Stephens, is thrown about fifteen yards and comes to rest on the propeller boss, now only partially recognizable, and on fire. The surrounding ground is also an inferno, the result of the spreading fuel spill. Himself a ball of flame, Stephens crawls out of the wreckage.

At once, he and the two mechanics are rolled and dragged clear of the flames. Three sailors are dead and Stephens is

MH Stephens

in severe shock, grievously burned about the face and hands and badly wounded in his right leg. The limb will have to be amputated.

Stephens does survive the horrific ordeal, and will be questioned by a Board of Inquiry as to his awareness of the position and condition of the bomb. In their findings, The Board states that he is not to be precluded from receiving compensation and Stephens is granted an award of £492, with a pension of £100 a year for life.

In November, he is surveyed and found fit for duty in England only. By April 1918 Stephens is the Air Officer on staff to Commander-in-Chief The Nore. His reports very strongly recommend him for promotion to Flight Commander. Just over two decades later Stephens will serve again in a non-flying commission with the Fleet Air Arm.

FEBRUARY 1917

01Feb17 – PFSLt Gabriel Henry George SMYTH (Toronto; b. France) – FSLt

Smyth graduates from Cranwell with a report of: 'VG Pilot, Keen Officer, but not much idea of discipline.' On the night of 26 January, he lost three months' seniority for misconduct in causing a disturbance, along with other officers, in the Duty Officer's Cabin.

An already shaky career continues with Smyth's assignment to East Fortune in Scotland, where he crashes BE2c 8720 and is placed on sick leave with injuries. He recovers only to write-off a brand new Sopwith Camel, B3854, at Bray Dunes in August. Sent to the Manston Fighting School as ground staff while

GHG Smith

RAeC Trust

convalescing, he is charged with being Absent without Leave in February 1918. Again, Smyth loses three months' seniority; but this time he is also severely reprimanded: 'My Lords Commissioners of the Admiralty direct CO at Manston to inform this Officer that the question of his retention in RNAS will be considered if another adverse report is received.'

Unluckily for Smyth, this reprimand will carry over into the new RAF. Placed on instructional duties, Smyth stalls a landing and crashes Caudron G.III trainer H8272, injuring his student in the process. This misstep takes place on the 4th of October 1918: Smyth is released from the air force the following day.

06Feb17 – A/SCdr Redford Henry MULOCK, DSO (Winnipeg) – CO 3 Naval

(From 21May16) The new naval scout squadrons are beginning to arrive on the Western Front. Number 3 Naval Squadron, commanded by 'Red' Mulock, relieves Naval 8, taking over their Sopwith Pups. Another new unit, 1 Naval together with Naval 8 (after being rested and re-equipped), will operate the very latest fighter, the Sopwith Triplane, a three-winged machine that boasts an incredible climbing ability. A third new squadron, 6 Naval, flies the Nieuport 17, an upgraded version of the 'Bébé'. By March 1917, these four units will all be operating 'in the field', one with each of the Army's four RFC Brigades. Yet another squadron, Number 10 Naval, also assigned the Triplane, will enter the fray by the middle of April.

The Germans have modernized their fighter *Jastas* with upgraded Albatros aircraft and they rule the skies east of the lines. Twenty-Three British fighter squadrons are facing them; but of these, it is only 3 Naval that is commanded by an Ace. Under Mulock's experienced leadership, his pilots, half of whom are Canadian, will receive credit for eighty successful combats to the loss of nine Pups. (Actual records will prove that 3 Naval destroys 20 and damages 24 German aircraft—a very credible performance nonetheless).

When the unit returns to the RNAS in June, General Trenchard of the RFC will write: 'The work of Squadron Commander Mulock is worthy of the highest praise; his knowledge of machines and engines and the way in which he handled his officers and men is very largely responsible for the great successes and durability of the Squadron.'

As the result this tribute, 3 Naval receives the following from the Vice Admiral, Dover: 'I am commanded by My Lords Commissioners of the Admiralty to acquaint you that they note with pleasure the letter from General Trenchard testifying to the very fine work performed by all ranks of Number 3 Squadron of the Royal Naval Air Service during their four months' service with the 5th Brigade of the Royal Flying Corps. I am to request that you will convey to Squadron Commander Mulock, and the Officers and men of this Squadron, Their Lordships' high appreciation of their good service.'

One of Mulock's English pilots, LH Rochford, gives a good 'snapshot' of his 3 Naval CO when he described him as: '...older than most of us and I was at once impressed by his strong personality. A man of medium height, he had a square, weather-beaten face with eyes that nearly always had a twinkle in them. Later I was to discover that he was a highly competent organizer and had a deep understanding of human nature ...He knew most of his pilots were mere boys and sometimes mischievous boys and he was always ready to turn a blind eye on these occasions so long as you did your job loyally and well.' *(Read 10Jul17)*

07Feb17 – FSLt Harold Wesley YATES (Mitchell ON) – INJ

Attempting to turn too close to the ground with insufficient speed, Yates crashes his Maurice Farman Longhorn Pusher, N5033, at Eastbourne. The aircraft is completely wrecked; Yates only slightly so with contusions of nasal cartilages, burns to the right arm and abrasions on his shins. Relinquishing his flying, he is appointed to the RNVR as an Armament Officer at Eastchurch. Not desirous of maintaining that commission, Yates is released in December.

HW Yates

RAeC Trust

17Feb17 – FSLt Gordon Thomas BYSSHE (Ottawa) – POW Turkey

Escorting a Sopwith Strutter during a bombing attack on a gunboat, Bysshe is shot down by *Ltn* Emil Meinecke over the Dardanelles. Crash-landing his 2 Wing Bristol Scout 8996, Bysshe is captured and imprisoned. An official Turkish communiqué on the 20th will confirm his new status and notes: 'The British aeroplane, armed with 2 M/C Guns is almost intact, ...will be available for use after slight repair in our possession.' A POW held initially in Constantinople, Bysshe will spend the remainder of the War at Afiou-Kara-Hissar in Turkey

GT Bysshe, in 1918 RAF uniform, after POW release

GWFM

During the Second World War, Bysshe's son, Sub Lt (Pilot) Arthur Gordon, Royal Canadian Navy Volunteer Reserve, is killed while training at USNAS Pensacola, Florida, in November 1944.

The German, Meinike, will find employment in Holland following the war as a mechanic, then as chief test pilot for the Fokker Aircraft Company. After 1945 he will work for the USAF during the Berlin Airlift before emigrating to St. Catherines, Ontario, in 1950.

25Feb17 – BREBACH RAID – FSLt Lewis Ewing SMITH (Mystic PQ) – POW/DOW

Smith is reported 'Missing' after his Sopwith Strutter 9739 fails to return from 3Wing's raid on the Breback Iron Works. Smith, a McGill graduate, was missing once before, following a raid on the Burbach Blast Furnaces in January, but managed to return safely. This time there is no sign of him until an extract from a German report on the 20th of March mentions that Smith was shot down by *Offst* Vohinecht of *Jasta* 24. The aircraft is reputed to have crashed at Auesmacher, 17 miles south of Saarbrucken.

Later still, it is learned that Smith had succumbed to wounds shortly after being taken prisoner. The loss of his potential service is a great misfortune for the RNAS. Smith's January 1st report had recommend him for early promotion and spoke highly of his ability to command as well as

LE Smith

MHR

his fighter pilot skills. Age 27, he is buried at Sarralbe, France. His Air Mechanic Gunlayer, R.S. Portsmouth, Cd'G, was also killed during the combat. The English crewman had earned his French Croix de Guerre while flying with **Raymond Collishaw**.

– FSLt Ernest POTTER
(Winnipeg; b. ENG) – Cd'GaP

Flying Stutter 9735, Potter is late starting for the Brebach raid. Unable to catch the main group, he forms a solo fighting patrol instead, engaging 4 Hostile Aircraft at Chateau Salires and sending one apparently Out Of Control. Although his Strutter is damaged in the combat, Potter force lands at Siechamps without injury to either himself or to his rating Gunlayer, LA Dell.

Potter has been described as a very able officer, with his ability to command rated as very good indeed: 'A Clever Flight Leader.' The French government awards him the Croix de Guerre avec Palme with the statement: 'Ex cut, la tête de son escadrille, sept expeditions de bombardement importante en territoire ennemi.' Astonishingly, for some reason perhaps known only to bureaucrats the medal will not be Gazetted until August 1918, almost nineteen months later.

Combat flying will have invalided Potter by May 1917 and he is given Canada Leave. The Department of Naval Service in Ottawa finds him physically unfit and terminates his Commission. In September 1917, obviously feeling there is more to be done, the resolute Potter rejoins as an Observer Sub Lieutenant.

– FSLt Clarence Alexander MAYWOOD
(Winnipeg) – Censure

An Admiralty report on the airborne failures of five machines during the raid on Brebach Iron Works reflects on the records of the pilots. Maywood is one who receives just such a criticism: 'TL consider his failure to carry on with the raid owing to defective revolution-counter unsatisfactory. He should have known by ear whether his engine was correct or

CA Maywood
RAeC Trust

not and as a matter of fact there was nothing wrong with his engine.'

This official censure of all five aviators is later formally withdrawn. However, it is disheartening for Maywood who is now posted to Prawle Point in Devon for maritime operations. In July, he requests to be relieved of flying duties and tenders his resignation in order to return to Canada to join CEF. Should the resignation be rejected, he asks for alternate employment in the RNAS. Maywood's OC requests his retention for Executive duties pending arrival of relief. By August 1917, the resignation is accepted.

MARCH 1917

01Mar17 – SLt Obs Charles Keith CHASE
(Toronto) – Action

With 2 Naval out of St. Pol, Observer Chase is in the midst of exposing photographic plates when his Sopwith Strutter is attacked by a formation of five hostile scouts—one taking up a position above the tail, three diving on the port side, and the fifth making a direct frontal attack. In an obviously well choreographed maneuver, the enemy aeroplanes to the front and rear dive and shoot simultaneously.

Chase was fortunate to have served as a Corporal with the Eaton Machine Gun Battalion of Toronto, and now, with a practiced eye, he holds his fire until the scout diving on his tail is within a few yards. He then empties a complete tray from his Lewis gun into the German pilot's face. The enemy fighter thereupon stalls, sideslips, and finally goes down in a spinning nosedive, smoke issuing.

At almost the same moment, the aeroplane attacking from the front receives a burst from the Strutter Pilot's Vickers gun, and appears to go down out of control. The British pilot, FLt CCR Edwards, now darts steeply for the lines and, although shot through the shoulder and both feet, succeeds in guiding the battle-damaged aircraft to a perfect landing at the Furnes Advanced Aerodrome.

On the 21st of April, both Pilot and Observer are Gazetted the British DSC and the French Cd'G for this action. Chase is, however, worn out and his Wing Commander reports: 'This Officer has done much good observing work over enemies' lines for which he has rec'd DSC & Croix de Guerre. The state of his nerves no longer permit him to carry out duties of observer efficiently. He wishes to qualify as Pilot in RNAS; if this is not practicable his experience would be valuable in connection with test flights in England for points in regard to equipment of machines.'

By June, Chase will be surveyed as medically Unfit for Flying. He carries out Ground Duties at Eastchurch until February 1918 when he is again declared 'Fit Flying Duty' and is sent to 6 Wing in the Mediterranean.

04Mar17 – FLt Harry Redmond WAMBOLT (Dartmouth NS) – MIA

HR Wambolt

RAeC Trust

Leading 'B' Flight of 3 Naval on a front line patrol, Wambolt encounters four Albatros scouts of *Jasta* 1. During the violent combat maneuvering, he falls out of his Sopwith Pup N6170 at 6,000' over Vis-en-Artois. *Ltn* Herbert Schroder claims a victory. Later the Geneva Red Cross will confirm Wambolt's death.

In his final Eastchurch Gunnery school report of 25 May 1916, Wambolt had been described as: 'Must learn to take matters more seriously. Very casual.' This was in reference to a visit made to the unit by King George V. When a mix up in names and introductions became obvious, Wambolt had boldly stepped forward and shaken the King's hand, announcing "Hank Wambolt, Your Majesty!"

Raymond Collishaw described the young Nova Scotian as fitting the traditional picture of a 'wild colonial boy.' Within a month of arriving at 3 Naval however, Wambolt had obviously taken his reports seriously and is: 'A perfect example of efficiency & good conduct. Excellent Officer in every way.' He had been promoted to Flight Lieutenant at the end of December 1916.

– FSLt James Percey WHITE (Winnipeg MB) – KIA

Also killed in this action, White is claimed by *Oblt* Hans Kummetz, the Commander of *Jasta* 1. Age 21, White is buried at Vis-En-Artois British Cemetery, Haucourt, Pas de Calais.

JP White

RAeC Trust

FSLt White had been an assistant instructor at the Eastchurch School during the summer of 1916. Before being posted to 3 Naval he was recorded to have: 'Made a very unpromising start, wrecking several M/C's. Is now a most capable Pilot, keen & industrious Officer.'

Both Wambolt and White will be Mentioned in Despatches. But for new Squadron Commander **Redford Mulock**, it is a sad initiation into battle for his 3 Naval. His other two Flights have also been in combat this day and he has lost one of his English pilots, FSLt LA Powell. On the positive side, Canadians **Raymond Collishaw** and **Jack Malone**, along with English unit-member Len Rochford, all future aces, have each brought down an enemy machine. The score is three for three.

12Mar17 – FSLt Charles McNICOLL (Westmount PQ) – U-boat

Out of Dundee, Scotland, in Short 827 8645, McNicoll drops four 16lb bombs on an enemy submarine just as she is submerging. This attack, close off Bell Rock, earns the Quebec-born pilot a Distinguished Service Cross, Gazetted in June.

From McGill University, McNicholl completed flying training at the Wright School in Augusta, Georgia, during January 1916. He has flown out of Dundee since September 1916 and in the Station's summary for that year was judged a 'VG Pilot. Very keen on 'G' Duties, and shows keenness on Executive work.' By July he is further written up as 'A reliable and conscientious Officer with good ability in handling men. Is acting as Armament Officer in an efficient manner.' These are rather good reports and in August he is promoted to

Flight Lieutenant and given a ship-borne appointment in HMS *Pegasus*. There, alas, he will run afoul of the regular Royal Navy.

On September 19th the Commander *Pegasus*, writes: 'I do not consider him suitable for service in seaplane carriers and request his transfer from this ship. His position of seniority requires that he be in charge of one hangar. Which position requires initiative, resource & organizing ability in all of which qualities he is lacking: the result is his department is suffering in consequence. I have no complaints to make as to his technical ability or knowledge as a pilot. I shall be satisfied if he can be relieved by a pilot with more experience in Seaplane work.' McNicholl, it appears, has incurred the Commander's wrath and in October will be sent to the Isle of Grain for experimental flying duties. In that Station's yearly report for 1918, he will be named a 'Most promising Test Pilot'.

12Mar17 – FSLt John Roderick ROSS (Winnipeg) – MID

Flying out of Calshot, Ross puts in a 'very creditable performance' in going to the rescue of a torpedoed vessel that is sending out SOS signals. Although having no previous experience in night flying, Ross remains out at sea in his single-engine Short Seaplane 3327 in search of information until nearly 8:00 PM. After more than two hours of patrol, he returns to base, making a perfect landing in the darkness. For his effort in finding the wreckage of SS *Memnon* and then directing patrol vessels to the survivors, Ross will receive a Mention in Despatches.

The Prairie pilot did not always arrive home in a dry condition. More than three months earlier, in November, flying Short 184, 8379, he bombed a U-boat. Landing at sea to report his attack to a British patrol vessel he then stalled on take off, side slipped and crashed. The aircraft had to be abandoned, and Ross and his air mechanic crewman, Redman, were picked up by HM ship. During salvage operations the next day, the aircraft was lost owing to a U-boat attack. However, the offending sub was sunk and its crew captured by the Royal Navy.

In another more recent incident, during January, Ross was beaching Short 184 seaplane 8071 when he damaged a float. Taken under-tow by a destroyer, the aircraft broke up and sank. Ross was again rescued; again unhurt, from a sinking fuselage.

By May 1917, Ross will be promoted to Flight Lieutenant and sent to Felixstowe for the Large America flying boat

course. Following qualification he goes to the Grain Experimental and Acceptance Depot as a Test and Ferry Pilot; but in December he will have yet another dunking. Testing Wight Tractor Biplane 9846, fitted as a seaplane prototype with modified undercarriage and enlarged wing tip floats, Ross only just lifts off from Portland NAS when the 250-hp Rolls-Royce Eagle engine implodes. He gamely attempts a turn into wind to force land but the new machine sideslips down from 200 feet and crashes near Chesil Bank. The aircraft is a wreck but, once again, Ross and his Observer, Lt FDJ Silwood, escape unhurt. In April of 1918, Captain JR Ross will be appointed Director of Parks and Depots for Ferry Duties.

18Mar17 – PFO Arthur Stuart GIRLING (Canada) – DOJ

After having joined RNAS this day, the young Canadian's chances of graduating will become slim just two weeks before finishing flight school in September. He will have managed to incur Their Lordship's severe displeasure for tendering a fictitious cheque to a prostitute - Officers do not write unfunded cheques.

Nonetheless, Girling is reported as a 'VG Pilot & good Officer' and will be granted a commission. Although recommended for seaplanes, he is sent instead to the Manston Fighting School for scouts and from there to service with 2 Wing in the Aegean. Despite his inauspicious start as an Officer, in the New Year's Honours List of 1919 Girling will be Gazetted the DFC for his efforts as a fighter pilot with 62 Wing in Italy, Macedonia and the Dardanelles.

19Mar17 – PFO Earl Leslie MacLEOD (Atchelitz BC) – Vendome

A school master in Vancouver, MacLeod had been accepted as a Candidate for the RNAS only to find all the flying schools booked solid. Following closure of the Toronto School he finally received a telegram from Naval Headquarters to proceed to directly to England:

> "I handed over my teaching duties in two hours and took the train east. I sailed on SS *Scandinavian* with a group of 51 RNAS pilots; all of them had their wings but me and they had considerable flying experience. I started ground school at the Crystal Palace in London and then went to Vendome in France for my flying instruction. I took several short flights as a passenger in Maurice Farmans and then met my flying instructor who took me up in a Caudron."

MacLeod's instructor believes that this latest pupil, like his Canadian classmates, has already flown, and after demonstrating a circuit and landing:

> "He could see no valid reason why he should risk his life as well as mine, and told me to carry on solo … (I) pushed the throttle wide open and let the plane take itself off, and up to the inordinate altitude— actually the meter registered no more than 3,000 feet. I was able to throttle back my aircraft, but then I became really alarmed about the difficulty I was experiencing keeping track of the location of the aerodrome, and, in the desperation of my predicament, I succeeded in getting down to the drome safely by trial and error, bumping a bit on my first landing. It was then that I had a feeling of elation. I took off again, did a circuit, and then landed again, this time smoothly."

Soon judged to have completed the primary flying standard, MacLeod returns to England and after advanced flying instruction at Cranwell, he is assigned to seaplanes. Operational out of Newbyn and Cattewater Stations near Land's End on Short and Hamble seaplanes he escorts convoys as they approach England.

> "We flew patrols … over the Irish Sea and along the coasts of Ireland and Wales to the Scilly Isles and almost to the French coast. We used our own submarines for bombing practice. My Observer and I made a run, and the small sub-calibre bomb hit the sub amidships, exploded, and left a small dent in the hull. To the crew inside the sub the noise was most distressing, so that was the last time we were allowed to bomb a live target."

MacLeod does bomb an enemy U-boat in March 1918 but the blast results are inconclusive. Following the War, he remains in the Canadian air forces and will retire an Air Commodore, OBE.

24Mar17 – FSLt William Smith OLIVER (Calgary; b. Toronto) – KIC

In Dover to pick up a new Sopwith Triplane, Oliver is conducting a flight test dive from 2,500 feet when the machine, as it was later described: 'broke up in the air, both sets of planes wrenched off and the fuselage came whistling down like a bomb.' The aircraft, N5473, had just been delivered from the factory and erected four days before. Age 25, Oliver is buried at St. James's, Dover, Kent. He had graduated from the Stinson School in Texas one year and two days previously.

Oliver has the sad distinction of being his squadron's first fatality. Number 10 Naval is just forming at St. Pol, one of the many airfields on the outskirts of Dunkirk. Initially equipped with obsolete Nieuport two-seaters, the unit is being upgraded to the Sopwith Triplane. In April, pilots from the disbanding 3 Wing will arrive in strength and the Squadron will be seconded to the Royal Flying Corps. By the 30th of August, 10 Naval will have suffered eighteen pilots killed. Ten of that number will be Canadian.

30Mar17 – FSLt Joshua Martin INGHAM, MID (Toronto) – KIA Greece

Number 2 Wing in the Mediterranean loses 'An exceptional gallant officer & good mess mate' when Ingham fails to return from a service flight out of the Island of Thasos. That evening Bulgaria's Sofija wireless reports '*Ltn* Rudolph von Eschwege shot down an enemy 'plane in battle…' Ingham had been flying Sopwith Strutter 5223 and was killed over Xanthia during a reconnaissance of the Philloppolis area. One month previously, he had been Mentioned for his part on an air attack on the Gereviz Seaplane base which had been conducted while under heavy AA fire. Aged 23, Ingham and his English Observer, SLt JE Maxwell, are buried at Dedeagath, Greece.

Von Eschwege has been nicknamed 'The Eagle of the Aegean' by RNAS and RFC pilots for his victories along the Macedonian Front. In November the 20-kill German Ace is literally blown out of the sky as he attacks a British spotting balloon. A trap is sprung when the basket, packed with explosives and a dummy observer, is detonated from the ground. The ruse takes down the German Halbertstad D.II. Allied pilots, who would have preferred that the 'Eagle' had died in fair combat, bury him with full military honours.

APRIL 1917

05Apr17 – FLt Robert Kenneth SLATER (Ottawa) – MIA/POW

The month of April gets off to a poor start for the newly constituted 6 Naval Squadron when they suffer their first casualty. Slater in Nieuport 17 N3202 is last seen going down in a spin over Arras. He has possibly been shot down by *Ltn* Eberhard Voss of *Jasta* 20 and it is not learned until early May that Slater is a Prisoner of War. The Geneva Red Cross's official German List has him as a prisoner at Karlsruhe. Later, he is incarcerated at Holyminden and will be repatriated to England in January 1919.

05Apr17 – FSLt Maurice Rooke KINGSFORD (Toronto) – INJ

After only two days in 6 Naval, Kingsford is returning from his first combat patrol when his Nieuport 17 N3191 has an engine failure. Perhaps not quite quick enough in establishing a glide, he crashes from 200 feet, dislocating the femur in his right leg. Hospitalized in England, Kingsford is not re-surveyed fit

MR Kingsford
RAeC Trust

until mid-July. He will eventually be sent to the Walmer Defense Flight and fly the Sopwith Pup, taking part in anti-Gotha Patrols. By the autumn, he is back in France operating Sopwith Camels before becoming eligible for Canada Leave in November 1917. A University of Toronto student and prior Lieutenant with the 30th Battalion, CEF, Kingsford will become an instructor on scouts at Manston Fighting School when he returns from leave.

05Apr17 – FSLt George Denison KIRKPATRICK (Toronto) – 6 Naval

No sooner has Upper Canada College student Kingsford been invalided out of 6 Naval than fellow UCC student Kirkpatrick is almost alphabetically assigned. Immediately upon arrival, he is sent up in a

Nieuport 17 test flight and, over the course of the next few months, he manages to survive the expanding air war. One of Kirkpatrick's survival adventures includes a synchronization surprise when his own machine gun shoots off the tips of his rotating propeller.

On the 8th of June, he will deliver one of the Squadron's new Sopwith Camels to the unit and by the 19th of that month conversion to the new fighter is completed. The Squadron is then moved to Dunkirk coast

GD Kirkpatrick
RAeC Trust

where they will be up against German naval airmen, specifically *Marine-Feldjadgstaffel* I, flying the new Albatross D.V. By mid-July, Kirkpatrick will be a deputy Flight Commander, often leading offensive patrols. These sometimes twice-daily flights exact a price. On the 18th of August he overturns Camel N6357 while taxiing in from a noon mission. But this is just a prelude. At 1600 that same day he leads another line patrol; then in the early evening takes Camel N6357 up for a test flight and crashes in a field. Taken to hospital he is diagnosed with neurasthenia. Remaining in nursing care until October, Kirkpatrick will be granted an extended Canada Leave in order to fully recover and indeed, he will not pass flight muster until May 1918. Assigned to Yarmouth for 212 Squadron RAF he will command 485 Fighter Flight at Burgh Castle before being demobilized in February 1919. Despite his time out for illness, he will persevere and end the War with nearly 360 solo flight hours to his credit—an impressive achievement given that not many aviators will attain the 300-hour mark.

08Apr17 – Canadian RFC ACE 2Lt William A. Bishop (Owen Sound ON)

Of interest, the 6 Naval Nieuport 17's are the same type of aircraft flown by Royal Flying Corps pilot 'Billy' Bishop when he makes Ace this day. He is awarded the Victoria Cross for a solo airfield attack in June 1917. Bishop will fly 208 operational missions and claim 72 victories by War's end.

09Apr17– FSLt Albert Edward 'Eddie' CUZNER (Ottawa) – Vimy Ridge

It is Easter Monday, and the Battle of Arras begins in earnest with the capture of Vimy Ridge by the Canadian Corps. A four-day preamble of artillery concentration has taken out many of the targets pre-registered by observation aircraft. As Canadian troops funnel out of the tunnels and trenches in the dawn light they time their advance through landscape cratered by a 'creeping barrage' of Allied shelling. The big guns execute a fire-plan carefully crafted from aerial photographs, keeping the German infantry and machine-gunners pinned down until the Canadians overrun the enemy trenches. The uphill assault on Vimy Ridge is also obscured by sleet and snow.

Flying conditions are deplorable but Naval 8 does manage to get airborne. Cuzner follows his Flight Commander into the artillery blustered skies and the twosome attempt troop support but the weather is atrocious and chances of mistaken identity of ground targets far too great. As it is the pair become lost and land at an abandoned airfield, spending a chilly night before launching for home the following day.

AE Cuzner, in Rugby togs

U of T

Eddie Cuzner is no stranger to the cold. A superb sportsman, he played both rugby and hockey for the University of Toronto, and managed the school's hockey team before leaving for Naval service. A school yearbook declares him 'a man of infinite jest'. Cuzner joined Naval 8 in early March as the Squadron was transitioning to the new Sopwith Triplane. *(Read 29Apr17)*

11Apr17 – FLt Lloyd Samuel BREADNER (Carleton Place ON) – Triple Victory

Tasked to escort a flight of RFC BE.2 bombers on a raid over Cambrai, a No. 3 Naval flight is led by Breadner. When a number of hostile machines attempt to attack the bombers, he engages the enemy in rapid succession, bringing three down; one in flames, one completely out of control, and the third in a spinning nose-dive with one wing broken off.

LS Breadner

WSU Library

His wingman **Joe Fall** is equally successful:

– FSLt Joseph Stewart Temple FALL (Cobble Hill BC) – Triple Victory

Fall's description of the event is no humdrum account:

"When BE2's were attacked at Cambrai I attacked HA head on at 8,000 feet. I saw many tracers go into his engine as we closed on one another. I half looped to one side of him, and then the HA dived with a large trail of blue smoke. I dived after him down to about 4,000 feet and fired about fifty rounds when he went down absolutely out of control. I watched him spinning down to about 1,000 feet, the trail of smoke increasing.

"I was immediately attacked by three more Albatros which drove me down to about 200 feet. We were firing at one another whenever possible, when at last I got into a good position and attacked one from above and from the right. I closed on him, turning in behind him and got so close to him that the pilot's head filled the small ring in the Aldis sight. I saw three tracers actually go into the pilot's head; the HA then simply heeled over and went into the ground. The other two machines cleared off.

"Having lost sight of all of the other machines and being so low, I decided to fly home at about that height (200 feet). A company of German cavalry going east along a small road halted and fired upon me; also several machine guns opened fire.

"After flying west for about five minutes I was again attacked by a Halbertstadt single-seater and as he closed upon me I rocked my machine until he was within fifty yards. I side-looped over him and fired a short burst at him. He seemed to clear off, then attacked me again.

"These operations were repeated several times with a slight variation in the way I looped over him, until within about five minutes of crossing the lines (flying against a strong wind), when he was about 150 yards behind me, I looped straight over him and coming out of the loop I dived at him and fired a good, long burst. I saw nearly all the tracers go into the pilot's back, just along the edge of the cockpit. He immediately dived straight into the ground.

"I then went over the German trenches filled with soldiers, and I was fired upon by machine-guns, rifles, and small field guns, in or out of range. There was a lot of small artillery firing and many shells bursting in and about the German trenches, somewhere in the vicinity of the Cambrai-Arras Road."

JST Fall

Fall, a farmer's son, later adds: "When I landed, the wings dropped down to the ground like a hen over a brood of chicks". His aircraft had been riddled by hostile gunfire, having the cross-braced landing wires shot apart. The wings, held intact only by the flying wires, collapsed on touchdown. For this triple victory, Fall wins the first of three Distinguished Service Crosses. He will go on to become the only triple DSC holder in aviation history. *(Read 19Dec17)*

Both of these Canadians make Ace on the 23rd of April. Breadner will spectacularly bring down a German Gotha bomber as one of his five. This is the first Gotha shot out of the sky over the Western Front—no easy feat in a tiny Pup. 'Bread' is later described in his RNAS Reports as: 'A hardworking & capable officer. Keen & intelligent with very good power of command. A daring pilot who inspires confidence in others. He has carried out his duties as officer in charge [...] with consistent keenness and initiative.' Perhaps not surprisingly, Breadner will rise to prominence as the Air Chief Marshal of the RCAF during the Second World War. *(Read May 1940)*

14Apr17 – FREIBURG REPRISAL RAID:

The torpedoing of the Hospital Ship *Asturias* on the 20th of March has enraged the Admiralty into carrying out a reprisal raid on the city of Freiburg, near Baden. Revenge is demanded by the British public for a range of German atrocities such as the execution of Nurse Edith Cavell and the sinking of the passenger liner *Lusitania*. To achieve maximum effect, the aircraft drop not only bombs but also propaganda, in the form of leaflets announcing the reason for the 'terror raid' on the German civilian population. The attack is conducted in two waves, both by 3 Wing just prior to it's becoming disbanded in order to provide further pilots for the new naval scout squadrons.

Significantly flying on this Raid are:

– FSLt John Edward SHARMAN (Oak Lake MB) – DSC

Sharman distinguishes himself in this final operation by 3 Wing. He is the sole member of the unit to fly in both attacks and will be Gazetted the DSC for: 'Devotion to duty during long distance air raids. After leading a flight in the morning he volunteers and flies a bombing machine with a second flight in the afternoon, again, acting as leader.'

A mining engineer from Manitoba, Sharman has flown with the Wing since its formation in mid

JE Sharman

1916. He was in the first large-scale bombing raid, against the Oberndorf munitions works in October, and by March 1917 was leading formations. On one such operation against the Burbach Iron Works, he quickly adapted and switched to the alternate target of Morchiengen airfield when strong headwinds were encountered. Prisoners captured later admitted that the raid had been very effective, as several aircraft stationed there were rendered useless.

(Read 14Jun17)

– FSLt Walter Ernest 'Pete' FLETT (Toronto) – DSC Action

Shortly after bombing the Freiburg town centre objective, Flett is engaged by three enemy machines—two single-seaters and one two-seater. His Gunlayer, Air Mechanic RG Kimberley, is wounded in the wrist but succeeds in bringing down two of the enemy before being again wounded, this time by an explosive bullet in the ankle. Flett's machine is now tattered with holes, and owing to the damage, navigation is difficult and the return journey very slow. Consequently he is again attacked, but his twice-wounded gunner again drives the enemy machine off.

In May, Flett will be Gazetted the DSC for conspicuous gallantry during the air raid and also awarded the Cd'GaP by the French. His Gunlayer is granted a very well-won DCM. For Flett, this is a vindication of his having previously incurred the displeasure of the Admiralty during the Burbach Raid on the 25th of February: 'T.L. consider his failure to carry on with the raid on Saarbrucke-Burbach Iron Works discreditable. He should have known how to adjust his carburettor at varying heights'. It had been an unfair pronouncement, as five aircraft had to turn back from that effort due to engine problems in the extreme cold.

WE Flett

UCC

Flett has been flying with 3 Wing since November 1916 and it has been a harsh winter. After the April raid, he is invalided from France and granted Canada Leave. He will remain sick for the duration of 1917 and the Director Naval Service in Ottawa will recommend a discharge due to physical unfitness/neurasthenia trauma. Flight Lieutenant Flett, DSC, Cd'GaP, is released from RNAS on the 25th of March 1918 with the privilege of retaining rank.

– FLt George Rivers Sanderson FLEMING (Toronto) – POW/DOW

Following his bomb drop, Fleming's Sopwith Strutter 9667 is hit by anti-aircraft fire over Freiburg. The tail of the aircraft blown off and Fleming sustains serious injuries in the crash. His Gunlayer, AG Lockyer, is dead. On the 26th of the month the Germans drop a paper in French lines reporting the Canadian pilot killed. Fleming is officially reported to have Died of Wounds as a Prisoner of War on the 17th of April: the Geneva Red Cross confirms this in September. Age 31, he is buried at Plaine National Cemetery, Bas-Rhin, France.

GRS Fleming

U of T

Another University of Toronto graduate, Fleming completed the Curtis Canada Flying School on the first of September 1915. By April 1916 he was with 3 Wing as it began to form at Eastchurch and was promoted Flight Lieutenant at the end of the year. Described: 'A very methodical Officer. Ability to command VGI.' It is high accolade from the Royal Navy that places a premium on the leadership ability of an officer. Allowed a special Canadian leave to deal with his late father's business, the Alwell Fleming Printing Company in Toronto, the younger Fleming had only just returned to flying duty when he is lost.

– FSLt Harold 'Gus' EDWARDS (Glace Bay, NS; b. ENG) – POW

During the afternoon attacks of the Freiburg reprisal raid, Edwards shoots down one enemy aircraft but he, in turn, falls under the guns of *Vzfw* Rudolph Rath of *Jasta* 35. This will be Rath's only victory as he is killed ten days later. Edwards, a Nova Scotia mining electrician crashes near Schlettstadt in his Strutter, N5117. His fate is unknown until again, the information arrives via a paper dropped by German aviators. Edwards is reported as unwounded and Prisoner of War in Freiburg.

During the morning's attack, Wing Commander CFN Rathbone had been shot down and taken POW. The Englishman was placed in a cell in Military Detention Barracks in Colmar. 'I looked through the peep-hole in the door of the cell and soon discovered that somebody in the opposite cell was trying to signal to me by means of the Morse code by flashing his hand across the peep-hole.

'The occupant turned out to be FSLt Edwards, a stout hearted Canadian who had been shot down a little later than myself. I was glad to have company and most of our time was spent in communicating by means of signals when the phlegmatic warden was not about. During the next eight days we were frequently marched to the Intelligence Officer who put us through the well-known process of pumping. He was, however, unable to obtain any information from us and although they kept Edwards and myself apart we always managed to communicate on our return through the peep-holes in the cell. At the end of eight days when pumping was supposed to be over Edwards was allowed to come into my cell during the day. My cell was larger than his and being a Lieutenant Colonel I was given a bed to sleep on whereas Edwards had the ordinary all boards. We were fed on two plates of thin soup and half a pound of bread per diem; no soap.'

By the end of August, Edwards will be incarcerated at Karlsruhe and writes:

> "I was shot down after lengthy engagement with several enemy machines. My Observer, JL Coghlan, was wounded in about 15 places and died a few minutes after we came down. My controls were shot away and I fell all the way completely out of control. Luckily we struck the ground in such a way that I was unhurt. Since then I have sombered away with a gnawing at the stomach like many others who have shared this fate".

Edwards does not 'somber' for long. He manages to escape twice and in one episode is at large for ten days before being recaptured after having walked 175 miles— all at night. Sent to a special camp for persistent escapers at Holzminden he applies himself to the prison library and increases his education. Repatriated after the War, Edwards joins **Raymond Collishaw**'s 47 Squadron in South Russia, earning two Czarist decorations before finally returning to Canada where he joins the Canadian Air Force. *(Read 1942)*

15Apr17 – PFO Joseph Louis LAVIGNE (Grand Mere PQ) – KIC

In flying training at Chingford, student pilot Lavigne has a catastrophic crash. His Grahame-White XV aircraft, 3610, loses engine power on takeoff. During the forced landing attempt the machine overturns and Lavigne is killed. His English instructor pilot Flt FW Merriam is injured.

LaVigne's fatal crash

FAAM, 19991/206/65

The 22-year-old French-Canadian had attended the Curtiss Flying School in Toronto but did not graduate before winter set in. He was accepted by the RNAS in December 1916 and completed the Crystal Palace ground school, arriving at Chingford Flying School in March. Lavigne is buried at Leytonstone, Essex.

20Apr17 – FSLt Donald Howe MASSON (Ottawa) – KIC

Coming out of a practice evasive roll manoeuver at 5,000 feet, Masson's Nieuport XI 'Bébé' 3991 breaks apart and falls. The 11 Naval Training Squadron pilot, aged 28, is buried at Dunkirk. Masson was a McGill man and had completed his RNAS 'Candidate' requirements at the Stinson Flying School in San Antonio Texas in March 1916. His Nieuport XI is an aging warhorse by this time and previously had been hit by flak and overhauled. That and other damages may have resulted in today's structural failure.

DH Masson

MHR

21Apr17 – FSLt John Joseph 'Jack' MALONE (Regina SK) – ACE

Canada's fourth naval Ace makes his fifth kill. It is one month after a spectacular triple victory in March. Malone has been flying the Sopwith Pup with 3 Naval since early February and he is noted for having excellent piloting skills.

During a dawn patrol on the 23rd of April, he repeats his triple talent. In Pup N6208 he engages an Albatros D.III and drives it down. Forty-five minutes later Malone attacks a second 'Alberti' and takes out the pilot. The third aircraft is struck from a distance of 60 feet and immediately descends out of control. Engaging a fourth hostile, Malone runs out of ammunition and lands at an advanced flying ground to rearm and return to the fray. *(Read 30Apr17)*

22Apr17 – FSLt Douglas Alex'dr Hardy NELLES, MID (Simcoe ON) – INT Holland

(From 02Aug15) Nelles does not return from a raid on St. Denis Westrem aerodrome. He is reported as last seen over Holland, apparently with engine trouble and descending rapidly. Indeed, his 5 Naval Sopwith Strutter 9376 has lost the air pressure system that pushes the fuel through to feed the engine and a landing is forced:

DAH Nelles

"I was on a bombing raid and we all—bombs, machine and self—land intact beside Oostburg which is close to Belgium and near the coast. I had come East as far as possible in the glide but was not certain which country I was in until I had time to notice the crowd which had collected about me almost before the machine had come to a standstill. Numerous soldiers were in the throng from whose uniforms I knew that I had been able to get sufficiently far East.

"A Dutch officer took me in charge. He knew no English and was so uncertain of my intentions when I took out my revolver, unloaded a few moments previous, to give it to him that he almost feinted with fright evidently thinking that I intended fighting my way, single handed, back to France. I was marched to the local military headquarters where I gave temporary parole and the outside world was informed of my presence. It was a very fine warm day so I removed as much of the warm flying clothing as I conveniently could. This left me bare-headed and attired in an old khaki uniform with high fur-lined boots. No doubt, I presented an odd spectacle walking through the main street of the village accompanied by the military."

The sorry Sopwith is later sold to the Dutch for £1,700 and becomes LA42 of the Dutch Air Arm. For Nelles himself, the War is effectively over. He is escorted to The Hague and joins other fliers, of both sides, who have landed in neutral Holland. The internees are allowed to find billets with private families; the German aviators stay on one side of the city, and the Allied lads on the other. In letters home to his lady friend and later wife, Nelles writes of tennis games, long bicycle rides, museum visits and teaching English to children. However, he reads of the names of friends in casualty lists and chafes at being put entirely 'out of the game.' Learning of his being promoted to Flight Lieutenant and having been awarded the Distinguished Service Cross, Nelles writes:

> "These honours for me have made me more anxious than ever to be back with the squadron. One has such a feeling of uselessness here."

His DSC is awarded in part: 'For conspicuously good work as a pilot of a bombing machine. He has taken part in 17 raids, and has also done a large amount of fighter patrol work.' He had been Mentioned previously for these efforts. Nelles will be granted a compassionate parole to travel to Canada to visit a sick parent in April 1918.

23Apr17 – FCdr Theodore Douglas HALLAM, (Toronto) – DSC – U-boat

(From 04Jun15) Hallam is now Officer Commanding the Felixstowe War Flight, consisting of Curtiss H.8 'Large America' flying boats. Today, in aircraft 8661 he and his English crew sight a submarine with three men in the conning tower. The boat makes no attempt to dive and four bombs are dropped. The weapons appears to badly damaged the submarine and it disappears 20 miles ESE of North Hinder Light Vessel. Two aircraft then search the area for over five hours without result.

Hallam is credited with a U-boat destroyed and will be awarded a Bar to his Gallipoli DSC for the exploit. In

December he is Gazetted a second Bar for sustained anti-submarine operations in flying boats. *(Read 19Dec17)*

24Apr17 – FSLt Fredrick Earle FRASER (Winnipeg) – DSC – U-boat

Flying as Second Pilot in Curtis H8, 8655, Fraser attacks an enemy submarine that is assailing the Italian S.S. *Portfino* near Weymouth. As the submarine submerges he drops a 100lb bomb within five or six feet of the conning tower. His second bomb falls a few feet further ahead. The U-boat goes to the bottom in 30 fathoms and it is not possible to observe the effect of the attack. However, the boat later rises to the surface and is permanently sunk by the destroyer HMS *Ambuscade*. Back at home station Calshot, his aircraft captain, FLt CL Scott, reports that Fraser: 'Carried out duties with great coolness.'

FE Fraser

RAeC Trust

Fraser had initially joined the RNAS as a Sub-Lieutenant Observer in December 1915. While serving with No.3 Wing in France, he took pilot training at Vendome and earned his Royal Aeronautical Certificate. Transferred to Probationary Flight Officer status, he completed his pilot course at Cranwell. Re-appointed a commissioned officer in March 1917, his Naval seniority is backdated, based on his former Observer time-in-rank. Having reported aboard at Station Calshot just yesterday, today's action has taken place on his very first war patrol.

Fraser will be Gazetted the DSC in July. By this time he is in Italy, flying with No. 6 Wing out of Otranto. In January 1918, suffering from a nervous condition and kidney complications he is given sick leave to Canada. Returning to active duty in June, he finishes the war at Prawle Point Naval Air Station.

28Apr17 – FSLt (A/FCdr) Raymond COLLISHAW (Nanaimo BC) – ACE

(From 05Jan1893) The fifth RNAS Scout squadron to enter battle is 10 Naval and in his new Sopwith Triplane N5490, Collishaw scores his fifth victory. Across the lines, a German *Leutnant*, one Hermann Goering, also achieves an Ace title today. Years later, the military careers of Collishaw and Goering will share another commonality: during 1941, Air Commodore Collishaw will command the RAF Desert Air Force against Nazi *Reichsmarschall* Goering's Luftwaffe in North Africa.

R Collishaw

VIMM

Collishaw scored his first two victories with 3 Wing in the Sopwith Strutter on October 25th, 1916. This double action left him disoriented and led to his innocent landing—and startled immediate takeoff—from a German airfield.

Assigned to Sopwith Pups with 3 Naval the following January, he brought down another two enemy machines before a bullet shattered his goggles, causing eye injury and frostbite. Upon return from sick leave in England, Collishaw was assigned to the newly forming 10 Naval and appointed an Acting Flight Commander:

> "The Squadron was pretty much a Canadian show... 13 of the 15 pilots being from the Dominion. [It was] ...also more or less a Three Wing reunion for all but two of the Canadians had previously flown with the bombing force."

Now leading B Flight of Naval 10, 'Collie' puts together a fighting team of five Canadians. Each will score five or more victories during the next twelve weeks. For ease of both flight formation and ground crew recognition they paint their Sopwith Triplane engine nacelles and wheel covers a black colour. Collishaw names his machine '**Black Maria**' *(Read 22Jul18)*

Collie's wingmen follow suit in personalizing their machines:

FSLt John Sharman, DSC (Oak Lake MB)
'**Black Death**' *(Read 22Jul17)*

FSLt Mel Alexander (Toronto)
'**Black Prince**' *(Read 06Jul17)*

FSLt Ellis Reid (Belleville ON)
'**Black Roger**' *(Read 06Jun17)*

FSLt Gerry Nash (Stoney Creek ON)
'**Black Sheep**' *(Read 06Jun17)*

The evocative names are stenciled in white on both sides of the khaki-coloured fuselage just forward of the cockpit. All told, the five-member '*Black Flight*' will shoot down 68 enemy aircraft by the end of July 1917. As a comparison, the famed French *Lafayette Escadrille*, comprised of thirty-eight pilots from the United States, accounted for 199 enemy aircraft over a period of two years.

29Apr17 – FSLt Lloyd Allison SANDS (Moncton NB) – Crashes

In a rather flamboyant accident, Sands crashes through the roof of the Wing Commander's office at Coudekerke. His Short Bomber 9491 is wrecked and written off. Sands has already been through two previous crashes: during training on August 23rd 1916 he had a Maurice Farman S.7 Longhorn engine failure *and* a Caudron G.III engine failure, *both* on the same day at Redcar. Having now flown operationally with 3 Wing in its one-and-only Handley-Page bomber, he is currently awaiting reappointment following the disbandment of the Wing, which is being demobilised in order to augment the new scout squadrons.

After training on the lighter machines, Sands will crash Sopwith Pup N6178 on landing and a month later smash up the same aircraft on takeoff. In between these two incidents he does send down two enemy aircraft out of control. When his new squadron, 3 Naval, re-equips with the latest fighter, the Sopwith Camel, Sands, unlike many others, has no problems in handling the gyroscopically inclined aircraft. *(Read 22Mar18)*

29Apr 17 – FSLt Hilary George NARES (Winnipeg) – INJ/REL

Testing collapsible floats on Sopwith Pup 9901, Nares is quite seriously hurt during a ditched-landing experiment. His aircraft is the first post-prototype Sopwith Pup and has been delivered to the Experimental Constructive Department at Grain Naval Air Station. The air bag inflation trials that injured Nares do eventually prove to be successful and the machine is shown to hold at anchor for six hours; however, the floats are never fitted on operational aircraft.

By July, the former McGill student has to resign, as the injuries have rendered him unfit and he is awarded a service gratuity of £150 for his efforts. Nares will join the Royal Canadian Navy Reserve and rise to the rank of Commander during the Second World War.

HG Nares
RAeC Trust

29Apr17 – FSLt Albert Edward 'Eddie' CUZNER (Ottawa) – MIA by the Red Baron

(From 09Apr17) Manfred von Richthofen shoots down his 52nd aircraft and kills a second Canadian naval aviator. By Richthofen's own combat report, Cuzner of Naval 8 dies a fiery death: 'Soon after shooting down a (bomber) near Rouex, we were attacked by a strong enemy one-seater force of Nieuports, Spads and Triplanes. The plane I had singled out caught fire after a short time, burned in the air, and fell north of Henin Lietard.'

Cuzner's is the first and only Sopwith Triplane (N5463) that the 'Red Baron' sends down. Richthofen is reported to have been very impressed by the incredible altitude-gaining agility of the three-winged 'Tripehound' and demands a similar type machine from German industry. The Dutch aircraft designer Anthony Fokker will provide the Dr.I Drideker in response. A year from now von Richthofen, in his notorious red Fokker Dr.1, will be engaged by a third Canadian naval airman and on that occasion, not emerge the victor.

29Apr17 – FSLt Arthur Percival HAYWOOD (Toronto) – WIA

The Naval 8 melee with Richthofen's *Jasta* 11 that has sent Cuzner down in flames escalates further when joined by 1 Naval's Sopwith Triplanes. During the dangerous mix, Haywood is wounded and his engine shot out, but he manages to glide to a forced landing near Bethune. Understandably confused as to his location and believing himself behind enemy lines he sets fire to his Triplane, N5441.

A pilot graduate from the Texas-based Stinson School, Haywood has been with 1 Naval Squadron since early January. Today's wound to the arm is a bad one and effectively takes him out of the war. Following discharge from hospital in October he is surveyed by the Admiralty and found unfit for flying. Given Long Leave to proceed to Canada, he returns in mid-1918 for resurvey but is invalided out of the air services on the First of November 1918.

30Apr17 – FSLt John Bampfylde 'Dan' DANIELL (Prince George) – Action

During a 3 Naval escort of RFC BE2c's to bomb Epinoy aerodrome, Daniell has his seat shot out from under him but manages to continue flying. However, in his struggle to stay airborne without cockpit structure, he becomes lost and lands at an aerodrome near Marieux.

Daniell, a newspaper editor from Prince George, BC, is a bit of a squadron character. His English Flight Commander, LH Rochford, remarks: 'On his return he told us in his own inimitable way the story of his adventure. The RFC squadron, who put him up for the night were having a party in the mess at which 'Dan' said he made three speeches, in all of which he told them that in escaping from the EA which attacked him he 'hopped lightly from cloud to cloud'.'

JB Daniell at Schweidnitz POW Camp

On the 11th of May, Daniell will be hosted by yet another squadron—but this time it is on the east side of the lines. Flying Pup N6464 he is shot down by *Vzfw* Robert Reissinger of *Jasta* 12, near Bourlon. Slightly wounded in the action, Daniell is captured and taken Prisoner of War. He is Reissinger's first victory and the German will score three more times before being brought down in a mid-air with an RFC machine in June.

Daniell is sent to the *Kriegsangeneren* Lager at Karlshrue and then to Trier and finally Schweidnitz. Although his war is over, he receives a MID for good work while serving with No 3 Squadron in the field and is promoted to Flight Lieutenant while in captivity. During his incarceration, Daniell will scrounge and publish a camp newspaper 'The Barb'.

30Apr17 – John Joseph "Jack" MALONE, MID (Regina) – KIA

(From 21Apr17) Now a ten-victory Ace with 3 Naval, Malone is shot down and killed in Sopwith Pup N6175.

Six days previously he had sent down a DFW two-seater near Morchies-Louverval. Malone's own engine then failed and he force-landed alongside his quarry. Both machines immediately came under German shellfire and were very soon destroyed while the former combatants scrambled for shelter together. Pilot *OffzSt*

JJ Malone

Max Haase is slightly wounded, but Observer *Ltn* Karl Keim dies shortly after taking to the ground cover.

The experience of crashing and seeing his opponent perish may have had a distracting influence on Malone: he scores again on the 26th but on this last day of April he is lost over Roumaucourt, West of Cambrai. *Ltn* Paul Billik of *Jasta* 12 claims the score, his first. Like all other aviators whose bodies are never recovered, Malone's name is engraved on the Arras Flying Services Memorial, Pas de Calais, France. He will be Gazetted a posthumous Distinguished Service Order (DSO) in May 1917. The German Billik will go on to shoot down a total of 30 Allied aircraft before a shot-out engine leads to his being captured in August 1918. In 1926, he will die in a Junkers aircraft accident in Berlin.

In February 1918, Malone's younger brother, **Charles Edward**, a Gunner with the 38th Battery, Canadian Field Artillery, transfers from the CEF in England to the RNAS. In spite of a training injury at Uxbridge, 2nd Lieutenant C.E. Malone will survive the War.

MAY 1917

01May17 – PFO Howard Eckhardt GRUNDY (Winnipeg) – KIC

Cranwell student pilot Grundy crashes his Bristol Scout. The machine, a Type C Number 1247, is badly wrecked and Grundy dies of injuries shortly after rescue. In November 1916, the then-25-year-old Manitoban had entered in the RNAS through the Department of Naval Service of Canada. He is buried at Cranwell (St. Andrew) Churchyard, Lincolnshire.

01May17 – FLt Donald Mitchell SHIELDS (Mount Albert ON) – WIA

Naval 8 is back in front line service having completed transition to the new Sopwith Triplane. Escorting RFC FEs, two of the Squadron's Canadian pilots are shot down this day when engaged by Albatros aircraft of *Jasta* 4 and *Jasta* 11.

Shields shoots down one enemy machine out of control before

DM Shields

RAeC Trust

being brought down himself by *Ltn* Kurt von Doring of *Jasta* 4. Crashing just inside Canadian lines near Vimy Ridge, Shields extricates himself from the wreckage and hides in a shell hole as German artillery destroys his Sopwith Triplane, N5434. Crawling to safety in a trench a few hours later, he is carried by his countrymen to a Casualty Clearing Station and stabilized. His wounds are listed as a dislocated shoulder and a fracture of the left tibia. Sent in a hospital ship from Calais to England, Shields will be ordered on three months' sick leave to

Canada. He will fly again in 1918 and survive the War.

His victor, von Dorking, also lives through the conflict and will become a Lieutenant General with the Luftwaffe in 1941.

– FSLt Edmund Daniel ROACH (Toronto) – KIA

(From 25Jan17) Flying Triplane N5474 'Gwen' in this same action near Seclin, Roach is brought down by *Ltn* Kurt Wolff of *Jasta* 11. The body of the 23-year-old Canadian is buried at the Cabaret-Rouge British Cemetery, Souchez.

The RN, unenthusiastic for flamboyant livery such as that of the German Flying Circus, does, however, permit pilots to paint the names of girlfriends on their machines.

Whoever *Gwen* was, is so far, unknown.

Wolff will have achieved 33 victories and be flying a new Fokker Dr.I Triplane when shot down by a 10 Naval Sopwith Triplane in the coming aerial battles of July.

ED Roach

Toronto Star, May 2, 1917

04May17 – FSLt Harry Stephen 'Sport' MURTON (Toronto) – POW

Another Canadian aviator becomes a 'Guest of the Kaiser': Murton, nicknamed 'Sport' at the UofT, is reported last seen flying west with full engine over Ecourt St. Quentin. Shortly after that sighting, his 3 Naval Sopwith Pup N6207 'Black Bess', loses an aerial combat to *Oberleutnant* Adolph von Tutscheck of *Jasta* 12, resulting in Morton's incarceration.

Almost one year later, in March 1918, Tutscheck, by then a twenty-seven-victory Ace, will be shot down and killed in his signature green-painted Fokker.

HS Murton

U of T

Recounting his POW time, Murton recalled what has to be one of the best 'small-world' stories in history:

> "I got a shot through the engine and I landed on top of a German artillery crew. A German asked me where I was from. I said 'Toronto.' He said 'Do you know a man named Vogt?' I said, 'Yes, he's the leader of the Mendelssohn Choir.' And the German said, 'I know. I took music under him for a couple of years'."

Murton, granted freedom at the Armistice, will sign on with the RAF and fly with Collishaw and the White Forces in Southern Russia during 1919 and 1920.

06May17 – FSLt Harold Spencer KERBY (Calgary) – ACE

(From 26Nov15) In 3 Naval, Sopwith Pup N6160, Kerby becomes an Ace sharing an Albatros D.III over Burlon Wood with FSLt **FC Armstrong**. One minute later, Kerby single-handedly sends down another D.III for his sixth victory. He had opened his scorecard weeks earlier, on the 24th of March, and will eventually tally-up nine enemy aircraft.

Bringing down any enemy machine, let alone achieving the mantle of 'Ace,' might seem improbable for Kerby in light of his release for physical unfitness after Gallipoli flying in 1916. Although re-entered and re-qualified by early 1917 with a recommendation for Home Service, Kerby had instead received an appointment to 3 Naval on the Continent.

It takes the German bomber raids on England to return him to United Kingdom Service in mid-summer. On the 12th of August, as part of the defense flight out of Walmer, he attacks a Gotha bomber and sends it down into the sea. Circling the wreckage, Kerby throws a life belt to one survivor clinging to the tail. British tabloids make a great fuss over the humanity of his life belt toss versus the atrocities exhibited by U-boat crews in their machine-gunning lifeboat survivors.

For his action in bringing down this homeland attacker Kerby is Gazetted a DSC. Later, he will be described by his Walmer Commanding Officer as: 'Very efficient 1st Lieut. Pilot of judgment & resource. Has twice attacked Gothas successfully, & several other hostile machines.'

Following a second, and this time healthier, Canada Leave in late 1917, Kerby returns again to England and is assigned instructional duties. Promoted Flight Commander, he becomes the CO of the new RAF School of Aerial Gunnery at Freistone and is awarded the Air Force Cross (AFC) for his work, cited in the New Years Honours List of 1919.

Granted a permanent commission in Royal Air Force after the Great War, Kerby will be selected to attend the first course of the new RAF Staff College. There follows a series of fascinating appointments: India 1923-29; Air Ministry 1929-34; Singapore 1935; Air Attaché, China 1936-39; AASF France 1939-40; Ireland 1941-42; AOC East Africa 1943-44; AOC Admin, Coastal Command 1944-46. Kerby, the 'washed out' RNAS Flight Sub Lieutenant of 1915 will leave the RAF in 1946 as an Air Vice Marshal, CB, DSC, AFC.

06May17 – FLt Gerald 'Guy' Duncan SMITH (Oakland CA, USA) – MIA – Indian Ocean

(From 17Aug14) Missing since the 21st of April, Smith and his Observer, Lt WCA Meade RN, are recovered by their ship, safe and well from a somewhat interesting engine failure escapade. Operating off HMS *Raven II* in the Indian Ocean, Smith had managed a successful forced-landing and then beached his Short 184 8018, on Male Island in the Maldives. After three days of searching, the Port Said HQ had issued a telegram stating that the crew were 'Missing believe drowned.' Smith however has lived up to his Confidential Report of the first of April in which the East Indies Reviewing Officer observed that the young American was a: 'Very Good and bold Pilot. To be relied upon in a tight place.' Even before joining the service, Smith had proven his mettle in 1914 as a civilian radio operator on a German merchant ship.

The great English author Rudyard Kipling will write about Smith's exploit in an article titled '*A Flight of Fact*' and it is published in Nash's and the Pall Mall magazines in June 1918. He tells of the airmen spending several weeks: 'having a convivial time in the best traditions of the Navy, until they are able to rejoin their ship, wearing massive beards, and the spectacular uniforms of the Pelunga army,—a cross between a macaw and a rainbow-ended mandrill...' Kipling's title is a play of words on '*Flight of Fancy*', a phrase he coined for the title of his 1905 tale of an imaginary trip by air from London to Quebec.

Guy Duncan Smith goes on to complete his war with the unique record of having served in six aircraft carriers: *Raven II, Anne, Ben-my-Chree, Northbrook, Empress,* and *City of Oxford.* He will receive the French Cd'G for Egypt service and ship development, and will be

Gazetted the DSC in July 1917 for his good work while serving with the East Indies Seaplane Squadron.

Perhaps due to his 'Loot' adventure of May 1917, Smith becomes involved in the spa business following the War. He operates the Rio Nido, a recreational resort on the Russian River in California.

HB Smith, aboard ship

FAAM 2000/112/080

Harold Beaumont Smith, Guy Duncan's younger brother, will also fly with the RNAS. Out of Yarmouth in England he will be Mentioned in Despatches in October 1917 for attacking a U-boat.

11May17 – FSLt Oliver Joseph GAGNIER (Montreal) – WIA

The fighting spirit of the Canadians can often lead to trouble. Flying Nieuport 17 N3189 near Villers Outreaux with 6 Naval, Gagnier only just survives a German trap. He reports:

"Saw 4 HA at about 4,000 feet. Climbed above them and tried to attract attention of [my] formation, but unable to do so, so [I] climbed above [the enemy] formation. Soon two detached themselves and moved up North. I circled twice and dived on one when very close to him. I pulled my trigger control lever, but the guns did not fire. I am

OJ Gagnier

RAeC Trust

certain the guns were cocked and loaded. I just avoided collision. Pilot was wearing a sweater and black flying helmet. Immediately afterwards, I heard bullets fired by the second machine and one shattered my left arm. I endeavoured to get down and away and managed to do so, although I lost consciousness on my way down. HA followed me down. I saw ground approaching, and knocked stick back. Machine hit and turned over. Machine gun fire on ground was very intense. I scrambled into a shell hole, and later made my way into the English lines, when I became unconscious."

Gagnier has flown into a setup and is claimed by *Ltn* Kurt Kuppers of *Jasta* 6, the second of his six victories. Evacuated to London's Guest Hospital, Gagnier's left arm is amputated. He will be on sick leave in Canada when the new Royal Air Force forms on April First 1918, and remains in the Dominion as an RAF Captain and administrative officer.

12May17 – FLt Philip Sidney FISHER, MID (Montreal) – DSC

Fisher is Gazetted for: 'Conspicuous skill as a seaplane pilot during last nine months. He has carried out many valuable reconnaissance patrols and several bomb attacks with good results.' Fisher, a McGill graduate, has been Mentioned by the Vice Admiral, Dover for his bombing attacks on enemy torpedo boats at Bruges and on seaplane sheds at Zeebrugge. When not flying the Short bomber seaplane in attack or recce work, he conducts patrols in a Sopwith Baby fighter seaplane.

In June, he is sent to fly Sopwith Camels, an aircraft type more suited to his aggressive fighting spirit; and by July, Fisher is an Acting Flight Commander with 4 Naval out of Dunkirk. Two months later while leading an offensive patrol he is very seriously wounded. A hostile two-seater is sighted and during the attack, a number of Albatros scouts are engaged. In the melee, a bullet explodes in his knee. Fisher struggles to return his Camel B3853, to Dunkirk; and is hospitalized immediately. The leg must be removed and he writes home that it was due to 'a collision with a German tracer bullet.' Fisher is Gazetted the Distinguished Service Order in November (for at least two confirmed victories) and takes Canadian sick leave when discharged from Peebles Hospital, Scotland, in April 1918.

Forced to relinquish his RAF commission on account of ill health caused by wounds, Fisher embarks on a career with Southam Newspapers. He is later President

& Managing Director, Canadian Daily Newspaper Publishers Association and will be awarded the CBE (Civil) in 1946. Further honours follow with the award of the Order of Canada in 1967, upgraded to Officer, Order of Canada in 1972.

14May17 – FSLt George Gladstone AVERY (Gates Cove NF) – MIA

Delivering a Wright Seaplane 9847 from Calshot to home base at Plymouth, Avery goes Missing. One month before, he had been rescued when his Short Seaplane, 9084, landed in the sea owing to engine trouble. But this time, Avery is not found. The C-in-C Devonport orders a continued search and two days later part of a float from 9847 is recovered: it bears indications of a fire in the air. Avery, 'a keen and zealous officer, rather young at present', had recently been recommended for promotion. He and his air mechanic crewman, WS Elliott, are presumed accidentally drowned. Their names are remembered on the Chatham Naval Memorial to the Missing in Kent.

14May17 – FSLt Robert 'Bob' LECKIE (Toronto; b. SCT) – Zeppelin

(From 06Dec15) Flying as Second Pilot to English FSLt JO Galpin in Curtiss H8 flying boat 8666 out of Yarmouth, Leckie is at the controls when they intercept Zeppelin L.22 at 4,000 feet off Terschelling. A backdrop of dark clouds affords opportunity to overhaul the dirigible from behind and above. Leckie takes full advantage then swoops down alongside the starboard gondolas, Galpin, manning the twin bow Lewis guns, pours incendiary bullets into the looming gasbag. As Leckie pulls ahead and swings about for another pass, a deep glow blossoms inside the Zeppelin and in seconds the incinerating fabric disappears, sending the skeletal frame plummeting into the sea where it sinks immediately.

One month later Leckie will intercept a second Zeppelin but this one escapes by ejecting water ballast and rapidly ascending to a safe altitude. Returning to Germany, it carries home the answer to the mystery of vanishing airships—the German Navy is still puzzling over the loss of Zeppelin L.22. As a direct result of such a revelation, the *Fregattenkaptian* (Chief) of the German Naval Airship Division orders all patrols to be carried out a minimum altitude of 13,000 feet. Such a height places strenuous respiratory demands on airship crew and drastically reduces the effectiveness of their long missions. This trade-off of higher altitude for greater airship safety leads to ineffective and inaccurate bombing raids. *(Read 05Sep17)*

14May17 – FSLt William Roy WALKER (West Kildonan MB) – MIA/POW

Flying Sopwith Pup A6158 with 3 Naval, Walker's propeller is destroyed by the marksmanship of *Oblt* Heinrich Lorenz, Commander of *Jasta* 33. Walker manages to glide to a landing and is captured at Douai. He is listed as Missing until the 3rd of July when officially reported a Prisoner of War. Although now out of action, Walker is Mentioned in Despatches for his good work 'in the field.' He is one of the few Canadians who took his initial flying training from the Christofferson School in Alameda, California.

20May17 – FSLt Charles Edward PATTISON (Winona ON) – WIA

Pattison shoots down an Albatros scout but sustains a gunshot wound to the chest during the combat. He crash lands his 10 Naval Triplane N5366 near La Lovie and is hospitalized. Following a Canada recovery, he regains his pilot status and volunteers for further active service.

Almost one year later, while retraining for the Front, Pattison does not survive a crash in Scotland. On the 2nd of April 1918, approaching the airfield at the converted Redcar Race Course near Edinburgh, his Sopwith Camel B5720 catches a telephone wire, nosedives, smashes, and burns. Pattison is severely injured and dies the following day. He is interred at the New Calton Burial Ground, Scotland.

20May17 – FSLt Henry George BOSWELL (Toronto) – U-boat

The 'Spider Web', a hexagonal patrol system established around the North Hinder Light Vessel, became operational on the 13th of April 1917 and today, five weeks after inauguration, it bears fruit. Flying as Second Pilot on Curtiss H-12 Large America 8663, Boswell is part of the crew that attacks submarine *UC-36*. The enemy craft is spotted at full buoyancy and does not respond to recognition signals. Flying directly overhead and banking tightly to run in on the diving wake of his adversary, Boswell releases two bombs. One strikes just forward of the conning tower, still above the surface. A large patch of oil is noted after the explosion. Returning to Felixstowe, the victorious flying boat makes a rather inglorious night landing in heavy swell and is lost, but the aircrew is rescued. Credited with the first aerial sinking of a German U-boat, the pilots are Gazetted the Distinguished Service Cross. After the War, German naval logs disprove the claim and it is learned that *UC-36* did survive the attack but did not return to homeport. It is presumed that she exploded while attempting to lay mines or suffered a structural failure from the aerial bombing.

Boswell, from McGill University, had joined the Princess Patricia Canadian Light Infantry in 1914. A worn-out trench veteran by 1915, he was discharged as medically unfit, and returned to Canada. In early 1916 he applied for the RNAS through the Department of Naval Service in Ottawa, taking his Candidate training at the Curtiss Flying School in Newport News, Virginia. Graduating with American license No. 514, he was sent to Windermere for seaplanes. The nighttime crash-landing following the U-boat attack causes yet another impairment to his health and he is sent home to Canada once again for convalescence.

23May17 – FLt Arthur Henderson ALLARDYCE (Vancouver) – Instructor

Appointed to Manston as an Instructor, Allardyce is first sent on loan to RFC Station Gosport by the Admiralty to study the successful pilot training system developed by Colonel Smith-Barry. Allardyce will have all good reports as an instructor, 'very keen'; however, the feverent pace of turning out new aviators brings on side effects. By February 1918 he applies for leave in Canada to regain his confidence. The Medical Officer at Manston considers application well founded and on April first, Allardyce is granted nine weeks leave of absence—but to make own arrangements for passage.

24May17 – PFO John Neptune GALLWEY (Toronto) – REL

Gallwey's appointment as a Probationary Flight Officer is terminated with the statement: 'Submission put forward to terminate commission as it is not considered that he is suitable for retention in the RNAS'. Two weeks later his records show an additional comment: 'No objection to this officer's being granted a commission in the RFC.' The Navy's opinion of the Army's air arm would seem obvious. A former Sergeant in the Canadian Expeditionary Force, Gallwey perseveres and will be recorded as a Lieutenant under the 'Aeroplane

and Seaplane Officer' category in the Royal Air Force List of April 1918.

25May17 – FSLt Langley Frank Willard SMITH (Phillipsburg PQ) – ACE

Another newly constituted scout squadron, 4 Naval, is working-up in Dunkirk on Sopwith Pups in preparation to convert to the latest fighter, the Sopwith Camel, and to replace 3 Naval 'in the field'.

The activity level of this training period escalates considerably when the Germans begin bombing raids on London. Flying Pup N6168 Smith achieves his fifth victory in grand style when he brings down a Gotha bomber. The nineteen-year-old will score eight times in this particular machine before he begins his transition to the Camel. Dunkirk Headquarters states that Smith is 'Deserving of special recognition' and he is awarded the DSC.

On the 13th of June, an alert is received that Hostile Aircraft are again dropping bombs on London; seven pilots are sent up to intercept. Smith is one of the last to launch from the French coast airfield and is not seen by the rest of the now-airborne formation.

LFW Smith

RAeC Trust

He is flying Camel N6362 and this is his first combat flight in the machine. Off Zeebrugge, several hostiles are encountered and driven back in the direction of Bruges. At about this time, a dark-coloured aircraft is sighted spinning down minus one wing. It is Smith. The new aircraft had just been rigged and delivered to 4 Naval the day previously from the Aircraft Depot Dunkirk and has broken up in the air, marking Smith as the first Camel casualty in France.

The young Ace had only been flying operationally for six weeks. Smith graduated with the highest RNAS flying marks 'Very Good Pilot Indeed' and arrived in squadron at the end of April. Albert, King of Belgians, confers on him both a posthumous Commander, Order of the Crown, and Croix de Guerre decoration.

The June 13th raid by Gotha bombers on London kills 162 people including 43 children. 'The Raid that Stirred the Country' creates a public outcry that leads to a doubling of the RFC and RNAS. Several front line fighter pilots are recalled from France to England for defensive patrols.

25May17 – FSLt Herbert Godfrey LESLIE (Victoria) – Action

During a German air attack on Folkstone Leslie engages in a spirited attack of the enemy raiders off Dover. This tests the limits of his mental and physical resources. He has suffered from the effects of Neurasthenia for over a year and in that time has crashed three aircraft; two at Westgate then

HG Leslie

FAAM 2000/065/0087

the complete write off of a third at East Fortune in Scotland. In August, Leslie applies to resign his commission. He is granted free passage home to British Columbia with a certificate of good conduct, a release gratuity of £150, and the rank of Flight Lieutenant.

26May17 – Lt Obs Cyril Lalande HAINES (Salmon Arm BC: b. ENG) – KIA Ostende

'Off to Ostende'
Observer Haines with pilot RS DeQuincey-Quincey
in a Nieuport 12

FAAM 2000/065/0122

Observer Haines, in DH-4 N5963 is flying escort to another DH-4 aircraft from his 2 Naval Squadron. The mission is to reconnoiter Ostende. When the lead aircraft returns the crew reports having last seen their escort machine over Oost Dunkirk Bains, one mile astern and heading for shore. Haines and his English pilot, SLt W. Houston-Stewart, are listed as Missing. Their bodies are later recovered by the Germans and buried at Zeebrugge, Belgium. Haines, age 21, has served in the RNVR since November 1915 and had taken his Observer training in early 1916.

27May17 – FSLt Alfred William 'Nick' CARTER (Calgary) – ACE

'Excuse Me' is Carter's personalized 3 Naval Sopwith Pup N6474. Today the four-victory aviator excuses himself to an Albatros D.III that is attacking RFC observation machines East of Bullecourt. Firing forty rounds and watching the tracers strike home, Carter sends the German down out of control for a fifth victory.

Nine days later, the term, Excuse Me, could be used to describe a most unusual accident as told by his English wingman, FSLt AB Ellwood: 'One of our favorite recreations was 'Contour-chasing' and we rarely came back from the lines much over twenty feet from the ground. On one occasion after taking off from our Advanced Landing Ground we had climbed to about 100 feet and were just starting to dive down when I saw the leader, FSLt Carter, suddenly go into a vertical dive. Something about the size of an envelope was falling in front of him and I remember momentarily having the insane impression that he had dropped a letter and was trying to recover it. He suddenly received a violent jerk backwards, and turning on his back floated gently to the ground from a height of about thirty feet. A large crowd of soldiers collected around the wreck, and as I flew round to see whether Carter was safe I narrowly missed a balloon cable.

'It turned out that he had struck the cable in the centre of his engine, snapped it, and wound it securely round his propeller shaft. As the cable tightened he had been jerked over on his back and the balloon had then let him down lightly, acting like a parachute. He escaped without a scratch, as did the occupants of the basket who had been all but ejected by the shock of the collision. This somewhat sobered our enthusiasm for low flying, at any rate in the balloon area.'

Number 3 Naval Squadron has been in Front Line service for several months and is now sent to the

Dunkirk coast for a rest. Carter, however, is assigned to 10 Naval to fill-in for casualties and will raise his score to 17 enemy aircraft. He does survive this War and becomes an RCAF Air Marshal during the next global conflict.

29May17 – FSLt James 'John' Lindsay GORDON (St Lambert PQ), &
– FSLt George Ritchie HODGSON (Montreal) – Rescue

Gordon and Hodgson are known at Felixstowe Air Station as 'The Heavenly Twins'. The Canadians are cousins and often fly together alternating Captain and Second Pilot roles. Today, their H-12 flying boat is dispatched on a missing-aircraft search with Gordon as first pilot and Hodgson as his second. Their crew consists of two naval ratings, a Mechanic and a Wireless Telegraphist, SF Anderson, and BH Millichamp.

On 24 May, a Short seaplane from Westgate went down in the North Sea with engine trouble. Rough seas tore off a wing; the seaplane turned turtle and sank leaving the pilot and observer clinging to a float that had broken away. Bad weather has hampered searching aircraft, and four days have passed without any knowledge of the missing crew. Again today, this time due to the fog, Gordon, Hodgson, and crew see little on their mission. Returning homeward, they come across a break in the gloom and spot the remains of the seaplane below.

Miraculously, the pilot and observer are still alive.

Because the rescue machine carries a bomb load in event of a submarine sighting, the 'Twins' must first jettison the weapons. One bomb hangs-up and will not release but Gordon elects to continue and safely lands the flying boat. The two survivors are pulled aboard and a takeoff attempted, however heavy seas prove too much and on a second attempt the plane's tail and starboard wing are smashed. Gordon then swings the crippled boat towards England and initiates a taxi through high waves.

JL Gordon
RAeC Trust

Following four hours of hard pounding, they manage to clear the fog bank and are spotted and towed. At Buckingham Palace in September, Gordon, Hodgson, and crew, are presented with the Board of Trade Silver Medal for Gallantry in Saving Life at Sea, a rare award for members of the air services.

Hodgson is no neophyte to receiving medals. The first Canadian to have won two Olympic Golds, he triumphed at the 1912 Stockholm games in the 400-meter and the 1,500-meter swim events. He will also achieve an AFC in November 1918.

Gordon will be promoted to Major, RAF, in August 1918 and take command of 232 Squadron at Felixstowe. He completes his war with an additional award of the DFC. Remaining in the services, Gordon becomes Director of the Canadian Air Force from 1922 to 1924 and Chief of Staff, RCAF, as an Air Vice Marshal in 1932.

JUNE 1917

02Jun17 – FSLt William 'Bill' LODGE (Arnprior ON) – INJ/REL

When Short 184 9083 crashes off the aircraft carrier HMS *Manxman*, pilot Lodge is hospitalized suffering from neurasthenia. He has been with the ship since January and is now found permanently unfit for further flying; months of sea-going flight operations have taken a harsh toll on his health.

Lodge first learned to fly with the Stinson School at San Antonio, Texas, in March 1916. Joining the RNAS, he completed the seaplane school at Calshot and was graded a: 'Good Pilot. Keen & Capable Officer.' In *Manxman*, his reports were also very favorable: 'Steady & Reliable. Good Initiative.' Resigning from the service, he will be granted a gratuity of £150 per year to 1919, followed by £42 per annum until November 1923.

02Jun17 – FSLt Wallace Earnest ORCHARD (Vancouver; b. Quebec) – WIA/DOW

On a 3 Naval stand-by at the Fremiscourt Advanced Landing Ground, Orchard is launched on reports of enemy reconnaissance aircraft working near the front lines. He locates and attacks the hostiles but is injured by a shot to the face. From accounts of mechanics who see him come back, it is gathered that he returns flying erratically, and when overhead the ALG, his machine's nose drops, sending it into a vertical dive from 200

WE Orchard

GWFM

feet. Orchard is found head-down inside the aeroplane and it is surmised that he must have fainted through loss of blood. Taken to a Field Dressing Station then to No. 29 Casualty Clearing Station at Grievillers, he dies during the night. Orchard never completely regains consciousness and is unable to recount anything about what has happened, except that he had been fighting.

On the 6th of July the late Vancouverite receives a Mention for his good work while serving with No. 3 Naval. Orchard, 28 years old, is buried at Grenvillers, France. N6194, his Sopwith Pup, is believed credited to *Flugmeister* Kunstler of Marine *Jasta* I.

02Jun17 – FSLt Arthur Clarke DISSETTE (Toronto) – KIA

Dissette is the C Flight Commander of 10 Naval and together with **Collishaw's** B Flight, he leads an escort for two reconnaissance aircraft. The mission is a wash when heavy clouds make photography impossible. But menace lies in wait in these same cumuli and Dissette fails to return. His Sopwith Triplane N6294 is broken up by gunfire and crashes and burns in a wood near Proven. A 'Tripe' is claimed by *Ltn* Gustav Nolte of *Jasta* 18.

Although only a Flight-Sub Lieutenant in rank, Dissette, at 31 years-of-age, has shown the maturity to lead. He first flew in combat with 3 Wing and during the Freiburg Reprisal Raid of the 14th of April, managed to nurse his Sopwith Strutter back over the French Lines after flak had disabled the engine. Posted to 10 Naval later that same month, he was described as: 'A good formation leader. 'Specially recom'd for promotion. Ability to command VG.'

Dissette is posthumously awarded the French Croix de Guerre. On the 6th of June, his father cables the Admiralty, asking that his son's body be sent home to Canada at family expense. Their Lordships will reply that, with regret, the request is impossible as his son was killed abroad.

03Jun17 – FSLt Percy Gordon McNEIL, Cd'GaE (Toronto) – MIA

McNeil is the Commander of A Flight of 10 Naval and late this morning he led a six-plane distant offensive mission that provided escort for RFC machines. Now, in the early evening, he takes up a three-plane close offensive patrol. Airborne, they encounter an Albatros force four times their number. While wingman **Leslie Hunter Parker** manages to shoot down one of the enemy, McNeil's Triplane N6297, is brought down by *OffzSt* Klein of *Jasta* 27. He falls near Moorslede but his body is never recovered.

Like Dissette, who was killed the previous day, McNeil was also low in rank for flight commanding but he too had proven himself capable. With 3 Wing in July 1916, he was reported as: 'Ability to command VGI, a steady and reliable Pilot. Capable Officer with a sense of responsibility. Recommended for promotion.' During April 1917 he had been decorated with the Croix de

PG McNeil

via M Pirie

Guerre avec Etoile by the President of the French Republic: 'A pris part a cinq bombardementd a grande distance, au cours desquels il a donne des preuves a adresse et de courage.'

Just days before his death McNeil wrote home:

"I have brought down a few Hun machines".

He had indeed—four victories. He is now Mentioned in Depatches and his name engraved on the Arras Memorial to missing airmen. A graduate of Toronto's Parkdale Collegiate, McNeil is also recorded in the school's memorial book titled *'Their Name Liveth'*.

The loss of two Flight Commanders in a space of just twenty-four-hours can only have had a devastating impact on 10 Naval. FSLt **Raymond Collishaw** is now the sole original flight leader remaining from the time of the Squadron's transfer to RFC command. With today's death of Percy McNeill, Collishaw's Black Flight deputy **John Sharman** takes over leadership of A Flight's red-motif Triplanes. 'Nick' Carter, of balloon cable-strike fame, is transferred from 3 Naval to take command of Art Dissette's blue-nosed C Flight.

Regarding the makeup of 10 Naval, Collishaw will later remark that there was a good deal of interchange amongst the pilots and that often patrols consisted of a mix of two or three machines from different flights. HQ at this point in time are demanding in their mission assignments and not concerned with flight compositions.

Simply put, the standing orders to the RFC and RNAS scout squadrons on the Belgian front are: 'Keep the German Air Service away!' The British are massing guns, troops, and supplies to attack the Messines Ridge and do not want the German High Command to obtain any reconnaissance reports of the buildup. British tunnellers have also been busy for the past several months, and during the early hours of June 7th, the Ridge will be blown to a literal hell by nineteen mines comprising one million pounds of detonation force. A twentieth mine remains buried and unexploded to the present day.

04Jun17 – FLt Alexander MacDonald SHOOK, MID (Tioga ON) – Camel First

(From 24Apr16) Number 4 Naval has just become operational with the new twin-machine-gun Sopwith Camel and to Shook goes the honour of scoring the aircraft's first victory when he sends down an Albatros D.III. This is his fourth EA destroyed; the next day, he crashes another German scout onto the beach between Nieuport and Ostende for his Ace-making fifth kill.

AM Shook

U of T

The gyroscopically unstable but highly maneuverable Sopwith Camel will set an Allied War record for 1,294 victories. Equally deadly to the hands of an inexperienced pilot, the machine is said to offer 'a wooden cross, a red cross or a Victoria Cross.' Shook will score twelve victories in the Camel.

Northwest of Ostende in early July, as a newly promoted Flight Commander he sends a twin-engine Gotha bomber down emitting clouds of black smoke. He

is specially Mentioned for this action as the bomber was enroute to attack England. When the French government recognizes him with the Croix de Guerre, the British react and Gazette him for the DSC.

In October, Shook will be wounded. While leading a patrol he observes a good many Albatros scouts near Ghistelles and fires several bursts at one, sending it into an inverted spin completely out of control. During the intense action that ensues, Shook is hit but manages to bring his Camel back to safe landing at the Bray Dunes airfield. When discharged from nursing care, he will be sent on Canadian leave, taking home the news that his younger brother, a Royal Flying Corps pilot with 46 Squadron, has just been shot down and captured.

While in Canada, Shook learns that he has been awarded the Distinguished Service Order for over 30 aerial combats. In the ceremony held at Buckingham Palace in January 1918, he is invested with both his August DSC and the DSO. Shook is described as a 'magnificent Flight Leader... Has flown over 230 hours over the enemy's lines... Much of the success achieved by his flight is due to his brilliant leadership.' *(Read 22Mar18)*

05Jun17 – FSLt Kenneth Gordon BOYD (Goderich ON) – MID Redemption

In Sopwith Triplane N5478, Boyd shares a victory with FCdr **Collishaw** and his 10 Naval Flight. However, Boyd is reported as 'Very steady & cautious, too much so for a fighting Pilot.' In early July he is transferred to 5 Naval, an anti-submarine patrol squadron, and by the end of August redeems himself, receiving a Mention for continuous flying: 'Often out at sea in land machines'. Becoming sick with exposure in September, he will run afoul of higher command for 'breaking out of hospital while under treatment' and receive a severe reprimand by Court Martial.

By mid 1918, Boyd is a Captain and Flight Commander in the new Royal Air Force, flying De Havilland DH-4's with 217 Squadron. On August 12th 1918 while leading a patrol of four machines from Dunkirk, he sights a submarine, half-blown, headed towards the Belgian port of Ostende. Setting up a line-astern attack Boyd drops his two 230lb bombs, hitting the port side of the undersea craft and rolling it over to starboard. Bombs from the other aircraft burst around the now bottoms-up boat and it sinks in 5 minutes, the hull peppered by about 500 rounds of ammunition fired from 100 feet. It is believed to be U-boat *UB-12,* which met her demise about this time in unknown circumstances, but this is never proven. Boyd will be awarded the Air Force Cross for the action.

06Jun17 – FSLt Gerald Ewart 'Gerry' NASH (Stoney Creek ON) – ACE

(From 28Apr17) Black Flight of 10 Naval is in heavy action this day with each member scoring at least once. Airborne in Triplane 5376 *'Black Sheep'*, Nash makes a fourth kill shooting down an Albatros D.III over Polygon Wood and then a few minutes later scores his fifth, also a D.III. *(Read 25Jun17)*

06Jun17 – A/FLt Ellis Vair REID (Belleville ON) – ACE

(From 28Apr17) Reid in Triplane N5483, *'Black Roger'*, sends down his fifth, leading to an award of the DSC which will carry the citation: 'For his work before Ypres, more particularly on June 6th, 1917, when he attacked and drove down a hostile scout, and on June 15th when he was leading a formation of three scouts and encountered ten enemy planes, two of which he drove down out of control.'

An architecture graduate from the University of Toronto, Reid had flown with 3 Wing on the April 14th Freiburg Reprisal Raid. **Raymond Collishaw** described his Black Flight wingman as being 'seriously inclined and a thinker.' *(Read 28Jul17)*

07Jun17 – FSLt John Harvey KEENS (Toronto) – WIA

On this, the first day of the Battle of Messines, Allied aircraft are out in force to provide cover for the advancing troops. Near Bousbechque, while engaged in air combat with *Ltn* Alfred Niederhoff of Jasta 11, Keens gets a bullet through the left lung. Straining to return home in his 10 Naval Sopwith Triplane N5361, he manages to land safely and rolls to a stop. After a few minutes his rating mechanic approaches and asks. 'Are you not going to get out of the aeroplane?'

When the reason for his dismount delay is recognized, Keens is rushed to No 14 General Hospital at Wintereux. Diagnosed 'dangerously ill' with a penetrating gunshot wound to the chest, he will be declared no longer a serious case by the end of the month. In August, he goes on Canada Leave with a compensation of £163 for the wound and will return to England in December to take up ground duties. Resurveyed Fit for Flying in

JH Keens

January 1918, Keens is employed on instructional duties for the balance of the War. Evaluated an: 'Efficient Instructor. Keen on his work and handles men well', he flies at the Aerial Gunnery School Leysdown, and is Gazetted for the Air Force Cross on the New Year's Honours List 1919. Discharged in February of that year he will return to Canada but serve again as a Group Captain RCAF in the next war with Germany.

07Jun17 – FSLt Hugh D. MacIntosh WALLACE (Blind River ON) – KIC

Scrambled to attack an overhead hostile aircraft, Wallace's engine chokes on take off and he tumbles fifty feet to an instant death. A 1914 graduate of the University of Toronto, Wallace had worked as a civil engineer in the construction of the Welland Canal prior to joining the naval air service in early 1916. He flew Sopwith Strutters with 3 Wing before being transferred to 1 Naval to fly the Sopwith Triplane in

HDM Wallace

March 1917. An experienced pilot, he was rushing aloft in new Triplane N6298, when the engine failure led to his fatal fall.

07Jun17 – PFO Weston Ward PITT (Kingston-Cardinal ON) – KIC

At RNAS Training Establishment Cranwell, the 23-year-old Pitt is killed in the crash of Bristol Scout 1790. A Court of Inquiry into the accident finds 'No blame attributable to anyone.'

11Jun17 – FSLt John Richard BIBBY
(Toronto; b. ENG) – KIC Malta

Bibby is killed while conducting a torpedo-drop trial in Malta. The experimental aircraft, a Short Type 310A 8317, is written off. An early graduate of the Wright Flying School in Augusta, Georgia, Bibby is buried at Malta's Cappuccini Naval Cemetery. A married RNAS Canadian, he leaves behind a war bride in Devon, England.

13Jun17 – FSLt Thomas Ralph SHEARER
(Pointe Claire PQ) – KIC

Returning from a patrol, Shearer's Sopwith Triplane N5374 inexplicably enters a spinning nosedive, crashing three miles from his 9 Naval home field. He is killed instantly. Investigation reveals that the pilot's heel had become jammed behind the rudder bar causing the accident. Another 3 Wing bomber pilot before being sent to scouts, Shearer had been successful in

TR Shearer

GWFM

the Sopwith Pup, bringing down two enemy machines in May.

Tom Shearer joined the RNAS via a so-called flying school in St. Augustine, Florida. The one aeroplane business had turned out to be a fraudulent operation but through the good graces of Admiral Kingsmill the Candidate students were re-interviewed in Ottawa and sent overseas to England for training.

14Jun17 – A/FCdr John Edward SHARMAN, DSC
(Oak Lake MB) – ACE

(From 14Apr17) Still flying his B Flight Triplane 'Black Death', 10 Naval C Flight Commander Sharman sends down an Albatros D.III out of control over Zonnebeke for his 'fifth'. He will be awarded a Bar to his DSC on the 20th of the month for his 'great courage and skill in attacking enemy aircraft'. A French Croix de Guerre is announced the same day.*(Read 22Jul17)*

14Jun17 – FSLt Leslie Hunter PARKER
(Leeds Village PQ) – MIA

With two victories to his credit, Parker does not live to score the hat trick. His 10 Naval Sopwith Triplane N5470 goes missing during an evening Offensive Patrol. The 20-year-old McGill student is believed to be the fourth victim of *Vzfw* Fritz Krebs of *Jasta* 6. Kerbs will double that number but is killed in combat one month later.

LH Parker

RAeC Trust

14Jun17 – FLt Basil Deacon HOBBS, DSC&Bar
(Sault Ste Marie ON) – Zeppelin

A Royal Navy wireless intercept indicates that two Zeppelins are on patrol covering minesweepers attempting to breach a British minefield north of Terschelling. Launched from Felixstowe in Curtis H8 Large America 8677, Hobbs spots one German airship at 1,500 feet off the Dutch coast of Vlieland. Climbing to 2,000 feet he attacks:

> "As we approached the Zeppelin we dived for her tail at about 100 knots. Her number L43 was observed on the tail and bow, also Maltese Cross in black circle. Midship gun opened fire with tracer ammunition and when about 100 feet above Sub Lieut Dickie [England] opened fire with Brock and Pomeroy ammunition as the machine passed diagonally over the tail from starboard to port. After two bursts the Zeppelin burst into flames. Cutting off engines we turned sharply to starboard and passed over her again; she was by this time completely enveloped in flames and falling very fast."

During the war, Hobbs receives two DSC awards for services in action against enemy submarines. In both cases, post-war German Naval records will show conclusively that no U-boats were destroyed on his dates of attack. But today, ashes on the surface of the sea leave no doubt as to his victory and he is Gazetted for the DSO on July 20th.

Hobbs goes on loan to the United States Naval Air Services as an instructor in 1918, and when the Schneider Cup air race recommences the next year, he returns to England and competes on behalf of the RAF.

In Canada in 1920, Hobbs joins the Canadian Air Force and is appointed Director of Air Operations in Ottawa. During 1924, as an RCAF pilot, he conducts the first long-range air survey over northern Saskatchewan and Manitoba. In 1927 the former Sault Ste Marie electrician resigns from the service in order to establish an importing business in Montreal, and will be re-commissioned as Group Captain RCAF during the Second World War. As Commanding Officer of Station Dartmouth, Nova Scotia, he is awarded the OBE for his work in convoy protection and anti-submarine patrols.

Twenty-four years after Hobbs' death in 1963, The Canadian Aviation Hall of Fame will induct him as a Member with the citation: 'This man truly reached for the stars and through his flying achievements and ability through peace and war brought honour to the aviation fraternity of Canada.' In 2006, the new Air Force HQ building in Winnipeg is dedicated to Group Captain B.D. Hobbs.

BD Hobbs
Wayne Robinson

17Jun17 – FSLt Hibbert Binney BRENTON (Vancouver) – Zeppelin

In the hours from midnight to morning, some 32 defense sorties are launched over England in an effort to bring down Zeppelins intruders. Following its bombing mission, Zeppelin L42 passes perilously near the East Anglia coastline and by dawn's first light it is spotted by five Yarmouth-based aircraft. One manages to close within 100 feet and open fire with nil damage result; however, this assault by English pilot FSLt Bittles has driven the dirigible to higher altitudes. Canadian Brenton, in Sopwith Baby N1108, next chases the Zeppelin, stalking it for 70 minutes but he is unable to get within firing range. Brenton is an 'Extremely

Good Seaplane Pilot & very capable Officer.' Appointed to the Isle of Grain for Test Flying duties in November, he will be further described as 'A good Test Pilot. A most trustworthy, reliable Officer.' Promotion to Acting Flight Commander takes place for Brenton in March 1918.

19Jun17 – FSLt James Edward POTVIN, MIDx2 (Goderich ON) – MIA

Out of RNAS Dunkirk, Sopwith Baby 1015 is on a special Mine Patrol when it encounters enemy aircraft. Lost in the ensuing action off the French coast near Nieuport, the body of its pilot, Potvin, is never recovered. His name is yet another to be engraved on the Chatham Naval Memorial.

Potvin had gone directly from the University of Toronto to take his flying certificate with the Stinson School at San Antonio, Texas. By the time of his death, he had two Mentions in Despatches to his credit. In April, he had flown a single-seater out in the Channel to search for a missing officer who had been forced down. Finding three enemy machines buzzing around the downed airman, Potvin had driven them off and stayed to spot for the rescue vessel. His second Mention was in connection with bombing raids on Bruges and Zeebrugge; including attacks on enemy torpedo boats tied up alongside the Zeebrugge Mole.

FLT. S. LT. JAMES E. POTVIN UNIVERSITY COLLEGE
JE Potvin
U of T

22Jun17 – FSLt Harold Laurence CROWE (Bridgetown NS & Toronto) – KIC

Returning to Prawle Point from a U-boat search off Devonshire, Sopwith Strutter N5604 is seen to nosedive into the sea about 500 yards from shore. There is no immediate trace of either pilot or aircraft and Crowe has undoubtedly drowned. His body later recovered by the trawler *Louis,* he is accorded full naval honours. The Prawle Point Naval Air Station mechanics construct a small airship covered with moss and flowers for the service.

HL Crowe

U of T

'Harry' was the 20-year-old eldest son of HJ Crowe. Accompanying his boy to England, HJ has spent the greater part of the last ten months with him. Now, he will take the remains home to be interred at Mount Pleasant Cemetery, Toronto.

A few short months later, HJ will himself pass away.

23Jun17 – FSLt John Norquay McALLISTER (St. Andrew MB) – KIC

Less than a month on Squadron, McAllister is killed when his Naval 8 Triplane N5442 sheds a wing and spins into the ground near Neuville St. Vaast on the Western Front. McAllister, a 'VGI' Cranwell graduate, had ridden Triplane N5355 through a successful crash landing on the 29th of May but no feat of airmanship can avert this day's airframe collapse. The 20-year-old is buried at Pas de Calais, France.

25Jun17 – FSLt Gerald Ewart 'Gerry' NASH (Stoney Creek ON) – POW

Airborne in Sopwith Triplane 5376 *'Black Sheep'* with **Collishaw's** 'B' Flight, Nash loses a fight against an Albatros D.III from Richthofen's *Jasta* II. Collishaw reports that his *Black Flight* wingman is: 'Missing from offensive patrol. Last seen brought down by hostile aircraft, believed to have landed under control.' The report is correct, Nash has indeed landed, but on the wrong side of the Lines near Lille. Slightly wounded, he is taken prisoner.

Nash had six victories to hid credit, but he has been sorely outclassed. His victor is *Ltn.* Carl Allmenroder, a 'Blue Max' recipient with 29 kills. Both victor and vanquished were born in the month of May 1896. The German himself will be mortally wounded two days later.

A telegram from the Geneva Red Cross on the 15th of August is the first word that 10 Naval receives of Nash's status; confirming that he is alive and indeed a POW. Shortly afterwards, Nash sends a request for certain clothes to be sent from his kit. He will be repatriated in December 1918 and return to his fruit growing business on the Niagara Peninsula. During the Second World War Nash will serve again, as a Group Captain, RCAF.

JULY 1917

05Jul17 – PFO Harold John FLYNN (Niagara Falls ON) – KIC

Student pilot Flynn is killed at the Manston Flying School in Kent. A Coroner's Inquest returns a verdict of 'Death by Misadventure' on the crash of the Maurice Farman 'Longhorn' Pusher Biplane, N5727: 'Accident caused through propeller breaking in the air, to some part of the machine or engine coming adrift & being caught in the propeller.'

Flynn was a Bonding Agent at the cross-border city of Niagara Falls when he joined the RNAS just three months ago. Twenty-three-years-old, he is buried at the Ramsgate and St. Lawrence Cemetery, Kent.

05Jul17 – FSLt Alexander Richard KNIGHT (Collingwood ON) – Crash

Prior to this crash on landing, Knight had been on an Ace-bound trajectory, scoring three victories in three months with Naval 8. His aircraft for all of these successes, Triplane N5477, will be resurrected but Knight,

AR Knight

RAeC Trust

although not injured, is suffering the cumulative effects of high altitude patrols. He becomes ill and is sent on Canada Leave in December, returning for duties as an instructor in April 1918.

A picture of the rigors of combat flying is revealed in Knight's own report of May 24th, at 14,000 feet on the outskirts of Douai:

"While on Offensive Patrol... we climbed East and attacked four Albatros scouts which were a little above, and when we opened fire they dived at us. I fired at one which was easily distinguishable by his Yellow fuselage and zig-zag strip along his side... A black EA then attacked me, head on. I fired about 30 rounds straight at him and then had to dive under him to prevent a collision. I saw two of the EA's spin out of the fight and the other two proceeded East. I saw my shots entering both the EA's fuselage."

With no additional explanation, there is a handwritten 'Doubtful' across the top of his report and Knight was not credited for any victories that day.

06Jul17 – FSLt William Melville ALEXANDER (Toronto) – ACE

(From 28Apr17) Flying *Black Prince*, 10 Naval Triplane N5487, Alexander scores victories four and five, both Albatros D.IIIs sent down out of control. His report reads:

"Encountered about 25 EA scouts near Deulemont—killed pilot of one and drove another down into sideslip and nosedive. Was then forced to dive to get away from two others."

WM Alexander

RAeC Trust

In later-life, Alexander will recall this victory—and how he had opened fire on his target from a distance of just forty feet—in vivid detail:

> "I saw the bullets streaming into the cockpit. I was very excited. Over the trenches our nerves were so taut that when we got back, landed and lifted our goggles, it was like having a 100lb weight eased off your back. Of the dogfights I remember the clatter of the engine, the high pop-pop-popping of the machine gun and the flic-flic-flic as slugs tore through the aircraft's fabric."

Mel Alexander will have scored all of his first eight victories in N5487 before switching to Sopwith Camels. In August he is Gazetted the DSC: '...has driven down seven enemy machines to date and has at all times shown great skill and daring.' His total war-tally will be 23 enemy aircraft by May 1918, at which point he is posted to Home Establishment.

Raymond Collishaw described Alexander as: "Highly intelligent and endowed with a good memory, Alexander would be an asset anywhere. With one year's experience on active service, he was an asset to No. 10 Naval Squadron when it was sent to work under RFC operational control in May 1917." Collishaw, himself, scores an outstanding six victories during this day's aerial actions.

In 1977, Ron Lowman, a staff writer with the Toronto Star newspaper compared Collishaw's Black Flight with a popular TV show titled *Black Sheep Squadron*: 'The exploits of the originals and their successors in Black Flight, and their wing mates in Naval 10[sic], which was helping the hard-pressed Royal Flying Corps squadrons on the Western Front, would likely terrify US Marine Corps Lieutenant Colonel Gregory (Pappy) Boyington's World War II Black Sheep. But the stories of a bunch of Marine misfits who blossomed into a classy fighter squadron in the Pacific theatre are lapped up by Canadian TV audiences while our own 'Black Sheep' are almost forgotten.'

07Jul17 – ACES

If Canada were to declare a National Fighter Pilot Day, this date would be a strong contender: An unprecedented five Canadian naval aviators become ACES:

– A/FLt Frederick Carr ARMSTRONG, Cd'GaE (Toronto ON) – ACE

In 3 Naval Sopwith Pup N6465, Armstrong destroys his fifth enemy aircraft—a *Marinestaffle* seaplane North of Ostende. The French Government has already honoured Armstrong with their Croix de Guerre avec Etoille in April. Promoted locally to Acting Flight Commander by the Vice-Admiral, Dover, 'Army' Armstrong will be Gazetted the DSC in November 'for several victories and for leading his Flight with very great skill & gallantry.' His eventual credit of Enemy Aircraft will be thirteen. *(Read 25Mar18)*

– FSLt James Alpheus 'Jimmy' GLEN, Cd'GaP (Enderby BC) – ACE

(From 30Jul16) During the 3 Naval offensive patrol led by Armstrong, Glen in Pup N6183 also sends a seaplane down into the water where it immediately sinks. This action will form the basis of his first DSC, awarded in April 1918.

By August, in spite of summer weather, Glen is hospitalized with frostbite and sent on Canada leave.

The Vice Admiral, Dover, recommends a special promotion for Meritorious War Services: 'He is a good formation leader & a daring fighter. Of a total of 278 hours flying, 127 hours was flown during battles of the Somme & Ancre & from 16Feb17 to 7Jul17 he destroyed 3 enemy M/C's, & drove down 4 others.'

Promoted to Flight Lieutenant, Glen's sick leave will be extended by DNS Ottawa until late December. He will be back in 3 Naval in January 1918, with an immediate appointment to Acting Flight Commander. *(Read 21Mar18)*

– FSLt Sidney Emerson ELLIS (Kingston ON) – ACE

A recent Cranwell graduate, Ellis has been with 4 Naval for only two months. Initially flying the Pup, he scored his first kill on the 25th of May. On July 4th, with the Squadron re-equipped in Camels, he became one of the first two Camel pilots to shoot down a Gotha bomber. Today, he brings down his fifth German.

SF Ellis

RAeC Trust

Ellis has gone from being a student at the Curtiss Flying School in Toronto to achieving Ace status in less than one year. Although it would appear that he is now competent on the new Sopwith machine, he falls victim to the Camel's unforgiving stall characteristics while at slow speed and low altitude. Taking off on July 12th in N6337, he enters just such a spin situation and is killed on impact. Age 21, the former Queen's University student is interred at the Adinkerke Cemetery, Belgium.

– FLt John Albert PAGE (Brockville ON) – ACE

Like Ellis, Page's time will be short. A 10 Naval pilot, he scores again on the 22nd of the month shooting down his sixth and seventh German machines, but during that tight aerial combat, he is killed by *Ltn* Otto Brauneck of *Jasta* 11. Page's Triplane N5478 falls near Messines. The young McGill Student is

JA Page

RAeC Trust

recorded as missing and death is presumed in view of a report dropped by a German aviator. In 1918, a letter from the Admiralty regretfully informs Page's father that the RNAS service gratuity is not payable to the estates of officers killed.

– FSLt Arthur Treloar WHEALY (Toronto) – ACE

Whealy's fifth victory is scored in Pup N6174. He has been on active service since August 1916 with 3 Wing near the Swiss border and is now with 3 Naval at the Dunkirk-end of the long trench line. Following a well-deserved Canada Leave during the winter he will return to fly the Camel. By the end of March 1918 his score stands at 14 of an eventual 27 victories and he is reported as having: '...had valuable experience, leading a fighting flight for a year. Has good command of men. A splendid Officer.' But, no gallantry awards will come his way until his 3 Naval is integrated into the new Royal Air Force as 203 Squadron. *(Read 31Mar18)*

What makes a great fighter pilot? It would appear to be the inimitable coupling of Situational Awareness with a Berserker Mentality—contradictory attributes to be sure, but a certain formula for success in aerial combat.

07Jul17 – FSLt Alfred Hartley LOFFT (St Mary's ON) – MID

Recently graduated as pilot, Lofft is undergoing scout training with the Manston War Flight when German bombers begin another series of raids on England. Although having just been checked out on the new Sopwith Camel, Lofft is sent up on an Anti-Gotha

AH Lofft

RAeC Trust

Patrol. He returns with engine trouble and makes a bad landing. He has, however, fought an enemy machine as far as Walcheren Island off the coast of Holland and is awarded a Mention for the good service. Another AGP results in a crash landing for him and by August Lofft is found unfit

for an overseas draft as he is suffering from a duodenal ulcer. Employed as an instructor he is rated as 'Efficient and Keen' but training new pilots does not help his stomach condition and in January 1918, Lofft will be honourably released from service due to ill health.

07Jul17 – FSLt Lionel Lodge LINDSAY, MID (Calgary) – Ditched/INJ

Allied scouts, one of whom is Lindsay in 12 Naval Camel N6460, intercept twenty-two Gotha bombers returning from a raid on London. Caught out over the water with an engine failure, he ditches one mile southwest of Nieuport and is rescued by a French Motor Torpedo Boat.

Sent initially to Chatham Hospital because of back injuries, Lindsay is moved to Greenwich Hospital in early September for a further four weeks.

LL Lindsay

RAeC Trust

Chafing at this confinement, the University of Toronto law student slips out for a night on the town. His escapade violates hospital regulations. As a result, and: 'In view of his bad conduct in breaking leave while under treatment', the bored airman is escorted back to Chatham Hospital where more control be exercised over him—away from the theatre nightlife of London.

Resurveyed fit, Lindsay flies out of the Isle of Grain seaplane base for the remainder of the war. Later, in 1919, he will serve in South Russia with Collishaw's 47 Squadron RAF and be awarded the Imperial Russian Order of Saint Stanislas.

08Jul17 – FSLt William Edgar ROBINSON (Winnipeg) – POW Tripoli

Described as: 'First Class Pilot & Good Officer. Is really hard working when he chooses', Robinson has been choosing hard work in Malta for the past four months.

Today, things get harder when, on anti-submarine patrol out of Calafrana, his machine's unreliable 160 horsepower Isotta-Fraschini engine fails. The FBA Type H pusher flying boat N1078 is one of

WE Robinson

Wayne Robinson

four surplus aircraft presented to the RNAS by the Italian Government. The French fleet receives wireless SOS signals from Robinson's Observer JCA Jenks, and in response, five vessels embark from Malta and search for three days.

The crew is feared lost after no discovery of any trace of men or machine. However, Robinson and Jenks have floated for several days before drifting ashore near Tripoli, North Africa. They survived their ordeal at sea by drinking the rusty liquid from the water-cooled engine's radiator. Once on land, Turkish Troops take them captive. Confined at Fort Misurata, the pair are treated with reasonable liberty, being occasionally allowed to visit the local market under escort.

In August, Prisoner of War Robinson is awarded the Croix de Guerre by the French for his anti-submarine efforts. On one specific mission he had diverted an

Allied hospital ship after spotting a U-boat in the vicinity. He will be repatriated in early February 1919.

Robinson is the first of three generations of pilots; his son and grandson will both fly with Air Canada and achieve Captain. Their roots in aviation go back to the very beginnings: Grandfather Robinson's 1915 pilot training contract with the Wright Flying School at Daytona bears the signature of none-other-than Orville Wright.

10Jul17 – SCdr Redford Henry MULOCK, DSO, MIDx2 (Winnipeg) – Rescue

(From 06Feb17) Mulock's 3 Naval is being pulled out of the Lines for a well-earned rest and re-equipment, and he sets out to the RNAS Depot at Dunkirk to establish his Squadron's new home. It is not a good day to travel: the base is being heavily shelled and treacherous fires are raging. The ammunition railhead is in particular peril when Mulock arrives on scene. He immediately proceeds to the vicinity of a burning train, accompanied by a doctor and three Air Mechanic Drivers. The Senior Officer, RNAS Dunkirk will report: 'Surgeon and one Driver took the first wounded man they found away in an ambulance, and after this I was unable to get any definite statements, as Squadron Commander Mulock is very reticent on the subject. I gather from the remaining drivers, however, that he went alone and searched the Dump for wounded and would not allow the drivers to accompany him.' For rescuing wounded and salving ammunition while under shellfire, Mulock will receive his third Mention and an expression of appreciation from the Army Commander.

In September, after handing over his Squadron to FCdr **Lloyd Breadner**, Mulock is appointed Senior Officer of the RNAS depot at Dunkirk. There he will play a major role in rebuilding a base that has been wiped out by shelling and bombing raids. He earns the French Legion of Honour and is Gazetted a Bar to his DSO. A promotion to Wing Commander will follow in January 1918. (Read 29Aug18)

12Jul17 – FSLt Denis Heywood DALY (Vancouver; b. ENG) – Crash

Coming in to land at a fast 80 knots, Daly in his 12 Naval Triplane N5369, hits a cornfield on the far side of the Petite Synthe aerodrome, and performs a complete somersault over the road. The fuselage from just behind his seat doubles itself below the undercarriage, rolling the empennage into a ball ahead of the engine. The landing essentially ties the machine into a knot but somehow Daly finishes up on his wheels. More incredibly, he emerges from the tangle sporting nothing worse than a cut chin and bruises and abrasions on his knees. His Triplane is not nearly as fortunate and, deemed damaged beyond reasonable repair, the St. Pol Aeroplane Depot, Dunkirk, deletes it from inventory.

DH Daly

GWFM

Formed from No. 1 Wing at the end of June as a Training Squadron, 12 Naval is reputed to average about one crash per flying day. Operating out of the tiny Petite Synthe aerodrome is the hazard, as the field's limited size and treacherous perimeter tend to put the wind up new pilots. Although falling in the inexperienced category, Daly had graduated from Cranwell in mid-June with the highest RNAS accolade—VGI Pilot—the equivalent grade of a 1st Class Flying Ability. But despite his aptitude, and his recent near-miraculous escape from serious injury, five days later Daly's luck runs out. On the 17th of July, he is killed transitioning to Sopwith Camels. His loss in B3822 is a recurrence of the all too common Camel crash—the gyroscopic stalling and spinning into the ground during a low level left hand turn out. Age 21, he is buried at the Dunkirk Cemetery.

13Jul17 – PFO Donald Badgerow MULHOLLAND (Toronto) – INJ

Sustaining injuries to the head, Mulholland is listed as 'Condition Hopeless' following a crash at the Manston Flying School. His machine, Maurice Farman Longhorn Pusher N5740 is a complete write-off. But Mulholland, a

DB Mulholland

U of T

former infantry Lieutenant with the 48th Canadian Highlanders, is made of strong stuff and a subsequent hospital report reads 'Condition satisfactory & has improved.' Sent back to Canada in September, a DNS Ottawa Medical Board will recommend an extension of sick leave in January 1918. By April, the Military Board Survey calls for Discharge from Service: 'Physically unfit from debility following aeroplane crash.'

15Jul17 – FSLt John Roy ALLAN
(Westmount PQ) – DSC

Flying a Handley Page bomber nicknamed '*Kewpie Doll II*', Allan destroys several railway freight cars that are transporting high explosives. Descending with engines at idle, Allan avoids alerting the flak batteries in the area and successfully releases his bombs at 3,000 feet. He continues his glide until clear of the target and escapes unscathed. The stealthy night raid on the Ostende marshalling yards by 7 Naval Squadron is an effort to deny supplies to the port's submarine base.

A DSC awarded for this action is well deserved. Allan is described by one of his crewmen many years later: 'As a pilot, he was little short of superb, and having flown with many different pilots at the controls. I use that adjective advisedly.' On the subject of avoiding flack during numerous raids: 'He had that aeroplane doing things no Handley was designed to do and not once were we forced to ditch our load, though on one occasion it meant going back over the target three times.' *(Read 12Apr18)*

17Jul17 – FSLt Fraser MacPherson BRYANS
(Toronto) – KIC – Midair

In simulated aerial combat over Hornsea, Bryans is killed in a mid-air collision. He is flying Sopwith Baby Seaplane 1102 in exercise with Curtiss Large America H-12 flying Boat No. 8657 operated by FLt **Basil Deacon Hobbs**.

The English Second Pilot of the Curtiss LA reports: 'Fighting practice with FSLt Bryans, who was just beginning to get pretty good on the Schneider Cup float seaplane. For nearly 20 minutes Bryans tried unsuccessfully to get under our tail, while Hobbs maneuvered the big boat in a masterly fashion. After the wash-out signal was given the LA circled over Harwich Habour gliding down for landing.

'Suddenly and without warning there was an appalling crash and a yell of pain from our Engineer who was sitting on the floor of the hull. For a split second the controls went absolutely soft, a large fore-and-aft movement of the wheel produced no effect. As they tightened up again, Hobbs shouted [to me] "Bring her down as slowly as you can!" while he stood up to look over the side at the crumpled mass of wreckage hurtling towards the water below.'

Bryans had apparently decided to get in a last attack after Hobbs had broken off the engagement. It is probable that he failed to allow for the rapid descent of the flying boat and his upper plane may have interfered with his range of vision. His aim proves all too accurate: the Sopwith strikes the Curtiss squarely on the heel of the step, exactly on the centre line. Fortunately LA 8657 was the instructional H-12 and had been specially strengthened for 'dud' landings by the addition of a two-by-six spruce plank. Had Bryans hit in any other location there would have been five deaths.

Hobbs smoothly lands his crippled flying boat and before beaching, taxies the rapidly sinking H-12 around until the last moment, looking for Bryans among the floating wreckage. But Bryans' machine has fallen into the harbour in several pieces, and it is weeks before his body frees itself from the cockpit section that had been dragged down with the engine.

Bryans graduated from the Chingford School in October 1916 with high standing in examinations. Graded a 'Very Good Indeed Pilot' he excelled as an aviator who was able to fly all types. Appointed to Felixstowe, his only setback was during a U-boat sighting while flying with Hobbs earlier this year on the 16th of April. The standard operating procedure in the event of a submarine spotting is for the Second Pilot to scramble out to the nose cockpit and guide the Pilot by hand signals to cross the undersea boat at right angles; the Wireless/Telegraphist operator would fire a Very flare recognition challenge; and the Engineer would standby with a camera to photograph any attack-bomb bursts for a sunk or damaged U-boat claim. If the

FM Bryans

RAeC Trust

correct color challenge-rocket was not returned, the Second Pilot would toggle off two 230lb bombs, aiming for a direct hit or a least a close straddle. Following the indecisive attack, Hobbs reported: 'Surprised the first U-boat of the season. It must be admitted that the surprise was mutual, for Bryans was so struck by buck fever that he did not reach for the bomb releases until his Hun had dived.'

Normally, airmen killed in England are buried at their air station cemetery. However in this case, The Lords Commissioners of the Admiralty agree to send Bryans' body home to Canada. The Toronto Daily Star will report on a double military funeral held for the son of Dr. WF Bryans, and the eldest son of Rev. FW Wilkinson, Lieut. Harold Reid Wilkinson, RFC. By sad coincidence, the two young officers, both aged 23, had lived just a few houses apart on Carleton Street and both had joined the Air Services in October 1916.

20Jul17 – FCdr George Gordon MacLENNAN, CdGaP (Eugenia ON) – KIA

Leading his 6 Naval 'A' Flight of all Ontarians, **George Kirkpatrick** and **Ford Strathy** of Toronto and **James Forman** of Kirkfield, MacLennan encounters three German two-seaters over Middlekerke. He dives his Camel N6360 towards the machine on the left side of the enemy 'vic' formation and sends it spinning. Sadly, when 'A' Flight reforms after the split-up action, they find that their lead is missing. MacLennan is claimed

by *Ltn* Hugo Jons of *Jasta* 20 who later reports that he has sent a 'Sopwith down, burning'—although the time submitted by the German does not correspond to the reported time of the Canadian Flight Commander's death.

'Chubby' MacLennan was a University of Toronto graduate Civil Engineer and,

GG MacLennan

at age 31, older than most of the scout pilots. However, he was judged to be: 'An Officer who ought to stand the wear and tear of flying. Has VG mechanical knowledge & his qualities as an Officer are good, hardworking'. The Flight members that he led with 6 Naval are not only all

from his home province, but are also all University of Toronto types.

Following a short spell as Assistant Instructor in March 1916, MacLennan had flown with 3 Wing. In April 1917 he was awarded the French Cd'GaP for his efforts in the Verdun area and on the Alsace-Lorraine Front. His leadership ability was recognized as: 'Ability to Command VG. Is a steady & reliable Pilot. Shows great presence of mind'. MacLennan is interred at Oostende, West-Vlaanderen, Belgium.

22Jul17 – FCdr John Edward SHARMAN, DSC&Bar, CdG (Oak Lake MB) – KIA

JE Sharman

(From 14Jun17) Sharman is leading his 10 Naval all-Canadian 'C' Flight consisting of **John Page**, **Charlie Weir** and **George Trapp**, when they encounter a hostile formation of Albatros. Entering combat, Sharman's personalized Triplane N6307 *Black Death* is observed to break up, possibly due to having taken a direct hit from an anti-aircraft or artillery shell. During the subsequent drift-down fighting, Sharman's wingman and Deputy Flight Leader, Page is also killed. Before the end of the year both Weir and Trapp will have also perished in combat.

Previously flying in the *Black* Flight, Sharman was awarded a Bar to his DSC on the 20th of June for his great courage and skill in attacking enemy aircraft. A French Croix de Guerre was announced that same day.

Raymond Collishaw described Sharman as:

'Medium stature, good looking... blonde. He had been raised on a farm... and consequently enjoyed robust health and strength. He was extremely ambitious both in the academic field and the air fighting game.'

'Had it not been for an unlucky chance—a factor against which he could not possibly guard—it is likely that he would have emerged as one of the top fighter pilots on the Western Front.'

When the War Graves are formalized following the Armistice, John Page's recovered body will be interred at Pont-du-Hem Military Cemetery, La Gorgue, France, to rest next to that of his Flight Commander John Sharman.

24Jul17 – FSLt Theodore Charles 'Ted' MAY (Toronto) – MIA

Eighteen-year-old May has been with 10 Naval only five days when he meets his death. The Squadron is decimated, down to ten pilots at this point, and as a result, the evening offensive patrol is only a three-plane effort. Led by **Mel Alexander**, with **Ellis Reid** and May forming up, a first takeoff attempt at 17:30 is hampered by heavy mist. Once the three machines do get airborne an hour later, they are involved in five indecisive engagements with gun stoppages being the hindrance.

TC May

Paul Donnellan

At 19:15 both Alexander and Reid see the wings on May's Triplane N5364 fold and the aircraft break up in the air. They are certain that this is not due to enemy attack; however, *Ltn* Helmut Dilthey of *Jasta* 27 makes a claim. May falls near Moorseele, south of Passchendaele. An old-boy of Toronto's St. Andrew's College, his body is never recovered and he joins the named on the Arras Flying Services Memorial.

25Jul17 – FSLt Harold Edgar MOTT (Winnipeg MB) – ACE

Mott's fifth victory is in Camel B3832. Almost three months before, he had opened his scorecard on the 2nd of May flying Pups with 9 Naval. His second victory, ten days later, was almost his last. He fired 50 rounds at close range and saw the tracers hit near the German pilot's seat, rendering the machine completely out of control. Mott was unable to follow it down as he himself was by then fighting off five other enemy aircraft. After a running fight of ten to fifteen minutes, the enemy fortunately made off.

HE Mott

GWFM

Battle fatigued by October, Mott is granted a Canadian sick leave and departs with a Report of having: 'Given great satisfaction. His work has been invariably good. Very good Command indeed. Strongly recommended for promotion.' The rank of Flight Lieutenant will be promulgated in January 1918, and at the same time, his medical leave extended by DNS Ottawa. Declared fit for ground duty in April, Mott is held in Canada and appointed to the RAF's Aerial Gunnery School at Beamsville, Ontario. He is allotted the heavy task of crash investigations.

27Jul17 – FSLt Roderick 'Rod' McDONALD (Antigonish NS) – ACE

McDonald's Squadron, Naval 8 has just transitioned to the Camel and in N6375, he sends down his fifth enemy machine. In November, before departing on a Canada Leave, McDonald's Squadron Commander writes: 'This Officer has been with Naval Squadron No. 8 since 20th March 1917 and has done conspicuous good work on the Lens-Arras Front. He is a very good Pilot and has proved himself in every way capable of taking Command of a Flight. He is a very keen and hardworking Officer'. McDonald will return to the Squadron in February 1918 and be immediately appointed an Acting Flight Commander. *(Read 08May18)*

28Jul17 – FSLt James Henry FORMAN (Kirkfield ON) – WIA

JH Forman

U of T

On this, his second patrol of the day, Forman remains at altitude when his Flight Commander leads a dive on a pair of enemy two-seaters. Forman's suspicion that this is a trap proves to be correct when three Albatros scouts enter the fray. He attacks one at very short range, firing a sharp burst before pulling clear to avoid a collision. The other two Albatros come after him and he receives a wound to his right shoulder. Endeavoring to get back across the lines, Forman force-lands in a bean field and overturns. Meanwhile, his 6 Naval Flight has accounted for one of the two-seater observation machines.

The day before, flying his same Camel N6358, Foreman had shot down his first EA, a slate-coloured Albatros D.V. Canadian wingman **Wilf Curtis**, watching the flaming Albatros fall and then plunge into the sea described the scene as 'spooky'.

In late September, Forman's shoulder has mended; he is declared fit for duty and sent to 1 Naval. This is a bit of a step backwards as that unit is still flying the Triplane. Nonetheless, he will shoot down a DFW.C in October and after the Squadron is equipped with Camels, he will bring down two more enemy aircraft in November. Forman's year-end Confidential Report writes him up as a: 'Very keen & zealous Officer and Pilot, with Good Active Service experience. Has ability to command.' He will achieve Ace status on April 12th 1918 and eventually tally up nine kills. *(Read 04Sep18)*

28Jul17 – F/Cdr Arnold Jacques CHADWICK (Toronto) – MIA/KIC

(From 02Oct16) Up until now the young Flight Commander had led a charmed existence. But today, with 4 Naval in Camel N6369, Chadwick is reported as 'Missing, believed Drowned.' His wheels caught a wave while he was flying too close to the water and the aircraft turned turtle.

Chadwick made Ace on June 3rd and was later recommended for a DSC with the write-up: 'He has destroyed eight enemy machines and has on three occasions forced down balloons. Has always fought with the utmost gallantry and pluck.' The medal is now Gazetted posthumously.

In order to keep German submarines penned up, the Royal Navy instituted a Belgian Coast Barrage, a minefield of over twenty miles parallel the shoreline between Zeebrugge and Ostend. The laying of the field commenced on the 25th of July and took three days. RNAS pilots were kept on continual patrol protecting the mine-laying ships from air attack by German torpedo-carrying seaplanes.

Chadwick had shot down one of these intruders on the 25th for his 11th victory. Today he may have been wave-top flying in celebration of the completion of the intense work. Several weeks later his body washes ashore near La Panne and is interred at Adinkerke, Belgium.

28Jul17 – FLt Ellis Vair REID, DSC, MID (Belleville ON) – MIA

(From 06Jun17) Reid destroys his 19th Enemy Aircraft but is himself shot down and killed by anti-aircraft flak.

One day before, in his signature Triplane *Black Roger*, Reid had sent down three Albatros D.Vs: today, his 10 Naval N5483 is one of the machines to fall from the skies. A Bar to Reid's DSC is to be awarded if he is reported as being a Prisoner of War but he remains among the Missing and is instead granted a second Mention.

EV Reid

U of T

31Jul17 – FCdr Kenneth Gordon MacDONALD (Victoria) – INJ

Although a highly qualified pilot, MacDonald makes the classic error after an engine failure on takeoff—he attempts to return to the airfield. His 9 Naval Triplane N6305 stalls on the turn back, flips into a spin and dives to the ground. MacDonald is extremely fortunate to only suffer a concussion.

A 1915 graduate of the Wright Brothers Flying School in Dayton, Ohio, MacDonald had arrived in France in November 1916. A 'Thoroughly sound Officer' his accident renders him much less so, and he is sent on Canada Leave. In May 1918 he will join 62 Wing in the Aegean Group

AUGUST 1917

14Aug17 – PFO Raymond Earl BRAY
(Victoria BC) – KIC

Bray is killed in an Avro 504 training accident at RNAS Cranwell, and the aircraft, Number 3320, deleted from service. Bray's rank is that of Probationary Flying Officer (PFO), a training title that has now replaced the Probationary Flight Sub-Lieutenant commission and is equivalent to today's Canadian Armed Forces Officer Cadet.

15Aug17 – Lieut Geo Richard Davidson WOOLER
(Canadian) – KIA

Serving with the 5th Infantry Battalion, Saskatchewan Regiment, Wooler is killed in the front-line trenches. He had been a Lieutenant with the CEF the previous August when he transferred to the RNAS. By October his Cranwell Commander reported: 'In my opinion, he is unlikely to ever become a first class Pilot, and request that his Commission be terminated. He is not recom'd for Observer or for Armament. I am satisfied with his conduct. He has requested he may transfer to Motor Boats, & informs me he can sail a yacht.'

Released as unsuitable in November, Wooler will twice attempt to rejoin. He is informed that it is impossible; and on the second try, is told that no further correspondence can be entertained regarding his re-instatement. Completely rejected by the Navy, the ever-keen Wooler re-enters the War through the Canadian Expeditionary Forces in England, and was posted back to the Western Front. He is buried at the Loos British Cemetery, Pas de Calais.

17Aug17 – FSLt Claver Victor BESSETTE
(Conneticut USA) – Disciplined

Acting as a mail censor on staff at RNAS Houghton, Bessette is brought up on a change of writing improper remarks on the letter of a rating to his sister; the Sailor quite rightfully complains. Bessette apologizes and a disciplinary board allows him to hold his commission, but it notes that he is: 'Not likely to make a good pilot

CV Bessette

on large Seaplanes. Lacks common sense & is liable to lose his head.'

Born in America to French-Canadian parents, Bessette does advance to train on the 'large seaplanes' at Felixstowe and earns reports as 'A good steady pilot, slow & painstaking, good with men.' Through these efforts, he will go on to earn one of the RAF's first Distinguished Flying Crosses in June 1918 for operational flying out of the Isle of Grain Naval Air Station.

17Aug17 – FSLt Rob't Franklin Preston ABBOTT,
MID (Yukon & Ottawa) – WIA

In Camel B3783 on a Fleet Protection Patrol over the Nieuport piers, Abbott comes under attack by hostile machines. Although badly struck in the thigh, he manages to make a return to his 3 Naval base.

The previous day, on a special mission in low in visibility, Abbott had found and attacked an enemy aerodrome at Uitkerke, firing about 500 rounds into the Bessoneaux-type hangars and earning a Mention in Despatches for the action. Today the gunshot wound he sustains is described as having penetrated above the femur, with a high likelihood of severe and likely permanent effects. The surgeon

RFP Abbott

recommends a total disablement of seven months with 'such gratuity as Their Lordships may see fit to award'.

Hospitalized until mid November, Abbott takes Canadian leave, returning in March 1918, anxious to continue service. He re-qualifies and is recommended for employment on short flights until his wounds harden. He performs test-flying duties out of Dunkirk but will be released due to ill health by October 1918.

Abbott's English Flight Commander Len Rochford, in an autobiography *I Chose the Sky,* recalled his young wingman: 'We called him Skimp and he was a tough, wiry Canadian with red hair. If I remember rightly he came from the Yukon where he had worked as a trapper. He had a forceful way of expressing himself, with many gestures, especially when he landed after being in a scrap over the lines.' One instance of these 'many gestures' had occurred following an earlier Fleet Protection mission, from which Abbott had to return early due to engine trouble. Taking off again to rejoin his flight, he saw three machines over Nieuport at 10,000 feet. Unable to distinguish their markings, he continued to climb and when ten miles offshore the three now-suddenly-recognizable enemy aircraft turned and attacked him. Abbott returned fire and drove down one before his own cowling was shot away, fouling his propeller and throwing his Camel into a nosedive. He regained control and force landed safely on a beach at Coxyde.

17Aug17 – FSLt Ford Stuart STRATHY (Toronto ON) – KIA

FS Strathy

RAeC Trust

Strathy meets his death going to the assistance of a Bristol aircraft being attacked by superior numbers. His 6 Naval Camel N6334 is shot down behind enemy lines near Zevecote.

Strathy, an Upper Canada College 'Old Boy' was 19 years old. He had been credited with one victory in July.

19Aug17 – FSLt Theodore Linscott GLASGOW (Toronto) – KIC

TL Glasgow

RAeC Trust

'A' Flight of 10 Naval is returning from a two-hour offensive patrol when Glasgow's Triplane N5464 suddenly falls out of formation and spins into the ground. A formation of about fifteen enemy machines is seen patrolling just east of the lines and Glasgow may have been distracted and inadvertently stalled his aeroplane. Age 19, the former Cadet from the Royal Military College at Kingston, Ontario, had been with the squadron just one month.

20Aug17 – PFO Lawrence CODE (Ottawa) – KIC

Code is killed in a smash-up landing of his BE2C Bristol Scout machine, A1771, at the RNAS Training Establishment Cranwell. He was 20 years of age.

20Aug17 – FSLt Charles Haddon WEIR (Medicine Hat AB) – POW/DOW

Five aircraft of 10 Naval's A Flight are on an afternoon offensive patrol when two machines are forced to turn back with mechanical problems. Over Langenmarck, five German Scouts jump the remaining three Triplanes. Weir's N5355 is last seen entering cloud on an evasive nosedive. Both he and his aircraft have been hit, and he is even more severely injured on the crash landing. Wier, a 'VG Pilot Indeed, Good & extremely keen Officer', dies shortly after being taken prisoner.

CH Weir

RAeC Trust

21Aug17 – Flt Charles Joshua WYATT
(Mount Brydges ON) &
– Obs SLt Albert Irving 'Fred' HUTTY
(Toronto) – Both KIC

A bad crash-landing of DH-4 N5983 claims the lives of both Pilot and Observer from 2 Naval Squadron based out of St. Pol. Twenty-four-year-old Wyatt and thirty-year-old Hutty are buried at the nearby Dunkirk Cemetery.

It is a poignant end to Observer Hutty's service. Although he was older than average for aircrew, in late 1915 he had been entered in the RNAS by the Department of Naval Service, Ottawa, as a Pilot Candidate. He went on to achieve his Royal Aeronautical Certificate at Eastbourne in February 1916 but his Confidential Report one month later read: 'This Officer is so bad that I consider it unwise to even allow him to risk his life. He is aware that he is a bad Pilot. As he possesses plenty of courage, I submit he might become Observer, for which duty he volunteers.' Hutty duly became an Observer Sub-Lieutenant, RNVR by the following March and was sent to Dunkirk a: 'Very keen, capable & determined Observer.' Today was his first day on Squadron.

CJ Wyatt

RAeC Trust

AI Hutty

RAeC Trust

22Aug17 – FCdr Gerald 'Gerry' Essex HERVEY
MIDx2 (Calgary) – DSC

Flying Pup 9901 out of Manston, England, Hervey attacks a formation of ten Gotha bombers over North Foreland. Firing 100 rounds from a 100-yard range, he observes the tracers enter the fuselage of Gotha IV 663, which falls into the sea off Margate. Hervey receives the DSC for the action. His Squadron Commander reports that he performs his duties with great zeal. 'Given every satisfaction as Instructor & Executive Officer. A courageous fighter.' Hervey will be recommended for promotion to Squadron Commander by the General Officer Commanding the 7th Brigade in April 1918.

A former accountant, Hervey began his score count when flying with No. 1 Wing, Dunkirk, in 1916. On the 9th of July he dove a Sopwith Pup from 14,000 to 10,000 feet and attacked three large hostile machines about two miles out to sea from Westende. He was apparently successful as one of the enemy aircraft fell out of formation and was last seen close to the sea, still in a nosedive. Hervey was well described by his 1 Wing CO as: 'A most promising Officer. Gets through with things.'

GE Hervey

RAeC Trust

Two of these 'things' earned Hervey Mentions from the Vice Admiral, Dover, in September 1916. Together with **C. B. Sproatt** he had attacked enemy aerodromes: Ghistelles Aerodrome on the 3rd and St. Denis Westrem on the 7th, earning a MID for each effort. After a period as a Flight Commander with 9 Naval in early 1917, he was posted to England as an instructor. His victory today is his fourth and last and he will be one-short of Ace on the balance sheet.

25Aug17 – FSLt Harold Harman BOOTH
(Toronto) – POW

Booth fails to return from a night bombing raid on St. Denis Westrem. He has been taken Prisoner of War after his 7 Naval Handley Page 3137 is shot down by flak near Ghent. His Observer is missing and his Gunlayer killed. During the attack, the Squadron drops four 250lb bombs, nine 65lb bombs, and sixty-to-eighty 12 lb bombs, with only the one aircraft lost.

By mid-September Booth will be reported as a POW at Karlesruhe and in December at Holzmidnen. A pre-war draftsman, Booth in later-life will become the Art Director of the Stroukoff Aircraft Corporation in the United States.

SEPTEMBER 1917

02Sep17 – FSLt Norman Douglas HALL (Nelson & Victoria BC) – POW

On his very first patrol with 3 Naval, Hall goes Missing In Action. The action is a Fleet Protection Patrol of five Camels and they encounter a considerable number of EA near Ostende. FCdr **Lloyd Breadner** attacks and destroys one EA, shooting its wings off, then he and his Flight send down another EA completely out of control. FSLt **Bill Chisam** attacks four Albatros scouts, shooting down one before being attacked by the others. Driven down to 50 feet Chisam escapes across the lines. The remaining 3 Naval pilots have several indecisive engagements: all are much shot about, become separated, and return home singly, save their new pilot Hall.

Hall had begun his operational flying with 3 Wing in February 1917. He got off to a good start and was presented with a medal by the Town Council of Dunkirk for bringing down a threatening German aeroplane on the 2nd of May. Wounded in Action on the 23rd of that month, Hall was appointed to 10 Naval following his recovery. He arrived in the unit on the 24th of July just as FSLt **Ted May** was killed when his Sopwith

ND Hall

RAeC Trust

Triplane broke up in the air. Two days previously, FCdr **John Sharman** had died when his Triplane had also come apart in flight, although probably from anti-aircraft fire. Hall refused to fly what he felt were combat-stressed machines—10 Naval's Triplanes—and he was immediately posted out to 3 Naval's Sopwith Camels.

In late September, Hall is reported to be a Prisoner of War at Karlsruhe. He is later held at Holzminden and then Schweidnitz.

03Sep17 – FSLt Gordon Beattie George SCOTT (Guelph ON) – MIA

Diving to assist a French Sopwith Triplane under attack by an enemy Albatros, Scott of 1 Naval is chased down by six others. Both Allied aircraft are shot out of the sky. *Ltn* Stapenhorst of *Jasta* II claims a 'Dreideker' over Wytschaete: Scott's Triplane N5381.

An honours graduate of the University of Toronto, the faculty sends a sympathetic letter to Scott's family and also asks for information to enter into the school's Roll of Honour. From his millinery-importing business in Guelph, Scott's father mails various clippings and writings, requesting:

GBG Scott

U of T

'Kindly be careful with Photo and return with letters and papers as we prize them very much.'

In correspondance home on August 17th Scott had penned:

> "Have had very many encounters with enemy machines since the beginning of this month, as the Huns have been much more active. I certainly was one of the luckiest chaps on the face of the earth the other day when I got back alive. We went away over with some RFC machines and encountered a Hun formation of twenty machines. They were albatros scouts. We dived on them. Then some got behind me and their machine guns began to cackle, cackle furiously. It was no good giving them a straight shot, so I twisted and turned and dived, spun and did all manner of things, but the cackle, cackle didn't seem in any way to be abated. However they didn't get their shots into me as I must have done plenty of turning. I had to turn and fight, saw three machines close at hand, with the others in the distance. I was quite low and about eight miles into Hunland. One of them got on to the tail of my machine—but then I could yarn to you a long time about these, but I'll cut

it short by saying that I had two more scraps before I got enough start to beat it like fury for home."

In another letter written the day before his luck does run out Scott had described a dawn patrol:

"It is now just half past seven, so you see I am quite an early bird this morning. Have just come down from an early morning patrol. We went up at five thirty to have an extensive view of Hunland—just before the sun came up there was a small cloud which had wonderfully rich colouring. We all remarked about it. Don't think, however, that we were the only ones to be up so early, for we encountered a bunch of French machines which we at first thought to be Huns. Not long after we got up high and the sun made an appearance. We finally decided to come down, so dived through the clouds. They were ten thousand feet thick and full of rain and hail. It seemed an age before I got through, although I was diving at from ninety to a hundred knots. A cloud is very dark with nothing but mist, and nothing can guide you except your instruments. The hail stung somewhat. I came out at three thousand feet, a little back of the Hun trenches, but soon got back to our spot."

An eloquent carved-stone monument at the historic Woodlawn Cemetery in Guelph commemorates the aviator: 'In memory of Flight Lieutenant Gordon B.G. Scott, RNAS, only son of Andrew and Margaret Scott.' There was no pilot's body to bury, but his parents are later interred below the sculpture.

05Sep17 – FSLt Stanley Harry McCRUDDEN (Toronto ON) – INJ

Attempting to land through a thick mist covering the airport at Mount St. Eloi, France, McCrudden crashes his Naval 8 Triplane N5366. He is severely injured and the machine broken. Both will be fit to fly again in 1918, and both are re-purposed in a training role. The aircraft goes to the Gunnery School at Eastchurch and McCrudden

SH McCrudden
RAeC Trust

becomes an instructor at Vendome with 205 Training Depot Squadron. Other than a ground collision when his Curtiss Jenny is hit by another JN-4, he will survive the war without further incident.

05Sep17 – FLt Robert 'Bob' LECKIE (Toronto; b. SCT) – Rescue

(From 14May17) Out of Yarmouth in H-12 'Large America' flying boat 8666, Leckie is paired with a DH-4 aircraft. The land-based De Havilland can out-climb a Zeppelin and the flying boat is along for navigation and water rescue if required. During this mission two Zeppelins are spotted covering mine sweeping operations. In an ensuing chase they lead the pair of RNAS aircraft into range of a German cruiser squadron. The DH machine is struck by anti aircraft fire and forced down with engine failure to pancake on rough seas. Leckie has also sustained flak damage but does not hesitate to land and rescue the crew. He knows that he may be unable to lift off again, and in the blustery winds and rising seas this proves correct: a wing is damaged, and an engine fails. Now, with six men aboard, they are forced to bail as the shell-pierced flying boat takes on water with the adverse weather developing into a full-fledged gale. Another chore is to take turns crawling out on the good wing to keep it down as flat as possible. Each dip of the wing soaks the individual at the tip.

R Leckie
RAeC Trust

Although the storm abates by the next morning, two more days of hardship and privation in the cold waters follow. The flying boat carries four homing pigeons and each is carefully husbanded and dispatched to carry an SOS position of the aircraft.

It is only the last bird, Pigeon No. NURP/17/F.16331, that makes the distance and tumbles to the beach near the Coast Guard Station at Cromar. The wee bird dies from exhaustion but it has saved the lives of the RNAS airmen. The naval vessel HMS *Halcyon* proceeds immediately to coordinates on the slip of rice paper.

In a letter home Leckie writes:

> "In a glass case in the wardroom may be seen a very pretty stuffed pigeon. Beneath, a little plate bears this inscription, 'A very gallant Gentleman', and who shall deny it?" *(Read 04Jun18)*

12Sep17 – PFO Russell Hammond BARKLEY (Toronto ON) – REL

Joining in January of this year, Barkley has discovered that the romance of flying is more nerve-wracking than recreational. He suffers weeks of insomnia at the Chingford Flying School and is deemed physically unfit. Barkley's mental state prior to the realities of flying is displayed in a cartoon he drew while in basic training at Crystal Palace. Instructions for the new Probationary Flight Officers dictate that the RNAS Eagle insignia is to be worn on each arm.

THE ADMIRALTY'S NEW ORDER.

"A bird must now be worn on each arm."

Barkley's cartoon: 'The Admiralty's New Order—
A bird must be worn on each arm'

FAAM

13Sep17 – FSLt John Richard WILFORD (Lindsay ON) – WIA/POW

Wounded and shot down over Wervicq in his 1 Naval Triplane N5429, Wilford survives the crash but is captured at Menin. Becoming a Prisoner of War, he is reported to be at Karlsrhue in early October and then at Holzminden by the end of the month. Wilford fell as the fifteenth victory of *Ltn* Kurt Wusthoff of *Jasta* 4.

14Sep17 – FSLt Anthony Anderson BISHOP (Kamsack SK) – KIC

Flying out of Dover, Bishop is killed when his Sopwith Strutter dives from a great height and crashes on the costal rocks of Kent. Structural failure is suspected after an investigation shows that the aircraft, N5508, was badly damaged in a previous accident.

AA Bishop

RAeC Trust

Bishop had graduated from Cranwell in July with a high recommendation for Seaplanes, however, in early August he had submitted a request to return to land machines.

19Sep17 – FSLt Edmund Victor Joseph GRACE (Westmount PQ) – MIA

An eight-machine offensive-patrol of Camels from 10 Naval encounters an equal-sized formation of enemy scouts over Hooge and a general engagement ensues. In the fifteen-minute fight, three EA are driven down, but the Allied side loses Grace. His machine, N6374, falls in flames southeast of Houthulst Wood. A 'Sopwith' is claimed by *Ltn* Hans Ritter von Adam, *Staffelfuhrer* (CO) of *Jasta* 6. Grace was a McGill University student and had joined squadron just two weeks previously.

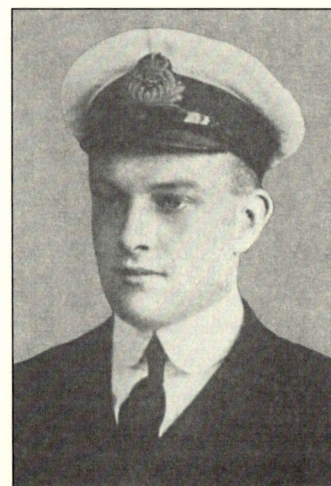

EVJ Grace

MHR

Ltn von Adam, with twenty-one victories, will, himself, be killed in aerial combat in two-months' time.

19Sep17 – FSLt Robert Earnshaw McMILLAN
(Jaguet River NB) – POW

McMillan is reported as being last seen going down 'under control' northeast of St. Julien after a fight with enemy scouts. He has been with 1 Naval just four days when his Triplane N5490 becomes the eighth victory for German Warrant Officer Fritz Kosmahl of *Jasta* 26. McMillan is captured at Menin, however, the RNAS will not learn that he is a prisoner until mid-October. He is held first at Karlsruhe and later at Holzminden.

20Sep17 – NUMBER 1 NAVAL

This day's fighting is in support of the Battle for the Menin Road Ridge. All objectives are won but the cost to Naval Squadrons is high. The Triplane is simply not suited for the role of low-level ground attack.

– SCdr R.S. Dallas, DSO, DSC&Bar
(Australia)

The new Squadron Commander of 1 Naval is the great Australian Ace, R. Stanley Dallas and in a letter home he writes:

> "I have lost some fine fellows. One sees them off on their mission laughing and joking but it is waiting for them to return that is the anxious part of it. They fight miles over the German lines and of course if they are hit or have their petrol tanks punctured they cannot get back.

> "On the day of the 20th[…] They went down to fifty feet over the German trenches and shot troops in shell holes, chased them into their dugouts and harried and demoralized them generally […] Some of the pilots paid the penalty and did not return but the Hun got such a dribbling that their noble sacrifice was justified […] I am not supposed to go over the lines myself but I don't think life would be worth living if I could not do so."

Three of SCdr Dallas' Pilots in action this day are:

– FSLt Edward William DESBARATS
(Montreal PQ) – POW

Desbarats has been two weeks on No. 1 Naval Squadron strength when he brings down his first German, sharing an enemy scout that falls completely out of control. But then, near Passchendaele, his Triplane N5459 is sent down. He has fallen under the same ordnance as **Robert McMillan** did the day before: that of *Jasta* 26's *Offizierstellvertreter* Fritz Kosmahl. Also taken prisoner,

Desbarats is incarcerated initially at Karlsrhue. He too is sent later to Holzminden and then Schweidnitz.

Kosmahl, the nine-victory Warrant Officer, sustains a stomach wound the following afternoon and will succumb to his injuries four days later.

– FSLt Ellis ANTHONY
(Maitland NS) – WIA

Conducting a strafing attack on ground troops near Zandvoorde, Anthony is hit but manages to nurse his 1 Naval Triplane N6300 back over the lines. The gunshot wound to his leg gives him a 'Blighty' for England and then a Canadian leave. Anthony has flown over the Western Front since December 1916 and is considered to be a very good scout pilot, with much fighting experience and two 'kills' to his credit. He is awarded an Admiralty gratuity of £81 for wound compensation.

E Anthony in CAF uniform 1920 – 1923   GWFM

Returning to England in early 1918, Anthony is employed flying home patrols out of the South Shields air station and will survive an engine fire and ditching in a Sopwith Strutter off Dungeness in July. He receives the Air Force Cross in January 1919 as recognition for a distinguished war service and will continue flying with the Canadian Air Force in the early 1920's.

– FSLt John Hilton WINN
(England) – MIA

An Englishman, Winn fails to return from low flying patrol. He has been involved in a fight with two enemy scouts and is never seen again. *Ltn* Wendelmuth of *Jasta* 8 claims the kill. Winn's 1 Naval Triplane N6292 is a former Naval 8 machine named '*Lily*' by her previous pilot—'because she was hard to get into.'

Although not a Canadian, Winn was an employee of the Bank of Montreal in London. His name is commemorated in the Bank's list of War Dead and is well worthy of being included in this manuscript.

20Sep17 – NUMBER 10 NAVAL

– FSLt Herbert James EMERY
(Edmonton)   MID

Tasked to attack German reinforcements on return flights over the lines, Emery especially heeds the orders and is Mentioned in Despatches: '... for taking part in general operations with conspicuous success; principally attacking enemy troops and transport from low altitudes.'

Although having only recently joined the unit at the end of July, Emery has already survived a crash on September 3rd and now, due to the high attrition rates for pilots on the Western Front, is flying as a Deputy Flight Commander. Described as 'Very Steady; Good Command' he will outlast the brutal year and be posted back to Home Establishment in January 1918.

– FSLt Edward Irvine BUSSELL
(Toronto) – MID

Also Mentioned in Despatches for firing at ground targets, Bussell has, by this time, been a 10 Naval pilot for just over a month. He will send down an Albatros D.III out of control three days hence, but his Camel B6216 is badly winged in the action and he crashes near Westroosebeke. Although having graduated as a 'very good pilot and very good and keen Officer', Bussell will become considered as 'Very erratic & uncertain', doubtless having been badly shaken by his crash and the continual low-level work. In January 1918 Bussell is returned to Eastchurch for

El Bussell, in CEF uniform
U o-f T

instructor duties. Later he flies with 97 RAF in the northwest of India.

– FSLt John Gerald 'Punk' MANUEL
(Edmonton) – Action

Since joining 10 Naval in early August, Manuel has flown the Triplane and brought down two enemy aircraft, both Albatros D.V fighters, for a double score on August 21st. Today, in one of the Squadron's new Camels, B3950, he crashes a German two-seater behind the German Lines in the Houthulst Forest. Strafing the enemy machine on the ground, he ensures that neither pilot nor observer escape alive. This is not the age of chivalry: had the observer survived, he could have succeeded in causing immense damage by ranging artillery shoots and calling-in barrages on Allied troops.

Manuel is one to know about such matters. He had joined the Canadian Field Artillery in October 1914 and served at the front with the 6th Howitzer Brigade. His Battery was Mentioned in Despatches in the Battle of St. Eloi and again during the Battle of the Somme, where Manuel was wounded. Leaving hospital in March 1917, he transferred to the RNAS and is now proving to be a fearsome airborne fighter.

In a raid conducted six days after downing the two-seater, Manuel drops two bombs on Abeele Aerodrome, damaging at least one machine. He then dives on, eliminating a machine gun firing at him, and attacks and scatters a party of 500 infantry, firing 250 rounds in all. He is awarded DSC on the 10th of December for the airfield action. Yet, despite the honours and ceremony at Buckingham Palace, the day turns bittersweet: Manuel learns that his older brother Larry, a pilot with the Royal Flying Corps, has been killed in action.

While on high patrol over Menin on the 18th of February 1918, five Albatros scouts appear. In the general engagement that follows, 'Punk' Manuel will score his fifth Victory.

In November 1964, **Raymond Collishaw** wrote: 'Manuel became a Flight Commander, 'C' Flight, and he was highly regarded by his fellow pilots and I think that we should know much more about him today. One has to recollect that Manuel's air fighting career, in 1917, embraced a period of extraordinary difficulty for No. 10 Naval Squadron: whence the squadron suffered some 59 casualties in the months June to October 1917. A man has to be of a robust character when he sees his pals follow, one after the other, into the maw of oblivion and at the same time, give forth his own best effort.' *(Read 10Jun18)*

– FSLt Herbert Seton BROUGHALL, MC
(Toronto; b. ENG) – POW

In a low-level bombing of motor transport and strafing of troop masses, Broughall's machine is shot to pieces. He crash-lands near the lines but his Sopwith Camel

B6226 does not come down near enough to the Allied trenches. He is captured shortly after his heavy landing in the shell-pocked Houthulst woods north east of Ypres.

Broughall is a graduate of Toronto's Upper Canada College and was attending Toronto University when war broke out. He has seen front-line service as a Lieutenant with the Royal Sussex Regiment and earned the British Army's Military Cross for gallantry in July 1916.

HS Broughall, in British Army uniform

UCC

By the time of his incarceration, he had been flying in active service for almost two months with 10 Naval.

In 1919, Broughall will begin a military career with the Royal Air Force and serve in South Russia, earning two Czarist decorations: the St.Anne 3rd Class with Swords and the St.Stanislaus 3rd Class with Swords. In 1924 he wins a DFC for service in Kurdistan. Commander of 12 Squadron RAF in 1935, Broughall will complete his service years as a Group Captain during World War II.

22Sep17 – FSLt Arthur Chadwick BURT (Brantford ON) – Ditched

During a fleet-protection overflight for monitors bombarding Ostende, a hostile seaplane is observed spotting and directing return fire. Burt and his two accompanying No. 4 Naval aircraft bring the EA machine down in the water. The German observer is killed, but not before he scores a hit. With engine pressure falling fast, Burt is obliged to ditch near the downed seaplane. His Camel B6213 soon sinks. Luckily for Burt and less so for his opponent, both are fished out of the water by a Royal Navy destroyer. Burt

AC Burt

RAeC Trust

will finish the war as a Captain (Flight Commander), RAF, with four victories.

Coming up just short of an Ace-making victory is not from lack of effort on Burt's part. Just recently, on the 14th of June, he had launched out of Manston in Triplane N5390, an experimental type with a 150-hp Hispano-Suiza engine and twin machine guns, in an attempt to catch Gotha raiders. A total of 74 aircraft from the RFC and the RNAS went up from various airfields but were incapable of reaching the altitude of the Gotha squadron. On another Anti-Gotha Patrol on August 13th, Burt attacked one of the intruders off North Foreland but both of his Vickers guns jammed after only thirty rounds. To add to the embarrassment, a centre section wire on his Camel B3844 snapped—possibly hit by an enemy bullet—and he had to make a forced landing.

22Sep17 – FLt Norman Ansley MAGOR (Westmount PQ), &
– FSLt Charles Edward Stafford LUSK (Toronto) – U-boat

Conducting an early morning patrol, the crew on Curtiss flying boat 8695 sight a large hostile submarine. Magor, accompanied by Lusk and two airmen, drops a pair of 230 lb bombs on the U-boat. The weapons explode just behind the conning tower and the boat submerges leaving a quantity of wreckage afloat.

CES Lusk

RAeC Trust

Magor's Operations Report reads: 'The submarine was observed to heel over and sink'. At first, the boat was thought to be UC72, but that vessel had been sunk two days earlier. The recipient of Magor's bombs was possibly UB32, which had failed to return from North Sea operations about this time.

On the 29th of September, again flying out of Felixstowe and with the same crew, Magor bombs yet another U-boat north of Dunkirk, but this time the weapons fall wide. However, for his services rendered in the September 22nd action, Magor is awarded the DSC. The Citation reads: 'Destroyed an enemy submarine

29 miles north by west of Ostend'. The Large America H8 aircraft that the crew have flown on these missions are part of an order of 50 built at the Curtiss aircraft plant in Toronto and shipped overseas to England. *(Read 24Apr18)*

23Sep17 – FSLt Gordon Stuart HARROWER, MID (Montreal) – WIA

When information is received that large formation of twenty-two EA is near the lines, fourteen aircraft of 3 Naval are sent to engage them. This comprises the total strength of serviceable aircraft in the Squadron. A general melee ensues and in the tumultuous swirl of aircraft, it becomes difficult to discern what is happening. There are a number of indecisive fights, the EA either diving or spinning away, but Harrower and another pilot each shoot down an EA completely out of control. This is Harrower's second victory, having previously driven down an EA on 27th of May; but in today's commotion, he is badly wounded. His serious injuries will hospitalize him until November, and upon release he is goes on extended Canada Leave.

Harrower, of McGill University, had learned to fly at the Stinson School in Texas and has previously been awarded a Mention in Despatches 'For very good work while serving with 3 Naval in the Field.' His Confidential Report states: 'Given every satisfaction. Daring Fighter, G.Pilot. Recom's for Promotion.' Returning from Canada in April 1918, Harrower will be resurveyed as fit for Home Service only. Promoted to Captain in the RAF, he takes his Release in August 1918 with the standard gratuity of £81.

23Sep17 – A/FCdr Stearne Tighe EDWARDS (Carleton Place ON) – ACE/DSC

Edwards is leading a Hostile Aeroplane Patrol with 9 Naval when he crashes an enemy Albatros scout into the sea. In a successive engagement, he spots another Albatros at very close range to the tail of one of his Flight. As the German pilot begins to shoot, Edwards attacks from above: the enemy machine falls on its back, enters into a vertical dive, and at 8,000 feet, the wings break off the doomed aircraft. These are Edwards' fourth and fifth victories, and they earn him a DSC.

After his medal is Gazetted in November, Edwards takes an earned Canada leave. He has been on Active Service since April 1916 and had been another of the original members of 3 Wing when it formed at Detling. His first victory was in a Sopwith Strutter with the Wing.

Following a Christmas at home Edwards will return to flying duties with 9 Naval in late January and commence a tally of victories with a final 'bag' of seventeen.

A railroad construction worker at the attempted Port Nelson harbour on Hudson's Bay when war broke out, 'Stearns' had walked 200 miles to the railhead between there and Winnipeg in order to enlist. *(Read 16May18)*

23Sep17 – FLt William Clarence JOHNSTON (Copper Cliff ON) – WIA

After three months of hazardous front-line flying Johnston sustains a bullet wound to the leg and damage to his 10 Naval Camel B3912. Crashing near Vlamertinghe., he takes leave of his squadron for a Canadian recovery.

24Sep17 – FSLt Ronald McNeill KEIRSTEAD (Wolfville NS) – ACE/DSC

In an action that is later recognized for conspicuous gallantry in aerial combat, FSLt Keirstead single-handedly engages four enemy aeroplanes. He destroys two of them for his fourth and fifth victories. On the 21st of October, flying his same 4 Naval Camel, N6370, he will score another double. During that engagement between British and German formations, he shoots the wings off one machine then dives on enemy scouts attacking a friendly aircraft, sending a second hostile down. For the actions on these two dates, Keirstead will be awarded the DSC in January 1918.

A graduate of the Ontario Agricultural College, the young Nova Scotian will rise to Flight Commander with a total of 13 victories and survive the War.

RM Keirstead

RAeC Trust

In the Second World War, Keirstead works as a Canadian Munitions Inspector only to be blinded by an accidental explosion during the demonstration of a new shell-striker device.

24Sep17 – FLt Harold Halsey ARUNDEL (Toronto) – Turret Ships

As a seaplane pilot with 2 Wing in the Eastern Mediterranean, Arundel was considered: 'A very keen pilot, will be good on fast machines.' Now retrained as a Sopwith Camel Turret Pilot, he will see service in two ships over the next few months: the Battle Cruiser *Renown* and the Dreadnought *Malta*. But by the end of January 1918, Arundel is brought down by Malaria and an indulgence pass to Canada has to be arranged.

HH Arundel

RAeC Trust

As a new concept, Turret pilots operate their aircraft from a planked flying-off deck constructed atop the guns of the 'Big Ships'. The duty is fraught with hazard as there is no return landing to be made onto these vessels. If an airfield is not within range, the aircraft must be ditched alongside the ship and the pilot pray for a sprightly lifeboat crew rescue.

25Sep17 – Alexander Forsyth MacDONALD, MID (London ON) – WIA

In Camel B3920 on a low-level ground attack over Passchendaele, 'Sandy' MacDonald suffers a gunshot wound to his left buttock. He crashes east of Ypres and manages to get away from the wreck. By now he is somewhat of an expert at forced landings, as this is his sixth since joining 9 Naval Squadron in May.

Two months earlier, in July, he had perforated an eardrum and was sent to Chatham Naval Hospital. While there, he incurred an 'Expression of TL's displeasure' by breaking his leave; by making statements as to hospital food; and for the insubordinate tone of a letter to the Surgeon General. MacDonald's future propensity for writing has no doubt taken root.

Returned Fit for Duty in early September, MacDonald is Mentioned in Despatches for his aggressive low-level trench strafing. Now shot from below, he again finds himself in hospital, this time at Greenwich. In January

1918 he is granted Canada Leave to get back in shape, returning to England as an instructor pilot.

During the 1920's MacDonald will serve as a Flight Lieutenant in the new Royal Canadian Air Force and, at the start of the Second World War, is the Chief Instructor in air navigation at No. 20 Elementary Flying School. He composes a classic flight training manual titled *'From the Ground Up'* in 1941—it has been constantly updated and is still in use today as a private and commercial pilot study guide in Canada. MacDonald completes his second war service as a Trans-Atlantic Ferry Command pilot.

26Sep17 – FSLt Ralph Edward CARROLL (Toronto) – MID

Carroll is Mentioned by Brigade reports for good work in ground and contact patrol during important infantry and artillery operations. He has scored three, possibly four victories.

RE Carroll

Paul Donnellan

In two months' time, on the 23rd of November, he will be injured in the crash of his 10 Naval Camel B6388. A concussion and wounds to forehead sends him on sick leave to Canada. While at home he is further hospitalized and on release is retained on Special Services in the Dominion in order to work with the Royal Air Force training buildup during 1918.

28Sep17 – FSLt Kenneth Vincent TURNEY (Trenton, ON) – KIC – Midair

Turney's 4 Naval Camel B3867, and Camel B3934 of FSLt EJK Buckley collide near Nieuport off the Belgian coastline. The aircraft fall, locked together, from 15,000 feet. Both pilots are killed.

Turney had scored two victories in his machine, a presentation aircraft from the British crown colony of Basutoland (now Lesotho) named *'Mokhachane.'*

28Sep17 – A/SCdr Ronald Francis REDPATH, CdG (Montreal) – Mutiny?

Today is Redpath's first as Acting Squadron Commander of 10 Naval. The unit has been decimated and rebuilt several times over the summer and now Australian CO BC Bell has been taken ill and sent to hospital. Tasked to send out a low level bombing and strafing attack on Rumbeke aerodrome, Acting SCdr Redpath duly dispatches six Camels. All return and report good results but have bombed from 2,000 to 3,000 feet. The RFC Wing Commander complains, as he feels that the results would have been better at low level. When he telephones orders for another strike, Redpath replies that his "pilot's aren't for it."

RF Redpath

RAeC Trust

The Wing Commander immediately visits the Squadron to confirm that Redpath is correctly representing his aircrew. He is told that they do not consider the probable results as being worthy of the risk to machines and pilots. Sensibly, as an outright refusal would bring dire consequences, the Wing Commander does not order out the mission. RFC HQ is notified however and 10 Naval is discretely transferred to another RFC Brigade and then back to the RNAS by November.

New CO Redpath may be guilty of excessive protection of his troops but he is no mutineer. He graduated a pilot in April 1916 and flew with 3 Wing, where he was recognized as having: 'Ability to command VGI being steady and reliable pilot. Successful flight leader.' On the 12th of October 1916 Oberndorf Raid Redpath had kept his flight from getting too far off course and drifting into Switzerland by aggressively taking the lead. His French Croix de Guerre avec Palme had been conferred by the President of the French Republic at a ceremony in April 1917 and Redpath was promoted to take over 10 Naval, based on his August 1918 report of being: 'Specially recommended for promotion. Very steady & capable Officer. Thoroughly able in command.'

Later, in November, when his Squadron CO returns from hospital, Redpath will be reduced to the rank of Acting Flight Commander and sent to Cranwell as an instructor. However, just prior to this, an October Confidential Report states that Redpath is a: 'Daring Pilot & Flight Leader. Can handle men.' By the spring of 1918, his 'Great zeal & ability' is recognized. He will become the Commanding Officer of 209 RAF in post-war days, and upon returning home, is made a Wing Commander and Director in the new Canadian Air Force.

29Sep17 – FSLt Hubert Haddler COSTAIN (Brantford ON) – Action

Costain graduated and joined 7 Naval bomber squadron at Dover in mid September, just as the German recommence raids on London. On this night, the enemy sends over several aircraft against the British capital; Waterloo Station suffers considerable damage and seventeen civilians are killed. As an immediate counter, 7 Naval launches their Handleys to bomb St. Denis Westrem Aerodrome and the returning Gothas find their home base severely mauled.

An English Gunner (Bill Hall) flew on this bombing mission and noted a new officer 'up front having a look around.' This was Costain, his future Pilot, and in his diary Hall would write about their numerous bombing raids together. He had inherited an aviator noted as being 'Very Steady, a good and keen Officer.'

On the 26th of February 1918, in aircraft 3136, Hall will note: 'Attempted bombing raid on Freves with ten 112lb bombs but the weather was fairly dud and as the pilot turned queer we landed after flying around the drome'. Costain had caught the Spanish Influenza that laid many squadron personnel low. Fortunately, his case is diagnosed as a 'Slight Flu' by the Hospital at Etaples and Costain is back flying in April with 216 Squadron RAF.

30Sep17 – FSLt William James BEATTIE (Stratford, ON) – KIC

Within one day of joining his first operational squadron, 1 Naval, Beattie is lost. A wing on his Triplane comes adrift in flight and the machine crashes just west of Bailleul. His CO, Dallas of Australia, reports: 'He went up to do a flight with another pilot and had looked at the country over which he would have to work. The other pilot landed but Beattie remained up in his machine to do a few practice evolutions and his machine collapsed. He fell about 4,000 feet and was killed almost on the spot… His body was taken to a clearing station and afterwards buried with naval honours.'

SCdr Dallas also writes to Beattie's mother: '...He had only joined this squadron the day before and was engaged in a practice flight when the accident happened. No person saw it happen but saw his machine coming down afterwards and perhaps he was attempting to perform some trick flying. It will be comforting to you to know that he suffered no pain and his body will be buried in a cemetery close to the aerodrome although I am not permitted to state the exact spot. The Squadron will look after his grave and I will later if possible let you know where it is...'

WJ Beattie, in CEF uniform

U of T

This letter is followed up by one from the Nursing Sister in Charge, No. 2 Casualty Clearing Station, BEF: '...I, myself went down to the Mortuary and laid him out for burial so that although so far from home he had a woman's hands to attend to him at the last. By now you will have received my letter sent off a few days after his death, enclosing a lock of his hair...' D. McPherson, Sister Queen Anne Nursing Service.

Beattie had visited his grandfather in Scotland during a leave whilst in flight training in England. His mother asks that his body may be sent to Scotland but as per British Expeditionary Force Standing Orders, this regretfully cannot be approved.

In July 1920, in response to a University of Toronto request for information in preparation of their War Record book, Mrs. AA Beattie writes of her son: '...He was then transferred to No. 1 Squadron on the 29th and on the 30th as you will see by the enclosed letters that was the finish of my poor boy. He was killed 22 days before he had reached his 20th birthday.

'...Letters enclosed will give you all the details of his death but please take care of them and return them all to me as soon as you are finished with them as they are all I have.'

30Sep17 – FLt Hugh Reston AIRD, MID (Toronto) – POW Constantinople

Flying as Second Pilot to FLt John Alcock (of later Trans-Atlantic fame), Aird is enroute from his Mediterranean airfield to bomb Constantinople when their Handley Page bomber 3124 is hit by AA fire, destroying the port propeller. Forced to alight in the waters of the Gulf of Xeros near Suvla Bay, the three

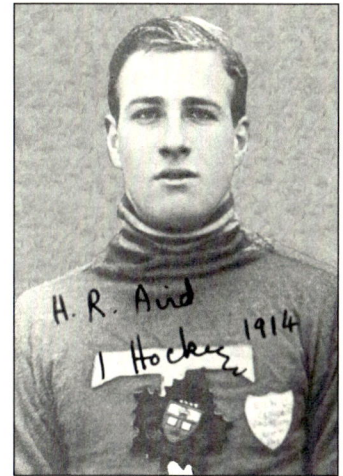

HR Aird

U of T

airmen float for two hours but their Very light flares fail to attract the attention of British destroyers. Eventually, when the aircraft begins to sink, they strike out for land and lie concealed during the night. Exhausted, cold, and hungry, they give themselves up the following day. Stripped of everything, even their boots, they are force-marched to a Turkish encampment. Finally, given slippers and ragged uniforms they are transported by ox-cart to Chanak.

A nearby German Air Force squadron tries in vain to have the prisoners transferred to their care. When that fails, a German airman tosses a note over Mudros airfield promising safe passage for any aircraft dropping gear for the three naval officers. As the English Wing Commander Smyth-Piggott prepares to deliver the parcel himself in a Sopwith Camel, ground crew sailors bet on his return—one half stating that: 'He won't come back.'—the other side claiming: 'Bet'cher he will!' In the event, not a shot is fired: the Commander makes the drop, waves to the Turks, and returns safely. Now more properly clothed, the captured crew is sent to a detention camp at Kedos in the Anatolia Mountains for the duration of the war. (The third crewman is Observer Lt SJ Wise of England).

Aird is the son of Sir John Aird, General Manager, Canadian Bank of Commerce. A forestry student at the University of Toronto, Hugh was a member of the Blues hockey team and the Toronto Granites, forerunners of the Toronto Maple Leafs. Conn Smythe, a classmate and later President of Maple Leaf Gardens, describes Aird as 'one of the greatest left-wingers of all time.'

Having joined the Eaton Machine Gun Company early in the War, Aird transferred to the RNAS and was subsequently appointed to No. 2 Wing in the Mediterranean. He earned a Mentioned in Despatches on the 23rd of February 1917 for attacks on Buck Bridge. Operating under heavy AA fire, he dropped three 100lb bombs from 1,500 feet, rendering the structure unsafe for traffic.

OCTOBER 1917

06Oct17 – FLt Charles William BAILEY (Winnipeg) – Ditched

Out of NAS Westgate on patrol in Short 184 N1278, Bailey and his crewman AM Alderton are in the South Falls area when their engine fails at about 500 feet. They descend somewhat precipitately near the South Knock buoy and release pigeons No. 2594 and No. 15123 with messages of their situation. Pigeons are assigned to aircraft in pairs, an experienced bird together with a 'squeaker'. Luckily in this case, the aircraft descent is spotted by HMS *Clacton Belle*, which takes the crew on board and then tries to tow the seaplane to Sheerness. The speed of tow and state of the sea prove too much for the machine however, and it overturns and is lost. Bailey will complete his War as the Officer Commanding 330 Flight, 231 Squadron, at Felixstowe.

07Oct17 – Marmaduke Pritchard PEARSON (Guelph ON) – DOJ

The two Pearson brothers from Guelph, Ontario, transfer from the Canadian Expeditionary Forces to the Air Services. Older brother 'Duke' opts for the RNAS and his younger sibling 'Mike' enters the RFC. In later life, Lester Bowles 'Mike' Pearson will become the Prime Minister of Canada. He recalls in his memoirs that there was 'Something about a Scottish Nursing Sister in Ayrshire' that influenced his elder brother's choice of service.

Duke, having served as a Lieutenant with the Canadian Field Artillery in France, will graduate from Cranwell in March of 1918 as a VGI Officer and is recommended for Scouts. In 1919 he returns to Canada with his Glasgow bride. They later immigrate to the United States where Duke enters the leather trade in Boston.

Of interest, Duke's brother Mike had served in Salonika during 1915 and 1916 as a Corporal with the Canadian

Army Medical Corps. Becoming an infantry Lieutenant in August 1917, he then joined the RFC. Injured at Hendon in December 1917 he returned to Canada as a ground school instructor.

08Oct17 – SLt Obs Wm Oliver Fielding HARDING (Canada) – Court of Inquiry

An unusual hearing is held aboard HMS *Phoserphine* in Mesopotamia. Harding is on charge for the accidental wounding of a fellow officer. The Court of Inquiry: 'Considers revolvers should not have been used from a Motor Car for sporting purposes. It is not thought necessary that further disciplinary action need be taken against this Officer.'

Harding is an Observer and has been serving with Number 14 Kite Balloon Section in country since November 1916. His 'dune buggy' hunting escapade is put aside and he is strongly recommended for promotion one month after the Inquiry. The former Canadian Expeditionary Force Corporal will complete his war service as a Captain, RAF.

09Oct17 – FLt Melville Cornelius WOOD (Winnipeg) – KIC HMS *Empress*

In what should have been a routine aircraft launch, four Short 184 machines are hoisted out from HMS *Empress* off Famagusta, Cyprus. The mission is to attack Adana in Turkey. The ship's log reports: 'A slight swell made it difficult for machines to leave the water, and in two cases bombs had to be dropped in order to enable machines to rise.

MC Wood

RAeC Trust

'No. 8018, FLt MC Wood, after some difficulty in getting off the water, and being apparently unable to climb above 700 – 800 feet, was observed to drop some of his bombs, and then return to the ship and alight, when the remaining bombs exploded, blowing the machine to pieces, and instantly killing the pilot.

'In consequence of this, No 1091, which had been

detailed to accompany 8018, returned to ship, and after patrolling for submarines while the wreckage of 8018 was examined, was hoisted aboard.'

Wood is given a burial at sea and his name commemorated on the Chatham Naval Memorial.

13Oct17 – A/FCdr Arthur Roy BROWN (Carleton Place ON) – ACE

An Acting Flight Commander with 9 Naval, 'Brownie' achieves his fifth victory. Before going on leave at the end of the month he will bring down yet another German machine. Gazetted for the DSC in November, the citation mentions his six victories and also a 'rescue operation'. In midst of a large dogfight in September he had to break away with both guns jammed. Observing another pilot attempting to fend off four EA, Brown had been unhesitant in diving to the rescue, whipping through the Germans, scattering them, and providing the English pilot with an escape.

His is a well-earned Canada Leave. One of the Carleton Place 'Hobo Quartet', Brown had broken his back in an Avro 504 crash at Chingford in May 1916. Hauled unconscious from the wreck, he was not surveyed fit until August that year, but graduated as a pilot one month later.

Although he has to revert from his Acting rank to that of Flight Lieutenant while in Canada, Brown will be substantiated as a Flight Commander on his return to 9 Naval in 1918. *(Read 21Apr18)*

21Oct17 – FSLt Anthony George Allen SPENCE (Toronto) – ACE

AGA Spence
RAeC Trust

Spence scores his fifth victory in 1 Naval Triplane N5449. He had graduated from Cranwell the previous March a 'VGI' Pilot and seems destined to become another great Canadian Naval Ace. However, a nosedive-type accident in November will inflict contusions to his right leg, arm, and shoulder. Spence is duly sent on Canada recovery leave, and will be again fit for Active Service in February 1918. His Squadron is now equipped with the Camel and Spence raises his victory tally to nine before being posted to Home Establishment for Instructing in May. He spends the remainder of the war at the School of Special Flying, Gosport, and will be demobilized in February 1919 with, most surprisingly, no Decorations.

21Oct17 – FSLt William Norman FOX (Toronto) – WIA

On a dawn offensive patrol, six Camels of B Flight, 10 Naval, encounter twelve Albatros scouts. In the ensuing engagement there are no decisive results but Fox, in aircraft B3919, receives a serious gunshot wound to his right leg. He is given long leave to Canada but the wound is substantial and in March 1918 the Military Medical Board in Ottawa will recommend further treatment. Fox had served six weeks in 10 Naval.

21Oct17 – FSLt Wilfred Austin 'Wilf' CURTIS (Haverlock ON) – ACE

During a combined attack with two other aircraft, Curtis sends down an enemy machine in flames. Twenty minutes later, he follows another enemy scout from 10,000 to 2,000 feet, sending it into a vertical dive that ends in a crash. These actions in 10 Naval Camel B6202 will form the basis for a DSC citation Gazetted in December.

WA Curtis, in CEF uniform
RAeC Trust

Curtis had a shaky start with the RNAS. A 2nd Lieutenant with the Canadian Essex Fusiliers, he transferred to naval aviation in August 1916. That November, he crashed at Ancaster, England, in Curtiss machine 8857. The accident left him suffering from shock, with wounds to the head and face. He was sent on Canada leave and once back in Cranwell graduated a VGI Pilot and 'Exceptionally keen & hardworking Officer.' His achievement of Ace status today will grow to 13 victories. *(Read 23Jan18)*

24Oct17 – FSLt Harold Cowasjee GOOCH
(Montreal; b. India) – INT Holland

During a routine patrol out of Felixstowe, Curtiss H-12 8693 comes down in the North Sea near Deurloo, Holland, due to an engine failure. The machine sinks off Weskaelle but will later be recovered by the Dutch. The Captain, FLt W. Perham, his Second Pilot Gooch and two Naval Airmen Mechanics are rescued by a Netherlands motor torpedo boat and landed at Flushing, Zeeland. They are interned by neutral Holland for the remainder of the war.

Gooch is a McGill student who entered the RNAS through the Department of Naval Service in Ottawa in late 1916 and graduated on seaplanes at Calshot in May 1917. Although born in the East Indies, Gooch is 'of pure European descent' and the son of 'natural born British subjects'. The Regulations for the Special Entry of Officers into the RNAS are very solid on this point; stating that 'In doubtful cases the burden of clear proof will rest upon the candidate'.

HC Gooch
RAeC Trust

The use of the Royal Canadian Navy against the Indian immigrant vessel *Komagata Maru* at Vancouver during the summer of 1914 displayed the strong but simplistic racist view held by most Anglophone peoples at this time. Rudyard Kipling's poem 'The White Man's Burden' reinforced the imperialistic sense of an obligation to rule over other cultures.

24Oct17 – FSLt John Elswood Chaffey HOUGH
(Winnipeg) – MIA

Only two weeks on squadron, Hough is reported Missing In Action when he fails to return from a patrol supporting a Houthulst Forest ground action. His Triplane N5476, is reported as last seen east of the Lines near Ghelavelt, where his 1 Naval flight dove on a formation of enemy scouts. *Ltn* Walter Blume of *Jasta* 26 enters a 'Tripe' combat claim—his fifth kill. Hough, aged 19, is named to the Arras Memorial. The German, Blume, will survive the war with 28 victories.

27Oct17 – FSLt Walter Morse CLAPPERTON
(Toronto; b. USA) – WIA

In an aerial combat with Vztw Kurt Wusthoff of *Jasta* 4, Clapperton's 1 Naval Triplane N5455 becomes the German Ace's 22nd victory. Clapperton sustains gunshots to his left side, which fracture his humerus and severely wounds his thigh. In late December, the hospital at Gillingham in Kent will advise that he is progressing slowly and that the condition still gives cause of anxiety. However, by September 1918, Clapperton will have recovered and be back in action with his old Naval unit, now 201 Squadron, RAF.

Wusthoff will go on to raise his tally to twenty-seven, and be awarded the 'Blue Max', before being similarly wounded and captured in mid-1918. The German's wounds are much more severe and it is not until 1922 that he regains the ability to walk. Wusthoff returns to flying but is killed in the summer of 1926 while participating in an aerobatic display at Dresden in honour of Germany's first Ace, Max Immelmann.

27Oct17 – FSLt William Moffat DAVIDSON
(Victoria) – INJ

A crash on landing at Petite Synthe, Dunkirk, leaves Davidson critically injured. He is admitted to No. 7 Casualty Clearance Station with a fracture to the base of his skull, and when stabilized nearly a month later, he is embarked for Chatham Hospital in England with a 'Mental Derangement.' Davidson had been flying his Naval 8 Flight Commander's aircraft, Camel N6378, when the accident occurred. This is the aircraft in which his Australian flight leader, R.A. Little, DSO, scored his first nine Camel kills, numbers 29 to 37, out of an eventual 47 total victories. (The leading Aussie Ace of the War, Robert A Little, DSO&Bar, DSC&Bar is KIA 27May18. His Grandparents resided in Toronto).

Davidson had arrived in the Squadron in early July and his September report read: 'Inexperienced at present. Very stout-hearted Scout Pilot, improving daily.' With this injury taking him out of service, his CO writes that Davidson: '…Has conducted himself to my entire satisfaction. A good & plucky pilot.'

In March 1918, his injuries will have been improved enough to admit him to the Peebles Royal Navy Hospital in Scotland and then onwards to Canada. Indeed plucky, Davidson will return by late June for duties as an instructor.

27Oct17 – FSLt George Heaven MORANG
(Toronto ON) – MIA

GH Morang

UCC

Missing in Action, Morang may have been shaken up by a crash the day before, and not quite up to the mark. Shortly after takeoff, he had returned to exchange his aircraft and then crashed on a rushed departure to catch up with his flight. Today, his machine, Camel N6371, is seen going down in a vertical flame northeast of Dixmunde. Out of an encounter with six Albatros of *Jasta 36, Ltn* Hans Bohning, makes the victory claim, his fourth of an eventual seventeen.

Morang had only recently been commissioned and had been in 10 Naval for just five days. While at Cranwell he was reported to the Commodore: 'for the offence of drunkenness and insubordination to his Superior officer.' Deprived of two months' seniority, Morang's promotion was withheld until early October.

The Barvarian, Bohning, will die in a gliding accident in 1934 during the secret buildup of the new Nazi Luftwaffe.

NOVEMBER 1917

03Nov17 – Handley Page Bomber Crash

HP Number 3116 bursts into flames just before landing at Manston Fighter Training Station. Three Officers are killed and three are severely injured: two Canadians are involved in the crash:

– FSLt Joseph Hesquith St. JAMES
(Edelson Junction PQ) – KIC

French-Canadian St. James had graduated from Cranwell in June and been recommended for Scouts as being 'Very Keen Indeed.' However he showed no aptitude for the small machines and was discharged to heavy-bomber training. This change of training proves fatal today.

JH StJames

RAeC Trust

Before entering the RNAS in December 1916, St. James was the owner-proprietor of the Dominion Motor Company of Montreal. An only son, his parents live in St Constant, Quebec.

(*Some lists show his name as Joseph Hesquith St.James DeBEAUVAIS*)

– PFO Vyvian Holcombe HERVEY
(Calgary) – INJ

Among the badly burned survivors is Hervey, a Probationary Flying Officer, who was along for a familiarization ride in the big machine. It will take a period of recovery at Aberdeen, Scotland, before Hervey is resurveyed fit for duty. He will go on to graduate from Cranwell in April 1918 with full honours of VGI Pilot and Officer: 'A very keen & capable pilot & should make a good fighter.'

VH Hervey, 'Camera Gun Practice - Freiston, 8Apr – 31 May 1918'

FAAM, B 0191A/0033

Vivian Hervey is the younger brother of Flight Commander **Gerry Hervey** and, following his brother's lead, does indeed make a good fighter pilot. Assigned to 56 Squadron RAF on SE5a scouts, he is wounded in August but returns to score a victory in September.

Captain Vyvian Hervey will himself be a Flight Commander in the last few weeks of the War.

05Nov17 – FSLt Andrew Austin CAMERON (Shelburne ON) – First Victory

Flying 10 Naval Camel N6341, Cameron scores his first victory. After sending down an Albatros scout out of control, the former Queens University student proudly writes about his experience in a letter to his father. The equally proud parent then forwards the letter onward to their local newspaper where a description of the exploit is published under the headline:

> *'AN AIR ENCOUNTER':*
>
> 'The squadron was about 10,000 feet in the air when it crossed the German lines. They were attacked by eight German planes from a height of about 12,000 feet. Four of them got on the tail of the leader of the British fliers. Austin tackled one of them and gave him some machine gun treatment. The Hun took a vertical nose dive with his engine running. Austin followed to an elevation of 2,000 feet, firing as he went. Here the German stalled his engine and another burst of machine gun fire sent him down sideways and he fell well within the British lines.
>
> 'Austin's machine was by this time going so fast that when he pulled it out of the dive the great force of the wind broke the main spar in the centre and the lower right wing buckled up and was only held by the fabric covering it. However, he managed to land safely, although far away from his own aerodrome. Not being able to get word of his safety back to his own camp that day, he was reported missing, and just got back 'home' in time to prevent word to that effect being cabled his father. All the British patrol returned safely, and although the flight's leader's machine was pretty badly shot to pieces, he was not touched himself.' *Orangeville Banner, 03Jan18.*

On the 18th of January, just three days after an engine failure and subsequent successful forced-landing in Camel B6380, Cameron attempts a turn at insufficient speed in the same aircraft and spins in from 200 feet. Sustaining a possible fracture to the base of the skull, his injuries are serious and will require a lengthy recovery period.

Following recuperation in Canada, a May 1918 medical board survey will declare Cameron fit for 'Observer Duties Only'. He nearly does not survive the war: on the anniversary of his November 1917 victory, and

only six days before the Armistice, his aircraft is shot up during aerial combat but his pilot manages to get to ground safely.

06Nov17 – FSLt Hubert Peter 'Bert' SALTER (Ottawa) – MIA/WIA/POW

A new Strutter pilot with 2 Naval, Salter's machine N5081, is shot down by Lombartzyde Flak Unit 514. He recounts:

> "I got lost owing to the clouds and fog and wandered over the lines and was hit by anti-aircraft ground fire. The machine was badly wrecked and why she didn't catch fire and burn to pieces is beyond me. Thanks to her crippled condition and also the clouds we were only hit once. We fell about 20 yards behind the German front trenches. My observer [HW White] was unwounded and I did not discover I was wounded, until I was being searched.
>
> "On the 9th I was taken to a base hospital and that evening operated on, and had a piece of iron weighing 3 or 4 oz taken from my right hip. The next day I was x-rayed and another piece was found, so on the 11th I was again operated on."

While a prisoner, Salter writes home that the treatment he receives has been the best, but in later years back in Canada he will state that he thought the doctor who operated on him was a butcher.

Officially declared Missing in Action, it will be mid-January 1918 before Slater's anxious family learns through the Geneva Red Cross that their son is a Prisoner of War. The months of stress and strain are devastating on his mother's health and she is doubtless immensely relieved to finally receive a letter from her boy reassuring her that all is well and that he is now in the *Offizier-Kriegsgefangenenlager* (Fallen Airman Prison Camp) at Karlsruhe:

> "When I arrived here, I found half a dozen R.N. pilots that I had trained with in England, also about the same number from Ottawa, two of whom had been schoolmates of mine, so you see I was not unknown."

11Nov17 – FSLt David Ross KERR
(Westmount PQ) – KIC

A flying accident in an Avro 504 takes the life of former McGill University student Kerr. The twenty-year-old had recently graduated from Cranwell and was undergoing advanced training at the Manston Fighting School when the fatal mishap occured.

DR Kerr

RAeC Trust

12Nov17–A/FCdr George Leonard TRAPP, MID
(New Westminster BC) – KIA

(From 11Dec16, Brother S.V – KIC) The morning started well for naval Ace Trapp when he brings down his sixth enemy machine; but a second mission turns the tables. SCdr Redpath reports: 'In the afternoon of this day, Pilot was killed while engaging an enemy two-seater. His Machine B6341 was seen to break up in the air and came down in pieces near Fortheim.'

Twenty-three-year-old Trapp has been shot apart by *Oberleutnant* Bruno Justinius of *Jasta* 35. Two days later Redpath writes to the Commanding Officer XIV Wing RFC: 'I wish to bring to your notice the name of Acting Flt Cdr G.L. Trapp, who was killed in an air combat on the 12th instant, as especially deserving of the DSC. This pilot has rendered very valuable service since joining the Squadron on 14 July 1917. His

GL Trapp

MHR

work has always been most steady and consistent, and he has achieved a considerable number of material successes of which a note is appended.' In the field, R.F. Redpath, Commanding Officer Naval Squadron No. 10.

The Wing Commander sends the letter to Headquarters, RFC, with the comment 'Forwarded and strongly recommended. Acting Flt Cdr G. L. Trapp's example as a patrol leader was invaluable. He is a great loss.'

A reply is received on the 17th: 'It is regretted that with the exception of the Victoria Cross, posthumous honours are not awarded.'

A third son of Thomas John and Nellie Kathleen Trapp, Donavan Joseph, transfers from the CEF to the RFC after PPCLI service on the Western Front. Flying with Billy Bishop's 85 Squadron he is shot down inside the German lines and declared Missing in Action on 19Jul18.

Raymond Collishaw pays a sympathy visit to the family during a Canadian leave and meets his future bride, the Trapp brothers' sister Neita.

13Nov17 – A/FCdr John "Jack" ROBINSON, MID,
(Toronto), &

– SLt Obs William Stuart ANDERSON
(Winnipeg) – Crash

(From 07Feb16) Robinson is recognized as a highly experienced aviator, and has been employed part-time as personal pilot to Albert, King of Belgium. In today's spectacular crash during a routine patrol, 2 Naval Strutter 9419 out of Dunkirk, spins down from 5000 feet and smashes into a canal between piers at Gravelines. The aircraft is completely destroyed and the two aviators are badly bruised but extremely fortunate to be alive.

Already overdue for Canada Leave, Robinson is now held in hospital to recover from a head laceration. Normally, any acting rank must be dropped when going on leave; however, Robinson is confirmed as Flight Commander by the time he is fit for travel to home. When he returns in early April, 2 Naval has been renumbered 202 Squadron in the Royal Air Force Order of Battle. Rejoining his old unit, Robinson will go on to earn one of the new air medals, the Distinguished Flying Cross, in June, and will be appointed the squadron's Commanding Officer in January 1919. His war medals will also include the Belgian Order of Leopold and the French Croix de Guerre.

Observer Anderson had been a transfer to 2 Naval from the RNVR in May '17. He is considered an: 'exceptionally promising Officer and a very determined & capable Photographic Observer'. He, like Robinson, will proceed to Canada for recovery and medical survey; however, his future assignment as Adjutant to the RAF's Central

Flying Training School at Camp Borden, Ontario, will keep him in the Dominion.

'*Captain J Robinson – Our machine photographed for the King of Belgium*'
Robinson with 202 RAF DH-4 A7845

FAAM, Album 35

22Nov17 – FSLt Ralph Gordon MacALONEY (Halifax) – MIA

Out of South Shields, MacAloney goes missing and feared drowned off the Coast of Northumberland. A naval signal on the 26th sums up the situation: 'This Officer left in Short Seaplane N1233 to patrol War Channel to 10 Miles NE of Longstone. Carrier pigeon picked up at Robin Hood Bay on 24Nov with the message "S'plane sinking, will float a little longer, MacAloney." No date or time on message. Search was made, but it is not considered there is any chance of rescue now.' MacAloney and his Airman Mechanic, FT Sprules, are lost.

23Nov17 – FSLt Byron William BROACH (Maidstone SK) – Crash

Engine failure causes Broach to force land his Naval 8 Sopwith Camel at Neuville St. Vasst and he survives the unplanned arrival. Becoming a post-war bush pilot, the 'thoroughtly reliable & keen' Broach is not so fortunate in 1933 when he is killed in an aircraft crash.

Born in 1891, Broach was over age for new RNAS regulations

BW Broatch

RAeC Trust

in 1917 requiring aviators be age 25 or under. The Department of Naval Service in Ottawa however, accepted his application on account of his exceptional record as an athlete.

28Nov17 – FLt Edward Stanley BOYNTON (Toronto) – MID Macedonia

While at home on Canada Leave, Boynton learns that he has been Gazetted a MID for his work with 2 Wing in Macedonia. Badly hurt in a June 1916 motorcycle accident shortly after completing his flight training, Boynton did not take up duties on Mudros Island in the Eastern Mediterranean until November that year.

Even so, he had not in fact, recovered sufficiently from his injuries as noted in reports: 'Keen & able but has been hampered by ill health. Good pilot & excellent bomb-dropper.' Boynton is too ill to remain in the Mediterranean. Sent home that August, he will be admitted to hospital in Toronto by March of 1918. In 1919, Captain ES Boynton, MID, is released with a gratuity of £327 for his war-related injuries.

DECEMBER 1917

04Dec17 – FSLt James Anthony 'Tony' MORELL (Toronto) – Ditching/INJ

An engine failure forces Morell to ditch his Pup N6182 in the Channel near the Kentish Knock Light Vessel. Rescued by a British Motor Torpedo Boat, he returns to duty after a short recovery from slight injuries. His Dunkirk-based squadron, 12 Naval, is a training unit and Morell is soon transitioning to larger Sopwiths. Two weeks later, on the 18th of December, he crashes at the Petite Synthe aerodrome in Camel B5652, the aircraft is so badly damaged that it is deleted from naval inventory. Morell is in almost the same condition, sustaining multiple bruises, contusions to his left hip, both knees and a shoulder blade. Initially conveyed to Peebles Hospital in Scotland, he is next sent to Canada until March 1918.

This will be Morell's second Toronto homecoming due to aircraft related injuries. In April 1917, just days after graduating, he had crashed Avro 504 N5255 at Cranwell. Sustaining serious head injuries he had been carried unconscious from that wreckage.

09Dec17 – FSLt Norman Ivan LARTER, MID (Toronto) – MIA, HMS *Riviera*

Seaplane Carrier HMS *Riviera* posts a Failed-to-Return notification on Short 184 N1678. Larter and his Chief Petty Officer crewman, Robbins, are missing. By March 1918, they will be officially listed as drowned.

NI Larter

Larter had completed his Royal Aeronautical Certificate with the Curtiss Canada School in early November 1916. Further qualifying on water-borne machines at RNAS Calshot, he was then appointed to Riviera the following June. On October 15th, flying Short 184 N1588, Larter and the CPO crewman, R. Nicholson, bombed a U-boat seven miles east of Start Point. Again, on the 3rd of December, he attacked a U-boat. His Observer Sub Lt crewman in this instance, CSA Sivil, dropped two 100lb bombs. In both actions the results were inconclusive but even so, had earned Larter a Mention.

12Dec17 – FSLt John George CLARK (Irma AB) – POW

Flying Camel N6330 with 10 Naval, Clark, a graduate of the Agricultural College Vermilion, Alberta, is a long way from the Prairies. On an offensive sweep today, his Flight passes Nieuport, flying five miles from shore, and then re-crosses the coastline around Ghistelles and Dixmunde. There they encounter six Albatros scouts at 14,000 feet—and a hot fight ensues.

The English Flight Commander, NM Macgregor, spotting an EA shooting on Clark, fires on it. The EA appeared to have gone down, but the FCdr is unable to verify that, owing to his now being fired upon by another EA. Winnipegger FSLt **Hugh Maund** attacks the machine targeting his Commander, chasing it off

but not scoring. Clark, meanwhile, has been shot down and captured unwounded.

Clark has a most interesting tale to tell of his experience on the ground as the guest of the enemy. His patrol had encountered the pilots of *Jasta 7*, led by *Ltn* Josef Jacobs, who writes in his diary: 'In the afternoon a second start with my *Kette* [Flight]. We had some fights without results. Finally *Ltn* Degelow attacked a Sopwith single-seater which he probably shot down.

'In the evening the Sopwith pilot was our guest, a 2/Lt Clark; he's a Canadian, 20 years old and makes a very nice impression. Next morning the Canadian was moved off.'

From POW camp Holzminden, 'Clarky' writes back to his squadron mates:

> "I have no one to blame but myself. I fought with the enemy aircraft after the fight pulled out and I must say I was getting along fine until my engine cut out absolutely. If it had been on the other side I could have glided to the lines easily but with two EA on my tail I could only go down. When I landed it was amongst a bunch of German soldiers and of course I couldn't do a thing.

> "The pilot who forced me down (I got three bullets through the 3-ply) came and took me to their aerodrome that night and one would never have known that we had been trying to kill one another shortly before. Then in the morning I was shown the machine which brought me down and incidentally, they were putting on a new rudder because I had shot the old one up a little.

> "[…] I forgot to say that the pilot who brought me down gave me his 'bird' [wings] for mine, so I have a souvenir anyway, also a picture of his machine. They were certainly a fine bunch of fellows."

Of the Germans, *Ltn* Carl Degelow will live through the war and gain a total 30 victories. He is the last airman-recipient of the 'Orden Pour le Mérite' in November 1918. His book, *With the White Stag Through Thick and Thin,* is an aviation classic. *Jasta 7* commander, *Ltn* Jacobs also survives the war achieving 48 victories and the Blue Max Order. Jacobs becomes a manufacturer and refuses to join the Nazi party in the 1930's moving his plant to Holland. Post-1945, Jacobs provides an important source for First World War historians before passing away at Munich in 1978.

12Dec17 – FSLt Joseph Leonard MORAN
(Ottawa) – KIC

At NAS Calshot, Moran perishes in a Franco British Aircraft (FBA) accident. He was performing a practice flight on Seaplane N2680 in the immediate vicinity of the Station when he is observed to stall. The machine nosedives into the water with Moran falling out from a height of about 150 feet.

Rescued immediately by the Station Steam Boat Controller, resuscitation attempts are applied but to no avail: Moran had been killed instantly upon striking the water's surface. An investigation will determine that the accident was due to over confidence on the part of the pilot. He had graduated a VGI Pilot in September and also a: 'Very good Officer, extremely keen, should do well. Recommended for Seaplanes.' Age 23, his body is returned to Canada and interred at Ottawa's Notre Dame cemetery.

JL Moran

DeWolfe/M Pirie

15Dec17 – PFO Kenneth Porter KIRKWOOD
(Toronto) – Halifax Explosion

Travelling on the SS *Orduna* out of New York, Kirkwood arrives in Halifax Harbour to await convoy escort to England. It is just over a week since the French cargo ship SS *Mont-Blanc*, loaded with munitions collided with the Norwegian SS *Imo* carrying relief supplies for Belgium. The resulting fire had led to what remains today the world's largest accidental explosion:

> "For the past few hours … we have been slowly steaming up the harbour, and allowing a ghastly panorama of destruction to slide past our gaze. Far out on the rocks near the sea we saw the first wreck, a beached ship half-submerged. Then we passed one after another until the Belgian relief ship presented itself, and further up a remnant of a large boat we took to be the munition ship. Ships were sunk in the docks and only masts appeared through the debris. Railway cars lay upturned and wrecked along the shore. One freight car had either floated or been hurled to the opposite shore. On land buildings lay in ruins. Whole hillsides are devastated and denuded, and the straight intersecting roads alone indicate the blocks of houses that used to be. The spectacle is pitiful. There is very little snow here now but a damp mist hangs over the hills. The relief parties still at work in the ruins looking for victims or helping refugees.

> "We lay in Halifax, without being permitted to go ashore, for a couple of days, and then steamed silently out into the Atlantic."

In later life Kirkwood pursues a career with the Canadian Diplomatic Service culminating with an appointment as the High Commissioner to New Zealand in 1956

16Dec17 – FLt Joseph GORMAN
(Ottawa) – KIC Italy

Flying with 6 Wing, Padova, Italy, Gorman is killed while testing Camel B6215. His engine stops at 200 feet above ground level and he makes the fatal mistake of attempting to turn back towards the aerodrome. It is a classic error: running out of both flying speed and altitude by initiating a turn, the aircraft suddenly stalls, flicks into a spin, and falls—with no chance of recovery. Over an hour of effort is needed to free Gorman from the tangled wreckage. Carried to the British Military Hospital, he passes in the early hours of December 17th without regaining consciousness.

An 'Efficient Officer & Splendid Pilot. Capable of command & takes great interest in his work. Specially recommended for promotion'; Gorman's death is keenly felt by his unit. Aged 28, and leaving behind a wife in England, he is buried at the Maggiore Roman Catholic Cemetery near Padova, some twenty miles east of Venice. According to Canadian relatives visiting the Great War Flying Museum in Brampton, Ontario, during 2005, Gorman was killed stunting a Camel for the King of Italy, who attended the funeral. There is no mention of this in official records.

19Dec17 – FSLt Samuel Spalding RICHARDSON (Montreal PQ) – MIA Belgium

A McGill Science grad, Richardson is lost when his 5 Naval DH-4 6008, is shot down by *Obflgm* Albin Buhl of the *Seefrontstaffel*. RNAS Air Gunner RA Furby is also killed in the engagement, which takes place just off Blankenberghe, on the Belgian coast. Officially declared Missing, the two are listed together on the Chatham Naval Memorial. Richardson, 23 years old, had been on Squadron strength

SS Richardson

MHR

for only two weeks. HM Motor Launch 23 will recover wreckage from his machine as well as his flying cap and goggles but finds no trace of either body.

19Dec17 – PFO Harry Bambrick ARCHIBALD (Truro, NS) – FSLt

Upon graduation from the Cranwell Flying School, Archibald is granted leave to Canada. A Lieutenant with the 107th Battalion CEF, he had transferred to the RNAS in July 1917, after serving for twenty-one months with the Canadian Army, thirteen of which were spent on the front lines of Flanders. His new appointment as a Flight Sub Lieutenant, coupled with his time in the trenches, entitles him to one month's clear leave. Many Canadian Army-types transferring to the RNAS will be granted this privilege from their accumulated time overseas. However, with this sort of approval to proceed to Canada, individuals must arrange their own passage. Following gunnery school, Archibald does manage to make his way home to Nova Scotia in January 1918. He returns to take Handley Page bomber training at Manston prior to joining his operational squadron workup at Stonehenge.

Archibald's brother, Walter Roy, an RFC/RAF pilot, will be reported as Missing, presumed killed, in October of 1918.

19Dec17 – BUCKINGHAM PALACE

In a Palace ceremony, King George V presents two Canadian airmen with double Bars to their previously-won Naval Distinguished Service Cross:

– FCdr Joseph Stuart Temple FALL, DSC (Cobble Hill BC) – Two Bars to DSC

(From 11Apr17) In an unprecedented and never-to-be-repeated aviation first, Joe Fall becomes the only holder of a triple DSC for aerial gallantry. He had been the highest-scoring Allied pilot during the month of September 1917 and, ultimately, he will be Canada's second-highest naval ace of the First World War, having brought down thirty-six enemy aircraft and two observation balloons— all in 1917.

Following a Canadian leave in early 1918, Fall will return to England to instruct and test fly with the school of aerial gunnery and fighting. For this experimental work he will be awarded a new decoration, the Air Force Cross and when the Great War ends he is granted a permanent commission in the RAF. *(Read 24Jul20)*

Thirty-six Victory Ace Joe Fall
relaxing at home on leave
Vancouver Island, BC, Winter 1917–1918

Mike Fall

– FCdr Theodore Douglas HALLAM, DSC (Toronto) – Two Bars to DSC

(From 23Apr17) The other Canadian to receive a first and second DSC Bar is Hallam. His initial DSC was for 1915 trench combat at Gallipoli with the RNVR. Now his second is for attacking U-boats together with a third bar for sustained anti-submarine operations.

TD Hallam

U of T

Promoted to Squadron Commander in 1918, Hallam will take command of the Experimental Squadron at Felixstowe. Demobilized in July 1919, his postwar personal reflections, *The Spider Web,* becomes the defining depiction of the RNAS anti-submarine patrols. Back in home in Ontario, he takes to civilian life as the General Manager & Secretary, Canadian Woolen & Knitting Goods Manufacturers. His background in flying and his business in fabric lends him to the invention of the airfield wind sock. Hallam is listed in the Canadian Who's Who 1936.

22Dec17 – FLt John Osborne 'Tiny' GALPIN, DSC, MID (Ottawa) – ASP

In a Large America flying boat out of Felixstowe, Galpin comes across not one, but two German U-boats. The first is sighed at a considerable distance and submerges before he can attack. The periscope of second is lost to view before a proper bomb run can be established. Climbing to 2,000 feet and circling, Galpin again spots the periscope and dives on it, releasing two 230lb bombs. Unhappily, both fail to explode.

Five months previously, Galpin was awarded the DSC for his actions in attacking and, it is believed, to have sunk a submarine. Now six months later, Galpin, known as 'Tiny' because of his comfortable proportions, feels that he is being followed by a Hoodoo (bad luck). He has recently been, yet again, 'let down' on the water. This time it is due to a double engine failure when dental platinum, requisitioned to make points for magnetos, has not proven durable. He holds the record for the greatest number of engine failures at sea and has become quite toughened to spending the night adrift—that being preferable to the alternative—sinking. Once, when the destroyer attempting to tow him collided instead, his flying boat was sent to the bottom.

Certain that he is cursed, Tiny poetically laments his state of affairs in *The Wing,* the Felixstowe Air Station newspaper:

CHEERIOH
The Seaplane is my Hoodoo,
I shall not fly another.
It maketh me to come down on roughwaters,
It spoileth my reputation.
Though I fly from the harbour,
It returneth by towing.
Its Magneto discomforts me.
Its tank runneth over.
Its rods and its engines fail me.
Yeah, even by mechanics is my name
held in laughter.
Though I strive to overcome them,
Its weaknesses prevail.
In the hour of my need its engines mock me
And bring me down with great bumpings,
And there is no health in it.
Verily, verily, if I continue to fly these things
I shall end by drowning,
For my friends desert me
And call me a Jonah
My luck smelleth to Heaven
And I am disheartened.
Therefore shall I turn my hand elsewhere
And become a Tram Driver.
For again I say unto you, that of all Pilots
I am the most unlucky,
Yea, D-----d unlucky.

Eventually, amused but sympathetic squadron mates, in a gesture aimed at ending Tiny's quandary, put a pebble in a small silk bag and present it to him as a talisman from Egypt. The power of suggestion banishes his hoodoo and the large Canadian goes from melancholy to mirth—often to the point of having to be restrained from speech making on Wardroom Guest Nights. *(Read 06Jun18)*

23Dec17 – FSLt Douglas Ross Cameron WRIGHT (New Westmister BC) – KIA

(From 15Nov16) Death is no respecter of the Christmas Season. Landing in mist and low cloud, Wright loses control of his aircraft, spins out of the murk and crashes onto his aerodrome.

The 10 Naval report reads: 'This Officer left on a low Fleet Patrol at 7:30am on Sopwith Camel B6201. Owing to unfavourable weather conditions patrol returned immediately. Pilot came down in a spin over aerodrome, and failed to get out of it before hitting the ground. He was killed instantaneously and machine completely wrecked. Death was due to the following injuries: 1) Punctured wound of frontal region with protrusion of brain substance. 2) Compound comminuted fractures of both legs and thighs. 3) Injuries to chest wall. It is impossible to state the cause of the spin which resulted in the accident, as no evidence is available on the point.'

In the present day, the cause would be identified as vertigo: an upset in flight with the loss of visual reference to the ground. Without adequate instrument training or experience on the physical effects of spatial disorientation, there is little chance of recovery.

Wright had been a Sub-Lieutenant Observer RNVR before transferring to the RNAS for pilot training in October 1916. The twenty-five-year-old is buried at Dunkirk, France.

25Dec17 – FSLt Fred Christie CRESSMAN (Peterborough ON) – MIA North Sea

'Tubby' Cressman is lost at sea with his Scottish Air Mechanic, GDR Shearer, after their Dundee-based Short 184 N1638 comes down about a dozen miles southeast of Fifeness.

When he left on patrol on Christmas Eve morning the weather conditions, unusual for the time of year, had been ideal. The mission consisted of two seaplanes, each with a crew of two, a fairly routine affair. Dispatch of a brace of machines has been found eminently desirable should one of them experience engine trouble—an unfortunately common occurrence. In such an event, the other crew can note the position of their comrades in distress and inform the home base by wireless as well as seek out a potential rescue vessel to signal by Aldis lamp.

Seeing that Cressman is forced down, the accompanying seaplane carried out the SOP for help. After signaling a nearby naval ship, they set off back to the crippled machine. In the meantime, a dense surface fog has settled, shrouding the water-bound aircraft.

From the Firth of Forth, destroyers, drifters and minesweepers are sent out to comb the area. After dark, a gale arises and by the early hours of Christmas morning, the sea is so rough that all ships are withdrawn. At dawn the gale is still blowing and the temperature described as being 'cold as charity'. Two aircraft deploy from Dundee but can make no headway against the wind.

As the mist set in and the sea rose, Cressman had released a carrier pigeon. It arrives back at NAS Dundee with the message:

> "Engine trouble. Position... S.O.S. Sea rough"

At noon on the 25th, an exhausted second bird arrives in the Air Station pigeon loft bringing:

> "Still right side up but expect to turn over at any moment. If help doesn't come soon I'm afraid we're for it, but we're making a good fight. Cheerio—Cressman."

FC Cressman

FAAM

The time is given as 0300, Christmas morning. With a true 'Nelsonian Touch', Cressman had died bravely, in the highest traditions of the Navy.

27Dec17 – PFO Howard Frederick BOND
(Montreal) – REL

Bond had achieved his Royal Aeronautical Certificate at Cranwell in July; however he was released before attaining his commission in early October: 'On account of nervousness & desire to give up flying'.

On this December date, the Admiralty receives a telegram from the Eagle Aviation Company of New York requesting information about his Termination of Appointment in view of the fact that they wish to employ him as an instructor pilot. There is no record of the Navy's reply. (If indeed there ever was one)

31Dec17 – FLt Kenneth Foster SAUNDERS
(Victoria BC) – DSC

For the second year-end in a row, Saunders receives an outstanding report. He has been instructing at Eastchurch since May 1916 and that year, the Commanding Officer's Report called him an: 'Excellent Pilot, & particularly fine Instructor. Tremendously keen & hardworking. He sets a magnificent example to all other Officers & I am more than satisfied with his work.'

Now at the close of another year, his reviewing officer writes: 'I cannot speak too highly of this Officer. His example and keenness have done much to keep the standard of work up to a high state of efficiency. He has shown great energy and skill both day and night in going up after hostile machines and on one occasion found and attacked a formation of Gothas by night. He has done 250 hours flying in the last six months which probably constitutes a record.' This latest commendation earns Saunders the DSC for zeal and devotion to duty. It is Gazetted in May 1918, and by November he is also awarded the AFC for his exceptional training work. *(Read 1923)*

FAAM 2000/112/080

HMS YARMOUTH *August 1917*
Turret-mounted flight launching platform

Courtesy of Special Collections and Archives, Wright State University

NUMBER 3 SQUADRON RNAS · BRAY DUNES · MARCH 1918

Left to Right:

Back Row:
JD Breakey, **AT Whealy, LD Bawlf, GB Anderson**, BH England, E Pierce, **LA Sands, KD MacLeod**

Middle Row:
RC Berlyn, H Nelson, **HF Beamish**, LH Rochford, **R Collishaw, FC Armstrong, JA Glen, HM Ireland**

Front Row:
Devereux, **WH Chisam,** FE Ellwood, GT Hayns (?), HF Haig, FTS Britnell

CHAPTER 4
THE YEAR 1918

FLIGHT & SQUADRON COMMANDERS

Through attrition and experience, many of the surviving Flight Sub-Lieutenants of 1916 and Flight Lieutenants 1917 have risen to the rank of Flight Commander and some are appointed to lead squadrons. **Raymond Collishaw** is one who has proven himself capable of this latter commission:

> "When I became Squadron Commander of No. 3 Naval Squadron early in 1918, I set out to try to obtain the best pilots possible passing out of the schools in England. Generals Trenchard and Salmond were much against any kind of selecting pilots for a super squadron along the lines of the 'Circus' but General Festing who was in charge of postings at HQ RFC and HQ RAF was a friend of mine so I nearly always got the people I asked for. In this way about 70% of the pilots throughout 1918 remained the Canadian average. ...All the ground crew were exclusively English." (*Archives letter 26Apr1962*)

Nineteen Eighteen is the year of victory for the Allies; but such an outcome looks bleak on March 21st. Reinforced with divisions transferred from the collapsed Russian Front, a *Kaiserschlacht*, better known as the Lundendorff Offensive, launches. The Germans are anxious to achieve victory before the American Expeditionary Force is battle-ready and British army trenches are breached on a seventy-mile front. For high-flying scout squadrons it requires a complete change of tactics, they must now carry out low-level attack missions to help stem the German advance.

April 1st, 1918, marks the 'integration' of the Royal Naval Air Service and the Royal Flying Corps into a first truly-global air power—the Royal Air Force. RNAS aviators on the Western Front are far too engaged in the German offensive to pay much attention. On other fronts there is sadness for the demise of naval traditions but fresh manners and mores nurture and grow in the new force.

The RAF initially adopts an Army rank structure; thus a Flight Sub-Lieutenant becomes a 2nd Lieutenant, a Flight Commander is titled Captain. Naval Squadrons are now led by Majors and take on a 200 series of numbering; Naval 3 becomes 203 Squadron RAF. Naval Wings are relisted in a 60's series; 2 Wing in the Mediterranean becomes 62 Wing RAF.

August 8th brings Allied success at Amiens. *'Der Schwarze Tag'*—the Black Day of the German Army. The Kaiser's War is essentially lost and the Canadian Expeditionary Force is used as shock troops to lead the 'Hundred Days Offensive' that pursues the enemy all the way to Mons by November 11th.

JANUARY 1918

02Jan18 – FLt Percy Exeter BEASLEY (Victoria BC) – Fit to Fly

In the early spring of 1917, Beasley was described by his 3 Wing CO as 'A very good long distance pilot; plenty of stamina.' At that time Beasley had been on bomber operations since joining the Wing in April 1916. He flew a Breguet V in the Frieburg Raid of 12 October 1916 and by July 1917 had lost the 'stamina'. He was sent home to British Columbia to recuperate.

Now reporting back fit, Beasley is initially employed shuttling various types of RNAS fighter aircraft from Manston to Dunkirk. He is asked for by **Raymond Collishaw** of the new St. Pol Seaplane Defence Squadron to become deputy leader of his Flight. Collishaw has also returned from Canada Leave and has resumed the 'Black Flight' theme leading 'A' Flight in Camel B6390 named *'Black Maria'*. Beasley flies his wing in Camel B3773 and christens it *'Black Bess'*. Other Canadians in the Flight, **WA Moyle**, and **WJ MacKenzie** fly *'Black P'*, and *'Black Prince'* respectively.

When the unit is established as 13 Naval in mid-January, Collishaw becomes the initial Squadron Commander and Beasley is promoted to be an Acting Flight Commander. Later he will command a flight with 211 Squadron of the new RAF before being posted to instruct at the Aerial Fighting and Gunnery School in England during July 1918.

03Jan18 – FSLt Andrew Gordon BEATTIE (London ON) – POW

Beattie is shot down in Camel N6351. His 10 Naval Squadron Commander reports 'This Officer was last seen taking part in an enemy engagement at 1:50pm near Lille. Intermittent snow storms throughout the day made flying difficult.'

Beattie has been brought to earth by the Albatros D guns of *Vzfw* Hans Oberlander from *Jasta* 30. Following a crash landing, Beattie is captured at Provin and in February he is reported as Prisoner of War. A 'Very steady & keen Officer with good command' Beattie had one victory to his credit when balance was made equal by Oberlander.

For Oberlander, the victory is his fifth. The new Ace will score only once more before being wounded out of action in May

04Jan18 – FSLt Albert James DIXON (Ottawa ON) – KIA

Naval 8 Camel B6278 fails to return from a mission this morning. During the patrol an enemy Rumpler two-seater is attacked and crashed, but immediately

AJ Dixon

DeWolfe/ M Pirie

afterwards Dixon is seen going down out of control East of the Lines over Neuvireuil-Oppy. Age 22, he is buried at Flers-en-Escrebieux, France.

FSLt Francis Edward DIXON,

is Albert's brother, and he only just survives the War. A serious skull injury was sustained in a December 1917 crash of Sopwith Baby Seaplane 8187 on the River Humber. Sent on a Canada Long Leave, 'Frank' is returned to his wife's care in Ottawa.

FE Dixon

RAeC Trust

04Jan18 – FLt Frederick Gordon HELLMUTH (Toronto) – SUNK

Returning sick to England after service in Italy and Malta, Hellmuth's hospital ship is sunk by U-55. Struck in the stern by the U-boat's torpedoes, the HMHS *Rewa*, 7,267 tons, goes down just short of her Cardiff destination. Surprisingly the casualties are very light considering the ship is transporting 279 cot-and-walking-wounded cases. Only two crewmen perish in the sinking.

In this War of unrestricted German submarine attacks

on Allied shipping there appears to be a specific targeting of British hospital vessels. The largest loss has been 48,000 ton HMHS *Britannic*, sunk off Gallipoli in 1916. She was a sister ship to the 1912 iceberg-fated *Titanic*.

The hospital ships *Portugal*, *Braemar*, and others have also been sent to the bottom: a clear violation of a German promise not to attack neutrals.

FG Hellmuth

U of T

Hellmuth has been flying with 6 Wing out of both Otrano, Italy, and the Malta Seaplane Station since April 1917, and is reported as a 'VG Pilot & capable Officer when he likes. Requires keeping up to the mark.' In February 1918 he is fit and is sent to Rosyth, Scotland, where he is soon considered 'A sound ferry pilot.'

In 2003, divers will discover the wreck of the *Rewa*, sitting upright in 60 meters of water 33 miles off Newquay, Cornwall.

07Jan18 – FSLt Cecil Roaf BARBER (Port Credit ON) – KIC

Based at Dunkirk, Barber and his Observer are killed in the crash of their 2 Naval DH-4 N6402. Barber joined the Dunkirk squadron in early December and by today's date had made 12 practice flights. This has proven him sufficiently good enough to be put on the Operational Duty List for the first time.

Together with his Observer, SLt HR Easby, he leaves the aerodrome for a local flight, but at about 500-600ft comes down in a spinning nosedive. There is little doubt that the two are killed immediately. The machine bursts into flames, and is practically burnt out before anyone from the aerodrome can reach the crash site near Fort Mardyck, over a mile away. The engine and all parts of airframe are completely destroyed. Aged 23, the remains of the former bond salesman for Dominion Securities are buried at Dunkirk.

08Jan18 – PFO Charles Schofield APPELBE (Parry Sound ON) – REL to RNVR

Appelbe achieved a Royal Aeronautical Certificate in June but is now Released into the RNVR. His Chingford CO reports: 'He is desirous of discontinuing flying and I am of opinion it would be dangerous not to do so owing to nervous trouble.

His application for transfer to Auxiliary Patrol is recommended. His conduct is entirely satisfactory.'

Applebe will go on to Command Motor Launch 246 in the Mediterranean.

CS Appelbe

RAeC Trust

14Jan18 – Rev. Albert Henry 'Fuzzy' WALKER (Toronto b. IRE) – DOJ for KBO

AH Walker

U of T

Born in County Mayo, Ireland, during 1883, Walker immigrated to Canada in 1906. He became quite the all-round student at the University of Toronto: President of the Athletic Association and Vice President of the Students' Council. He founded The Wycliffe Magazine, named for his Anglican College.

Ordained as a Deacon in 1914, Walker took vows as a Priest the following year. Now, against the wishes of his bishop, he enters the War as a combatant. Age 35, he is Canada's second oldest naval aviator.

Trained as a Kite Balloon Officer, Walker will be appointed to Number 1 Balloon Base at Malta. An active scout balloon pilot, he travels between Gibraltar and Port Said helping protect shipping from submarines stalking the Mediterranean. He will also serve at Alexandria, Imbros Island, and, at the end of the War, in the captured Turkish capital Constantinople.

In October 1918 he will find that he has been mistaken for a Canadian 2nd Lieutenant, one A.H. Walker of the Cheshire Regiment who has been noted to have Died of Wounds by the *Canada* magazine. This weekly photo journal is the main source of war news in the Dominion: worried parents and friends searching for information from the Front very carefully peruse the its pages. One can only imagine the distress such name confusions must have caused. Safely home in 1919, Walker takes up religious appointment in St. Catherines. In 1964 the diocese of Lincoln and Welland Counties, Ontario, will honour Canon Walker for fifty years of ministry.

– FSLt Gilbert Ord LIGHTBOURN (Toronto) – KBO Malta

Fuzzy Walker may have been influenced in going to War by fellow Wycliffe classmate Lightbourn. A Lieutenant in the 180th Battalion of the CEF up until August 1917, Lighbourn had served in the unhealthy environment of the trenches, and on transfer to the RNAS was found fit for Kite Balloon or Airship work only. Graduating as a KB Officer he was sent to the Malta Group for Mediterranean work.

Post War, Lightbourn also renews his holy orders and becomes the Rector of Trinity Anglican Church in Aurora ON. He will resign and join the Royal Canadian Air Force in April 1940. For his subsequent service as the Senior Protestant Chaplin for the RCAF Overseas, Lightbourn will be made an Officer of the Order of the British Empire (OBE) in January 1946.

18Jan18 – PFO Harold BRICKER (Preston ON) – INJ

Attempting to make a forced landing Bricker stalls, sideslips and nose dives in from about 25 feet near his training base at Vendome. He sustains a fracture of the nose, a wound on right cheek and another on the right thigh. His machine, Curtis JN-44 8817, is completely wrecked and declared a total write-off. In spite of these setbacks, Harold Bricker will graduate and be recommended for scouts. Following Fighting School training at Manston he is assigned to 219 RAF.

– FSLt William Ralph BRICKER,

Harold's brother, has already graduated from Cranwell and is at Calshot for Seaplane training. However this

is not a successful marriage of man and machine. William Bricker refuses to fly the water-borne aircraft. The Report states; 'It is not considered that this Officer will make an efficient seaplane pilot. He is keen to be employed on Handley Page aeroplanes & to see action in France. He appears to be of a somewhat nervous disposition and would prefer to resign his commission rather than continue flying Seaplanes.' William Bricker's naval appointment is terminated on the 24th of January.

20Jan18 – FSLt William JOHNSTON (Westmount PQ; b. IRE) – MIA

When news that the German cruisers *Goeben* and *Breslau* have left Constantinople and are sailing out of the Dardanelles Straits, all local RNAS, RFC and Greek aircraft are 'scrambled'. Harrassed by the Allied aircraft, *Breslau* zigzags into a minefield and is sunk. The larger *Goeben* also strikes the mines but is able to make a run back to the Straits.

W Johnston

At this point, two Sopwith Baby Seaplanes launch off HMS *Ark Royal* and determinedly make their attack. Encountering some ten enemy seaplanes, Johnston, in N1445, is flamed by *Ltn* Emil Meinecke. A Greek Navy Sopwith Camel breaks up the enemy formation and the second Sopwith Baby carries out his bomb run with 65-lb weapons but misses the crippled cruiser. *Goeben* runs aground just inside the Dardanelles and for the next few days, aircraft attempt to further destroy the German raider.

Dublin born Johnston was a McGill student who joined the RNAS in March 1917. His Cranwell graduation report was an excellent VGI, naming him a 'VG & Keen Officer.' Johnston had completed his Seaplane instruction at Calshot and was recommended to 2 Wing in the Mediterranean in October 1917.

22Jan18 – FLt David Moair 'Bill' BALLANTYNE (Winnipeg) – *Goeben*

(From 03Oct16) From Marsh Aerodrome, Mudros Island, Ballantyne is another Canadian scrambled against the grounded German cruiser *Goeben*. Bombing from a DH4 he carries out three attacks in two days. Today he flies with two other DH4s and is accompanied by two Camels for fighter protection. The following day Ballantyne conducts two separate bombing attacks scoring two direct hits on his second run. However, not only are the 65-lb and 112-lb bombs far too light against the vessel's heavily armoured deck, the *Goeben* is further shielded by inclement weather. Towed afloat on a high tide, she retreats to the Turkish capital never to sally forth again. Jane's Fighting Ships of World War One states that: '*Goeben* has probably had more narrow escapes from destruction than any other Dreadnought or Battle Cruiser in existence.'

22Jan18 – PFO Harold Thomas COO (Toronto) – KIC Midair

At the RNAS Training Establishment Vendome, France, Coo is lost in Caudron C5290, when he and another Caudron C5284, PFO H.C. Langstone, collide in mid air. Coo was 21 years old.

Although his parents register a request for their son's body to be returned to Toronto, he is laid to rest at the Vendome town cemetery. Between February 1917 and December 1918, twenty-one pilots assigned to this training establishment will be buried here. The names of these airmen are engraved on the Vendome War Memorial along with the names of local soldiers who fell. A sculpture depicting the bodies of a French Poilu and a British Airman clasping hands rests at the foot of the memorial.

22Jan18 – FLt Charles Eldridge BURDEN (Toronto) – KIC

(From 21Nov15) The dreaded term 'Pilot Wastage' does not only apply to novices killed in training accidents or to combat casualties shot down in enemy action. Burden is a staff pilot at the Air Warfare Station Manston and is killed while testing Strutter N5524. This particular aircraft had a history of its engine cutting out while descending and this time the machine nose-dives all the way into the ground. Death from misadventure is the Inquest verdict.

A well-tried veteran, Burden had flown Sopwith Strutters in 3 Wing from July of 1916 and again with 1 Wing from March of 1917.

He had just returned from Canada Leave to take up his new duties at Manston.

CE Burden

23Jan18 – FLt George Benson ANDERSON, MID (Ottawa ON) – ACE

Anderson has been 'in the field' since November 1916, scoring his first victory in April 1917 and slowly building up to this fifth, a DFW.CV over Houthulst Forest. He achieves the Ace mantle in Camel B3940. Anderson's Mention in Despatches was given in July 1917 for good work while serving with No. 3 Squadron; he is reported as a 'Daring & Steady Pilot; a good scout fighter.'

23Jan18 – FCdr Wilfred Austin 'Wilf' CURTIS, DSC (Haverlock ON) – DSC BAR

(From 21Oct17) Leading a 10 Naval offensive patrol, Curtis follows three two-seater enemy machines and an enemy scout through clouds. The Germans emerged and are joined by five other scouts in a possible ambush setup. Curtis dives and fires into one of the two-seaters from about 40 feet behind. The German machine falls over on its side entering a spin and is observed to break up in an accelerating spiral.

The Dunkirk Commanding Officer recommends a Bar to Wilf Curtis's DSC for continuous skill & bravery as a fighting pilot. The award is Gazetted in March by which time Curtis is home in Canada. The Vice Admiral, Dover has requested that he be granted leave: 'He has done fine work while suffering complaints of headaches & sickness whilst in the air, & it is considered he should be granted a rest to avoid a nervous breakdown.' The Medical Department of the Admiralty survey Curtis and agree, finding him unfit for flight duty. In late February he sailed from Liverpool on Canadian 'Long Leave'. *(Read Sep1947)*

**– FSLt Ross Allison BLYTHE
(Toronto) – KIA**

RA Blythe
RAeC Trust

Amidst 10 Naval's 'tumbling-sky' clash with the nine hostiles, Blythe's Camel, B5663, collides with one of the enemy Albatross scouts. Mangled into a knot they fall to earth and are observed to impact simultaneously. Aged 25, Blythe has been on unit strength only one week.

He is buried at Perth Cemetery, near Ypres.

**25Jan18 – Lieut James Garnet SCOTT, RNVR
(St. Catherines ON) – RIP**

Cause of death is unknown but Scott has possibly become a first victim of the so-called Spanish Influenza a 'bug' that is beginning to be seen in epidemic proportions.

JG Scott
U of T

Scott flew with the RNAS in early 1916 achieving his Aeronautical Certificate, however, by middle of that year, the University of Toronto Honours Science graduate had transferred to the RNVR as an Engineering Officer.

**28Jan18 – FLt Cecil Gordon BRONSON, Cd'G
(Ottawa) – POW/DSC Turkey**

Bronson and his Observer are shot down in their 2 Wing Short 184 N1582. A letter, dropped on Imbros Island by a German Seaplane in March, is from Bronson and states that he and Observer, OL L.H. Pakenham-Walsh, Cheshire Regiment, are unhurt and have been taken prisoner by Turks.

The past December Bronson was awarded the French Croix de Guerre for Syrian reconnaissance flights along the Palestine coast and for spotting for the guns of French naval vessels. Four days prior to being shot down he had pressed forward a 'determined night bombing attack' against the German cruiser *Goeben*. Described as a 'Very plucky pilot', the award of a DSC is announced several months later.

FEBRUARY 1918

**05Feb18 – FSLt Robert Mattieu BERTHE
(Ottawa ON) – On Charge**

Berthe of 17 Naval, Dunkirk, is today brought before a Disciplinary Court on Charges of being 'Drunk on Shore' and creating disorder to the 'Prejudice of Good Order and Naval Discipline'. He pleads guilty and as there is nothing otherwise against him in records he is permitted to keep his commission but given a severe reprimand.

In June, as a DH-4 pilot in 217 Squadron, Berthe will Make up for his errors by bombing a U-boat. But, then in July he crashes into a hangar on takeoff, wrecking two aircraft although he and his Observer emerge unhurt. Even so, Captain R.M. Berthe is awarded the French Croix de Guerre avec Palme in November 1918.

**08Feb18 – FCdr John Augustus BARRON, MID
(Stratford ON) – USA**

(From 19Sep16) Unrestricted German U-Boat activity is now trans-Atlantic. Barron is sent from 6 Wing in Italy to the United States to assist in establishing anti-submarine airship patrols off the North American east coast. In June he is given further orders to travel onward to Ottawa and help in the planning and development of a new Royal Canadian Naval Air Service. His job title is Air Station Site Selection and Development Officer. By September, the new RCNAS takes in airship and aeroplane pilot trainees but the War ends before any of the new Flight Cadets become operational.

Granted a permanent commission in the Royal Air Force following the Armistice, Captain Barron will return to Europe and serve as a member of the Inter-Allied Aeronautical Control Mission in Berlin. When he returns yet again to Canada for technical work with the Canadian Air Board in 1920, it is specifically to advise on lighter-than-air-craft. A War Gift of equipment from

Britain includeds a number of airships and balloons. Other than proposals to establish routes down the MacKenzie River, or forestry patrols from Fort Francis, nothing happens and apparently, the only use made of the airships is the rubberized fabric—to patch hangar roofs at Camp Borden.

Barron will retire from the service in 1925, but will commission again in the Second World War, becoming the Chief Ground Instructor at No. 10 EFTS in Mount Hope, a British Commonwealth Air Training school in Ontario.

15Feb18 – FLt Claude Chester PURDY (Prince Albert SK) &

– Ensign Albert D. STURTEVANT, United States Navy – Both MIA

In a two aircraft escort for a convoy near the North Hinder Light vessel, Curtiss Large America H-12 N4338 is lost in action. The section of Felixstowe-based flying boats is jumped by a flight of Brandenburg fighter seaplanes out of the Zeebrugge *Seeflug Station*. Curtiss consort N4339 escapes but Purdy's boat is crippled and brought down by the German crew *Flgm* Urban and *Ltn* R Ehrhard of *SFS I*. Purdy, his American Second Pilot Sturtevant, and their English crewmen, Air Mechanic SJ Hollidge and Boy Mechanic AH Stephenson, are presumed drowned.

Purdy was a Queens University graduate and an accountant with Canadian Bank of Commerce. He entered the 1914-18 conflict as a Lieutenant with Earl Grey's Own Rifles in late 1915 but took leave to undergo flight training with the Glen Martin School in Los Angeles.

Ensign Sturtevant, Purdy's co-pilot, had enlisted in the USN Reserve Forces with the First Yale University Unit and was commissioned in March 1917. After flying school in Florida he was given orders in October for overseas duty to 'learn the drill' on an attachment with the RNAS. He is the first US Naval Aviator to be lost in combat and is awarded a posthumous Navy Cross: 'For distinguished and heroic service as an aviator attached to the RAF Station at Felixstowe, England, making a great many offensive patrol flights over the North Sea, and was shot down when engaged gallantly in combat with an number of enemy planes.' The United States Naval vessel USS *Sturtevant* is commissioned in his honor in September 1920. She will be tragically lost steaming into a secret minefield in April 1942. A second Destroyer, DD-240, is next named for the young American aviator.

CC Purdy
CB of C

18Feb18 – FCdr Cecil Hill DARLEY, DSC (Toronto, b. ENG) – DSC BAR

In a 14 Naval Handley Page bomber, Darley carries out two low level attacks on the St. Denis Westrem Aerodrome. It is the longest double operation by the RNAS to date.

For this effort and for: 'Zeal and determination in carrying out numerous night bombing raids on enemy aerodromes, docks, & etc ...' He is awarded a Bar to his first DSC which was won on the night of July 2nd 1917. On that mission, he pressed home an attack on Bruges in spite of having an engine seized, managing to fly home and achieve a safe night landing.

A civil engineer, Darley learned to fly with the Curtiss School in Toronto during August 1915. He is living up to his December 1915 Eastchurch School graduation report:

CH Darley
RAeC Trust

'Promises to be a very good pilot, being very keen, plucky & skillful. He has flown about 17 hours, some of it in fairly bad weather, on Bristols, Bleriots, Farman, Curtiss & Sopwiths. Has flown across country to Westgate and to Detling. As an officer he is very good, being smart, intelligent & reliable. Recommended for any service at home or abroad.' *(Read 28May18)*

18Feb18 – PFO James Bruce BINNY
(Canadian; b. SCT)
– REL – With TL's Regret

A former Captain in the 4th Canadian Infantry Battalion, Binnny is Released, with an Admiralty expression of regret. The Vendome Flying School reports that he has 'Tried hard to get on, but admits that his nerves are entirely gone & that whenever he goes in the air he is afraid of losing his head. This is probably accounted for by his having 3 years service in the Canadian Army, with a long period of very hard Active Service, as a result of which he was sent home from the front as no longer fit.' Binny is granted a free passage to Canada and is directed to apply for re-entry into the RNAS on his return to England. He has been recommended for Appointment to Executive duties.

18Feb18 – PFO Robert George Grant NAIRN
(Ontario; b. SCT) – REL – Application

Like Binny, Grant is also a CEF transfer to the RNAS. He has completed 28 months active service in France as an Infantry Lieutenant and is not quite accepting of the 'undergraduate' restrictions that the Navy places on Midshipmen-rank pilots: 'This Officer arrived late for morning flying & was ordered to do 2 hours extra drill. He complained & sent in his resignation evidently in a fit of temper, & I submit that it should not be accepted. In other respects he had done well both as regards flying & general work.' While this Confidential Report is being processed through channels, Grant graduates and humbly requests that his application to relinquish the RNAS commission be cancelled. It is a good call on his part and going on to complete the fighting school at Manston he is graded 'VGI Pilot & Officer. Recommended for Scouts. Very keen & full out. Should do very well.'

20Feb18 – PFO Alan Wesley TUCKWELL
(Regina) – REL – Attitude

Tuckwell is yet another CEF Officer who served in France before resigning his Lieutenant's commission to join the RNAS. Early in the new year he runs afoul of the Commander of the Eastbourne Flying School who reports: 'This Officer was brought up before me for insolent behaviour and inattention at lectures. I gave him 14 days stoppage of leave. He stated he would rather resign than accept punishment, and wrote his resignation. Previous to this he had been cautioned by

me for careless flying resulting in a M/C being wrecked. He has been twice wounded while in the CEF. Under these circumstances it is probable that his resignation was actuated by a sense of injustice.'

Because of his disrespectful attitude, the Eastbourne CO submits that Tuckwell's temporary Appointment be terminated. Considered undesirable for continued flying instruction, he is released.

20Feb18 – PFO John Inglis SANDERSON, MM
(Toronto) – Greenwich

The influx of Canadian Army and Naval veterans into the RNAS also includes those who have been decorated for bravery. Sanderson was a Gunner with the 34th Artillery Battery and has just commenced his RNAS Officer Training at Greenwich. The Citation with his Military Medal is 'For distinguished and gallant conduct. He assisted in running the (telephone) line forward from our old front line and maintained the same as long as possible. When the line was smashed beyond repair, he acted as a runner, bringing the messages from Hugo Trench to the old line. He afterwards established a signaling lamp and operated same until late in the evening. All the work was done under practically continuous shell fire, as well as machine-gun and rifle fire.'

Sanderson had served in the Front Lines for 18 months and survived his MM trench-action, and all others, unwounded. The air services will not afford him the same good fortune. Graduating into the new Royal Air Force, he flies Sopwith Camels with 70 Squadron until badly injured on September 18th, when he is brought down by engine failure, smashing his left leg and fracturing his skull on the crash landing. Almost one year later, when the Prince of Wales visits Canada in August 1919, Sanderson is invited to attend a Toronto military ceremony to be presented with his Decoration by the future King however; his injuries persist and preclude his participation.

Other Probationary Flight Officers with previous combat experience and meritious service medals are:

– PFO James MARSHALL, MM
(Belleville ON)

Yet another Military Medal recipient is Marshall, a Bombardier from the Canadian Field Artillery. He will graduate from flight training in late October 1918 with Royal Aeronautical Certificate 7642.

– PFO Robert Edwin SPROULE, DSM (Westmount PQ)

A Chief Motor Mechanic on Costal Motor Boats, Sproule received his Distinguished Service Medal with the RNVR.

One more entry into the RNAS at this time is a rather quiet Royal Naval Lieutenant surnamed Windsor. He is Prince Albert, future King George VI, and he joins at Cranwell. As a Captain in the new Royal Air Force he will become the OC 4 Squadron, Boy Wing.

20Feb18 – FLt John Graham IRELAND (Montreal) – Crash Dundee

When the port aileron of his Short 184 N1670 fails in flight, Ireland has no option but to attempt a force landing on the water. Without adequate longitudinal control the Dundee-based machine brushes a wingtip and crashes on touchdown. Ireland waves off naval salvage vessels as bombs are still attached and the risk to personnel is too great. When the aircraft sinks the crew is finally rescued.

Ireland has flown out of Dundee for most of the War. His initial reports in January 1917 stated that his: 'General conduct is fair, but he does not fully appreciate the duties of a Commissioned Officer. Will probably learn. A good Pilot.' This was followed in April with: 'A fair Officer, at present does not understand his responsibilities or Service methods. He is keen on flying.' By July Ireland has gotten the gist of the message: 'Has improved very considerably as an Officer and is a keen & reliable Patrol Pilot.'

After Canada Leave in April 1918, Ireland is appointed CO of 318 Flight, part of 257 Squadron RAF. In the Honours List of November he is Gazetted the AFC for his efforts. He will serve as a Group Captain RCAF during the Second World War.

23Feb18 – PFO James William McVEAN (Dresden ON) – INJ

Learning to fly Camel B5718, McVean crashes at Cranwell Aerodrome. The machine is completely wrecked and McVean listed in critical condition with a lacerated scalp, chest injury, and broken breastbone. But, the former Lieutenant of the Canadian Reserve Cyclist Company is a hardy soul and pulls through to graduate a 2nd Lieutenant in the RAF.

23Feb18 – FSLt Harold MacKenzie REID (Belleville ON) – KIC – Midair

An RNAS airship is making a slow pass over the Eastchurch Flying School when Reid joins alongside. Unfortunately another pilot, FLt CHM Chapman has had the same idea and, blindsided, the two aircraft collide near the dirigible. Both aviators are killed. Reid's body is allowed to be returned to Canada and is interred at his hometown cemetery in Ontario.

Reid was a new flying instructor at the school. After graduating a VGI Pilot in June 1917 he had done a 'Camel' tour on the Western Front with Naval 8, gaining four victories to his credit. His first two kills were rather spectacular. With only a week on Squadron he dove through a formation of five enemy aircraft destroying two that collided trying to avoid him, the wings of one falling off and the other crashing into a house.

MARCH 1918

09Mar18 – FLt Daniel Fairman ELLIS (Winnipeg) – INJ by Prop

Killingholme-based Curtiss H-8 'Large America' pilot Ellis is injured in a propeller accident when his machine No.8669 comes down just off Corporation Pier in Hull. Both his legs are believed broken and he is rushed to the local RN hospital.

A flying boat pilot since September 1916, Ellis had bombed a black object resembling a submarine in October 1917. On that occasion, his starboard 230 lb bomb failed to release; his port bomb exploded 20 yards short. A whirl and disturbance of water was seen but nothing further.

Today's accident is his second active service injury. In December 1917 he was hurt in the crash of Norman Thompson Seaplane 8341. When discharged from the Service in March 1919 Ellis will be granted an injury pension of £200 per year for life.

10Mar18 – PFO Albert Walter Gordon CROSBY (Uxbridge ON) – DOI

Student pilot Crosby was severely injured in BE2c 8302 crash at Spittlegate on the 27th of February. The 22-year-old former bank clerk had lingered but passes away this day at Belton Park Hospital. Crosby is one of five Probationary Flight Officers who die while at Cranwell during March 1918. His name is entered with 46 others on the Roll of Honour at the Air Station's St.Michaels's Church in Linconshire.

10Mar18 – FSLt Harold Randolph CASGRAIN (Montreal) – POW

Although no action is reported for 12 Naval today, Camel B3905 fails to return from a local formation practice flight with two other aircraft. Last seen in by the leader of formation over frontlines, Casgrain had slipped under the guns of *Ltn* Hans vonHaebler of *Jasta* 36 and has fallen into enemy hands. Later this month the German, Haebler, himself, will perish from air combat wounds but not before he lands his Fokker DR.1 Triplane virtually intact inside British lines.

10Mar18 – FSLt Herbert Bethune KERRUISH (Fergus ON) – U-boat

Launched from HMS *Campania* in Fairey Seaplane N1009, Kerruish and his Warrant Officer crewman sight the conning tower wake of a U-boat lurking 8 miles ahead of their ship. They drive the boat underwater with two 110lb bombs, one of which turns out to be dud. In June pilot Kerruish is given a Mention in Despatches for this attack attempt.

Leaving his studies at the University of Toronto, Kerruish joined the Canadian Expeditionary Force as a Lieutenant before transferring to the RNAS in December 1916. Assigned to East Fortune for flying with the Grand Fleet, he has operated from both HMS *Clive* and *Campania*. Kerruish is assessed as having a 'VGI ability to command' – A high praise rarely given out by regular Royal Navy ship Captains to their aviators.

11Mar18 – FSLt Colin Gordon MacDONALD (Charlottetown) – KIA

Flying DH-4 N5965 as an escort to another DH-4 on a Fleet Patrol and Costal Reconnaissance over Zeebrugge, MacDonald becomes separated. The aircraft that he was flying alongside later reports that both had climbed for height along the French Coast near Dunkirk. The lead machine had trouble with the wireless gear for signaling the Fleet and, after concentrating on the repair, found that their escort was missing. Four days later the remains of MacDonald's 2 Naval aircraft is picked up at sea five miles north of Dunkirk. Brought into harbour the wreckage is examined and found to have crashed on its back. The engine, petrol tanks and guns have all been wrenched completely clean of the machine. Although there is no trace of it having been shot down a victory is claimed by *Leutnant zur See* Bertram Heinrich of *Marine Feld Jasta* I.

MacDonald has been with 2 Naval Squadron for less than a couple of months. 'A keen and capable Officer, a VG Active Service Pilot;' his recovered body is buried at Coxyde, Belgium, along with that of his Air Mechanic Gunner, PJ Capp, also lost during the mission. The ten-victory German Naval ace Heindrich will be shot down by Canadian FCdr **Alexander Shoo**k later this month.

12Mar18 – FSLt George Chisholm MacKAY (Mimico Beach ON) – ACE

After scoring his first three victories in December 1917, MacKay finally reaches the much-vaunted score of five enemy aircraft brought down.

GC MacKay

U of T

The son of a Presbyterian Church pastor, MacKay did not get off with much of a flying start in the RNAS. He failed to graduate from Cranwell twice before finally making the grade in September 1917 with a 2nd class pass. He was however recognized as a 'VG Pilot' and recom-mended for Scouts. By early November he had survived the deadly acclimatizing process of front-line flying. On one occasion he joined a formation of aircraft thinking they were British—when they turn out to be German he stoutly shot one down before escaping.

At the end of March MacKay is assessed by his 13 Naval Squadron as having: 'VG Ability to command, keen & reliable Officer. Can take charge of a flight.' Given a flight command in early June shortly after a 9th victory he learns of being Gazetted for a new RAF decoration: the Distinguished Flying Cross. *(Read 10Nov18)*

13Mar18 – FSLt William Seborne ANDERSON (Lambeth ON) – INJ

Delivering Camel B2544 from the Mediterranean Islands of Mudros to Stravos, Anderson crashes on landing. Suffering a broken thigh and other injuries, he is trapped in the machine until ground crew cut through the wreckage to extract him. One of London, Ontario's Western University students, Anderson was flying with 2 Wing on the Aegean Front. He is sent home to Canada for an extended convalescence.

16Mar18 – FLt. William Hardgrove CHISAM (Edmonton) – ACE

With No. 3 Naval in Camel B7222, Chisam fires a burst of 50 rounds at an enemy two-seater. The tracers enter the EA, which dives vertically and is seen to crash by a battery observation post. This is Chisam's fifth of an eventual seven victories.

It is also a vindication. One year prior, flying a 3 Wing Strutter in March 1917, Chisam had incurred the displeasure of Their Lordships of the Admiralty: 'TL

WH Chisam

WSU

consider his failure to carry on with raid on Brebach Iron Works on 4th of March discreditable. He should have known how to adjust his carburetor at varying heights.' In acknowledging the receipt of Their Lordship's opinion, Chisam stated that he had been informed by the Wing's 'E' Officer that his engine was a continual cause of slight trouble.

Now he is reported as an 'Extremely good Pilot, daring Fighter.' Wounded previously, he had managed to return to flying, however, a hand wound on the 26th of March disables him from further active service. His final writeup reads 'A VG War Pilot, has splendid ability to command, a conscientious Officer.' In spite of such a reporting, no decorations are awarded.

16Mar18 – PFO David William DAVIES (Victoria) – FSLt

Graduating from Cranwell a: 'VGI Pilot, VG Officer. Good and Steady, has plenty of common sense, recommended for bombers,' Davies is sent on DeHavilland training at Manston, then posted to 217 Squadron, RAF, in May. He will be awarded the Belgian Croix de Guerre in recognition of various adventures he undergoes between June and September of 1918.

He begins scoring by shooting down a Pfalz D.III in June but while going on to inflict much bombing damage on the enemy, he will only achieve 'ace' by writing-off his own DH-4 aircraft. In July he crashes on landing in D8400 at Crochte, then is badly shot about in A7964. In August he has to force-land in a cornfield and smashes A8056. During the month of September he hits a ridge after an anti-submarine patrol and breaks off the undercarriage of A8081; later that same month he is once more badly shot about, this time on a raid on Thourout, and crash lands at Morshoek, near Abincourt.

17Mar18 – PFO Clarence Edward SHERLOCK (Lethbridge AB) – INJ

The novice Alberta Pilot is fortunate to survive walking into a revolving propeller. On cross-country training out of Vendome he is pre-flighting his Caudron G.III at the American Aerodrome at Tours when he sustains a scalping on the crown of his head.

On the 19th of August luck will run out for the former Canadian Field Artillery Bombardier. Flying Avro 504 E2929 as an Instructor, 2Lt Sherlock is killed in a Midair collision over Cranwell. His Flight Cadet student (SA Scott) and the crew of DH-6 B2787 are also lost (South African Lt. NCS Campbell & Flt Cdt CE Wiltshire).

18Mar18 – FSLt Gordon Tracy STEEVES (Hillsboro NB) – MIA/POW

During High Offensive Patrol a general engagement takes place when a 10 Naval flight of eight is attacked by a similar-sized group of Albatros scouts. Steeves, in Sopwith Camel B3781, does not rejoin formation after the inconclusive combat. Last observed flying eastward, he is brought down south of Roulers by *Ltn* Emil Thuy of Jasta 28. Not until mid-May is it learned through the Geneva Red Cross that Steeves is a POW. He will serve again during the Second World War as a Wing Commander with the RCAF. Thirty-eight victory German Ace Thuy also survives the War and is active in aviation until 1930 when he is killed in a flying accident at Smolensk, Russia, while secretly training pilots for the new Luftwaffe.

20Mar18 – PFO Cecil Clarence FRANKLIN (Port Rowan ON) – KIC

Looping Bristol Scout 3054 at 3,000 feet proves fatal for the young student pilot. He has insufficient altitude to recover and is killed. Aged 20, Franklin had been a chemist back in his home Province of Ontario. He is buried in the Cranwell Churchyard.

21Mar18 – A/FCdr James Alpheus 'Jimmy' GLEN, Cd'GaP (Enderby BC) – WIA

(From 07Jul17) The morning opens with a sharp, short artillery and poison gas barrage by the Germans as they launch their Lundendorff Offensive. During aerial combat with an Albatros two-seater East of Bapaume, Glen is wounded in the nose and mouth but crashes the EA on the British side of the lines four miles East of Bapaume. Nursing his head wound, Glen manages to return and land safely at his Mount St. Eloi aerodrome. His No. 3 Naval machine, Camel B7185, is unscathed by the combat.

JA Glen

This same day, it is announced that the King has approved the award of a DSC to Glen 'for exceptional abilities & courage as a fighting pilot.' Number 3 Squadron is now Commanded by **Raymond Collishaw** who, although extremely busy with the German onslaught, will, within days write to the Admiralty: 'With reference to the award by Commander in Chief of Distinguished Service Cross is it possible that this may mean a Bar to the Distinguished Service Cross considering this officer's conspicuous work since he was originally recommended for a decoration. He was wounded by an enemy two-seater which was brought down this side of the lines but owing to shortage of experienced pilots in the squadron he continued flying in spite of his wound. During the recent low flying operations this officer reported most of the useful reconnaissance which was forwarded to First Army Intelligence.'

At first, the Rear Admiral, Honours Committee, states that it appears to be a case of overlapping recommendations. However, a further review leads to the Gazetting of a DSC Bar for Glen in June 1918: 'For exceptional gallantry and skill as a Flight Leader when engaging enemy aircraft. He has destroyed or driven down out of control many enemy machines.' Glen will finish the War with fifteen victories and will remain

with the RAF until 1938.

– Lt **David Kenneth Glen**, brother to Jimmy also flies with the RNAS. The younger Glen has been overseas with the CEF since August 1915. A former Lance Sergeant he is described by the seaplane school at Lee on Solent as 'VGI Pilot & reliable. As Officer VGI'. David Glen will serve his war as an instructor at Calshot and will be Mentioned in Despatches.

22Mar18 – FLt Lloyd Allison SANDS (Moncton NB) &

– FSLt William Arthur MOYLE (Paris ON) – KIC – MIDAIR

(From 29Apr17) This is a tragic day for **Collishaw's** 3 Naval. Two of his Canadian pilots apparently collide during an attack on enemy aircraft at 15,000 feet over St. Quentin. Accompanying wingmen report the machines falling with opposite wings folded. The Camels, Moyle's B7219 and Sands' B7216, tumble into no-mans-land; the bodies of the pilots are never recovered. Both are aged 23 and both will be listed on the Arras Memorial.

Moyle had been a Lieutenant with the Canadian Infantry before his entry into Naval aviation, where he graduated as: 'VGI Pilot; VG & capable officer. Can command men but lacks (flying) experience.' Collishaw called him a 'Keen Active Service Pilot.'

WA Sands

Sands was better known to his Squadron Commander as they had entered the Navy a month apart in early 1916 and shared a Front Line apprenticeship together in 3 Wing. In a letter to Sands' New Brunswick family, Collishaw writes:

'We were all very proud of him and he earned such a good name that whenever a job was ordered for our squadron to do, he was usually the one selected to carry it out. Twice he was congratulated by the General commanding our army for work well done.

'No other officer ever did his work more thoroughly and well. He had accounted for six Huns before they got him, and I only wish he had been spared to carry on the good work. There never was a cleaner, more gentlemanly boy in France, and his great bravery has always been very much admired by every pilot. During the Somme battle in March this officer attacked enemy troops in the open many times in a very gallant manner.'

Collishaw has embellished the record of 'Huns' brought down by Sands but the matter is a small one. He was writing the most difficult of letters, that of a Squadron Commander to the bereaved family of one of his pilots.

22Mar18 – FCdr Alexander MacDonald SHOOK, DSO, DSC, CdG (Tioga ON) – 3 Victories

(From 04Jun17) In one day Shook takes down three German aircraft. The first is an Albatros D.V flown by *Leutnant zur See* Bertram Heinrich, the Naval Ace of Marine Field Jasta I who shot down CG MacDonald. Heindrich crashes and survives the wounding only to be killed in August by Canadian WS Jenkins, an RFC/RAF Pilot with 210 Squadron.

Today's victories raise Shook a total of 12 and he is soon after sent to England for instructional duties. Promoted to Acting Major in the new RAF, he is given charge of the Leysdown Air Station. By September, Shook's rank is confirmed and he takes command of No. 2 School of Aerial Observation at Manston. Transferred to the unemployed list in March 1919, he is Gazetted the AFC in June that year for his training school work. Returning to Canada a highly decorated aviator, Shook will be appointed Secretary of a newly constituted Canadian Air Board. However, the effects of multiple wounds received during his extended wartime flying will oblige him to resign from the Board due to ill health. Even so, he does live to a good age, dying at Bala, Ontario, in 1966.

25Mar18 – FCdr Frederick Carr ARMSTRONG, DSC, Cd'GaE, MID (Toronto ON) – MIA

(From 07Jul17) 'Army' Armstrong falls in flames near Ervilliers. While leading five aircraft on a bombing and trench strafe he observed massed troops attacking and dove to disband them. Re-crossing the lines his machine is seen to go down.

For the past four consecutive days, since the start of the Lundendorff Offensive, Armstrong has shot down an aircraft a day bringing his total victories to 13. The 'tall, fair-haired Canadian' of No. 3 Naval was 23-years-of-age. His name is yet another to be

FC Armstrong
RAeC Trust

inscribed among the Missing on the Arras Memorial.

In a Command Confidential Report from Dunkirk issued earlier this month, Armstrong had been recommended for promotion to Squadron Commander:

'He has helped to gain for his Squadron the high reputation it has...' His own CO, Collishaw, describes him as 'A most fearless flight leader and very daring war pilot. Has splendid command of men.'

28Mar18 – FSLt John George CARROLL (Wynyard SK) – MIA

Flying a DH-4 with 5 Naval out of Dunkirk, Carroll is Canada's last RNAS casualty before the First of April amalgamation with the RFC to become the Royal Air Force. Claimed by *Oblt* R vonGreim of *Jasta* 10, Carrol was 21 years old. He and his gunner Air Mechanic, G.E. Duffey, are named to the Arras Memorial.

31Mar18 – FSLt Arthur Treloar WHEALY (Toronto) – DSC

(From 07Jul17) While the Western Front is reeling from the German Spring Offensive Whealy's Squadron CO, Collishaw, pushes through a recommendation for a DSC 'For most consistent determination, bravery and skill with which he has carried out numerous low flying harassing attacks during the battle on Third and Fifth Army fronts. He has fired a total of 13,000 rounds into massed enemy troops, transport, etc., inflicting heavy casualties. His Flight Commander (**FC Armstrong**) was killed in one of the early attacks, and during the remainder of these patrols he led the flight and, by his splendid example and gallantry a great many minor hostile operations were hampered and frustrated with severe loss during the massed enemy attacks in open fields between Bapaume and Albert.'

The decoration receives the King's approval. Less than a month later Whealy is recommended for a Bar to the medal as a '...brilliant fighting pilot.' That too is Gazetted and before taking up a Home Establishment training appointment in September, 27 victory Whealy is further recommended for, and will be awarded, the DFC.

SCdr Collishaw's words are well chosen in describing the tenacity that his Acting Flight Commander has shown and perhaps best sums up the Canadian Naval Aviation experience on this, the last day of the RNAS:

> 'He has had invaluable experience on every front, from Switzerland to the sea, has flown about 200 hours on active service and has always shown exceptional stamina and initiative in action against the enemy.'

AT Whealy, watching Armourers "bombing-up' his Sopwith Camel

LAC, detail of A 472/e010836812

APRIL 1918

01Apr18 – Capt Frederick Everest BANBURY (Wolseley SK) – KIC

Taking off in Camel B7247 from his Flanders airfield, it is believed that Banbury suffers a heart attack or passes out. His machine stalls and spins into the ground.

Banbury had been a law student at the University of Toronto and took his flying training with the Curtis School at Newport News, Virginia, achieving the highest grade in the history of the establishment. Joining 9 Naval Squadron in February 1917, he attained Ace status by September 17th and was promoted to Acting Flight Commander for Meritorious War Service a: 'very keen & capable Officer. Thoroughly competent to take charge.'

A well-deserved two-month leave to Canada brought him home to his parent's house in Regina on Christmas morning 1917. Returning to duty, he was

rushed through a quick recurrent due to the anticipated German offensive.

He survived a Camel midair over Dover on the 20th of March and was back in action with his old Squadron the next day. Five days later he shot down an enemy Aviatik at 12,000' feet during a high patrol over Becelaire. It was his eleventh and final victory.

FE Banbury

U of T

Banbury's 9 Naval, now renumbered 209 Squadron, bury their first Royal Air Force casualty at Hazelbrouk Military Cemetry in Flanders. A cross, made from the propeller of an aeroplane initially marks his resting place. Banbury is Gazetted a posthumous DSC with the citation reading, in part, that he displayed 'continuous skill and ability as a Pilot…'

01Apr18 – 2Lt Orval Patrick ADAM (Westport ON) – MIA

In December 1917, Adam had crashed into a cemetery at Dover while transferring Sopwith Pup N6180 from Dunkirk. He was shaken and had sustained cuts on his face. It was his third flying injury and followed close behind a letter that he wrote to a friend in Ottawa remarking:

> "I'm soon off to the west front and suppose in another month or so I shall be pushing up daisies in France."

Sadly, his words are prophetic and on this initial day of the new RAF, flying Sopwith Camel B3798 with 203 Squadron, Adam goes Missing. His English Flight Commander, LH Rochford, writes: '[I] led my flight in the evening on an escort for 18 Squadron carrying out a reconnaissance. We encountered no EA but on our return from this patrol Adam was missing. None of us had noticed him leave our formation or being attacked but it was reported later that he had crashed and been killed near Loos on the German side of the lines. One of the last RNAS pilots to join the Squadron, he had shown promise and had shot down in flames a DFW two-seater.'

Orval Patrick's 'shown promise' was described in his Squadron's pre-RAF March 1918 report: 'A very daring war flyer. Will be valuable with experience. A superior Officer & has ability to command'. His crash site is shelled by German artillery and his body never recovered.

03Apr18 – Capt Harold Harrison GONYON (Chatham ON) – U-boat

Leading a section of DH.4's on an anti-submarine patrol out of Dunkirk, Gonyon spots an enemy U-boat with its conning tower awash. Attacking from 700 feet he releases one 230lb bomb that hits just ahead of the submerging conning platform. As the submarine disappears quantities of air bubbles and patches of oil are observed and another bomb is dropped. Gonyon's wingman also spends his two weapons on the swirling waters. Air station Dunkirk is only ten miles away and after re-bombing their machines the flight returns and drop four additional weapons on observed oil slicks and a floating spar. The RAF reports that an enemy submarine is destroyed: 'There appears to be no doubt'.

A DFC is Gazetted to Gonyon in early June. By this time he has left Dunkirk's 217 Squadron to recover from being wounded by a rifle grenade. Unhurt in an engine failure crash landing in No-Man's-Land he abandoned his aircraft only to be hit on the head by an unexploding grenade. Dazed but ambulatory, Gonyon escaped to the Allied lines as his machine was destroyed by shellfire.

In July he will report to a new unit, 233 Squadron at Dover, where he serves as both a pilot and the Station Adjutant. In February 1919 he is considered for the new Air Force Cross (AFC). While this award is not Gazetted, the recommending document gives a measure of the man: 'This Officer returned from France on July 20th 1918, and from then until the present day has been untiring in his efforts on submarine and mine patrols on DH-9 machines. Not only has he kept up his flying and shown a good example in the air but also does a great amount of work on the ground when he might (be) resting …as a Flight Commander and leader few equal him. His work in the air and on the ground always deserves the highest praise.'

07Apr18 – Lt Douglas Charles HOPEWELL (Ottawa) – POW

In an aerial engagement with the German Ace *Ltn* Paul Billik, Hopewell comes out second best and is brought down. He force lands his 208 Squadron Camel B6417 northeast of Loos and is rapidly brought into custody by German troops. Hopewell's victor is the Commander of *Jasta* 52 and he is Billik's thirteenth victory of an eventual thirty-one. The German Ace, himself, will be taken a Prisoner of War in August.

11Apr18 – 2Lt Merton Tyndale McKELVEY (Homefield MB) – WIA/POW

Flying Camel B5750 with 210 Squadron, McKelvey is shot down East of Armentieres. Wounded in the ankle, he is easily captured and taken to Limburg POW Camp. It is just one month to the day since he was previously wounded in action. Now he is the eight victim of *Ltn* Albert Dietlen of *Jasta* 58 who is shot down the following morning.

McKelvey, rated a VGI pilot, has been 'very steady and reliable' with his squadron since joining 10 Naval in late September 1917. On the night of 25th of February he flew a Special Mission in company with his Deputy Flight Commander, Hinchliffe. The pair left just before midnight carrying four 16lb bombs each. Together they attacked Abeele Aerodrome from 300 feet and bombs were observed to burst amongst the sheds and hangars. McKelvey was held by searchlights for a considerable period and was subjected to very heavy machine gun fire. Both machines, however, returned safely.

11Apr18 – Lt Earle Fraser McILRAITH (Lanark Park ON) – Ditched

A one-time rural schoolteacher, McIlraith has his hands full this night. During a raid on Zeebrugge his Handley Page bomber 3129 is caught in searchlights and badly shot about, causing the loss of one engine. The horsepower of the remaining Rolls-Royce is insufficient to sustain level flight and there is no option but to put down in the sea. Successfully ditching just off Fort Mardyck near Dunkirk, McIlraith and his 214 Squadron crew Lt WH Matthews & Lt A Clark are rescued. The 1919 New Year's Honours List will Gazette McIlraith with the DFC.

12Apr18 – Capt John Roy ALLAN, DSC
(Westmount PQ) – MIA

– 2Lt Maxwell Cline PURVIS
(Bolton ON) – INJ

(From 15Jul17) One night later, Allan, a Flight Commander with 215 Squadron, is also forced to ditch his Handley Page following yet another raid on Zeebrugge. It is the failure of an engine on Bomber 1462 that brings him down in the early morning darkness. Unlike McIlraith the night before, Allan is unable to extricate himself from the sinking wreckage and drowns. His Second Pilot, Max Purvis and English Observer Capt P. Bewsher, DSC, are picked up by friendly craft seven miles off Ostende. Soon after this mission, Purvis is given an aircraft

JR Allan

command. Slightly wounded at the end of August, he does survive the War.

21Apr18 – Capt Oliver Colin LeBOUTILLIER, MID
(New Jersey USA) – ACE

All three Flights of 209 RAF are on a patrol of the Allied Lines when Flight Commander 'Boots' Le Boutillier finally scores his fifth victory. It has been nearly ten months since his fourth successful engagement. However there is little time for celebration as the eleven Camels now run into the twenty-seven machine *Jagdgeschwader* of von Richthofen—The 'Flying Circus' of variously coloured aircraft. In the ensuing action, Germany's Ace of Aces is killed. His death ignites a controversy that continues to the present day—'Who shot the Red Baron?'

LeBoutillier has a ringside seat as his fellow Flight Commander Roy Brown of Carleton Place, Ontario, brings his guns to bear on Richthofen. During a newspaper interview in 1973 LeBoutillier will state:

"To my dying day I'll say Brownie shot him down, Capt. Roy Brown. I'm convinced of it. By God, it was so evident. I saw the shots going into the cockpit.

How could it be anything else? There is absolutely no doubt Brownie shot him down. He was probably dead before he hit the ground.

"The Australians saw the red triplane and started firing like hell at him. Then when he was down they jumped in and scavenged the airplane. It isn't up to me to say they didn't fire at him and maybe they hit the wings. But they claimed him. The Australians will always say, 'We got him.'"

LeBoutillier was born in New Jersey to an English father and a French-Canadian mother. He had crossed into Canada in 1916 and entered the RNAS through Ottawa's Department of Naval Service. A Columbia University student and Wright Brothers Mineola Flying School trainee he was easily accepted into the Royal Navy. He finishes the War with ten aerial victories.

Remaining an aviator, LeBoutillier will work as a barnstormer and a skywriter. A Hollywood stunt pilot, he flies in eighteen movies, including such aviation classics as 'Hell's Angels' and 'Wings'. In August 1931 LeBoutillier becomes the first pilot to land and takeoff atop a moving car, an act that is now an airshow staple. Later 'Boots' is chief test pilot for the Lockheed brothers and gives the famous aviatrix Amelia Earhart her first instruction in twin-engined aircraft. LeBoutillier will amass some 19,000 flying hours before retiring as a Civil Aviation Authority inspector. He dies in 1983 at Las Vegas, Nevada.

– Capt Arthur Roy BROWN, DSC
(Carleton Place ON) – RED BARON

(From 13Oct17) Brown dives after a red-painted Fokker Triplane that is about to kill a novice member of his flight, 2Lt Wop May (former RFC, Carberry MB). In the ensuing three-way chase, Brown shoots and distracts the German pilot, driving him down into the gun sights of Australian soldiers. *Rittmeister* Manfred von Richthofen, the eighty-victory 'Red Baron,' is dead. Roy Brown will be credited in aviation history as the man

AR Brown

who was pivotal in sending down the Red Fokker. Later, forensics determine that Australian infantry gunners may have fired the fatal round.

In Action since early 1917, Brown is now diagnosed as being completely fatigued. He is taken out of battle to become an instructor in England. Wop May, the pilot saved by Brown, becomes an Ace himself and later a famous Canadian pioneer bush flier.

At an International Aerobatic Championship event some fifty plus years after the Great War, the German team members were strutting about in beautifully tailored scarlet flight suits, driving a brand new red Mercedes station wagon bearing an artistic notice that proclaimed them to be 'Sons of the Red Baron.' The Canadian team, not so well equipped, wore nondescript military surplus flying gear and drove a beat-up older Chevy wagon. In the true spirit of competition, the Canucks propped a grease-penciled cardboard sign in their car window declaring that they were the 'Sons of Roy Brown!'

– Lt William John MacKENZIE (Port Robinson ON) – WIA

Following his Flight Commander, Roy Brown, into combat, MacKenzie is wounded in the neck. His Camel B7245 is badly shot about by *Vzfw* Edgar Scholz of the Richtoften 'Circus'. This all takes place during time Brown is chasing after the Red Baron.

By early October, MacKenzie has recovered from his wounds and is back in Squadron as a Flight Commander himself in time for the last push against the Germans. Much of the work is in low bombing raids against enemy troops in conjunction with the advancing Belgian Army. During this eriod he destroys one Fokker biplane and shoots down a second out of control. His tally from previous work gives him four confirmed victories at Armistice.

In May 1919, Captain MacKenzie is listed in Belgian Army Daily Orders for the award of the Croix de Guerre 'for valuable services rendered in connection with the war'. The following month the British gazette him the DFC.

21Apr18 – Lt Charles Robert Reeves HICKEY (Parksville BC) – ACE

Hickey had served as a Trooper with his father, Major R.H.F. Hickey, in the 11th Canadian Mounted Rifles before transferring to the RNAS in February 1917.

CRR Hickey

CFB Comox Museum

Appointed to 4 Naval in July he scores his fifth victory today. In the action he forces down a Rumpler two-seater near Wulpen and lands alongside to protect his prize from a growing crowd of Belgian civilians. When a timed 'infernal machine' in the German aircraft explodes several bystanders are killed and Hickey is injured. Recovering from burns to his face and hands he is back in action a month later

His Combat Report of a seventh victory on the 12th of July is about: 'Six Pfalz Scouts painted yellow fuselage, sky blue underside of planes. Armament two Spandua Maxims.'

His narrative reads:

"While travelling towards Middelkerke from Ghistelees at 18,000 feet, we observed one EA off Middelkerke, three EA higher up off Nieuport and two more attacking a DH.4 off Coxyde at about 14,000 feet. I turned left and dived towards the two latter EA, opening fire at about 100 yards. EA turned and dived towards Nieuport and I followed close on his tail. EA apparently hit by my first burst as all he did to evade my fire was to side-slip.

"I kept firing intermittent bursts taking careful aim each time. When at 1,000 feet off Nieuport Piers, I closed on EA and fired a long burst at very close range. EA dropped vertically and caught fire on the right hand side of his cockpit. In a few seconds its fire had spread and machine fell into the sea. One plane floated for a few minutes but shortly nothing remained on the surface. Altogether I fired 450 rounds." *(Read 03Oct18)*

21Apr18 – Lt David Leland 'Barney' BAWLF (Winnipeg MB) – KIC

DL Bawlf

Bawlf is killed in Sopwith Camel B3795 when he sideslips into a spin during formation join-up just after takeoff. He has been in 203 Squadron for only one month, arriving with a First Class flying assessment from Cranwell: 'Ready and quick to learn. Should do extremely well as fighting pilot.'

'Barney' is one of three brothers to serve in the RNAS. Older brother Louis, a veteran pilot who is also with 203 RAF, keenly feels his death.

– FLt Louis Drummond BAWLF

has been at the front for over nine months. His Squadron Commander, **Major Collishaw**, describes him as: 'A most daring & resourceful War Pilot. Has every ability to command & lead a fighting flight. An exceptional officer with superior command of men.' Having four victories to his credit, Bawlf has been Mentioned for good work while serving with No. 3 Squadron in the field. He achieves Ace status on the 22nd of July when he destroys a German DFW.C and is posted to Home Establishment instructing by August.

– FSLt Clarence Nicholas BAWLF

is the third brother and flew with 2 Wing in the Eastern

CN Bawlf

Ray Pollard

Mediterranean. He was released from the service with his appointment terminated in 1916.

A 'keen and very willing' Officer, Bawlf came into trouble concerning sums of money handed to him by Greek Officers for the purchase of gear and clothing in Malta. Returned to Canada he attempts to join the RFC but is turned down 'Until this Greek matter is cleared up.'

22Apr18 – FSLt Stuart GRAHAM (Wolfville NS; b. USA) – U-boat

Out of Naval Air Station Cattewater, Devon, in Short 184 N2832, Graham bombs a submarine just off the Eddystone Lighthouse. Four weeks later he attacks yet another U-boat. For these actions he is awarded the AFC in November 1918.

From the Annapolis Valley of Nova Scotia, Graham had joined the Canadian Mounted Rifles in 1915. As a 'dismounted' machine gunner, he was wounded at Ypres several months later. On recovery, the young Lance Corporal had successfully applied for pilot training with the RNAS. *(Read 22Jul20)*

22Apr18 – Lt Charles St. Clair PARSONS (Toronto) – POW

Engaged in bombing and machine-gunning an enemy trawler, Parsons crashes his 217 Squadron DH-4 A8063 alongside the Zeebrugge Mole. Together with his Gun Layer, G.S. Gladwin, the two share the dubious pleasure of being rescued up by the very same trawler they had been trying to sink.

Parsons had served as an Infantry Lieutenant with the 8th Battalion CEF for two years before joining the

RNAS. He graduated as a VGI Pilot in March 1917: 'Shows excellent judgment & should do well.' Now taken aboard the vessel that he was strafing he does do well in surviving the rescue to become a Prisoner of War.

CS Parsons

RAeC Trust

Parsons' action is in lead-up support of a Royal Navy blockship attempt to seal off the U-Boat entrance to the Bruges Shipyard Canal at Zeebrugge. The Admiralty is alarmed to have learned that over thirty U-Boats a month are launching and returning from here on missions down the Channel. Still others are making their way up around Scotland to hamper supply and troop ships arriving in Britain. In the early hours of the 23rd, a daring diversionary attack is made on the Mole by a landing party of Royal

Marines from HMS *Vindictive*. At the same time, three old cruisers, filled with concrete are scuttled in the entrance to the canal leading to the submarine pens. A similar blocking of the Ostend arm of the Bruges Canal is unsuccessful but will be re-attempted in May.

24Apr18 – Capt Norman Ainsley MAGOR, DSC (Westmount PQ) &
– Ensign Stephen POTTER, United States Navy – Both KIA

(From 22Sep17) During a running airfight between two British flying boats and seven German fighter seaplanes, Magor and his three-man crew are shot down just off the North Hinder Light Vessel. Their Canadian built Curtiss Large America H-8 8677 is claimed German naval ace *Oberleutnant* Christiansen and *Vizeflugmeister* Wladicka of SFLI. The tactic used by Christiansen is to open fire on the flying boat from behind with his Branderburg seaplane's fixed forward gun, killing the RAF stern gunner. Then, pulling up in parallel formation to the unwieldy flying boat Christiansen gives his Petty Officer Observer, Wladicka opportunity to shoot out an engine. The incendiary bullets set the machine afire.

Magor desperately tries to land on the water but, unable to turn into wind, he catches a wing tip and tumbles. His cart-wheeling aircraft bursts into flames. The Germans report seeing three men swimming 'But the sea was too bad to allow of our machines alighting in the hope of saving them.'

The second Curtis Flying Boat escapes back to friendly shores and learning of their loss, Allied pilots plot to avenge the blow. The following afternoon they 'set off on a proper hurrah party for the North Hinder'. Eight 'boats' from Felixstowe and various machines from Great Yarmouth sweep the sea but sight nothing. Similar patrols the next day also fail to find an enemy before bad weather sets in for several weeks.

Magor, a 27-year-old importing merchant from Montreal, and his USN Second Pilot and RAF crew, perish in the cold waters. Cpl RA Lucas & AM JG Strathearn. The recovered bodies are buried at Southhampton's Holybrook Memorial Cemetery, Hampshire. Magor is Mentioned in Despatches.

A month previously, on the 19th of March, Magor and Ensign Potter had fought two German Seaplanes and Potter, manning the forward machine-gun, had shot one down in flames. This 'First' by an American

naval aviator is recognized during the Second World War when the US Navy names Fletcher-class destroyer DD-538, the *Stephen Potter*. Born in Saginaw, Michigan, Potter was a member of the Second Yale University Unit that entered naval aviation in April 1917.

25Apr18 – Capt Gerald Atkinson MAGOR, MID (Westmount PQ) – POW/DOW

Three days ago, on April 22nd, *Ltn* Hans Weiss of *Jasta* 11 shot down Norman Ainsley Magor's younger brother, Gerald. Dragged from the wreckage of his 201 Squadron Camel B6428 and taken Prisoner, Gerald dies of wounds on this, the day after Norman is killed in the North Sea action.

GA Magor

MHR

The brothers had trained together at the Wright Flying School in Augusta, Georgia. Gerald earned his American Aeronautical Certificate No. 397 on the 17th of January 1916 and older brother Norman his AAeC No. 402 on the 28th. They parted ways in England, Norman going to North Sea Flying Boats and Gerald to the Mediterranean to fly with 2 Wing. In April 1917, Gerald, a McGill University graduate, was given an outstanding report as being 'An exceptional Officer in every sense, being gallant, intelligent and a brilliant and safe pilot.'

One month later he was almost killed. During a raid on the Drama air station, his Sopwith Stutter N5532, was struck by AA fire over Angista. Initially knocked out Gerald regained consciousness and managed to land his machine safely. The Salonika Casualty Clearing Station declared him dangerously ill with a gunshot wound to head. He was sent to England for skull surgery and thence on Canada Leave with a Mention in Despatches for distinguished services. Returning to active air service in February 1918, Gerald re-qualified at the Manston Fighting School and was posted to Dunkirk for 1 Naval Squadron.

The Magor brothers, Norman aged 27 and Gerald 21, died within 24 hours of one another on two different

War Fronts. In February 1920, a gratuity of £327 in compensation for the wounds that Gerald received together with prize monies from Norman's anti submarine work are probated and sent to their father.

25Apr18 – Capt Stanley Wallace ROSEVEAR, DSC&Bar (Port Arthur ON) – KIC

SW Rosevear

FAAM, Album 153

Failing to pull Camel B6231 out of a dive on a practice ground shoot, Rosevear, a 25-victory Ace, is killed. For an aviator of his experience it is difficult to believe that this was a 'target fixation' accident and his death is more likely due to sheer and utter exhaustion.

Rosevear had only joined the RNAS in January 1917 and his rise to Flight Commander has been nothing short of spectacular. He arrived in 1 Naval by late June and had achieved his fifth victory by the middle of October, earning himself the DSC. He won a Bar to the award in March of 1918 for attacking a formation consisting of eight enemy machines, and destroying two in the process. During the German Spring advance he was in continuous heavy action scoring a triple kill on March 21st, the first day of the offensive. Although he scored a 'double' just three days before his death, the majority of his flying for the past month has been in extremely hazardous low-level strafing duties over the trenches.

Described as a very skillful and dashing fighter pilot, Rosevear is personally complimented by Winston Churchill, who states on learning of the aviator's death: 'Next to Major Bishop he was probably Canada's foremost Aviator.' The British Telegraph newspaper publishes the quote under an obituary headline: 'Rival of Major Bishop.'

The 'rival' comments are not entirely correct as naval aviators such as **Ray Collishaw** and **Joe Fall** are higher scorers. However, in ten months' service at the Front, the 22-year-old Rosevear had excelled. A graduate of Port Arthur College and a University of Toronto student, he is buried at St Hilaire Cemetery, Pas de Calais. His obituary is published in the Toronto Evening Telegram on the 29th of April and again on the 27th of May 1918.

A younger brother, A. B. Rosevear, will fly with 213 Squadron RAF.

MAY 1918

02May18 – Lt William Hartley ROBINSON (Toronto) – KIC

Accidentally killed in Italy flying Camel B3840 with 66 Squadron RAF, Robinson's life is cut short before he can live up to his potential.

The former Canadian Artillery Sergeant had joined the RNAS in November 1917 and by March 1918 had earned a glowing graduation Report: 'Proficiency as pilot VGI 100%. VGI Officer, recom'd for Scouts. Has shown wonderful judgment, should do extraordinarily well. Has shown a remarkable natural

WH Robinson

GWFM

ability for flying.' Perhaps part of Robinson's ability came from his pre-service knowledge of automobiles as the Editor of the Canadian Motorist magazine. He is buried at Montecchio Precalcino, Italy.

02May18 – Lt Hazel LeRoy WALLACE (Lethbridge AB) – ACE

In 201 Squadron Camel B6359, Wallace brings down an Albatros C north of Albert for his 'Fifth'. By early August, he is a Flight Commander and wins the DFC for leading an attack on Epinoy Aerodrome. When the medal is Gazetted the citation states: 'A gallant and most capable leader, who in many engagements has displayed marked ability and courage, notably in a recent attack on an aerodrome when he led his flight against the group of hangars allotted to him at an altitude of between 100 to 200 feet. By direct hits he destroyed three enemy aeroplanes and set fire to a hangar by machine-gun fire.'

Wallace attended the Curtiss School at Newport News but had flown his 400 minutes by October 1916 without achieving a certificate. However, DNS Canada fortuitously recommended him as a Probationary Pilot and he graduated from Cranwell in May 1917. A low-flying Ace, Wallace survives the war with a fourteen-victory tally. All of his actions, in some 108 offensive patrols and special missions, are flown in Sopwith Camels.

02May18 – Lt Merril Samuel 'Sammy' TAYLOR (Regina SK) – ACE

Shooting down an all-white Fokker Dr.I south of Cerisy establishes Taylor as an Ace. He is flying Camels with

209 Squadron and he has done very well in bringing down this particular enemy Triplane. The machine is flown by *Ltn* Hans Weiss of *Jasta* II, himself a victor over 16 Allied machines including that of Canadian Gerald Magor.

MS Taylor

U of T

Taylor had written a letter home on the 26th of April:

> "During the past month air activity has been very lively, and a push on the ground means a corresponding scrap in the air. Our squadron, on account of our present situation, has taken part in holding the Hun in his big Push. We have consequently been in a few wonderfully exciting scraps, but have invariably come out on top. I am sure you will be pleased to hear that the renown Baron von Richthofen was bested by one of our chaps a few days ago. The victor is a Canadian boy who belongs to this squadron. It makes me proud to think that I took part in the scrap, although I had nothing to do with bringing down the Baron. All the credit goes to Brownie. I hope you won't think I am 'swanking' in telling you this, but I imagine you like to hear a little about our work. I hope I may

be able to tell you about the whole scrap some day."

Taylor's letter is very much along the writing style of 'Boys Own' books that were popular with Edwardian lads and it is written to a fellow student at the University of Toronto. This friend will become the compiler of the school's *Trinity War Book* in 1921 and the publication will include Taylor's letter. Unfortunately, also attached is a notation about Taylor becoming Missing in Action on the 7th of July: '...Was leading his patrol on return from trip over the lines on Amiens front when it was attacked by a number of EA. They fought back to the British front line and he had brought down one EA when his own plane was hit and shot down. Fell at Corbie, east of Amiens and he was killed.

'...He joined the Methodist Church when only a lad, and lived up to his professions, being not only a fearless aviator but a thorough conscientious Christian. He was enthusiastic about his work and wrote most affectionate and reassuring letters home. His brother, Neil J. Taylor, also in the Air Force, was a prisoner in Germany for a long time.' (Brother Neil of the Royal Flying Corps lost an eye when shot down. On repatriation in December 1918, Neil returns to school and becomes a lawyer.)

Sammy Taylor was shot down by *Ltn* Franz Buchner and is the 8th of Buchner's eventual 40 victories. Had Taylor emerged the victor it would have been his eighth. The award of a posthumous French Croix de Guerre is Gazetted.

08May18 – Capt Roderick McDONALD (Antigonish NS) – MIA

(From 27Jul17) In his personalized Camel D1852 '*DUSTY II*' Flight Commander McDonald, an eight victory Ace, is bested in aerial combat. He is caught out over Provin by *Vzfw* Julius Trotsky of *Jasta* 43. It is Trotsky's second and last victory, as he is himself is killed nine days later in an action with 40 Squadron, RAF.

McDonald was with Naval 8, now 208 RAF, for just over a year. Surprisingly he is never decorated in spite of a splendid war record. In the 1931 history of the unit, *Naval Eight*, McDonald's last CO, Major Chris Draper wrote: 'I lost Macdonald... one of those low flying stunts that H.Q. were then in serving out with increasing frequency... in May 1918. A fine big-hearted Canadian whom the Squadron could ill afford to spare.'

10May18 – Capt Albert Henry MUNDAY (Toronto; b. AUS) – Zeppelin

As Second Pilot in Felixstowe F2A N4291 'Old Blackeye', Munday's job is to man the forward machine gun should a target be presented. Today the large shape of a Zeppelin is spotted over the Heligoland minefields. While his aircraft commander, TC Pattinson, maneuvers the flying boat Munday begins shooting. The Zeppelin jettisons its bombs and dumps fuel tanks to rise upwards out of firing range. After an hour's chase the F2A crew has to break off action because of engine trouble. They alight briefly on the water to permit the engineer to repair a broken fuel pipe and narrowly escape several German destroyers that close in on them.

AH Munday

RAeC Trust

A DFC is awarded to the Pilot for this action and Munday receives a Mention. Although credited with the destruction of Zeppelin L-62, German records show that particular airship blown up by lightning on the 10th of May when she entered cumulonimbus cloud. The Zeppelin Munday was firing at, and reportedly shot down, was L-56.

Based at Killingholme, Munday is promoted to aircraft commander during the summer just as the Station is in transition to the United States Navy. On the 6th of June with Ensign RU Mill USN as Second Pilot, he bombs a German submarine 15 miles east of Spurn Head.

Munday was born in Australia and educated at Eaton in England. He came to Canada to complete his academics at Queens University and then worked for the Toronto Telegram newspaper. A Militia Trooper, he had entered the RNAS in March 1916 but the following April was injured in a Nieuport crash while with 12 Naval. Back in Canada on recovery leave with a gratuity of 364 days' pay for injuries sustained, a total of £327, he wrote a book on 'practical aviation' titled *The Eyes of the Army and Navy*, and published in October 1917.

Returning to England in January 1918, Munday requested Seaplanes. His new flying environment did not get off to a successful start when he wrecked Short

N1362. Rescued by HMS *Ouse*, he persevered and eventually graduated.

Post-war, Albert Munday will earn a Doctorate in Journalism at Columbia University and will write several aviation books in addition to his 1917 work. These are a novel, *No Other Gods*; and two military publications, *Practical Flying in War & Peace*, and *Captain of the Sky*. A founder of the Toronto Flying Club, Munday will help to organize the Canadian Aeronautical League in the 1930s. *(Brother Edward – Read 05Aug18)*

10May18 – Lt Gordon Fraser ROSS, RNVR (Toronto) – KIA

In a Naval attack on Ostend, the old HMS *Vindictive*, filled with concrete, is sunk inside the harbour mouth to block submarine exit and entry to the Bruges Canal. During the raid action Lieutenant Ross, a former RNAS pilot, is killed. Second in Command of Motor Launch 254, he dies while rescuing the crew of block ship. As his launch approaches *Vindictive*, Ross is spraying the enemy with Lewis-gun fire when an overhead shell-burst strikes him down. A shell fragment enters his left breast and exits through the right thigh, inflicting mortal wounds.

Ross had gained his flying certificate, AAeC 347, at the Wright Flying School in Daytona in October 1915. He passed his Probation period as a Flight Sub Lieutenant and was assigned to No. 3 Wing in April 1916 and then to East Fortune, Scotland, in July. There he put forward his resignation. The Reviewing Officer wrote: 'He has recently had 3 flying accidents, & has lost all confidence. He is no longer efficient as a flying Officer, but in other respects has shown himself keen, hardwork-

GF Ross

via M Pirie

ing & reliable. He has applied to transfer to Motor Boats & can be recommended.'

Ross was duly released from his RNAS Commission and accepted as a Sub-Lieutenant, RNVR, for Motor Patrol Service. He had been in action during the blockade of the opposite end of the Bruges Canal at Zeebrugge in April. Following that attempt to 'put a cork in the bottle',

Ross sent a letter home:

> "I have not written you for a long time, but if you read your papers you will understand. We find ourselves the heroes of the day. I myself was in the thick of the Zeebrugge 'straff' and can tell you that while it lasted it was hell. ...[But] We were not even hit with a bit of shell."

The Admiralty actions have raised the morale of a British population stunned by the German advances in Flanders. The Zeebrugge and Ostend raids do not completely cork U-boat movement but the audacity of the attack is glorious. Faith and confidence in the Royal Navy is at a wartime high. For his part in the Ostend Raid, Ross will receive a posthumous MID.

His Motor Launch Captain, Lt. GH Drummond, wounded by the same withering fire that killed Ross, managed to place vessel alongside *Vindictive* and take off forty of the crew. He collapsed from his wounds and Lt. VAC Crutchley, one of those rescued, took command and with leadership, seamanship, and baling-bucket squads kept the sinking ML afloat until all were picked up by HMS *Warwick*. Drummond and Crutchley are each awarded the supreme British medal for gallantry, the Victoria Cross.

As Ross's launch backed away from *Vindictive*, ML 276, Commanded by Canadian Lt. Rowland Richard Louis Bourke, DSO, RNVR, laid up alongside the block ship to further search for survivors. Finding none they withdrew but on hearing calls in the water again entered the shell-splashed harbour and eventually found three badly wounded seamen clinging to an upended skiff. This rescue under such dire circumstances earns Bourke the Victoria Cross. Turned down by the CEF in 1914 for defective eyesight, 'Rowley' Bourke had earned his DSO during the previous Ostend raid for saving 38 men from that block ship, HMS *Brilliant*.

11May18 – Capt John Edmund GREENE (Winnipeg) – ACE

Flying Camel D3357 with 213 RAF, Greene becomes an Ace shooting down an Albatross D.V over Westende and then scoring his sixth kill, another D.V—all in less than a minute.

Greene graduated from the Manston Fighting School in October 1917. He was immediately sent to Dunkirk for the Seaplane Defense Squadron, the unit designated as No. 13 Naval in January 1918. Now achieving Ace, he is granted the DFC in June.

By August, Greene is a Flight Commander and his Squadron CO writes up an outstanding Report: 'This Officer has great ability to command and is very trustworthy. He has complete command of his men and understands them thoroughly. In the air his abilities as a leader and fighter cannot be too highly praised. He has been in command of a flight for one month and carried out his duties with complete satisfaction. *(Read 14Oct18)*

16May18 – 2Lt Willard E. COWAN (Hamilton ON) – POW

In 208 Squadron Camel D9540, Cowan is last seen at 500' feet apparently under control but with two enemy aircraft on his tail. These hostiles are from *Jasta* 30 and when captured, Cowan is hosted by the unit and meets his victor, *Ltn* Hans Georg von der Marwitz.

Cowan joined the RNAS September 1917, transferring from the Canadian Army Medical Corps. He has been in 208 Squadron for less than two months. A German photograph shows Cowan, looking very relieved to be alive, enjoying a cigarette with von der Marwitz, Commanding Officer of the Jasta. The German has fifteen victories by the Armistice but is killed in an aeroplane accident in May 1925.

16May18 – Capt Stearne Tighe EDWARDS, DSC (Carleton Place, ON) – Last Victory

(From 23Sep17) Edwards is a Flight Commander with 209 Squadron and today brings down Fokker Dr.1 Triplane *G/5Bde/8*. The German pilot, *Ltn* Hubner of *Jasta* 4, is captured and taken POW. In the excitement, Edwards becomes lost and lands near Corbie. Although a highly experienced front-line pilot with 16 victories, he is by now running on sheer nerves alone. Becoming disoriented over familiar fields brings respite: Edwards' condition is recognized and he is sent back to England to be hospitalized for mental exhaustion. A Bar to his DSC is awarded: 'For conspicuous bravery and most brilliant leadership of fighting patrols against enemy aircraft.' The citation also notes that Edwards: '...has at all times shown the greatest gallantry and a fine offensive spirit.' This is one of the final DSCs awarded to a naval pilot, as the new RAF shortly thereafter initiate a new decoration—The Distinguished Flying Cross (DFC).

In early July Edwards is appointed to Number 2 School of Aerial Fighting as an instructor but before reporting for this assignment he joins his Carleton

Place hockey teammate **Roy Brown** on leave. The two war-weary Canadians take a relaxing weeklong canoe trip near Reading to recuperate from the stresses of Front Line fighting. Then, just days after returning to the flying school at Marske, Yorkshire, Edwards watches as his pal takes off and crashes.

In a letter to Brown's family he writes:

> "He was just getting off the ground on his second flight here. At about 200' his engine stopped and since there were trees and telegraph wires in front of him, he tried to turn back to the aerodrome. He lost his speed on the sharp turn and he fell from about 60' feet vertical to the ground. Luckily the ground was soft, but it was bad enough. The engine somehow was thrown on top of the wreckage, although it was a Camel he was flying and its weight was more or less on his head and neck.

> "I saw it all from where I stood and thought he must be killed instantly. The red ✚ hut was not 100' away and no time was lost. Both collarbones are broken, four ribs I think, one of which has pierced his lung. His jaw may or may not be broken. There is a cut or rather a hole in the inside upper corner of his eye, which they thought at first had pierced the brain, but it had not and will probably not be serious. There is also a cut on his forehead and of course many smaller cuts and bruises on his face and body.

> "The station doctor gave up all hope for him immediately and I brought a specialist down who arrived that evening and said the same thing so you see things looked pretty blue. However he has gradually improved and it is the opinion of three doctors that he will now pull through. He is being well looked after and has three nurses for himself."

Edwards becomes a fourth nurse for his Hobo Quartet best friend, and Roy Brown does indeed pull through. Post-War he remains active in aviation and is the editor of the *Canadian Aviation* Magazine during the 1930's. Edwards now returns to his new duties that place him in charge of training American fighter pilots. *(Read 12Nov18)*

18May18 – Lt Herb't Howard Snowdon FOWLER (Bowmanville ON) – ACE

Fighting his Camel C8266, Fowler out-maneuvers an Albatros D.V and brings his victory score to five. Four days later he brings down a sixth enemy aircraft before going on leave. He has been with 8 Naval, now 208 RAF,

since August 1917 and has flown more than 166 hours over the lines. In February 1918 he was temporarily grounded with ear trouble but now the condition is even more serious. During a medical examination in England, Fowler is found to have become almost totally deaf from recurring frostbite and rapid altitude pressure changes. He is released from the flying service and sent home to Canada in July. Some of his hearing will restore itself in later life.

Fowler had become a pilot with the Curtiss School in Toronto, earning RAeC 4051 in December 1916. He completed his Crystal Palace – Chingford – Cranwell training in June 1917 and his first victory was an Albatros D.V over Pont a Verdin on 05Feb18.

18May18 – 2Lt James Mills JOHNSTON (Athens ON) – KIC

Recently-graduated RNAS PFO Johnston has just been commissioned a 2nd Lieutenant in the new RAF. He is at the Temporary Duty Squadron in Cranwell awaiting his first operational posting when he dies in an aircraft crash. Stalling Avro 504 N5803, the machine enters an unrecoverable spin.

It is a third and fatally final crash for the young Ontarian. His first accident had occurred in France shortly after he transferred from the Canadian Expeditionary Force and completed Greenwich ground training. Flying Caudron G-III C5296 at RNAS Training Establishment, Vendome in February he hit a ridge, and damaged the aircraft. Two months later, in Curtiss JN4 8837, he misjudged his landing distance and crashed. Sustaining a lacerating wounds to his face and suffering from moderate shock he was admitted to the Station Sick Quarters. On this third occasion the stretcher carries his body to the Station morgue.

JM Johnston
Queens U

– Douglas Butterworth JOHNSTON,

his younger brother, was a McGill Student and Sergeant in the Canadian Militia. He too joins the RNAS and is initially trained at Greenwich and Vendome. After 'Wings' Graduation at Cranwell, Douglas is posted to 25 RAF Squadron. He will return alive and well to Canada and take up studies at the University of Toronto, and graduate as a dental surgeon.

19May18 – 2Lt John Seymour FORGIE
(Toronto) – Action

During a bombing raid over Blankenburge at 14,000 feet, a flight of Airco DH-9s from 211 Squadron are set upon by several enemy aircraft. One Albatros scout dives under the British leader's tail while the leader is engaged with other EA's. Forgie maneuvers his aircraft, B7661, positioning his gunner to fire about 30 rounds into the Albatros, and it nose-dives away vertically. Further observation is impossible owing to enemy action but 88 Squadron reports that the EA was seen to crash into a wood and catch fire.

Forgie was a transfer from the Canadian Cyclist Company to the RNAS in September 1917. The Army Lieutenant excelled in flying and graduated VGI from Cranwell in February. Due to his previous service he is granted one month's leave of absence in Canada. Making it known that he is not desirous of taking the home leave Forgie goes directly to Manston for DeHavilland aircraft training. He will be twice wounded in action during the summer but does survive the War.

21May18 – Observer Lt James Weierter ADAMS
(Ottawa ON) – CRASH

Returning from a raid on Frankfurt-am-Main, Adam's Handley Page 1466 has to force land just short of its 216 Squadron home base at Ochey. On touchdown the large twin-engine bomber catches fire and is burned out. All three crewmembers survive the crash. Observer Adams is later awarded the French Croix de Guerre for his war efforts in numerous bombing attacks.

23May18 – PObs Oscar Melville ARMSTRONG
(Toronto ON) – INJ

Probationary Observer Armstrong is badly hurt when his pilot sideslips at 700' and accidentally dives into the sea. Based with 209 Training Depot Squadron at Lee-on-Solent, the pair were airborne in a Short 184 seaplane. The aircraft 9068 is written off but both airmen survive and Armstrong will graduate as an Observer.

28May18 – Capt Cecil Hill DARLEY, DSC&Bar,
(Toronto; b. ENG) – DFC

(From 18Feb18) It is just a few weeks after the Royal Navy's Blockade ship sinkings when Marshal Foch, Supreme Allied Commander for the Western Front, learns of enemy congestion in the ports of Bruges and Zeebrugge from French naval air reconnaissance. He asks his British Commander, Sir Douglas Haig, to concentrate squadrons for intensive bombing in order 'to conclude the work so happily begun by the British Navy.' To carry out this request, British Army HQ replies that all available squadrons are being immediately placed at the disposal of the Vice-Admiral, Dover Patrol.

Tonight Darley leads the raid on the Zeebrugge Submarine Pens. Handley Page aircraft are not speedy, traveling at only 70 to 80 mph, and defensive ground fire can be 'very unpleasant'. In the early morning hours

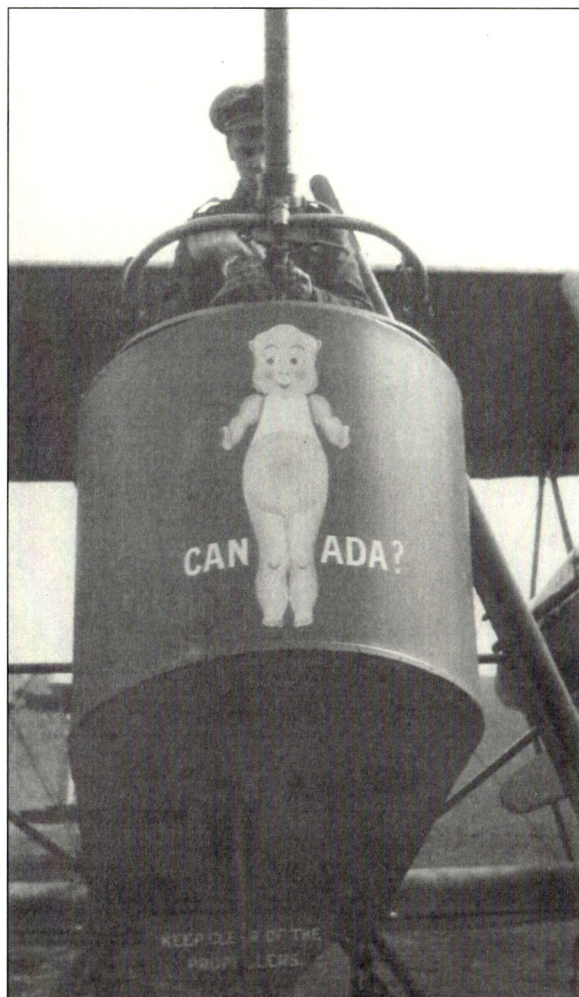

Early Nose Art: (Can-adian?)
The business end of a Handley Page Bomber

FAAM, 1998/047/0185

Darley approaches from the sea with both engines at idle. Gliding down silently in the darkness over the heavily defended target he releases at a height of 200'. Of his three 520lb bombs, one explodes close to a lock gate and the other two detonate inside the lock. Ten minutes later a second silent HP attacks.

Described as a 'Brilliant HP Pilot' by his peers, Darley is awarded the DFC for this action. *(Read 28Sep19)*

28May18 – Capt Hugh Bingham MAUND (Winnipeg; b. ENG) – WIA

Maund, a four-victory pilot will not achieve the title of Ace. Today, in Camel D3410, he is wounded in the hands and put out of active service. In addition to his four kills, Maund had also shot a Kite Balloon into flames and, although his guns were jammed, led his flight to smoke and drive down two more balloons just one week before sustaining today's injuries.

A Lieutenant with the 8th Battalion CEF, Maund joined the RNAS in November 1916. His graduation was setback by a flying accident and head injury but he more than made the grade in June 1917 as a 'VGI Pilot, Good & very keen Officer'. He was initially assigned to the new 6 Naval but this unit was disbanded in August 1917 in order to provide pilots for the severely decimated and understaffed 10 Naval. Soon in the fray, Maund proved his mettle on the 19th of September. In a matched engagement of eight Sopwith Triplanes with eight Albatros scouts near Hooge, Maund opened fire on one coming at him head-to-head. He saw tracers hit the engine and pass along fuselage. The EA slid underneath and fell out of control.

In spite of today's wounds to his hands, Maund will again fly and by January 1919 be in command of 204 Squadron.

JUNE 1918

03Jun18 – Major Bert Sterling WEMP (Tweed ON) – CO 218 RAF

(From 25Apr16) During February 1918 Wemp was appointed Commanding Officer of Number 2 Naval Squadron in France. Now, two months later he is selected to form 218 Squadron, a new RAF bomber unit. Dunkirk Command describes Wemp as: 'A most capable hard-working & zealous Squadron Commander. A good leader of men with good command & a skilful

& determined Active service pilot.' On the 3rd of June 1918, Wemp becomes one of the first Canadians to be awarded the new RAF decoration of a Distinguished Flying Cross (DFC). *(Read 01Jan30)*

04Jun18 – Lt Albert Gerald HODGSON (Vancouver) – WIA/INT

A mixed group of five flying boats are sent out from Felixstowe and Yarmouth to investigate possible Zeppelin activity over the north Dutch Islands. Hodgson is taken along as an additional pilot and observer. Since he is only just checked out on the F-2a Flying Boat.

AG Hodgson in RAF uniform
RAeC Trust

During the mission his aircraft is forced down on the water by a broken fuel feed pipe, and while attempting a fix the boat is attacked by several enemy seaplanes. Other RAF machines form a flying 'wagon circle' around their water-bound colleague and drive off the assailants. One of the boats, flown by Ensign Eaton, USN, breaks away and enthusiastically chases the enemy only to be shot down.

As the Germans will obviously return with reinforcements, the patrol leader orders Hodgson's Captain to taxi to the nearby Dutch shore and burn his machine. The remainder of the patrol are shepherding the downed craft towards Holland when they come under attack by a second wave of enemy seaplanes. Two hundred yards offshore of Terschelling, Frisian Islands, Hodgson's aircraft is struck and set afire by a Brandenburg fighter. Although surface-bound, the disabled flying boat gamely fights back and brings down one of the enemy. Hodgson, his Captain, RFL Dickey, DSO, and the crew, are interned in Holland.

But Hodgson has been badly wounded in the fracas and loses a leg. Due to this amputation he is now considered a non-combatant and paroled back to England on recovery. He returns to Canada to continue his pre-War law studies and will become a well-known Vancouver barrister.

In the summer of 1915, Hodgson was a non-graduate of the well intentioned but unpractical Aero Club of BC. This single-seat, single-aircraft operation by patriotic Vancouver citizens only graduated two aviators out of the 15 who joined. Financially a failure, the students subsisted through the kindness of the Commanding Officer of the 58th Battalion CEF who placed them on unit strength entitling pay and allowances. Hodgson, like many of the others anxious to join the British air forces, had made his own way overseas in late 1916.

– Captain F/Cdr Robert LECKIE, DSO, DSC (Toronto) – Action

(From 05Sep17) Leckie is the patrol leader of the mission that costs Hodgson his leg. When the reinforced squadron of Germans arrived back on scene, Leckie aggressively led his two remaining flying boats into a head-on attack. Driving through the enemy formation, he lost his wireless aerial on the upper wing of the first German. Splitting the enemy grouping, Leckie banked heavily to port, leading his machines in line astern to cut off three seaplanes of the attacking unit's right wing. These Germans then received the concentrated firepower of the flying boats' bow and port guns. The biggest seaplane battle of the war develops. Two EA are observed shot down and although the RAF patrol almost loses another member to yet another fuel line failure, all three return to the English mainland when the action breaks off. By flying skills and adept gunnery they have brought down a total of six German seaplanes. Leckie critically writes in his report:

> "It is obvious that our greatest foes are not the enemy but our own petrol pipes."

As a result of this day's action, it is decided that flying boats should have 'dazzle-painted' hulls in order to distinguish them more easily in air-to-air combat. *(Read 05Aug18)*

06Jun18 – Captain John Osborne 'Tiny' GALPIN, DSC, MID (Ottawa) – Shot Down

(From 22Dec17) On patrol in Curtiss H-12b N4345, Galpin is attacked by four Brandenburg seaplanes and is shot down by *Obflugm* Metzing and *Flgm* Walker. Galpin manages to force land his damaged Large America Flying Boat but it overturns on water contact. Aboard is Lieutenant Colonel Robertson, Station CO of Felixstowe who has been acting as Galpin's Second Pilot. As the dampened crew clamber a-top their upturned keel, a Brandenburg lands and taxies alongside. The enemy Chief Petty Officer pilot tells them that they are close to the English coast and asks if they would like to be taken to Zeebrugge as Prisoners of War or prefer to take their chances on being rescued by the British. His rank concealed by a Sicdot Flying suit, Colonel Robertson declines their offer of 'hospitality'. The German snaps a photograph, waves a cheerful farewell and takes off. The downed crew is rescued the following day by flying boats from Felixstowe.

Galpin, noted as a: 'Very hardworking & zealous Officer. G.Command. First class Pilot' is promoted to Major in August and assigned Command of 231 Squadron. By September he will be Gazetted the DFC.

09Jun18 – Lt William Fletcher SALTON (Ottawa; b. IRE) – KIC Adriatic

Taking off on an Adriatic raid, Salton's DH-4 D1773 crashes. He is killed and his Air Mechanic gunner, SW James, injured. Their Squadron, 224 RAF, is based at Otrano, and carries out anti-submarine patrols, reconnaissance along the enemy coast, and bombing of Austrian submarine bases.

Salton had been a Lieutenant with the CEF and served at the Front with the 225th Battalion. He entered the RNAS in March 1917 and was sent to No. 6 Wing

WF Salton

Italy in November. He was described as a: 'VG Pilot, fair Officer only, is improving & needs experience.

10Jun18 – Capt John Gerald MANUEL, DSC (Edmonton) – KIC – Midair

(From 20Sep17) Leading new 2nd Lieutenant, FC Dodd, into action, Manuel is killed when the inexperienced wingman skids into him. The 210 Squadron Camels are diving to attack hostile aircraft over Neuve Chapelle when the midair smash occurs and they fall in pieces.

Manuel had achieved his fifth kill on the 18th of February 1918 and was now a thirteen-victory Ace. He had been out of action from early May when a Very pistol cartridge exploded blowing out the side of his cockpit and injuring his hand. Back to work in June, he scored his 12th and 13th kills the day before the deadly midair. His combat report of these actions reads:

> "At 8:30 am while leading a flight on O.P. I observed 7 Pfalz scouts at 8,000 ft over Ploegsteert Wood and dived to attack. Shortly after, 7 more Pfalz and 3 Triplanes came up from the East and a general engagement ensued. Eventually 2 Pfalz became detached and dived East. I followed to 1,500 ft firing 200 rounds at the first one from 100 to 40 yds. Range. E.A. stalled, then spun down OOC. The second one then turned, but as he turned I fired a burst of 50 rounds at 30 yds range and E.A. dived straight into the ground and was seen to crash N.E. of Ploegsteert Wood."

Manuel has been put up for a second gallantry award to his DSC. In the event, the recommendations become the basis for a posthumous Mention in Despatches. He is buried at Y Farm Military Cemetery, Bois-Grenier.

11Jun18 – Lt George Mathewson SCOTT (Westmount PQ) – KIC – Agean

Landing on the Aegean island of Mudros, Scott's wingtip catches a flagstaff and his DH-4 D1774 tips into a fiery crash. Both Scott and his Boy Wireless Telegraphist, H. Boyles, are killed.

GM Scott

MHR

Scott had graduated from Cranwell flying school the previous October. Considered at first for instructing he was then described as: 'A Canadian, dull & sick most of the time. As Officer moderate. Not of the type likely to make a good instructor.' On this sour note he was sent to 2 Wing in the Aegean. At the time of his death Scott was flying with the Mobile Squadron at Mudos.

– 2Lt Gordon Douglas Scott,

his older brother, is a CEF transfer to the RNAS. Injured while training at Vendome in early August he does live to return to home to Quebec.

21Jun18 – PFO William Stanley Gordon BARKER (Winnipeg MB) – KIC

A trainee pilot, Barker is killed flying with 205 Training Depot Squadron at RAF Station Vendome, France. His Sopwith Pup C325 catches fire at 3,000 feet and Barker is thrown out at 150 feet near Crucheray. His aircraft burns up on ground impact. The 20-year-old Manitoban is buried at Loir-et-Cher.

26Jun18 – 2Lt John William DOWLING (Vancouver BC) – KIC

Dowling is accidentally killed in Camel C25 at No.4 Flying School of Aerial Gunnery and Fighting in England. His aircraft spins in while banking near the ground. Dowling, a twice-wounded CEF Soldier, entered the RNAS in November 1917. He is interred at the Freiston Churchyard, Lincolnshire.

JW Dowling
Sporting two Wound Stripes above his RNAS Eagle

FAAM

29Jun18 – Lt Henry James ELLIOT (Edwards ON) – KIA Aegean

The twenty-five-year-old Ontarian is killed whilst flying Camel B5670 with 62 Wing, Aegean Group. He had graduated as a VGI Pilot from Cranwell the previous

HJ Elliott

RAeC Trust

August was posted to the Eastern Mediterranean in November.

Elliot served for two years with the Canadian Army Service Corp's Motor Transport and was a Sergeant at the time of his transfer to the RNAS. He is buried at Lancashire Landing, Gallipoli.

JULY 1918

02Jul18 – 2Lt Alexander MacBeth SUTHERLAND (Winnipeg) – KIA

A former Sergeant with the Canadian Field Artillery, Sutherland's senior non-commissioned background stood him well at the RNAS and RAF training schools. He entered through Greenwich in September 1917 and graduated from Cranwell as a 'Very Good Officer.' He has natural flying skills and is given the highest rating as a 'V G Pilot Indeed.' Posted to 65 Squadron in late May 1918, it is now less than six weeks later when his Camel D9404 is lost in action.

Twenty years-of-age, he is buried at Caix, France.

AM Sutherland
In the first RAF uniform,
Single bar on cap denotes
2nd Lieutenant

GWFM

03Jul18 – 2Lt William Francis TWOHEY (Chatham ON) – KIC

WF Twohey in CEF uniform

U of T

At 202 Training Depot Squadron, BE-2c 9473 crashes and Twohey is lost due to injuries incurred. He is interred with the growing number of crosses at the St. Andrews Cranwell Churchyard, Lincolnshire.

Twohey had previous military service as a Lieutenant with the Canadian Field Artillery.

04Jul18 – Lt. Sydney ANDERSON (Vancouver BC) – WIA/DFC

Anderson earns his DFC the hard way—becoming wounded in the action. Operating Felixstowe F-2A flying boat N4513 on a War Flight patrol with 232 Squadron, Anderson and two accompanying aircraft, N4297 and N4540, engage in combat with four enemy seaplane fighters over Zeebrugge. The 38-year-old Ace, Friedrich Christiansen, commander of the German Naval Air Station at Zeebrugge, leads the Brandenburg machines. Although Anderson's crew manages to account for one fighter, N4513 itself is forced down in the water. Anderson is hit, as are his English Second Pilot Lt KL Williams and Boy Mechanic AEV Hilton. His Gunlayer, Airman Cokeley, has been killed.

The flying boat, although taken in tow by the Royal Navy, sinks and is lost. For pitting his slow 'boat' against the faster fighters, Anderson will be Gazetted the DFC in September. The War Flight of Felixstowe and its offshoot at the Scilly Islands comprise a most highly trained group of flying boat aviators. They rightfully nickname themselves 'Pukka Boat Pilots'.

06Jul18 – Lt Edwin Curtis Robinson STONEMAN (Toronto) – Adriatic Action

In Albania the Italian Corps have commenced an offensive against the Austrians. All Otranto-based pilots and aircraft not required for anti-submarine patrols are tasked in support of the campaign. Today, Stoneman, a DH-4 bomber pilot with 224 Squadron attacks the Kuchi Bridge. The structure is Austria's only line of supply and communications and it is taken out. For this and other raids on Austrian bases in Albania and Montenegro, Stoneman will be awarded the Al Valore Militare—the Italian Silver Medal for Military Valor.

Stoneman was a 'Very Good Indeed' graduate of Cranwell in March of 1917. However, after being posted to 11 Naval, he became quite ill and damaged several aircraft during the summer. Sent back to Cranwell for a suitability check as to his ability as an efficient pilot 'or just unlikely to be of use in air fighting,' Stoneman is reassessed as being 'thoroughly steady' and goes to Seaplanes at Calshot. In December 1917 he was appointed to 6 Wing in the Eastern Mediterranean.

ECR Stoneman
via J Straw

In the January 1919, New Year's Honours List, Captain Stoneman will be further recognized with the award of a DFC for Service on the Albanian, Montenegrin & Austrian Frontiers

06Jul18 – Lt Donald HAMMOND (Toronto) – News

In the Canada Illustrated Weekly, it is reported that:

> 'Miss Teddie O'Neil, a review actress, was last week awarded 750 Pounds damages for breach of promise of marriage. The judgement was given against Flt Sub Lt Donald Hammond, a Canadian, who did not appear to defend the action'.

Hammond is in Canada. He had flown with Naval 8 in March and April 1917 and was diagnosed with Neurathsenia in May. Following a recovery leave in Canada he returned to ground duties in October, being declared permanently unfit for flying. His resignation was accepted in February 1918.

08Jul18 – 2Lt Charles HOMEWOOD (Canadian; b. ENG) – KIC

Taking off in Avro 504 C5843 Homewood enters into a stall condition and his machine spins into the ground. He does not survive the impact and is buried at Frittenden in Kent. A former Private in the Canadian Expeditionary Force, Homewood had graduated as a pilot and was putting in time with 207 Training Squadron at Chingford when the accident occurred.

One month previously, while in Avro 504, D7657, a propeller had fatally injured his Instructor (FBG Smith, MC). Student Homewood was unhurt in that accident. This time though, caught in a spin from 300 feet, he is not so fortunate.

10Jul18 – Lt Charles Bryson RIDLEY (Toronto) - WIA/POW

Described as being 'very keen and full out.' Ridley graduated from RNAS flying training into the RAF and was sent to Manston for fighters. Assigned to 43 Squadron, a former RFC unit that had formed in Stirling, Scotland in 1916, he was soon in the thick of things on the Western Front. Wounded in early June, he is hit again today during an engagement with three EA. His Sopwith Camel engine is also damaged and Ridley has to put down in enemy territory. He is imprisoned for the duration at Seidletz. Repatriated following the Armistice, he takes on medical studies at the UofT and graduates as a physican in 1923.

'C. B. Ridley
Auxi-le-Chateau'
FAAM, Album 153

13Jul18 – Lt Cecil Guelph BROCK (Winnipeg; b. ENG) – ACE

It has been a painful but determined route for Brock to achieve Ace. He joined 1 Naval in late May 1917 and was operational in Sopwith Triplanes during the opening of the Third Battle of Ypres. By August

1917 he had scored three victories but was wounded three times and detailed to ground duties at Naval Air Station Wormwood.

Turning down a Canada Leave he requalified at Manston in early March 1918. Assigned to 209 RAF he was airborne in the Red Baron engagement of the 21st of April. Now with 3 Squadron in Camel D7835 he makes his fifth victory.

13Jul18 – 2Lt Henry Hunt WALKER (Fort William ON) – Flu Canada

On Canada leave, Walker dies of illness while in his hometown at the head of Lake Superior, Ontario. He is an early victim of the Spanish Influenza, a pandemic that will sweep the world, mainly claiming healthy young adults. An estimated 50 million die of the disease.

Walker, civilian accountant, had been a Sergeant in the Canadian Forestry Corps before commissioning with the Infantry. Transferred to the RNAS in March 1918, his previous military service from November 1915 had permitted a Home Leave on completion of initial flying training. He is interred at the Thunder Bay (Mountain View) Cemetery.

13Jul18 – 2Lt Evan Francis KERRUISH (Port Elgin ON) – KIC

EF Kerruish

U of T

'Keen Steady Pilot' Kerruish had recently completed a DH4 bomber course at Manston as well as torpedo weapons training in HMS *Vernon*. Assigned to No. 1 Torpedo Squadron at East Fortune, Scotland, he is killed in the crash of Bristol F-2b B8937. The 250 horsepower machine stalls and spins on takeoff. Aged 20, the former 153 Battalion CEF Signaler is buried at Catterick, Yorkshire.

15Jul18 – Lt George Powell ARMSTRONG (Toronto ON) – DOI

GP Armstrong

RAeC Trust

Armstrong dies of burns received in a flying accident two days previously. His passenger, 2Lt H. Higgins of New York City, died in the crash. The aircraft, BE2c 8422, was operated from the 202 Depot Squadron, a training establishment set up for Handley Page bomber pilots and crew. Armstrong is buried at Cranwell.

15Jul18 – Obs 2Lt Charles William DODDS (Canadian; b. ENG) – INJ Egypt

Observer Dodds is injured when his Pilot stalls avoiding an Arab dhow on takeoff at Alexandria Harbour, Egypt. Their Short Admiralty 184 seaplane 8020 crashes into yet another vessel. Fortunately the two 64 Wing aviators survive their dunking and their injuries.

18Jul18 – Obs2Lt Jas Garvey Marshall FARRALL (Vancouver; b. IRE) – KIA

A patrol of two Short 184 aircraft from 406 Flight, Westgate, rendezvous with an escort of two Camels out of Manston. Just four miles southeast of Kentish Knock they encounter six Brandenburg Seaplane fighters of 'Flanders 1' led by the now ten-victory German Naval Ace Christiansen.

In the confusing melee that follows, the Sopwith pilots mistake a Short that is shot down for an enemy machine and a retreating Brandenburg for a Short so they leave the scene. With that, the Germans are the clear winners. *Oberleutnant zur See* Christiansen shares his eleventh and twelfth kills, the two Shorts, with his wingmen.

The Observer in N2937 is 2nd Lieutenant Farrall of Vancouver: there are no survivors from either aircraft. A photograph of a downed Short, taken by one of the Brandenburg aviators, substantiates the action.

19Jul18 – Lt Stephen Arthur DAWSON
(Albertson PEI) – Tondern Raid

In 1916, Admiral Jellico, Commander in Chief of the Royal Navy's Grand Fleet had observed the attempts by HMS *Vindex* and HMS *Engadine* to launch aircraft. The cumbersome lowering of Seaplanes over the side at sea confirmed his opinion that efforts should be devoted to starting aircraft from the deck of ships.

Now such a vessel has been built. HMS *Furious*, a highly-modified battle cruiser with a flat forward deck, is ready for active service launch operations. A target of the Zeppelin sheds at Tondern is selected and the pilots are chosen. Dawson, who has just completed his scout training at Manston, is recognized as having a 'First Class flying ability.' The aviators complete deck takeoff qualification at Turnhouse in Scotland and also practice bombing the outlines of the Tondern sheds marked out on the airfield grounds.

SA Dawson

MHR

In the event, HMS *Furious* launches seven Camels, each armed with two 60lb bombs. Off at 0315 first light they easily hop into the air with the combined ship/wind speed over the flight deck of 34 knots. All are airborne within nine minutes towards Tondern, some 80 miles across open water. Briefed to act independently over the target, the Camels 'Caught Fritz properly napping' and Naval Zeppelins L.54 and L.60 are destroyed. But low skud clouds and poor visibility does not help the return. Only three pilots reach *Furious* and rather than attempt the ship's hazardous aft landing deck, they ditch alongside to be picked up. One aviator is believed to have run short on fuel and is Missing. The three others, recognizing their fuel constraints, land in nearby neutral Denmark.

Dawson in Naval Camel 2F1 N6823 force lands at Holmslands Klit. He manages to secure civilian clothing but is taken into custody at a railway station. Brought to a hotel with the other two pilots who have been arrested in uniform, Dawson simply walks out and escapes in his non-military garb. The other two are eventually released

and all three make their way back to Britain via Sweden.

Thus ends the world's first true aircraft carrier air strike on an enemy air base. All of the aircraft are lost as well as one pilot but *Furious* is safely back at her Rosyth moorings in the Firth of Forth by 04:00 the following morning. A planned future raid using Strutters is never carried out. The RNAS has been absorbed into the RAF and there are now other priorities…

Former McGill student Dawson is assigned to 73 RAF in Flanders. On the 10th of August he becomes Missing in combat west of Chuignottes. Camel D1783 is claimed by *Oblt* Harald Auffahrt of *Jasta* 29, the eighteenth of his twenty-nine kills. The rumored award of a DFC to each of the Tondern Raiders is never officially promulgated.

20Jul18 – Lt Charles Wilfred LOTT
(Brussels ON) – KIC

Lott is a seaplane pilot at Kalafrana, Malta, when he is lost—reportedly crashing and drowning in Sopwith Dolphin scout machine B6871.

The 'Keen and Promising Pilot' had graduated from the Navy's Lee on Solent Seaplane School in October 1917 and was written up as: 'Did well in Bends & Hitches, Practical Armament, Rigging, First Aid, Practical Engine Work; but not so well in Boat Work, Seaplane Flying, Signals, Rifle Drill, Meteorology, Navigation, Rules of the Road, Compass Chart Reading, and Photography.'

Aged 22, Lott is buried at Pieta, Malta.

CW Lott

FAAM, Album 13

22Jul18 – Major Raymond COLLISHAW, DSO, DSC (Nanaimo BC) – 50th Victory

(From 28Apr17) Together with his senior Flight Commander Len Rochford, Collishaw takes off just before dawn for a strike on the German Dorignies Aerodrome near Douai. Each Camel carries four 25lb bombs and Rochford does the first pass, setting a hangar on fire and using up all his machine gun ammunition. Collishaw hangs back just enough to catch aircraft being wheeled out of hangars. He then sweeps over the camp and drops his bombs. Spotting a night recce machine returning to land he shoots it down for his 50th victory.

Rearmed and returning to assess damage two hours later, Collishaw is assailed by three Albatros fighters. He sends one down into the Scarpe River and then escapes home. Soon letters of congratulations arrive from Major General JM Salmond, Commander of the RAF in France, and from Lieutenant General AW Currie, Commander of the Canadian Corps. It is believed that Collishaw was recommended the Victoria Cross and Rochford a DSO for the raid. However, the medals awarded are a Bar to the DSO for Collishaw and a DFC for Rochford. *(Read May1919)*

24Jul18 – 2Lt Frederick Alfred CASH (Hamilton ON) – KIC

Cash meets death during a flight training mission with the Grand Fleet School of Air Firing & Gunnery at East Fortune, Scotland. His Sopwith Pup 9946 develops a spinning dive from which he cannot recover. Cash, a 22-year-old University of Toronto student, is interred at Preston Kirk Parish Churchyard, East Lothian.

25Jul18 – 2Lt George Bamfield McSWEENEY (Toronto ON) – KIC

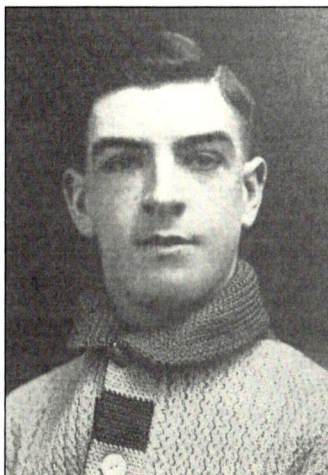

Flying in an aircraft with the engine mounted at the rear is fraught with danger. The pilot has no heavy metal protection in front to absorb any crash impact. Indeed, he is sitting in little more than a doped canvas 'bathtub'

GB McSweeney
via M Pirie

enclosure, with the ever-present chance that the engine can crush forward.

Flying FE-2b Pusher Biplane A6596, McSweeney is thus killed. He had been training with the No.1 School of Navigation and Bomb Dropping, and is buried at Durrington Cemetery, Wiltshire.

25Jul18 – Lt Ralph Waldon ROBINSON (Komoka ON) – WIA/DOW Holland

Nineteen-year-old Robinson is last seen above clouds at 12,000 feet off Nieuport. His 218 Squadron DH-9 B7667 crashes at sea and Robinson is most severely injured. Rescued by the Dutch, he dies of his wounds while in their care on the 11th of August and is buried at Petten in the Netherlands. The body of his Gunlayer, HA Claydon, washes ashore in later days.

27Jul18 – FSLt Stanley Alexander GRANT (Montreal PQ) &
– Obs SLt Frank Russell BICKNELL (Dunville ON) – MID Aegean Action

The Aegean Group consists of isolated and scattered units stationed from the island of Lemnos near the Dardanelles to the island of Crete in the Aegean Sea. RAF 62 and 63 Wings together with Flights of Greek Naval aviators make up the strength of the Group. All are short of aircraft and the numbers are further reduced when a 'lucky' enemy bomb destroys a hangar containing seven Sopwith Camels. In retaliation, the Talikna Seaplane Station, Lemnos Island, is tasked for a night bombing attack on the German airfield at Galata, on the Dardanelles Peninsula. Grant and Bicknell are paired for the operation.

Pilot Grant will later write in his diary:

> "Too bad we haven't practiced night flying and bomb dropping, but it will be bright moon-light. Had too much weight to get off. Made three runs dropping 1st 3 sixteen lb bombs, then 1 sixty-five and then was off on my first real active service over enemy territory.

> "Had no trouble picking up our objective. Passed Suvla Point where so many Australians died. Saw 2 extra bright stars which queued us for some time. Crossed Gallipoli at 4000 feet, which seemed to be a sea of mountainous ridges. Dropped to 2000, made a run, but Bick hadn't sights fixed. Returned and dropped two 100lb bombs almost on hangars and one 16lb some distance away. Circled round

again dropping to 1000 and gave them some Lewis gun. They replied with regular hail of machine gun, which pierced planes and finally drilled the radiator. Fine spray and water came back, and began to think of landing in the Straits. Bick climbed up on top, but couldn't stop leak, but as engine was going alright, decided to make Xeros. To do this I had to climb 1500 to clear the mountains. I made about 2000 but was beginning to loose it, before reaching the hills, which we just managed to scrape over thro' a gap. Engine and height were now going rapidly, so tried to get as far from shore as possible, and be picked up. Bick fired his distress signals and then got out Aldis lamp. Engine was behaving badly now, so shut off petrol, and opened the throttle. This seemed to finish her, appeared to crumble up and nose dived into sea."

Bicknell recalled the engine overheat:

"We crashed … in the Gulf of Xeros and remained afloat by hanging to the small tail float which we had managed to hack off with pocket knife before the plane sank about one hour after landing at mid-nite."

Stripped of their clothing for swimming, the two exhausted crewmen, "in our shirts and wrist watches only" are picked up by the Greek destroyer *Leon* as they floated towards the Turkish shore. They are Mentioned in Despatches for the night's efforts.
(Read Bicknell 28Jun19)

29Jul18 – Lt Obs Leonard Arthur CHRISTIAN (Armstrong BC) – OBS ACE

Returning from a bombing raid, 206 Squadron machines are attacked by about 20 Fokker D.VII biplanes. Inside of two minutes Observer/Gunner Christian shoots down one EA that is seen to crash, and sends down another in flames near Menin-Wervicq. Eight minutes later he shoots down a third West of Courtrai. These are Christian's fifth, sixth and seventh victories, all scored with the Lewis gun mounted on the rear cockpit frame of the DH-9. During this mission, he is flown by an English Pilot, L.R.Warren, in aircraft B7596. He had scored his previous four kills with his Canadian Flight Commander, **George Leslie Eugene Stevens**.

'Leo' Christian was a farmer and a horse breeder from British Columbia. Joining the Royal Naval Air Service in 1917 he developed a fear of heights during pilot training and yet bravely requested to serve as an Observer. Graduating as a: 'Moderate Observer & Officer', Christian has done extremely well and will have 9 German aircraft to his credit by August 1918. In September he is Gazetted for a DFC recommended in June: 'Since joining his squadron this officer has taken part in forty-seven bomb raids, displaying at all times keenness and determination, and rendering his pilot most valuable support. He has accounted for four enemy aeroplanes, destroying two, and driving down two out of control.' During World War II, Christian will serve with the Royal Canadian Air Force.

29Jul18 – Capt James Butler WHITE (Manitoulin Island ON) – ACE

White makes his fifth kill of an eventual 12 victories with 208 Squadron. He will have one strange encounter on the 14th of August while diving on an enemy two-seater. The German Observer looks around when White opens fire but does not return shots. He has perhaps been mesmerized by a structural failure that immediately comes to White's attention—the Camel's left-hand lower wing has buckled. White keeps his cool and delicately rights his machine and lands without further damage.

Gazetted the DFC and Mentioned in Despatches by War's end, White is repatriated to Canada in April 1919. He becomes a mortgage broker and will eventually rise to the position of President of the Toronto Stock Exchange.

JB White

FAAM

31Jul18 – 2Lt John Eckford GOW
(Kingston ON) – POW/DOW

During an evening patrol, 204 Squadron's Sopwith Camels enter into a heavily mixed melee with two formations of Fokker biplanes. The Squadron suffers the loss of three pilots missing and one wounded in the engagement. Gow, in Camel D3394, is one of the Missing.

Owing to the nature of the fight with the ten enemy Fokker D.VIIs a close observation of the events was impossible. It is thought probable that Gow followed an enemy machine too far down and was hit by machine gun fire from the ground. He was last seen over Roulers and had crashed on the enemy side of the lines. Taken prisoner, he dies of wounds on the 10th of August. Aged 19, Gow had served as a Gunner with the Canadian Field Artillery and was recommended for the RNAS by Colonel Walter Gow, Deputy Minister of Canadian Military Forces Overseas.

AUGUST 1918

05Aug18 – Capt Robert 'Bob' LECKIE, DSO, DSC
(Toronto; b. SCT) – 2nd Zeppelin

(From 04Jun18) Leckie is carrying out his turn on the roster as Duty CO of Yarmouth base this evening when a Zeppelin raid is perceived. He signals an alert and the Air Station personnel rush from pubs and a concert in town to scramble after the airships. One DH-4 Pilot, Major Egbert Cadbury, sprints into a ready cockpit of machine A8032. Quickly turning over his temporary command of the station to the nearest officer, flying boat captain Leckie clambers aboard sans flying gear to act as Cadbury's gunner. They immediately take off and jettison their bombs in order to gain altitude efficiently.

The intrepid duo climbs to over 16,000 feet and find and attack Zeppelin L.70. Leckie concentrates his explosive bullet fire on the bow and rakes the airship aft, shooting down this, the most recently built pride of the German lighter than air fleet. Aboard is *Fregattenkapitan* Peter Strasser, Commander in Chief of German Zeppelins.

Turning their attention to the remaining two Zepps, Cadbury closes on L.65 for another head-on pass, giving Leckie a clear shot. The gunfire begins to perforate the giant airship but then the weapon jams. In the rushed takeoff, Leckie had not brought along gloves and now his badly frostbitten fingers cannot clear the cross-feed jam in the pitch darkness. L.65 somehow does not

ignite and escapes. At this point, in the inky blackness and miles from land, the DH-4 engine fails. Descending through layers of thick cloud the machine is eventually restarted and following an anxious half-hour, the crew sight the flares of a night landing ground. There follows a near midair collision on touchdown, after which the victorious pair discover that their 'jettisoned' bombs had failed to release.

Cadbury, later Sir Egbert of Fry-Cadbury, and Leckie, later Air Marshal, RCAF, are each Gazetted for the Distinguished Flying Cross: 'These officers, attacked and destroyed a large enemy airship, which recently attempted a raid on the northeast coast, and also succeeded in damaging a second airship. The services rendered on this occasion were of the greatest value, and the personal risk was very considerable for aeroplanes a long way out from land.'

In 1995, Robin Leckie, RCN Air Branch retired, and son of Robert Leckie, wrote

> "My father told me that Strasser's body had been found floating in the wreckage and on his person, a copy of the zeppelin code book. The papers were taken and the body was dumped back into the sea and the minesweeper crew sworn to secrecy. My father's comment was 'What a rotten way to treat a gallant enemy'." *(Read 07Oct20)*

– Observer Lt. Edward Richard MUNDAY
(Toronto) – MIA

In the mad dash to launch and intercept the Zeppelins over Yarmouth Naval Air Station, two aircraft, a Sopwith Camel and a DH-9, are lost in the thick cloud and poor conditions that prevail and obscure detail. Aboard the DH-9, D5802, Observer Munday and his English Pilot, DGB Jardine become missing. Brother **Albert Munday**, a Flying Boat Captain, telegrams their mother in Toronto.

> "Edward adrift North Sea; may have been picked up. Doing everything possible."

The Pilot's body washes up on the West coast of Jutland in late September but Edward Munday is never found. Age 31, he is another name listed on the Naval Memorial at Chatham.

Edward was a Legal Accountant in Winnipeg when he joined the Canadian Expeditionary Force at the start of the war. A Signals Corporal with the 34th Fort Garry Horse, he served two years in France before transfer to the RNAS. A third brother, Walter Munday, was also a Trooper with Fort Garry Horse and joined the Royal Flying Corps in December 1917.

Following the War an interesting account from *Kapitanleutnant* Walter Dose of Zeppelin L.65 tells of being hit by 312 bullets and that four of his interior ballonets were perforated like sieves 'So that the homeward journey was not a special pleasure.' As Leckie was only able to get off a short burst before his gun jam, both he and pilot Cadbury are of the opinion that the damage was inflicted by Jardine and Munday flying the DH-9 just below them.

07Aug18 – 2Lt George Kendall 'Ken' LUCAS (Markdale ON) – Ditched off Albania

In a raid against Austro-Hungarian forces at Durazzo Harbour in Albania. Lucas is tasked to follow the attacking DeHavilland and Camel aircraft in his Short Seaplane and rescue any of the land machines obliged to alight in the sea. On return, it is the Short that is brought down by a cracked cylinder and Lucas veers off in the direction of nearby destroyers. An attempt is made to tow the seaplane to Brindisi but an angry sea wrenches it unsalvageable:

GK Lucas

Betty Lucas Stewart

"We wanted to save some of the gear before sinking the machine so we had her pulled up alongside and a demolition party sent aboard. The way in which that party went to work proves that the British Navy still retains the taint of the buccaneering days of long ago... They broke off, pulled off and sawed off everything detachable. Up went dashboard instruments, wireless gear, pails of petrol, half the propeller, signaling apparatus etc, etc. However upon returning to the ship, instead of a huge heap of miscellaneous articles lying on the deck, there was only part of our wireless gear. Everything else had disappeared as souvenirs. It took considerable persuasion at Brindisi to even coax the more valuable parts of our gear out of the various hiding places. The machine gun, for instance, was recovered from beneath the floor of the first Lieutenant's cabin.

"After we had abandoned the remains of our old

Short, the Captain thought that this would be grand opportunity for a little target practice... The first shots missed the mark by a hundred yards and even those that did eventually hit, merely tore large holes in the canvas. Our target practice was the occasion for much ironical cheering from the Australian Destroyer that had stood by to see the fun.

"The Captain, nettled by the attention of our Australian friends, decided to turn heavier guns on the poor old Short and blow the – – thing out of the water. He'd show them. This was accordingly done, but with the same results.

"The Australians were now giving us advice on 'how to sink a seaplane.' Our Captain now sent out his redoubtable wrecking party in a small boat, with orders to fire the machine. After much promiscuous pouring of petrol about, the conflagration was finally started and finally consumed all the canvas on one wing. Wild cheers from Australia. The wrecking gang were provided with axes and hatchets to chop her to pieces... This they did in a truly through manner—but still she floated—upside down.

"The Captain, now thoroughly out of patience, drew the ship off about half a mile and amid the hat waving and cheers from Australia, rammed old man Short at full speed. This was too much, and with a last saucy flip of her toes, she gurglingly gave up the ghost."

Many years later, in September 1932, 'sometime Flight Lieutenant in the RNAS, Barrister at Law of Osgood Hall Toronto,' Lucas will give up his life to save his infant daughter Betty from drowning at Pointe Au Baril, Georgian Bay in the 37th year of his age. His father, the Hon I.B. Lucas, former Attorney General of the Province, erects a tablet there in commeration.

07Aug18 – Capt William James PEACE (Bartonville ON) – DFC

It is the night before the opening of the Battle of Amiens and the flying weather is atrocious. However Peace of 207 Handley Page Squadron is detailed for an unusual mission. The British Army intend a surprise use of tanks to capture the important railway network town and call for a bomber to fly low along the front lines to camouflage the noise of mechanical movement. After two takeoff attempts, Peace manages to get his heavy machine airborne despite the dense clouds and rain.

Flying by compass he reaches the Lines and patrols for three hours.

Peace is Gazetted the DFC in November for: 'A very fine performance, calling for high courage and perseverance, in face of the difficulties due to weather conditions.' Group Captain WJ Peace will be CO of RCAF Station Jarvis in 1943.

08Aug18 – Capt Gordon Aird FLAVELLE (Lindsay ON) – DFC

When Peace lands just after midnight, Flavelle endeavors to get his Handley Page bomber off the ground. It also takes several attempts in the hazardous conditions of low cloud and heavy driving rain.

Flying at extremely low altitudes in the black and turbulent skies, Flavelle also patrols up and down the front lines for three hours. His exhaustive efforts drown out the noise of the tanks being started up and moved forward en mass. Coupled with a heavy morning mist the assault is an outstanding success. It is truly a 'Black Day' for the German Armies. In November Flavelle too is Gazetted the DFC for this unique camouflage operation.

Flavelle had flown his first operational flight in the HP the previous October. With a grand total of 53 flying hours he had only 11 on the big bomber at that time. He noted in his logbook: "Dropped bombs on target but could not see the results for clouds. Lost ourselves on way back. Crashed machine near St. Dizier. Nothing left but tail and part of fuselage… Self thrown clear. Hit head and left shoulder cutting head slightly." The large 7 Naval machine, 3140, was indeed a write-off.

11Aug18 – Capt John Playford 'Jack' HALES, MID (Guelph ON) – ACE/KIA

The Ontario Agricultural College graduate flew with 9 Naval during 1917 and had scored four times. By January 1918 having been on active duty and flying constantly for 19 months, Hales requested a Canada Leave. The applica-

JP Hales

U of T

tion was not approved and he was told to resubmit after two years service.

Following a 'rest' as a ferry pilot out of Dunkirk, he had returned to the flying fray with an appointment to 203 RAF. Twelve days after scoring this fifth victory, Hales is brought down by anti-aircraft fire during a trench attack near Bray. The 25-year-old Ace is buried at the Meaulte Military Cemetery in the Somme.

11Aug18 – Lt Stuart Douglas CULLEY (Montreal; b. USA) – Zeppelin Kill

Zeppelins off the Frisian Coast are annoying the Royal Navy's Harwich Striking Force. The airships are able to observe British transport and troop shipping movements without coming into range of the Force's guns. The Zeppelins scout ahead for U-boats but stay clear of attacks by British-based aircraft. The Navy decides to take its aircraft to the airships

A rudimentary take-off deck is conceived utilizing a forty-foot barge. The scow contraption can be towed by HMS *Redoubt* at just over 30 knots. Onboard, a skid landing-geared Sopwith Camel is carried to 'slide-launch' along channels built into the pine-planked deck. Colonel Charles Samson, one of the four original pilots in the RNAS, does the trial run. Tied back to avoid falling into the blades, a naval airman is harnessed to the scow's bow and swings the Sopwith's propeller. The engine catches, the airman is pulled aside and Sampson signals 'chocks away'. Disastrously, a sudden crosswind raises his wing and slips a skid out of its channel. Sampson cartwheels over the bow and is overrun by the barge. He is fortunate to only just escape drowning, suffering broken fingers, a cracked rib and concussion.

Culley immediately volunteers to go but on a wheeled machine in order to avoid the drag of the skids. He has no previous training at this type of take-off, nor will there be any practice run. The Harwich Force is now at sea, closing on the Fresian Coast and launching Motor Torpedo Boat attacks. A Zeppelin soon appears, taking the MTB bait.

Armed with twin Lewis guns mounted on the upper wing and loaded with incendiary magnesium bullets, Culley successfully launches. Exactly one hour after rising from the deck, and slowly climbing with the sun at his back, he is at the absolute maximum ceiling of his machine and just below the enemy. Pulling his joystick back, Culley opens fire, stalling his aircraft:

"Rose to 18,700', attacked Zeppelin from 300 ft below.

Fired 7 rounds from No. 1 gun, which jammed, and a double charge from No. 2."

The two million cubic feet of flammable hydrogen in the 645 foot long aerial dreadnaught ignites. The airship's bow breaks away and the blazing mass rotates to stand vertically upwards and then plunge seawards, tail first. Culley's aircraft is completely out of flying speed and falls away. He recovers to view the smoke trail of the burnt out airship:

"Blown into the shape of a huge question-mark"

Flying straight to the Dutch coast, then south to the Texel and back out to sea, Culley seeks a rendezvous at Terschelling Bank. It takes time to find the flotilla and when he does spot the force, he loops and rolls overhead before carrying out a pre-planned ditching. "When I landed in the water alongside the destroyer *Redoubt* I had just under one gallon of petrol left in my reserve tank, the main having been exhausted. The Camel was so light I could hardly get her down at the exact spot."

Observing from his Flagship, Admiral Tyrwhitt sends out a Fleet Signal. 'Hymn Number 24 Verse 7' that sends the Watch Officers on countless bridges scurrying to obtain a Hymnal and read:

"Oh happy band of pilgrims,
Look upward to the skies,
Where such a light affliction
Shall win so great a prize."

The Admiral will refer to the feat of airmanship as "The grandest and bravest thing I have ever seen in my life." Culley is recommended for a Victoria Cross but is in the event he is appointed 'The Poor Man's VC'—a DSO for services rendered.

Aircraft N6812 is retrieved from the water in fair shape and is to this day exhibited at London's Imperial War Museum. Zeppelin L.53 is the last German airship to be destroyed during the War. The crew of 19 perishes with the exception of the single parachutist who is picked up, relatively uninjured, by a Dutch fishing vessel. The day is not without British casualties; the six 'bait' MTBs fail to torpedo any enemy craft and all are lost to *SFS* seaplane attack.

In 1964, an RNAS Museum was proposed for the Royal Navy's Fleet Air Arm at Station Yeovilton. When asked for information about the incident that had eventuated his name, Culley, now a business man in Milan, Italy, wrote:

"I made a once only effort, and thereby created a bit of naval air history. There are two service points I would be glad if you made clear as they were two

records for those days: a) There was ONE German survivor who dropped by parachute from 19,000' and I saw him come out of the Zeppelin. I am quite sure that was a parachute record for those days. b) My takeoff run was exactly 5 feet according to Colonel Samson who watched the takeoff. That I feel sure is a take off which I doubt has ever been equaled even by catapults."

Remaining with the RAF following the First World War, Culley will see service mainly in the Middle East and India. He is Mentioned in 1935 for the Mohmand Operations; and receives another MID in 1941 for the Syrian Campaign. He retires as a Group Captain.

20Aug18 – Four Canadians are promoted Major, RAF, and appointed Anti-Submarine Squadron Commands:

– **Major Robert LECKIE, DSO, DSC (Toronto, b.SCT) – 228 RAF**

– **Major John Osborne 'Tiny' GALPIN, DSC, DFC (Ottawa) – 231 RAF**

– **Major Cecil John CLAYTON, MIDx2 (Victoria) – 230 RAF**

Clayton takes over the newly formed 230 Squadron at Felixstowe. He has been a seaplane and flying boat pilot since early 1917 and had received a Mention for action on September 3rd 1917. That day, flying as Second Pilot in Large America seaplane 8676, Clayton was part of a two-aircraft bombing run on an enemy submarine off North Hinder. The boat was fully blown and traveling about 14 knots in a northerly direction. The number U4 was deciphered with the second numeral unread and two men were seen in the conning tower. Canadian pilot **TD Hallam** led the attack placing the submarine upwind and keeping the sun's position behind the flying boats.

In January 1919, Clayton will be Gazetted a DFC for his war services.

CJ Clayton

With the cessation of hostilities his Squadron applies

a peacetime colour scheme to their Felixstowe F-5 flying boats and are involved in an ambitious plan to start transport services to the Azores, the USA and Egypt. One F-5 makes a successful 14-hour endurance trial before the project is abandoned. Clayton will leave the RAF in October 1919 and study dental surgery back in Canada.

– Major John Keith WAUGH, DSC (Whitby ON) – 241 RAF

(From 25Apr16) Waugh becomes CO of 241 Squadron at Portland. In March 1919 he receives correspondence from his Toronto Alma Mater: 'On behalf of the University and the Faculty of Applied Science, we wish to congratulate you on being awarded the Distinguished Service Cross, and on being Mentioned in Despatches. The University has been highly honoured in the services rendered by its five thousand and more members who have taken their part in this war, and we are specially gratified when these services have received recognition in the award of well merited honours.' Remaining in RAF service, Squadron Leader Waugh is killed in a flying accident at Heliopolis, Egypt, in April 1931.

– Lt Alexander MacGregor ANDERSON (Toronto ON) – DFC

On the Western Front, 218 Squadron is short of Observers and Anderson flies this day's contact patrol 'in the back seat' of a DH-9. He does valuable recce work and then rescues his wounded pilot when they are forced down. One month later, flying as pilot, Anderson encounters a Fokker D.VII over Stalhille Aerodrome and he shoots it down. His DFC for these actions will be Gazetted in November.

AM Anderson

U of T

22Aug18 – 2Lt James Brightwell CUNNINGHAM (Ottawa) – KIC

JB Cunningham

DeWolfe/M Pirie

An overturn upon landing at Wavans in France takes Cunningham's life. His Observer, SGT EB England, is injured but escapes from the wreckage of DH-4 F6169.

Graduating from Cranwell in April Cunningham was with 205 Squadron. He had been a Clerk with the Department of Militia & Defence in Ottawa.

23Aug18 – 2Lt. Joseph Philip CORKERY (Regina) – KIC Italy

On Adriatic service Corkery is killed in a DH-9 crash at Cattaro with 224 RAF. Before transferring to naval aviation in November 1917 he had served in France as a Private with the 15th Canadian Field Ambulance.

29Aug18 – Capt Harold Mervyn IRELAND, MID (Toronto) – DFC

Leading a large DeHavilland-9 formation across the trenches into Belgium, Ireland runs into adverse winds and obscuring cloud. Detailed for a long-range bombing raid on enemy docks, he carefully studies his compass and making due allowance for the strong winds he continues the 211 Squadron mission. Arriving at a point he judges to be correct, a break opens in the clouds proving his navigation spot-on. The dockyard is effectively blasted.

Ireland is Gazetted the DFC for this work and for having led some 43 long-distance raids 'of which he has shown judgement, skill and determination of a very exceptional nature.' His MID had been awarded a year previous for good work with 3 Naval in the field. When the Canadian Air Force is formed in late 1918, Ireland will be one of those chosen for manning Number 2 Squadron, CAF. He admirably suits the directive that 'as far as possible it is desired to have Officers who have good records with the RAF and have had a certain amount of active service flying in France and in other theatres of the war.'

29Aug18 – Lt Col Redford Henry MULOCK, DSO&Bar (Winnipeg) – 82 Wing IAF

(From 10Jul17) 'Red' Mulock is tasked to form a new Wing with the Independent Air Force (IAF) of the RAF. This 'Independent' force is the strategic bomber section of the new RAF and functions without coordination or orders from the Army or Navy. The objective of forming Mulock's 82nd Wing is to strike at the German industrial heartland around Cologne.

RH Mulock, note year of service chevrons on right sleeve
CAHF

In October Mulock will be promoted to the rank of full Colonel and given charge of establishing and training 27 Group, a special force to consist in part of Handley Page V/1500 'Super' aircraft, designed to attack deep into enemy territory from Norfolk in the British Midlands. These latest, and by 1918 standards, monstrous, four-engine machines give the RAF a cross-Channel capable bomber and Mulock is just the man to make them operational. By early November he has worked up one of his squadrons to bomb Berlin. At the eleventh hour the mission is scrubbed and German capital saved by the Armistice. Only one of the aircraft ever does see action when a Handley Page V/1500 bombs Kabul during the Afghan War of 1919. The origins of the Second World War's 6 Bomber Group of the Royal Canadian Air Force take root in the IAF. *(Read03Jun19)*

30Aug18 – 2Lt Persival Howard GOODHUGH (Westmount PQ) – POW/DOW

On his 15th operational mission with 46 Squadron, Goodhugh is declared Missing In Action during operations over the Fourth Army Front. He is last seen in combat under eight EA south of Peronne at 2,000 feet fighting his Camel B9271. Taken prisoner he dies of wounds in a German military hospital.

Goodhugh was one of the first Canadians to join the colours. The former Bank Clerk had entered the CEF in November 1914 and by the time of his transfer to the

RNAS in December 1917 he was an Acting Sergeant with the 17th Canadian Machine Gun Corps.

SEPTEMBER 1918

03Sep18 – 2Lt Frederick Arthur HUYCKE (Peterborough ON) – MIA

Huycke, the youngest of four serving sons of Judge Edward Huycke of Peterborough is Missing. He had come overseas as a Lieutenant in the Canadian Field Artillery and transferred RNAS in March 1918.

Recently graduated from the seaplane flying school at Calshot, Huycke was on a familiarization flight with his new unit, 239 Squadron out of the Torquay Harbour Devon.

His aircraft, Short 184 N2962, and his English instructor, AG Bishop, are all lost. A Court Inquiry places the blame on an error of judgment.

FA Huycke
U of T

04Sep18 – Capt James Henry FORMAN, DFC (Kirkfield ON) – POW

(From 28Jul17) Leading a squadron-sized offensive patrol, Forman is shot down at Douai and taken prisoner. It is a day of very heavy losses for 70 Squadron as eight of the twelve Allied machines are brought down in this single combat. Forman's group has encountered some thirty Fokkers of *Jagdgeschwader* III. Highly involved in wearing down the enemy ground forces, the RAF's doctrine of offensive flying brings it up against large formations of experienced and competent German pilots.

Forman had become an Ace on the 12th of April with 201 Squadron and on the 2nd of July was Gazetted the DFC for eight victories, three in flames and five OOC. Rated as 'A skillful patrol leader' he scored a ninth in August with his new unit. Released and repatriated to Canada in January 1919, Forman will serve with the RCAF in the

1920's and again as a Flight Lieutenant Administrative Officer during the Second World War.

04Sep18 – 2Lt Hugh Angus SUTHERLAND (Hamilton ON) – KIC – Midair

Sutherland is accidentally killed in a midair crash out of RAF Turnhouse. His Sopwith Pup B8012 collides with Stutter 9894 over the Firth of Forth. One occupant of the Strutter, 2Lt R Payne, is injured and the other, Flt Sgt A Wright, is killed. Twenty-year-old Sutherland was training for flight deck operations in HMS *Furious*. A former Canadian Expeditionary Force Sapper, he is buried in Scotland.

04Sep18 – Lt Victor Algar BISHOP (Vancouver; b. SCT) – Crash in Canada

On home Leave, Bishop crash-lands a Hoffar H-2 aircraft on a downtown Vancouver, British Columbia, rooftop. The impact penetrates the ceilings of a house at the corner of Bute and Alberni Streets but he, fortunately, escapes serious injury.

Bishop had transferred to the RNAS from the Seaforth Highlanders of Canada and on graduation was permitted the now standard home leave for two years previous service. Reported as a 'Keen Officer. Shows promise of becoming a good Instructor', the perhaps too keen Bishop had accepted a test flying opportunity over his hometown.

05Sep18 – Lt Herbert Wm MacKarsie CUMMING (Toronto) – KIC

Leaving Dunkirk and climbing steeply to pick up his 204 Squadron formation, Cumming's Camel F3242 stalls and spins. The twenty-year-old University of Toronto student crashes and dies from the injuries.

Cumming was not an in-experienced Camel driver, he had been flying the challenging machine for over one year, sustaining injuries with Naval 8 in October 1917 and surviving being badly shot-up and crash-landing in August with 204 Squadron.

WM Cumming

U of T

12Sep18 – Major Ambrose Bernice SHEARER, Cd'G (Neepawa MB) – CO 227 RAF

Number 227 Squadron is being formed at Pizzone, Italy, and Shearer is appointed Commanding Officer. The unit is to be equipped with a mixed bag of twin-engined Caproni bombers and single-engined DH-9 machines. However, they never become fully operational by War's end. The Squadron will be disbanded by December.

Shearer is fortunate to have lived through the conflict to this point. During flying training he had an engine fail on a Curtiss JN-3 in January 1916 and the same aircraft, 3423, brought him crashing down again ten days later, this time to a complete write-off of the machine. Operational with 3 Wing, Shearer was badly injured in the accidental explosion of 23 January 1917 when **MH Stephen's** Strutter had a bomb hang-up and release on the ramp.

It took two months in hospital and a Canadian Long Leave before Shearer was surveyed and found fit again by October 1917. Re-training at the Manston Fighting School he suffered a broken jaw in a Sopwith Strutter accident at Pegwell Bay in Kent. Regardless of all his injuries, by April 1918 FCdr Shearer was recognized as: 'Excellent Officer & Pilot. Handles men well. Recommended for promotion to Squadron Commander in due course.'

During the summer of 1918, Shearer flew with the Adriatic Group in Taranto, Italy. He led bombing missions against Cattaro, a round trip across 400 miles of water. In one instance, bucking headwinds, he took four-and-a-half hours to reach the target. With insufficient fuel to return he traversed the Austrian lines and landed on an Italian held beach at Valona in Albania.

Shearer finishes the War with awards of both the Italian Silver Medal for Military Valor and the Italian Croce de Guerra in addition to his 1917 earned French Croix de Guerre. Although offered a permanent commission in the RAF, he will return to Canada in 1920, become a Squadron Leader in the Canadian Air Force and eventually take command of the Air Station at Dartmouth, Nova Scotia.

During the Second World War Group Captain Shearer is initially the Director of Works and Buildings and then completes the War as an Air Vice Marshal, AOC, Number 2 Training Command.

14Sep18 – Lt Roland Wallace HEINE
(Moncton NB) – POW

The Independent Air Force has been tasked to support the French and American attack on the St Mihiel Salient at the Lorraine Front. The main drive of the bomber force is to take out the Metz-Sablon railway network. During this evening's raid 216 Squadron loses Handley Page 3131, shot down over Metz. Aircraft Captain Heine, his Second Pilot, 1st Lieut. FF Jewett, United States Air Service, together with English Observer/Gunner, Lt. EA Marchant, are all captured by the German authorities. Heine, a married insurance manager from New Brunswick, had only just joined the RNAS in January of this year. His time of incarceration will be short as the War rolls to an end.

16Sep18 – Lt William Benson 'Scottie' CRAIG
(Smiths Falls ON) – ACE

A very fierce fighter pilot, Craig had begun a victory count just a month ago, on the 15th of August, with two kills. Today, in Camel D3374, he brings down his third, fourth and fifth victims. He will go on to score another double and a single for a total of eight.

A schoolteacher, 'Scottie' Craig joined the RNAS from the Canadian Field Artillery in October 1917. He graduated a 2nd Lieutenant in the new RAF in early May 1918 and completed the Manston War School by the middle of that month, reporting to Dunkirk for 204 Squadron. (*Read 26Sep18*)

16Sep18 – Lt Varian Sweetnam GREEN
(Calgary) – Action

228 Squadron, Yarmouth, launches Green in Felixstowe F-2A Flying Boat N4549. Together with another F-2A and a DH-9, the patrol will attempt to set a trap for enemy machines operating out of Zeebrugge. The idea is to fly about 40 miles to the south and lure the enemy after the slow 'Boats'. Once the trap is baited, a wireless signal would be sent to bring land machines from Dover to wipe up.

Five seaplane hostiles are duly encountered and the wireless message goes out. However, only one DH-4 out of five launched makes the rendezvous and that machine fails to spot the enemy. The entrapment is now reversed and becomes a one-sided engagement with advantage to the Brandenburg seaplanes of the *Seefrontstaffel*. Green's aircraft is shot up but he claims an enemy brought down as it is seen to be aflame. The second Yarmouth flying boat has a loss of engine revs and alights on the water near the Shipwash Light Vessel. Fortunately for all, the German machines choose to break off the engagement at this time and depart to the east. It is Naval Station Yarmouth's last engagement with the enemy.

Green was a McGill student who served as a Militia Lieutenant from 1914, joining the RNAS in October 1917. He graduated with the highest marks: 'VGI Seaplane Pilot & Officer. Recomd. for Large Boat Patrol. Should make a remarkably good patrol pilot. Always stays in the air as long as possible.'

In June 1970, in a re-enactment celebration of the 50th Anniversary of the First Trans-Canada Flight, Green pilots his personal twin-engine Cessna 337 Skymaster. Passing through Ottawa he meets once again with retired Air Marshal **Robert Leckie**, his former 228 Squadron Commander.

17Sep18 – Capt Frederic Ross JOHNSON, DSC, MID
(Westmount PQ) – POW

The evening of the 16th/17th September is an all-out commitment for the night bomber squadrons of the Independent Air Force. The industrial targets are near the German Rhine cities of Cologne, Frankfurt and Coblenz and twenty-four aircraft are launched. During the operation seven Handley Pages are lost to enemy fire and three others crash on the Allied side of the lines. It is the heaviest losses of Handley Pages during the War.

Johnson, with 100 Squadron, has just released his

FR Johnson

RAeC Trust

bomb load on the Frescaty Zeppelin sheds when an engine fails. The machine cannot sustain level flight and can only be coaxed a few miles before the inevitable forced landing.

The three aviators, including Lt RC Pitman of Saskatoon, burn their aircraft and intrepidly set off on foot for Switzerland. On the run for four nights they are finally captured in a state of hunger and exhaustion.

Johnston was one of the first Canadians to be trained on the Handley Page in January 1917. 'Very keen Officer.

Good at handling men & excellent Pilot. Zealous & reliable with sound technical knowledge.' Assigned to Dunkirk for 7 Naval he was Mentioned for good work on a bombing raid on Aertrycke Aerodrome in July 1917 and awarded the DSC for bombing Thourout in September. In January 1918 his good copybook is blotted when he is Court Marshaled for an 'Act to the prejudice of good order and Naval discipline in assisting a Temporary Flight Sub-Lieutenant to evade Admiralty Regulations for the censorship of private correspondence.' Pleading guilty Johnson is sentenced to a Reprimand from the Vice Admiral of the Dover Patrol. Even so, he is appointed an Acting Flight Commander and placed in temporary charge of 15 Naval during March 1918.

He further clears his name during a rare opportunity on the night of the 15th/16th August. Returning from a raid, Johnson spotted a set of exhaust flames. Realizing that they were from a German bomber following flares to Friesdorf aerodrome he dove to attack and his observer opened fire:

> "After a burst of about 45 rounds the machine crashed alongside the flare path, the searchlight on the ground immediately put its beam on to this machine which was observed to be a total wreck."

17Sep18 – 2Lt Ernest Graham GALLAGHER (Leamington ON) – INT Switzerland

Gallagher is a Second Pilot in Handley Page D4588 with 115 Squadron, a unit that has only just arrived in France. During this night's Independent Air Force bombing raids against the various German targets, his aircraft is hit by flak but manages to reach the southern border and limp into Switzerland. The crash-landing crew are immediately interned by the neutral Swiss.

20Sep18 – 2Lt Milton George CRUISE (Port Dover ON) – KIA

A 203 Squadron patrol and ensuing dogfight ends disastrously for Cruise. His Camel E4409 is shot out of the sky over Haynecourt. The civilian Automobile Mechanic and later Private in the Machine Gun Corps of the CEF is buried at Queant Road, Buissy.

20Sep18 – 2Lt Ernest Gordon RALPH (Toronto ON) – POW

An unsuccessful aerial combat with five EA northeast of Dixmunde brings down Ralph in his 204 Squadron Camel D3387. Less than two month's imprisonment follows. *(Also Listed as E.G. Rolph)*

20Sep18 – First United States Navy ACE Lieut. David Sinton INGALLS, (Ohio USA)

USN Lieutenant Ingalls is on exchange with 213 Squadron RAF and scores his fifth victory of an eventual six. Awarded the British DFC and an American DSC he is the only United States Navy Ace of the First World War. American born **Edward Rochfort Grange** of Michigan and **Oliver Colin 'Boots' LeBoutiller** of New Jersey are both Naval Aces who flew with the RNAS.

21Sep18 – 2Lt Frederic Ivor ATKINS (Winnipeg MB; b.SCT) – INJ

With 249 Squadron, Dundee, Atkins is badly injured while flying as Second Pilot in Curtiss H-16 'Large America' N4070. The aircraft hits a ship's mast on the River Tay, crashes and bursts into flames. The flying boat captain and the two enlisted airmen are all killed. Atkins is the sole survivor.

25Sep18 – 2Lt Ralph Vyvian GORDON (Kamloops & Victoria BC) – KIA

On a bombing raid over the lines from Charmes, several enemy machines attack Gordon, shooting away some of his DH-4's landing wires. He succeeds in

RV Gordon

returning to his 55 Squadron IAF base but, without the taut wire structure his aeroplane collapses upon touchdown.

The heavy landing fractures the skull of the 22-year-old University of Toronto science graduate and he dies of injuries that evening. He is buried at his airfield cemetery.

U of T   Gordon had held a Lieutenant's certificate with his Woodstock College COTC but enlisted in the ranks of the 88th Battalion CEF and served in the Signals Section. He went overseas in May 1916 and was transferred to the 25th Battalion in France that November.

With extraordinary resilience, Gordon had seen more of the war than many, having served through the battles of the Somme, Vimy Ridge, Hill 70 and Passchendaele.

He moved his fight from the ground to the air in March 1918 when he entered the RNAS—where his battles would end in just six months.

25Sep18 – Lt James Campbell SORLEY (Ottawa) – KIA

RAF 213 Squadron is in heavy action and scores one Fokker but at the cost of two pilots killed and another taken prisoner. Sorley is one of the dead.

JC Sorley

Before transferring to the RNAS Sorely had been with the CEF in France since September 1915. He served before Wytschaete, at St. Eloi, Ypres, and on the Somme. After the Battle of Courcelette he was sent to England to be commissioned and became an instructor in signaling. Transferring to the RNAS in January 1918 Sorley was offered a flying instructor's position following pilot graduation. He refused and requested a return to the Western Front—To fly in overhead support of his old trench mates. He joined 213 Squadron on the 24th of August. Now only a month later Sorely is lost on the Belgian Front near Ostend

26Sep18 – 2Lt Orley Landon MALCOM (Toronto) – KIA

Bombing the Metz-Sablon railway junction 99 Squadron and 104 Squadron of the Independent Air Force come under heavy air attack. Malcom of 104 IAF, in DH-9 D7232, is seen spinning down out of control and both he and his Observer, GV Harper, are killed. The IAF is strongly committed to supporting Allied preparations for an attack on the Hindenburg Line but losses to the day-bomber squadrons are high. Six DH-9 aircraft that cross the line this day will fail to return; survivors report combat with upwards of 30 to 40 Enemy Aircraft.

Malcom, being groomed as a flight leader, was heading the second formation seven of aircraft from his squadron. He fell under the guns of *Leutnant* Johannes Klein, a sixteen-victory ace of *Jasta* 15.

26Sep18 – Lt George Edwy Caldwell HOWARD (Toronto) – KIA

In Camel C75, Howard has just completed a special mission escorting bombers when his formation enters into combat over Blankenberghe on the West Flanders coastline. A fierce fight in a stiff westerly breeze ensues and Howard is shot down by *Flgm* Karl Engelfield of German Navy Fighter *Jasta* V.

Howard was no stranger to action. He had joined 4 Naval in July 1917 and received a shrapnel bullet through his left thigh that September. Following a recovery leave in Canada, he requalified as a scout pilot at the Manston Fighting School in February 1918 and immediately applied to rejoin his squadron. The 22-year-old Torontonian is buried where he fell in West Flanders.

GE Howard

– Lt William Benson 'Scottie' CRAIG
(Smiths Falls ON) – KIA

Scottie Craig

FAAM, B0191A/0065

(From 16Sep18) Along with Howard, 204 Squadron today loses Craig. In Camel D3374, Craig is brought down by German Chief Petty Officer Christian Kairies of *Marine Feld Jasta* V. Twenty-three year old Ace Craig will be posthumously awarded the DFC in November.

Of the German Naval airmen: *Oberflugmeister* Kairies, seven victories, is killed five days later; *Flugmeister* Engelfield, five victories, survives the war.

26Sep18 – Captain John Foster CHISHOLM, DSC, DFC, (Westmount PQ) – INT

Leading an early morning bombing attack, with the Zeebrugge Mole, Harbour, and Lock Gates as objectives, Chisholm is shot down over Bruges. His 218 Squadron DH9 aircraft is hit by AA fire at 7,000 feet. Firing a white flare to signal his plight, Chisholm falls out of formation. His radiator is holed: the coolant sprays out and causes the engine to seize. Gliding to overhead

'Petite Synthes June 1918'
JF Chisholm (holding mascot)
and AM Anderson (see 21Aug18)

FAAM Album E 01085

Flushing and circling over the town to lose height, Chisholm is fired upon by Dutch troops. He lands on the beach in front of the Grand Hotel, but in order to miss a breakwater, has to steer the machine into the sea. The aircraft will be repaired and become Dutch Air Force deH466—the pilot becomes a rather short-time guest in Holland.

Chisholm had earned his DSC: 'in recognition of his services on 6th of December 1917 when he made a photographic reconnaissance to the vicinity of Zeebrugge, & for the great skill and determination with which he has carried out his duties at all times.' Chisholm's DFC was only just Gazetted on the 21st of September. By that time he had brought down four enemy aircraft.

Returning to McGill University after Armistice, Chisholm will become a prominent lawyer and a King's Council in Montreal.

26Sep18 – 2Lt William Joseph KELLY
(Brantford ON) – KIC

With 205 RAF, Kelly is struck by a propeller and killed. A Sapper from the Canadian Engineers, Kelly came to the RNAS in November 1917. He was fortunate to have survived an accident during flight training—at Vendome in March while practicing steep turns in Curtiss JN-4 8877 he had lost flying speed at 200 feet. Failing to recover control, his aircraft entered a slow spin, crashing in a complete wreck. Pilot Kelly sustained moderate shock, lacerations to the upper and lower lips, and general body bruising with a wound to his right knee. Today, the 21-year-old loses his life to the spin of a prop.

27Sep18 – 2Lt William Allison Weldon CARTER
(Fredericton NB) – Cambrai Crash

The Battle of Cambrai commences and Canadian Infantry and tanks assault the Canal du Nord on the Hindenburg Line. 201 RAF is tasked to carry out low bombing and firing at ground targets during this advance. Four Camels are detailed for each Army Corps.

Carter's Flight finds that smoke from the covering barrage has caused a thick haze over their objectives, so they return to the lines and follow up the advancing infantry and tanks, assisting at hold-up points by firing bursts into machine-gun emplacements and trenches from very low altitude. Carter drops his bombs on an point offering particularly strong resistance and then observes the Canadian infantry capture the defenders. He then empties his remaining ammunition into the trenches in front of the tanks. During this entire time he is under intense ground fire and finally when the petrol lead on his machine is shot away, Carter comes crashing down into the bursting shellfire. His Squadron mates believed that he is picked up by one of the Tanks. However the 'battlefield battleship' that they see from the air does not pass close enough to recognize the downed airman and make good a rescue.

Uninjured after his Camel flips over and comes to an inverted stop Carter drops out and starts running west through the barrage. Coming across a wounded British soldier he begins to carry him back to safety. At one point they enter and share a shell hole with two disarmed Germans awaiting capture. One Hun presents his Iron Cross to Carter rather than let it be taken for a souvenir by some prison guard. Transferring his wounded man to the Germans, Carter escorts them back to the Allied trenches

Awaiting transport, the airman goes exploring and finds the Hindenburg Line, empty of combatants. Going down into a deep shellproof dugout littered with discarded equipment, he gathers souvenirs to take back to the Squadron. When the local shelling stops, he emerges and makes his way to base. On arrival Carter reverses his cap, hangs his Iron Cross, and—festooned with two Lugers and Zeiss binoculars—advances looking like a comic Hun.

27Sep18 – 2Lt Roy Victor CURTIS
(Toronto) – Action

Roy Curtis is the younger brother of Naval Ace **Wilf Curtis**, DSC & Bar. Joining the RNAS at the end of 1917, Roy is now flying with No. 3 Squadron, RAF, and proving himself as aggressive an aviator as his sibling. The Squadron 'Canadian' Report for September notes RV Curtis on this day dropping three bombs and firing 300 rounds on enemy troops and transport on the Cambrai-Masnieres Road. One transport is knocked out and troops dispersed. Two days later Curtis drops four bombs on a fully inflated enemy balloon on the ground. He also fires 200 rounds at another enemy balloon as it is being pulled down.

Again in October and November, Roy Curtis will figure in the Squadron's 'Canadian' write-ups. His last action in the War is on the 1st of November when he drops four bombs on six motor transports and scatters 150 troops from the side of a road. He then shoots 300

rounds into an active machine gun emplacement causing it to cease firing.

28Sep18 – Lt Bliss Edward 'Dutch' BARNUM
(Kingston ON) – Action

Barnum has a very busy day with 204 Squadron. In the absence of his Flight Commander, he leads his Sopwith Camel flight on four successive bombing raids. This morning opens the last campaign in Flanders as the Allies push to finally break the German Army's spirit. For 204 the big battle starts around Dixmunde and Ypres:

- At 06:35AM a Squadron takeoff is made in a tremendous rainstorm but returns when the formation cannot be kept together.
- At 10:40AM Barnum leads 6 Camels and bombs Thourout.
- At 1:30PM he attacks the Cortemack Railway junction, and finally;
- At 4:14PM he takes off to bomb and shoot up Leek.

In late October, Barnum receives an appointment to HMS *Furious*. His 204 Squadron Commander writes: '[…] since the 28th of September Lieutenant Barnum has acted as leader in eleven successful low bombing raids. In these he has shown marked courage and devotion to duty, descending at times to 50 feet altitude. In addition, this officer has destroyed four enemy machines.'

The Queen's University student will end of the War with these four victories, just short of Ace. He is recognized on the King's Honours List of December 1918 with the award of a DFC.

28Sep18 – 2Lt Charles Reynold MOORE
(Toronto ON) – POW

The final Allied ground battles for Flanders may have opened, but early-morning flying missions have to contend with violent storms as well as enemy gunfire. Departing at 0600 to escort a spotting machine on a 'shoot' at Rayersyde, Moore, in DH4 A8066, is last seen diving through clouds about two miles over the lines. He has encountered very heavy weather, the visibility is zero, and it is the meteorological adversary that forces him down near Nieuport. The retreating German Army quickly captures Moore and his Observer, 2Lt E. Darby. His Squadron, 202 RAF, has lost three aircraft, two of them to the weather.

An unusual entry for the RNAS, Moore joined as a transfer *from* the Royal Flying Corps. Graduating in April 1917 a VGI Pilot and Officer 'Keen and full out', he was recommended for instructing. This appointment ended badly at the Instructor School at Redcar: on the 28th of April Moore's engine on Avro 504 B8618, failed on a climbing turn near the ground. He continued the turn, stalled, side slipped and spun in. He was slightly injured but his Airman passenger, WAC Easter, was killed. Shortly after the accident Moore applied for operational flying.

28Sep18 – Lt Alexander MacKay STEVENS (Moose Jaw SK) – MIA

Stevens is flying another DH-4 machine that 202 Squadron loses this day, but not due to weather. Caught out by five enemy scouts over the Engel Ammunition Dump target, Stevens and his Observer, 2Lt WHL Halford, are shot from the sky. Their aircraft, A7849, is combat-claimed by *Ltn* F Piechulek of *Jasta* 56. There is no known grave for the former McGill engineering student and Canadian Field Artillery Lieutenant. Both he and his Observer will be named on the now far too long list of missing airmen for the Arras Flying Memorial.

28Sep18 – Lt Bernard Hill STATA (Ottawa) – KIC

Also providing air support this 'start day' of the final Allied Campaign in Flanders, 218 Squadron loses four DH-9 machines; three to enemy ground fire. The Squadron casualties include the first American Marine Aviator to be Killed In Action, 2Lt CC Barr USMC on exchange with the RAF, who will die of wounds on the 6th of October.

Stata 'Petite Synthes June 1918'
FAAM, E 01085

Stata is flying the fourth DH-9, D1085, and is brought down by a violent thunderstorm cell. Patrolling in low-level support of the Belgian Army, his aircraft breaks up and spins in near Wulveringhem. A 'Very Good Indeed Pilot & Officer', the 24-year-old Stata and his 18-year-old 2Lt Observer, CVR Browne, are both dead.

29Sep18 – Lt Alan Geoffrey WHITE (Victoria BC) – KIA

Five DH-9s of 211 Squadron are on a bombing raid on Courtrai when they encounter some forty hostile aircraft over Ypres-Cambrai. In the running fight that ensues all five allied machines are hit and three are very fortunate to make it back to home base. White's D3039 is last seen smoking and out of control. He and his Observer, 2nd Lt JB Blundell, are killed.

White's death brings the former-RNAS Canadian casualties during 'Black September' to a close. Twelve are Killed or Missing. Eight have been Interned by neutrals or taken Prisoner of War by the Germans. The long War is not yet over.

OCTOBER 1918

01Oct18 – 2Lt Robert Ellerton THOMPSON (Toronto) – MIA

At age 18, Thompson is one of the youngest Canadian Fighter pilot casualties of the War. The Port Hope Trinity College student becomes Missing during an 80 Squadron action over Bellicourt. The remains of Camel F6026 and pilot Thompson are never recovered.

02Oct18 – Captain William Fulton CLEGHORN, DFC (Toronto ON) – KIA

(From 26Apr16) At 1800 on the first of October, the Belgian Army HQ was informed that reserves of food for advanced troops are exhausted and that getting supplies forward by morning is doubtful. Roads in the region of Houthulst Forest have incurred considerable damage from the effects of artillery fire, rain, and previous convoys. With the route rendered impassable it is decided to deliver 15,000 rations to the cut-off troops by air.

The supplies, in sacks padded with earth, are thrown overboard at an agreed spot—dangerously close to the German positions at Stadenberg. By 1325 hours on the 2nd, the 218 Squadron mission is a success;

but at the cost of Cleghorn's life. His Observer, FH Stringer, DSC is taken prisoner when their aircraft, DH-9 E8958 is brought down but Cleghorn's body is never found.

WF Cleghorn
'Petite Synthes June 1918'
FAAM, E 01085

'Cleggy' had scored two victories during his time with 218 Squadron and he had been awarded the DFC in August for his part in some 59 bombing raids.

For several years, Cleghorn's food drop mission was displayed in a dramatic diorama at the British Airborne Museum outside London near Farnborough.

03Oct18 – Capt F/C Chas Robert Reeves HICKEY, DFC (Parksville BC) – KIC Midair

(From 21Apr18) A midair collision in cloud takes the life of Hickey, a Flight Commander with 204 RAF. His Camel D6626, is impacted by Camel B8189, flown by 2Lt S.E. Matthey.

A member of 4 Naval since July 1917, Hickey was an outstanding ace with 21 victories. Together with **Collishaw** of Nanimo and **Fall** of Cobble Hill these three fighter pilots from the Cowichan Valley of Vancouver Island account for a total tally of 117 enemy aircraft.

Hickey has been in combat for over a year and was awarded the DFC. A Bar to this gallantry medal is posthumously Gazetted in November. This second DFC was proposed by his Squadron Commander in mid September with the commentary: 'Since being recommended in June last for award of the Distinguished Flying Cross, this Officer has destroyed seven enemy machines and driven nine down completely out of control and has been engaged in ten indecisive combats.

His skill and devotion to duty have made his Flight very successful. On 16 September 1918 while leading his Flight he destroyed two and drove down two enemy machines, his Flight getting several Huns down and sustaining no casualties.' Hickey was further described as a 'Very determined air fighter. Good disciplinarian. Was in charge of Squadron Headquarters for three

months and the production of work under his command was very satisfactory.'

Hickey scored nine of his victories in Camel C74. On the 30th of September this Sopwith airframe is deleted due to general fatigue. It may well be that Hickey himself was in an exhausted state when he and a member of his Flight collided three days later.

CRR Hickey
CFB Comox

The 21-year-old Vancouver Islander is buried at Coxyde Military Cemetery, Belgium, and a commemorative plaque is placed at St. Anne's Anglican Church, in his hometown of Parksville.

07Oct18 – 2Lt Herbert David LACKEY (Ottawa) – KIA

After operations in a dangerous low-bombing offensive patrol with 70 RAF, Lackey's Camel E7176 fails to return. He is last seen near Lichtervelde and is at first listed as Missing. When his body is eventually recovered, the 22-year-old is buried at Harlebeke in Belgium. Two Leutnant Pilots from *Jasta* 40 claim a Camel kill over Ghent.

14Oct18 – Capt John Edmund GREENE, DFC
(Winnipeg) – KIA

(From 11May18) After scoring a morning victory, his 15th, shared with USN exchange officer Lieut Kenneth MacLeish, Greene is leading his flight of 213 Squadron Camels on a second mission of the day when they are attacked by 17 Fokker D.VIIs over Pervyse. Green's aircraft, D3409, is brought down by German Naval Ace Reinhold Poss, Commanding Officer of *Marine Feld Jagdstaffel* IV. Crashing at La Panne, Greene fractures his skull and dies soon after in hospital. Two others from his flight have also been killed.

In front line action for a year now, Greene had to have been feeling the fatigue and strain of constant combat. As it was, German Ace Carl Degelow of *Jasta* 40 had crashed Greene on the 4th of October. Surviving that episode has only gained the 24 year-old Canadian Flight Commander ten days. It is noteworthy that eight of Greene's victories were achieved against the much-vaunted Fokker D.VII aircraft type. On October 2nd alone, he had scored a triple, destroying three of these machines.

– Lt William Thomas OWEN
(Toronto) – MIA

Owen is one of the losses from Greene's Flight in the encounter with the German Marine *Jasta*. The odds of a single flight against a squadron are over three against one and have proved overwhelming. Although Owen had graduated a VGI Pilot and VGI Officer from Cranwell in February, he is no match against his victor, *Flugmeister* Gerhard Hubrich. Camel D3378 falls as the ninth kill of this eventual 14-victory ace. Hubrich will fly and fight again during the Second World War. As a Major in the Luftwaffe he is believed to have shot down two Allied aircraft.

Owen had earned Canada Leave from his previous service in the trenches as a CEF Sapper and took the trip home following his Cranwell 'wings' presentation. Returning to England he had been injured during a training flight on the 5th of July. These events led up to his late arrival in 213 Squadron only three weeks before this fateful combat with the veteran German naval pilots.

– Lieut Kenneth MacLEISH, USN
(Illinois, USA) – KIA

US Naval aviator Kenneth MacLeish is on exchange with the RAF in order to gain fighter combat experience. He has previously served with 218 RAF Squadron as a DH-9 Bomber pilot. A member of Greene's Flight, MacLeish too is lost—But the bad day is not yet over for the unit, as three others will be declared Killed or Missing by evening. MacLeish's body will not be found until the 26th of December when it is discovered by a Belgian landowner returning to his wrecked farmyard near the village of Schoore.

MacLeish is posthumously awarded the United States Navy Cross for 'distinguished service and extraordinary heroism' and is buried at the Flanders Field American Cemetery in Waregem, Belgium. USN destroyer DD-220, the USS *MacLeish*, is named in his honor in December 1919. His story is told in *The Price of Honor—The World War One letters of Naval Aviator Kenneth MacLeish*, published by the Naval Institute Press of Annapolis, Maryland. The preface poem 'On a Memorial Stone' is written by Archibald MacLeish, a Pulitzer Prize winner and Kenneth's brother.

14Oct18 – 2Lt Osborne John ORR
(Nanaimo BC) – ACE

While 213 Squadron suffers a day of carnage, Orr of 204 RAF has a better operation, bringing down a German 2-seat observation aircraft for his fifth victory. Orr began his score with a pair of Fokker D.VII's on August 12th followed by two more enemy fighters that same month. In September his Sopwith Camel was hit by AA fire but he managed to sideslip into the ground and survive the subsequent crash. Today, in Camel D9613, he enters the ranks of the Aces. His name however will not be among those who survive the War. Orr is Killed in Action nine days later when he is shot down near Termonde, Belgium. He is awarded a posthumous DFC in the New Year's Honours List of January 1919.

Born in Nanaimo, British Columbia, Orr is believed to have found pre-War employment south of the border in Cleveland, Ohio, before re-entering Canada to join the RNAS. The immense pity of Orr's death is that the conflict is almost over. His Irish-Canadian wife Virginia is recorded to have crossed into the USA from Canada on the 12th of October, destination Cleveland. The young couple was planning their lives together and Virginia positioning herself to greet his return.

Orr's body is never recovered and he will be added to the Arras Flying Services Memorial. This design by Sir Edward Lutyens consists of a cloister of Doric Columns facing west. Orr's name and those of over 1,000 men of the Royal Naval Air Service, the Royal Flying Corps and the Royal Air Force, who have no known grave, are carved and commemorated on stone panels within the cloister. These airmen have all 'Gone West.'

28Oct18 – 2Lt Justin Thomas Joseph Mc'ANULTY (Westmount PQ) – Action in Italy

Strongly supported by the RAF, Italian and British forces have the Austro-Hungarian army in retreat. With the Hapsburg Empire falling into dissolution, the Hungarian units mutiny and refuse combat. However the Austrians bravely plan to hold the line behind the twenty-foot dikes of the Livenza River. Meanwhile the Camels of 66 Squadron create chaos with the enemy troops as they fall back and attempt to regroup.

Today McAnaulty reports seeing infantry milling about a crossroads and he attacks at low level claiming 'many casualties'. His strafe is one of several carried out by his Squadron and the river obstacle is easily breached by the Allied Armies the next day. The chasing and harassing continues and Mc'Anaulty attacks congested columns of: 'a large amount of transport and troops, stationary and facing east.' When he drops his bombs: 'The majority were direct hits.' On the 2nd of November he and a wingman will machine-gun troops they find 'engaged in destroying bridges and roads, also burning villages behind them.'

29Oct18 – 2Lt Wallace Ward McBAIN (Atwood ON) – Shot Down

This is the decisive day of the Italian Campaign, with the Austrian army attempting to make their stand along the Livenza. However, a supporting Czech regiment breaks and runs when they are strafed from above. A resolute enemy, they are panicked by this three-dimensional attack. The gap that is created opens the way for the Allies, but there are also casualties to the aerial machines.

McBain of Number 28 Squadron is shot down near Pordenone and his Sopwith Camel smashed on impact. Unscathed, McBain is now 'strafed' by the very infantry he had been machine-gunning. Scrambling

WW McBain
U of T

into a farmer's home he is fortunate to find a family willing to hide him until the Allies arrive.

Hard-bitten British soldiers following-up are aghast at the aerial destruction rained down on their enemy. One English general goes so far as to state that '... this form of warfare should be forbidden in future.' On the 4th of November, an Armistice is accorded to this sector of the Great War.

29Oct18 – 2Lt Kenneth Bruce WILKINSON (Toronto) – Recce Mission

The Germans are falling back and building new airfields. Wilkinson of 110 IAF and his Observer, Sgt. A.H. Banks, are tasked to carry out reconnaissance of a purported new landing ground at Thal but they find nothing. Operating their DH-9a F1060 at the fairly safe altitude of 20,000 feet, they expose several photographic plates including two of new construction they spot at Buhl airfield. This field is the home to three *Jastas* that have been inflicting severe casualties to the daylight bomber squadrons of the Independent Air Force. Consequently, 99 Squadron IAF is dispatched to bomb Buhl the following afternoon.

Wilkinson will fly postal duties with the army of occupation following the Armistice and return to Toronto in the summer of 1919.

30Oct18 – Lt Henry Gordon CLAPPISON (Hamilton ON) – ACE

After scoring his first three victories in Camel F3243 Clappiston ran into a brick building on landing with that machine. Quite unhurt, he makes his fifth kill today with Camel D9600, becoming the last Canadian Naval Ace of the War. Not until the Pacific Fleet Campaign of 1945 will another Dominion aviator be able to claim this ultimate fighter pilot title.

Although just joining 204 Squadron in August, Clappiston has scored all five of his victories against

HG Clappison
RAeC Trust

the better-built Fokker D.VII. On November first, he outfights a sixth D.VII. This Fokker is described as having black stripes on the wings and a white tail. Clappison sends it down in an uncontrollable spin over Soffeghem.

On the 4th of November 1918, he becomes a Flight Commander with the Squadron and will be recognized by the Belgians with the award of a Croix de Guerre. These are not his last promotions or awards. Clappiston will serve with the RCAF, reaching the rank of Air Commodore and receiving the OBE in 1946.

31Oct18 – 2Lt Arthur Henry WILLIAMS
(Toronto) – KIA

A pilot with 204 RAF flying Camel F3103, Williams is lost in combat over the Western Front. Although he had entered the RNAS in early 1916, Williams was released due to insufficient education. Back in Canada, he completed an additional year of school and then joined the RFC, graduating as an RAF pilot in April 1918. Flying with the former 4 Naval Squadron and dying twelve days before the war ends, Williams can quite honestly be considered as the last Canadian Naval aviator Killed In Action during the Great War.

31Oct18 – 2Lt Lynn Newton BISSELL
(Algonquin ON) – KIC

With 201 TDS, East Fortune, Scotland, Bissell classically stalls his Bristol F-2b B8942 in a climbing turn and sideslips to the ground. The aircraft's practice smoke bombs explode and both Bissell and his passenger are killed. The number of pilots lost in this unfortunately all-too-frequent takeoff accident is very high—but are nowhere close to the numbers killed in action.

NOVEMBER 1918

02Nov18 – 2Lt Richard Walter JOHNSON
(Regina; b. ENG) – Flu

A former Saskatchewan schoolteacher, Johnson dies of sickness in England. He served as an Ordinary Seaman in the RCNVR before entering the RNAS at Greenwich in March 1918. At the Chingford Flying School he was weakened by Neuritis and spent three weeks in the Chatham RN Hospital. Appearing to have recovered he is with 7 Reserve Depot Squadron at time of death.

04Nov18 – 2Lt George Alfred HODGETTS
(Ottawa) – Action

This date is recognized by First World War Historians as the last great British and Canadian offensive of the War. The Allied soldiers breach the Sambre Canal and finally snap the resistance of the German Armies who fall back in full retreat. Today also marks of the last large air battle. Poor weather conditions of the past few days break into fine flying conditions and the *Jagdstaffeln* pilots, although surely knowing the end is near, stoutly come up to fight and protect their ground troops.

80 Squadron RAF sends its first mission up at 0600 as the misty morning clears. Hodgetts is in that launch and for his effort is badly shot up over Foret de Mormal. He is, however, unwounded and limps his damaged Camel F2139 home safely. By the end of the day, another four members of 80 Squadron have been shot-out-of-battle and one is killed in this final intense effort by the German air services.

A total of 25 Allied airmen die in today's Western Front fighting; 15 others are brought down and taken Prisoner of War for what can only be the very shortest of incarcerations. During the next four days the inclement weather returns and there is little action. The retreating German armies are given a respite from aerial attack.

04Nov18 – Lt Jewitt Rice SMITH, Cd'G
(Canadian; b. USA) – DFC

On this night of 4th/5th November, Smith and his Observer, 2Lt CA Moth, start out to bomb a railway station in Germany. After two hours, an engine problem compels them to return to their 218 Squadron base. Gamely obtaining another DH-9A machine they set out once more well aware of an impending gale warning. They reach the objective and score three direct hits. On the return they encounter the forecasted storm yet manage to land in the face of a 60 mile-an-hour wind. This very determined second flight effort has taken six hours and fifteen minutes. Both aviators are Gazetted the DFC in February 1919.

Smith is the second-youngest Canadian pilot to have entered the RNAS. Born in the USA to Canadian parents on the 26th of April 1900, he falsified his age in order to join the CEF. As a Signals Sapper and not quite seventeen Smith was wounded at Vimy Ridge on the 11th of April 1917. Awarded the French Croix de Guerre in July that year, he subsequently transferred to Naval aviation in December.

The strength of the pan-European storm that challenged Smith is revealed the following morning when the gale reaches Scotland's Firth of Forth. The 18,000-ton aircraft carrier HMS *Campania*, is blown into a collision with the battle cruiser *Glorious* and sinks.

Dazzle-painted HMS Campania sinking in the Firth of Forth, 05Nov18

FAAM 1995/038/0004

10Nov18 – 2Lt Clarence Earl YOUNG (Kingston ON) – KIC

Young is killed in SE-5a E1323 during fighter training at the RAF's Central Flying School Cranwell. A product of the last pre-integration RNAS course that had commenced on the 24th of March, he has the melancholy distinction of being the last wartime aviation casualty for Canada. Before joining the RNAS, Young had served as a Sergeant with a Canadian Army Medical Corps at the Kitchener Military Hospital in Brighton.

10Nov18 – Capt George Chisholm MacKAY, DFC (Mimico ON) – Last Kill

(From 12Mar18) In Camel D9648, MacKay leads his Flight on 213 RAF's the last combat mission of the War. During the patrol he brings down his 18th enemy aircraft, scoring Canada's final aviation victory of the four-year conflict.

Having survived over 300 hours of combat flying, MacKay is the leading ace of his squadron, a unit that has accounted for over 110 enemy aircraft while still maintaining a ground attack role. MacKay has not been unscathed. On the 15th of September he had been taken out of action with a bullet wound to the neck but has returned for the closing days of the War.

In addition to his DFC and five Mentions in Despatches, MacKay's efforts are well recognized by both French and Belgian governments. He is appointed as a Chevalier,

Order of Leopold, by Belgium, and presented the Croix de Guerre avec Palme by France.

In post-war debriefings with German officials, it is discovered that the Kaiser and his entourage had visited the Zeebrugge in the spring of 1918 and were chased off the pierhead by a Sopwith Camel strafe. A date-time comparison finds that the pilot was none other than GC MacKay

11Nov18 – WAR ENDS

Canadian troops enter and capture Mons and an Armistice is declared at the morning's Eleventh Hour. Globally, over six million (6,181,000) armed forces personnel have been killed and a further twelve million (12,570,000) wounded in the conflict. Sadly the losses continue:

12Nov18 – Capt Stearne Tighe EDWARDS,DSC & Bar (Carleton Place, ON) – KIC

ST Edwards

RE 19551-4

(From 16May18) At Number 2 Fighting School in Marske, Edwards crashes a Sopwith Pup during an exuberant aerobatic display celebrating the War's end. The victory stunting costs him his life. The 16-victory fighter pilot lingers for ten days under the care of his hometown pal **Roy Brown** before passing.

Twenty-five year old Edwards is buried at Tadcaster Cemetery in Yorkshire. He is Canada's first peacetime military aviator casualty.

12Nov18 – 2Lt David Phillip BRENNAN
(Ste Hyacinthe PQ) – Flu

Brennan succumbs to the Influenza epidemic that is now sweeping the world. A bank clerk before the war, Brennan had joined the RNAS in early January 1918.

DP Brennan

In May the young student pilot struck a ridge on landing and overturned in Caudron G-III N3285 at Vendome. Despite the mishap, he did achieve his 'wings' by July and was serving at Yarmouth Air Station at the time of his death.

18Nov18 – 2Lt Reginald Keith LITTLE
(Thornhill ON) – KIC Midair

In a aerial collision Observer Little is killed along with his English Pilot CE Wodehouse. The aircraft, BE-2c 9954, is operating out of the Eastchurch Observer's School when the accident happens over Uxbridge.

A bank clerk, Little had enlisted with the 19th Cameron Highlanders of Winnipeg in 1915. He was in the firing lines by February 1916 and shell-shocked at Ypres in June. He recovered and returned to battle only to be badly wounded at the Somme that September. After more than a year in hospital he regained his health sufficiently to be commissioned the RNAS during February 1918. Little is buried Kingstone, Somerset, leaving behind a young widow, his English warbride.

21Nov18 – 2Lt Arthur Mark McELHINNEY
(Ottawa ON) – KIC

Flying with 205 Training Depot Squadron at Vendome, McElhinney is killed in when his Camel, E1493, spins into the ground upside down. Today the maneuver would be called an inverted spin. In any case it is an airborne situation that requires altitude in order to recover and McElhinney lacks the luxury of a safe height. The War is over but the demands of an Armistice Air Force require best efforts. McElhinney has died learning a professional standard geared towards maintaining a lasting peace.

21Nov18 – Capt Rudolf Dawson DELAMERE
(Toronto ON) – German Naval Surrender

(From 07Feb16) From an overhead perch in his flying boat, Delamere observes a most historic event—the German Naval Surrender.

RD Delamere, aloft over the Firth of Forth on 21Nov18

Sailing less than majestically into the Firth of Forth, the German High Seas Fleet, filthy from being harbour bound since the Battle of Jutland, arrives in Scotland to surrender. Two lines of Allied vessels form a gauntlet for the German ships to sail through. British, French, American and Australian warships represent their respective nations. Canadian course-mates of the Midshipmen lost at Cornel in 1914 are standing watch in Royal Navy ships. They may be chagrined at having no Royal Canadian Naval vessels on guard station this day; *but RCN has not fired a single shot in anger throughout the entire conflict.*

These same Lieutenants and Sub-Lieutenants will rise to prominent occasion some twenty years later when they lead the Royal Canadian Navy during her finest years—the Battle of the Atlantic 1939 to 1945—the longest continuous military campaign of the Second World War.

25Nov18 – Major Walter Brodgin LAWSON, MID (Barrie ON) – Canadian Air Force

(From 17Aug15) For quite some time, Canadians have been demanding greater national recognition of their RNAS, RFC and RAF airmen who now comprise nearly twenty percent of the British pilot strength. However, the Air Ministry has long stated that reallocating Canadian aviators would disrupt War efforts and that in any case, there is a severe shortage of trained Canadian ground crew. In August, after much political intrigue and military muddling, the RAF concedes to setting up two Canadian squadrons, one fighter and one bomber unit. During September the Canadian Government finally approves the creation of the Canadian Air Force (CAF), to comprise initially of two squadrons.

By November 20th No. 1 Squadron, with Sopwith Dolphin fighters, was formed. Today, No. 2 Squadron CAF, is started up at RAF Station Upper Heyford as a Canadian-manned day-bomber unit flying DeHavilland DH-9 machines. Lawson is appointed the Commanding Officer.

Lawson is a fine choice for leadership of the Bombers. As a 1913 RMC graduate and a 1915 entrée into the RNAS he has an excellent military and aviation background. After recovery from illness contracted in Mesopotamian service, he became an instructor and was in charge of Leysdown, a sub-station of RNAS Eastchurch Flying School. Described as 'Extremely reliable & hardworking Officer - Has done excellent work I/C Leysdown'; Lawson reverts from Flight Commander rank to Flight Lieutenant in order to volunteer for Active Service. He trains at Stonehenge on the Handley Page bombers and is sent thence to 215 Squadron in France by June 1918.

Once in action, Lawson becomes a paradigm of courage and determination for the young pilots of the Squadron, consistently bombing and machine-gunning his targets at low altitude—and at night. An example is the 25th of August raid on the Badische Works in Mannheim. Leading another bomber, Lawson approached the target at 5,000 feet and began a silent glide four miles back, an altitude calculated to place the Handley Page at a blast-safe 1,000 feet over the objective. Arriving at the 1,000-foot marker still half a mile short of the target factory, Lawson opted to glide onward, finally releasing the bombs dead centre from 200 feet. His aircraft 'lurched and reared' through the explosive force as he powered up into the night. Most fortunately for the crew, searchlights, now alerted by the engine noise, lite up and outlined smoke stacks and steeples directly in

the path of the bomber. Threading his way through the obstacles, Lawson circled the target area sweeping the works and the searchlights with machine-gun fire while the second bomber glided into attack.

On June 3rd, 1919, Major Lawson is Gazetted for the Distinguished Flying Cross. Later that same month the Canadian Government will decide against continuing with a permanent peacetime Air Force and all flying operations are ceased. By February 5th, 1920, both Squadrons will have been disbanded. Thus ends Canada's first attempt at an air service.

Lawson returns to Canada and becomes involved with mining engineering. In 1928 he takes a refresher flying-course with Western Canada Airways but is killed in a deHavilland Tiger Moth crash at Winnipeg.

DECEMBER 1918

05Dec18 – 2Lt. Edward Dudley WARREN (Winnipeg MB) – KIC

Another peacetime casualty, Warren is killed in flying boat crash with 228 RAF at Yarmouth. According to his attestation papers he had been recommended by fellow Winnipeger **'Red' Mulock** for RNAS entry in February.

19Dec18 – Lt Thomas Barton SIMPSON (London ON) – KIC

After looping-the-loop near Fairlop Airdrome in Essex, Simpson is seen to dive towards a wood. His body is found under the smashed machine, a 54 Squadron aircraft.

Courtesy Fleet Air Arm Museum, Album 35

'JUNE 1918 CONCERT PARTY'

A poignant photo. Major Bert Wemp, future Mayor of Toronto (on the left), and his Senior Flight Commander, Captain WF Cleghorn, pose with an all-male entertainment troupe.

'Cleggy' is killed on 02Oct18 dropping food supplies to cut-off Belgian Forces in the Houthulst Forest.

Douglas Munn

PEACE DAY, MALTA HARBOUR

Douglas Munn

FLYING BOAT READY TO CELEBRATE
A Victory garland of flowers adorns the nose

Courtesy Fleet Air Arm Museum, Album 461

'NS 7 & 8 LEAVING FOR PATROL AT 9 AM ON PEACE DAY'

Great Britain-based North Sea-class airships

Courtesy Fleet Air Arm Museum, Album 461

'NS3 FLYING OVER LAND'

Date unknown, illustrates the the crew
in an exposed perch.

JL Gordon, RCAF CAS 1932 – 1933
CAHF

LS Breadner
RCAF CAS 1940 – 1943

DND

H Edwards, AOC RCAF Overseas
SK Edwards

R Collishaw, AOC RAF Desert Air Force 1940 – 1941

CAHF

R Leckie, RCAF CAS 1943 – 1947
CAHF

WA Curtis, RCAF CAS 1947 – 1953
CAHF

CHAPTER 5

THE YEARS 1919 TO 2003

AIR COMMANDERS

T he first year of peace opens with the King's New Year's Honours List Gazetting awards around the British Empire. When the 1919 medals to Canadian Naval airmen are tabulated with those previously won the figures reveal that eight pilots have been recognized with the Distinguished Service Order; two of who received Bars. In addition, 42 Distinguished Service Crosses with eleven first Bars and two second Bars have been Gazetted. Now 'integrated' with the Royal Flying Corps, the naval fliers have earned a substantial number of the new Royal Air Force awards, some 40 Distinguished Flying Crosses and 24 Air Force Crosses.

To the victors go the spoils… but other than the decorations, it is not much of a world that greets demobilizing aviators and trench survivors. A nation of eight million peoples, Canada had over six hundred thousand serve in uniform from August 1914 to November 1918. Ten per cent of the Canadian Expeditionary Force to Europe have died or become missing; twenty per cent of the Canadians who joined the RNAS have paid that ultimate sacrifice.

The soldiers and airmen left the Dominion as boys and became men in far off lands. Those that return find the ravages of the influenza pandemic has caused almost as many Canadian deaths as did the War and now the veterans must try to integrate into communities that have absolutely no concept of the horrors that were faced overseas. Many of the returnees are suffering both physically and mentally.

Nor are wars over for some. Major Raymond Collishaw has been granted a permanent commission with the RAF and will command a squadron in South Russia. His mission is to assist the Czarist White forces against the Bolshevik Red Army. Canadians are also flying in North Russia and on the Caspian Sea.

Still others will remain in service throughout the Second World War. The Royal Canadian Air Force will be led by an unbroken succession of former RNAS Officers appointed Chief of Air Staff from 1940 to 1953. In civilian flying, the first Bush Pilot; the first Canadian to fly the Atlantic and the author of the primary Flight Training manual still in use today are all x-RNAS types. Among other high achievers are a Mayor of Toronto; a President of the Toronto Stock Exchange; and a Professor Emeritus at the Mayo Clinic in the United States.

To this day, the lads' 'local' in London, England, retains a war log. There one can peruse their high-spirited comments and view their happily scrawled cartoons. The Old Cheshire Cheese Pub is located in Wine Office Court just off Fleet Street and was made famous by Samuel Pepys in the 17th century.

The 943 naval aviators truly represented Canada—not just from sea to sea; but from a horse and buggy Victorian past into a Twenty-First Century aerospace future. In 2003, the last Canadian pilot to serve in the Royal Naval Air Service dies at the remarkable age of one hundred and six.

THE YEARS 1919 TO 2003

01Jan19 – AWARDS:

In this New Year's Honours List, eight former RNAS Canadians receive the RAF's **Distinguished Flying Cross** and another seven are decorated the Air Force Cross. Among them, and not previously identified in these pages, are:

– Capt Walter Robert KENNY
(Ottawa) – DFC Action

Since joining the RNAS in December 1915, Kenny, a furrier, has completed three tours of anti-submarine flying and his DFC is in recognition of this accomplishment. The majority of his activities were performed out of Dundee and Turnberry on the chilly eastern shores of Scotland. Also acting as an Air Station executive officer, Kennedy had been described in 1918 as 'A capable & efficient First Lieutenant with superior organizing qualities & is a sound seaplane pilot.' His leadership abilities will carry over to another war and by 1942 he is an Air Vice Marshal with the RCAF.

WR Kenny

RAeC Trust

– Capt David Fraser MURRAY
(Victoria) – DFC

A teacher from Victoria, Murray flew with 62 Wing. His unit was the mobile 'F' Squadron and operated out of the islands of Thasos, Imbros, and Thermi-Mitylene. Murray made quite a number of successful missions using his own homemade bombsight affixed to the side of his DH-4. The DFC is awarded for his distinguished Aegean service.

Distinguished Flying Medal

– Corporal Mechanic Richard BROCK
(Hamilton ON; b. ENG) – DFM

(From 24Oct14) Instituted in June 1918 at the same time as the DFC, the Distinguished Flying Medal is awarded to enlisted personnel. Of the 102 DFMs Gazetted in the First World War, only one goes to a Canadian: engine mechanic Brock.

Before joining the RNAS in March 1916, Brock's trade had been that of magneto repairer. Assigned as a Fitter to the Polegate Airship Station, he flew in the costal patrol dirigibles. He was a member of the three-man crew of SSZ 39 that had remained aloft for a record fifty-one hours from the 11th to the 13th of August 1918.

Sadly, on the 12th of July 1919, 26-year-old Brock will suffer a heart attack and drown while visiting a lady friend at Muskoka Lakes, Ontario.

(Note: without explanation, Brock is also listed as R.B. Belzard in some records)

19Jan19 – Obs 2Lt Wellesley Malcom C. BABER
(Canadian; b. ENG) – 'Splash!'

Observer Baber was the wartime censor of 'Splash!' the Calshot Seaplane station magazine. For the Souvenir Number of January 1919 (price: sixpence) he writes in the foreword: "It will be noticed that a feature of this issue is the splendid collection of aerial photographs included, and I am certain that no one will be slow to take advantage of this opportunity of procuring these photographs (they are otherwise practically unavailable), which we shall be able to place above our beds (not bed *boards*) when we once more become humble civilians."

16Feb19 – 2Lt Clarence Victor CLARK
(Hespler ON) – KIC

Clarke is killed in a crash while flying with 50 RAF Squadron at Bekesbourne in England. The North Bay, Ontario, civil servant entered the RNAS in January 1918.

18Feb19 – 2Lt John Horace 'Horry' BROWN
(Carleton Place ON) – Flu

Roy Brown's younger brother – who as a CEF Lieutenant had served in the trenches for sixteen months, was wounded, recovered, joined the RNAS and survived a training crash – now succumbs to the Influenza that has swept the globe. By its end, the pandemic will have garnered a death toll larger than that of the Great War. An estimated 3% of the world's population dies.

John Horace Brown graduated a VGI Pilot and Officer, and was described as a 'Keen and full out.' He flew with 93 RAF on the new Sopwith Dolphin fighters; however, the unit did not become operational before the end of the war and was disbanded in November 1918. Twenty-two-year-old Brown is buried at St. Fillan's Cemetery, Lanark.

180

Other Influenza losses this spring are:

– PFSLt William McNeil GRAY of Toronto

who served from December 1915 until Released as medically unfit in July16.

RIP the 22nd of January 1919.

WM Gray

– 2Lt Ernest Russell PERCIVAL,

a postal clerk from London, Ontario, had flown DH-9's with 205 Squadron at Cattewater. RIP the 13th of March 1919.

05Apr19 – Italian Decorations

– 2Lt James Alexander MUNN, MID (Kensall ON) – Cd'G Italy

Munn flew his war from HMS *Riviera* with the Malta Group. Some of his time was spent assisting the Italian troops that were trapped in Tripoli and other towns along the Libyan coast by Turkish-led Sanusi tribesmen. For the work he is awarded the Italian Croce di Guerra, and in July 1919 the Libyan Medal 'For services rendered in connection with the Italian forces at Misurata.'

(A forgotten episode of the First World War, this situation would have been made forever memorable

JA Munn, airborne with cap well-secured

Douglas Munn

had the Caliph of Islam's call for a religious war, or Jihad, been followed. Only the Libyan locals, backed by Ottoman officers, responded. Their North African neighbours and the Muslims of Egypt, India, Caucasus, and Turkistan remained apathetic or held out for British and French promised independence after the War. Now, the spring of 1919, the Versailles Peace Conference in Paris is busily redrawing the map of Europe but will only etch 'lines in the sands' of the Middle East.)

Munn, a Sergeant in the Canadian Army Dental Corps before entering the RNAS in November 1917, will graduate from the University of Toronto as a dental surgeon in the early 1920's. Fourteen other RNAS veterans also enter the dental profession postwar.

– Lt Archibald Leslie HUETHER (Guelph ON) – Bronze Medal Italy

This same date, Huether is awarded the Italian Bronze Medal for Military Valour. He has flown

with the RAF's 66 Wing and rendered 'Valuable services in connection with the War.'

Permitted an early release in October 1918 to resume his studies in medicine, Heuther returns to his alma mater in Toronto and then opens up practice in his birthplace of

AL Huether

U of T

Guelph, Ontario. Years after his death his beautiful heritage house is pulled down to provide parking for a funeral home.

A total of twenty Canadian naval aviators become physicians.

– 2Lt Haddow MacDonnell KEITH (Toronto) – MD

Outstanding in the medical field will be Keith who was a pilot with 266 RAF in the Aegean. He will retire in 1964 as Doctor Emeritus, Mayo Clinic.

02May19 – Grant Armstrong GOODERHAM, MID (Toronto ON) – Drowned

(From 22May16) Placed on the RAF Unemployed List in April 1919, 27-year-old former Flight Commander Gooderham returned to Canada exhausted in body and spirit. Going missing from home he is found drowned in Toronto Bay: the very same waters where just four years earlier he had graduated with the first class at the Curtiss School.

GA Gooderham

After several months of intense combat flying and a diagnosis of neurasthenia in early February 1917, Gooderham was deemed fit again by that March. He was then attached to the Naval Testing Squadron and Mentioned in Despatches for his early front line actions: 'For consistently good work for the last ten months in carrying out coastal reconnaissance's and fighter patrols for our own and French machines.' He returned to the Front in early June with 6 Naval Squadron and the following month, flying Sopwith Camel N6373 brought down an Albatross D.V although his own machine was badly shot up in the process. Gooderham's July 1917 report called him an 'Experienced Air Fighter.'

From a health perspective, he had returned to active service flying far too soon and was surveyed Unfit by September. His request for two months' Sick Leave to Canada was approved along with an additional two months extension into 1918. But once more Gooderham was far too anxious to serve. Towards the end of December he cabled from Toronto: 'Will report London first available boat.' Not yet in good health, he was surveyed as fit for duty but with a proviso: 'In view of the nature of his complaint (neurasthenia) it is recommended he be employed for 2 Months Ground Work.'

Resurveyed yet again as fit for flying duties in March 1918, Gooderham was detailed to Redcar to instruct. There he was written up by his Commanding Officer as: 'Reliable Officer, VG Command. Has shown much improvement in his flying, but is much out of practice owing to his having been sick 6 months. I consider that he should be sent to another station where he could practice on service machines. Will make a very good Instructor.' Spending this suggested additional time at Cranwell, Gooderham was further recommended for promotion to Flight Commander. He remained involved with technical and instruction work through to the close of the war.

Another veteran Flight Commander drowns in 1924:

– George THOM, AFC (Merrit BC)

A Scot who emigrated to Canada in 1910, Thom, like Gooderham, was an early Curtiss Toronto Flying School graduate. He flew with 5 Wing in 1916 and completed that year with Naval 8. Selected for the new 10 Naval Scout Squadron Thom was grounded due to neurasthenia during the spring of 1917. After recuperation, he trained as an Instructor and then taught at Cranwell. He was Gazetted the AFC in 1919.

G Thom

Thom is lost when his canoe overturns on Alberta's Peace River rapids while prospecting for oil.

May1919 – Major Raymond COLLISHAW, DSO&Bar (Nanaimo) – South Russia

(From 22Jul18) Collishaw had been involved in the initial formation of the CAF in England when the Armistice was signed. After taking Canadian leave, he returned with plans to attempt a trans-Atlantic flight using an RAF Bomber; however, events in Russia forestall this project. The British Parliament decides to assist the Czarist White Forces against the Bolshevik Reds in the Russian Civil War. One expeditionary unit is already in North Russia and another patrols the Caspian Sea. Collishaw is given command of Number 47 Squadron RAF for an operation in South Russia and

R Collishaw

GWFM

he recruits many of his old RNAS mates to man the unit. Operating a mixed bag of Sopwith Camels and DeHavilland DH-9s, they are pitted against some of their former German *Jasta* adversaries who are now piloting for the Reds.

"To understand what happened toward the end of 1919 in South Russia, it is important to comprehend that General Denkin's (White) Armies then occupied a vast area 1500 miles deep into Russia and that it was spread over a width of about 1000 miles. The spread was about equally divided between … three Armies, with the Volunteer Army (mostly ex-officers in the ranks) on the left between Odessa and Kharkof, with the Don Cossack Army between Kharkof, Rostov and the Kuban Cossack Army responsible for everything east of Rostov, including the Caspian Sea.

"No. 47 Squadron operations had been confined to co-operation with the Kuban Cossack Army while the Don Cossack Army and the Volunteer Army had NO co-operation of any kind. They relied upon cavalry reconnaissance.

"The success or failure of the whole venture hinged upon the good will of the Kuban and Don Cossack peoples. The principal aspiration of these peoples was to sustain freedom from Moscow domination

and once General Denkin announced his objective to restore the Ancient Regime, he put the writing on the wall.

"The Cossacks were organized into clans not unlike the ancient Scottish clans … with the collapse of Czarism these clans had grasped individual independence and thus they were very loosely held by the respective Commanders in the Field. Denkin's 'Back to the Ancient Regime' threatened their newly won independence and so they all 'Downed Tools.'— As events turned out the Bolsheviks broke up the clan system and everyone lost his independence." *(23Jun64 Letter to R.V. Dodds)*

Initially the campaign had gone well but the conflicting Czarist and Cossack intentions opens the field for the Reds. A general retreat turns into a rout and 47 Squadron, operating off an armoured train, is forced into a wild race to escape via the railroad. They reach Novorossisk on the Black Sea following a heart-wrenching trip with several hundred Allied Russian officers' wives and children. Many of these families suffer and die from Typhus and Collishaw himself falls desperately ill and nearly succumbs to the fever.

Awarded the OBE and three Czarist medals for his trials, Collishaw will spend his next two years commanding squadrons in Iraq. In 1923 he takes a long leave and marries Neita Trapp of New Westminster BC. Continuing in RAF service, a 1929 posting returns him to his naval roots as the Senior Air Officer aboard the new aircraft carrier HMS *Courageous*. Promoted Group Captain in 1935, Collishaw is just settling into command of the large air station at Upper Heyford in Oxfordshire when Mussolini invades Abyssinia. In light of his early 1920's Middle East experience, the RAF sends Collishaw to the Sudan. When the dangers subside he is appointed CO of the RAF station at Heliopolis near Cairo. Joined by his wife and two daughters he describes these years as "the most pleasant of all those that I spent in uniform." *(Read 10Jun1940)*

Neita Collishaw, née Trapp

U of T

20May19 – 2Lt Robert Geo Kerr MORRISON (Chesterville ON) – Caspian Crash

Operating off HMS *Alader Youssanoff*, a 2,000-ton tanker converted to seaplane carrier, Morrison crashes into the Caspian Sea. In a climbing turn just after takeoff the engine fails at 200 feet. The immediate crash landing sinks the aircraft but most fortunately for both Morrison and his Observer 2Lt HG Pratt, the bombs they carry do not explode.

The Caspian Sea measures just over 600 miles from north to south and averages about 200 miles in breadth. A small British force holds the Western shore at Baku and Petrovosk. They are attempting to reinforce the White Russians in this area against the Bolsheviks on the Eastern shore. The Allied effort is stiffened with two-dozen Russian merchant ships that form the Royal Navy's Caspian Flotilla. Of these vessels, the *Alader Youssanoff* is commissioned as an HM Ship and fitted out to carry two Short Admiralty 184 Seaplanes.

RGK Morrison

U of T

Morrison's machine, N9079, is suspected to have had water in the petrol causing carburetion problems. His mission was to bomb the Bolshevik fleet at Alexandrovsk Harbour on the eastern side of the Caspian. The rescued aircrew will attempt the raid again the following morning, taking off at 0530 hours. They share the remaining Short 184, N9080, with two other aircrew pairs. It is no small effort. Each time the machine alights in the water it must be hoisted out, rearmed and refueled aboard, then hoisted back over the side for the next raid. The numerous bomb drops strike several vessels and create mayhem in the enemy harbour.

At the end of the day, the Rear Admiral Black Sea dispatches the Admiralty (in part): 'I have the honour to call particular attention to the services rendered by the following officers of the Royal Air Force who between them carried out five raids in one seaplane on the same day, with excellent results, and attempted a sixth...' He mentions Morrison and also Canadian 2Lt Pilot **Howard Grant Thompson** (Dorchester ON) and Lt Observer **Frank Russell Bicknell** (Dunville ON). *(Read Thompson & Bicknell 28Jun19)*

03Jun19 – AWARDS:

– Colonel Redford Henry MULOCK, DSO&Bar, (Winnipeg) – CBE

(From 29Aug18) Aviator Mulock is, at this time, involved in a totally different role. Due to delays in demobilization, unrest is building in the ranks of the enlisted airmen who are anxious to get home and find work. 'Bolshie' type strikes begin taking place at aerodromes around England and Mulock is given full powers to settle the problems. With his native ability to grasp the essence of a situation, Mulock resolves the troubles by dealing with ringleaders man-to-man, explaining the difficulties besetting the government's transition from wartime to peacetime purposes. For these calming actions together with his very distinguished wartime services, Mulock is recognized with an appointment to Commander, Order of the British Empire (CBE).

Speaking in England in 1919 to the pilots of the newly formed Canadian Air Force, Mulock had offered eloquent counsel on the type of military aviation that the Dominion should maintain after the war.

> "...Don't forget that every Canadian in the air services wanted to fight—you couldn't keep him on the ground. That was to the credit of you fellows, but now it reacts. [sic] We have no highly trained technical men, no experienced equipment men. If this Canadian Air Force goes across to Canada, as some of you are proposing, you must have an organization from the ground up—not the other way. We've got the best flying men in the world, and they're a great future asset to the Dominion—but don't forget that there are such things as aerodromes, a supply system for spares, and, above all, a real Air Policy. Someone has got to go to Ottawa with a clearly defined plan."

Mulock's words are prophetic. In the Canadian capital an Air Board has been created as a governing body for civil aviation and the handling of air defense. However, there is no air policy. Aircraft are not a problem since the British government has gifted more than 100 war surplus machines and sundry supplies. The United States has also been benevolent and donated their twelve flying boats used in Nova Scotia – those the Air Board pragmatically uses for civil operations, essentially 'Bush Flying'. The Board also re-establishes the Canadian Air Force but true to pre-war Canadian military heritage, not as a permanent structure but rather an air militia giving summer refresher courses to former RNAS, RFC and RAF pilots. It is the precursor of what will become the Royal Canadian Air Force (RCAF) in 1924.

The first choice for a commander of the new CAF is Mulock: however, the Colonel expresses no desire to remain in military aviation. Leaving the RAF he returns to Canada and is involved in the peacetime aviation industry, although he does enter the RCAF Reserve and will rise to the rank of Air Commodore. In 1935, he becomes an executive with Canadian Airways and during the Second World War is a member of the Honorary Advisory Air Council. Redford Henry Mulock passes away at age 82 in Montreal during 1961.

RH Mulock

CAHF

– Major Arthur Raymond LAYARD (Ganges BC; b. ENG) – OBE

The simple citation for this Order of the British Empire reads 'In recognition of distinguished services rendered during the War'. The sentence scarcely speaks of the magnitude of Layard's contribution to the Technical Branch of the RNAS. Born on the Isle of Wight, England, in 1888, he attended the Naval Academy, Gosport, gaining a Diploma in Mechanical Engineering. Then, prior to immigration to Canada, he apprenticed for two years at the Cowes shipyards.

In August of 1915, Layard left his new home in Ganges, British Columbia, and with wife and child, returned to England to commission with the RNVR. At first, his work was in airship construction at the Kingsnorth Airship Station; subsequently in 1916, he was appointed to Pembroke, Wales, as the Airship Station Engineering Officer. His duties included gas, power, transport and airship building maintenance but he also found time to carry out over 100 hours on Submarine Scout and Costal Class Airship flight-testing. In 1917 Layard was sent to 6

Wing, Italy, as Senior Engineering Officer. Promotion to Major, RAF, followed in 1918 together with Command of the Adriatic Group Depot.

Layard will serve in RCAF as an aeronautical engineer from 1940 to 1945, rising to Group Captain and commanding No.6 Repair Depot, Trenton. He dies in Ganges, on the 5th of April 1967.

During the Cold War, the Air Branch of the Royal Canadian Navy will commission an Experimental Squadron, VX10, and the unit will emulate much of the technical spirit of Layard.

21-27Jun19 – with Lawerence of Arabia

– Lt James Durkin VANCE (Toronto) &

– Lt Harry Alexander YATES (Ingersoll ON)

Vance and Yates are both veteran RNAS Handley-Page pilots. They are now on special duty assignment transporting VIP diplomats to and from the Versailles Peace Conference in Paris. Although a lasting peace is the objective, the talks are in a shambles over the Middle East. Promises made by Lawrence of Arabia to the Arabs are not being honoured. The British have reverted to pre-war 'Gun-boat' diplomacy and have send a more modern fleet, 51 Handley-Page bombers, to Egypt. In the past, aircraft were shipped to Cairo; but now, in the interests of expediency, they are flown. It is hardly a time-saving endeavor. Departing in April, only 26 will arrive at the destination by the end of October. Colonel T.E. Lawrence is aboard the first bomber. It crashes at Rome and the two pilots are killed, Lawrence is hospitalized.

JD Vance

RAeC Trust

Back in England, Vance and Yates are given two hours' notice to launch with an urgent passenger for Cairo. He is a Mr. H. St J. Philby who will become the British Administrator in Mesopotamia. The 'steady and reliable' pilot pair flight plan via Paris, Lyon, Marseilles and Rome. Colonel Lawrence has continued his flight in another machine and has carried on through Albania, Athens and finally, Crete. It is there at Souda Bay, on that Greek Island, that Vance and Yates catch up to the famous desert fighter, who is found awaiting aircraft repairs. Passenger Philby invites Lawence to continue in his aircraft.

The trip so far has not been without incident. Bad fuel, a forced landing, puncture repairs, and the latest, a split propeller, have plagued the operation. An unreliable fuel pump has the two mechanics, Stedman and Hand, continually wobble-pumping gasoline to the engines during flight. At Souda Bay, the crew cannibalizes another bomber for its propeller and continues on, crossing the Mediterranean for Libya. Yates will later recall: "Four hours out of sight of land and not a darn ship in sight. Decidedly not my idea of a good time." In spite of unreliable compasses they make their planned landfall at the Bay of Sollum. Lawrence passes a note forward 'Most Excellent. You have had no drift at all.'

The last leg is across 500 miles of desert in an aircraft that is now in very bad shape, control lines frayed and fuel pumps still inoperative. The crew are equally frayed and almost completely exhausted. Yet intrepidly they carry on, facing and surmounting the final challenge of a night landing at Cairo. Lawrence of Arabia has spent the flight writing the Foreword to his book '*The Seven Pillars of Wisdom.*'

For what is Gazetted as 'Conspicuous ability and determination...' Vance and Yates are each awarded the Air Force Cross. Their two mechanics are decorated with Air Force Medals.

Vance had flown his war with 214 RAF on the Handley-Page. During a June 1918 raid on Zeebrugge he was brought down to a water landing and floated adrift into Holland where he was interned. With the Armistice he returned to flying duties in England. Following his AFC Award Vance will go home to Canada and become a pioneer bush pilot. A flying accident at Great Bear Lake in 1930 will take his life.

Yates had learned to fly the Handley Page at Stonehenge and then had been retained as an instructor. He applied for Active Service but his Commanding Officer noted: 'Services of this Officer cannot be conveniently spared.' On his return to Canada in the early 1920's Yates becomes a medical doctor. He retains his interest in flying and is the Chairman of the Board of the Royal Canadian Flying Club Association during the 1960's.

28Jun19 – Obs Lt Frank Russell BICKNELL, MID (Dunville ON) and

– 2Lt Howard Grant THOMPSON, MID (Dorchester ON) – Caspian Sea Crash

(From 20May19) Hoisted out of HMS *Alader Youssanoff* for Caspian convoy escort duties, the Short 184 crew is unable to get airborne off the less buoyant fresh water sea. This problem has plagued operations in these waters and, following an accepted non-standard procedure, the two Canadians jettison a 112 pound bomb to lighten the load. This time the weapon explodes blowing the aircraft in half—but, incredibly, only slightly injuring the crew. His Britannic Majesty's seaplane N9082 is completely destroyed.

By September, British forces will withdraw from the Caspian/Caucuses region, ending the Royal Navy and Royal Air Force intervention in South Russia. The small air squadron, Number 266 is disbanded. In December both Bicknell and Thompson will be awarded the DFC for their contribution: 'Bombing Alexandrovsk Harbour and sinking four Red Navy ships.' The pair is probably the only Canadian aircrew to have both sunk an enemy destroyer and to have been bombed out of their aircraft—and lived to tell the tale.

Observer Bicknell is further awarded a White Russian medal: The Order of St. Stanislaus 2nd Class with Swords. He will return home in 1920 to resume his pre-war studies at the University of Toronto and become a dental surgeon.

FR Bricknell
via J Straw

'Spike' Thompson, also a U of T student, had been in his second year of Mechanical Engineering. Joining the 135 Battalion Middlesex Rifles in 1915 as a Signaler, he transferred to the RNAS in November 1917. On his return to Canada, Morrison re-enters the army militia and rises to the rank of Colonel by 1941. A large oil painting of this 'Father of the Royal Canadian Electrical and Mechanical Engineers' hangs in the Regimental Officers Mess in Kingston, Ontario.

In 1945 Thompson wrote:

> "It is RCEME's guiding principle that their men are soldiers first and foremost. It is their proud boast that they can repair every type of equipment from a watch or radio to a gun or tank."

Thompson Drill Hall, McNaughton Barracks, Kingston, is named in his honour.

Col HG Thompson

U of T

20Jul19 – FLt Archibald James RANKIN (Edmonton) – INJ North Russia

An Allied expedition to North Russia in 1918 had been sent to secure and guard large stocks of war supplies delivered from Britain. With the Bolshevik seizure of power in October 1917 there was substantial alarm that this military equipment would fall into their hands. The job of an Allied force codenamed 'Elope' to Archangel and a similar 'Syren' force to Murmansk was to encourage and re-train a Russian army to form a new Eastern Front. When the Allies capture Archangel in a battle with the local Bolshevik troops, the action precipitates the Reds looking upon the British as the new enemy. German advisors are sent by Berlin to aid, abet and train the Bolshevik forces.

Early in 1919 Rankin was sent to Archangel, North Russia, as part of a relief force to bring out Allied troops. Now, he is assigned to His Majesty's Ship *Pegasus*, a converted merchantman weighing 3,070 tons and accommodating nine seaplanes. The vessel operates the aircraft off the Dvina River in support of the White Forces.

Today Rankin is injured when his Fairey IIIB Seaplane N9251 crashes into an ammunition-lighter during takeoff. His machine is a write off and his Observer 2Lt J. Gondre drowns. For Rankin the Russian campaign is over, although he will subsequently make the RAF his career, ultimately rising to the rank of Air Commodore.

20Aug19 – Lt Claude Melvin LeMOINE (Toronto) – KIC Russia

With Force 'Elope' in Archangel, LeMoine spins in during a test flight. He was operating Short 184 N9090 out of HMS *Pegasus* on the Dvina River. His Observer, F/Sgt HW Quantrell, is severely shaken; LeMoin lingers for three days before dying from his injuries:

25Aug19 – Capt Dugald MacDOUGALL, DFC (Lockport MB) – Killed in Russia

A seaplane pilot who has been serving in North Russia for over a year, MacDougall is killed when an ammunition barge blows up alongside his ship, HMS *Glowworm*. Twenty officers and men are lost in the catastrophe at the Archangel-Obozerskaya dockyard near Berezniki.

Assigned to the Russia zone in June 1918, MacDougall flew his first missions in July off HMS *Nairana*. On the 7th of August that year he was airborne for over two hours, engaged in escorting a flotilla of paddle steamers conveying Allied troops up the River Dvina. For this work during the capture of Archangel he was subsequently decorated with the Distinguished Flying Cross and two Russian honours, the Order of St Stanislas and the Order of St Anne. Although wounded in September 1918, MacDougall volunteered to remain in North Russian service after the Armistice.

By now, the Allied intervention into Russia had become a completely indecisive, and pathetic, sideshow. The White Russian troops tended to mutiny and switch allegiance to the Bolsheviks; moreover, there is not much support from the population on a home front still mourning losses from the Great War. At the end of the summer it is painfully obvious that with the escalating civil war the mission has become impossible: and all surviving Allied troops are withdrawn from ravaged Russia as another winter sets in.

28Sep19 – Captain Cecil Hill DARLEY, DSC&B, DFC (Toronto; b. ENG) – KIC Rome

(From 18Feb18) Piloting a Vickers Vimy enroute from England to Egypt, Darley crashes in Italy. The highly decorated English-Canadian was departing Bracciano, near Rome, on a leg of a new London-to-Cairo operation. The heavily laden Vimy hits a tree on takeoff and bursts into flame: Darley is burned to death. His brother and co-pilot, Major Charles Curtis Darley, is awarded Albert Medal for attempting to rescue his sibling from the flames. Charles suffers burns that put him in hospital for

18 months. Brother Cecil is buried at Rome's Testaccio Protestant Cemetery.

After the War, Cecil Darley, best known for the May 1918 novel low-level attack on the Zeebrugge Lock Gates, moved into pioneering flying work with the RAF. In May 1919 he flew out of Ramsgate, England, to Madrid, Spain, via a forced landing at Pau due bad weather in the Pyrenees. Attempting a first non-stop flight Madrid-London return, his Handley Page machine started to disintegrate at 5,000 feet over Bay of Biscay, possibly owing to delaminating effects of the sun in Spain. They ditch safely and are rescued by fishing boats. Darley is awarded the Spanish Cross of Military Merit for this aeronautical attempt.

His brother Charles Darley, a 1913 Royal Flying Corps pilot, was shot down and made POW in October 1915 by the first German Ace, Max Immelmann. On recovery from his Vimy crash burns in Italy, Charles Darley will remain in the RAF and attain Air Commodore rank by 1938. However he is further injured by a crash in India and invalided from RAF in 1939 only to be re-employed in the Air Ministry during the Second World War.

23Jan20– Edward Weldon BERRY
(Langley BC) – RIP

A classic 'After-The-War' loss, former Lt Berry dies of heart disease at home in Langley, British Columbia. The Canadian Field Artillery Corporal had entered the RNAS in January 1918 and the strains of flying had taken a severe toll on his heart and health.

– John Frederick Joseph KIERNAN
(Montreal) – RIP

By the end of this year, another post-war death of an ex-RNAS Officer will be that of Kieran who succumbs to rheumatic fever. He is buried at Notre Dame Des Neiges Cemetery in Montreal. A former clerk, he had joined the RNAS through the Canadian Department of Naval Service, then

JFJ Kiernan

RAeC Trust

graduated from Cranwell in April 1918 into the RAF. As a new 2nd Lieutenant he was assessed: 'VG Pilot & Officer, rec'd for bombers. Is Keen & anxious to do well.' Kiernan went on to fly the DH-4 Bomber.

23Mar20 – Capt George Harold BOYCE, AFC
(Ottawa ON) – Crash

Boyce has remained in the RAF and today, while Spotting for a torpedo drop by a Sopwith Cuckoo aircraft of the Development Flight at Gosport, he survives a crash when his Avro 504 spins into the North Sea. Serving with 6 Wing out of Otranto, Italy in 1917, Boyce was noted for having 'Very good Executive ability.' He had been awarded the AFC and was granted a permanent commission by the RAF for his early carrier test flying in HMS *Argus* and *Furious* during 1918. Boyce will build a career in the British air service and retire an Air Commodore.

22Jul20 – Stuart GRAHAM, AFC
(Wolfville NS; b. USA) – Bush Pilot

(From 22Apr18) The former RNAS pilot, now flying a Curtiss HS-2L for Laurentide Air Service, stakes the first mining claim made by use of an aircraft. Demobilized from the service in early 1919, Graham returned to Canada convinced of the great potential for civilian air operations. He secured financing to purchase two of the Curtiss flying boats from the disbanded RCNAS in Halifax and flew them to Grand Mere, Quebec, for use in forestry fire patrol, mapping, and transportation.

S Graham 1963

CAHF

More than just a 'bush pilot', Graham's influence will span the nation when he becomes Comptroller of Civil Aviation in 1928. His expertise will extend even farther afield during the Second World War when he designs airfields for the British Commonwealth Air Training Plan. He garners acknowledgment for this effort in 1945 when he is named an Officer of the Order of the

British Empire (OBE). From 1951 until his retirement from active flying in 1963, Graham serves as an aviation advisor for the United Nations International Civil Aviation Organization.

Recognized as Canada's first professional peacetime aviator, Graham is inducted into the Canadian Aviation Hall of Fame with the citation: 'His vision, foresight and application of airborne skills, despite adversity, during the birth of civil aeronautics, have been of outstanding benefit to Canadian aviation.' Stuart Graham died in 1976 and was posthumously awarded the Trans-Canada (McKee) Flying Trophy in 1991. Today Graham's Curtiss HS-2L flying boat *La Vigilance* can be viewed at the National Aviation Museum in Ottawa.

24Jul20– FLt Joseph Stuart Temple FALL, DSC (Cobble Hill BC) – Air Race

(From 19Dec17) At the first post-war air show, the 1920 Hendon Aerial Pageant, Fall leads an aerobatics formation of five Sopwith Snipes. It could be said that Joe Fall is Canada's first-generation 'Snowbird Lead'. Today he takes part in an Aerial Derby that races a course of 200 miles. The double circuit tracks from Brooklands Aerodrome via Epsom, West Thurrock, Epping and Hertford to the London Aerodrome at Hendon.

Flight Lieutenant Fall will serve in Iraq and Egypt in the early 1920's and then as a test pilot with the experimental unit at

GCapt JST Fall

Mike Fall

Farnborough. When the Second World War looms, now-Wing Commander Fall is appointed CO of the RAF Station in Malta. This is followed by promotion to Group Captain and a posting to Alexandria, Egypt. A rather too-close neighbor at the time is a German chap named Erwin Rommel.

In 1943, G/Capt Fall returns to Canada and assumes command of No 33 Flying Training School at Carberry, Manitoba. He retires from active service in 1945 and finally goes home to the Cowichan Valley of Vancouver Island. Operating a dairy farm Fall works long hours

and raises champion Jersey milk cows. In 1988, at age 93 he finally succumbs to the polio that he had contracted in a mid-East tour during the 1920's. Fall's outstanding flying achievements aside, his living with post polio syndrome alone speaks volumes about the caliber of this most determined and amazing man.

07Oct20 – LtCol Robert LECKIE, DSO (Toronto; b. SCT) – Trans Canada Flight

(From 05Aug18) In 1919, Leckie was appointed Commanding Officer of Number 1 Wing of the newly created Canadian Air Force. His Wing consisted of the Sopwith Dolphin fighter squadron and the DeHavilland DH-9 bomber squadron. Subsequently, when the Canadian Parliament decided against continuing with a permanent air force and opted for a militia style CAF Leckie accepted a commission with the RAF. Now he is back in the Dominion, on loan from the RAF to the recently established Canadian Air Board as their Director of Flying Operations.

In an effort to boost public opinion and give recognition to the potential of aviation, Leckie and Major **Claire MacLaurin** have planned an across Canada flight. Today, accompanied by his Dartmouth Station commander Major **Basil Deacon Hobbs**, Leckie sets out from Nova Scotia for MacLaurin's west coast station at Vancouver, British Columbia. He flies as far as Winnipeg, arriving on the 10th of October. Other pilots and aircraft continue the 3,635-mile trip and arrive on the 17th of the month. The adventure is beset by aircraft breakdowns and weather stoppages – nonetheless, it is proven feasible to cross the country by air.

By 1923, Leckie will return to RAF duties in the UK and serve in a variety of appointments, including time in the aircraft carriers HMS *Hermes* and *Courageous* as CO of the RAF flights aboard. In 1935 he is appointed RAF Director of Training and promoted to Air Commodore. His next commission is that of Air Officer Commanding Mediterranean with headquarters at Malta. He will be again loaned to Canada in yet another war. *(Read January 1944)*

29Mar21 – Capt Daniel M. Bayne GALBRAITH, DSC&Bar (Carleton Place ON) – Killed

(From 16Nov16) The new 'Weekend Warrior' styled Canadian Air Force suffers its first casualty when Galbraith is fatally injured in a motor vehicle accident near Camp Borden, Ontario. The second Canadian to

become a naval ace, Galbraith had finished the war with a total of six in the bag.

In December, the thirteenth Canadian Parliament is convened. It proves an unlucky number for Canada's fledgling military air service. The new Prime Minister, William Lyon Mackenzie King, charges that the British gift of aviation supplies is simply a dumping of war surplus. A pre-war militia corporal from Waterloo County, Ontario, the PM has no place for the CAF reservists and cuts funding to the air service. Aviation for the military finds no champions in a country still grieving her war losses. The CAF summer refresher courses for 1922 are cancelled.

15Apr21 – Lt Elmer Garfield FULLERTON, CAF (Pictou NS) – Bush Test Flight

Fullerton and another CAF pilot are 'on loan' to Imperial Oil Limited to carry out a northern flight from Edmonton up along the Mackenzie River of the North West Territories. Oil has been discovered on Bear Island just south of the Arctic Circle. Piloting two German-built Junker monoplanes, named the 'Rene' and the 'Vic', the pioneering airmen have both become snowbound with broken propellers at Fort Simpson.

Resourcefully the aviators and their mechanics set up shop with the local Hudson's Bay trading post and Roman Catholic Mission. Using sleigh boards and moose glue they engineer a hand-made propeller for Fullerton's machine 'Vic' and today he successfully takes to the air.

His bush flying skills become well noted and in 1922, although the trip is cancelled, Fullerton was chosen by explorer Raold Amundsen for a North Pole attempt. In his later career, Fullerton instructs and passes along his valuable knowledge to new aviators. He is also the designer of the RCAF Tartan, officially adopted in 1942. Fullerton, the RNAS trained pilot, is inducted into the Canadian Aviation Hall of Fame in 1974. The hand-carved wooden propeller is on permanent display at the Canadian Aviation and Space Museum in Ottawa.

11Sep22 – Major Clarence 'Mac' MacLAURIN, DSC (Lachine PQ) – KIC Vancouver

(From 10Jan16) Superintendant of Jericho Beach Air Station in Vancouver, MacLaurin has just lifted off in HS-2L G-CYEA enroute to Sumas Lake when the engine radiator begins to boil. As he commences banking for an immediate return landing, Air Mechanic AC Hartridge

points out a gasoline leak across the hot manifold. Reported later by Hartridge, MacLaurin had immediately cut the engine to avoid a fire while continuing his turn. The flying boat stalls and plunges into the waters off

C MacLaurin

P Donnellan

of Point Grey. Mechanic Hartridge is badly injured but survives; MacLaurin and his passenger John Duncan, the engineer in charge of the Sumas Lake Reclamation Project, are killed.

MacLaurin's death is a significant loss for the nascent Canadian Air Force and he is mourned at air stations across the country.

In 1918, to assist in setting up the new Royal Canadian Naval Air Service, MacLaurin had been relieved of his Bembridge Air Station command on the Isle of Wight and sent to Ottawa. Promoted to the rank of Acting Wing Commander he travelled via Washington DC, stopping there to advise on airborne anti-submarine operations. The United States Navy consequently built naval air stations in Nova Scotia at Baker Point in Sydney and at Kelly Beach in Dartmouth. The objective was to turn these units and their aircraft over to RCNAS pilots as they became available after training. By August 1918 MacLaurin was appointed Director of the RCNAS and following the Armistice he remained a one-man Naval Air Service.

The Canadian government selected MacLaurin as a founding member of their new Air Board when it was formed in December 1919. A lumberman, he proposed an aerial forest survey experiment in Quebec confirming that the use of aircraft increased productivity. When given the privilege of selecting the base of his choice, MacLaurin requested Jericho Beach. It was there that he conceived and helped plan the October 1920 trans-Canadian flight. In the two years before his death, MacLaurin was a veritable driving force in Canada's new air militia.

Mac's English war bride, Frances Luisa (Pitita) had died of Influenza at Ottawa in February 1920 and he had escorted her body home to the Isle of Wight for burial.

In October 1922 he is laid to rest beside her 'In Death Not Divided'. Their only child, a son, dies in a traffic accident in the 1930's.

1923 –Kenneth Foster SAUNDERS, DSC (Victoria BC) – Bush Pilot

(From 31Dec17) Saunders has brought his RNAS instructional skills and hard-flying outlook back to Canada. Becoming the Chief Pilot of Fairchild Aerial Surveys out of Grand Mere Quebec, he leads the early bush flying along the north shore of the St. Lawrence River for Canadian (Quebec) Airlines until joining the Department of Transport in 1936.

He retires after forty-two years of flying service as the Regional Superintendent of Alberta, the Northwest Territories and the Yukon, Saunders is known for being a strict disciplinarian tempered with a fair mixture of fatherly advice and humour. He will be elected posthumously to the Canadian Aviation Hall of Fame in 1997: '...his ability to adapt the airplane to commercial tasks in the north set the scene for the years of bush flying that followed.'

KF Saunders 1960s

CAHF

1929 – William 'Bill' TEMPLETON (Vancouver) – Airport Manager

(From 23Apr11) Following his 1916 RNAS training in England, Templeton operated out of the Malta Seaplane Station. However, like many who served in the Mediterranean theatre of the War, Templeton was grounded by malaria and invalided out of the service. During 1920 he re-commissioned as a Pilot Officer with the embryonic Canadian Air Force at Jericho Beach. Again his malaria flared, and again he was forced to give up flying.

But, Templeton's biggest contribution to aviation in Canada is yet to come about. This year he is tasked to take charge over the City of Vancouver's airfield on Lulu Island. The

W Templeton in 1916

RAeC Trust

famed aviator Charles Lindberg has refused to land on the rough pasture and this has embarrassed the city into providing proper leadership. Templeton oversees the relocation and construction of a new airport on nearby Sea Island and will go on to serve as manager for over twenty years. In 1940 the field becomes an important West Coast RCAF Station. Today it is known as the Vancouver International Airport.

01Jan30 – Herbert 'Bert' Sterling WEMP, DFC, OL, Cd'G – Mayor of Toronto Inagural

(From 03Apr18) A Toronto city Alderman, Wemp had thrown his hat in the ring for the Mayoralty. On Election Day many of Wemp's aviator friends launched from the Toronto Flying Club airfield and flew over the city in a 'V for victory' formation as the voters headed to the polls. The former RNAS airman and RAF Squadron Commander was an easy winner.

During the campaign, the incumbent, a fiery Orangeman, had challenged Wemp to a debate. Knowing that such an undertaking would only degenerate into a shouting match, Wemp ignored the man. Later, at a political rally, the mayor called his rival a coward. Such a damning and false accusation raised the ire of the Toronto *Evening Telegram* and the newspaper published an almost unprecedented full front page photo of Wemp dressed in his Great War uniform, replete with pilot wings and a host of medals. An editorial demanded: 'Was he a coward when bombing the German Fleet or the Zeebrugge submarine base – five times?'

Much is made of the fact that the Prince of Wales, later King Edward VII, had presented Wemp with the one of the first DFCs awarded to a Canadian and that the King of Belgium had honoured Wemp as a Chevalier of the Order of Leopold. A third country, France, conferred upon him the Croix de Guerre.

HS Wemp

GWFM

During the Second World War Wemp will go overseas to Europe as a War Correspondent and will be awarded the Civil OBE for his reporting from the Italian Front.

09Oct30 – James Erroll Durnsford BOYD (Toronto) – Trans-Atlantic Flight

(From 03Oct15) After spending most of the Great War in Holland as an internee, Erroll Boyd returned to home determined to continue flying. Throughout the 1920s and into the 1930s he inaugurated many of the first official air mail flights in North America and also set a world record flying time from New York to the tiny island of Bermuda. However, it is his successful attempt today that places him as the very first Canadian to fly the Atlantic.

Returning by ocean liner to Toronto, Boyd is welcomed by cheering crowds and a large dinner at the Royal York Hotel with the new Mayor, **Bert Wemp,** officiating the ceremony. Boyd will become the aviation editor of the Toronto's Star Weekly magazine and in 1938 forms the Aviation Scouts of Canada, a forerunner of the Air Cadet movement. He continues his flying as a test pilot in the United States during the Second World War and recruits veteran pilots for Trans-Atlantic Ferry operations. Ross Smyth of Air Canada chronicles the life of Boyd in his 1997 book titled *The Lindbergh of Canada.*

Sep1933 – David Douglas FINDLAY (Carleton Place ON) – Flight to Turkey

(From 23Sep16) Following demobilization in 1919, Captain Findlay returned to his former status as a student at Queens University in Kingston. Graduating in 1922, he joined his family business, the Findlay Foundry, a stove and furnace works in Carleton Place, Ontario. In the fall of 1933 he makes good his dream to return to his RNAS roots in the Eastern Mediterranean. Flying a DeHavilland Puss Moth out of England, he and his wife travel to Constantinople (now Istanbul) and back. A serial entitled *'Europe Revisited'* is published in the October and November 1934 issues of *Canadian Aviation.*

> "…We left Brindisi to fly the 400 miles to Athens. Between the 'heel' of Italy and the west coast of Greece there is over 50 miles of open Adriatic. About 8,000 feet above the mathematical middle, the engine, which had never missed a pop, suddenly started to backfire and lose revs badly. Do what I would I couldn't clear the obvious stoppage in the petrol system. We were losing height, so I turned downwind and pointed the nose for the nearest bit of Italy. Then followed twenty sweating minutes of wondering if land or zero on the altimeter would arrive first. Land won. We crossed the cliffs at 1,000 feet and sat down in a cornfield, the only possible place in miles. I got out, lit a cigarette and basked in the glow that follows a forced landing pulled off successfully."

After the "most abounding but inquisitive hospitality" by his corn farmer host, and the "courteous appearance of an Italian engineer officer", the problem is solved and the snag traced back to a "little hole in the chamois at Brindisi." Findlay continues on to Athens where he reunited with "no fewer than five Greek officers, gentlemen all, who had flown with our squadron in 1916." His next stop is Salonika "on the edge of the old RNAS stamping ground" to await Turkish flight clearance.

> "The appointed day arrived and we left on the 400-mile flight to Constantinople. We passed over a cultivated field that was the old Stavros

aerodrome. Then along the Struma and bad lands of Pilav Tepe, where the Bulgars shot George Abbott's old Short seaplane full of holes and even punctured the Inspector of Civil Aviation himself. Then a side jaunt out to Thasos to see the old aerodrome. It's in vineyards now, but there were the dugouts, the bomb dump and the imprint of the drainage trenches that once surrounded our Bessoneaux.

"Along the coast, up toward Gallipoli, the trenches are still well preserved, particularly in high land, where there is no cultivation. We flew back over the Peninsula and up the Dardanelles. At Suvla and Gaba Tepe, the trenches and shell holes still scar the hillsides. It was eerie and unnatural to fly with one's wife over sheep grazing on those very hills that once belched forth enough fire and hate to keep one dodging and wondering where the next one would burst."

The Findlays visit six European countries and fly about 7,000 miles in total. From the vantage point of his home hearth, the former RNAS pilot will note to himself: "… next time, take your own (fuel) funnel." David Findlay serves as a Group Captain RCAF during World War II.

Sep1939 – Former 2Lt Russell Welland FROST (Hamilton ON) – AWOL

RW Frost

RAeC Trust

Attempting to join the RCAF at the outbreak of the Second World War, Frost is surprised to learn at the recruiting centre that he is on the books of the RAF as having deserted in late 1918. Having entered the RNAS in January 1918 and graduating as a pilot in the new RAF, he had flown with 155 Squadron (along with the Duke of York, later King George VI). During his time in squadron Frost crash-landed while ferrying an aircraft and although injured, he thought himself fortunate to come down in a good location – as he had described in a letter home, the pretty daughter of the household that rescued him provided nursing care.

Just after the Armistice, Frost learned that his father was gravely ill with the Flu and he managed to board a ship that was departing immediately for Canada. Without proper discharge papers, he was consequently listed as being Absent Without Leave. Now, some twenty years later his administrative indiscretion catches up. However, Frost perseveres to clear his record and by this War's end he will be Honourably released as a Wing Commander with the Royal Canadian Air Cadet Corps.

10Apr40 – History Repeats: *Konigsberg* – Norway – Lt(P) Alexander B. FRASER-HARRIS (Halifax NS)

(From 11Jul15) In a repeat of history, Royal Navy aviators sink the new Nazi Cruiser *Koningsberg*. Damaged by Norwegian costal batteries before that country fell, *Konigsberg* is tied up for repair in the recently captured Bergen Harbour. Two RN Fleet Air Arm Squadrons, 800 and 803, from Lossiemouth in Scotland are tasked to attack the vessel. Operating at the extreme limit of their Skua fighter aircraft range, a sixteen aircraft formation launches at night on the risky undertaking. Arriving at daybreak they dive bomb from out of the rising sun, each dropping a 500lb bomb. Only one Skua fails to return.

Lieutenant (Pilot) Fraser-Harris scores a hit on *Konigsberg's* forecastle. His is one of the four bombs that strike the cruiser. Other weapons hit the dock and explode sideways through the vessel. A historic record is set: The first sinking of a major warship in wartime by aerial bombing. For some reason, dive-bombing is a method that had been disparaged by Royal Air Force Bomber Command.

Fraser-Harris will continue to fly with the Fleet Air Arm for the remainder of the war before transferring to the Royal Canadian Navy in 1945. He becomes the first Canadian Naval Aviator to command an aircraft carrier, HMCS *Magnificent*, the 'Maggie' in 1956. Promoted to Flag rank he pushes hard for the recognition of naval aviation as a vital, versatile, and indivisible component of the fleet. The 'Father of Canadian Naval Aviation', Commodore Fraser Harris is inducted as a Member of the Canadian Aviation Hall of Fame in 2004.

May1940 – AirM Lloyd Samuel BREADNER (Ottawa) – CAS RCAF

(From 11Apr1) Described as bon vivant with a practical mind, Air Marshal Breadner had served with the RCAF throughout the 1920s and 1930s, and trained at Britain's Imperial Defence College in 1936. Becoming the Canadian Chief of Air Staff (CAS) in May 1940 he leads the RCAF during the first years of the Second World War. The Dominion air force will reach a peak wartime census of more than two hundred thousand personnel operating 78 squadrons, 35 of them based overseas.

LS Breadner, 1917
CO 3 Naval

GWFM

In January 1944 Breadner will be appointed the Air Officer Commanding the RCAF Overseas. On retirement in May 1945 he is promoted Air Chief Marshal, the first Canadian to hold this rank.

His only son, Donald Lloyd Breadner RCAF, a DeHavilland Mosquito pilot, is killed during the War.

10Jun1940 – ACmdr Raymond COLLISHAW, RAF (Nanaimo) – War with Italy

(From May 1919) Collishaw's halcyon years in Cairo are interrupted by the second global conflict. Promoted to Air Commodore in 1939, he takes over the Egypt Group that is soon known as 'The Desert Air Force.' When Mussolini declares war this day, 'Collie' reacts with his old fighter pilot skills, striking first and fast. His meager force consists of Blenheim bombers, Gladiator bi-plane fighters and old Bombay transports converted to drop weapons. The single Hurricane fighter in his arsenal is nicknamed 'Collie's Battleship' and appears at irregular intervals over the enemy convincing them of squadrons of the eight-gun aircraft. The Desert Air Force utterly demoralizes the Italian Regia Aeronautica in North Africa, reducing it to defensive operations only and destroying nearly 1,100 aircraft.

Collishaw completely wins the day. Among his accomplishments he re-establishes the neglected concept of Army Air Cooperation and gains the respect and admiration of the men on the ground. British Army General Sir Richard Nugent O'Connor is the field commander for the Western Desert Force that completely destroys the much larger Italian army.

When the last of the enemy troops surrender in the early morning of 7th February 1941, O'Connor address a special order of the day to Collishaw. 'I wish', he writes. 'To record my very great appreciation of the wonderful work of the R.A.F. units under your command, whose determination and fine fighting qualities have made this campaign possible. Since the war began you have consistently attacked the enemy air force ... dealing him blow after blow, until finally he was driven out of the sky, and out of Libya [Cyrenaica], leaving hundreds of derelict aircraft on his aerodromes. In his recent retreat from Tobruk you gave his ground troops no rest ...'

The joint Army-Air victory has nearly pushed the Axis out of Africa, forcing the Nazi leader Adolph Hitler to dispatch General Erwin Rommel and his Afrika Korps to attempt a force reversal.

However, in spite of this outstanding victory over an entire enemy air force, Collishaw runs afoul of the new Commander of the RAF Middle East, Air Marshal Arthur Tedder. Collie had followed his First World War instincts, when the pilots were not tethered by radio and radar and aggressively ran their own show once airborne. Tedder believes in detailed planning and preparation and finds Collishaw impulsive in overlooking 'proper' administration.

Sent to Scotland to command a Fighter Group Collishaw is promoted to Air Vice Marshal but retires, it is said involuntarily, from the RAF in July 1943 and returns to British Columbia. *(Read 28Sep76)*

1942 – AirM Harold 'Gus' EDWARDS (Glace Bay, NS) – AOC RCAF Overseas

(From 14Apr17) By this third year of the Second World War, the RCAF has well over 10,000 aircrew personnel serving overseas and these numbers are rapidly expanding. The Canadian government does not want their airmen absorbed into the RAF but wishes to have them operate under a Canadian command structure. Air Marshal Edwards is appointed AOC in Chief, RCAF Overseas, and given charge of carrying out this 'Canadianization.'

Edwards finds that it is an: "utterly frustrating process dealing with high-minded Brits", and in Canada, certain other individuals prove equally unsupportive. During September 1942, speaking, he believes, off the record Edwards states:

> "Some people are talking a lot of bloody nonsense about splitting the Empire. If Canadians who see it from that point of view want to be mugs all their lives, that's their business. I can see no reason against Canadianization."

His words are made public and bring down a barrage of critique – but also very strong support. It is recognized that while combat control must be run by a single agency, the efficiency and indeed, the wellbeing of Canadians, is best carried out in cohesive formations.

AVM Edwards at Traflgar Square in September 1943, addressing a crowd gathered to view the first Canadian-built Lancaster (KB700) delivered to England

SK Edwards

To this end, Number 6 (RCAF) Bomber Group is formed in January 1943 and will eventually comprise of fifteen squadrons. The manpower on the ground and in the air is 'all-Canadian.'

The RCAF overseas command also includes the Middle and Far East Canadian contingents and demands rigorous travel. At the end of 1943, Edwards, a 'Man of hope & forward looking mind' is replaced by Air Marshal **Lloyd Breadner**. Once back in Ottawa, Edwards turns down a largely ceremonial post of inspector general of the air force and retires. Always keen on his airmen's welfare, he devotes himself to the RCAF Benevolent

Fund, serving as president and chairman of the board. Ill-health from the First World War and work strains of the Second bring Edwards' life to a close in 1952 at age 59. He has the legacy of being instrumental in developing the RCAF into a truly Canadian air force – Not an RAF adjunct. His biography *GUS, From Trapper Boy to Air Marshal* was written by his daughter Suzanne K. Edwards and published in 2007.

Jan1944 – AirM Robert LECKIE (Toronto; b. SCT) – CAS RCAF

(From 07Oct20) With **Lloyd Breadner** leaving for overseas duty in December 1943, Air Marshal Leckie takes over the leadership of the RCAF. He had returned to Canada as an Air Commodore on loan from the RAF in 1940 to become Director of Training for the country. From this appointment he transferred to the RCAF and developed the training role into the British Commonwealth Air Training Plan (BCATP).

Due to the success of 'The Plan,' US President Franklin D. Roosevelt calls Canada 'the aerodrome of democracy': a high praise indeed for what are largely Leckie's leadership efforts. From across the former British Empire, 131,522 Aircrew (Navigators, Bombers, Wireless Air Gunners, Air Gunners and Flight Engineers), including 49,707 pilots are trained to 'wings'.

Bob Leckie, CB, DSO, DSC, DFC, CD, the man who shot down two Zeppelins, retires from the RCAF in September 1947. An active retiree, he plays a prominent role in Canada's Air Cadet movement. When he passes in 1975, a *Toronto Star* obituary states that Leckie's BCATP was: 'an administrative task as arduous as organizing D-Day itself and arguably as important as that in the winning of the War.'

Sep1947 – AirM Wilfred Austin CURTIS (Havelock ON) – CAS RCAF

(From 23Jan18) Just as he had succeeded **Breadner**, **Bob Leckie** hands control over to Curtis as Chief of Air Staff, RCAF. By the time Curtis retires in January 1953, four former RNAS aviators will have led the country's air force for over one dozen of its most critical years.

During his watch, Curtis expands the recently demobilized air force to participate in the Korean War, and he fulfills a strong commitment to the North Atlantic Treaty Organization in the opening years of the Cold War. His creation of an overseas RCAF Air Division will place twelve F-86 Saber squadrons in

Europe. Curtis also encourages development of the Canadian aircraft industry with production orders for the Avro CF-100, an all-weather interceptor designed to protect against feared Russian bombers. It is the genesis of Canada's part in what will go on to become known as the North American Air Defense Command (NORAD). Wilf Curtis, CB, CBE, DSC & Bar, ED, was one of the early supporters of the CF-105 Avro Arrow.

28Sep76 – AVM (Ret'd) Raymond COLLISHAW (Nanaimo BC) – RIP

(From 10Jun1940) Age 82, the Naval Ace of Aces dies in West Vancouver, BC. Upon leaving the RAF he had successfully applied himself to mining engineer ventures. When his 1916 frostbitten eyes began to fail him in the field he retired once again and took up historical aviation research, working with the *Cross & Cockade* journal. In a letter to former RNAS aviator **Charlie Geale** in 1969, Collishaw wrote:

> "I have compiled a Register of some 17,500 names and dates of British, French and German Air casualties of the 1st War. If you have any queries to do with a particular casualty, I can probably give the answer."

In aviation circles there is debate over whether Collishaw's victories had been understated as Royal Naval Air Service fighter pilots received somewhat less publicity than their Royal Flying Corps counterparts. Some historians credit him with more kills than the Red Baron or the top Allied Ace Canadian Billy Bishop. However, if a strict verification were applied, his score, as with all RNAS, RFC and RAF victories, would invariably be lower.

Collishaw is one of Canada's least-remembered heroes. Regardless, he continues to be honoured in small ways. On the 2nd of October 1999, through the untiring efforts of Ted Brothers, Chairman of the Vancouver Island Military Museum, the Nanaimo airport named their passenger terminus the Nanaimo-Collishaw Air Terminal. The city's Royal Canadian Air Cadet unit is named 205 Collishaw Squadron; and the Kamloops, BC, Air Cadets parade with 204 Black Maria Squadron. Collishaw was inducted into the Canadian Aviation Hall of Fame at the Hall's official opening in 1974.

His memoirs, titled *Air Command, A Fighter Pilot's Story* is first published in 1973 in England and finally released in Canada during 2008 as *The Black Flight*. In the last pages of the book Collishaw states:

> "I feel that my days of command in North Africa, when we had to outwit and outfight a numerically superior enemy by a combination of deception, superior tactics and fighting spirit, represented by far my best effort. Yet if I am known at all to my fellow Canadians and others it is through more carefree days, when as a young fighter pilot, with the limited responsibilities of a Flight and Squadron Commander on the Western Front, I had the good fortune to shoot down a number of the enemy without in turn being killed."

On the subject of command, Collishaw held continual leadership appointments from his first flight command with 10 Naval in 1917 until retirement in 1943. He led seven Squadrons, six Stations and four Groups:

> "Experience in command impressed upon me one thing above all else. The commander, to be successful, must, above all, be able to impart to those under him a spiritual stimulation."

1982 – Francis Gilmer Tempest DAWSON (Chester NS) – RIP

(From 09Jul15) Although he was released from the RNAS in 1915 due to his poor health from service in the Dardanelles, Dawson, Canada's first naval aviator was far from leaving flying activities. Returned to England from the Aegean, he entered into a partnership with Richard (later Sir Richard) Fairey and became the founding Director and the principal financier of the Fairey Aviation Company. Described as shy and modest by nature, Dawson stayed out of the limelight in the new venture but worked with a fervent interest in the business until he retired in 1933. During the Second World War he was employed in Ottawa with the Department of Munitions and Supply, travelling to the United Kingdom in 1943 to work on sonar experiments with the Navy. Three of his children also serve in the 1939-45 conflict. Son John joins the Royal Canadian Navy and retires in the 1960's as a Captain. Two daughters serve for the duration as Canadian WREN officers.

Postwar, Dawson returned once again to Nov Scotia and bought property in Chester, near his father's birthplace. When 'Wuffy' dies at age 88 in Ireland during a visit, The British *Times* newspaper describes him as: 'One of the last links with the early days of aviation.' In keeping with his wishes, his ashes are scattered over the Channel from a Sea King helicopter of the Fleet Air Arm.

In the early 1930's, Dawson had purchased three soggy cabbage fields and drained them for Fairey Aviation.

The site was named The Great Western Aerodorome: it continues to operate to this day as an airport (and construction site) – and is now more commonly known as Heathrow International.

03Jan2003 – Henry J. Lawrence BOTTERELL, LdH, (Ottawa) – RIP

At the grand old age of 106, Henry Botterell, a Canadian Royal Naval Air Service veteran and the world's last living First World War pilot, passes away peacefully at a veterans care facility in Toronto.

author's collection

208 RAF · CHRISTMAS 1918

The pilots wear a mixed-bag of RNAS, RFC and RAF uniforms.

Henry Botterell in his Naval uniform, standing far left side. Squadron Commander Chris Draper, also in Naval Dress is seated center.

Canadian Ace JB White is on the CO's right.

CHAPTER 6
THE LAST OF OUR FIRST

HENRY BOTTERELL
1896 - 2003

"I have a vivid thing about a German officer in a sort of wagon with six horses, three pairs, hauling a gun. I was in the air and he was snapping [his whip], trying to get the best out of his horses to get back from that position, it was well over the lines. I regret to say that I hit the horses and they fell down, you know, they collapsed, got all tangled up. OHHH! I wasn't very pleased about that . . . Kind of a sickening feeling seeing the poor darned horses: they were lovely horses they had. They fell and piled up."

Although rarely speaking of it for most of his life, eight decades after his Sopwith Camel attack on an enemy gun caisson, Henry Botterell was still haunted by the memory of the stricken horses. Pulling up from his strafing-run, the young Canadian pilot had glanced over his shoulder at the agony he had inflicted—an image that was seared into his mind.

This was not the stuff of *Snoopy and the Red Baron*—the impression that comes to mind today when someone mentions a Sopwith Camel. This was human conflict at its bloodiest: the First World War 1914-1918. While Canadians fighting in the trenches of the Western Front had a one in ten chance of being killed: an aviator flying overhead had a likelihood of one in five. In spite of these tremendous odds against his longevity however, Henry John Lawrence 'Nap' Botterell would live to see three centuries: from Queen Victoria's Diamond Jubilee through to the centenary year of the Wright Brother's first powered flight.

The son of a civil servant, Henry was born in Ottawa on the 7th of November 1896, and was just six weeks old when his father died. While his mother worked, his grandmother, Annie Botterell, raised him, together with his two brothers and two sisters. Attending Lisgar Collegiate Institute, Henry was nicknamed 'Nap' by fellow students who thought he looked like Napoleon. Following his schooling, he took employment at the Bank of British North America (later absorbed into the Bank of Montreal) as a clerk. By this time, the conflict that came to be known as the Great War had begun and young Canadian men were volunteering their service.

Henry's older brother, Edward, a Toronto Argonaut footballer, joined the 48th Highlanders along with many of his teammates. The battalion went overseas with the First Contingent of the Canadian Expeditionary Force in October 1914. After months in the trenches, and just before receiving his Captaincy, Lieutenant Edward Botterell was killed by a German sniper in June 1916.

Henry, then nineteen, was anxious to do his bit. His oldest sister Edith, a secretary for Admiral Kingsmill, RCN Chief of Naval Staff, encouraged her brother to enter the supposedly safer Royal Naval Air Service. Accepted as a 'Candidate' he shipped out to England and entered the Royal Navy on the 14th of March 1917, with the Midshipman rank of Probationary Flight

Officer, RNAS. Completing the compulsory naval indoctrination at the air service training depot in London's Crystal Palace he started his actual flying at Air Station Chingford, Essex, in May 1917. Henry soloed after four hours and twelve minutes: "I learned on the Grahame-White. It was like a big box kite in shape and did 35 knots or something." His initial instructor was Flight Lieutenant **Harwood Arnold** of Queen Charlotte Islands, who had won Canada's first aviation DSO for his role in sinking the enemy raider *Konigsberg* in German East Africa.

Henry went on to win his wings at Cranwell aerodrome, flying Avros, Bristol Scouts, and Sopwith Strutters. With a grand total of fifteen hours and nineteen minutes he earned Royal Aeronautical Club certificate number 5093. Commissioned a Flight Sub-Lieutenant, Henry was selected for 'scouts', as the early fighters were known. Sent to advanced training at RNAS Freiston in late August he learned bombing and gunnery. Next came RNAS Dover and an introduction to the Sopwith Pup. It was an inauspicious start: on his first flight he lost a tire and had to land without it. This was no easy feat as Dover was a very small field with a take-off over the cliffs and a haphazard landing pattern. After a total of two hours on Pups, bringing his solo time to a near forty hours, Henry was deemed combat ready.

Henry's photo on his Royal Aero Club certificate #5093
Courtesy RAeC Trust

Appointed to 12 Naval Squadron at Petite Synthe near Dunkirk, Henry's first flight in France took place on September 17, but he had to land immediately because of a broken engine inlet valve. After ground running his machine the next morning, he took off again, but this time the motor completely failed:

> **"It was in a Sopwith Pup, my engine conked out and I crashed just after takeoff. I wasn't too high, about 200 feet, but I stalled and spun and hit pretty hard. I broke a leg and lost some teeth and gashed my head. It was not a very noble effort but I guess everyone had a few."**

Following convalescence at the Peebles Hydro Hospital in Scotland, Henry was demobilized as disabled. While standing-by in London to be repatriated to Canada, a chance meeting with fellow pilots on a 'run ashore' inspired him to rejoin the navy. This was April 1918, and by now the RNAS and the Royal Flying Corps had been integrated into the Royal Air Force. Henry became a Lieutenant, RAF, under Major **Lloyd Breadner**, DSC, of Ottawa, (later Air Chief Marshal, RCAF), at RAF Station Manston, Kent. There, Henry completed a ten minute dual hop in an Avro and then flew solo. That same day he also did two flights in a Pup. By the week's end, Captain **Daniel Galbraith,** DSC & Bar, from Carleton Place, Ontario, sent Henry off on his first flight in a Sopwith Camel. The Camel, getting its name from the hump created by two machine guns mounted over the engine cowling, was giving Allied pilots an edge on the Western Front. Notoriously difficult to control, the Camel coupled a short fuselage with a powerful engine, creating a vicious gyroscopic tendency. In the hands of a capable pilot like Henry it was a dynamic fighting machine.

Sent back to France, Henry was now assigned to 208 Squadron RAF in May of 1918. His Squadron Commander was the Englishman Chris Draper, who became famous in the early 1950's as the 'Mad Major' for flying under twelve London bridges in protest to being retired and declared redundant. Delegated to 'C' Flight, Henry joined Canadian aces **Herb Fowler** of Bowmanville and **'JB' White** of Manitoulin Island.

The Western Front at this time was in the height of a fierce confrontation: *Kaiserschlacht*, the

Botterell in his Sopwith Camel

Courtesy Bottrell Family

'Emperor's Battle,' as the Germans called Field Marshal Ludendorff's Spring offensive. A short period —after the collapse of Russia and before the fresh American troops pouring into France became combat ready—was Germany's window of opportunity to win the War.

Henry flew through this intensive period of offensive patrols, returning from many with an aircraft pierced by bullet holes or Archie (flak) damage.

Commenting on the 16,000-to-18,000-foot high altitude patrols Henry stated:

> **"The aircraft was a little bit soggy after 15,000', after 12,000' actually. But you had the advantage of going over high up and coming back diving down where they weren't expecting you. You could watch through the holes, the apertures, of the clouds. The thing was; we used to have one person pop out as a decoy. You have to have a little courage. But you got in and got out before you were mowed down yourself."**

> **"I had good hands,"** he said, assessing his own abilities in a dogfight. **"I didn't have the fighting acumen of some, like Billy Bishop. I was just a bank clerk. I wasn't one of the very best, but I had my share of action."**

On July 10, his logbook records:

> **"Saw EA [enemy aircraft] and hid in the clouds. Dived straight down at EA and fired short burst from 50 yards. Guns jammed. Pulled away about 20 ft from Hun. Over Estaires at 4,000 to 5,000 ft, so returned to lines. Enemy observer believed killed."**

In August, the Allies counterattacked and the Squadron was caught up with the Arras-area push. Henry now became active in low-level bombing and ground-strafing missions. In contrast to those fighting in the trenches, who might go 'over the top' perhaps once every two or three weeks, Henry's logbook is a chronicle of peril as he went over the Lines two and sometimes, three times, daily:

> **"August 26 – 1st mission – Low bombing. Dropped four bombs on lorries on Douai road near Brebieres. Fired 150 rounds into trench on outskirts of Brebieres. Bullet hit pressure tank and air pipe.**

> **"2nd mission – Flew machine on gravity from Izel to Tramcourt and flew another machine back.**

> **"3rd mission – Low bombing. Dropped four bombs on Jigsaw Wood. Bullet hit and broke trailing edge of left bottom plane, penetrated cowl and cracked windshield. Engine missing."**

On August 29, in an outstanding single-handed performance and 'kill', Henry attacked and shot down a German artillery observation balloon. An assault on a balloon was a plucky and impressive effort. The 'gas bags' were double-skinned for protection against bullets and were heavily defended by anti-aircraft emplacements. These AA guns were ranged to the exact height of the observation platform and could concentrate their fire on an attacking aircraft with devastating results. However, in spite of the defensive barrage, balloons were most desirable targets. They spotted for artillery and could direct very accurate 'shoots'. The long stalemate of trench warfare had turned the conflict into a gunner's war and shelling caused more casualties than any other weapon.

That day, Henry was carrying four 20lb bombs to attack the railway station at Vitry, fifty miles into enemy-occupied territory. On the outbound leg, he saw the balloon near Arras. After dropping his bombs, he flew back to the location only to find the German ground crew frantically winching his target down. Defying heavy anti-aircraft fire, Henry dove and let loose some 400 rounds, setting the balloon's gas alight. As the 'sausage' began to crumple, the German observer took to his parachute and leapt from the wicker basket. Henry banked to avoid him:

> **"I flew around him and gave him a wave but he wasn't very sociable. He didn't look too enthusiastic. In my recollection, he looked petrified. He thought he was a cooked goose, but you didn't shoot down a fellow in a parachute. We wouldn't do that. It wasn't done in those days. Well, I waved at him anyway."**

When queried about the anti-aircraft defenses, Henry simply states:

> **"Yes, there was quite a bit of fire from the ground."**

Asked about another flight during which a bullet ripped through his ear and smashed his goggles, Henry replied:

> **"Yes, I was shot. Just look at the bump on my head."** In fact, he had briefly lost consciousness, recovering just in time to avoid crashing.

Nor were his bad landing days over. On September 19, two years and a day after his first accident, Henry crashed and overturned a new Camel and this time emerged unscathed. His diary records that the next day he played rugby, however, it also notes that: **"Major Draper was very annoyed when I went over on my nose."**

Henry's diary provides details of how he spent November 11:

> **"The CO woke us up to tell us about the Armistice. We had a big dinner with pheasant and hare, shot locally."** The next day, he took off in a new Sopwith Snipe and recorded: **"I flew low over Mons and waved at the troops."**

During his seven months on active service the young Canadian had flown 267 hours. 'Pilot Wastage' was incredibly high—in that same seven-month period 208 Squadron, made up of three 6-pilot flights, suffered the loss of six pilots killed in action: two killed accidentally, seven taken prisoner of war, three wounded in action and two injured accidentally.

Until the peace treaty at Versailles was concluded, the Allies kept a military watch along the Rhine. Henry's Squadron moved to Belgium and maintained cease-fire patrols. While flying a Snipe to visit a friend near Brussels in March 1919 Henry almost added himself to the casualty list. Temporarily unsure of his position, he pulled out a map. Thrusting it back into his flying boot he failed to notice that the terrain was rapidly rising. As a result he hit a fence post with his lower left wing and broke the rear spar, carrying away a piece of fencing which had become embedded in the airfoil.

Later that year, Captain Henry Botterell returned to Canada and resumed the banking career he had left for the war. His total time in the air was 324 hours and he never flew an aircraft again. A treasured souvenir, smuggled home in three parts was the nine-foot propeller from his Sopwith Snipe. The other trophy brought home—the offending piece of Belgian fence—Henry donated to the Canadian War Museum in Ottawa.

Married in 1929 to the former Maud Goater, Henry later moved with his wife and their two children from Ottawa to Montreal. Their son Edward recalls his athletic father cross-country skiing the Maple Leaf trail on winter weekends and bicycling around Montreal's West Island in the summer. Henry was also an avid tennis player and sailor, joining the Royal St. Lawrence Yacht Club in 1946. During the Second World War, he commanded an Air Cadet squadron in Lachine, Quebec. A man of many dimensions, he also played violin in amateur orchestras, sang tenor in his church choir, and enjoyed listening to the Toronto Symphony. He continued to swim at the Montreal Athletic Club until he slipped on icy steps at the age of 98.

Eighty years after the event, Henry's balloon action became the subject of a painting called *'Balloon Buster'* by well-known aviation artist Robert Taylor. That same year, 1998, former Captain Botterell was recognized with the award of France's Chevalier de la Legion d'Honneur, a token of gratitude from that nation to all remaining First World War veterans who had served in (or over) French soil.

On his 106th birthday, the 7th of November 2002, Henry Botterell was inducted an Honourary Member in the Canadian Naval Air Group (CNAG). National Chairman, John Eden, made the presentation in the company of Henry's son Edward of Toronto and daughter Frances Marquette from Texas. Henry participated fully in the ceremonies and even partook of a 'wee dram' when his daughter Frances produced a Texas-sized flagon of wine for the guests. The event had been made possible through the good offices of CNAG Members Gordon Moyer of Ottawa and Joe MacBrien of Toronto.

This was to be Henry's last public appearance. Entering a slow downward spiral, he suffered a heart attack on New Year's Day 2003 and passed away 48 hours later, on the 3rd of January.

Addendum:

On January 13th, a Service of Thanksgiving in memory of Henry John Lawrence Botterell was conducted in The Warriors Hall of Sunnybrook & Women's College Health Science Center on Bayview Avenue, Toronto. Nearly 300 people gathered in honour of their fallen comrade and friend. The military was well represented by both past and serving members, including air cadets. It was observed by some of the Veterans that no political figures had deigned to attend. The religious service included a rousing chorus of 'Onward Christian Soldiers' and concluded with the 'Navy Hymn' and its aviation verse.* Those who were closest Henry in his final years then paid fond tributes:

Ms. Ann Morris, Director of the hospital:

"We admitted Henry six years ago at age 99. He was remarkable for his age; keen to know how the hospital ran. He had an antique desk that he kept well organized. 'Well, I was a banker.' He said and wore a shirt and tie every morning. His only worry on moving in was setting up his computer.

"He always greeted the ladies of the staff with a kiss on the back of the hand, a gentleman. When I brought him a card for his 100th birthday I noticed several others – all the same. But Henry was not disconcerted. 'They don't make too many of them,' he said.

"He shared a room with 'Ace' Irving, a Second World War RCAF Air Gunner, and they were the characters of the ward with Henry playing the straight man. He enjoyed dogs and sports. Music was also very important and was to be listened to with a glass of sherry. He joined the veterans music group, the Troubadours, and played drum. On his 105th birthday he played and sang.

"When I asked him the secret of his longevity he said 'I do what I'm told.' But in truth, he wanted to do the best for everyone; he was the last of a breed, a truly gracious gentleman. He lived by humanitarian principals through wars; he maintained a positive spirit and he had a wry sense of humor."

Second World War Veteran Lloyd Queen:

"He was a father figure to the younger vets; we all looked up to him, a comrade in arms who knew the terror of war... and the consequences -- he had spent six months in Peebles hospital. When we saw his logbook and asked him about fear he simply said he was OK once he got airborne.

"Our Mary, a longtime volunteer in the veterans' wing once asked him what she could get for him and he said 'Nothing.'

'Well', she said, 'What can I give you?'

'A hug' he said.

"Last June the Lieutenant Governor of Ontario visited and Henry was introduced as 103. In a loud stage whisper he said 'One hundred and three! I'm a hundred and five. You've taken away the best two years of my life!'"

Arthur Plumb, 84, served as an infantry platoon commander with the Lincoln and Welland Regiment in the Netherlands and Germany during the Second World War:

"Henry was a leader, true role model for every Canadian. We're not grieving his passing, we're not celebrating his longevity but rather what he did between his birth and his death. We as Canadians need to stop hiding our lights under a bushel. Henry was a man for whom we can be very proud."

Last to speak was **Henry's son Edward**, namesake of the brother who was killed in 1916. After jokingly chiding Ann, Lloyd and Art for unceremoniously 'ripping off' his speech, Edward remarked on the recent change of the title of the Hospital:

"This will always be Sunnybrook Veterans Hospital. An institution like this reflects its leader and a wonderful staff of social workers, therapists and volunteers. It is a true home for almost 550 vets. I wish to thank you publicly.

"There was mention of Dad's affinity for the ladies. In 1999 he was Guest of Honour at the 75th Anniversary of the RCAF. I traveled with both him and Ace [Irving] to the Ottawa dinner. At one quiet point in the ceremonies, Ace, who was blind, said:

'What's he doing?'

'He's still kissing hands.' I said.

'How does he get away with that?' asked Ace.

'Well, that last lady said she swooned. What does that mean?'

'I don't know' said Ace, 'But you find out and we'll do it together!' "

Postscript:

Doctor Thomas P. Hackett, a Harvard graduate and a professor of psychiatry at Massachusetts General Hospital, studied First World War fighter pilots for years. His research, which included interviews, found that these men had 'a wealth of optimism and a want of fear'.

Time after time, Dr. Hackett observed common traits of a positive attitude, a sense humor and the ability to reduce or abolish worry or fear. Even in times of great stress, 'They could turn off the juice'. These same fighter pilots, some of who developed coronary or cancer later in life, denied being frightened. They minimized the seriousness of illness and displayed calm, fatalistic attitudes. They viewed intensive care unit equipment as beneficial, rather than disturbing.

This optimism proved advantageous as the former aviators survived hospitalization in greater numbers than civilian peers who, worrying constantly, were unable to decrease personal distress.

Hackett also found that another life-prolonging characteristic of the group was fitness and activity. All were athletic to some degree and kept in good shape. None reported psychiatric illness and all recovered in time from periods of depression following such later life events as the loss of a spouse.

*THE NAVAL HYMN

FIRST VERSE:

Eternal Father, Strong to save,
Whose arm hath bound the restless wave,
Who bid'st the mighty Ocean deep
Its own appointed limits keep;
O hear us when we cry to thee,
for those in peril on the sea.

AVIATION VERSE:

O Spirit, Whom the Father send
To spread abroad the Firmament;
O wind of heaven, by Thy Might,
Save all who dare the eagle's flight;
And keep them by Thy watchful care
From every peril in the air.

16Sep1997 – This author had the privilege of meeting and interviewing Henry, then aged 102. Ever the courtly gentleman, his first comment was an invitation to join him in his evening ritual—a glass of rum and ginger. His longevity was a credit not only to his luck in 1917–18, but to the character of the man: his enduring faith, good nature, sense of humor and positive outlook (and perhaps that nightly elixir).

The notes above are from this interview and were used by the Canadian Broadcasting Corporation Radio show 'Sounds Like Canada' in an memorial episode titled 'We'll Remember Henry Botterell' during January 2003.

Henry would have been delighted that the notes were read and embellished by a lady, Ms. Shelagh Rogers.

EPILOGUE

Canada's Naval Aviation Heritage 1945–2010
'Hammy' Gray and 'Rapid Robert' Welland

O n August 9th, 1945, Lieutenant Robert Hampton GRAY, DSC, RCNVR (Nelson, BC) led a flight of eight Corsair fighter-bombers off the deck of HMS *Formidable* against airfields and shipping around the Onagawa Wan Bay of mainland Japan. In the face of intense anti-aircraft fire, 'Hammy' pressed home an attack, crippling and sinking the destroyer *Amakusa*. In these same moments his Corsair was hit—flipping inverted, it plunged into the waters. For this supreme sacrifice, Gray was posthumously awarded the British Commonwealth's highest military honour, the Victoria Cross.

A gallant company of Canadian naval airmen had flown from the 1940 raids on the *Konigsberg* in Norway, through to the last days of the Second World War. Hampton Gray is a brilliant representive of these 'shipmates' and of their contribution to the Royal Navy's Fleet Air Arm during the conflict—and what a contribution it was. The Dominion provided not just pilots and observers, but had crewed two aircraft carriers, HMS *Nabob* and HMS *Puncher*. Other Canadian ships companies and squadrons were working up to take larger carriers to the Pacific when atomic bombs on Hiroshima and Nagasaki frightfully—and fortunately—finished the war.

These same sailors and airmen had gained a hard-won naval technical expertise and were recognized by the Canadian Cabinet's creation of a permanent RCN 'Air Branch'. A British Light Fleet carrier was commissioned HMCS *Warrior* in early 1946 and brought two squadrons, Supermarine Seafire fighters and Fairey Firefly bombers, to Dartmouth, Nova Scotia. The local RCAF Station was re-designated HMCS *Shearwater* and has been the center for Canadian naval air ever since. In 1948, *Warrior* was exchanged for a more modern HMCS *Magnificent*, carrying Hawker Sea Fury fighters and Grumman Avenger antisubmarine aircraft.

The 1939-1945 War also provided seasoned sailors for Canada. Outstanding in these ranks was Robert Philip WELLAND (Oxbow, SK). 'Rapid Robert,' so named for his superb and speedy destroyer handling, had joined the Navy in 1936. He was 'blooded' in HMCS *St Laurent* at the Dunkirk evacuations and awarded the DSC when '*Sallie*' sank a German U-Boat. Given command of HMCS *Assiniboine* at age 25, Welland became the youngest destroyer captain in the Atlantic and was CO of the larger HMCS *Haida* on the Murmansk Convoy Run by the end of the War. [*Haida*, Canada's most famous naval vessel, is today a maritime museum, permanently moored on public display at Hamilton, Ontario.]

In 1950, now Commander Welland, took HMCS *Athabaskan* on deployment to Korea. In '*Athabee*' he was awarded a Bar to his DSC for an outstanding performance in the Chinampo Operation and appointed an Officer of The Legion of Merit by the United States of America.

Promoted Captain in 1953 and appointed Director of Naval Training, he 'invented Venture,' a journeyman naval college that turned-out officers and aviators for the fleet. Welland himself had applied to transfer to the RN Fleet Air Arm in the early 1940's and been thwarted by his Admiral:

'Welland, it takes six years to train a Naval Officer to Command and only six months to train a pilot.

We've spent years preparing you to take a ship to sea. Here's what I think of your request form…'

And with that the Flag Officer had torn up the paper. Welland had his first ship inside of a year.

By 1963, Bob Welland was CO of HMCS *Shearwater* and the Air Station now operated over 100 aircraft supporting the latest Canadian aircraft carrier, HMCS *Bonaventure*. Here, he finally learned how to fly, taking lessons from the training squadron and even soloing the twin-engined Grumman CS2F Tracker anti-submarine aircraft before he was ordered to cease and desist by Ottawa Admirals.

In the *'Bonnie'* Canadian naval aviation reached its heyday. This vessel sported an angled deck, a mirror landing apparatus, a modern steam catapult and a carrier control approach radar. The ship was an all-weather, day-night capable, aviation platform.

Anti-Submarine Warfare became the expertise of the RCN. The fighter side of the fleet, aging McDonnell Banshee jets, gave way to a Helicopter/Destroyer concept that Canada developed and led in the North Atlantic Treaty Organization nations. As a former destroyer Captain, Welland was at the forefront of many of these new ASW innovations, including the introduction of large Sikorsky Sea King helicopters to small decks using the 'Beartrap' landing system in all sea states.

Welland's next promotion to Commodore was followed by a stint as Senior Canadian Naval Officer Afloat and he took the fleet to sea in 1963 without waiting for parliamentary approval during the Cuban Missile Crisis. By this precipitous action he solidly anchored the northern flank of the Atlantic against a Russian Submarine threat.

Promoted Rear Admiral in 1964, Welland became the youngest 'two-star' in the Army, Navy or Air Force. When these three military organizations were integrated as the Canadian Armed Forces in 1966 he was vocal in opposition and retired. He founded a successful air traffic control company and served as a Director of the Canadian Air Industry Association.

Unlike the wartime expedient 'shotgun' marriage of the RNAS and the RFC into the RAF in 1918, the political ménage-a-trois of Canada's three armed forces was a radical experiment. The paying off of the Flagship *Bonaventure* in 1969 as a cost-cutting exercise did little to further morale. However, naval aviators are nothing if not flexible and two of them became Chiefs of Defense Staff in the new single force. At the junior officer, NCO, and enlisted level, former RCN sailors and RCAF airmen accommodated each other on helicopter detachments at sea.

In his Memoirs, Welland wrote:

> **"Serving in a ship is not like working in business. In the Navy you make lifelong friends; being one of a ship's company seems to bind you to your mates, forever."**

Bob Welland died during the Centennial Year of the Royal Canadian Navy, 2010.

> The Legacy of these two outstanding Naval Officers, Hampton Gray and Robert Welland is being carried into the second century of Canada's Maritime Command by a modern fleet of frigates that will operate new CH–148 Cyclone Helicopters, the Sea King replacement. Canadian Forces Base *Shearwater* remains home to the naval aviation community and is now known as 12 Wing of Air Command. These ships and aircraft were active in the recent Gulf Wars and they continue to patrol the high seas. They 'fly the flag' of the early RNAS Canadians who operated similar missions during the Great War.

RNAS GLOSSARY

1st Lieut
    First Lieutenant, RN term for a unit's Adjutant/Administrator
2Lt Second Lieutenant (RAF)
2LtObs Second Lieutenant Observer (RAF)

A/ Acting (Rank)
AA anti-aircraft
AAeC American Aeronautical Club (Certificate)
AB Province of Alberta, Cities: Calgary, Edmonton
a/c aircraft
ACE Victory over Five Enemy aircraft
ACM Air Chief Marshal
ACmdr Air Commodore
AD Aircraft Depot
ADD Aircraft Depot Durkerque
ADM Admiralty (document)
Adm Admiral (Rank)
AEA Aerial Experiment Association
AFC Air Force Cross
AGP Anti-Gotha Patrol
AirM Air Marshal
ALG Advanced Landing Ground
AM Air Mechanic
ARD Aeroplane Repair Depot
ASD Aroplane Supply Depot
ASP Anti-Submarine Patrol
AUS Australia
AVM Air Vice Marshal
AWOL Absent Without Official Leave
AZP Anti-Zeppelin Patrol

Bar Medal awarded twice or more
BC Province of British Columbia, cities: Vancouver, Victoria
BCATP British Commonwealth Air Training Plan (WW2)
Bde Brigade
BM Bronze Medal (Italy)
Bttn Battalion

CAF Canadian Air Force (1919-1923)
Capt Captain
CAS Chief of Air Staff
CB Companion, Order of the Bath
CBE Commander, Order of the British Empire
CCS Casualty Clearing Station

CDA Canada
CdG *Croix De Guerre* Medal (/France, /Belgium, /Italy)
Cdr Commander
CEF Canadian Expeditionary Force
CFA Canadian Field Artillery
CinC Commander in Chief
CO Commanding Officer
COL Crashed on Landing
Col Colonel
Cpl Corporal
CPO Chief Petty Officer

Dal Dalhousie University, Halifax NS
DFC Distinguished Flying Cross
DFM Distinguished Flying Medal
DNS Department of Naval Service (Ottawa)
DOI Died of Injuries
DOJ Date of Joining
DOW Died of Wounds
DOS Died of Sickness
DS Dental Surgeon
DSC Distinguished Service Cross
DSM Distinguished Service Medal
DSO Distinguished Service Order

EA Enemy Aircraft
EFTS Elementary Flying Training School
ENG England

Fitter Engine Mechanic
FAA Fleet Air Arm
FAI Federation Aeronautique
FBA Franco-British Aviation (Company)
FCdr Flight Commander
FLt Flight Lieutenant
FSLt Flight Sub Lieutenant
Flu Influenza, Spanish Flu Pandemic 1918
FTL Forced to Land

G Gunnery
GB Great Britain
GCapt Group Captain

HA Hostile Aircraft
HD Home Defence (UK based Squadron)
HE Home Establishment (UK)
HMAS His Majesty's Australian Ship

HMCS	His Majesty's Canadian Ship
HMS	His Majesty's Ship
Hon	Honourable (as in Released)
HP	Handley Page (bomber)
HQ	Headquarters
Hydro	Hydro Aeroplane, later Seaplane
i/c	in charge
INJ	Injured
INS	Instructor
INT	Interned by a neutral country; eg, Holland, Switzerland
IRE	Ireland
KIA	Killed in Action – Combat
KIC	Killed in Crash – Accident
KBO	Kite Balloon Officer or Dirigible Pilot
Later	Referring to Post War activities
Ld'H	*Legion d' Honneur* (France)
LCdr	Lieutenant Commander
LCol	Lieutenant Colonel
Lt	Lieutenant
MBE	Member of the British Empire
MB	Province of Manitoba, Capital Winnipeg
MC	Military Cross
m/c	Machine as in Aeroplane
McG	McGill University Montreal
MID	Mention in Despatches
MD	Medical Doctor
ML	motor launch
MM	Military Medal
MN	Merchant Navy
MIA	Missing In Action
MTB	motor torpedo boat
MV	motor vessel
NAS	Naval Air Station
Naval	Naval (Squadron)
NB	Province of New Brunswick: cities St John, Moncton, Fredericton
NF	Dominion of Newfoundland
NS	Nova Scotia, capital Halifax
Obs	Observer
OC	Officer Commanding
OBE	Order of the British Empire
OOC	Out of Control
OIC	Officer in Command

ON	Province of Ontario, cities Ottawa, Toronto
P/	Probationary
PE	Prince Edward Island, Capital Charlottetown
PFO	Probationary Flying Officer (1917–1918)
PFSLt	Probationary Flight Sub Lieutenant (1914–1916)
PQ	Province of Quebec, cities Montreal, Quebec City
PO	Petty Officer
POW	Prisoner of War
PPCLI	Princes Patricia's Canadian Light Infantry (First to War)
Pte	Private
Queen's	Queen's University, Kingston ON
RA	Royal Artillery (British Army)
RAdm	Rear Admiral
RAN	Royal Australian Navy
RAeC	Royal Aeronautical Club (Certificate)
RAF	Royal Air Force
RAMC	Royal Army Medical Corps
RCAF	Royal Canadian Air Force (1924–1966)
RCEME	Royal Canadian Electrical & Mechanical Engineers
RCN	Royal Canadian Navy (1910–1966)
RE	Royal Engineers (British Army)
REL	Released from Naval Commission
Regt	Regiment
Ret'	Retired
RFC	Royal Flying Corps
Rigger	Airframe Technician
RIP	Rest in Peace (Died)
RMC	Royal Military College, Kingston ON
RN	Royal Navy
RNAS	Royal Naval Air Service
RNVR	Royal Naval Volunteer Reserve
RP	Repair Park
RR	Railroad
S	Student, School/University unknown
SCdr	Squadron Commander
SCT	Scotland
Sgt	Sergeant
SK	Province of Saskatchewan, Cities Regina, Saskatoon
SLdr	Squadron Leader
SLt	Sub Lieutenant

GLOSSARY

Sqn Squadron
SS steamship

T/ Temporary
TechO Technical Officer
TDS Training Depot Squadron
TL's Their Lordships (of the Admiralty)
TE Training Establishment

UCC Upper Canada College, Toronto ON
UK United Kingdom
UofT University of Toronto
USA United States of America
USAS United States Air Service
USNAS US Naval Air Service
USN United States Navy
USS United States Ship

VAD Voluntary Aid Detachment (nursing staff)
VAdm Vice Admiral
VC Victoria Cross
VGI Very Good Indeed

WCdr Wing Commander
WF Western Front
WIA Wounded in Action
WO Warrant Officer
WRNS Women's Royal Naval Service
WW2 World War Two

XO Executive Officer

Some German Terminology

Flgm *Flugmeister:* Naval Airman
Hpt *Hauptmann:* Captain
JG *Jagdgeschwader:* Wing
Jasta *Jagdstaffel:* Squadron
Ltn *Leutnant:* Second Lieutenant
Ltn z S *Leutnant zur See:* Flt Sub Lieutenant
MFJ *Marine-Feld Jasta:* Naval Fighter Squadron
Obflgm *Oberflugmeister:* Naval Chief Petty Officer
Oblt *Oberleutnant:* Flight Lieutenant
OffzSt *Offizierstellvertreter:* Warrant Officer
Rittm *Rittmeister:* Cavalry Captain
SFS *Seefrontstaffel:* Naval Seaplane Squadron
SflS *Seeflug Station:* Naval Air Base
U-Boat *Unterseeboot:* German Submarine
Vzflgm *Vizeflugmeister:* Naval Petty Officer
Vzfw *Vizefeldwebel:* Sergeant Major
ZEP *Zeppelin:* German Airship

APPENDICES

APPENDIX A MINI-GLOSSARY

Column E: Educational Facility: D–Dalhousie; M–McGill; O–Oxford; Q–Queens;
    R–Royal Military College; S–Student, School Unknown;
    T –University of Toronto; U–Upper Canada College.

Column DOJ: Date of Joining the RNAS

Column P: Previous Service B–British Army; C–Canadian Expeditionary Force;
    P–Royal NorthWest Mounted Police;
    N–Royal Canadian Navy/Royal Navy.

Column RANK: Highest Rank during First World War

Column DEC: Highest Decoration during First World War

Column BOOK: Where mentioned in this Book–by Date

SURNAME	GIVEN NAMES	FROM	E	DOJ	P	
ABBOTT	George Samuel	ON -Ottawa		8-Nov-15		
ABBOTT	Robt Franklin Preston	ON -Carleton Place	S	7-Nov-16		
ADAM	Orval Patrick	ON -Westport		19-Apr-17		
ADAMS	James Ignatius	ON -Toronto		7-Jan-18		
ADAMS	James Weierter	ON -Rockliffe	S	19-Apr-17	C	
ADDERLEY	Peter Broughton	Canadian b.ENG		30-Nov-16	R	
AGUR	Phillip Balland	BC -Summerland		24-Nov-17	C	
AIRD	Hugh Reston	ON -Toronto	T	8-Nov-15	C	
AITCHISON	David Bancroft	ON -Hamilton	T	8-Dec-17	C	
ALEXANDER	James Morrow	ON - Toronto	S	28-Jul-15		
ALEXANDER	William Melville 'Mel'	ON - Toronto		23-Mar-16		
ALFORD	Charles Ross	SK - Saskatoon		7-Feb-17		
ALLAN	Hugh	PQ - Montreal	M	10-Jun-16	C	
ALLAN	John Roy	PQ - Westmount		20-Jul-16		
ALLARDYCE	Arthur Henderson	BC - Vancouver		16-Mar-16		
ALLELY	George Howard	ON - Lindsay	S	19-Apr-17		
ANDERSON	Alexander MacGregor	ON - Toronto	T	4-Nov-17	C	
ANDERSON	George Benson	ON - Ottawa		26-Mar-16		
ANDERSON	Gordon Noble	ON - Brampton	T	5-Oct-17	C	
ANDERSON	Sydney	BC - Vancouver b.USA		14-Mar-17		
ANDERSON	William Seborne	ON - Lambeth	W	19-Apr-17	C	
ANDERSON	William Stuart	MB - Winnipeg		27-May-17	N	
ANTHONY	Ellis	NS - Maitland	S	3-Feb-16		
APPELBE	Charles Schofield	ON - Parry Sound	Q	7-Feb-17		
ARCHIBALD	Harry Bambrick	NS - Truro		1-Jul-17	C	
ARMSTRONG	Arthur Owen	ON - Toronto		4-Feb-18	C	
ARMSTRONG	Frederick Carr 'Army'	ON - Toronto	U	1-Dec-15		
ARMSTRONG	George Powell	ON - Toronto		19-Apr-17	C	
ARMSTRONG	Harold John	ON - Toronto		5-Jan-18	C	
ARMSTRONG	Oscar Melville	ON - Toronto		23-Nov-17		
ARNOLD	Harwood James	BC - Q.Charlottes b.ENG		28-Jan-15	N	
ARTHUR	Harold Francklyn	NS - Halifax	S	7-Jan-18		
ARUNDEL	Harold Halsey	ON - Toronto		16-Dec-15		
ASH	Selby Harrison Hale	BC - Victoria		10-Nov-16	C	
ATKINS	Frederick Ivor	MB - Winnipeg b.SCT		30-Nov-17		
AULT	Wellington Cameron	ON - Toronto		16-May-16		
AVERY	George Gladstone	NF - Gates Cove		16-Dec-15		
BABER	Wellesley Malc'm Colb'n	Canadian b.ENG		29-Dec-17	C	
BADGLEY	John Beresford	PQ - Montreal	S	14-Dec-17	C	
BAILEY	Charles Leonard	ON - Toronto	U	29-Feb-16		
BAILEY	Charles William	MB - Winnipeg b.ENG		1-Sep-16		
BALL	Robert Notman	ON - Woodstock		14-Mar-17		
BALLANTYNE	David Moair	MB - Winnipeg b.SCT		3-Feb-16		
BANBURY	Frederick Everest	SK - Wolseley	T	28-Jun-16		
BARBER	Cyril Roaf	ON - Port Credit		14-Mar-17		
BARKER	Wm. Stanley Gordon	MB - Winnipeg	S	7-Jan-18		

NAME	RANK	DEC	BOOK	Notes
ABBOTT, GS	Capt		**30-Nov-16**	WIA -2Wing Eastern Med. Later DoT Canada
ABBOTT, RFP	Lt		**17-Aug-17**	WIA -3Naval. REL-25Oct18 Invalided
ADAM, OP	Lt		**1-Apr-18**	MIA -203RAF. INJ-04Dec17 Crash.
ADAMS, JI	2Lt			Home Establishment Service in Great Britain.
ADAMS, JW	LtObs	CdG	**21-May-18**	Crash -216 RAF HandleyPage
ADDERLEY, PB	PFO			REL -2May17 'Lost nerve but Good Conduct'
AGUR, PB	2LtObs			29TDS 'Nov18. Fm CMR. Was RNWMP
AIRD, HR	FLt	MID	**30-Sep-17**	POW -Constantinople 2Wing AA Fire .
AITCHISON, DB	Lt			110 RAF(IAF) DH9a Doctor1923
ALEXANDER, JM	PFSLt		**12-Sep-15**	KIC -Midair at Eastchurch. 1st US Lic. 1st Killed.
ALEXANDER, WM	Capt	DSC	**6-Jul-17**	ACE -10 Naval Black Prince
ALFORD, CR	PFO			REL -17Apr17 'Most unsuitable'
ALLAN, H	FSLt		**7-May-15**	Lusitania. **12Jun16** -Request. KIC -3N 06Jul17
ALLAN, JR	Capt	DSC	**15-Jul-17**	DSC -7Naval.**12Apr18** -MIA Zeebrugge 215RAF.
ALLARDYCE, AH	Capt		**23-May-17**	INS -Manston Smith-Barry instructional system.
ALLELY, GH	Lt			Eastchurch '17. Pilot&Obs INS Nov18
ANDERSON, AM	Lt	DFC	**21-Aug-18**	DFC -218RAF
ANDERSON, GB	Capt	MID	**23-Jan-18**	ACE -3 Naval
ANDERSON, GN	PFO			INJ/REL -Vendome. Lost Flying Nerve.
ANDERSON, S	Capt	DFC	**4-Jul-18**	WIA/DFC -Felix'tw Flying Boat vs EA Seaplanes.
ANDERSON, WSea.	Lt		**13-Mar-18**	INJ -2Wing crash Stravos
ANDERSON, WStu.	LtObs		**13-Nov-17**	INJ -Dunkirk. RAF Camp Borden ON'18
ANTHONY, E	Capt	AFC	**20-Sep-17**	WIA -1 Naval. Ditched 13Jul18 -S.Shields. CAF
APPELBE, CS	SLt		**8-Jan-18**	REL -to RNVR. CO of HML 246 in Med.
ARCHIBALD, HB	Lt		**19-Dec-17**	FSLt -Redcar'17. Handley Page'18
ARMSTRONG, AO	2Lt			RAF Blandford -Nov'18. Brother to 'Army'
ARMSTRONG, FC	FCdr	DSC	**7-Jul-17**	ACE -3Naval. **25Mar18** -MIA. +CdGaE(F)
ARMSTRONG, GP	Lt		**15-Jul-18**	DOI -Cranwell BE-2c crash. Died of Injuries
ARMSTRONG, HJ	PFO			RAF Chingford
ARMSTRONG, OM	2LtObs		**23-May-18**	INJ -Sideslip into sea Lee-on-Solent.
ARNOLD, HJ	FLt	DSO	**11-Jul-15**	DSO -Konigsberg. KIC -20 Mar18.**10Apr40**-FAA Norway
ARTHUR, HF	2Lt			INJ -Infantry 6Dec17. Tx RNAS
ARUNDEL, HH	Capt		**24-Sep-17**	Turret Ships -2Wing. Was Mudros '16. Ill -Malaria'18
ASH, SHH	Lt			Transferred to RAF in Canada April'18
ATKINS, FI	2Lt		**21-Sep-18**	INJ -Hit Ship mast. Rest of crew killed.
AULT, WC	Capt			REL -Honourably Ju18. Was 6Wing'17
AVERY, GG	FSLt		**14-May-17**	MIA -Plymouth. Lost in the Channel
BABER, WMC	2LtObs		**19-Jan-19**	'Splash' -Calshot Newsletter
BADGLEY, JB	2Lt			Vendome. Canada Magazine 12Jan18&06Jul18.
BAILEY, CL	Capt			4Wing'16; 6N+4N'17 -3Victories. INS 207RAF'18
BAILEY, CW	Capt		**6-Oct-17**	Ditched -Westgate. Felixstowe'18 -OC 330Flt.
BALL, RN	Lt			INJ -Manston Sep'17. 9N'18. 61Wing'18
BALLANTYNE, DM	Capt	DFC	**3-Oct-16**	Episode. 2Wing'17. **22Jan18** -Bomb *Goeben*
BANBURY, FC	Capt	DSC	**1-Apr-18**	KIC -209 RAF. ACE -13Sep17
BARBER, CR	FSLt		**7-Jan-18**	KIC -2 Naval Dunkirk, DH4 Crash.
BARKER, WSG	PFO		**21-Jun-18**	KIC -205 TDS S.Pup Fire. Pilot thrown out.

SURNAME	GIVEN NAMES	FROM	E	DOJ	P
BARKLEY	Russell Hammond	ON - Toronto		19-Jan-17	
BARNUM	Bliss Edward 'Dutch'	ON - Kingston	Q	19-Apr-17	
BARRON	John Augustus	ON - Stratford		17-Mar-15	N
BARRY	William Sarsfield	PQ - Montreal b.IRE		19-Jan-17	
BARTON	Fredrick Wm 'Eric'	British Columbia		1-Apr-17	
BATCHELOR	Arthur Trelawany	Canadian		21-Feb-18	C
BATH	Henry James	ON - Oakville		1-May-16	
BAWLF	Clarence Nicholas	MB - Winnipeg		11-Feb-16	
BAWLF	David Leland 'Barney'	MB - Winnipeg	S	15-Sep-17	C
BAWLF	Louis Drummond	MB - Winnipeg		14-Dec-16	C
BEAL	Arthur Potter	ON - Lindsay		19-Apr-17	C
BEASLEY	Percy Exeter	BC - Victoria		31-Oct-15	
BEATTIE	Andrew Gordon	ON - London		14-Mar-17	
BEATTIE	William James	ON - Stratford	T	14-Mar-17	C
BECKER	Clarence 'Clair'	AB - Medicine Hat		17-Nov-16	
BEDARD	Wm. Omeara	Canadian b.IRE		24-Feb-18	
BELL	Arthur Phelps	ON - Belleville		19-Apr-17	
BENDER	Hugh Wm.	PQ - Montreal	S	3-Feb-18	
BERRY	Edward Weldon	BC - Langley		15-Jan-18	C
BERTHE	Robert Mattieu	ON - Ottawa		19-Apr-17	
BESSETTE	Claver Victor	USA- Conneticut		12-Feb-16	
BEST	Lewis Edward	BC - Victoria		5-Jun-17	C
BEWELL	Robert Lloyd	SK - Regina		4-Jul-17	C
BIBBY	John Richard	ON - Toronto b.ENG		12-Feb-16	
BICKNELL	Frank Russell	ON - Dunnville	T	19-Apr-17	
BICKNELL	James Nathan	ON - Toronto	T	14-Mar-17	C
BIGGAR	Earl Lachland	ON - Mohawk	T	19-Apr-17	C
BINNY	James Bruce	Canadian b.SCT		21-Oct-17	
BISHOP	Arthur Anderson	SK - Kamsack		19-Jan-17	
BISHOP	Victor Algar	BC - Vancouver b.ENG		2-Oct-17	C
BISSELL	Lynn Newton	ON - Algonquin	S	6-Jan-18	C
BLACK	Hugh	USA - New Jersey		8-Dec-17	
BLACKBURN	Albert Ernest Edward	NS - Lower Truro		30-Dec-15	
BLAIR	Thomas Howard	ON - Toronto b.IRE		18-Sep-17	N
BLAKENEY	Thomas Lewis	ON - Ottawa	S	8-Dec-17	C
BLYTH	Ross Allison	ON - Toronto		20-Jul-16	
BODDY	Andrew John	ON - Toronto		15-Nov-15	
BOND	Howard Frederick	PQ - Montreal		11-Mar-17	C
BONE	Geo. Henry Kavanagh	Canadian		16-Jun-16	N
BONE	John Turner	AB - Calgary	M	21-Mar-15	
BONHAM	Robert Lincoln	ON - Jerseyville	Q	3-Nov-17	C
BOOTH	Harold Harman	ON - Toronto		8-Aug-16	
BOOTH	John Rudolphus	ON - Ottawa		6-Jul-16	
BOSWELL	Henry George	ON - Toronto		27-Jun-16	C
BOTTERELL	Henry John Lawrence	ON - Ottawa		14-Mar-17	
BOUDREAU	Joseph Emery	NB - East Bathurst		7-Jan-18	

NAME	RANK	DEC	BOOK	Notes
BARKLEY, RH	PFO		**12-Sep-17**	REL -Unfit, Insommnia. Bird Cartoon
BARNUM, BE	Lt	DFC	**28-Sep-18**	Action -204RAF 4 Victories. Furious Nov'18
BARRON, JA	Capt	MID	**17-Mar-15**	DOJ -Dirigibles. **19Sep16** -Italy. **8Feb18** -RCNAS
BARRY, WS	PFO			REL -18Aug17 'No idea of discipline.'
BARTON, FW	PFO			REL -22Aug17 'Totally Unsuited'
BATCHELOR, AT	PFO			REL -17Mar18 'Medically Unfit'
BATH, HJ	FLt	MID		U-Boat 10May18. Resigns Sep'18 -To Avoid RAF.
BAWLF, CN	FSLt		**21-Apr-18**	Brother. REL 23Jun17 -2Wing. 'Greek Matter'
BAWLF, DL	Lt	MID	**21-Apr-18**	KIC -203RAF Spun in. Two Brothers in RNAS
BAWLF, LD	Capt		**21-Apr-18**	Brother. ACE -22Jul18 203RAF.
BEAL, AP	Lt T			REL -4Oct17 Airsick. To RNVR -Italian Svce
BEASLEY, PE	Capt		**2-Jan-18**	Fit to Fly. 3W'16. 6N'17. 13N & 211RAF'18
BEATTIE, AG	FLt		**3-Jan-18**	POW -10Naval - Lille.
BEATTIE, WJ	FSLt		**30-Sep-17**	KIC -1Naval S.Triplane wing adrift.
BECKER, C	Lt			6Wing'17. Slough'18. Edmonton Av Museum.
BEDARD, WO	PFO			Uxbridge -May'18
BELL, AP	Lt			228 RAF -Yarmouth. Leckie as CO
BENDER, HW	2Lt			Greenwich -Feb'18
BERRY, EW	Lt		**23-Jan-20**	DOS -Heart Disease.
BERTHE,RM	Capt	CdG	**5-Feb-18**	On Charge -17N. CdGaP(France) -08Nov18
BESSETTE, CV	Capt	DFC	**17-Aug-17**	Disciplined -Mail Censor. DFC 03Jun18.
BEST, LE	Lt	AFC		269RAF -Aboukir; Egypt. AFC -8Feb19
BEWELL, RL	Lt			Dunkirk DH-4 Pilot 26Feb18
BIBBY, JR	FLt		**11-Jun-17**	KIC -Malta Torpedo trials. NOK Wife ENG
BICKNELL, FR	Lt Obs	DFC	**27-Jul-18**	MID -Aegean Raid. **28Jun19** INJ/DFC Caspian Sea
BICKNELL, JN	Lt			Yarmouth -North Sea & Ferry Piloting. 273 RAF
BIGGAR, EL	PFO			REL -4Aug17 'Incapable Pilot, Unsuitable Officer'
BINNY, JB	PFO		**18-Feb-18**	REL - With TL's Regret. Offered Exec duties
BISHOP, AA	FSLt		**14-Sep-17**	KIC -Dover. Sopwith Strutter
BISHOP, VA	Lt		**4-Sep-18**	INJ -Vancouver Canada Crash. Hoffar H-2
BISSELL, LN	2Lt		**31-Oct-18**	KIC -East Fortune Stall/crash. Bristol F2b
BLACK, H	PFO			Vendome -Mar'18.
BLACKBURN, AEE	PFSLt		**4-Aug-16**	REL -to RNVR for Motor Launches.
BLAIR, TH	Lt			2Wing'17. Aegean Group'18. Was PO RNAS
BLAKENEY, TL	2Lt			245RAF. Irish Sea Patrol
BLYTH, RA	FSLt		**23-Jan-18**	KIA -10Naval Camel Midair w/EA Albatros
BODDY, AJ	FSLt		**27-Apr-16**	KIC -Killingholme - Sopwith Baby Wrecked
BOND, HF	PFO		**27-Dec-17**	REL -'Nervousness'. New York INS application.
BONE, GHK	Major			Tech O -Eastchurch'Dec17
BONE, JT	FSLt		**18-Nov-15**	KIA -1Wing. Zeppelin Shed Attack. 1stCdn KIA.
BONHAM, RL	PFO			Vendome -Mar'18
BOOTH, HH	FLt		**25-Aug-17**	POW -7 Naval AA Flak Ghent
BOOTH, JR	FSLt			REL -7Feb17 Unfit - Neurasthenia
BOSWELL, HG	Capt	DSC	**23-May-17**	U-Boat - '*Spider Web*' Felixstowe.
BOTTERELL, HJL	Capt	LdH	**2003-Jan**	RIP. INJ -18Sep17 Dunkirk. Balloon Kill 29Aug18.
BOUDREAU, JE	2Lt			55RAF.

SURNAME	GIVEN NAMES	FROM	E	DOJ	P	
BOUEY	John Jos. Laurence	MB - Winnipeg		14-Mar-17	C	
BOVILL	Fredrick Oscar	Canadian b.ENG		25-Feb-18	C	
BOWIE	Neil Hugh	Canadian		28-Mar-17	C	
BOYCE	George Harold	ON - Ottawa		19-Jan-17		
BOYD	James Erroll Durnsford	ON - Toronto		22-May-15	C	
BOYD	Kenneth Gordon	ON - Goderich		3-Feb-16		
BOYNTON	Edward Stanley	ON - Toronto		30-Dec-15		
BRADLEY	Erfort Rayal	ON - Toronto	Q	7-Jan-18		
BRAY	Raymond Earl	BC - Victoria		27-Apr-17	C	
BREADNER	George	MB - Winnipeg		12-Feb-16		
BREADNER	Lloyd Samuel	ON - Ottawa		28-Dec-15		
BRENNAN	David Philip	PQ - Westmount		7-Jan-18		
BRENNAN	Francis Patrick	Nova Scotia		9-Mar-18	C	
BRENTON	Hibbert Binney	BC - Vancouver		24-Feb-16		
BRICKER	Harold	ON -Preston	S	5-Oct-17	C	
BRICKER	William Ralph	ON -Waterloo		7-Feb-17		
BRIDEN	Douglas Moon	ON -Haileybury		14-Dec-16		
BRIMER	Charles Torryburn	ON - Toronto		7-Jun-16		
BRISSENDEN	Albert Oswald	NS - Halifax b.Singapore		3-Oct-15		
BROATCH	Byron William	SK - Maidstone	S	19-Jan-17		
BROCK	Cecil Guelph	MB - Winnipeg b.ENG	T	28-Oct-16	C	
BRONSON	Cecil Gordon	ON - Ottawa	M	12-Feb-16		
BROUGHALL	Herbert Seton	ON - Toronto	T	3-Dec-16	B	
BROWN	Archibald Moffatt	MB - Deloraine	S	31-Oct-17	C	
BROWN	Arthur Roy	ON - Carleton Place	S	15-Nov-15		
BROWN	Hugh Dalgleish	Canadian b.SCT	S	9-Jan-18	C	
BROWN	John Horace	ON - Carleton Place	S	5-Oct-17	C	
BROWN	Wm. Henry	ON - New Listcard		9-Jan-18	C	
BROWN	Wm. Norman	ON - Toronto		23-Jan-16		
BROWNE	Frederick Collins	ON - Alvinstone		7-Feb-17		
BRUCE	George Nigel	ON - Toronto	T	6-Dec-15		
BRYAN	Mervyn Joshua Marshall	MB - Souris		20-Sep-15		
BRYANS	Fraser MacPherson	ON - Toronto	T	26-Sep-16		
BRYDON	Ronald Kerr	ON - Toronto	U	22-Jul-17	C	
BRYERS	Brandon Hamilton	MB - Winnipeg	T	24-Apr-17	C	
BUCKLEY	George	ON - Toronto		24-Oct-17	C	
BURDEN	Charles Eldridge	ON - Toronto	T	8-Nov-15	C	
BURLAND	Gordon Hamilton	ON - Grimsby		30-Dec-15		
BURT	Arthur Chadwick	ON - Brantford	T	26-Sep-16	C	
BURTON	George Tait	ON - Toronto	T	28-Jan-18	C	
BUSH	Richard Eldon	Canadian b.ENG		11-Jul-15	N	
BUSSELL	Edward Irvine	ON - Toronto	T	14-Mar-17	C	
BUTCHART	Lynn Whitten	ON - Toronto		28-Oct-17	C	
BUTTERS	Geo. Mitchell	PQ - Montreal	S	17-Jan-18	C	
BUTTERWORTH	Chs. Hampden Stanley	ON - Ottawa		30-Dec-15		
BYSSHE	Gordon Thomas	ON - Ottawa		22-Mar-16		

NAME	RANK	DEC	BOOK	Notes
BOUEY, JJL	FSLt			14Naval HP's. REL -21Jan18 Defective Vision.
BOVILL, FO	PFO			Eastchurch -Mar'18.
BOWIE, NH	FSLt			FSLt 03Oct17. DiscipCourt 01Mar18-AWOL
BOYCE, GH	Capt	AFC	23-Mar-20	AFC. 6W'17. Furious'18. Crash'20. ACmdr RAF
BOYD, JED	Capt		3-Oct-15	INT -5W Zeebrugge. **09Oct30**-1st Cdn X-Atlantic
BOYD, KG	Capt	AFC	5-Jun-17	MID -5Naval. U-Boat 12Aug18 217RAF.
BOYNTON, ES	Capt	MID	28-Nov-17	MID -2 Wing Macedonia.
BRADLEY, ER	2Lt			HMS Campania -'18.
BRAY, RE	PFO		14-Aug-17	KIC -Cranwell. Avro 540
BREADNER, G	Capt		23-Oct-16	Ditched -HMS Campania -Deck flying trials
BREADNER, LS	Major	DSC	11-Apr-17	3 Victories. ACE -23Apr17. **May1940** -CAS RCAF
BRENNAN, DP	2Lt		12-Nov-18	Flu -Yarmouth. Crash May'18 -Vendome.
BRENNAN, FP	Lt			190TDS Reading Jun'18.
BRENTON, HB	Capt		17-Jun-17	ZEP -L42. Test Flight, Isle of Grain'18.
BRICKER, H	Lt		18-Jan-18	INJ -Vendome JN4 Stall & crash.
BRICKER, WR	FSLt		18-Jan-18	Brother. REL -24Jan18 Refused Seaplanes
BRIDEN, DM	FSLt			REL -22Aug17 Unfit. Neurasthenia.
BRIMER, CT	FSLt		4-Dec-16	MIA -Channel patrol Bembridge.
BRISSENDEN, AO	FSLt		29-Feb-16	Probation. Crashed 3 times. REL -Unfit Jan'17
BROATCH, BW	FSLt		23-Nov-17	Crash -Naval 8. BushPilot KIC'33
BROCK, CG	FSLt		13-Jul-18	ACE -209RAF - WIA three times.
BRONSON, CG	Capt	DSC	28-Jan-18	POW -Dardanelles. +CdG(F) Syria Ops
BROUGHALL, HS	Lt	MC	20-Sep-17	POW -10N. S.Russia'19. DFC'24. GpCapt-RAF
BROWN, AM	2Lt			REL -4Jun18 TempermentallyUnfit. To 'E' Officer
BROWN, AR	Capt	DSC	13-Oct-17	ACE -9 Naval. **21Apr18** -Red Baron driven down.
BROWN, HD	2Lt			3TDS Nov'18.
BROWN, JH	Lt		18-Feb-19	Flu 93 RAF. Was INJ 19Jan18 JN-4 Crash. (Roy's Brother)
BROWN, WH	2Lt			Chingford -Mar'18
BROWN, WN	FSLt			INJ/REL -23Jan18 fm Naval8. INJ -Twice
BROWNE, FC	2Lt			REL -11Aug17 Airsick.
BRUCE, GN	PFSLt			REL -17Jul16. To Army'17; then RNVR'18
BRYAN MJM	Capt			Eastbourne Observer School Pilot
BRYANS, FM	FSLt		17-Jul-17	KIC Midair -Hornsea. Sopwith Baby & Flying Boat
BRYDON, RK	Lt			207 RAF HP Bombers
BRYERS, BH	PFSLt			REL- WIA 7Naval. Army Colonel DSO WW2
BUCKLEY, G	PFO			REL -16Feb18 Lost Confidence.
BURDEN, CE	FLt		21-Nov-15	Crash -Hendon. **22Jan18** -KIC Manston
BURLAND, GH	PFSLt			REL -11Jun16 Unfit as pilot. To RNVR
BURT, AC	Capt		22-Sep-17	Ditched -4Naval. Rescued OK.
BURTON,GT	PFO			Roehampton -Jan'18. Kite Balloons
BUSH, RE	FLt		24-Mar-16	INJ -Westgate. KIC -Fishguard 22Apr17.
BUSSELL, EI	Capt		20-Sep-17	MID -10Naval. 97RAF -NW India'18
BUTCHART, LW	Lt			122RAF. DH-9
BUTTERS, GM	2Lt			102RAF. FE2b
BUTTERWORTH, C	Capt		12-Oct-16	WIA/POW -3W Oberndorf Raid. Son FAA -DSC 1945
BYSSHE, GT	FSLt		17-Feb-17	POW -2W Turkey. Son FAA -KIC 1944

SURNAME	GIVEN NAMES	FROM	E	DOJ	P	
CALDER	George McKay	AB - Medicine Hat	S	14-Dec-16		
CALDER	Paul Bancroft	AB - Edmonton	S	26-Jan-18	C	
CALNAN	Lindley Bell	ON - Picton	T	5-Nov-17	C	
CALVERT	Charles Wm. Leonard	ON - Toronto b.USA		20-Dec-16		
CAMERON	Andrew Austin	ON - Shelburne	Q	19-Apr-17		
CAMERON	John Alistair	ON - Toronto		30-Dec-15		
CAMPBELL	Ewan Sutherland 'Pete'	ON - Toronto	T	22-Nov-16		
CAMPBELL	Robert Alexander	ON - Blytheswood		10-Jan-16		
CARLEY	William Alexander	ON - Fenlon Falls		19-Jan-17		
CARLIN	Owen Gordon Marquis	PQ - Westmount	S	5-Feb-18	C	
CARR	Guy Beresford	Canadian b.USA		19-Feb-16	C	
CARROLL	John George	SK - Wynyard	S	19-Apr-17		
CARROLL	Ralph Edward	ON - Toronto	T	10-Nov-16		
CARROLL	William John	ON - Kingston	S	3-Nov-17	C	
CARTER	Alfred Williams 'Nick'	AB - Calgary	Q	23-May-16		
CARTER	Bayard Marshall	SK - Saskatoon	S	17-Feb-18	C	
CARTER	Wm. Allison Weldon	NB - Fredericton		28-Oct-17	C	
CASGRAIN	Harold Randolph	PQ - Montreal b.ENG		7-Feb-17		
CASH	Frederick Alfred	ON - Hamilton	T	7-Jan-18	C	
CATTO	John Maurice	ON - York Mills	T	8-Dec-17	C	
CHADWICK	Arnold Jaques	ON - Toronto		30-Dec-15		
CHAPMAN	Henry Spencer	BC - Manawa		13-Oct-17	C	
CHASE	Charles Keith	ON - Toronto		21-Oct-16	N	
CHESTER	John Francis Vickers	ON - Toronto	T	19-Apr-17	C	
CHISAM	William Hargrove	AB - Edmonton b.ENG		3-Jan-16		
CHISHOLM	John Foster	PQ - Westmount	M	29-Feb-16		
CHRISTIAN	Leo Arthur	BC - Armstrong		19-Apr-17		
CLAPPERTON	Walter Morse	ON - Toronto b.USA		7-Feb-17		
CLAPPISON	Henry Gordon	ON - Hamilton	T	8-Dec-17	C	
CLARK	Harold Joseph	ON - Pickering		5-Oct-17		
CLARK	John George 'Clarky'	AB - Irma	S	19-Apr-17		
CLARKE	Clarence Victor	ON - Hespler	S	7-Jan-18		
CLAYDON	Ernest	MB - Winnipeg		30-Jan-18	C	
CLAYTON	Cecil John	BC - Victoria	T	6-Sep-16		
CLEGHORN	William Fulton 'Cleggy'	ON - Toronto		16-Dec-15		
CLELAND	John Geo. Paxton	BC - Penticton		17-Jan-18	C	
CLELAND	Robert John	ON - Niagara Falls		15-Nov-17	C	
COCHRANE	Gilbert Wynn	ON - Toronto	S	7-Jan-18		
CODE	Lawrence	ON - Ottawa		19-Apr-17		
COLLISHAW	Raymond	BC - Nanaimo		10-Jan-16	N	
COLQUHOUN	Humphrey Alexander	ON - Hamilton		10-Dec-15	C	
COLT	Samuel Porter	Canadian		23-Dec-16	C	
COMBA	Geo. Leslie	ON - Almonte		10-Jan-18	C	
COMSTOCK	William Henry	ON - Brockville	S	14-Dec-16		
CONNOLLY	Harold James	ON - Toronto	T	19-Jan-17	C	
COO	Harold Thomas	ON - Toronto		5-Oct-17		

NAME	RANK	DEC	BOOK	Notes
CALDER, GM	PFSLt			REL -23May17 'Totally Unsuitable for Flying'
CALDER, PB	2Lt			CRASH -6Oct18 ShotDown&Escapes 203RAF
CALNAN, LB	FSLt			KBO -HMS Canning. Grand Fleet.
CALVERT, CWL	Lt			WIA -26Sep17 S.Triplane 1Naval
CAMERON, AA	Lt		5-Nov-17	1st Victory -10Naval. INJ-18Jan18. Later OBS
CAMERON, JA	PFSLt			REL -24May16 -Invalided with Regret & Pension
CAMPBELL, ES	Lt			Crash -27Oct17. REL 31May18 -Invalided
CAMPBELL, RA	FSLt			INJ -22Sep16 +REL 31Dec17 Unfit fm Crash
CARLEY, WA	PFO			REL -30May17 Recom for MG Corps
CARLIN, OGM	2Lt Obs			KBO - Roehampton Feb'18
CARR, GB	CaptObs			KBO - HMS King George V '18
CARROLL, JG	FSLt		28-Mar-18	MIA -5Naval DH4 Dunkirk
CARROLL, RE	FLt	MID	26-Sep-17	MID. INJ -10 Naval 23Nov17. RAF Canada '18. Later MD.
CARROLL, WG	2Lt			Cranwell Graduate Mar'18
CARTER, AW	Capt	MBE	27-May-17	ACE -10N. +Crash -Hit Cable. AirM RCAF
CARTER, BM	2Lt			INJ -11Oct18 209RAF Camel hit trees.
CARTER, WAW	2Lt		27-Sep-18	Cambrai Crash - 201 RAF +Escape.
CASGRAIN, HR	FSLt		10-Mar-18	POW -12 Naval
CASH, FA	2Lt		24-Jul-18	KIC -East Fortune. Sopwith Pup spun-in.
CATTO, JM	2Lt			115 Independent Air Force -Sep'18.
CHADWICK, AJ	FCdr	DSC	2-Oct-16	Escape. ACE -03Jun17. **28Jul17** -MIA 4Naval.
CHAPMAN, HS	Lt			Ayr, Scotland -March '18
CHASE, CK	CaptObs	DSC	1-Mar-17	Action -2Naval. 6Wing Adriatic'18. +CdG(F)
CHESTER, JFV	PFO			REL -8Oct17 Due Airsickness. Later MD
CHISAM, WH	FLt		16-Mar-18	ACE -3 Naval. WIA-Twice. No Decorations
CHISHOLM, JF	Capt	DSC	26-Sep-18	INT -218RAF AA Fire Bruges. 4 Kills. +DFC. Lawyer
CHRISTIAN, LA	LtObs	DFC	29-Jul-18	OBS ACE -206RAF on DH-9. RCAF WW2
CLAPPERTON, WM	Lt		27-Oct-17	WIA -1Naval S.Triplane. 201RAF '18
CLAPPISON, HG	Capt	CdG	30-Oct-18	ACE -204RAF. INJx2. ACmdr OBE RCAF WW2
CLARK, HJ	2LtTech			INJ -9Mar18 Cranwell Avro504B Crash.
CLARK, JG	FSLt		12-Dec-17	POW -10 Naval. Hosted by German Squadron
CLARKE, CV	2Lt		16-Feb-19	KIC -50 RAF
CLAYDON, E	2Lt			Greenbrough Mar'18
CLAYTON, CJ	Major	DFC	20-Aug-18	CO -230 RAF +MIDx2. Later DS
CLEGHORN, WF	Capt	DFC	25-Apr-16	WIA -HMS Conquest. **2Oct18** -KIA 218RAF
CLELAND, JGP	2Lt			86 RAF -Jun'18. Fm CAMC
CLELAND, RJ	PFO			REL -30Mar18 Illness. Was Lt CEF
COCHRANE, GW	2Lt			REL -2Nov18 Ill health.
CODE, L	PFO		20-Aug-17	KIC -Cranwell -Smashed landing
COLLISHAW, R	Major	OBE	05Jan1893	**28Apr17, 22Jul18, May1919, 10Jun40, 28Sep76**
COLQUHOUN, HA	PFSLt			REL -5Jun16 Resigned
COLT, SP	Lt	MID		INJ -2Mar17 Vendome. 2Wing.
COMBA, GL	Lt			Crash -09Aug18 Eastchurch - at sea
COMSTOCK, WH	Lt			Yarmouth'17. 228 RAF '18.
CONNOLLY, HJ	PFO			REL -9Feb18 Dissatisfied w/Discipline.
COO, HT	PFO		22-Jan-18	KIC -Midair Vendome.

SURNAME	GIVEN NAMES	FROM	E	DOJ	P	
COOK	Byron Leslie	ON - Brockville	T	11-Nov-17	C	
COOK	Maynard Stephen	ON - Ottawa	M	11-Nov-17	C	
COON	Henry Augustus	ON - Kingston		7-Dec-16		
COOPER	Hugh Eldon	BC - New Westminster		15-Nov-17		
CORKERY	Joseph Philip	SK - Regina		27-Nov-17	C	
CORSTORPHINE	James Barron	USA - Hawaii		7-Jan-18		
COSTAIN	Hubert Haddler	ON - Brantford		14-Mar-17	C	
COURTENAGE	Ross Allen	ON - Brantford	T	1-Sep-15	C	
COWAN	Willard E.	ON - Hamilton		13-Sep-17	C	
COWLEY	Arthur Thomas Noel	BC - Victoria	M	30-Jul-15		
CRADOCK	Charles John	ON - Toronto		23-Nov-17		
CRAIG	Norman McLeod	ON - Fergus		8-Mar-17	C	
CRAIG	Wm. Benson 'Scottie'	ON - Smiths Falls		5-Oct-17	C	
CREAGHAN	Gerald Francis	New Brunswick	M	23-Jul-16	C	
CRESSMAN	Fredrick Christie 'Tubby'	ON - Peterborough		16-Oct-16		
CRICK	Wm. Aubrey	ON - Seaforth		8-Dec-17		
CRONYN	James Kerr	ON - Toronto	U	1-Mar-16	C	
CROSBY	Albert Walter Gordon	ON - Uxbridge		5-Oct-17		
CROSS	Ronald Horace	ON - Toronto		30-Nov-17	C	
CROSSLEY	Charles Carleton	ON - King City		23-Nov-17		
CROWE	Harry Lawrence	ON - Toronto b.ENG	T	28-Sep-16	C	
CRUISE	Milton George	ON - Port Dover		27-Nov-17	C	
CULLEN	Herbert Francis	USA - Hawaii	S	27-Jan-18	C	
CULLEY	Stuart Douglas	PQ - Montreal b.USA		19-Apr-17		
CUMMING	Herbert Wm. MacKarsie	ON - Toronto	T	14-Mar-17		
CUMMING	Kenneth Wm.	SK - Mitchelton		20-Jan-18	C	
CUNNINGHAM	James Brightwell	ON - Ottawa		15-Nov-17	C	
CURTIS	Harry Croyle	PQ - Montreal b.Bermuda		8-Dec-17	C	
CURTIS	Roy Victor	ON - Havelock		22-Dec-17	C	
CURTIS	Wilfrid Austin 'Wilf'	ON - Havelock		11-Aug-16	C	
CUTLER	Roderick Orrison	BC - Vancouver		17-Jan-18	C	
CUZNER	Albert Edward	ON - Ottawa	T	3-Sep-16		
DALY	Denis Heywood	BC - Vancouver b.ENG		26-Nov-16	C	
DANIELL	John Bampfylde	BC - Prince George		10-Apr-16		
DARLEY	Cecil Hill	ON - Toronto b.ENG	O	1-Sep-15		
DAVERN	Wm. Albert Nethery	ON - Toronto	U	17-Nov-16		
DAVIDSON	Arthur Greenwood	ON - Dundas	T	15-Dec-17	C	
DAVIDSON	John George McNeil	Canadian b.SCT		21-Nov-17	C	
DAVIDSON	Reginald Francis	NS - Bridgewater		7-Feb-17		
DAVIDSON	William Moffatt	BC - Victoria		31-Dec-16		
DAVIES	David William	BC - Victoria		5-Oct-17		
DAVIS	Ammon Victor	ON - Toronto	T	7-Jan-18	C	
DAVIS	Clayton Gordon	ON - Hamilton		20-Dec-16		
DAVIS	Gerald Alfred	Canadian b.ENG		28-Sep-17	C	
DAVY	Arthur Cecil	PQ - Montreal		24-Nov-17	C	
DAWSON	Francis Gilmer Tempest	NS - Chester	M	16-Sep-14		

NAME	RANK	DEC	BOOK	Notes
COOK, BL	2Lt			WIA during CEF Service. 44 RAF
COOK, MS	Lt			151 RAF. VGI Pilot&Officer. Later MD
COON, HA	PFO			REL -9May17 Unsuitable
COOPER, HE	2Lt			Turret Ship Pilot.
CORKERY, JP	2Lt		**23-Aug-18**	KIC -Italy. 224 RAF Adriatic.
CORSTORPHINE, JB	PFO			Sick -Appendicitis Feb'18
COSTAIN, HH	Lt		**29-Sep-17**	Action - 7Naval. 216 RAF Apr'18,
COURTENAGE, RA	FSLt			REL -13Apr16 'Indifferent&Incapable.'
COWAN, WE	FSLt		**16-May-18**	POW -208 RAF
COWLEY, ATN	Capt		**2-Aug-15**	Crash -Toronto. **06May16** -POW. AVM RCAF
CRADOCK, CJ	PFO			Crash -18Apr18 Eastbourne. REL-11Jul18
CRAIG, NM	FSLt			62Wing. HMS Ark Royal.
CRAIG, WB	Lt	DFC	**16-Sep-18**	ACE -204 RAF. **26Sep18** -KIA. DFC Postumous
CREAGHAN, GF	FSLt			INJ/REL -Mar'17 Cranwell. REL -14Aug17
CRESSMAN, FC	FSLt		**25-Dec-17**	MIA -Dundee. Lost at Sea - Xmas
CRICK, WA	Lt			46 RAF -Shot up 09Oct18. Later DS
CRONYN, JK	FSLt			REL -19Dec16 With TL's Regret. Tried Rejoin
CROSBY, AWG	PFO		**10-Mar-18**	DOI -from Cranwell Crash 27Feb18
CROSS, RH	2Lt			205 RAF -1May18 Crashed on takeoff.
CROSSLEY, CC	2Lt			Crash -23Mar18 Vendome. 67 Wing Nov'18.
CROWE, HL	FSLt		**22-Jun-17**	KIC -Prawle Point Nosedive into sea.
CRUISE, MG	2Lt		**20-Sep-18**	KIA -203 RAF
CULLEN, HF	2Lt			46 RAF Aug'18.
CULLEY, SD	Capt	DSO	**11-Aug-18**	ZEP -L53 Kill. Launched from towed barge
CUMMING, HWM	Lt		**5-Sep-18**	KIC -204 RAF Spun-in. WIA -20Oct17 Naval 8
CUMMING, KW	2Lt			201 RAF. Fm CAMC.
CUNNINGHAM, JB	2Lt		**22-Aug-18**	KIC -205 RAF Overturned Landing
CURTIS, HC	2Lt			INJ -30Jul18 201RAF Camel crash.
CURTIS, RV	2Lt		**27-Sep-18**	Action - 3RAF. Brother to 'Wilf'
CURTIS, WA	FCdr	DSC	**21-Oct-17**	ACE -10Naval. **23Jan18** -DSC Bar. **Sep'47** -CAS RCAF
CUTLER, RO	2Lt			Crash -22Aug18 230 RAF
CUZNER, AE	FSLt		**9-Apr-17**	Vimy -Naval 8. **29Apr17** -KIA Richthofen's 52nd.
DALY, DH	FSLt		**12-Jul-17**	Crash -12 Naval S.Triplane. KIC - 17Jul17
DANIELL, JB	FLt	MID	**30-Apr-17**	Action - 3 Naval. WIA/POW -11May17
DARLEY, CH	Major	DSC	**18-Feb-18**	DSC Bar. **28May18** - DFC. **28Sep19** -KIC Rome.
DAVERN, WAN	FSLt			U-Boat bombed -21Sep17. Yarmouth
DAVIDSON, AG	2Lt			Vendrome Mar'18. Later DS
DAVIDSON, JGM	PFO			Vendome Feb'18. From CAMC.
DAVIDSON, RF	PFO			REL -7Aug17 'Unlikely Pilot'
DAVIDSON, WM	Lt		**27-Oct-17**	WIA -Naval 8 Petite Synthe. INS'18
DAVIES, DW	Capt	CdG	**16-Mar-18**	Action -217RAF. CdG(Belgium)'19
DAVIS, AV	2Lt			Vendrome Mar'18
DAVIS, CG	PFO			REL -11Aug17 Airsick
DAVIS, GA	PFO			Cranwell Apr'18. From PPCLI -14Months France.
DAVY, AC	PFO			REL -22Mar18 Vendrome. To RNVR.
DAWSON, FGA	FLt		**16-Sep-14**	DOJ -1st. **09Jul15** -Gallippoli REL. **1982**-RIP.

SURNAME	GIVEN NAMES	FROM	E	DOJ	P	
DAWSON	Stephen Arthur	PE - Alberton	M	5-Sep-17	C	
DAY	Chester Sessions	PQ - Montreal		15-Jul-17	C	
DAY	Cyril	ON - Toronto b.ENG		24-Sep-15		
DAY	Wm. Dennis	ON - Toronto		23-Nov-17	C	
DEACON	Percival Alan	ON - Toronto	T	23-Nov-17		
DEAN	Oliver James	SK - Regina	M	15-Nov-17	C	
DEAN	Robert Theodore Morgan	ON - Toronto		6-Dec-15		
DELAMERE	Rudolf Dawson	ON - Toronto	T	30-Jul-15		
DELORME	Emile D.	ON - Ottawa	S	19-Apr-17		
DEMPSEY	George Allan	ON - Ottawa		14-Dec-17	C	
DENNISTOUN	Robert Peel	MB - Winnipeg		15-Nov-17		
DESBARATS	Edward Wm.	PQ - Montreal		14-Mar-17		
DEVLIN	Brian	ON - Ottawa		8-Jul-16		
DEVLIN	John Roland Secretan	ON - Ottawa	S	10-Dec-15		
DINGWALL	Gordon Caufield Wilson	ON - Toronto		3-Feb-16		
DISSETTE	Arthur Clark	ON - Toronto	T	3-Feb-16		
DIXON	Albert James	ON - Ottawa		3-Dec-16		
DIXON	Francis Edward	ON - Ottawa		7-Feb-17		
DIXON	Rob. Frederick James	ON - Toronto		7-Jan-18		
DODDS	Charles William	Canadian b.USA		24-Nov-17	C	
DONALDSON	Geo. Roland Trevelyan	ON - Toronto	S	7-Jan-18	C	
DONALDSON	Wm. Darrell Ethelfred	ON - Ottawa	T	30-Nov-17		
DOVER	Melville Grant	MB - Winnipeg		6-Dec-15		
DOWLING	John William	BC - Vancouver		25-Nov-17	C	
DOWNEY	Augustine Sherwood	Canadian		2-Mar-18	C	
DRUMMOND	Chas. Barclay DeTollie	PQ - Montreal		12-Jan-16		
DRUMMOND	Harold	ON - Toronto	T	9-May-16	C	
DRUMMOND	Paul Crathern	PQ - Montreal	S	3-Feb-18		
DUBUC	Marcel Camil	PQ - Montreal	M	29-Feb-16		
DUKE	Gordon Ezra	ON - Toronto		1-Dec-15		
DUNHAM	Lawrence James	ON - Brockville		4-Dec-16		
DUNN	Frank Robertson	NS - Sidney		5-Oct-17		
DUNN	Garner Welsley Ja Geo J.	MB - Winnipeg	S	29-Sep-17	C	
DUPIS	Hubert Richard	PQ - Montreal		19-Apr-17	C	
DUVAL	Joseph Irenee	ON - Buckingham		23-Nov-17	C	
EADES	Herbert William	BC - Revelstoke b.ENG		30-Dec-15		
EDMONDS	William Brodie	ON - Toronto	T	16-Dec-15		
EDWARDS	Harold 'Gus'	NS - Glace Bay b.ENG		3-Feb-16		
EDWARDS	Stearne Tighe	ON - Carleton Place		31-Oct-15		
ELLIOT	Henry James	ON - Edwards		19-Apr-17	C	
ELLIS	Daniel Fairman	MB - Winnipeg		29-Jan-16		
ELLIS	Frederick James	ON - Ottawa		15-Dec-17	C	
ELLIS	Russell Ogden	ON - Toronto		5-Oct-17		
ELLIS	Sidney Emerson	ON - Kingston	Q	29-Jul-16		
ELY	Robert Frederick	BC - Victoria		5-Aug-17	C	
EMERY	Geo. Perceval	ON - Toronto		17-Dec-17	C	

NAME	RANK	DEC	BOOK	Notes
DAWSON, SA	Lt		**19-Jul-18**	RAID -Tondern HMS *Furious*. KIA -10Aug18
DAY, CS	PFO			REL -9Oct17 Lost Nerve.
DAY, C	FSLt			REL -28Dec15 Unfit as Pilot.
DAY, WD	PFO			138 RAF
DEACON, PA	PFO			REL -22Mar18 Unsuitable as Pilot.
DEAN, OJ	2Lt			219 RAF.
DEAN, RTM	PFSLt			REL -17Jul16 Inefficient Pilot.
DELAMERE, RD	Capt	DSC	**21-Nov-15**	Crash -Hendon. **7Feb16** -Zanzibar. **21Nov18.**
DELORME, ED	PFO?			REL -22Jan18 Appt terminated
DEMPSEY, GA	PFO			Chingford -Mar'18
DENNISTOUN, RP	2Lt			210 RAF Nov'18. Law Student FatherDJAG.
DESBARATS, EW	FSLt		**20-Sep-17**	POW -1 Naval Passchendaele
DEVLIN, B	FSLt			REL -2Nov16 Neurasthenia
DEVLIN, JRS	Capt	DSC	**4-Jan-17**	DSC -Salonica, Bulgaria. +AFC RAF Canada. +MID.
DINGWALL, GCW	Lt			Dunkirk 6N -11Dec16. Eye INJ Feb'17
DISSETTE, AC	FSLt	CdG	**2-Jun-17**	KIA -10 Naval. Acting Flight Commander
DIXON, AJ	FSLt		**4-Jan-18**	KIA -Naval 8
DIXON, FE	Lt		**4-Jan-18**	Brother to AJ. INJ -6Dec17 Killingholme.
DIXON, RFJ	2Lt			HMS *Furious*.
DODDS, CW	2LtObs		**15-Jul-18**	INJ - Egypt. Stalled avoiding vessel. 64 Wing
DONALDSON, GRS	2Lt	MID		Eastchurch Mar'18
DONALDSON, WDE	2Lt			Turret Pilot.
DOVER, MG	Capt		**6-Dec-15**	DOJ. **23Aug16** -Palestine Action.
DOWLING, JW	2Lt		**26-Jun-18**	KIC -School of Aerial Gunnery
DOWNEY, AS	PFO			Greenwich Mar'18
DRUMMOND, CBD	Capt			INJ -May'17 Naval 8. AdminO then REL -9Jul18
DRUMMOND, H	FSLt		**20-Nov-16**	REL -'Unsuitable -Slovenly.' To Army Singapore
DRUMMOND, PC	2Lt			Airships Aug'18.
DUBUC, MC	Capt			HMS *Engadine*'17. East Fortune -Ins'18
DUKE, GE	FSLt		**10-Jan-16**	KIC -Eastbourne. Short S-38 Control Failure
DUNHAM, LJ	Lt			INJ -Aug'17. AWOL. Courtmartial REL -22Dec17
DUNN, FR	2LtObs			REL -23Jan18. Reappointed as Observer
DUNN, GWJGJ	FSLt			East Fortune Mar'18. For Grand Fleet
DUPIS, HR	PFO			REL -4Aug17 'No Confidence'. Manston NAS
DUVAL, JI	2Lt			Scilly Islands Sep'18.
EADES, HW	Capt			REL -5Jun16 to RNVR as TechO. Crash13Oct18
EDMONDS, WB	PFSLt		**18-Jul-16**	REL -To CEF. WIA Ypres July'17. Later MD
EDWARDS, H	Capt		**14-Apr-17**	POW -Frieburg 3W. Russia'19. **1942** -AirM RCAF
EDWARDS, ST	Capt	DSC	**23-Sep-17**	ACE -9 Naval. **16May18** -Last Kill. **12Nov18** -KIC
ELLIOT, HJ	Lt		**29-Jun-18**	KIA -62Wing Aegean Group
ELLIS, DF	FLt		**9-Mar-18**	INJ -Propeller accident Killingholme
ELLIS, FJ	2Lt			Chingford Mar'18. Pilot 11Aug18
ELLIS, RO	Lt			VGI Pilot -Mar'18. To 219 RAF.
ELLIS, SE	FSLt		**7-Jul-17**	ACE -4Naval. KIC -Camel spun in 12Jul17.
ELY, RF	PFO			REL -3Nov17 Appt terminated
EMERY, GP	2LtObs			Eastchurch. Tech O Apr'18.

SURNAME	GIVEN NAMES	FROM	E	DOJ	P	
EMERY	Herbert James 'Jimmy'	AB - Edmonton	M	8-Mar-17	C	
EVANS	William Bernard	BC - Victoria		11-Aug-15		
EVERSON	Stanley Farewell	ON - Oshawa		17-Nov-16		
EYRE	Robert Thornton	ON - Toronto	T	5-Nov-16		
EYRES	James Arthur	AB - Eyremore	T	28-Oct-17	C	
FALL	Joseph Stewart Temple	BC - Cobble Hill		29-Jan-16		
FARIS	Edwin MacKay	ON - Brantford	T	4-Nov-17	C	
FARNCOMB	Hugh Frederick	ON - Trenton	T	23-Nov-17		
FARQUHAR	Arthur Westlake	ON - Toronto		7-Jul-16		
FARRALL	James Garney Marshall	BC - Vancouver b.IRE		3-Dec-17	C	
FENTON	Edw.Chas. F. 'O'Connor'	Canadian b.IRE		12-Jul-17	C	
FERGIE	Thomas Francis	PQ - Montreal	M	22-Sep-16		
FINDLAY	David Douglas	ON - Carleton Place	Q	28-Mar-16		
FISHER	Philip Sidney	PQ - Montreal	M	27-Oct-15	B	
FITTON	Anthony Hugh	ON - Simcoe	S	19-Oct-17	C	
FITTON	Horace Cecil Malone	ON - Simcoe		6-Nov-16		
FITZGERALD	Maurice Richard	ON - Toronto	T	8-Dec-17		
FITZGERALD	Terence Duncan	ON - Hamilton		17-Dec-17	C	
FitzRANDOLPH	Archibald Menzies	NB - Saint John	U	3-Jun-16	N	
FLAVELLE	Gordon Aird	ON - Lindsay	S	19-Jan-17	C	
FLEMING	Geo Rivers Sanderson	ON - Toronto	T	1-Sep-15		
FLETT	Walter Ernest 'Pete'	ON - Toronto	U	18-Apr-16		
FLYNN	Harold John	ON - Niagara Falls		19-Apr-17		
FORBES	John Grahame	Canadian	S	2-Feb-18	C	
FORGIE	John Seymore	ON - Toronto		30-Sep-17	C	
FORMAN	James Henry	ON - Kirkfield	T	17-Nov-16	C	
FOSS	Donald Burrowes	QB - Sherbrooke		9-Jan-18	C	
FOSS	Roy Holmes	QB - Sherbrooke	M	5-Jan-18	C	
FOWLER	H'bert Howard Snowdon	ON - Bowmanville		7-Dec-16		
FOX	Wm. Norman	ON - Toronto		14-Mar-17		
FRANKLIN	Cecil Clarence	ON - Port Rowan		5-Oct-17		
FRASER	Alexander Gordon	ON - Lancaster	S	18-Nov-17	C	
FRASER	Donald Scott	Ontario		24-Mar-18	C	
FRASER	Fredrick Earle	MB - Winnipeg		16-Dec-15	N	
FRASER	Jack Frederick	AB - Calgary		23-Nov-17		
FRASER	Norman Graham	ON - Toronto		17-Dec-16		
FREEMAN	Kenneth Chesborough	ON - Wallaceburg		6-Dec-15		
FROST	Russell Welland	ON - Hamilton	T	7-Jan-18	C	
FULLERTON	Elmir Garfield	NS - Pictou		29-Jan-18	C	
GADBOIS	Paul Oliver	PQ - Montreal		29-Feb-16		
GAGNIER	Oliver Joseph	PQ - Montreal	M	15-Aug-16		
GALBRAITH	Daniel Murray Bayne	ON - Carleton Place	S	15-Nov-15		
GALLAGHER	Ernest Graham	ON - Leamington		7-Jan-18	C	
GALLWEY	John Neptune	ON - Toronto		25-Feb-17	C	
GALPIN	John Osborne 'Tiny'	ON - Ottawa		26-Nov-15		
GARLAND	Albert Howard	ON - Hespler		7-Jan-18		

NAME	RANK	DEC	BOOK	Notes
EMERY, HJ	Lt	MID	20-Sep-17	MID -10 Naval. INJx2. Instructor 29TDS'18
EVANS, WB	PFSLt			REL -10Apr16 'Unlikely as Pilot.'
EVERSON, SF	FSLt			INS - 29Jan18 Stonehenge on Handley Page
EYRE, RT	Lt	AFC		U-Boat -Bombed Dec'17. AFC -Jun19 INS
EYRES, JA	Lt			INJ -9May18 Dunkirk. 218RAF
FALL, JST	Capt	DSC	11-Apr-17	3 Kills. ACE -3N&9N. **19Dec17**-DSC&2Bars. **24Jul20** RAF
FARIS, EM	2Lt			210 RAF
FARNCOMB, HF	2Lt			Crash -27Mar18 Cranwell. INJ -30Sep18
FARQUHAR, AW	Capt			Calshot'16. Dover'17. 217 RAF'18.
FARRALL, JGM	2LtObs		18-Jul-18	KIA -Westgate Short 184.
FENTON, ECF	Lt			VGI Pilot -Mar'18. INS Chingford
FERGIE, TF	Lt			INJ -6Jun17 Dover, Concussion. REL -01Aug17
FINDLAY, DD	Capt		23-Sep-16	Dardanelles 2Wing. **Sep1933** -Turkey. GCapt RCAF
FISHER, PS	Capt	DSO	12-May-17	DSC -Dunkirk. WIA -24Sep17 Leg Lost.
FITTON, AH	2LtObs			REL- 26Feb18 From Pilot to Observer.
FITTON, HCM	FSLt			Calshot - Seaplanes. Brother to A.H.
FITZGERALD, MR	2Lt			205 RAF
FITZGERALD, TD	LtObs			KBO -Kite Balloons Malta.
FitzRANDOLPH, AM	Capt			RNVR Obs to Pilot. Bombed Brit Sub -21Mar18
FLAVELLE, GA	Capt	DFC	8-Aug-18	DFC -Tank Camouflage Ops 207RAF
FLEMING, GRS	FLt		14-Apr-17	POW/DOW -Frieburg Raid. 3Wing
FLETT, WE	FLt	DSC	14-Apr-17	WIA/DSC -3W Frieburg. REL-Sick 25Mar18 +CdG
FLYNN, HJ	PFO		5-Jul-17	KIC -Manston. Maurice Farman 'Longhorn'
FORBES, JG	PFO			Greenborough.
FORGIE, JS	2Lt		19-May-18	Action -211 RAF. WIA -3Aug18.
FORMAN, JH	Capt	DFC	28-Jul-17	WIA -1Naval. ACE -12Apr18. **4Sep18** -POW
FOSS, DB	PFO			28 RAF. With Bro RH from 7th Cdn SeigeBatt.
FOSS, RH	PFO	CdG		28 RAF. Awarded Italian Croiche di Guerra
FOWLER, HHS	Lt		18-May-18	ACE -Naval 8. REL -18Feb18 Deaf
FOX, WN	Lt		21-Oct-17	WIA -10 Naval. Camel combat.
FRANKLIN, CC	PFO		20-Mar-18	KIC -Cranwell Crash
FRASER, AG	2Lt			58 RAF
FRASER, DS	2Lt			DOJ -Last to Join prior RAF. INJ -30Jul18 CFS.
FRASER, FE	Capt	DSC	24-Apr-17	DSC -U-Boat. RNVR Obs to Pilot Jan'17. 6W'18
FRASER, JF	2Lt			56 RAF
FRASER, NG	Capt	MBE	17-Dec-16	PFSLt -Curtiss Canada. MBE -NRussia'19. +AFC
FREEMAN, KC	PFSLt		13-Jun-16	REL - Unsatisfactory/Resigned. Court Charges
FROST, RW	2Lt		1939-Sept	AWOL -Since 1918 -155 RAF. WingCdr RCAF
FULLERTON, EG	PFO		15-Apr-21	Bush Pilot Imperial Oil. Carved Prop. CAHF
GADBOIS, PO	FSLt		9-Jul-16	INJ -Slipped into Prop. Invalided '17
GAGNIER, OJ	Capt		11-May-17	WIA -6N Arm amputated. AdminO'18 Canada
GALBRAITH, DMB	Capt	DSC	15-Jul-16	DSC+CdG. **16Nov16** -ACE. **29Mar21**- Killed in Auto
GALLAGHER, EG	2Lt		17-Sep-18	INT - 115 RAF HP Bomber Shot down- Flak.
GALLWEY, JN	PFO		24-May-17	REL -'Unsuitable' But -No objection to joining RFC
GALPIN, JO	Major	DSC	22-Dec-17	ASP -Felixstowe. **6Jun18** -Shot Down. CO 231 RAF '18
GARLAND, AH	2Lt			WIA -17Oct18 46RAF. INJ 16Aug17

SURNAME	GIVEN NAMES	FROM	E	DOJ	P	
GEALE	Charles Norman	ON - Peterborough	T	21-Jul-15		
GERARD	Harold William	BC - Vancouver	S	11-Nov-17	C	
GIBEAULT	Joseph Oscar Raoul	ON - Alfred		3-Feb-16		
GILBERT	Albert Victor	ON - Kingston	T	18-Dec-17	C	
GIRLING	Arthur Stewart	Canadian		18-Mar-17		
GIRVIN	Patterson	ON - Ottawa	T	1-Nov-17	C	
GLASGOW	Theodore Linscott	ON - Toronto	R	2-Sep-16		
GLEN	David Kenneth	BC - Enderby		6-Apr-17	C	
GLEN	James Alpheus 'Jimmy'	BC - Enderby		16-Dec-15		
GLENNY	Wilton Ross	ON - Little Britain		19-Apr-17		
GONYON	Harold Harrison	ON - Wallaceburg		30-Jun-16		
GOOCH	Harold Cowasjee	Canadian b.India	M	17-Nov-16		
GOODACRE	Kenneth Roy	USA - Massachusetts		5-Aug-17		
GOODERHAM	Grant Armstrong	ON - Toronto	T	12-Jul-15		
GOODHUE	Clifford Chase	PQ - Sherbrooke		13-Sep-16		
GOODHUGH	Persival Howard	PQ - Westmount		6-Jan-18	C	
GORDON	James 'John' Lindsay	PQ - St Lambert	M	18-Jan-16		
GORDON	Ralph Vyvian	BC - Kamloops	T	19-Feb-18	C	
GORMAN	Joseph	ON - Ottawa		5-Dec-15	C	
GOW	John Eckford	ON - Kingston	S	4-Dec-17	C	
GOWLAND	William Charles	ON - Toronto		6-Dec-15		
GRACE	Edmund Victor Joseph	PQ - Westmount	M	19-Jan-17		
GRAHAM	Stuart	NS - Wolfville b.USA		5-Oct-17	C	
GRAHAM	Wm. Darling	MB - Melita		19-Apr-17		
GRANGE	Edward Rochfort	ON - Toronto b.USA	T	22-Sep-15	C	
GRANGE	Geo. Reginald	ON - Napanee		15-Nov-17	C	
GRANT	Bernard McK	ON - Toronto		17-Jun-16		
GRANT	Stanley Alexander	PQ - Montreal		14-Mar-17		
GRAY	William McNeil	ON - Toronto		30-Dec-15		
GRAY	George Stewart	ON - Meaford	T	6-Dec-15		
GREEN	Varian Sweetnam	AB - Calgary	M	5-Oct-17	C	
GREENE	John Edmund	MB - Winnipeg	S	19-Dec-16		
GREGORY	Edmund Neil	ON - Lindsay	S	19-Apr-17		
GRIER	Douglas Eric Monro	ON - Toronto		19-Jan-17		
GRIER	Edmund Geoffrey	ON - Toronto	U	23-Nov-17		
GRIEVE	Gavin Hutchinson	ON - Springfield		24-Nov-17	C	
GRIFFITHS	Wm. Reginald Mathews	Canadian		22-Feb-17	C	
GRIGG	Victor Samuel	ON - Toronto	T	28-Oct-17	C	
GRIMSHAW	Albert	ON - Toronto		8-Dec-17		
GRUNDY	Howard Eckhardt	MB - Winnipeg		9-Nov-16		
GUBBINS	Hugh Power Nepean	Canadian b.ENG		25-Nov-17	C	
GUILD	James Duff	MB - Kemnay		14-Mar-17		
GUNTHER	Roy Alfred	ON - London		7-Jan-18	C	
GWYTHER	Ralph Edwin Wm.	BC - Vancouver		27-Nov-17	C	
HAIG	Donald Alexander	ON - Toronto		14-Mar-17	N	
HAINES	Cyril Lalande	BC - Salmon Arm		9-Nov-15	N	

NAME	RANK	DEC	BOOK	Notes
GEALE, CN	Capt		17-Dec-15	Ditched. Later Instructor Flying Boats
GERARD, HW	PFO			Cranwell Apr18
GIBEAULT, JOR	PFSLt			REL -23Aug16 - Crash 22Jul16 -Too Nervous
GILBERT, AV	PFO			REL -27Mar18 Physically Unfit.
GIRLING, AS	Lt	DFC	18-Mar-17	DOJ - Bad Cheque Incident. Aegean -63Wing.
GIRVIN, P	2Lt			55 RAF -DH-4. Later DS
GLASGOW, TL	FSLt		19-Aug-17	KIC -10 Naval S.Triplane spun into ground. RMC
GLEN, DK	Lt	MID	21-Mar-18	Bro to J.A. MID -01Jan19 209RAF.
GLEN, JA	Capt	DSC	30-Jul-16	Action 3W. **7Jul17** -ACE 3N. **21Mar18** -WIA
GLENNY, WR	Capt?			2Wing -E.Med Struma Front. Later MD
GONYON, HH	Capt	DFC	3-Apr-18	U-Boat -217RAF. WIA -30May17.
GOOCH, HC	Lt		24-Oct-17	INT -Holland. Felixstowe North Sea Patrol
GOODACRE, KR	PFO			REL -28Oct17 Tx to Aux Patrol RNVR
GOODERHAM, GA	Capt	MID	22-May-16	Action -1Wing. **02May19** -Drowned Toronto
GOODHUE, CC	PFSLt			REL -3May17. 'Giddiness in the air but zealous Officer'
GOODHUGH, PH	2Lt		30-Aug-18	POW/DOW -46RAF. Only 1day in Sqdn.
GORDON, JL	Major	DFC	29-May-17	Rescue -Felixstowe. BofT Medal. AVM RCAF
GORDON, RV	2Lt		25-Sep-18	KIA -55 RAF.
GORMAN, J	FLt		16-Dec-17	KIC -6 Wing Italy -Camel. NOK-Wife ENG.
GOW, JE	2Lt		31-Jul-18	POW/DOW -204RAF. Died 10Aug18.
GOWLAND, WC	FSLt			REL -16Jul16 Poor pilot
GRACE, EVJ	FSLt		19-Sep-17	MIA -10 Naval over Ypers -1 week on Squadron
GRAHAM, S	Lt	AFC	22-Apr-18	U-Boat -Cattewater. **22Jul20** -1st Bush Pilot. CAHF
GRAHAM, WD	FSLt			REL -2Nov17 Heart Attack
GRANGE, ER	FCdr	DSC	4-Jan-17	DSC -Triple Victory -Naval 8. WIA/ACE. +CdG.
GRANGE, GR	Lt			Crash -16Apr18. Vendome
GRANT, BM	Lt	MID		WIA -RNVR.
GRANT, SA	Lt		27-Jul-18	MID -Aegean Action. 62 Wing
GRAY, WM	PFSLt		18-Feb-19	FLU. REL -10Jul16 to RNVR as TechO.
GRAY, GS	FSLt			INJ/REL -18Dec17 Invalided out. CC Pub
GREEN, VS	Lt		16-Sep-18	Action -Seaplane dogfight -Yarmouth
GREENE, JE	Capt	DFC	11-May-18	ACE -203RAF. **14Oct18** -KIA. +MID
GREGORY, EN	Lt			10Naval/210 RAF
GRIER, DEM	PFO			REL -3Aug17 Medically Unfit.
GRIER, EG	PFO			INJ -27Mar18/REL -18May18 Vendome.
GRIEVE, GH	PFO			Calshot Apr'18
GRIFFITHS, WRM	FSLt			Served Killingholm/Calshot/Fisguard
GRIGG, VS	2Lt			Turret ships. REL -23Oct18 to Med Studies.
GRIMSHAW, A	PFO	MID		MID Aug17
GRUNDY, HE	PFO		1-May-17	KIC -Cranwell, Bristol Scout Crash
GUBBINS, HPN	PFO			Calshot May'18
GUILD, JD	Lt	DFC		Houton Bay.
GUNTHER, RA	2Lt			97 RAF + IAF.
GWYTHER, REW	2Lt			INJ -2May18 209TDS Lost control in rough air
HAIG, DA	LtTech			REL -15Mar17 to RNVR as Armn't Officer
HAINES, CL	LtObs		26-May-17	KIA -Ostende, 2 Naval DH4.

SURNAME	GIVEN NAMES	FROM	E	DOJ	P	
HALES	John Playford 'Jack'	ON - Guelph	T	12-Oct-16		
HALL	Norman Douglas	BC - Nelson	S	26-Aug-16		
HALL	Robt Fred'rk Bainbridge	PQ - Montreal		17-Oct-17	C	
HALL	Sidney Herbert	Canadian	S	7-Feb-18	C	
HALLAM	Theodore Douglas	ON - Toronto	T	7-Dec-14	N	
HALLICK	Wm. Gordon Albion	ON - Ottawa	S	8-Dec-17	C	
HALLIDAY	Garnet Roy	BC - Victoria		7-May-16		
HAMILTON	Frederick Cecil	ON - Toronto		23-Nov-17		
HAMMOND	Donald	ON - Toronto	S	24-Sep-16		
HANEY	Wilfred Smith	ON - Sarnia	S	24-Nov-17	C	
HARDING	Thomas Lawrence	ON - Pickering		5-Oct-17		
HARDING	Wm. Oliver Fielding	Canadian		3-Mar-16	C	
HARLAND	Arthur Cecil	Canadian		23-Aug-15		
HARMAN	John Alfred	ON - Uxbridge	T	9-Dec-15		
HARRIS	Charles Roland	ON - Ottawa		5-Oct-17		
HARROP	Benjamin Nelson	SK - Indian Head	S	16-Dec-15		
HARROWER	Gordon Stuart	PQ - Montreal	M	17-Jan-16		
HARTT	John Chas. Naismith	ON - Toronto	S	12-Nov-17	C	
HARVIE	James Gray	Alberta	T	24-Feb-18	C	
HAY	Douglas Archibald	ON - Owen Sound		13-Jul-15		
HAYWOOD	Arthur Percival	ON - Toronto		9-May-16		
HEINE	Roland Wallace	NB - Moncton		7-Jan-18		
HELLMUTH	Frederick Gordon	ON - Allendale	T	1-Dec-15		
HENDERSON	Frederick Cecil	ON - Toronto	T	1-Sep-15		
HENDERSON	Wm. Ross Sutherland	ON - London	S	29-Dec-17	C	
HENNESSY	Martin John Paul	ON - Haileberry	S	30-Nov-17		
HENRY	Everett Wm.	ON - Warkworth	S	5-Jan-18	C	
HERIOTT	Victor Leslie	ON - Toronto		14-Mar-17		
HERVEY	Gerald Essex 'Gerry'	AB - Calgary		30-Sep-15		
HERVEY	Vyvian Holcombe	AB - Calgary		7-Feb-17	C	
HEWSON	George Cyril Vane	ON - Port Hope	T	24-Sep-15	C	
HICKEY	Charles Robert Reeves	BC - Parksville	S	4-Feb-17	C	
HILL	Henry McLaren	MB - Hilton	S	10-Jan-16		
HILL	Lloyd Allan	Canadian		23-Jan-18	C	
HOBBS	Basil Deacon	ON - Sault Ste Marie		27-Dec-15		
HOBBS	Joseph William	ON - Sault Ste Marie		31-Oct-15		
HODGETTS	George Alfred	ON - Ottawa	S	8-Dec-17	C	
HODGSON	Albert Gerald	BC - Vancouver		28-Nov-16		
HODGSON	George Ritchie	PQ - Montreal	M	18-Jan-16		
HOLLAND	Clyde Wallace	NS - Halifax	D	17-Feb-18	C	
HOLLEY	James Henry	MB - Winnipeg		15-Nov-17	C	
HOLMES	Thomas Byron	ON - Toronto	T	20-Dec-16		
HOMEWOOD	Charles	Canadian Forces b.ENG		18-Dec-17	C	
HOPEWELL	Douglas Charles	ON - Ottawa		19-Apr-17	C	
HOPPER	Arthur Burton	ON - Merwall		16-Oct-17	C	
HOUGH	John Elswood Chaffey	MB - Winnipeg		7-Feb-17		

NAME	RANK	DEC	BOOK	Notes
HALES, JP	Capt	MID	**11-Aug-18**	ACE -203RAF. KIA 23Aug18 - AA Fire.
HALL, ND	Capt		**2-Sep-17**	POW -3 Naval. Refused to fly 10 Naval S.Triplanes
HALL, RFB	Lt			241RAF.
HALL, SH	2Lt			243 RAF.
HALLAM, TD	Major	DSC	**7-Dec-14**	RNVR. **4Jun15** WIA Gallipoli. **23Apr17** U-Boat. **19Dec17**
HALLICK, WGA	PFO			Chingford.
HALLIDAY, GR	Capt			Great Yarmouth
HAMILTON, FC	Capt?			REL -1918 Appt term
HAMMOND, D	FSLt		**6-Jul-18**	Notoriety. REL -11Feb18 Naval 8 Neurasthenia
HANEY, WS	Lt			South Russia '19; 221 RAF Petrovsk
HARDING, TL	2Lt			INJ -3Jul18
HARDING, WOF	CaptObs		**8-Oct-17**	Court of Inquiry. -KBO Mesopotamia Nov'16.
HARLAND, AC	PFSLt		**18-Nov-15**	REL - 'Too slow & dull witted'
HARMAN, JA	FLt		**31-Aug-16**	INJ -Detling. Again 2Wing'17 -REL
HARRIS, CR	PFO			REL -27Feb18 to RNVR for Observer
HARROP, BN	Capt		**16-Dec-15**	DOJ. Malta Group -HMS *Riviera*, & *Vindex*
HARROWER, GS	Capt	MID	**23-Sep-17**	WIA -3 Naval
HARTT, JCN	2Lt			Calshot.
HARVIE, JG	2LtObs			Eastchurch Mar'18
HAY, DA	PFSLt		**19-Sep-15**	Lost at Sea -WhitleyBay. Only 2 days in unit
HAYWOOD, AP	Capt		**29-Apr-17**	WIA -1Naval. Invalided & REL -Nov'18
HEINE, RW	2Lt		**14-Sep-18**	POW -216 RAF.
HELLMUTH, FG	Lt		**4-Jan-18**	SUNK -HMHS *Rewa*. 6W-Malta'17. Rosyth '18
HENDERSON, FC	Capt		**11-Jan-17**	SUNK -HMS *Ben-my-Chree*.
HENDERSON, WRS	2Lt			Adriatic Gp for 66+64 Wing.
HENNESSY, MJP	2Lt			229 RAF.
HENRY, EW	2Lt			54TDS. Fm Cdn Gen Hosp-Cpl. Later MD
HERIOTT, VL	PFO			REL -21Aug17 'Defective Eyesight'
HERVEY, GE	Capt	DSC	**22-Aug-17**	DSC -Manston. Was 1Wing & 9Naval. +MIDx2
HERVEY, VH	Capt		**3-Nov-17**	INJ -HP Crash. WIA -13Aug18 -56RAF SE5a.
HEWSON, GCV	Major		**2-Apr-16**	INJ -5 Wing. Again 20Dec16 -1Wing
HICKEY, CRR	Capt	DFC	**21-Apr-18**	ACE - 204RAF. **3Oct18** -KIC Midair.
HILL, HM	PFSLt			REL -8Jun16 -Unsuited
HILL, LA	2LtObs			KBO -Kite Balloons
HOBBS, BD	Major		**14-Jun-17**	ZEP -L43; WIASep'17; U-Boat(s) +DSC&B. RCAF
HOBBS, JW	Capt	DSO		RCNAS by 1918. Cousin? to B.D.
HODGETTS, GA	2Lt		**4-Nov-18**	Action -80 RAF.
HODGSON, AG	Lt		**4-Jun-18**	INT -Westgate F2A Patrol Holland. Lawyer BC
HODGSON, GR	Capt	AFC	**29-May-17**	Rescue -Felixstowe +Board of Trade Medal.
HOLLAND, CW	2Lt			33 TDS Later MD
HOLLEY, JH	Lt			55 RAF.
HOLMES, TB	FSLt			REL -9Jan18 -Neuresthenia
HOMEWOOD, C	2Lt		**8-Jul-18**	KIC -207 TDS Avro504 Crash
HOPEWELL, DC	Lt		**7-Apr-18**	POW -208RAF
HOPPER, AB	LtObs			KBO -Grand Fleet -Ballons.
HOUGH, JEC	FSLt		**24-Oct-17**	MIA -1 Naval. Only 2 weeks in Unit

SURNAME	GIVEN NAMES	FROM	E	DOJ	P	
HOUNSOM	Albert 'Bert' Ernest	ON - Toronto	T	8-Dec-17	C	
HOWARD	Geo. Edwy Caldwell	ON - Toronto	T	19-Jan-17	C	
HUDSON	Walter Drew	ON - Toronto	T	9-May-16	C	
HUETHER	Archibald Leslie	ON - Guelph	T	14-Mar-17	C	
HUGHES	Garnet Nelson	ON - Picton		14-Nov-15		
HUGHEY	George Malcom	BC - Kamloops		30-Oct-17	C	
HULL	Allan Herbert	SK - D'Arcy		4-Dec-17	C	
HUTCHISON	Frederick Lorne	ON - Staffa	T	8-Dec-17	C	
HUTTY	Albert Irving 'Fred'	ON - Toronto		1-Dec-15		
HUYCKE	Frederick Arthur	ON - Peterborough	T	30-Nov-17	C	
INCE	Arthur Strachan	ON - Toronto		13-Jul-15		
INDERWICK	Charles Cyril	ON - Perth b.ENG		17-Nov-16		
INGHAM	Joshua Martin	ON - Toronto		11-Feb-16		
INGRAM	William Urquhart	Canadian b.ENG		12-Oct-17	C	
INGS	Frederick Walker	AB - Nanton	S	8-Dec-17	C	
IRELAND	Harold Mervyn	ON - Toronto		9-May-16		
IRELAND	John Graham	PQ - Montreal		12-Feb-16		
IRWIN	Wilfred James Hunter	ON - Markham	T	5-Oct-17	C	
JACK	Harold David	ON - Toronto		19-Apr-17		
JACKSON	James Edwin 'Ted'	ON - Port Perry	S	7-Jan-18		
JAMIESON	Ronald Campbell	Canadian		8-Jan-18	C	
JEFFRIES	William Claude	ON - Toronto		19-Jan-17		
JENCKES	Paul Worthington	PQ - Sherbrooke		10-Nov-16		
JOHNSON	Frederick Ross	PQ - Westmount		19-Jul-16		
JOHNSON	Joseph Harvey	ON - Kenora	T	19-Apr-17		
JOHNSON	Richard Walter	SK - Regina b.ENG		30-Dec-17	N	
JOHNSTON	Douglas Butterworth	ON - Athens	T	7-Jan-18	C	
JOHNSTON	James Mills	ON - Athens	Q	23-Nov-17	C	
JOHNSTON	William	PQ - Westmount b.IRE	M	14-Mar-17		
JOHNSTON	William Clarence	ON - Copper Cliff		7-Nov-16		
JONES	Clarence Audley	BC - Kelowna	T	8-Sep-17	C	
JONES	Nathaniel Unsworth	ON - Goderich	T	7-Feb-17	C	
JUNOR	Victor Robert McBeth	ON - Hamilton		19-Apr-17		
KEENS	John Harvey	ON - Toronto	U	1-Dec-15		
KEIRSTEAD	Ronald McNeil	NS - Wolfville	T	19-Jul-16		
KEITH	Haddow Macdonnell	ON - Toronto	T	8-Dec-17	C	
KELLY	Maurice Vincent	MB - Winnipeg		21-Dec-16		
KELLY	Wm. Joseph	ON - Brantford		22-Nov-17	C	
KENNEDY	John Winder	PQ - Westmount		30-Sep-17	C	
KENNEDY	Patrick Sylvester	ON - South Porcupine	M	27-Dec-15		
KENNY	Walter Robert	ON - Ottawa		16-Dec-15		
KERBY	Harold Spencer	AB - Calgary	T	21-Mar-15		
KERR	David Ross	PQ - Westmount	M	19-Apr-17	C	
KERR	John Beverly	ON - Chatham	T	19-Apr-17		
KERRUISH	Evan Francis	ON - Port Elgin	S	10-Oct-17	C	
KERRUISH	Herbert Bethune	ON - Fergus	T	14-Dec-16	C	

NAME	RANK	DEC	BOOK	Notes
HOUNSOM, AE	2Lt			249/257RAF -Crash 16May18
HOWARD, GEC	Lt		26-Sep-18	KIA -204RAF. WIA -3Sep17 w/4Naval
HUDSON, WD	PFSLt			REL -10Aug16 to CEF. WIA Apr17 Vimy
HUETHER, AL	Lt	BM	5-Apr-19	BM -Italy. REL -Oct18 to Medical studies.
HUGHES, GN	FSLt		25-Apr-16	INJ/REL Neurasthenia. 5Wing
HUGHEY, GM	2Lt			Frieston 8Apr-3May18. 42RAF Nov18
HULL, AH	PFO			Redcar for INS May'18
HUTCHISON, FL	2Lt			240 RAF -Dundee.
HUTTY, AI	Lt Obs		21-Aug-17	KIC -2 Naval -1st Day on Squadron
HUYCKE, FA	2Lt		3-Sep-18	MIA -239 RAF Torquay.
INCE, AS	CaptT		11-Jul-15	1st Curtis Grad. **14Dec15**-DSC. REL to RNVR.
INDERWICK, CC	PFO			REL -20Mar17 Unfit.
INGHAM, JM	FSLt	MID	30-Mar-17	KIA -2Wing Greece, by Eagle of Aegean
INGRAM, WU	2Lt			INS Portholme Meadows
INGS, FW	2Lt			209RAF.
IRELAND, HM	Capt	DFC	29-Aug-18	DFC -211 RAF. No.2 Sqn CAF
IRELAND, JG	Capt	AFC	20-Feb-18	Crash -Dundee. GCapt RCAF
IRWIN, WJH	Lt			WIA -10Group +CrashJan18. 241RAF
JACK, HD	Lt			East Fortune, Scotland
JACKSON, JE	PFO		16Jun1900	DOB - Youngest to Join. 28 RAF
JAMIESON, RC	2Lt			256 RAF Sep'18. Last Crse 24Mar18.
JEFFRIES, WC	FSLt			WIA -10Oct18 -Independent Air Force
JENCKES, PW	FSLt			REL -18Dec17 1Naval. Breakdown. To RNVR.
JOHNSON, FR	Capt	DSC	17-Sep-18	POW -100 RAF. +MID.
JOHNSON, JH	Lt			207 RAF. REL -Oct18 to Medical Studies.
JOHNSON, RW	2Lt		2-Nov-18	FLU -7 Reserve Depot Sqdn
JOHNSTON, DB	2Lt		18-May-18	(brother to JM) 25RAF 14Sep18. Later UofT - DS
JOHNSTON, JM	2Lt		18-May-18	KIC -Vendome Avro504k -Stalled &spun.
JOHNSTON, W	FLt		20-Jan-18	MIA -2 Wing Attack on *Goeben*.
JOHNSTON, WC	FSLt		23-Sep-17	WIA -10 Naval
JONES, CA	Lt			INJ -Eastbourne. REL -Oct18 Invalided
JONES, NU	PFO			REL -20Aug17 Appt term Later DS
JUNOR, VRMcB	PFO			REL -25Oct17 Lost Nerve.
KEENS, JH	Capt	AFC	7-Jun-17	WIA -10Naval. S.Triplane. Group Capt RCAF
KEIRSTEAD, RMcN	Capt	DSC	24-Sep-17	ACE -4Naval.
KEITH, HM	2Lt			266 RAF -Aegean. Dr. Emeritus Mayo Clinic 1964
KELLY, MV	Lt			INJ -May'17 -Cranwell
KELLY, WJ	2Lt		26-Sep-18	KIC -205 RAF Struck by Prop.
KENNEDY, JW	Lt			218 RAF
KENNEDY, PS	FSLt		26-Sep-16	KIC -Midair -Cranwell Bristol/Avro Accident
KENNY, WR	Capt	DFC	1-Jan-19	DFC -Dundee. AVM RCAF
KERBY, HS	Major	DSC	26-Nov-15	Sick -Gallipoli. **6May17** -ACE. AVM RAF
KERR, DR	FSLt		11-Nov-17	KIC -Manston Avro 504 Crash
KERR, JB	PFO			REL -8Aug17 - Refused to Fly. Later MD
KERRUISH, EF	2Lt		13-Jul-18	KIC -East Fortune Bristol F-2b.
KERRUISH, HB	Lt	MID	10-Mar-18	U-Boat. HMS Campania. MID 03Jun18.

SURNAME	GIVEN NAMES	FROM	E	DOJ	P
KIDNER	Arthur Wm. Colston	AB - Calgary		22-Nov-15	
KIERAN	John Fredr. Joseph	PQ - Montreal		5-Oct-17	
KINGSFORD	Maurice Rooke	ON - Toronto	T	15-Dec-15	C
KIRKPATRICK	George Denison	ON - Toronto	T	7-Feb-16	C
KIRKWOOD	Kenneth Porter	ON - Toronto	T	8-Dec-17	C
KNIGHT	Alexander Richard	ON - Collingwood		26-Aug-16	
LaBEREE	Edwin Eugene	ON - Ottawa		3-Dec-16	
LACKEY	Herbert David	ON - Ottawa	S	7-Jan-18	
LANGDON	Edwin Thomas	ON - Ottawa		3-Nov-16	
LARTER	Norman Ivan	ON - Toronto		7-Nov-16	
LAUGHLIN	Norman James	ON - Bellfountain	T	7-Jan-18	C
LAVIGNE	Joseph Louis	QB - Grand Mere		2-Dec-16	
LAWRENCE	Thomas Reginald	ON - Woodstock	S	7-Jan-18	
LAWSON	Albert H'brt Stanton	SK - Little Current		30-Apr-16	
LAWSON	Walter Brodgin	ON - Barrie	R	31-May-15	C
LAYARD	Arthur Raymond	BC - Ganges b.ENG		6-Aug-15	
LEARY	Albert Edward	ON - Toronto	T	7-Jan-18	C
LeBOUTILLER	Oliver Colin 'Boots'	USA - New Jersey		21-Aug-16	
LECKIE	John Stuart	ON - Toronto		14-Mar-17	
LECKIE	Robert 'Bob'	ON - Toronto b.SCT		6-Dec-15	
LEE	Carlton George	MB - Winnipeg		11-Mar-17	C
LeMOINE	Claude Melvin	ON - Toronto	S	8-Dec-17	
LESLIE	Herbert 'Hugh' Godfrey	BC - Victoria		3-Nov-15	
LESLIE	Norval Wilfred	MB - Winnipeg	S	11-Feb-16	
LEWIS	Mostyn	PQ - Montreal	M	16-Dec-15	
LICK	Cecil Havelock	SK - Davidson		14-Mar-17	C
LIDDLE	Thomas Robson	ON - Grimsby		1-Dec-15	
LIGHTBOURN	Gilbert Ord	ON - Toronto	T	19-Aug-17	C
LINDSAY	Lionel Lodge	AB - Calgary	T	19-Dec-16	
LITTLE	Reginald Keith	ON - Thornhill		9-Feb-18	C
LITTLEJOHN	Donald	SK - Saskatoon		23-Nov-17	C
LODGE	William 'Bill'	ON - Arnprior		20-Mar-16	
LOFFT	Alfred Hartley	ON - St. Mary's		7-Nov-16	
LOTT	Charles Wilfred	ON - Brussels		14-Mar-17	
LOWNDES	Wilbur James	Canadian		23-Nov-17	
LUCAS	George Kendall	Ontario		2-Dec-17	C
LUSK	Chas. Edward Stafford	ON - Toronto	U	26-Sep-16	
LYE	Harry Arthur	MB - MacGregor	S	4-Dec-17	C
MacALONEY	Ralph Gordon	NS - Halifax		14-Mar-17	
MacDONALD	Alexander Forsyth 'Sandy'	ON - London		5-Sep-16	
MacDONALD	Alexander Gordon	ON - Ottawa	T	15-Nov-17	
MacDONALD	Angus Grant	ON - Ottawa		11-Apr-16	
MacDONALD	Colin Gordon	PE - Charlottetown		8-Jul-17	C
MacDONALD	James Allister	ON - London		8-Dec-17	
MacDONALD	Kenneth Gordon	BC - Victoria	S	31-Oct-15	
MacDOUGALL	Dugald	MB - Lockport		4-Dec-17	C

NAME	RANK	DEC	BOOK	Notes
KIDNER, AWC	FSLt			INJ/REL -31Jul16 Physically Unfit
KIERAN, JFJ	Lt		23-Jan-20	DOS -Rheumatic Fever on 18Dec20. DH-4 Pilot
KINGSFORD, MR	Capt		5-Apr-17	INJ -6Naval
KIRKPATRICK, GD	Capt		5-Apr-17	6Naval. Later 212 RAF. OC 485Flight
KIRKWOOD, KP	2LtObs		15-Dec-17	Halifax Explosion Aftermath. Later Diplomat
KNIGHT, AR	FLt		5-Jul-17	Crash -Naval 8. INS -Eastbourne'18
LaBEREE, EE	PFO			REL -5Jul17 'Owing to Temperament'
LACKEY, HD	2Lt		7-Oct-18	KIA -70 RAF
LANGDON, ET	PFO			REL -24May17. Appointment Terminated
LARTER, NI	FSLt	MID	9-Dec-17	MIA -HMS Riviera Short184
LAUGHLIN, NJ	2Lt			Turret Ships. Later DS
LAVIGNE, JL	PFO		15-Apr-17	KIC -Chingford Grahame-White XV accident
LAWRENCE, TR	2Lt			38 RAF.
LAWSON, AHS	Capt		7-Jan-17	WIA -Naval 8. 'Extremely plucky Pilot'
LAWSON, WB	Major	DFC	17-Aug-15	Mesopotamia. **25Nov18** -CO 2 Sqdn CAF
LAYARD, AR	Major	OBE	3-Jun-19	OBE - Technical Officer
LEARY, AE	PFO			INJ/REL -4Apr18 Medically Unfit.
LeBOUTILLER, OC	Capt	MID	21-Apr-18	ACE - 209 RAF. Hollywood Pilot -1920s. Lockheed - 1930s
LECKIE, JS	FSLt			REL -19Feb18 Appt term
LECKIE, R	Major	DSO	6-Dec-15	**14May & 5Sep17, 4Jun & 5Aug18, 7Oct20, Jan1944**
LEE, CG	Lt			214 RAF -Slough 1918. Was Grounded 5Wing.
LeMOINE, CM	Lt		20-Aug-19	KIC -Archangel, Russia
LESLIE, HG	FLt		25-May-17	Action. REL 4Sep18 -Invalided Neurasthenia
LESLIE, NW	FSLt			REL -25Jul17 Phsy Unfit. G'Yarmouth
LEWIS, M	Capt		12-Oct-16	INJ -Obs drowned. RNVR Upavon'17
LICK, CH	Lt			WIA -203 RAF. Was also WIA 8Dec17
LIDDLE, TR	FSLt		30-Apr-16	KIC -Chingford
LIGHTBOURN, GO	FSLt		14-Jan-18	KBO -Kite Balloons Malta. GCapt RCAF OBE
LINDSAY, LL	Lt		7-Jul-17	Ditched/INJ -12Naval. S.Russia'19
LITTLE, RK	2Lt		18-Nov-18	KIC -Uxbridge.
LITTLEJOHN, D	2Lt			Technical Officer.
LODGE, W	FSLt		2-Jun-17	INJ/REL -Invalided 22Aug17. HMS Manxman
LOFFT, AH	FSLt	MID	7-Jul-17	MID -Westgate. REL 16Jan18 -Ill Health.
LOTT, CN	Lt		20-Jul-18	KIA -Malta Group -Sopwith Dolphin
LOWNDES, WJ	PFO			REL -14May18 Two Landing Accidents
LUCAS, GK	2Lt		7-Aug-18	Ditched -Albania. Lawyer 1920s
LUSK, CES	Capt		22-Sep-17	U-Boat -Magor's co-pilot.
LYE, HA	2Lt			INJ -3Aug18
MacALONEY, RG	FSLt		22-Nov-17	MIA -South Shields Short184
MacDONALD, AF	Capt	MID	25-Sep-17	WIA -9 Naval Ypres. Author: From the Ground Up
MacDONALD, AlexG	Major			INJ -11Apr18 Blois, Loire -American Hosp.
MacDONALD, AG	Lt			INJ -22Mar18 2Wing Mudros
MacDONALD, CG	FSLt		11-Mar-18	KIA -2Naval DH-4 over North Sea.
MacDONALD, JA	2Lt			210 RAF.
MacDONALD, KG	Capt		31-Jul-17	INJ -9 Naval. 62Wing'18
MacDOUGALL, D	Capt	DFC	25-Aug-19	Killed -North Russia. WIA-15Sep18.

SURNAME	GIVEN NAMES	FROM	E	DOJ	P	
MacINTOSH	Alister Bartholomew	AB - Calgary		24-Oct-16	N	
MacKAY	George Chisholm	ON - Mimico Beach	T	14-Mar-17	C	
MacKENZIE	Wm. Herbert	BC - Victoria		11-Dec-15		
MacKENZIE	Wm. John	ON - Port Robinson	T	19-Apr-16		
MACKIE	Frederick John	MB - Winnipeg		14-Dec-16		
MacLAURIN	Clarence 'Claire'	PQ - Lachine		21-Jul-15		
MacLEAN	Gerald Arthur 'Gerry'	ON - Toronto	U	2-Oct-15	C	
MacLENNAN	George Gordon 'Chubby'	ON - Eugenia	T	11-Nov-15		
MacLEOD	Earl Leslie	BC - Atchelitz		19-Jan-17		
MacLEOD	Kenneth Dawson	PQ - StAnneDeBellevue	S	7-Feb-17		
MacNAUGHTON	Gordon Philip	ON - Galt		7-Feb-17	C	
MacPHERSON	George Lucas	ON - Toronto	T	19-Apr-17		
MacPHERSON	Marshall Donald	ON - London	S	8-Dec-17	C	
MAGOR	Gerald Atkinson	PQ - Westmount	M	17-Jan-16		
MAGOR	Norman Ansley	PQ - Westmount		12-Feb-16		
MAIR	Ian	BC - Sydney		15-Aug-17	C	
MAITLAND	James Steel	PQ - Montreal b.SCT		16-Dec-15		
MAJOR	Frederick Annis	ON - Whitevale	S	30-Nov-16		
MALCOM	Orley Landan	ON - Toronto		4-Jan-18	C	
MALET	Francis Arthur Rivers	BC - Vancouver b.ENG		18-Sep-15	C	
MALONE	Chas. Edmund	SK - Regina	S	9-Feb-18	C	
MALONE	John Joseph 'Jack'	SK - Regina		15-Jul-16		
MANSELL	Frederick William	Alberta		24-Jun-16	N	
MANUEL	John Gerald	AB - Edmonton		7-Mar-17	C	
MARSHALL	George Reginald	ON - Toronto		2-Oct-16		
MARSHALL	James	ON - Bellville		19-Feb-18	C	
MARTIN	James Sherwood	BC - Vancouver	S	11-Apr-17		
MASSEY	Arnold Bonnell	ON - Toronto	S	14-Mar-17		
MASSON	Donald Howe	ON - Ottawa	M	21-Mar-16		
MATHESON	Wm Malcom Colin	MB - Winnipeg		11-Feb-16		
MAUND	Hugh Bingham	MB - Winnipeg b.ENG	S	6-Nov-16	C	
MAY	Theodore Chas.	ON - Toronto	S	21-Nov-16		
MAYWOOD	Clarence Alexander	MB - Winnipeg		11-Feb-16		
McALLISTER	John Norquay	MB - St. Andrews	S	17-Nov-16		
Mc'ANULTY	Justin Thomas Jos.	PQ - Westmount	S	30-Nov-17		
McARTHUR	Robert Kendall	PQ - Montreal	S	14-Dec-16		
McBAIN	Wallace Ward	ON - Atwood	T	23-Nov-17	C	
McCALL	Robert Simpson	Canadian Forces b.SCT		24-Nov-17	C	
McCLINTON	James	ON - Goderich		19-Jan-17		
McCOLL	Duncan Black	ON - West Lorne		7-Jan-18		
McCRIRRICK	Norman	Ontario	S	12-Apr-17	N	
McCRUDDEN	Stanley Harry	ON - Toronto		17-Aug-16		
McDIARMID	Neil Howard	BC - Victoria	M	22-Nov-15		
McDONALD	Roderick 'Rod'	NB - James River Stn.		15-Sep-16		
McDOUGALL	Ronald John	NS - Port Hawkesbury		4-Oct-15		
McELHINNEY	Arthur Mark	ON - Ottawa		8-Dec-17		

NAME	RANK	DEC	BOOK	Notes
MacINTOSH, AB	PFO			REL -17May17 to RNVR
MacKAY, GC	FCdr	DFC	12-Mar-18	ACE -213 RAF. **10Nov18** -Last Victory. Later DS
MacKENZIE, WH	Major	AFC	30-May-16	U-Boat. INS -E.Fortune 1918.
MacKENZIE, WJ	Capt	DFC	21-Apr-18	WIA - 209 RAF. +CdG(Bel)15Jul19
MACKIE, FJ	Lt			62Wing -E.Med. Macedonia
MacLAURIN, C	Major	DSC	10-Jan-16	OC -Bembridge. **11Sep22** -KIC Jerico Beach BC
MacLEAN, GA	FSLt		27-Apr-16	INJ/REL -Joins RFC -INJ twice, Capt RAF 1918.
MacLENNAN, GG	FCdr	CdG	21-Jul-17	KIA -6 Naval
MacLEOD, EL	FLt		19-Mar-17	Vendome Solo. WWII -Air Commodore RCAF OBE
MacLEOD, KD	FSLt			3 Naval '17. Grain Experimental Flight '18
MacNAUGHTON, GP	PFO			REL -28Jul17 Medically unfit
MacPHERSON, GL	Lt			WIA -13Sep18 97 IAF
MacPHERSON, MD	2Lt			241 RAF.
MAGOR, GA	Capt	MID	25-Apr-18	POW/DOW -201RAF Camel combat.
MAGOR, NA	Capt	DSC	22-Sep-17	U-Boat. **24Apr18** -MIA Felixstowe.
MAIR, I	CaptT			RNVR att. RNAS. Calshot TechO. REL -Aug '18
MAITLAND, JS	Capt	AFC		INS -Lee-on-Solent.
MAJOR, FA	PFO			REL -15May17 Unfit
MALCOM, OL	2Lt		26-Sep-18	KIA -104 IAF Bombing Metz-Sablon RR.
MALET, FAR	FSLt		12-Nov-16	KIA -HMS Riviera, Shoots off own Prop.
MALONE, CE	2Lt			INJ -7Aug18 Uxbridge. Brother to J.J.
MALONE, JJ	FSLt	DSO	21-Apr-17	ACE -3Naval. **30Apr17** -MIA
MANSELL, FW	CaptT			TechO. Was CPO Armoured Cars. 6W -Apr'18
MANUEL, JG	Capt	DSC	20-Sep-17	Action -10N. ACE-Feb'18. **10Jun18** -KIC Midair
MARSHALL, GR	Capt			Calshot
MARSHALL, J	2Lt	MM	20-Feb-18	MM - Bombadier Artillery -CEF Service
MARTIN, JS	SLt			REL -28Jan18. Became OBS -Nil Graduate
MASSEY, AB	Lt	AFC		AFC 02Nov18 -Houby experimental work.
MASSON, DH	FSLt		20-Apr-17	KIA -11Naval, Nieuport XI
MATHESON, WMC	FSLt		10-Jul-16	*Manxman*. REL -Neurasthenia 1918.
MAUND, HB	Capt		28-May-18	WIA -210 RAF. CO 204 RAF Jan'19
MAY, TC	FSLt		24-Jul-17	MIA -10 Naval. Age18
MAYWOOD, CA	FSLt		25-Feb-17	Censure -Brebach Raid, 3Wing. REL -Resigned.
McALLISTER, JN	FSLt		23-Jun-17	KIC -Naval 8 S.Triplane wing failure
Mc'ANULTY, JTJ	2Lt		28-Oct-18	Action - 66 RAF Italy
McARTHUR, RK	PFO			REL -9May17 Lost nerve
McBAIN, WW	2Lt		29-Oct-18	Action -28 RAF Italy. Later DS
McCALL, RS	PFO			Fm 72Bttn CEF. Was Customs Clerk
McCLINTON, J	PFO			REL -30May17 Appt Term. Later DS
McCOLL, DB	2Lt			97 RAF.
McCRIRRICK, N	LtObs			REL- 25Jan18 Medical - Reinstated RNVR
McCRUDDEN, SH	Capt		5-Sep-17	INJ - Naval 8 S.Triplane Crash. INS 205TDS'18
McDIARMID, NH	FSLt		13-Feb-16	INJ/REL -Honourable. Re-REL May '18.
McDONALD, R	Capt		27-Jul-17	ACE -Naval 8. **8May18** -MIA. Nil Decorations
McDOUGALL, RJ	PFSLt		14-Nov-15	Crash & REL - 'Shows no promise'
McELHINNEY, AM	2Lt		21-Nov-18	KIC -Vendome 205 RAF.

SURNAME	GIVEN NAMES	FROM	E	DOJ	P	
McFADDEN	John Alexander	ON - Ottawa		5-Oct-17	C	
McGILL	Andrew Kirk	ON - Glansworth	T	23-Nov-17		
McGILL	Frank Scholes	PQ - Montreal	M	23-Jul-15		
McGREGOR	Oswald Fitzgerald	PQ - Westmount		20-Dec-16		
McILRAITH	Earle Fraser	ON - Lanark Park	S	19-Apr-17		
McKELVEY	Merton Tyndale	MB - Homefield		14-Mar-17		
McLACHLAN	Howard Thorold	ON - Listowel		14-Mar-17		
McLACHRIE	David Ryland	ON - Toronto		6-Nov-17	C	
McLAUGHLIN	Reginald StClair	MB - Winnipeg	S	9-Jan-18	C	
McLEAN	Harry Logan Frazer	ON - Toronto		7-Jun-16		
McLELLAN	Frank Melville	NS - Springhill Mine		19-Apr-17		
McLEOD	Geo. Egerton Stuart	NB - Saint John	M	15-Nov-17	C	
McLEOD	Henry James	ON - Kingston	S	1-Dec-17	C	
McLEOD	Wm. Angus	ON - Toronto	S	8-Dec-17		
McMILLAN	Robert Earnshaw	NB - Jocquet River		19-Jan-17		
McNAUGHTON	Gordon Philip	ON - Galt		7-Feb-17	C	
McNAUGHTON	Gordon Vivian	Canadian		6-Mar-18	C	
McNEIL	Percy Gordon	ON - Toronto		30-Dec-15		
McNICOLL	Charles	PQ - Westmount	M	12-Feb-16		
McPHERSON	Arthur Dougal	ON - Sarnia b.SCT		7-Jan-18		
McSWEENEY	Geo. Bampfield	ON - Toronto	S	7-Jan-18		
McTAGGART	Mayne Donald	BC - Vancouver	S	11-Jan-18	C	
McVEAN	James William	ON - Dresden		30-Sep-17	C	
MERRIMAN	Horace Owen	ON - Hamilton	T	6-Dec-15		
MIDDLETON	Edward Elwood	ON - Ottawa	S	7-Jan-18	C	
MILLER	Clarence Percy	ON - Windsor		7-Jan-18	C	
MILLER	Geo. Gersham	ON - Woodford		15-Nov-17		
MILLS	Frederick Stanley	ON - Toronto		30-Dec-15		
MILLS	Harold Cowley	Canadian		22-May-16	C	
MILLS	Herbert Clifford	MB - Winnipeg	S	19-Oct-17	C	
MILLS	Ross Alexander	AB - Calgary	S	19-Mar-18	C	
MINNES	Wm. Grant	Ontario		17-Mar-18	C	
MITCHELL	Forest Henry	NS - Halifax		18-May-15	N	
MONK	Andrew Douglas Biggam	MB - Winnipeg		5-May-17	C	
MOORE	Clarence Earl	ON - Fort William		1-Dec-15	R	
MOORE	Chas. Reynolds	ON - Toronto		9-Dec-17		
MOORE	Maurice Eardley	SK - Saskatoon	S	6-Dec-17	C	
MORAN	Joseph Leonard	ON - Ottawa	S	13-May-17	C	
MORANG	George Heaven	ON - Toronto		7-Feb-17		
MORELL	James Anthony	ON - Toronto	S	27-Jul-16		
MORRIS	Walter George	Ontario	T	13-Feb-18		
MORRISON	Robert Geo. Kerr	ON - Chesterville	T	8-Dec-17	C	
MORSE	Gerald Morton	MB - Winnipeg	M	20-Sep-15	C	
MOTT	Harold Edgar	MB - Winnipeg	M	10-Aug-16		
MOYLE	William Arthur	ON - Paris		19-Apr-17	C	
MULHOLLAND	Donald Badgerow	ON - Toronto	T	19-Apr-17	C	

NAME	RANK	DEC	BOOK	Notes
McFADDEN, JA	2Lt			No 2 Group.
McGILL, AK	2Lt			239 RAF.
McGILL, FS	Capt		23-Jul-15	DOJ -Hydro Certificate. 230 RAF. AVM RCAF
McGREGOR, OF	PFO			REL -22Aug17 Unfit Flying.
McILRAITH, EF	Capt	DFC	11-Apr-18	Ditched - Zeebrugge 214 RAF.
McKELVEY, MT	Lt		11-Apr-18	POW -210 RAF. WIA -11Mar18
McLACHLAN, HT	PFSLt			REL -19Jun17 'Unsuitable'
McLACHRIE, DR	2Lt			Eastchurch -Gunnery INS
McLAUGHLIN, RStC	2Lt			57 TDS.
McLEAN, HLF	FLt	MID		WIA -E.Fortune. MID 06Oct17
McLELLAN, FM	Lt	DFC		DFC 01Jan19 -Imbros. 222 RAF
McLEOD, GES	LtObs			OBS -Adriatic Group. TechO Apr'18.
McLEOD, HJ	2Lt			INJ -21Mar18 Vendome.
McLEOD, WA	2Lt			141 RAF.
McMILLAN, RE	Lt		19-Sep-17	POW -1 Naval S.Triplane
McNAUGHTON, GP	PFO			REL -28Jul17 Appt term
McNAUGHTON, GV	PFO			RNAS Course 17Mar18.
McNEIL , PG	FLt	CdG	3-Jun-17	MIA -10Naval. Acting Flight Commander. +MID
McNICOLL, C	Capt	DSC	12-Mar-17	U-Boat. Dundee. HMS Pegasus. Isle of Grain
McPHERSON, AD	Lt			INJ - May'19
McSWEENEY, GB	2Lt		25-Jul-18	KIC -FE2b. School of Navigation&Bombing.
McTAGGART, MD	2Lt			61 RAF
McVEAN, JW	2Lt		23-Feb-18	INJ -Cranwell Camel Crash
MERRIMAN, HO	Capt T		2-Nov-16	REL -to RNVR as TechO. Microphone Records'19.
MIDDLETON, EE	2Lt			80 RAF. AVM RCAF OBE
MILLER, CP	2Lt			10 Group.
MILLER, GG	PFO			REL -27Mar18 Medically Unfit.
MILLS, FS	Capt	DSC	24-Nov-16	Romanian Service. Eastbourne'17
MILLS, HC	MajorT			RNVR -Tech O -WhiteCity -Mech Engineer
MILLS, HC	2Lt			INJ -Sep'18 Calshot.
MILLS, RA	2Lt			KBO Balloons
MINNES, WG	2LtObs			Last RNAS Course 24Mar18, Reading.
MITCHELL, FH	Lt		5-Dec-16	POW/DOS -RNVR Armoured Cars. Dardanelles
MONK, ADB	Lt			SE Area
MOORE, CE	Capt		1-Dec-15	DOJ. 2Wing, Eastern Mediterranean - '16- '17. 202 RAF '18
MOORE, CR	2Lt		28-Sep-18	POW -202 RAF Caught in storm. Tx From RFC
MOORE, ME	PFO			INJ -Apr18/REL -Aug18.
MORAN, JL	FSLt		12-Dec-17	KIC -Calshot FBA
MORANG, GH	FSLt		27-Oct-17	MIA -10Naval. Was INJ -5Jul17
MORELL, JA	Lt		4-Dec-17	Ditching/INJ -12 Naval. Crashes again 18Dec17
MORRIS, WG	2Lt			33 RAF.
MORRISON, RGK	2Lt	MID	20-May-19	Caspian Crash - S. Russia
MORSE, GM	FSLt			REL -30May17 To RNAS Armoured Cars
MOTT, HE	Capt		25-Jul-17	ACE - 9Naval. RAF Canada '18 -Beamsville ON
MOYLE, WA	FSLt		22-Mar-18	KIC -Midair 3 Naval with FSLt Sands
MULHOLLAND, DB	2Lt		13-Jul-17	INJ -Manston. REL -Invalided Jan'18

SURNAME	GIVEN NAMES	FROM	E	DOJ	P	
MULOCK	Redford Henry 'Red'	MB - Winnipeg	M	21-Jan-15	C	
MULVIHILL	Rene Michel	ON - Arnprior		15-Nov-17		
MUNDAY	Albert Henry	ON - Toronto b.AUS	Q	25-Mar-16	C	
MUNDAY	Edward Richard	ON - Toronto		30-Oct-17	C	
MUNDELL	John Aird	ON - Elora		19-Jan-17		
MUNN	James Alexander	ON - Kensall	T	27-Nov-17	C	
MUNRO	David John Best	PQ - Montreal	S	30-Nov-17	C	
MURPHY	Clarence W.	ON - Toronto		9-Sep-17	C	
MURRAY	David Fraser	BC - Victoria		17-Nov-16		
MURTON	Harry Stephen 'Sport'	ON - Toronto	T	11-Feb-16	C	
NAIRN	Robert George Grant	Ontario b.SCT		23-Sep-17	C	
NARES	Hilary George	MB - Winnipeg	M	11-Feb-16		
NASH	Gerald Ewart	ON - Stoney Creek		3-Feb-16		
NASH	Harold Chester	ON - Hamilton	T	6-Dec-15		
NELLES	Douglas Alex'dr Hardy	ON - Simcoe	T	3-Nov-15	C	
NESBITT	William	PQ - Montreal	S	5-Oct-17		
NICHOLSON	Leo Edward	MB - Winnipeg		10-Nov-16	N	
NIGHTINGALE	Alfred James	ON - Mount Dennis		30-Jul-15		
NODWELL	Geo Rose	ON - Grand Valley	T	22-Jul-17	C	
NORCROSS	Ashley Christopher	QB - Lennoxville	M	29-Jan-18	C	
NUNN	Roy Earl	ON - St. Annes Place		18-Oct-17	C	
NURSE	Louis William	ON - Toronto		6-Oct-15		
OAKLEY	Harold	PQ - Montreal		11-Dec-17	C	
O'LAUGHLIN	Harry Merrick	ON - St. Catherines		10-Jun-17	C	
OLIVER	William Smith	AB - Calgary		22-Mar-16		
O'NEIL	Victor Joseph	ON - Ottawa		5-Oct-17		
ORCHARD	Wallace Ernest 'Wally'	BC - Vancouver		18-Jan-16		
O'REILLY	Arthur John	BC - Victoria		29-Jul-15	N	
ORR	Osborne John	BC - Nanaimo		Nov -1917		
OWEN	Edward Rosser	Canadian Forces b.ENG		8-Sep-17	C	
OWEN	William Thomas	ON - Toronto b.USA		4-Nov-17	C	
PADMORE	Brian Read	NS - Liverpool		1-Dec-15		
PAGE	Herbert Joseph	BC - Saturna Isl b.ENG		3-Sep-15		
PAGE	John Albert	ON - Brockville	M	15-Nov-15		
PARKER	Chas. Alexander	ON - Ottawa	M	8-Dec-17	C	
PARKER	Leslie Hunter	QB - Leeds Village	M	16-Dec-15	C	
PARSONS	Charles St.Clair	ON - Toronto	T	28-Oct-17	C	
PATTERSON	James Dyck	Saskatchewan b.SCT		12-Sep-17	C	
PATTISON	Charles Edward	ON - Winona b.SCT		10-Jan-16		
PAUL	Robert John	ON - Winona		16-May-16		
PEACE	William James	ON -Bartonville	M	19-Apr-17	C	
PEARCE	Arthur Henry	BC - Vancouver b.ENG		5-Feb-16		
PEARSON	Marmaduke Pritchard	ON - Guelph	T	7-Oct-17	C	
PEBERDY	Warner Hutchins	ON -Toronto b.ENG	O	20-Jul-15		
PECK	Hugh Adderley	PQ - Montreal	M	23-Jul-15		
PEERS	Jack Wilson	ON - Toronto		15-Nov-17		

NAME	RANK	DEC	BOOK	Notes
MULOCK, RH	Colonel	CBE	20-Jan-15	**8Jul15-21May16-6Feb17-10Jul17-29Aug18-3Jun19**
MULVIHILL, RM	2Lt			233 RAF.
MUNDAY, AH	Major		10-May-18	ZEP L-62. INJ -20Apr17. NewsWriter
MUNDAY, ER	LtObs		5-Aug-18	MIA -G'Yarmouth on AZP
MUNDELL, JA	PFO			REL -10Jul17 Airsick
MUNN, JA	2Lt	CdG	5-Apr-19	CdG + Libyan Medal -Italy. Later DS
MUNRO, DJB	2Lt			HMS Furious.
MURPHY, CW	Lt			INJ -10Jul18 Calshot
MURRAY, DF	Capt	DFC	1-Jan-19	DFC -62 Wing Aegean.
MURTON, HS	Capt		4-May-17	POW -3Naval. Later S.Russia w/Collishaw
NAIRN, RGG	Lt		18-Feb-18	REL Application -Not Accepted.
NARES, HS	FLt		29-Apr-17	INJ/REL - to RNVR Isle of Grain. Cdr RCN WWII
NASH, GE	FLt		6-Jun-17	ACE -10 Naval Black Sheep. **25Jun17** -POW
NASH, HC	FSLt			REL -3Jun16 to Medical Studies.
NELLES, DAH	Capt	DSC	2-Aug-15	Crash - Toronto. **22Apr17** - INT Holland, 5 Naval
NESBITT, W	PFO			209 RAF.
NICHOLSON, LE	LtObs			HMS *Manxman*. RNVR Apr16-Mar17 OBS 01Apr17
NIGHTINGALE, AJ	FLt		14-Dec-15	MIA/OK. **2Dec16** -POW Palestine
NODWELL, GR	FSLt			REL & Rtn to Medical studies
NORCROSS, AC	2Lt			RD 10Aug18. Was CFA.
NUNN, RE	2Lt			REL -2Nov18
NURSE, LW	FSLt		15-Nov-15	Report & REL -'Objectionable habits…'
OAKLEY, H	Lt			WIA -Jun'18
O'LAUGHLIN, HM	FLt			246RAF 18Sep18
OLIVER, WS	FSLt		24-Mar-17	KIC -Dover -New aeroplane for 10N
O'NEIL, VJ	PObsO			REL -26Feb18to RNVR as Observer
ORCHARD, WE	FSLt		2-Jun-17	WIA -Died of Wounds 3 Naval
O'REILLY, AJ	CaptObs		16Feb1873	DOB -Oldest. **29Jul15**-DOJ. Kite Balloons
ORR, OJ	2Lt		14-Oct-18	ACE -204 RAF. KIA -23Oct18. DFC 01Jan19
OWEN, ER	LtObs	MID		OBS -237 RAF. MID 01Jan19
OWEN, WT	Lt		14-Oct-18	MIA -213 RAF
PADMORE, BR	CaptT			REL -18Sep16 Unfit flying. Joined RNVR
PAGE, HJ	FSLt		15-Feb-16	MIA -Yarmouth North Sea Patrol.
PAGE, JA	FLt		7-Jul-17	ACE -10Naval. KIA w/Sharman -22Jul17
PARKER, CA	Lt			24 TDS.
PARKER, LH	FSLt		14-Jun-17	MIA -10 Naval S.Triplane
PARSONS, CStC	Lt		22-Apr-18	POW -217RAF Zeebrugge Ops.
PATTERSON, JD	FSLt			Italy Service.
PATTISON, CE	Capt		20-May-17	WIA -10N. Crash 2Apr18 Redcar, Dies of Injuries
PAUL, RJ	FLt			Felixstowe
PEACE, WMJ	Capt	DFC	8-Aug-18	DFC -Tank Camouflage Ops. 207 & 58RAF. GCapt RCAF
PEARCE, AH	Lt	DFC		DFC 3Jun18n??
PEARSON, MP	Lt		7-Oct-17	DOJ. Brother LB 'Mike' RFC later Prime Minister.
PEBERDY, WH	FLt		8-Aug-15	Crash. MIA -2 Wing Macedonia 14Jan17.
PECK, HA	Capt		23-Jul-15	DOJ -Hydro Certificate. 253 RAF
PEERS, JW	PFO			REL -6Apr18 Unsuitable. Crash Twice

SURNAME	GIVEN NAMES	FROM	E	DOJ	P	
PENTY	Walter Smith	Canadian		18-Feb-16		
PERCIVAL	Ernest Russell	ON - London		23-Nov-17		
PERCIVAL	Roger Stickney	ON - Ottawa		15-Nov-17		
PETERS	Chas. Rowley	ON - Port Dalhousie		23-Nov-17		
PHILLIPS	Allan MacMillan	ON - Cornwall	T	8-Dec-17	C	
PINKERTON	Geo. McGill	ON - Toronto		21-Jan-18	C	
PITT	George Albert	Saskatchewan b.ENG		10-Jun-17	C	
PITT	Weston Ward	ON - Kingston		7-Dec-16	C	
POTTER	Ernest Coombe	MB - Winnipeg		3-Sep-15		
POTVIN	James Edward	ON - Goderich	T	29-Apr-16		
POULIN	Clement John	ON - Ottawa		19-Jan-17		
POWER	William Cope	MB - Winnipeg		19-Jun-15	N	
PRENDERGAST	William Killoran	ON - Toronto	T	28-Oct-17	C	
PRIME	Frederick Horace 'Holly'	ON - Toronto	T	1-May-16		
PRINGLE	Kenneth McKinnon	ON - Toronto	T	7-Feb-17		
PURDY	Claude Chester Wm.	SK - Prince Albert	Q	23-Aug-16	C	
PURVIS	Maxwell Cline	ON - Bolton	T	29-Jul-17	C	
RALPH	Ernest Gordon	ON - Toronto	T	8-Dec-17	C	
RAMSAY	Francis Malcolm	ON - Inglewood	S	30-Nov-17		
RAMSAY	John Albert	ON - Hamilton	T	8-Dec-15	C	
RAMSDEN	Victor Hubert	ON - Toronto		6-Dec-15		
RANEY	Grant	ON - Ottawa	O	19-Apr-17		
RANKIN	Archibald James	PQ - Montreal		3-Feb-18	C	
RANKIN	Kenneth Smith	ON - Ottawa		19-Mar-18	C	
REA	Cecil Arthur	Canadian b.IRE		21-Jul-15	N	
READE	Harris Hooper	ON - Ottawa	S	3-Feb-17	C	
REDPATH	Ronald Francis	PQ - Montreal	M	1-Dec-15		
REES	Lewis Austen	ON - Toronto		21-Dec-15		
REID	Archibald Cumberland	MB - Winnipeg	M	2-Aug-16		
REID	Ellis Vair	ON -Belleville	T	10-Jan-16		
REID	Frank Roy	MB - Minnedosa		10-Dec-17	C	
REID	Harold MacKenzie	ON - Bellville		19-Jan-17		
REID	Howard Vincent	NF - St. Johns		24-Jun-15	C	
REID	Hugh Wilfred	ON - Toronto	T	14-Mar-17	C	
REID	Wm. Ralph	ON - Seaforth		1-Dec-17	C	
RICHARDSON	Harold Richard Forbes	ON - Ottawa	T	27-Nov-17	C	
RICHARDSON	Robert Reginald	ON - Guelph		15-Jul-17	C	
RICHARDSON	Samuel Spalding	PQ - Montreal	M	19-Apr-17		
RICHARDSON	Tracy	USA - Missouri		19-Jan-17	C	
RIDLEY	Chas. Bryson	ON - Toronto	T	5-Oct-17		
RITCHIE	Henry Scott	ON - Toronto	T	7-Feb-17		
ROACH	Edmund Daniel	ON - Toronto		5-Jul-16		
ROBERTSON	John Ross	ON - Blenheim	T	12-Jan-18	C	
ROBINSON	John 'Jack'	ON - Toronto	T	30-Sep-15		
ROBINSON	John Burdwell	ON - Niagara Falls		11-Oct-16		
ROBINSON	Ralph Waldon	ON - Komoka	S	5-Oct-17		

NAME	RANK	DEC	BOOK	Notes
PENTY, WS	PFSLt			REL -5Jul16 Falsified Age.
PERCIVAL, ER	2Lt		18-Feb-19	FLU -205 RAF. Cattewater
PERCIVAL, RS	2Lt			REL -23Oct18 Unfit. Bro to E.R.?
PETERS, CR	2Lt			46 RAF.
PHILLIPS, AM	2Lt	DFC		DFC - 02Nov18. 217 RAF. 4 Victories. Later DS
PINKERTON, GMcG	2Lt			205 RAF
PITT, GA	Lt			Immigrated to SK
PITT, WW	PFO		7-Jun-17	KIC -Cranwell, Bristol Scout trainer
POTTER, EC	Capt	CdG	25-Feb-17	CdGaP -Brebach Raid. Invalided. ReJoins as OBS.
POTVIN, JE	FSLt	MID	19-Jun-17	MIA -Dunkirk S.Baby. MID Apr'16 for Rescue
POULIN, CJ	PFO			REL -19Jul17-Neurasthenia
POWER, WC	LCdr		19-Jun-15	DOJ -RNVR Technical Officer -1 Wing.
PRENDERGAST, WK	CaptObs			Italy Service. Later DS
PRIME, FH	Capt	AFC		AFC -3Jun19
PRINGLE, KM	PFO			REL -22Jun17 'Nervous Disposition'
PURDY, CCW	FSLt		15-Feb-18	MIA -Felixstowe Flying Boat vs Branderburg Fighters
PURVIS, MC	Lt		12-Apr-18	WIA -w/JR Allan 215N. WIA again 31Aug18
RALPH, EG	2Lt		20-Sep-18	POW -204 RAF. Also listed as ROLPH
RAMSAY, FM	2Lt			62 Wing.
RAMSAY, JA	PFSLt			REL -3Jun16 to CEF. Wrecked 3 machines.
RAMSDEN, VH	Capt			Dundee. 10Group1918
RANEY, G	Lt	BM		INJ 1Oct18. Bronze Medal Italy 5Apr19
RANKIN, AJ	FLt		20-Jul-19	INJ - North Russia. AirCommodre RAF OBE+AFC
RANKIN, KS	2Lt			KBO. Roehampton.
REA, CA	FLt			CPO RNAS Arm'd Cars Prior. As Pilot 'Keen & Capable'
READE, HH	Lt			'Fair Pilot Only'. 19Mar18 - to ferry duties
REDPATH, RF	Major	CdG	28-Sep-17	Mutiny A/SCdr 10 Naval. WCdr CAF 1921
REES, LA	FLt			Scilly Islands
REID, AC	Capt	AFC		AFC 2Nov18, MID 01Jan19. Dunkirk service.
REID, EV	FLt	DSC	6-Jun-17	ACE -10Naval. **28Jul17** - MIA. +MIDx2,
REID, FR	PObs			REL -16Mar18 Heart Disorder
REID, HMacK	FSLt		23-Feb-18	KIC -Midair Eastchurch
REID, HV	Capt A		30-Dec-15	Gallipoli. From Royal Newfoundland Rgt. RAF Canada - '18
REID, HW	TPFO			REL -27Aug17 to Imperial Tank Corps
REID, WR	2Lt Obs			256 RAF. Crashed 3 times. Became Observer
RICHARDSON, HRF	2Lt			HMS *Pegasus* -Grand Fleet. Later DS
RICHARDSON, RR	Lt	AFC		AFC -2Nov18. Was WIA w/CEF
RICHARDSON, SS	FSLt		19-Dec-17	MIA -5Naval DH4 Belgium
RICHARDSON, T	FSLt			WIA -21Aug17 then REL-19Oct17
RIDLEY, CB	Lt		10-Jul-18	WIA/POW -43RAF. Was WIA 4Jun17. Later MD
RITCHIE, HS	PFO			REL -17Aug17 Nervous Breakdown
ROACH, ED	FSLt		1-May-17	KIA -Naval 8 S.Triplane Combat
ROBERTSON, JR	2Lt			WIA -15Aug18 204RAF. Airways Inspector 1930
ROBINSON, J	Capt	DFC	7-Feb-16	Africa. **13Nov17** -Crash. OL(Belgium)
ROBINSON, JB	FLt			AAeC 609 from Curtiss School NY
ROBINSON, RW	Lt		25-Jul-18	WIA/DOW 11Aug18 Holland. -218RAF

SURNAME	GIVEN NAMES	FROM	E	DOJ	P	
ROBINSON	Wesley Fletcher	SK - Davidson	Q	19-Apr-17		
ROBINSON	Wm. Edgar	MB - Winnipeg	U	27-Dec-15		
ROBINSON	Wm. Hartley	ON - Toronto		20-Nov-17	C	
ROSENBAUM	Lionel	ON - Toronto b.Quebec		19-Jan-17		
ROSEVEAR	Stanley Wallace	ON -Port Arthur	T	19-Jan-17		
ROSS	Alexander	ON - Toronto	S	15-Dec-17	C	
ROSS	Gordon Fraser	ON - Toronto		31-Oct-15		
ROSS	John Roderick	MB - Winnipeg		29-Jan-16		
ROUGHSEDGE	John Haslam Kennett	ON - Ottawa		14-Mar-17		
ROWLAND	Donald Percival	MB - Winnipeg		31-Aug-16	N	
RUBINOVICH	Trewin Joseph	PQ - Westmount	S	8-Dec-17		
RUSSELL	Arthur Herbert Keith	ON - Ottawa	T	23-Nov-17	N	
RUTHERFORD	Cyril Burkitt	ON - Toronto		11-Dec-17	C	
SADD	Frederick Russell	Canadian b.ENG		15-Jul-15	C	
SALTER	Hubert Peter	ON - Ottawa		7-Feb-17		
SALTON	Wm. Fletcher	ON - Ottawa b.IRE		14-Mar-17	C	
SANDERSON	John Inglis	ON - Toronto		30-Jan-18	C	
SANDS	Lloyd Allison	NB - Moncton		3-Feb-16		
SAUNDERS	Kenneth Foster	BC - Victoria		3-Nov-15		
SCOTT	George Mathewson	PQ - Lakeside	M	19-Apr-17		
SCOTT	Gordon Beattie George	ON - Guelph	T	28-Oct-16		
SCOTT	Gordon Douglas	PQ - Westmount	M	7-Jan-18	C	
SCOTT	Gordon Tree	ON - Hespler		25-Sep-17	C	
SCOTT	Harry Albut	ON - Kingston		7-Feb-17		
SCOTT	James Douglass	SK - Regina		1-Dec-15		
SCOTT	James Garnet	ON - St. Catherines	T	3-Feb-16		
SCOTT	Norman Mackie	ON - Ottawa	U	27-Aug-16	C	
SCOTT	Wm. Alan	ON - Collingwood	T	16-Jan-18	N	
SHARMAN	John Edward	MB - Oak Lake	T	3-Feb-16		
SHARPE	Charles Thomas	ON - Toronto	T	7-Jan-18		
SHAW	Frederick Barr	ON - Forest		5-Oct-17		
SHAW	James	ON - St. Catherines	S	7-Jan-18		
SHAW	James Alexander'Alley'	AB - Edmonton b.IRE		1-Jan-16		
SHAW	Wm. Alfred	NS - Halifax	S	15-Nov-17	C	
SHEA	George Nelson	ON - Toronto	U	19-Jan-17		
SHEARER	Ambrose Bernice	MB - Neepawa		6-Oct-15		
SHEARER	Thomas Ralph	AB - Calgary	Q	23-May-16	C	
SHERLOCK	Clarence Edward	AB - Lethbridge		27-Nov-17	C	
SHIELDS	Donald Mitchell	ON - Mount Albert		22-Aug-16		
SHIRRIFF	Quintin Speirs	ON - Toronto		3-Feb-16		
SHOEBOTTOM	Lionel Robert	ON - London	T	14-Mar-17	C	
SHOOK	Alexander Macdonald	ON - Tioga	T	5-Nov-15		
SIMMERS	Joseph Adolph	ON - Toronto	T	3-Nov-17	C	
SIMPSON	George Howard	ON - Toronto		13-Oct-15		
SIMPSON	Thomas Barton	ON - London	S	15-Nov-17	C	
SINCLAIR	James Leonard Alexd'r	ON - Toronto		3-Feb-16		

NAME	RANK	DEC	BOOK	Notes
ROBINSON, WF	Lt			REL -26Oct18 to University. Shot up16May18. 204 RAF
ROBINSON, WE	Capt	CdG	8-Jul-17	POW -Tripoli. Turkish capture. CdG -29Aug17
ROBINSON, WH	Lt		2-May-18	KIC -66 RAF Italy Camel crash. Was Journalist
ROSENBAUM, L	FSLt			REL -3Nov17 Appt terminated - Crashed Calshot
ROSEVEAR, SW	Capt	DSC	25-Apr-18	KIA -210 RAF Camel crash. ACE -Oct17
ROSS, A	2LtObs	MID		KBO -Kite Blns. Gibralter
ROSS, GF	Lt	MID	10-May-18	KIA -Ostende Raid. Was REL -25Aug16 to RNVR.
ROSS, JR	Capt	MID	12-Mar-17	MID -For Rescue, Calshot.
ROUGHSEDGE, JHK	Lt			12 Naval. Later INS Chingford
ROWLAND, DP	CaptObs			Was RNVR. Later Admin O
RUBINOVICH, TJ	PFO			INJ -14Jun18 Vendrome Crash.
RUSSELL, AK	Lt			INJ -29Jul18 Italy. 273RAF. Lawyer NB. ACmdr RCAF
RUTHERFORD, CB	2Lt			Turret Pilot. HMS *Indomitable*
SADD, FR	Capt			KBO - OC Canning 1918.
SALTER, HP	Lt		6-Nov-17	MIA/WIA/POW -2Naval AA hit.
SALTON, WF	Lt		9-Jun-18	KIC -224 RAF DH-4 Adriatic.
SANDERSON, JI	2Lt	MM	20-Feb-18	MM -CFA Gunner. WIA -70RAF.
SANDS, LA	FLt		29-Apr-17	Crash -3 Wing. **22Mar18** -KIC Midair 3 Naval
SAUNDERS, KF	Capt	DSC	31-Dec-17	DSC -INS Eastchurch. +AFC. DoT Canada. CAHF
SCOTT, GM	Lt		11-Jun-18	KIC -Aegean 62Wing DH-4 Landing.
SCOTT, GBG	FSLt		3-Sep-17	MIA -1Naval S.Triplane
SCOTT, GD	Lt		11-Jun-18	(brother GM) INJ -2Aug18 Vendome.
SCOTT, GT	Lt	MID		212 RAF -MID 03Jun19
SCOTT, HA	Lt T			REL -24Sep17 To TechO RNVR
SCOTT, JD	FSLt		20-Sep-16	KIC -3 Wing Luxeuil.
SCOTT, JG	Lt		25-Jan-18	Flu. Was REL 11Jun16 -to TechO RNVR
SCOTT, NM	Capt			218 RAF'18, INS Vendrome '17
SCOTT, WA	2Lt			37 RAF by Jul18. Fm RNCVR
SHARMAN, JE	FCdr	DSC	14-Apr-17	DSC -3W. 14Jun17 -ACE 10N. 22Jul17 -KIA
SHARPE, CT	2Lt			INJ -6May18 Sheppey. 204 RAF. Colonel -Lorne Scots
SHAW, FB	Lt	CdG		INJ -Cranwell BE2c CdG -100RAF.
SHAW, J	2Lt			209RAF Nov18.
SHAW, JA	Capt			4Wing 1916, Naval8 1917, PrawlePt 1918.
SHAW, WA	2Lt			44TDS Nov18. Ap21740
SHEA, GN	PFO			REL -14Aug17 Unsuitable
SHEARER, AB	Major	MID	12-Sep-18	WIA -Adriatic. CO 227 RAF. AVM RCAF
SHEARER, TR	FSLt		13-Jun-17	KIC -9 Naval S.Triplane. Previous INJ.
SHERLOCK, CE	2Lt		17-Mar-18	INJ by propeller. Then KIC Midair -19Aug18 Cranwell
SHIELDS, DM	FSLt		1-May-17	WIA -Naval 8 S.Triplane -Hid on Vimy Ridge
SHIRRIFF, QS	Capt			Naval 10 -Sick 17Jul17 Ulcers
SHOEBOTTOM, LR	Capt	DFC		116 RAF -DFC 2Jul18
SHOOK, AM	Major	DSO	24-Apr-16	MID. **04Jun17** -1stCamel ACE. **22Mar18** -Triple Victory
SIMMERS, JA	2LtObs			Adriatic Group, 67 Wing, 271 RAF.
SIMPSON, GH	Capt	MID	13-Oct-15	PFSLt -Dayton. Scapa '16 '17. Russia '18. Later Bush Pilot
SIMPSON, TB	2Lt		19-Dec-18	KIC -54 Trn Sqdn.
SINCLAIR, JLA	Capt			INS -HP's Cranwell Apr '18; 2Wing Oct '16

SURNAME	GIVEN NAMES	FROM	E	DOJ	P	
SINCLAIR	Kenneth Younie	ON - Meaford	T	15-Aug-17	C	
SINCLAIR	Wilfred Maurice	ON - Toronto	S	24-Jan-18	C	
SKELTON	Hugh Fleming	BC - Victoria		15-Jan-18	C	
SLATER	Robert Kenneth	ON - Ottawa		8-Apr-16	C	
SMITH	Cyril Boyd	ON - London	T	26-Jan-18	C	
SMITH	Edgar Donald	ON - St Thomas	S	23-Nov-17		
SMITH	Ernest Spurgeon	NS - North Sidney	S	7-Oct-17	C	
SMITH	Frank Homer	ON - Toronto	T	12-Jul-15	C	
SMITH	Gerald Duncan 'Guy'	USA -California b.ENG		6-Sep-15		
SMITH	Gordon Beverly	ON - Toronto	S	30-Sep-17		
SMITH	Harold Beaumont	USA -California b.ENG		18-Feb-16		
SMITH	Jewitt Rice	Canadian b.USA	S	8-Dec-17	C	
SMITH	Kenneth Myron	ON - Toronto		30-Dec-15		
SMITH	Langley Frank Willard	PQ - Phillipsburg		29-Jun-16		
SMITH	Lewis Ewing	PQ - Mystic	M	30-Sep-15	C	
SMITH	Russell Douglas	MB - Winnipeg		1-Feb-17	C	
SMITH	Wallace Neil	ON - Sudbury		30-Nov-16		
SMITH	Wm.Alexander	MB - Winnipeg		8-Jul-17	C	
SMITHERINGALE	Charles Robert	BC - Vancouver		16-Oct-17	C	
SMYTH	Gabriel Henry George	ON - Toronto b.France	S	25-Aug-16		
SNIDER	Delford Roy 'Doc'	ON - New Berlin	Q	19-Apr-17	C	
SNIDER	Garnet Harold	MB - Portage La Prairie		27-Aug-16	C	
SOMERVILLE	Cavanagh Nixon	ON - Georgetown		18-Nov-15		
SORLEY	James Campbell	ON - Ottawa	T	28-Dec-17	C	
SOUTER	Walter Alexander	ON - Hamilton		23-Nov-17		
SOUTER	Wm. Russell	ON - Hamilton		23-Nov-17		
SOUTHGATE	Frank Leslie	Canadian b.ENG		18-Dec-17	C	
SPEAR	Robert Elmer	MB - Winnipeg		11-Feb-16		
SPENCE	Anthony George Allen	ON - Toronto	T	28-Oct-16		
SPROATT	Charles Beverley	ON - Toronto	T	1-Dec-15		
SPROULE	Robert Edwin	PQ - Westmount		12-Sep-17	N	
St.JAMES	Jos. Hesguith	QB - Delston Junction		14-Dec-16		
STANYON	Leonard Leslie	ON - Toronto	U	19-Jan-17		
STATA	Bernard Hill	ON - Ottawa		5-Oct-17		
STAUFFER	Joseph Stanley	ON - Galt	S	19-Apr-17		
STEEVES	Gordon Tracy	NB - Hillsboro	S	19-Apr-17	C	
STEPHENS	Maurice Hugh	ON -Toronto b.ENG		30-Dec-15		
STEPHENS	Robert Greaves	QB - Alymer East		7-Jan-18		
STEPHENS	Thomas Gordon Mair	ON - Toronto		1-Sep-15		
STEVENS	Alexander MacKay	SK - Moose Jaw	M	15-Nov-17	C	
STEVENS	Geo. Leslie Eugene	ON - Peterborough		6-Sep-15		
STEVENS	Wilfred George	AB - Calgary		19-Dec-17	C	
STEVENSON	James Milner	Prince Edward Island		30-Dec-17	C	
STEVENSON	Robt. Lancelot	MB - Winnipeg	S	15-Dec-17	C	
STEWART	Spurgeon Walter	ON - Brockville	S	15-Nov-17		
STINSON	Robert Kenneth	ON - Tamworth		7-Jan-18		

NAME	RANK	DEC	BOOK	Notes
SINCLAIR, KY	FSLt			REL -2Apr18 to Medical studies Later MD
SINCLAIR, WM	2Lt			INJ -Eastchurch. Stalled Avro 504
SKELTON, HF	2Lt			55 TDS
SLATER, RK	FLt		5-Apr-17	MIA/POW -6 Naval
SMITH, CB	2Lt			INJ -Mar18 Greenborough
SMITH, ED	PFO			257RAF.
SMITH, ES	Lt			INS -Calshot then 245RAF -Nov18.
SMITH, FH	FSLt		13-Nov-15	REL -1 Wing to RNVR. WingCdr RCAF WW2
SMITH, GD	FSLt	DSC	1-Oct-14	Leipzig. **06May17** -MIA/OK Indian Ocean.
SMITH, GB	PFO			REL -17Nov17 AWOL. Greenwich
SMITH, HB	Capt	MID	6-May17	(brother G.D) Yarmouth MIA-24Oct16, Rtn OK.
SMITH, JR	2Lt	DFC	4-Nov-18	DFC -Bombing. 218 RAF
SMITH, KM	FLt			2 Wing 1916/Sick/Grain 1918
SMITH, LFW	FSLt	DSC	25-May-17	ACE -4 Naval Gotha victory. KIA-13Jun17
SMITH, LE	FSLt	CdG	27-Nov-15	Crash -Hendon. **25Feb17** -POW/DOW -3Wing.
SMITH, RD	FSLt			REL -11Sep17 Airsick. Returned Army
SMITH, WN	FSLt			REL -2Nov17 Appt Term. Was 2 Wing.
SMITH, WA	PFO			REL -23Jan18 Father died. Sent on CA Lve.
SMITHERINGALE, CR	2Lt			Cranwell Mar18. Dentistry -UBC
SMYTH, GHG	FSLt		1-Feb-17	FSLt -Graduate. INJ Twice. AWOL. REL Oct'18
SNIDER, DR	Lt			Discipline Court Feb'18. 214RAF. 2 ASD Apr'18.
SNIDER, GH	FSLt			REL -29Dec17 Cattewater. RIP Golden BC
SOMERVILLE, CN	PFSLt		16-Jan-16	DOS -Died Of Sickness -Augusta, Georgia.
SORLEY, JC	Lt		25-Sep-18	KIA -213 RAF
SOUTER, WA	2Lt			Calshot Jun18. Bro to W.R.
SOUTER, WR	2Lt			Cranwell Mar18. Brothers joined same date
SOUTHGATE, FL	2Lt			No.1ASD -Electrical Engineer
SPEAR, RE	Capt			HMS Ark Royal in E.Med with 2W & 63Wing
SPENCE, AGA	Lt		21-Oct-17	ACE -1Naval. INJ 8Nov17. 211RAF
SPROATT, CB	Capt	DSC	7-Sep-16	MIDx2 -5Wing Dunkirk.
SPROULE, RE	2Lt	DSM	20-Feb-18	DSM -Fm RNVR + WIA. Cranwell Mar18.
St.JAMES, JH	FSLt		3-Nov-17	KIC -Manston. Handley Page bomber crash.
STANYON, LL	PFO			REL -2Jun17 Physically unfit
STATA, BH	2Lt		28-Sep-18	KIC -218RAF Severe storm.
STAUFFER, JS	2Lt			INJ -23Sep17 Manston
STEEVES, GT	FLt		18-Mar-18	MIA/POW -10Naval Camel Combat. WCdr WW2
STEPHENS, MH	Capt		23-Jan-17	INJ -3Wing Bomb hang-up. Lost leg.
STEPHENS, RG	2Lt			73RAF.
STEPHENS, TGM	FLt	MID	8-Feb-16	Crash(es). To East Indies. INJx2. MID2x.
STEVENS, AM	Lt		28-Sep-18	MIA -202 RAF Combat.
STEVENS, GLE	Capt			WIA -22May18 206 RAF -Shot up.
STEVENS, WG	2Lt			55TDS -Nov'18.
STEVENSON, JM	2Lt			WIA -27Sep18 54RAF -Shot up, Camel rtn OK.
STEVENSON, RL	2LtObs	MID		238 RAF -MID 01Jan19.
STEWART, SW	2Lt			Reading -May'18.
STINSON, RK	2Lt			Eastchurch -Jun'18.

SURNAME	GIVEN NAMES	FROM	E	DOJ	P	
STITT	John Grover	MB - Rossburn		29-Jan-18	C	
STOCK	Alfred Percy	ON - Peterborough		12-Aug-17	C	
STONEMAN	Edwin Curtis Robinson	ON - Toronto	T	28-Oct-16		
STRATHY	Ford Stuart	ON - Toronto	T	5-Nov-16		
STRATTON	Kenneth Vern	ON - Alymer	T	17-Sep-16	B	
STROUD	Geo. Levi	ON - Woodville		7-Jan-18	C	
SULLIVAN	Jacob Jeremiah	ON - Preston		5-Oct-17		
SUSSAN	Walter James	ON - Ottawa		15-Nov-15		
SUTHERLAND	Alexander MacBeth	MB - Winnipeg		15-Sep-17	C	
SUTHERLAND	Hugh Angus	ON - Hamilton	S	8-Dec-17	C	
SUTHERLAND	John Alexander	ON - Ottawa		23-Nov-17		
SYMMES	Henry Woodruff	ON - Niagara Falls	S	15-Nov-17	N	
SYMMES	John Arnold	ON - Niagara Falls	S	15-Nov-17	C	
TAYLOR	Joseph Watson	ON - Guelph	T	8-Dec-17	C	
TAYLOR	Merril Samuel	SK - Regina	T	19-Jan-17	C	
TEETZEL	Hugh Mowbray	ON - Chatham		9-Dec-17	C	
TEMPLE	Wm. Horace	ON - Toronto		7-Jan-18		
TEMPLETON	William	BC - Vancouver		10-Dec-15		
THOM	George	BC - Merritt b.SCT		3-Dec-15		
THOMPSON	Howard Grant 'Spike'	ON - Dorchester	T	28-Nov-17	C	
THOMPSON	Robert Ellerton	ON - Toronto	S	7-Jan-18		
TIDEY	Aubrey Mansfield	BC - Vancouver		27-Dec-17	N	
TINGLEY	Paul Roy	NS - Wolfville		8-Jan-18	C	
TODD	Allan Switzer	ON - Toronto		6-Sep-15	C	
TOMKINS	John	ON - Kingston		19-Apr-17		
TRAPP	George Leonard	BC -New Westminster	M	19-Jan-17		
TRAPP	Stanley Valentine	BC -New Westminster		16-Dec-15		
TRELEAVEN	Clarence Wesley	ON - Toronto		8-Dec-17	C	
TUCKWELL	Alan Wesley	SK - Regina		28-Oct-17	C	
TURNEY	Kenneth Vincent	ON - Trenton		20-Dec-16		
TWOHEY	Wm. Francis	ON -Chatham	T	30-Nov-17	C	
TYLER	Reginald Charles	MB - Winnipeg b.ENG		19-Dec-16		
URQUHART	Chas. Geo.	BC - Vancouver		23-Feb-18	C	
URQUHART	Henry Archibald	ON - Ottawa		19-Jan-17		
Van ALLEN	Kenneth Marsden	ON - Brantford	T	30-Sep-15		
VANCE	James Durkin 'Jimmy'	ON - Toronto		19-Apr-17	C	
VAUGHAN	John Fred'rk Simpson	ON - Ottawa		3-Nov-16		
VENNING	Robt. Blaine Norris	ON - Ottawa		19-Jan-17		
VETTER	Edward Leo	Canadian		8-Feb-18		
VEZINA	Thomas Donat	ON - Toronto		8-Dec-17		
VINCENT	Francis John	MB - Crystal City		24-Sep-16	N	
WAAGE-MOTT	Robt. Wm. Rex	BC - Victoria		19-Oct-17	C	
WALKER	Albert Henry 'Fuzzy'	ON - Toronto b.IRE	T	14-Jan-18	C	
WALKER	Harry Hunt	ON - Fort William		10-Mar-18	C	
WALKER	Major Benson	ON - Hamilton		1-Dec-15		
WALKER	William Roy	MB - West Kildonan		24-Nov-15		

NAME	RANK	DEC	BOOK	Notes
STITT, JG	2Lt			50 TDS
STOCK, AP	Lt	MID		62 Wing, 222 RAF -MID 01Jan19
STONEMAN, ECR	Capt	DFC	6-Jul-18	Adriatic Action. 224 RAF. +SM(Italy)
STRATHY, FS	FSLt		17-Aug-17	KIA -6 Naval
STRATTON, KV	Lt			INJ/REL -Jan17 10 Naval & Invalided out.
STROUD, GL	2Lt			Pilot by July 1918.
SULLIVAN, JJ	2Lt			REL -21Sep18. Manston for DH4 but Resigned.
SUSSAN, WJ	Capt	MID	18-Oct-16	REL - Invalided. Rejoins'17. 62Wing'18 -Greek MC
SUTHERLAND, AM	2Lt		2-Jul-18	KIA -65 RAF Sopwith Camel.
SUTHERLAND, HA	2Lt		4-Sep-18	KIC -Midair Turnhouse.
SUTHERLAND, JA	2Lt			INJ -10Jul18. 205TDS.
SYMMES, HW	2Lt			Calshot Apr'18. From RN
SYMMES, JA	2Lt			Vendome -Feb18.
TAYLOR, JW	2Lt			INJ -29Oct18. 115 IAF. Taylor-Forbes Co.
TAYLOR, MS	Capt	CdG	2-May-18	ACE -209RAF 'Fearless'. MIA 07Jul18
TEETZEL, HM	2Lt			Vendome -Mar18. Fm CADC
TEMPLE, WH	2Lt			43RAF -Aug18.
TEMPLETON, W	FSLt		23-Apr-11	Aviator. REL-1917 Sick Malta. **1929** -Vancouver Airport
THOM, G	Capt	AFC	2-May-19	Drowned -1924. AFC Jun'19 -INS Cranwell.
THOMPSON, HG	Lt	DFC	28-Jun-19	INJ/DFC -Caspian Sea. Army Col WW2 RCEME
THOMPSON, RE	2Lt		1-Oct-18	MIA Age 18. -80 RAF
TIDEY, AM	Capt	AFC	27-Dec-15	Obs -RNVR. Retrained Pilot Jan'17. AFC Jun'19
TINGLEY, AM	2Lt			53 TDS -Nov18. Fm CAMC
TODD, AS	FLt		4-Jan-17	MIA -Naval 8 -vonRichthofen's 16th&1st Cdn
TOMKINS, J	Lt			Nil Information
TRAPP, GL	Capt	MID	13-Nov-17	KIA -10Naval. ACE -28Sep17. ALL 3 Bros Killed
TRAPP, SV	FSLt		11-Dec-16	KIC -Naval 8. -Sister married Collishaw
TRELEAVEN, CW	PFO			Greenwich Feb'18
TUCKWELL, AW	PFO		20-Feb-18	REL - 'Poor Attitude'. From CEF-was WIA twice.
TURNEY, KV	FSLt		28-Sep-17	KIC -Midair - 4 Naval Camel
TWOHEY, WF	2Lt		3-Jul-18	KIC -Cranwell 205 TDS BE-2c.
TYLER, RC	Capt			Calshot Jul '17. 'Keen & Sound Instructor'
URQUHART, CG	2Lt			Greenwich Mar '18
URQUHART, HA	Lt			62 Wing Apr'18; 2N Wing '17
Van ALLEN, KM	FSLt		4-May-16	POW/DOW -5Wing
VANCE, JD	Lt	AFC	21-Jun-19	AFC -Flight to Egypt. INT'17 Holland. KIC'30
VAUGHAN, JFS	PFO			REL -1May17 Med Unfit. Money £75 returned
VENNING, RBN	PFO			REL -20Oct17 'Entirely unable theoretical.'
VETTER, EL	Capt			Uxbridge May'18
VEZINA, TD	2Lt			22 Group
VINCENT, FJ	Capt			HMS *Riviera*, Malta. Was PO Mechanic RNAS
WAAGE-MOTT, RWR	LtObs			KBO - Malta. Also shown as Mott.
WALKER, AH	Lt		14-Jan-18	DOJ. KBO - Malta. Clergyman -Ordained'14
WALKER, HH	2Lt		13-Jul-18	Flu -Died in Canada
WALKER, MB	CaptT			Malta'16. USA Duties'17. TechO Apr'18 RAF
WALKER, WR	FLt	MID	14-May-17	MIA/POW -3 Naval S.Pup

SURNAME	GIVEN NAMES	FROM	E	DOJ	P	
WALKEY	Roy Maunder	ON - Toronto		7-Jan-18		
WALLACE	Hazel LeRoy	AB -Lethbridge		9-Oct-16		
WALLACE	Hugh Douglas MacIntosh	ON - Blind River	T	3-Feb-16		
WALLACE	Nevil Hunter	ON - Comber		7-Jan-18		
WALLACE	William Ross	PQ - Westmount	S	7-Feb-16		
WALLER	Edward Bloomfield	ON - Toronto		8-Nov-15		
WALTON	Arthur McBurney	ON - Toronto	U	18-Aug-16		
WAMBOLT	Harry Redmond 'Hank'	NS - Dartmouth		1-Dec-15		
WARD	Walter Thomas	BC - Vancouver		12-Sep-17	N	
WARREN	Edward Dudley	MB - Winnipeg	S	9-Feb-18	C	
WASHINGTON	Frederic Paul Laurence	ON - Hamilton	T	7-Apr-16		
WATERHOUSE	Geo. Kerby	ON - Kingston		5-Oct-17	C	
WATSON	James Curtis	BC - Victoria		29-Oct-15		
WAUGH	John Keith	ON - Whitby	T	3-Nov-15		
WEBBER	Thomas William	ON - Toronto		30-Sep-15		
WEBSTER	Harold Leslie	PQ - Montreal		15-Dec-16		
WEIR	Charles Haddon	AB - Medicine Hat		26-Nov-16		
WEIR	Roderick McLean	ON - Toronto		21-Jan-16		
WELCH	Frederick Joseph	Manitoba		8-Dec-17	C	
WELCH	Herbert John	BC - Vancouver		23-Nov-17	C	
WELSH	Richard William	ON - Toronto		19-Oct-17	C	
WEMP	Herbert 'Bert' Sterling	ON - Tweed		1-Sep-15		
WHEALY	Arthur Treloar	ON - Toronto	T	29-Feb-16		
WHITAKER	Ronald Frank	Canadian b.ENG		17-Jan-18	C	
WHITE	Allan Geoffrey	BC - Victoria	S	7-Jan-18	C	
WHITE	James Butler	ON - Manitoulin Island		17-Feb-17	N	
WHITE	James Percy	MB - Winnipeg	M	7-Feb-16		
WHITFIELD	Roy Clark	ON - Hamilton		20-Dec-16		
WHITTIER	Douglas H.	BC - Victoria		6-Oct-15		
WICKENS	Percival	ON - Brockville b.ENG		22-Nov-16		
WILFORD	John Richard	ON - Lindsay	T	30-Dec-16		
WILKINSON	Kenneth Bruce	ON - Toronto	T	27-Jan-18	C	
WILKINSON	Thomas Cameron	PQ - St.Lambert		12-Feb-16		
WILKS	Arthur York	PQ - Westmount		29-Feb-16		
WILLIAMS	Arthur Henry	ON - Toronto		10-Jan-16		
WILLIAMS	George Knox	ON - Toronto	T	3-Sep-15	C	
WILLIAMS	Joseph Clarke	NS -Westchester		24-Jan-18		
WILSON	Elgin Edward	ON - Niagara Falls		19-Apr-17		
WILSON	Hugh Allen	PQ - Westmount	M	9-May-16		
WINDRUM	William (J.)	ON - Lindsay	S	5-Oct-17		
WINN	John Hilton	England		13-Mar-17		
WISER	Henry James	ON - Prescott		19-Jan-17		
WOOD	Frank 'Woody'	ON - Toronto	T	19-Apr-17	C	
WOOD	Lionel Eliner	MB - Winnipeg		21-Jul-17	C	
WOOD	Melville Cornelius	MB - Winnipeg	S	6-Dec-15		
WOODS	Arthur	ON - Elmira	S	19-Jan-17		

NAME	RANK	DEC	BOOK	Notes
WALKEY, RM	2Lt			HMS *Furious* & *Campania*.
WALLACE, HL	Capt	DFC	2-May-18	ACE -201 RAF. Was WIA -05Nov17 1Naval.
WALLACE, HDM	FSLt		7-Jun-17	KIC -1Naval. S.Triplane.
WALLACE, NH	Lt			Vendome Mar'18
WALLACE, WR	FSLt		20-Jul-16	KIA -Calshot. Died of Wounds
WALLER, EB	Capt		15-Nov-16	Force Lands -HP 3Wing. 215 RAF'18
WALTON, AM	FSLt			REL -1Aug17 -Discip Problem.
WAMBOLT, HR	FLt		4-Mar-17	KIA -3 Naval. Fell out at 6,000'
WARD, WT	2LtObs			REL -27Dec17 To OBS. Egypt HMS Engadine
WARREN, ED	2Lt		5-Dec-18	KIC -228 RAF.
WASHINGTON, FPL	Capt			63 Wing -Mudros.
WATERHOUSE, GK	Lt			63 Wing.
WATSON, GK	Capt		25-Sep-16	Ditched -Dunkirk. Felixstowe'17
WAUGH, JK	Major	DSC	25-Apr-16	FSLt. **20Aug18.** OC 241 RAF. KIC-Egypt '31
WEBBER, TW	PFSLt		23-Mar-16	REL - 'Unsuitable'. Becomes Instructor in Canada.
WEBSTER, HL	Capt			HP Bombers. Courtmartial for mail censor
WEIR, CH	FSLt		20-Aug-17	POW/Died of Wounds -10 Naval
WEIR, RM	PFSLt			REL -6Sep16 'Lack of keenness and control'
WELCH, FJ	PFO			REL -17Mar18 to RNVR TechO
WELCH, HJ	2Lt			RN College 7Nov18 Later MD?
WELSH, RW	Capt			Crash 19Jan18 -Vendome.
WEMP, HS	Major	DFC	19-Nov-15	Crash. **25Apr16** -Action. **3Jun18** -DFC. **1Jan30**
WHEALY, AT	Capt	DSC	7-Jul-17	ACE -3 Naval. **31Mar18** - DSC. +DFC+MID
WHITAKER, RF	PFO			Greenwich Jan'18. Fm Forestry Corps
WHITE, AG	Lt		29-Sep-18	KIA -211RAF Bombing Courtrai.
WHITE, JB	Capt	DFC	29-Jul-18	ACE - 208 RAF. Pres. Toronto Stock Exchange
WHITE, JP	FLt		4-Mar-17	KIA -3 Naval
WHITFIELD, RC	PFSLt		20-Dec-16	Last Curtiss Grad. REL '17 - Concussion/Neurasthenia
WHITTIER, DH	FSLt		20-Jul-16	KIC -3Wing. Bristol Scout attempting loop.
WICKENS, P	Capt	AFC		AFC -Calshot
WILFORD, JR	Capt		13-Sep-17	WIA/POW -1 Naval S.Triplane
WILKINSON, KB	2Lt		29-Oct-18	Recce -110 IAF
WILKINSON, TC	Capt			South Shields - Fall '16
WILKS, AY	Capt		16-Jul-16	Crash -Calshot. 2Wing 'F' Sqdn '17. 62 Wing '18
WILLIAMS, AH	2Lt		31-Oct-18	Last KIA -204RAF. REL & Rejoined RAF
WILLIAMS, GK	FSLt		10-Jun-16	KIC -MIDAIR 3Wing w/French machine.
WILLIAMS, JC	2Lt			J.C. Williams Tech Officer on RAF List
WILSON, EE	PFO			REL -02Aug17 'Refused any more ascents'
WILSON, HA	Capt	AFC		23 Group. +Russian Order of SteAnne.
WINDRUM, WJ	Lt	MID		MID -01Jan19. Saskatchewan aviation pioneer 1920s
WINN, JH	FSLt		20-Sep-17	KIA -1Naval. Bank of Montreal in England
WISER, HJ	Capt	DFC		63Wing Aegean DFC 3Dec18
WOOD, F	Lt	CdG		AdriaticGp, 6Wing'17; CdG Italy. Later DS
WOOD, LE	Lt			HMS *Pegasus* &*Argus*.
WOOD, MC	FLt		9-Oct-17	KIC -Cyprus, HMS *Empress*. Landing Accident
WOODS, A	Lt			70 Wing 7Nov18

SURNAME	GIVEN NAMES	FROM	E	DOJ	P	
WOODS	Leslie Neville Wilmot	Canadian Forces b.ENG		19-Oct-17	C	
WOODWARD	Arthur Gerald	BC - Victoria	M	6-Nov-15		
WOODWARD	Arthur Hill	Canadian Forces b.ENG		30-May-17	C	
WOOLER	Geo Richard Davidson	Canadian		5-Aug-16	C	
WORTHINGTON	Lancelot Patrick	AB - Westerdale		8-Jan-18	C	
WRIGHT	Douglas Ross Cameron	BC - New Westminster		21-Oct-16	N	
WRIGHT	Frederick Wm.	ON - Tottenham	T	18-Dec-17		
WYATT	Charles Joshua	ON - Mt Bryges b.ENG		6-Dec-15		
YATES	Harold Wesley	ON - Mitchell		7-Feb-17		
YATES	Harry Alexander	ON - Ingersoll	U	19-Jan-17		
YEATES	Ralph Howard	Canadian		9-Feb-16	C	
YOUNG	Alexander McBain	BC - Prince Rupert		27-Sep-16		
YOUNG	Clarence Earl	ON - Kingston	S	16-Mar-18	C	

CL Bailey

UCC

RN Ball

RAeC Trust

EL Biggar

U of T

ES Campbell

Paul Donnellan

RA Campbell

RAeC Trust

JG Harvie

U of T

NAME	RANK	DEC	BOOK	Notes
WOODS, LNW	2Lt			Served in France w/Cdn Cavalry.
WOODWARD, AG	Capt		**1-Apr-16**	Crash. Later 2Wing. Salonica/Dardanelles
WOODWARD, AH	FSLt			HP W/T Cranwell & WEE Hendon
WOOLER, GRD	Lieut		**15-Aug-17**	KIA - 5th Bttn CEF. REL -17Nov16 -Tried 2x to rejoin
WORTHINGTON, LP	2Lt			WIA -15Sep18 204 RAF
WRIGHT, DRC	SLt		**15-Nov-16**	OBS RNVR. To Pilot. **23Dec17** -KIA 10 Naval
WRIGHT, FW	2Lt			212 RAF. Overcame Neurthesia. INS Later MD
WYATT, CJ	FLt		**21-Aug-17**	KIC -2 Naval. DH-4 Crash Landing Dunkirk
YATES, HW	Lt T		**7-Feb-17**	INJ - to RNVR as Tech O. REL Dec'17
YATES, HA	Lt	AFC	**21-Jun-19**	AFC -Lawrence Flight Egypt 58RAF. Later MD
YEATES, RH	PFSLt			REL -7Aug16 to SLt RNVR Hermione Greenwich
YOUNG, AM	FSLt			REL -20Oct17. 3 Crashes, Lost Confidence
YOUNG, CE	2Lt		**10-Nov-18**	KIC -CFS. Last RNAS Course 24Mar18.

CJ Poulin

RAeC Trust

VT Sharpe

U of T

LR Shoebottom

U of T

JA Simmers

U of T

KY Sinclair

U of T

WJ Windrum

Windrum Family

APPENDIX B:

RNAS PROBATIONARY FLIGHT OFFICERS TRANSFERRED TO RFC

From Public Records Office Ledger ADM/273 RNAS Officers February to April 1916:

'Canadians entered as Temp'y Pro Flt Officers & App'td "President" Add'l for RNAS as from dates shewn against their names to 09Apr17 Inclusive, From which date their App'mts Terminate on Transfer to RFC'

Baker, Albert Nathaniel; Rodney ON
– 73RAF; KIA 25Apr18

Barbeau, Victor A

Bisonette, Charles Arthur

Boland, Lloyd Winton; Ottawa

Bradner, Leighton Stuart; Westmount PQ
– WIA 06Nov17

Bryant, Harry E

Buck, Stanley Ernest – 52 RAF

Bulmer, George William; Toronto
– 22 RAF, MC

Cameron, William Harold; Shelburne ON

Campbell, William Alexander; Durham ON

Chapdelaine, Aime; Ottawa

Chapman, John Wm; London ON – 49 RAF

Charron, Leo Rosario; Ottawa – 49 RAF

Clements, Wilbert Norman; Calgary

Cote, Joseph Arthur Robert; Levis PQ
– 46RAF; RIP FLU 28Oct18

Crossau, Ernest Percy

Cunningham, James Nelson
– 56 RAF; KIA 19Oct18

Cunningham, Micheal F
– 27RAF; KIA 06Jun18

Davidson, Joseph Jocelyn; Humber Bay ON

Davies, Harold Edgar; Toronto
– 84 RFC; POW 13Jan18

Dickie, Edward Gordon; Chatham ON
– 84 RFC; KIA 30Nov17

Dow, Alan Gladstone; Ottawa
– 63TDS; KIC 17Aug17

Drummond, John E

Durant, Wilfred Ellis; Chesterville ON
– 29RAF; KIA 02Jul18

WE Durant

U of T

Ferguson, John Alvin Arthur; Unionville ON
– 62 RAF; WIA/POW13Mar18
– RIP 27Oct20 in Toronto

Firby, George A

Gould, Walter Harvey Russell; Uxbridge ON
– 70 RFC; KIA 26Sep17

Gray, George Robert 'Robin'; Victoria BC
  – 84 RFC; POW/DOW 31Oct17

GR Gray

Bill & Robbie Hughes

Holcombe, Cecil H; St AnneDeBelv. PQ

Irwin, William Roy 'Sambo'; Ripley ON
  – 56 RAF; ACE 10Aug18, DFC&Bar

Johnson, George Owen; Woodstock ON
  – 84 RAF; ACE 18Mar18, MC, CdGaE
  – Air Vice Marshal

Johnston, Byron Sydney; Courtright ON
  – 60 RAF

Kilbourne, Watson Hector; Winnipeg
  – 57 RAF; POW 16Aug18

Lauriers, Joseph Leo D

Leduc, John-Charles Romauld; Montreal
  – 63 TDS; KIC 07Nov17

Lick, Cecil Haverlock; Davidson SK
  – 203 RAF; WIAx2

Little, Robert Hazen; Teulon MB

Lyon, Henry Alva; Ottawa

Macfarland, Foster M

Magill James J

McArthur, Clarence V

McCormick, Roy M

McCormick, William G

McCracken, Edward CJ

McDonald, Hugh J

McLean, Donald Gordon
  – KIA 04Feb18

McLintock, John Lawrie; Toronto
  – 19 RFC; KIA 29Feb18

McRae, Daniel A

Moore, Orville A

Morton, Edward Basil Gowan; Barrie ON
  – 98 RAF; KIA 16Jul18

Mulvaney, John B.

Nethercott, Fred A

Niverville, Albert

Noyes, Gerald Haighton; London ON

O'Loughlin, John J

Phillips, Joseph L

Primeau, Cecil W

Robinson, Charles W

Ryan, Richard W

Scobie, Cadwell G

Stuart, William Grey; Calgary
  – From RNWMP; WIA 13Dec17

Tempest, Paul V

Thompson, David Stuart, Canfield ON

Thompson, Herbert E

Turner, Harold W

Waddell, Samuel Percival; Britton ON

Watts, Henry J

Wilson, Frank K

Windover, William E
  – 110 RAF; POW 21Oct18

In total, sixty-nine RNAS Probationary Flight
Officers are transferred.

APPENDIX C:

RNAS · Died On Active Service · By Date

RNAS

1915

12Sep	JM Alexander	KIC
19Sep	DA Hay	MIA
18Nov	JT Bone	KIA

1916

10Jan	GE Duke	KIC
16Jan	CN Somerville	DOS
15Feb	HJ Page	MIA
27Apr	AJ Boddy	KIC
30Apr	TR Liddle	KIC
04May	KM vanAllen	POW/DOW
10Jun	GK Willliams	KIC
20Jul	DH Whittier	KIC
21Jul	WR Wallace	WIA/DOW
20Sep	JD Scott	KIC
26Sep	PS Kennedy	KIC
12Nov	FAR Malet	KIA
04Dec	CT Brimer	MIA
11Dec	SV Trapp	KIC

1917

04Jan	AS Todd	MIA
14Jan	WH Peberdy	MIA
06Feb	FH Mitchell	POW/DOS
25Feb	LE Smith	KIA
04Mar	HR Wambolt	KIA
04Mar	JP White	KIA
24Mar	WS Oliver	KIC
30Mar	JM Ingham	KIA
15Apr	JL Lavigne	KIC
17Apr	GRS Fleming	POW/DOW
20Apr	DH Masson	K IA
24Apr	RE Bush	KIC
30Apr	AE Cuzner	KIA
30Apr	JJ Malone	MIA
01May	HE Grundy	KIC
01May	ED Roach	KIA
15May	GG Avery	MIA
26May	CL Haines	KIA
02Jun	AC Dissette	KIA
02Jun	WE Orchard	WIA/DOW
03Jun	PG McNeil	MIA

04Jun	WW Pitt	KIC
07Jun	HDM Wallace	KIC
11Jun	JR Bibby	KIC
12Jun	LFW Smith	KIA
13Jun	TR Shearer	KIC
14Jun	LH Parker	MIA
19Jun	JE Potvin	MIA
22Jun	HL Crowe	KIC
23Jun	JN McAllister	KIC
05Jul	HJ Flynn	KIC
06Jul	H Allan	KIC
12Jul	SE Ellis	KIC
17Jul	FM Bryans	KIC
17Jul	DH Daly	KIC
21Jul	GG MacLennan	KIA
22Jul	JA Page	KIA
22Jul	JE Sharman	KIA
24Jul	TC May	MIA
28Jul	AJ Chadwick	MIA
28Jul	EV Reid	MIA
14Aug	RE Bray	KIC
15Aug	GRW Wooler	KIA with CEF
17Aug	AG Dow	Drowned (RFC)
17Aug	FS Strathy	KIA
19Aug	TL Glasgow	KIC
20Aug	L Code	KIC
21Aug	AI Hutty	KIC
21Aug	CH Weir	MIA
21Aug	CJ Wyatt	KIC
03Sep	GBG Scott	MIA
14Sep	AA Bishop	KIC
19Sep	EVJ Grace	MIA
19Sep	JH Winn (ENG)	KIA
22Sep	KV Turney	KIC
26Sep	WHR Gould	KIA with RFC
30Sep	WJ Beattie	KIC
09Oct	MC Wood	MIA
18Oct	MF Cunningham	KIA with RFC
24Oct	JEC Hough	MIA
27Oct	GH Morang	MIA
31Oct	GR Gray	POW/DOW with RFC
03Nov	JA StJames	KIC
07Nov	JCR Leduc	KIC with RFC
11Nov	DR Kerr	KIC

13Nov	GL Trapp	KIA
22Nov	RG MacAloney	MIA
30Nov	EG Dickie	KIA with RFC
09Dec	NJ Larter	MIA
12Dec	JL Moran	KIC
16Dec	J Gorman	KIC
19Dec	SS Richardson	MIA
23Dec	DRC Wright	KIA
25Dec	FC Cressman	MIA

1918

04Jan	AJ Dixon	KIA
07Jan	CR Barber	KIC
20Jan	W Johnston	MIA
22Jan	CE Burden	KIC
22Jan	HT Coo	KIC
23Jan	RA Blyth	KIA
25Jan	JG Scott	Flu
04Feb	DG MacLean	KIA with RFC
15Feb	CCW Purdy	MIA
23Feb	HM Reid	KIC
29Feb (RFC)	JL McLintock	KIA
10Mar	AWG Crosby	DOI
11Mar	CG MacDonald	KIA
20Mar	HJ Arnold	KIC
20Mar	CC Franklin	KIC
22Mar	WA Moyle	MIA
22Mar	LA Sands	MIA
25Mar	FC Armstrong	KIA
28Mar	JG Carroll	MIA

RNAS amalgamation to RAF

01Apr	OP Adam	KIA
01Apr	FE Banbury	KIC
02Apr	CE Pattison	KIC
12Apr	JR Allan	KIA
21Apr	DL Bawlf	KIC
25Apr	GA Magor	POW/DOW
25Apr	NA Magor	MIA
25Apr	AN Baker	KIA with RFC
25Apr	SW Rosevear	KIA
02May	WH Robinson	KIC
08May	R McDonald	MIA
10May	GF Ross	KIA with RNVR

18May	JM Johnston	KIC		23Aug	JP Hales	KIA
03Jun	WS Durant	KIA		29Aug	PH Goodhugh	KIA
		with RFC		03Sep	FA Huycke	MIA
06Jun	JN Cunningham	KIA		05Sep	HWM Cumming	KIC
		with RFC		05Sep	HA Sutherland	KIC
09Jun	WF Salton	KIC		20Sep	MG Cruise	KIA
10Jun	JG Manuel	KIC		25Sep	RV Gordon	KIA
13Jun	GM Scott	KIA		25Sep	JC Sorley	KIA
21Jun	WSG Baker	KIC		26Sep	WB Craig	KIA
26Jun	JW Dowling	KIC		26Sep	GEC Howard	KIA
29Jul	HJ Elliott	KIA		26Sep	WJ Kelly	KIC
02Jul	WE Durant	KIA		26Sep	OL Malcom	KIA
		with RFC		28Sep	AM Stevens	MIA
02Jul	AM Sutherland	KIA		28Sep	BH Stata	KIC
03Jul	WF Twohey	KIC		29Sep	PH Goodhugh	POW/
07Jul	MS Taylor	MIA				DOW
08Jul	C Homewood	KIC		29Sep	AG White	KIA
13Jul	EF Kerruish	KIC		30Sep	FR Reid	KIA
13Jul	HH Walker	Flu		01Oct	RE Thompson	MIA
15Jul	GP Armstrong	KIC		02Oct	WF Cleghorn	KIA
16Jul	EBG Morton	KIA		03Oct	CRR Hickey	KIA
		with RFC		07Oct	HD Lackey	KIA
18Jul	JGM Farrall	MIA		14Oct	JE Greene	KIA
20Jul	CW Lott	KIA		14Oct	WT Owen	MIA
24Jul	FA Cash	KIC		19Oct	WV Bedwell	Flu
25Jul	GB McSweeny	KIC				with RCNAS
25Jul	RW Robinson	KIA		23Oct	OJ Orr	KIA
05Aug	ER Munday	MIA		28Oct	JAR Cote	Flu
10Aug	SA Dawson	MIA				with RFC
10Aug	JE Gow	DOW		31Oct	LN Bissell	KIC
		(from 31Jul)		31Oct	AH Williams	KIA
19Aug	CE Sherlock	KIC		02Nov	RW Johnson	Flu
22Aug	JB Cunningham	KIC		10Nov	CE Young	KIC
23Aug	JP Corkery	KIC				

POSTWAR to 1922

12Nov18	DP Brennan	Flu
12Nov18	ST Edwards	KIC
18Nov18	RK Little	KIC
21Nov18	AM McElhinney	KIC
05Dec18	ED Warren	KIC
19Dec18	TB Simpson	KIC
16Feb19	CV Clarke	KIC
18Feb19	JH Brown	Flu
13Mar19	ER Percival	Flu
17Mar19	CM LeMoine	KIC
02May19	GA Gooderham	Drowned
25Aug19	D MacDougall	Killed
28Sep19	CH Darley	KIC
23Jan20	EW Berry	DOS
18Dec20	JFJ Kieran	DOS
29Mar21	DMB Galbraith	Crash
06Apr22	C MacLaurin	KIC

Total Numbers:

August 4, 1914 to November 11, 1918: 179

(1915: 3, 1916: 14, 1917: 72, 1918: 90)

Immediate Postwar Period: 17

Total Losses: 196

Final stanza, 'On a Memorial Stone'
By Archibald MacLeish

...And generations unfulfilled,
The heirs of all we struggled for,
Shall here recall the mythic war,
And marvel how we stabbed and killed,
And name us savage, brave, austere, –
And none shall think how very young we were.

APPENDIX D:

Decoration and Medal Awards

I. ROYAL NAVY AWARDS

CBE – Commander, Order of the British Empire

01Jan19	Colonel RH Mulock, DSO&Bar

OBE – Officer, Order of the British Empire

03Jun19	Major (Technical) AR Layard
12Jul20	Major R Collishaw, DSO&Bar, DSC, DFC

MBE – Member, Order of the British Empire

03Jun19	Capt AW Carter, DSC
22Dec19	Capt NG Fraser, AFC

DSO&B – Bar to Distinguished Service Order

26Apr18	WCdr RH Mulock, DSO
21Sep18	T/Major R Collishaw, DSO, DSC

DSO – Distinguished Service Order

08Dec15	FSLt HJ Arnold
22Jun16	A/FCdr RH Mulock
23May17	FSLt JJ Malone
20Jul17	FLt BD Hobbs, DSC
08Nov17	FCdr R Collishaw, DSC
17Nov17	FCdr PS Fisher, DSC
01Jan18	FCdr AM Shook, DSC
17May18	FCdr R Leckie, DSC
11Aug18	Lt SD Culley

DSC&2B – 2nd Bar to Distinguished Service Cross

19Dec17	FCdr JST Fall, DSC&Bar
19Dec17	FCdr TD Hallam, DSC&Bar

DSC&B – 1st Bar to Distinguished Service Cross

16Feb17	FLt DMB Galbraith, DSC
22Jun17	FCdr TD Hallam, DSC
11Aug17	FLt JE Sharman, DSC
30Nov17	FLt BD Hobbs, DSO, DSC
19Dec17	FCdr JST Fall, DSC
16Mar18	FCdr WA Curtis, DSC
17Apr18	FCdr CH Darley, DSC
17Apr18	FLt SW Rosevear, DSC
07Jun18	FLt JA Gleln, DSC
21Jun18	Capt AR Brown, DSC
21Jun18	Capt ST Edwards, DSC
21Jun18	Capt AT Whealy, DSC

DSC for RNVR Service – Attached RNAS

15Dec15	Lt TD Hallam

DSC – Distinguished Service Cross (48)

24Feb16	FSLt AS Ince
25Oct16	FSLt DMB Galbraith
16Feb17	FLt ER Grange
21Apr17	SLt CK Chase
12May17	FSLt PS Fisher
12May17	FSLt WE Flett
12May17	FSLt DAH Nelles
12May17	FSLt JE Sharman
23May17	FLt LS Breadner
23May17	FSLt JST Fall
22Jun17	FSLt HG Boswell
22Jun17	FSLt JRS Devlin
22Jun17	FSLt FE Fraser
22Jun17	FSLt BD Hobbs
22Jun17	FSLt R Leckie
22Jun17	FSLt C McNicholl
22Jul17	FLt R Collishaw
22Jul17	FLt GD Smith
11Aug17	FLt AJ Chadwick
11Aug17	FSLt EV Reid
11Aug17	FLt CH Darley
11Aug17	FCdr AM Shook
11Aug17	FSLt LFW Smith
28Aug17	FSLt JR Allan
29Aug17	FLt AW Carter
14Sep17	FCdr WM Alexander
14Sep17	FLt JO Galpin
01Oct17	FCdr C MacLaurin
01Nov17	FSLt CB Sproatt
02Nov17	FLt AR Brown
02Nov17	FCdr ST Edwards
02Nov17	FLt HS Kerby
17Nov17	FCdr GE Herveyt
17Nov17	FSLt FR Johnson
17Nov17	FSLt SW Rosevear
30Nov17	FCdr FC Armstrong
19Dec17	FLt WA Curtis
19Dec17	FLt NA Magor
19Dec17	FSLt JG Manuel
22Jan18	FLt RD Delamere
22Feb18	FLt JF Chisholm
22Feb18	FSLt RM Keirstead
26Apr18	FLt JA Glen
01May18	FLt FS Mills
01May18	FLt KF Saunders
26Apr18	FCdr FE Banbury
26Apr18	FLt AT Whealy
01May18	FCdr JK Waugh

II ROYAL AIR FORCE AWARDS

DFC&Bar – 1st Bar to Distinguished Flying Cross

02Nov18	Capt CRR Hickey, DFC

DFC – Distnguished Flying Cross RAF (44)

03Jun18	Lt CV Bessette
03Jun18	Capt HH Gonyon
03Jun18	Lt JE Green
03Jun18	Lt GC MacKay
03Jun18	Capt AH Pearce
03Jun18	Capt J Robinson, MIDx2
03Jun18	Capt HS Wemp
02Jul18	Capt CH Darley, DSC&B
02Jul18	Capt JH Forman
02Jul18	Lt LR Shoebottom
03Aug18	Capt WF Cleghorn
03Aug18	Major R Collishaw, DSC&B
03Aug18	Lt CRR Hickey
01Sep18	Capt R Leckie, DSO DSC
21Sep18	Capt S Anderson
21Sep18	Capt JF Chisholm, DSC
21Sep18	Lt Obs LA Christian
21Sep18	Capt JO Galpin, DSC
21Sep18	Capt JL Gordon
02Nov18	2Lt AM Anderson
02Nov18	2Lt WB Craig
02Nov18	Lt GA Flavelle
02Nov18	Capt HM Ireland
02Nov18	Lt WMJ Peace
02Nov18	Lt AM Phillips
02Nov18	Capt HL Wallace
03Dec18	Lt BE Barnum
03Dec18	Capt JB White
03Dec18	Capt AT Whealy, DSC&B
01Jan19	Capt DM Ballantyne
01Jan19	Capt CJ Clayton, MIDx2
01Jan19	Lt AS Girling
01Jan19	Lt JD Guild
01Jan19	Capt WR Kenny
01Jan19	2Lt D MacDougall
01Jan19	Lt EF McIlraith
01Jan19	Lt FM McLennan
01Jan19	Lt DF Murray
01Jan19	2Lt OJ Orr
01Jan19	Capt ECR Stoneman, SM (Italy)
01Jan19	Capt HJ Wiser
03Jun19	Capt WB Lawson
03Jun19	Capt WJ MacKenzie
08Feb19	Lt JR Smith, CdG
22Dec19	Lt FR Bicknell, MID
22Dec19	2Lt HG Thompson

AFC – Air Force Cross RAF (27)

02Nov18	Capt KG Boyd, MID
02Nov18	Lt S Graham
02Nov18	Capt GR Hodgson
02Nov18	Capt JG Ireland
02Nov18	Lt AB Massey
02Nov18	Capt AC Reid
02Nov18	Lt RR Richardson
02Nov18	Capt KF Saunders, DSC
02Nov18	Capt HA Wilson
01Jan19	Capt E Anthony
01Jan19	Capt JST Fall, DSC&2Bars
01Jan19	Capt NG Fraser
01Jan19	Capt JH Keens
01Jan19	Major HS Kerby, DSC
01Jan19	Capt JS Maitland
01Jan19	Capt P Wickens
08Feb19	Lt LE Best
03Jun19	Capt JRS Devlin, DSC
03Jun19	Lt RT Eyre
03Jun19	Major WH MacKenzie
03Jun19	Lt FH Prime
03Jun19	Major AM Shook, DSO, DSC
03Jun19	Capt G Thom
03Jun19	Capt AM Tidey
21Jun19	Capt JD Vance
21Jun19	Capt AH Yates
10Oct19	F/O GH Boyce

III FOREIGN AWARDS

Although not listed here it is notable that RNAS Canadians garnered a fair number of Decorations from grateful Allied nations.

The largest number of non-British awards was from France. These ranged from over two-dozen Croix de Guerre medals up to a Chevalier, Legion D'Honneur. Both Belgium and Italy also awarded their Cd'G's to Canadians along with other decorations and Imperial Russia gave out some of the last of her Czarist Orders.

APPENDIX E:

SENIOR OFFICERS

RNAS AIRMEN WHO ROSE TO SENIOR COMMAND
1919 TO 1953

CAF – Canadian Air Force 1919-1923
WCdr RF Redpath, OC CAF 1921

RCAF – Royal Canadian Air Force 1923-1939
AVM JL Gordon, CAS 1932-33   CAHF*
ACmdr RH Mulock   CAHF*

Royal Canadian Navy 1939-1945
Commander HG Nares

Canadian Army 1939-1945
Col B H Bryers, Toronto Scottish
LtCol CT Sharpe, Lorne Scots
Col HG Thompson, RCEME

RAF – Royal Air Force 1939-1945
ACmdr GH Boyce
GCapt HS Broughall
ACmdr EI Bussell
AVM R Collishaw   CAHF*
GCapt SD Culley
GCapt JST Fall
AVM HS Kerby
ACmdr AJ Rankin

RCAF – Royal Canadian Air Force 1940-1967
ACM L Breadner, CAS 1940-43
AirM AW Carter
ACmdr HG Clappiston
AVM ATN Cowley
AirM WA Curtis, CAS 1948-53   CAHF*
AirM H Edwards, AOC RCAF O'Seas 1941-43
GCapt DD Findlay
WCdr RW Frost
GCapt BD Hobbs   CAHF*
GCapt JG Ireland
AVM GO Johnston
GCapt JH Keens
AirVM WR Kenny
GCapt AR Layard
AirM R Leckie, CAS 1944-47   CAHF*
GCapt GO Lightbourn
ACmdr EL MacLeod
AVM FS McGill
AVM EE Middleton
WCdr AH Munday
GCapt GE Nash
GCapt WMJ Peace
ACmdr AHK Russell
AVM AB Shearer
WCdr FH Smith
WCdr GT Steeves

Plus Emigrated to Canada Post-WWI
AVM EW Steadman,   CAHF*

RANKS
ACM	Air Chief Marshal
AirM	Air Marshal
AVM	Air Vice Marshal
ACmdr	Air Commodore
Col	Colonel
GCapt	Group Captain
Cdr	Commander
LtCol	Lieutenant Colonel
WCdr	Wing Commander

APPOINTMENTS
CAS	Chief of Air Staff
AOC	Air Officer Commanding
OC	Officer Commanding

"A true leader is one who takes a genuine joy in the accomplishments of his people."
Anon

*Named to the Canadian Aviation Hall of Fame

APPENDIX F:

FIGHTER ACES

THE CANADIAN NAVAL ACES OF THE FIRST WORLD WAR BY DATE OF THEIR FIFTH VICTORY

5th Victory Date / Name / Total / Notes

1916			
21May16	Mulock, RH	5	
16Nov16	Galbraith, DMB	6	
1917			
07Jan17	Grange, ER	5	
23Apr17	Breadner, LS	10	
23Apr17	Fall, JST	36	
28Apr17	Collishaw, R	60	
21Apr17	Malone, JJ	10	(KIA)
02May17	Wallace, HLeR	14	
05May17	Taylor, MS	7	(KIA)
06May17	Kerby, HS	9	
25May17	Smith, LFW	8	(KIA)
27May17	Carter, AW	17	
05Jun17	Shook, AM	12	
03Jun17	Chadwick, AJ	11	(KIC)
06Jun17	Nash, GE	6	(POW)
14Jun17	Sharman, JE	6	(KIA)
06Jul17	Alexander, WM	23	
06Jul17	Reid, EV	19	(KIA)
07Jul17	Armstrong, FC	13	(KIC)
07Jul17	Ellis, SE	5	(KIA)
07Jul17	Glen, JA	15	
07Jul17	Page, JA	7	(KIA)
07Jul17	Whealy, AT	27	
25Jul17	Mott, HE	5	
27Jul17	McDonald, R	8	(KIA)
13Sep17	Banbury, FE	11	(KIC)
23Sep17	Edwards, ST	17	(KIC)
24Sep17	Keirstead, RM	13	
28Sep17	Trapp, GL	6	(KIA)
13Oct17	Brown, AR	10	
17Oct17	Rosevear, SW	25	(KIA)
21Oct17	Curtis, WA	13	
21Oct17	Spence, AGA	9	

5th Victory Date / Name / Total / Notes

1918			
23Jan18	Anderson, GB	5	
18Feb18	Manuel, JG	13	(KIA)
12Mar18	MacKay, GC	18	
16Mar18	Chisham, WH	7	
18Mar18	Johnson, GO (RFC)	11	
12Apr18	Foreman, JH	9	(POW)
21Apr18	Hickey, CRR	21	(KIA)
21Apr18	LeBoutillier, OC	10	
11May18	Greene, JE	15	(KIA)
18May18	Fowler, HHS	6	
27Jun18	Little, RH	5	
13Jul18	Brock, CG	6	
22Jul18	Bawlf, LD	5	
28Jul18	Christian, LA (Obs)	9	
29Jul18	White, JB	12	
10Aug18	Irwin, WR (RFC)	11	
11Aug18	Hales, JP	5	(KIA)
16Sep18	Craig, WB	8	(KIA)
14Oct18	Orr, OJ	5	(KIA)
30Oct18	Clappiston, HG	6	

53 Aces, scoring 635 Victories for a loss of 20 Killed

Three British subjects living in Canada pre-War and who returned directly to join the RNAS:

03Jul17	–Eyre, CA	6	(KIA)
06Dec17	– Ridley, CB	11	
08Mar18	–Findlay, MH	14	

In what distant deeps or skies
Burnt the fire of thine eyes?
On what wings dare he aspire?
What the hand dare seize the fire?

The Tyger
William Blake

BIBLIOGRAPHY

There exists a unique challenge writing a book such as this: Namely—Too Many Rabbit Trails. The subject is so vast and absorbing that one spends days (and nights) delving into detailed areas that, in the end, have little to do with the search for a particular character. Used bookstores are treasure houses that cannot be bypassed; journals must be read, stray articles are to be devoured (a Botterell Rum and Ginger assists the digestion). Below are some of these delights:

Books specifically by or about RNAS Canadians:

Collishaw, Raymond with R.V. Dodds. *Air Command: A Fighter Pilot's Story.* London, Kimber 1973. Republished in Canada by CEF Books 2008 as: *The Black Flight*

Costello, W. Brian (Mayor). *A Nursery of the Air Force: Carleton Place Airmen.* Canada, Forest Beauty 1979

Edwards, Suzanne K. *Gus: From Trapper Boy to Air Marshal.* Renfrew, ON, General Store 2007.

Hallam, T. Douglas. *The Spider Web: The Romance of a Flying Boat Flight, by PIX* (pseudo.) Edinburgh, Blackwell 1919

Houghton, George W. *They Flew Through Sand,* (Collishaw in the Western Desert). Cairo, Schindler 1942

Pettit, Brian. *Saturday's Hero.* Nanaimo BC, Waratha Press 2001

Smith, Guy Duncan. *The Aerial Crusader.* Oakland CA, GD Smith, DSC, (Self-Published) 1919

Smyth, Ross. *The Lindbergh of Canada: The Erroll Boyd Story.* Ontario, General Store Publishing 1997

Canadian Chronologies & Compendiums:

Bank of Montreal. *Memorial of the Great War. 1914–1918: A Record of Service.* Canada, Printed Privately 1921

Canadian Bank of Commerce. *Letters from the Front, Vol I & II. Being a Record of the Part Played by Officers of the Bank in the Great War 1914–1918.* Toronto, Privately Printed 1920-21

Carroll, Warren. *Eagles Recalled: Air Force Wings of Canada, Great Britain and the British Commonwealth 1913–1945.* Atglen PA, Schiffer Military History 1997

Cooke, OA. *The Canadian Military Experience 1867–1967: A Bibliography.* Ottawa, Minister of Supply & Services 1979

Douglas W.A.B. *The Creation of a National Air Force: The Official History of the Royal Canadian Air Force Volume II.* Ottawa, Minister of Supply and Services Canada 1986

Ellis, Frank H. *Canada's Flying Heritage.* Toronto, University of Toronto Press 1954

Fuller, Griffin & Molson. *125 Years Of Canadian Aeronautics 1840–1965.* Willowdale ON, Canadian Aviation Historical Society, Best Printing 1983

Halliday, Hugh A
Chronology of Canadian Military Aviation. Ottawa, Canadian War Museum 1975; and, *Not in the Face of the Enemy,* Toronto, Robin Brass Studio 2000.

Mathieson William D. *My Grandfather's War, Canadians Remember the First World War, 1914–1918.* Toronto, Macmillan 1981

McGill Honour Roll 1914-1918. Montreal, McGill University 1926

Nicholson, G.W.L. *Canadian Expeditionary Force 1914-1919: Official History of the Canadian Army in the First World War.* Ottawa, Queen's Printer 1962

Nelson, K.J. *The Royal Air Force Awards 1918 – 1919.* Canada, Kenneth James Nelson CD 2000

Oswald Mary E (Editor). *They Led the Way, Canada's Aviation Hall of Fame Members.* Wetaskiwin, Alberta 1999

Payne, Stephen (Editor). ***Canadian Wings,*** *A Remarkable Century of Flight.* Vancouver, Canadian Aviation Museum, Douglas & McIntyre 2009

Roll of Service 1914-1918. G. Oswald Smith (Editor). University of Toronto, 1921

Wise, Sydney F. ***Canadian Airmen and the First World War.*** *The Official History of the Royal Canadian Air Force Volume I.* Ottawa, Minister of Supply and Services Canada, 1980

Young AB (Editor): ***War Book of Upper Canada College.*** Toronto, Printers Guild Ltd, 1923

Selected Bibliography:

ADMIRALTY. ***Naval Air Service training manual, November 1914.*** London: HMSO, 1915

Aten, Marion. ***Last Train Over Rostov Bridge.*** (Collishaw in Russia). New York, Julian Messner 1961

Balfour, Harold. ***An Airman Marches,*** *Early Flying Adventures 1914-1923.* Aeolus, Greenhill 1985

Baring, Maurice. ***RFC HQ, 1914–1918***. London, Bell 1920

Bartlett CPO. ***In the Teeth of the Wind,*** *a Naval Pilot on the Western Front 1916–1918.* London, Barlett, Nick (Editor), Cooper 1974. Also published as ***Bomber Pilot 1916–1918***

Bashow, David L. ***Knights of the Air,*** *Canadian Fighter Pilots in the First Air War.* Toronto, McArthur 2000

Bell–Davies, Richard (VC). ***Sailor in the Air.*** London, Peter Davies 1967

Bewsher, Paul ***Green Balls,*** *The Adventures of a Night-Bomber.* Aeolus, Greenhill 1986

Bickers, Richard Townsend. ***The First Great Air War.*** London, Hodder & Stoughton 1988.

Bishop, William Arthur. ***Courage In the Air,*** *Canada's Military Heritage.* Whitby ON, McGraw-Hill Ryerson 1992

Boutilier, James A. ***RCN in Retrospect, 1910–1968.*** University of British Columbia Press 1982

Brown, Dave. ***Faces of War.*** Canada, General Store Publishing House 1998

Carpenter Alfred (VC). ***The Blocking of Zeebrugge.*** Plymouth, Mayflower Press 1921

Chatterton, E. Keble. ***Severn's Saga,*** *The Konigsberg Adventure.* Plymouth, Mayflower Press 1938

Cooksley, Peter G. ***The RFC/RNAS Handbook 1914-18.*** England, Sutton 2000

Corley-Smith. ***Barnstorming to Bush Flying***, *BC's Aviation Pioneers.* Victoria BC, Sono Nis 1989

Cronin, Dick. ***Royal Navy shipboard aircraft developments 1912-1931.*** Tonbridge, Kent, Air Britain 1990

Dick, Ron and Dan Patterson. ***The Early Years,*** *Aviation Century.* Canada, Boston Mills 2003

Draper, Christopher. ***The Mad Major.*** *Autobiography, Major C. Draper, DSC.* England, Air View 1962

Flight Lieutenant (pseud.) ***Hints for Flight Sub Lieutenants, RNAS.*** London, 1916

Fredette, Raymond H. ***The First Battle of Britain 1917–1918.*** London, Cassell 1966

Gamble, C.F. Snowden. ***The Story of a North Sea Air Station.*** Oxford University Press 1928

Gardam, Colonel John, OMM, CD. ***Seventy Years After 1914-1984***. Stittsville ON, Canada's Wings 1983

Gardiner, Ian. ***The Flatpack Bombers***, *The Royal Navy & the Zeppelin Menace.* England, Pen & Sword 2009

German, Tony. ***The Sea is at Our Gates***, *The History of the Canadian Navy.* Toronto, McLennan & Stewart 1990

Gibson, Mary. ***Warneford VC.*** Yeovilton, Friends of the Fleet Air Arm Museum 1979

Gray, Larry. ***We Are the Dead***, *Carleton Place Losses First World War.* Burnstown ON, General Store 2000

Granatstein JL. ***Who Killed Canadian History?*** Toronto, Harper Collins, 1998

Greenhous Brererton. **A Rattle of Pebbles,** *WWI Diaries of 2 Canadian Airmen.* Ottawa, Canadian Government Publishing 1987

Guttman, Jon. ***The Origin of the Fighter Aircraft***. Pennsylvania, Westholme 2009.

Hart, Peter. ***Aces Falling,*** *War Above the Trenches, 1918.* Great Britain, Weidenfeld & Nicholson 2007; and, ***Bloody April,*** *Slaughter in the Skies over Arras, 1917.* Great Britain, Weidenfeld & Nicholson 2005

Hart, Peter & Nigel Steel. ***Tumult in the Clouds,*** *The British Experience of the War in the Air, 1914–1918.* England, Hodder and Stoughton 1997

Hellwig, Adrian. ***Australian Hawk over the Western Front,*** *A Biography of Major RS Dallas.* London, Grub Street 2006

Hobbs, David. *Aircraft Carriers of the Royal and Commonwealth Navies*. London, Greenhill 1996

Jones, HA. *Over the Balkans and South Russia, 1917-1919*. Aeolus, Greenhill 1987

Kealy, JDF & EC Russell. *A History of Canadian Naval Aviation, 1918-1962*. Ottawa, Queen's Printer 1965.

Kemp, Peter. *Fleet Air Arm*. London, Jenkins 1954

King, Brad. *Royal Naval Air Service, 1912-1918*. Aldershot, Ed. Barry Ketley, Hikoki 1997.

Kinsey, Gordon. *Seaplanes – Felixstowe, The Story of the Air Station 1913–1963*. England, Dalton 1978

Layman, RD. *The Cruxhaven Raid, The World's First Carrier Air Strike*. England, Conway 1985; and, *Naval Aviation in the First World War*. England, Chatham 1996

Levine, Joshua. *On a Wing and a Prayer, Pioneering Aviation Heroes of WWI*. London, Collins 2008

Lewis, Cecil. *Sagittarius Rising*. New York, Harcourt 1936*

Liddle, Peter H. *The Airman's War 1914–18*. Poole, Blandford 1987

Livock, GE. *To the Ends of the Air*. London, HM Stationary Office 1973

Longmore, Sir Arthur. *From Sea to Sky*. London, Butler and Tanner 1946

MacFarlane, John and Robbie Hughes. *Canada's Naval Aviators* Victoria BC, Maritime Museum of British Columbia 1994

Malinovska, Anna & Mauriel Joslyn. *Voices in Flight, Conversations with Air Veterans of the Great War*. Great Britain, Pen & Sword Aviation 2006

McGreal, Stephen. *Zeebrugge & Ostend Raids 1918*. Great Britain, Pen & Sword 2007

Milberry, Larry. *Aviation In Canada, The Pioneer Decades*. Toronto, CANAV Books 2008

Milner, Marc. *Canada's Navy, The First Century*. University of Toronto Press 1999

Moore, W. Geoffery. *Early Bird*. (FCdr WG Moore OBE, DSC, RNAS) London, Putnam 1963

Morris, Alan. *First of the Many, the Story of Independent Force, RAF*. London, Jarrolds 1968

Morrow, John H. *The Great War in the Air*. Washington, Smithsonian Institution Press 1993

Mowthrope, Ces.
Battlebags, British Airships of the First World War. England, Sutton 1995; and,
Sky Sailors, The Story of the World's Airshipmen. England, Sutton 1999

Johnston ED (Editor). *Naval Eight*: *A History of No. 8. Squadron R.N.A.S.* London, The Signal Press, 1931

O'Connor, Mike. *Airfields and Airmen* (Battleground Series). England, Pen & Sword Books 2001–2005

O'Kiely Elizabeth. *Gentleman Air Ace, the Duncan Bell-Irving Story*. BC Canada, Harbour 1992

Patience, Kevin. *Konigsberg, a German East African Raider*. Zanzibar Publications 2001

Piggott, Peter. *Flying Canucks: Famous Canadian Aviators*. Toronto, Hounslow 1994

Pioneering Aviation in the West, As Told by the Pioneers. British Columbia, Canadian Museum of Flight & Transportation, Hancock 1992

Pollard AO (VC). *The Royal Air Force, A Concise History*. Plymouth, Mayflower 1934

Popham, Hugh. *Into Wind*: *a History of British Naval Flying*, London, Hamish 1969

Puleston WD. *The Dardanelles Expedition, A Condensed Study*. Annapolis MD, USNI 1927

Reynolds, Quentin. *They Fought for the Sky*. Toronto, Clark 1957

Richardson, Leonard A, RFC. *Pilot's Log, Letters Home and Verse*. Compiled by Elizabeth Richardson-Whealy, St. Catharines, Canada 1998

Roberts, Leslie. *There Shall Be Wings, A History of the RCAF*. Toronto, Clarke Irwin 1959

Rochford, Leonard H. *I Chose the Sky*. (Foreword by R. Collishaw) London, Kimber 1977

Rosher, Harold. *In the Royal Naval Air Service*. Arnold Bennett (Editor), London, Chatto & Windus 1916

Rossano, Geoffrey L. *The Price of Honor, The World War One Letters of Naval Aviator Kenneth MacLeish*. Annapolis, MD, Naval Institute Press 1991

Sampson, Charles. *Fights and Flights*. Ernest Benn Ltd 1930

Saunders HStG. *Per Ardua, The Rise of British Air Power 1911–1939*. Oxford University Press 1944

Seuter, Murray. *Airmen or Noahs*. Pitman and Sons 1928

Smith, Graham. *Taking to the Skies* 1903-1939. Newbury Berks, Countryside 2003

Snowden-Gamble, Charles. *The Story of a North Sea Air Station* (Yarmouth). London, Spearman, 1967. First Published 1928.

Snowie, J.Allan. *The Bonnie,* HMCS Bonaventure, Canada's Last Aircraft Carrier. Boston Mills ON 1987

Soward, Stuart E. *A Formidable Hero,* Lt RH Gray VC. Toronto, CANAV 1987
Reprinted Rothesay NB, Neptune 2005;
Hands To Flying Stations, Canadian Naval Aviation 1945–1969. Vols I & II.
Victoria BC, Neptune 1993 & 1995

Sullivan, Alan. *Aviation In Canada 1917-1918,* ... Work of the RAF... Imperial Munitions Board and Canadian Aeroplanes Ltd. Toronto, Rous & Mann 1919

Tallman, Frank. *Flying the Old Planes,* In the Cockpit of 25 Historic Aircraft. New York, Doubleday, 1993

Taylor, John WR. *Fairey Aviation.* Great Britain, Chalford 1997

Tennant J.E. *In the Clouds Above Baghdad,* Being the Records of an Air Commander. Nashville, Battery 1992 (Originally pulished 1922)

Treadwell, Terry C. *The First Naval Air War.* Great Britain, Tempus 2002;
Airships of the First World War. Compiled with Alan C Wood. Great Britain, Tempus 1999; and
The First Air War. A Pictorial History 1914–1919. With AC Wood. Barnes & Noble 1996

Thompson, Roy. *Wings of the Canadian Armed Forces 1913-1972.* Dartmouth, Nova Scotia 1973

Van Der Vat, Dan. *The Ship that Changed the World,* The Escape of the Goben to the Dardanelles in 1914. (Revised) Edinburgh, Birlinn 2000

Welland, Robert. *Advice,* on Politics, Society and Naval Affairs. Surrey BC, Allega 2006.

Westrop, Mike. *A History of No. 10 Squadron RNAS;* and, **A History of No. 6 Squadron RNAS** Atglen, PA, Schiffer 2004.

Whitehouse, Arthur 'Arch'. *Years of the Sky Kings.* Garden City NY, Doubleday 1960*

Williams, Geoffrey. *Wings over Westgate.* The story of a front line Naval Air Station during World War I. England, Kent County Library 1985.

Wragg David. *Wings Over the Sea:* a History of Naval Aviation. Newton Abbot, Devon : David and Charles, 1979.

Young, Desmond: *Rutland of Jutland.* London, Cassell 1963

Yeates V. *Winged Victory.* Jonathan Cape Published 1934; Buchan & Enright 1985*

Allied Compendiums

Cronin, Dick, *Royal Navy Shipboard Aircraft Developments 1912–1931.* UK, Air Britain 1990

Franks, Norman: *Nieuport Aces of World War 1;*
Sopwith Camel Aces of World War 1;
Sopwith Triplane Aces of World War 1;
Sopwith Pup Aces of World War 1. London, Osprey Aircraft of the Aces Series 2000–2005

Franks, Guest & Bailey. **Bloody April... Black September.** London, Grub Street 1995
Above the Lines (German Aces 1914-1918), London, Grub Street 1993

Flying Officers of the United States Navy 1917–1919. Atglen PA, Schiffer 1997

Hayward, JB. *Naval and Air Force Honours and Awards.* London, JB Hayward 1919; and
The Royal Air Force List, April 1918. London, JB Hayward 1918

Henshaw, Trevor. *The Sky Their Battlefield.* Air Fighting and the Complete List of Allied Air Casualties from Enemy Action in the First World War. London, Grubb Street 1995

Hobson, Chris. *Airmen Died in the Great War 1914–1918.* The Roll of Honour of the British and Commonwealth Air Services of the First World War. London, Hayward 1995

Jane's Fighting Aircraft of World War 1. Great Britain, Studio Editions reproduction 1990

Jane's Fighting Ships of World War 1. Great Britain, Studio Editions reproduction 1990

Martyn, Errol W. *For Your Tomorrow*. Christchurch, New Zealand, Volplane 1998

Nieuports in RNAS, RFC and RAF Service. Great Britain, Cross & Cockade International, The First World War Aviation Historical Society 2007

Raleigh, Walter. *Official History of the War*; *The War in the Air, Vol 1 to 6*. Originally Pub 1922. Reprint by The Naval & Military Press Ltd and Imperial War Museum

Robertson, Bruce et al. *Sopwith – The Man and His Aircraft*. England, Air Review 1970

Roskill, SW(Editor): *Documents Relating to the Naval Air Service, Volume I: 1908–1918*. London, Navy Records Society 1969

Revell, Alex. *British Single-Seater Fighter Squadrons on the Western Front in World War I*. Atglen PA, Schiffer 2006

Sanger, Ray. *Nieuport Aircraft of World War One*. Great Britain, Crowood Press 2002

Shirley, Noel C. *United States Naval Aviation 1910–1918*. Atglen PA, Schiffer 2000

Shores C, N Franks & R Guest. *Above the Trenches*. *A Complete Record of the Fighter Aces and Units of the British Empire Air Forces 1915–1920*. Canada, Fortress 1990. Supplement1996.

Shores, Christopher. *British and Empire Aces of World War 1*. Osprey Aircraft of the Aces Series 2001

Smith, Myron J. *World War I in the Air*, *A Bibliography and Chronology*. USA Smith 1977

Sturtivant & Page. *Royal Navy Aircraft Serials and Units, 1911 to 1919*. Tonbridge, Air-Britain 1992

Thetford, Owen. *British Naval Aircraft 1912–58*. London, Putnam 1963

Williamson, HJ. *The Roll of Honour*, *RFC & RAF 1914-1918*. England, Naval & Military Press 1992

Journals & Magazines

Canadian Aviation 1930's (Various)

Canadian Aviation Historical Society (Various)

Canadian Society of Military Medals & Insignia (Summer 1995)

Crowsnest, Royal Canadian Navy (Various)

Cross & Cockade (Various)

Over The Front (Various)

Roundel, Royal Canadian Air Force (Various)

Sentinel, Canadian Armed Forces (Various)

Finally, there are the writings of Canadian Donald Jack and his series THE BANDY PAPERS, being the Journals of Bartholomew Bandy. The five-volume set begins with *Three Cheers for Me,* and takes the reader through the fictional life of Bandy, a First World War Aviator, his humorous encounters and tumultuous tribulations. The stories are artfully woven to the realities of a young man at war—a 'Catch-22' series for Canadians.

Aviation Classics–Best Reads

INDEX

INDEX

GERMAN AVIATORS

2010 – J. Allan SNOWIE
(Bellingham WA; b. SCT) – Author

Having previously published about the Army and about the Navy, Allan began this book on an Air theme. He traced down RNAS Canadians during the 1990's expecting to find a couple of hundred or so. The search turned up 943 and became a 'Hobby Outta Control' for over the next dozen years.

A former RCN pilot, Allan was flying overseas for Air Canada, and able to conduct research in England during layovers and to seek out information across Canada.

Retiring from the airline in 2005 as an Airbus 330/340 Supervisory Captain and Instructor, he bought a reproduction *Nieuport XI* 'for futher research, of course' and flew the machine from Nanaimo, British Columbia, to CFB Shearwater, Nova Scotia, during the 2009 Centennial of Flight in Canada. He cheated a wee bit with a trailer across the Rockies and part of the Prairies but did fly into the Oshkosh airshow.

His ever-patient 'ground-crew' on the adventure was his bride Cynthia and she has also been instrumental in the production of this book—from research, to layout, to final draft.

The couple lives in Bellingham, WA. Allan volunteers at the airport's Heritage Flight Museum and hopes to take the local Escadrille Nor'West to France for the 100th Anniversary of Vimy Ridge in 2017.

Cynthia remains to be sold on that one.

Fleet Flypast
Esquimalt BC
September 2010

Jeff Phillips Photo
bcam.net

Photo by Lyle Jansma
www.jansmadesign.net

ESCADRILLE NOR'WEST OF THE HERITAGE FLIGHT MUSEUM

BELLINGHAM, WASHINGTON

These are two of fourteen Nieuport XI replica aircraft
built by Chapter 292 Experimental Aircraft Association
of Independence, Oregon.